AMENIA FREE LIBRARY

3 8020 00014 2459

W9-BRS-772

946.081
VAI

Vaill, Amanda

Hotel Florida

	DATE DUE		
JUN 1 4 2014			
JUN 2 0 2014			
APR 0 6 2015			
JUL 2 7 2015			

AMENIA FREE LIBRARY
3300 Rt 343
Amenia, New York 12501

ALSO BY AMANDA VAILL

Somewhere: The Life of Jerome Robbins

Everybody Was So Young:
Gerald and Sara Murphy—A Lost Generation Love Story

Seamen Schepps: A Century of New York Jewelry Design (coauthor)

HOTEL FLORIDA

HOTEL FLORIDA

TRUTH, LOVE, AND DEATH
IN THE SPANISH CIVIL WAR

AMANDA VAILL

FARRAR, STRAUS AND GIROUX

NEW YORK

Farrar, Straus and Giroux
18 West 18th Street, New York 10011

Copyright © 2014 by Amanda Vaill
Maps copyright © 2014 by Jeffrey L. Ward
All rights reserved
Printed in the United States of America
First edition, 2014

Grateful acknowledgment is made for permission to reprint the following material:

Previously unpublished writing from the papers of Arturo and Ilsa Barea, including memoirs by Valentin Pollak, copyright © 2014 by the Estate of Arturo and Ilsa Barea; used by permission of Uli Rushby-Smith.

Previously unpublished writing by Robert Capa and Gerda Taro copyright © 2014 by the International Center of Photography, The Robert Capa and Cornell Capa Archive.

Previously unpublished writing by Martha Gellhorn from the Martha Gellhorn Collection, Howard Gotlieb Archival Research Center at Boston University, copyright © 2014 by the Estate of Martha Gellhorn; used by permission of Alexander Matthews.

Previously unpublished writing by Ernest Hemingway in the Ernest Hemingway Collection, John F. Kennedy Library, copyright © 2014 by the Ernest Hemingway Foundation and Hemingway Foreign Rights Trust; used by permission of the Foundation and of Scribner Publishing Group. All rights reserved.

Library of Congress Cataloging-in-Publication Data
Vaill, Amanda.
    Hotel Florida : truth, love, and death in the Spanish Civil War / Amanda Vaill. — First Edition.
        pages   cm
    Includes bibliographical references and index.
    ISBN 978-0-374-17299-2 (hardback) — ISBN 978-0-374-71203-7 (ebook)
    1. Spain—History—Civil War, 1936–1939—Biography.   2. Hotel Florida (Madrid, Spain)   3. Couples—Spain—Biography.   4. Hemingway, Ernest, 1899–1961.   5. Gellhorn, Martha, 1908–1998.   6. Capa, Robert, 1913–1954. 7. Taro, Gerta, 1911–1937.   8. Barea, Arturo, 1897–1957.   9. Kulcsar, Ilsa, 1902–1973.   I. Title.

DP260.V35 2014
946.0810922—dc23   2013035338

Designed by Jonathan D. Lippincott

Farrar, Straus and Giroux books may be purchased for educational, business, or promotional use. For information on bulk purchases, please contact the Macmillan Corporate and Premium Sales Department at 1-800-221-7945, extension 5442, or write to specialmarkets@macmillan.com.

www.fsgbooks.com
www.twitter.com/fsgbooks • www.facebook.com/fsgbooks

1   3   5   7   9   10   8   6   4   2

For those who died in Spain, or left their hearts there;

and for Tom

You could learn as much at the Hotel Florida in those years as you could learn anywhere in the world.   —Ernest Hemingway

Cómo se pasa la vida,
Cómo se viene la muerte.
Tan callando:
Cuán presto se va el placer,
Cómo, después de acordado,
Da dolor,
Cómo, a nuestro parecer,
Cualquier tiempo pasado
Fué mejor.
                              —Jorge Manrique

For what is a man profited, if he shall gain the whole world, and lose his own soul?   —Matthew 16:26

CONTENTS

SPAIN

Atlantic Ocean

Bay of Biscay

FRANCE

Santander
Guernica
Irun •Biarritz

ASTURIAS
CANTABRIA
Bilbao
NAVARRE
PYRENEES
Perpignan

GALICIA

BASQUE COUNTRY *RIOJA*
Le Perthus

LÉON
Ebro
CATALONIA

SIERRA DE GUADARRAMA
Saragossa
•Lérida
Barcelona

Jarama
Manzanares
Guadalajara
ARAGON
Tortosa

Brunete•
•Madrid
Teruel
Sègre

Tajo
Toledo•
Morata de Tajuña
Turia
VALENCIA

MALLORCA
MENORCA

PORTUGAL

Tagus

CASTILE

EXTREMADURA
Valencia
•IBIZA

Badajoz•
Almadén•

•Peñarroya
MURCIA

Mediterranean Sea

•Cordoba

ANDALUSIA
Cartagena

Málaga•
Almería•

Atlantic Ocean

Tangier•
•Tetuán

Melilla•
ALGERIA

MOROCCO

© 2014 Jeffrey L. Ward

0 Miles   100   200

0 Kilometers   200

NATIONALIST-HELD TERRITORY, 1936–1939

SEPTEMBER 1936

OCTOBER 1937

JULY 1938

FEBRUARY 1939

CHRONOLOGY

1931 King Alfonso XIII leaves Spain, ushering in the Second Republic, a coalition of Socialists and liberal middle-class Republicans; the new government gives women the vote, legalizes divorce, cuts the size of the army

1932 General José Sanjurjo attempts a right-wing coup against the Spanish Republic; Anarchist uprisings take place in Andalusia, Aragon, the Basque country, and Madrid

Franklin Delano Roosevelt elected president of the United States; U.S. unemployment at 25 percent

1933 Adolf Hitler becomes chancellor of Germany; all political parties except National Socialists (Nazis) are banned; the first Nazi concentration camp is opened at Dachau

Spanish right-wing parties win a majority in the Cortes

1934 General Francisco Franco leads suppression of miners' rebellion in Asturias

Austrian Civil War causes street fighting in Vienna and other cities; conservative premier Dolfuss outlaws the Social Democrats and Austria becomes a proto-fascist state

1935 Andrés Nin and Joaquin Maurin form the Workers' Party of Marxist Unification (POUM) in Catalonia

Prime Minister Benito Mussolini sends Italian troops to invade Abyssinia

Stalin initiates the first purge of what will be called the Great Terror

1936 *February* Newly formed Popular Front coalition of Socialists, Communists, and Republicans narrowly wins Spanish general elections; the new government relieves Francisco Franco of his command and posts him to Canary Islands

March Hitler reoccupies the Rhineland

May Popular Front wins general election in France; Léon Blum narrowly escapes assassination by fascist militia, becomes premier

July Concerted military uprisings take place all over Spain; Franco flies from Canary Islands to Morocco to take charge of the Army of Africa and invade the Spanish mainland; the government arms civilians to combat the mutiny

August European nations, joined by the United States, declare a Non-Intervention Agreement for Spain; Nationalist (rebel) army, aided by secret gifts of war materiel from Germany and Italy, advances steadily; Socialist leader Francisco Largo Caballero becomes premier of Spain

September Spanish rebels take Toledo and San Sebastian; Franco is appointed supreme political and military commander of the rebels

October Spanish gold reserves transported to Russia; first International Brigades arrive in Spain

November Nationalist forces advance to outskirts of Madrid, but are halted; government relocates to Valencia; Germany and Italy recognize Franco

1937 *January* Moscow trials of Old Bolsheviks and current army officers begin; U.S. Congress forbids all arms sales to Spain

February Nationalists take Málaga, begin offensive in Jarama Valley

March Government forces push back Nationalists at Guadalajara

April German Luftwaffe bombs Guernica

May May Days in Barcelona; Juan Negrin replaces Largo Caballero as premier

June Bilbao falls to Nationalists

July Battle of Brunete; USSR enters Sino-Japanese War

August Fighting begins on Aragon Front

October Government forces take Belchite in Aragon; Nationalists win control of north; government moves from Valencia to Barcelona

December Teruel offensive begins. In China, Japanese besiege and take Nanking

1938 *January* Government forces take Teruel

February Nationalists retake Teruel

March Nationalists retake Belchite, start drive to Mediterranean; Italian planes begin bombing Barcelona; France reopens border with Spain; Germany annexes Austria in the Anschluss

April Nationalists take Lérida, then Vinaroz, cutting the Republican zone in two; Franco privately signs the Anti-Comintern Pact with Japan, Italy, and Germany

June Léon Blum resigns as French premier and is succeeded by Édouard Daladier; French border with Spain closed

July Spanish government begins counteroffensive along the Ebro

September Munich conference among France, Britain, Germany, and Italy permits Hitler's annexation of Czech Sudetenland

October Spanish government agrees to withdrawal of all foreign volunteers; International Brigades have farewell parade in Barcelona; in China, Hankow falls to Japanese

November Rio Segre offensive; Battle of the Ebro ends in government defeat and retreat back across river; in Germany, Kristallnacht results in destruction of 7,500 Jewish shops and 400 synagogues

December Franco begins offensive on Catalonia

1939 *January* Nationalist troops take Barcelona

February Fall of Catalonia; Britain and France recognize Franco

March Franco marches into Madrid; Germany annexes all of Czechoslovakia, demands the free city of Danzig in Poland

April Franco announces the end of military hostilities, makes public his agreement to the German/Italian/Japanese Anti-Comintern Pact

PRINCIPAL CHARACTERS

THE SPANISH
For the government (also known as Republicans, Loyalists)
Julio Álvarez del Vayo, foreign minister of the Spanish Republic, September 1936–May 1937 and April 1938–March 1939
Arturo Barea Ogazón, patent engineer, press censor, would-be writer
Luís Companys, president of the Generalitat (autonomous government) of Catalonia
Francisco Largo Caballero, Socialist leader, prime minister of the Spanish Republic, September 1936–May 1937
Enrique Líster, Soviet-trained commander of the 11th Division of the Popular Army, later of the 5th Army Corps
José Miaja, Loyalist general and chief of the Defense Junta of Madrid
Colonel Juan Modesto, Communist commander of the Fifth Army Corps, later of the Army of the Ebro
Constancia de la Mora y Maura, aristocrat, Communist, deputy (from May 1937) and then propaganda chief of the Spanish Republic, October 1937–February 1939
Dr. Juan Negrín, Socialist leader, finance minister, and later prime minister of Spain, May 1937–March 1939
Andrés Nin, anti-Stalinist Catalan communist, founder of the POUM
Indalecio Prieto, socialist leader, rival of Largo Caballero, Spanish minister of defense, May 1937–March 1938
José Robles Pazos, Spanish translator of John Dos Passos
Luis Rubio Hidalgo, propaganda minister of the Spanish Republic, September 1936–October 1937
José (Pepe) Quintanilla, chief of Madrid's secret police, brother of the artist Luis Quintanilla

For the rebels (also known as the Nationalists)

Luis Bolín, right-wing conspirator, later Nationalist propaganda chief

Francisco Franco Bahamonde, youngest general in the Spanish Army, later leader of the Nationalist rebellion

THE AMERICANS

Virginia (Ginny) Cowles, Hearst newspaper syndicate correspondent

John Dos Passos, novelist and journalist

Sidney Franklin, American matador, friend and factotum to Ernest Hemingway

Martha Gellhorn, novelist and journalist

Ernest Hemingway, novelist and journalist

Josephine (Josie) Herbst, American novelist and leftist journalist, friend of Hemingway and Dos Passos

James Lardner, American journalist, correspondent for the Paris bureau of the *Herald-Tribune*, son of the American novelist Ring Lardner

Archibald MacLeish, American poet and magazine editor, friend of Hemingway and Dos Passos

Herbert L. Matthews, Madrid correspondent for *The New York Times*

Robert Hale Merriman, American professor of economics, commander of the Abraham Lincoln Battalion, later chief of staff of the Fifteenth International Brigade

Maxwell Perkins, Hemingway's editor at Charles Scribner's Sons

Liston Oak, American Communist working for the Spanish Republican Propaganda Ministry; secretary of the League of American Writers

Franklin Roosevelt, president of the United States of America, 1933–1945

Eleanor Roosevelt, his wife, journalist and activist

Vincent (Jimmy) Sheean, foreign correspondent of the *Herald-Tribune*

THE BRITISH

Eric Blair, a.k.a. George Orwell, English investigative journalist and POUM militiaman

Claud Cockburn, Spanish correspondent for *The Daily Worker*, editor and correspondent for *The Week*

Sefton (Tom) Delmer, Madrid correspondent for *The Daily Express*

Diana (Dinah) Forbes-Robertson, a writer, married to Vincent Sheean

THE RUSSIANS

Vladimir Gorev, special military attaché of the Soviet Union and Madrid station chief of the GRU (Soviet military intelligence)

General Emilio Kléber, a.k.a. Manfred (or Lazar) Stern, commander of the Eleventh International Brigade, November 1936

Mikhail Koltsov, Russian journalist, Spanish correspondent for *Pravda*

Alexander Orlov, NKVD station chief in Madrid (later Valencia), 1936–1938

Joseph Vissarionovich Stalin, general secretary of the Communist Party, 1922–1952

Marshal Kliment Voroshilov, people's commissar for defense, USSR

THE OTHERS

Ted Allan, leftist Canadian journalist

André (Endre) Friedmann, a.k.a. Robert Capa, Hungarian photographer

Carlos Contreras, a.k.a. Vittorio Vidali, Trieste-born NKVD agent and founder of the Loyalist Fifth Regiment

Louis Delaprée, Madrid correspondent for *Paris-Soir*

John Ferno, a.k.a. Fernhout, Dutch Communist cinematographer

Joris Ivens, Dutch Communist film director

Colonel Hans Kahle, exiled Prussian Communist, after 1936 commander of the Eleventh International Brigade, later divisional commander in the Republican Popular Army

Alfred Kantorowicz, Polish émigré journalist, information officer of the Chapaiev Battalion of the Thirteenth International Brigade

Geza Korvin Karpathi, Hungarian photographer and filmmaker, boyhood friend of Endre Friedmann (Robert Capa)

Otto Katz, a.k.a. André Simone, refugee German Communist, propagandist, founder of the Agence Espagne

Ilse (later Ilsa) Kulcsar, née Pollak, Austrian journalist, socialist activist, and translator

Leopold (Poldi) Kulcsar, Austrian journalist and clandestine political operative

General Pavol Lukács, a.k.a. Maté Zalka, Hungarian-born, Moscow-trained commander of the Twelfth International Brigade

André Malraux, French novelist, art theorist, founder of the Escuadrilla España

Randalfo Pacciardi, Italian antifascist, commander of the Garibaldi Battalion of the Twelfth International Brigade

Gustav Regler, German Communist refugee, political commissar of the Twelfth International Brigade

Kajsa Rothman, Swedish guide and interpreter employed by the Loyalist propaganda department

Karol Swierczewski, a.k.a. Colonel [sometimes General] Walter, Polish-born, Soviet-trained commander of the Fourteenth International Brigade

Gerta Pohorylle, a.k.a. Gerda Taro, Polish-born German photographer

A NOTE ON SPELLING

Although current usage calls for Catalan or Basque spelling for proper and place names in those regions, I have followed contemporary (1930s) practice in rendering them in Castilian Spanish—or, in a few cases where contemporary sources did likewise, in anglicized orthography. Thus today's Lleida becomes Lérida; Gernika becomes Guernica; Andreu Nin becomes Andrés Nin; but the Catalan Catalunya becomes the anglicized Catalonia (not the Castilian Cataluña), and the Castilian Zaragoza becomes Saragossa. However, the state government of Catalonia is referred to as the Generalitat (not Generalidad), since that is the how both Arturo Barea and John Dos Passos refer to it. Also, when writing of Robert Capa's assignment in China, I've given his location as Hankow (as it was spelled at the time).

AUTHOR'S NOTE

"It is very dangerous to write the truth in war," said Ernest Hemingway, "and the truth is very dangerous to come by." *Hotel Florida* is about that danger, and how it is faced by three couples—Hemingway and his fellow writer Martha Gellhorn, the photographers Robert Capa and Gerda Taro, and the press officers Arturo Barea and Ilsa Kulcsar—whose paths cross in Madrid while they are covering the Spanish Civil War; it is also about whether, for each of them, living the truth becomes just as important as telling it, to the world, to each other, and to themselves.

From its beginning in 1936, when right-wing, conservative rebels staged a military mutiny against the elected left-wing government, the Spanish Civil War became a kind of historical flash point: as one of its most passionate propagandists, the British journalist Claud Cockburn, wrote in his autobiography, almost no one can "agree with any generalization anyone makes about Spain. I personally disagree with about half the generalizations I made about it at the time." A war that seemed to start as a struggle between the haves and the have-nots, it reflected—and quickly became subsumed in—the worldwide clash of ideologies that would culminate, only months after hostilities ceased in Spain, in World War II. In such an atmosphere, the shadow line between truth and falsehood sometimes became faint indeed: your friend could be your enemy, and honesty could get you (or someone else) killed.

Negotiating that landscape was particularly hazardous for journalists, who were able to cover this war more closely and thoroughly than they had any previous conflict, certainly more than the Great War of 1914–1918, in which (as Philip Knightley discusses in *The First Casualty*, his critical history of war journalism) correspondents and photographers were banned from the front. With millions of readers, viewers, and listeners getting their news from the new media of radio, documentary film, newsreels, and illustrated magazines, Spain became a place where reputations, and even fortunes, could be made. But those doing the making tended to be foreign nationals, outsiders; and when the war was over, if they lived, they could go home, to enjoy the reputations or the fortunes. If they bent the truth one way or the other, they faced few real consequences. The Spaniards, at least those on the losing side, weren't so lucky.

Hotel Florida is not a history of the Spanish Civil War; there have been many such, on all ideological sides of the issue, and I would have nothing to add to their number. It is a narrative examination of the Civil War experiences of my six subjects, and some of their close confederates, which attempts to offer contrasting and close-up views of their tangled wartime destinies. But although *Hotel Florida* is a narrative, not an academic analysis, it is not fiction, or even fictional. It is a reconstruction, based on published and unpublished letters, diaries, and personal accounts, official documents, recovered reels of film, authoritative biographies, histories, and contemporary news media, all cited in detail in the source notes. These sources, some of which have only recently become available, have enabled me to offer new versions of events covered differently elsewhere; but to preserve the narrative texture of the book, discussion of the differences, for those curious about them, has been largely confined to the notes.

In his poem "Remembering the Thirties" Donald Davie wrote of how his own post–World War II generation dismissed the passionate commitments of their elders as the stuff of "high-brow thrillers," preferring instead "a neutral tone" in action and in writing. And yet, he asked, mightn't it be better "To praise a stance impressive and absurd / Than not to see the hero for the dust"? I hope that in these pages some of the dust is blown away and the heroes—whoever they are—are visible.

HOTEL FLORIDA

PROLOGUE

On July 18, 1936, at Gando in the Canary Islands, a short, balding, barrel-chested man in a gray suit, carrying a Spanish diplomatic passport in the name of José Antonio de Sagroniz, boarded a private seven-seater de Havilland Dragon Rapide aircraft that had arrived at Gando three days previously and had been waiting on the tarmac for him ever since. The plane had been chartered for the substantial sum of £2,000 ($156,000 today), anonymously deposited into a special account in Kleinwort's Bank in London, and it had been flown to the Canaries under conditions of greatest secrecy from Croydon Aerodrome in England. Before taking off from Gando, its pilot, Cecil Bebb, a sometime British military intelligence officer, had been instructed to make sure of the identity of his passenger by giving him the bottom half of a playing card and asking the passenger to supply the top half—which would have been peculiar orders if the passenger were an ordinary diplomat, and this were a routine charter flight.

In reality, however, Bebb's passenger was Francisco Franco Bahamonde, at forty-four the youngest general in the Spanish Army and former commander of the Foreign Legion during the ill-fated Rif rebellion against Spanish and French rule in Morocco. A vocal critic of his country's five-month-old Socialist government, he had been sequestered in the Canary Islands as military commandant after being dismissed from his post as military chief of staff. And now he was on his way from exile in the Canaries, almost a thousand miles by sea from Spain, to rejoin his old troops in Spanish Morocco and lead them to the mainland as part of a carefully plotted military coup against Spain's democratically elected regime.

The republic whose government Franco and his coconspirators wanted to overthrow had been established only in 1931, when the first free elections in nearly sixty years led to the abdication of King Alfonso XIII. Spain had spent centuries under the control of the landed aristocracy, the Catholic Church, and, more recently, the new industrial oligarchy; in an effort to break that control, the new republic's constitution, passed in December 1931, granted women the vote, legalized divorce, discontinued state funding of religious orders, made free primary education compulsory, and supported the concept of autonomy for the nation's linguistically disparate and historically independent regions. "This young and eager Spain has at last arrived at its majority," the republicans claimed; but its government was so unschooled in practical politics, and included so many conflicting elements—from the reform-minded Socialists to the conservative anti-monarchists to the radical anarchists and in between— that a unified, consistent approach to Spain's chronic problems of worker disenfranchisement, illiteracy, poverty, and industrial underdevelopment proved impossible to achieve. And the country's vested interests—the army, the holders of the vast estates called *latifundias*, the mine- and factory owners, and the Church—viewed most steps toward reform as the beginnings of Communist revolution, a not-uncommon reaction in the Europe of the 1930s. Many among them saw an alternative in the vision of the ascendant fascist leaders Benito Mussolini and, increasingly, Adolf Hitler.

These established forces started pushing back against the government's policies almost at once. There were reports of *latifundistas* in the south starving out their tenant farmers by simply refusing to put acreage under cultivation, or hiring cheaper labor from elsewhere, and of workers who dared to unionize and strike being attacked by the Civil Guard. The conservative press began referring to the government as a cabal of Jews, Masons, and Bolsheviks; and within the army, which was conservative and monarchist to begin with and resistant to the new government's efforts to trim its inflated officer ranks, a small cabal started to plot against the Republic.

The anti-Republicans were helped by the old paradox of reform: when enough pressure for change builds up, lifting the lid off the kettle just a little doesn't reduce the pressure—it makes the contents explode. In the first year of the Republic there were agrarian revolts, church burnings, and an anarchist uprising, all of which created a climate of fear and turmoil and stimulated the right to action. Although the government managed to squash a mutiny by General José Sanjurjo late in the summer of 1932, in the 1933 parliamentary elections the right-wingers of the Catholic CEDA party (Confederación Española de Derechas Autónomas) won nearly twice the number of seats in the Cortes, the Spanish parliament, as the Socialists; and the Radical Republicans, who had become estranged from the left, definitively broke with them and joined the other anti-Republicans in a coalition of the right. With the Socialists out of power, the socialist trade union, the UGT, fearful that the new government would dismantle recent reforms, called a general strike; and the president of the Catalan regional assembly declared wealthy, industrialized Catalonia an autonomous state within the Republic. Then, in October 1934, an armed labor rebellion broke out in Asturias, where thirty thousand workers took over mines and factories, destroyed property, and killed factory owners and priests.

The man the government summoned to put down this uprising was Francisco Franco, newly promoted to army chief of staff; and his principal weapon was the fighting force with which he'd battled the Rif rebels in Morocco: the mercenaries of the Army of Africa, soldiers for whom slaughter was a job, who didn't need to think twice about what it meant to kill fellow citizens, because the miners of Asturias *weren't* their fellow citizens. "The war in Morocco," Franco remarked to a journalist covering his Asturian action, "had a certain romantic air, an air of reconquest. But this war is a frontier war and its fronts are socialism, communism, and whatever attacks civilization in order to replace it with barbarism." By the time reconquest was achieved, between one and two thousand people had been killed, of whom about 320 were military or government personnel.

In the aftermath of the events of October 1934, many left-wing politicians were imprisoned—one of them, Francisco Largo Caballero, spent the time reading the works of Marx and Lenin for the first time—and the president of the Catalan assembly, Luís Companys, was sentenced to death. All were ultimately freed in a vain attempt to restore some kind of equilibrium to the Republic; but by now the only equilibrium seemed to be the balance of suspicion and hatred between left and right.

In February 1936, a left-wing coalition called the Popular Front, led
by the former prime minister Manuel Azaña, a left-Republican *litterateur*,
and including both Socialists and Communists, faced down the right-
wing Antirevolutionary Coalition (sometimes referred to as the National
Front), a loose confederation of the CEDA and the monarchists, in a close
and bitterly fought election. Feelings ran high: during the campaign bishops told Catholics to vote for the Antirevolutionaries or risk purgatory,
while Largo Caballero threatened civil war if the right won. He had been
making similar statements since 1932, but his comments did nothing to
defuse tension. When the Popular Front prevailed (by a popular margin
of only 1.1 percent, although they won 263 of the 473 seats in the Cortes), the narrowness of the victory undercut the new coalition's mandate;
and the withdrawal of substantial amounts of capital from the country
by edgy investors shook the economy, already weakened by the effects of
worldwide depression, to its core. The Cortes became a hive of angry
rhetoric, while outbreaks of violence by the armed militias of a trium-
phalist left and a resentful and provocative right took that anger into the
streets.

It was against this background that the government tried to push
through a program that included military and agrarian reforms and Catalan autonomy, as well as freedom for the political prisoners taken during
the past several years—at which point leading figures on the right began
to talk seriously, and secretly, with a cadre of disaffected army generals
about seizing power. And Spain's fate became a matter of increasing interest outside its borders: to men and women in Europe and the United
States who eyed the power of Soviet Russia and its Communist revolution
with apprehension, or who watched in horror as Hitler and Mussolini led
their followers to ever more aggressive actions against their compatriots
and their neighbors; as well as to the leaders of Germany, Italy, and
Russia, who saw in Spain a template for their own futures.

In June, Francisco Franco had written from his post in the Canary
Islands to the prime minister, Santiago Casares Quiroga—a detached,
ascetic-looking man who had taken over the office when Azaña became
president—protesting the recent removal of some of his fellow right-wing
officers from their posts in the government's military house-cleaning. He
warned his superior that he was risking "the discipline of the army" by the
government's actions; however, he suggested, if he himself were put in su-

preme charge of the military, he might be able to assure its loyalty. Casares Quiroga never answered the letter.

The stage was now set for a carefully orchestrated military uprising, first in the colonial outposts of Melilla, Ceuta, and Tetuán in Spanish Morocco, then in garrisons around the Spanish mainland. The plotters apparently envisioned a quick military takeover: not a prolonged civil war that would last nearly three years; cost nearly four hundred thousand lives; destroy villages, towns, and substantial parts of cities; put thousands of citizens in political prisons for decades; lay waste to the country's economy; and leave scars in the national psyche that still hurt seventy-five years later. But they did intend—unilaterally, by force—to overthrow their country's legally elected government and replace it with one of their devising.

So when the hired Dragon Rapide crossed into Spanish colonial airspace, Francisco Franco opened his suitcase and changed from his gray business suit into a khaki uniform, winding around his waist the red-and-gold tasseled sash of a general in the Spanish Army. Shortly thereafter, the plane touched down on the tarmac at Tetuán, where rebel troops had already stormed and secured the airfield, and Franco proceeded by motorcade between lines of saluting Moorish soldiers to the office of the high commissioner. Soon all the world would hear his proclamation:

> Once more the Army, reunited with the other forces of the nation, has found itself obliged to respond to the wishes of the great majority of Spaniards who, with infinite bitterness, have seen disappear that which unites us in a common ideal: SPAIN. At stake is the need to restore the empire of ORDER within the REPUBLIC . . . [and] the principle of AUTHORITY, forgotten in these past years . . .
> To execute these tasks rapidly
> I order and command:
> *Article 1.* Martial law is declared in the whole territory and all armed forces in consequence are militarized . . .

Ten days later, an American newspaperman, Jay Allen, who had happened to be in Gibraltar when the uprising began, managed to get to Tetuán and interview Franco in the high commissioner's mansion. "There can be no compromise, no truce," the general told Allen then. "I shall advance. I shall take the capital. I will save Spain from marxism at whatever cost."

"That means," Allen asked, for clarification, "that you will have to shoot half Spain?"

Franco smiled. "I said whatever the cost."

The Spanish Civil War had begun.

PART I

"THEY ARE HERE
FOR THEIR LIVES"

July 1936: Madrid

Arturo Barea lay on the brown, pine-needled floor of a forest in the Sierra de Guadarrama, northwest of Madrid, with his head in his mistress's lap. It was midafternoon on Sunday, July 19, and the resinous air was loud with the sound of cicadas. Tall, thin, with slicked-back dark hair, the eyes of an El Greco saint, and the mouth of a sensualist, Barea was drowsy with the heat, the wine he and Maria had had with their picnic lunch, and the lovemaking afterward; he longed to close his eyes and give himself over to sleep. But Maria had other ideas. She wanted to talk. Not, this time, about how much she wanted him to leave his wife and children and make an honest woman of her after six years as his secretary and occasional bedmate, a subject that usually ended in stalemate and tears. Today she wanted to know where Barea had been last night, all night: what he had been doing that had kept him both away from home and away from her bed. But the events and sensations of the last twelve hours were too raw, too immediate to discuss; he sensed that the equipoise of his life was about to spin irrevocably out of control, and he was too exhausted to deal with the consequences.

At thirty-eight, Barea had constructed a life that was a delicate balancing act. He'd grown up poor: his father, an army recruiter, dead at forty, had left his family penniless; his mother had had to wash soldiers' dirty laundry in the Manzanares—breaking the ice with her wooden beater on cold winter mornings—and work as a servant for her well-to-do brother in order to keep the children out of the orphanage. The brother had taken an interest in little Arturo—sent him to school at the Escuela Pía, treated him to the circus, and the cinema and the bookstalls in the Plaza de Callao, and encouraged his dreams of studying engineering (he was less

enthusiastic about the literary ambitions that fueled Arturo's many contributions to the school's magazine, *Madrileñitos*). But then he, too, had
died and his wife wanted no more to do with her sister-in-law and her
children. So Arturo, still a scrawny teenager, had to go to work, first as a
jeweler's apprentice; then, after studying for and passing accountancy ex-
ams, as a clerk at the Madrid branch of the Crédit Lyonnais.

A quick learner, he soon began to see raises in his modest paycheck;
if he'd wanted to play the toady he could have climbed the bank's career
ladder in a hurry. But he was proud and thin-skinned—a dangerous
combination—and he chafed under the cavalier treatment of his bosses
while also feeling shame at the humble origins he knew they disdained.
He flirted with an alternative ambition—writing—but submitting prose
pieces to the Madrid weeklies and hanging around the *tertulias*, the freewheeling discussions in various literary cafés, seemed to lead nowhere. He
joined the Socialist general trade union, the UGT, when he was twenty;
and despite feeling out of place when he appeared at union meetings in
his *señorito's* suit and tie, he felt more solidarity with the workers in their
blouses and rope-soled shoes than he did with the frock-coated bank directors who glared over their pince-nez at him. It was as much their patronizing attitude as his disgust at what he considered unjust profiteering
that led him to storm out of the bank—calling it "a pig sty"—the day the
Great War was declared in 1914; and although he would manage, against
all odds, to become a boss himself, with a patent agent's office high above
the most fashionable part of the Calle de Alcalá, he still sided with the
workers over the fat cats. "I'm no use as a capitalist," he would say.

Not that he wasn't happy to have the capitalist's salary, and the gold
cédula personal, the identity card showing him to be in one of the top income brackets, that went with it. But he'd insisted on installing his family in a large flat on one of the narrow, crooked streets in Lavapiés, the
working-class barrio where he'd grown up, rather than in one of the bourgeois districts his wife, Aurelia, hankered after. He liked the idea of living
in both worlds while belonging to neither, which he'd managed to do, in
part, by staying out of the political struggles of the past decade. True,
he'd joined the Socialists in 1931, when the new republic was declared,
and that year he'd helped a friend organize a new clerical workers' union;
but otherwise he'd confined himself to the sidelines, even during the
bienio negro, the two dark years following the right's electoral victory in

1934. Although he decried the corruption and exploitation he frequently saw in his position as a patent agent, he told himself he was too insignificant a cog in the economic machinery to do anything about it.

Last February's national elections, however, had stirred him to action. He'd set up a Popular Front committee in the village outside Madrid where he spent weekends with his family—something that hadn't gone unnoticed by the local landowners and the officers of the Guardia Civil, the rural police force who often acted as the gentry's enforcers. And as the political situation had deteriorated in the ensuing months, with brawls and shootouts and rumors of coups and countercoups, culminating in the twin assassinations of a socialist lieutenant in the Assault Guards, José de Castillo, and the fascist opposition leader José Calvo Sotelo the week before, he'd realized he was going to have to choose sides.

Even so, he hadn't been prepared for what had happened the previous night. Madrid had been on edge all day, everyone keeping one ear cocked to the radio—easy to do when the government had placed loudspeakers at every street corner—because, sandwiched incongruously between sets of *norteamericana* dance music, there had been fragmentary news bulletins telling of mutiny in isolated military garrisons. *No need for panic; the government has the situation well in hand.* But rumors flew, and then there were reports of another outbreak, and another. Apparently there was street fighting in Barcelona. People started gathering in bars and cafés, on the streets. What if the government didn't have the situation in hand? What if these mutinies were the start of a purge of the left, like Franco's Asturian campaign? If the army turned on ordinary citizens, who would defend them? After supper with his family, Barea had gone across Calle del Ave Maria to Emiliano's bar, his local, where the radio was playing Tommy Dorsey's "The Music Goes Round and Round" at top volume and people were shouting at one another to be heard. He'd just ordered a coffee when the announcer's voice broke in: *the situation has become serious, and trade unionists and members of political groups should immediately report to their headquarters.*

The bar had emptied in seconds as terrified workers, afraid that troops quartered in one of the garrisons around the city would start firing on them, took to the streets calling for arms for self-defense. Barea had pushed his way through the mob to the Socialists' center, the Casa del Pueblo, in Chueca, on the other side of the Gran Via, where scores of union volunteers were clamoring to be turned into a defense force. Although he had little stomach for fighting—four years of military service in Morocco during the Rif rebellion had cured him of that, leaving his nostrils full of the stench of the rotting corpses he'd seen when he entered the besieged town of Melilla—he had less appetite for conciliation, and less still for defeat at the hands of the fascists. So he'd spent all night at the Casa del Pueblo, teaching men who had never handled a gun in their lives how to load and fire an old Mauser like the one he'd carried in the Engineers' Battalion. If the fascists tried to take Madrid, they'd have to fight for it. Or they would if the government decided to release arms to the militia so they *could* fight.

In the meantime, the government, meeting in emergency conclave, had dissolved, formed, and reformed, with some ministers urging compromise with the rebels, others retaliation, until just before dawn the announcement came: "The Government has accepted Fascism's declaration of war upon the Spanish people." There were cheers at the Casa del Pueblo; and then the sun rose in a cloudless sky, and just like that, everyone went home or to the café for breakfast. Leaving the Casa del Pueblo, Barea had found the streets silent and deserted; it seemed just a hot summer Sunday like any other. Perhaps, Barea permitted himself to hope, the rebels would now back down and life would return to normal—whatever that was. Unable to think what else to do, he decided to take Maria to the Sierra for the day, as he'd promised to on Friday, a lifetime ago.

Now he was regretting that decision: he wondered what had been going on in the capital, and in the rest of the country, since the morning, but Maria wasn't someone he could share his apprehensions with. When she'd first come to work at the patent office six years ago, he'd hoped he could discuss his ideas, convictions, and hopes with her as he couldn't with Aurelia, for whom his politics stood in the way of the social connections she wanted to forge, and who felt it was unmanly of him to want a wife who was a friend as well as a bedfellow. He'd made Maria his confidant as well as his secretary; and although the confidences eventually turned into trysts and he and Maria became lovers, Aurelia ignored the arrangement, since in her view it was permissible for a man to have affairs as long as there were no illegitimate children. But Maria didn't want to be Barea's soul mate; she just wanted to change places with Aurelia. Now, he reflected sourly, he was entangled with two women but in love with neither of them.

Enervated by the realization and anxious about what was happening in the world outside their wooded hillside, Barea rose to his feet. There was a five o'clock train back to the city, he said, and he wanted to be on it. Maria poutingly accompanied him down the hill to the little village in the valley, where they stopped for a beer at the station café and Barea chatted briefly with an acquaintance he found there, a printer he'd met at Socialist party meetings who spent summers in the village for his health. A couple of Civil Guards officers, their coats open and their patent-leather tricorne hats on the table, were playing cards by the window; just as Barea and Maria were leaving to catch the train, one of them rose, buttoning his coat, and followed them out into the road. Blocking their path, he asked Barea for his papers—and raised his eyebrows when he saw the gold cédula. How was it that a señorito like Barea was acquainted with a Red union man like the printer? he asked, suspicious. Something told Barea to lie and say they'd been boyhood friends; so although the officer patted him down for weapons, he let them go.

Later, Barea would learn how close a call he'd had: the next day the Guards took over the little village in the name of the rebels, and shot the printer by the side of the road. For the moment, though, all he knew was that when their train drew in to Madrid's North Station, he and Maria found themselves in a city transformed. Outside the station, traffic had come to a near-standstill, with trucks full of singing trade unionists going one way, fancy cars full of wealthy Madrileños and their luggage headed the other, toward the north and the border with France. There were roadblocks on the streets; people were saluting official Party cars as they passed with raised, clenched fists; and rifle-toting milicianos demanded Barea's and Maria's papers at every street corner. Over everything hung a pall of acrid smoke, the source of which he didn't discover until he'd dropped Maria off at the apartment she shared with her mother, brother, and younger sister, and hurried toward the Calle del Ave Maria. There he discovered the neighborhood's churches—including the one attached to the Escuela Pía, where he'd gone to school as a boy— engulfed in flames, the crowds gathered in front of them cheering as the ancient stones hissed and crackled and domes or towers crumbled into the streets. Some of the bystanders told him that fascists had been firing on the populace from the church towers, or storing arms in the sacristies; "and," said one, resorting to the slang description of the dark-cassocked priests, "there are too many of those black beetles anyhow." Barea had no great love for the organized church—its hand-in-glove relationship with big landowners, big bankers, and big ship-owners, its institutional wealth in a land so full of poverty, its anti-intellectual orthodoxy—but this wholesale destruction sickened him. He went home to Aurelia and the children with a heavy heart.

The next morning, he was awakened at first light by the sound of shouting in the street. Running downstairs, he learned that during the night a huge crowd had arrayed itself around the Montaña Barracks, a fortress overlooking the Manzanares a little over a mile away on the west of town, where rebel officers had barricaded themselves with five thousand troops and a cache of weapons. It was thought that the officers had been preparing to launch a concerted attack on the capital with other rebel garrisons in the city; but now air force officers loyal to the Republic had begun bombing the barracks, and cannons mounted on beer trucks had been brought to fire at the walls. Both eager and afraid to find out what would happen there, Barea hitched a ride with some *milicianos* to the Calle de Ferraz, which ran alongside the barracks parade grounds where he'd drilled sixteen years ago as a conscript bound for Morocco.

He found the fortress ringed by what looked like thousands of people; the air was crackling with rifle fire and the explosive rattle of machine guns. Quickly he dodged behind a tree—it was crazy to be here without a weapon, he realized, but he couldn't imagine being anywhere else when so much hung in the balance. In front of him two men were arguing over whose turn it was to shoot an ancient revolver at the barracks' massive walls; farther off, an officer of the Assault Guards, the urban police, was ordering that a 7.5-centimeter field gun be moved from place to place so the rebels in the fortress would believe their attackers had many cannon instead of few. Suddenly a white flag fluttered at one of the barracks windows; scenting surrender, the crowd surged forward, sweeping Barea along with it. But just as suddenly, machine-gun fire erupted from the walls; on either side of Barea attackers crumpled and fell to the ground. People screamed, ran, regrouped. Then, incredibly, they turned as one and with the aid of a huge battering ram threw themselves upon the barracks gates, which burst open under the onslaught.

The assault carried Barea himself inside the walls. In the barracks yard all was chaos: people shouting, running, firing. Looking up to one of the galleries ringing the yard, he saw one of the invaders, a huge Goliath of a man, pick up one soldier, then another, and hurl them like rag dolls from the parapet to the pavement below. In the armory, *milicianos* were seizing crates full of rifles and pistols and passing them out to their waiting comrades. Across the yard, a grimmer sight met his eyes: in the officers' mess, dozens of uniformed men—some of them hardly older than Barea's eldest son—lay in pools of their own blood.

Barea left the barracks, the exhilaration he'd felt during the assault ebbing away. Outside, on the grassy parade ground, there were hundreds more corpses, both men and women, lying motionless under the midday sun. Making his way into the public gardens on the Calle de Ferraz, all he could think of was how quiet it was.

For the next few days Barea went through the motions of normal life. He showed up at the office, where he and his chief decided that, despite the unexplained disappearance of some of their colleagues, and the absence of mail service, they'd try to keep things running for as long as anyone had patents to register or protect. He came home at night to Aurelia and the children. But things were emphatically not normal. In some of the offices in their building on the Calle de Alcalá, business owners had deserted their companies, taking their assets out of the country; others, known to be fascist sympathizers, would probably have their companies seized. In either case, the staff or a union committee would soon be running things, not the bosses—or so said the *milicianos* who turned up in the building on Tuesday, going from office to office, checking who was there and what they did. Everywhere you looked, in fact, there were more of these volunteer soldiers—men and women, dressed in blue boiler suits and tasseled caps, rifles slung over their shoulders, all of them throwing the clenched-fist salute of the Popular Front. Truckloads of them left for the Sierra in the mornings to skirmish with rebel forces who were trying to advance on Madrid from the northwest; others stayed in the city, stopping people at checkpoints on the street, asking for papers. On his way home one evening Barea had to dodge gunfire while some of them chased a suspected fascist over the rooftops; when he got back to Lavapiés it was to find more of them raiding the apartment of some rebel sympathizers and flinging the contents out the windows onto the street.

On Wednesday night, the government broadcast an announcement that the insurrection was all but defeated, and Barea went out for a celebratory toast at the Café de la Magdalena, the old flamenco cabaret, with his brother Miguel. But he was repelled by the café's crowd of pimps and prostitutes, and the boozy laborers, each with a new pistol jammed into the belt of his coveralls, half of them singing the "Internationale," the Communist anthem, as if it were a drinking song, the other half drowning the Communists out with Anarchist slogans and threatening to start a fight. So he and Miguel went to Serafín's tavern on Calle del Ave Maria, where Barea found himself talking to a stranger who said he'd spent the day rounding up fascists before taking them to the Casa de Campo, the wild, heathlike park on the other side of the Manzanares that used to be the king's hunting preserve and was still home to wild animals. "We led them out like sheep," the man boasted. "One shot in the neck and that was that."

Suddenly the sultry summer night felt chilly. "But that's all the government's affair now, isn't it?" Barea asked.

"Pal," said the stranger, looking at him with hard eyes, "—the government, that's us."

Barea paid his bill and left. As he turned toward home he heard shouts and running footsteps at the top of the street; then a shot rang out, followed by more footsteps that faded into the distance. Some *milicianos* came from the corner to investigate. In the middle of the street lay a man wearing the black-and-red scarf of the anarchist FAI, a bullet hole in the center of his forehead. One of the *milicianos* held a lighted match in front of the man's mouth; it didn't flicker. "One less," said the officer.

Afterward, Barea couldn't sleep. He got out of bed and went out onto the balcony: the city was pulsating with heat and the sound of people's radios, turned to top volume. *I can't keep drifting*, he told himself. In less than a week the fascists' rebellion had triggered the very revolution they had spent the past five years resisting. And working together, the armed workers and the government's own forces had prevented an immediate fascist victory. Despite the government's optimistic claims, however, it was clear that the revolt was far from finished. This was a civil war, not just between the rebels and the government, but among the factions supporting the government; it wouldn't be over until Spain had been transformed—whether into a fascist or a socialist state, Barea wasn't certain. But he knew he had to make a stand. Not with the pseudo-soldiers of the militia, or the self-appointed vigilantes; still less with the rabble he'd seen earlier in the café. *They won't fight*, he thought; *but they'll steal and kill for pleasure.* He'd have to find his own way to be of use. Sitting on the balcony, he vowed to isolate himself in that work, whatever it was, away from the straitjacket of getting and spending, away from the claims of Aurelia and Maria, until the battle was won or lost. He didn't know, couldn't know, how much this effort would change him—what he would lose by it, and what he would gain. But he did know he had to dedicate himself to it. *A new life*, he told himself, *has begun.*

July 1936: London/Paris

Martha Gellhorn hated getting up for breakfast. But when you're some-one's houseguest, and the someone wants you to have breakfast with him every day, it's only good manners to oblige—particularly if you're an ambitious young writer and your host is a famous man of letters who has found you a publisher and personally negotiated an unusually favorable contract with him on your behalf.

H. G. Wells, the British author of the science fiction classics *The Time Machine* and *The War of the Worlds* and the bestselling *The Outline of History*, among many other books, was, at seventy, old enough to be the twenty-seven-year-old Gellhorn's grandfather. He was also short, pot-bellied, red-faced, with a raggedy toothbrush mustache and a rather high squeaky voice, certainly not obvious suitor material for a long-legged, well-heeled blond American girl from St. Louis who, by her own account, "had a constant supply of attractive young gents" vying to take her out. But they had met while both were staying with Franklin and Eleanor Roosevelt at the White House—Gellhorn's mother, Edna, a prominent St. Louis social reformer and clubwoman, was a friend of the First Lady's—and he'd formed an extravagant crush on her. He called her "Stooge," advised her on her writing, paid her a small retainer to keep him up to date on news and trends in America, and sent her flirtatious letters, some decorated with suggestive drawings, outlining various amorous wish-fulfillment scenarios ("A sunny beach . . . Stooge very much in love with me and me all in love with Stooge, nothing particularly ahead except a far off dinner, some moonlight & bed—Stooge's bed"). And Martha, who in the summer of 1936 was both between jobs and between men, privately admitted she was flattered by his attentions.

Restless and hungry for life, she'd left her mother's alma mater, Bryn Mawr College, at the end of her junior year to become a freelance writer, covering the city desk for the *Albany Times-Union* and writing travel stories for the *St. Louis Post-Dispatch*, before transplanting herself to Paris in the spring of 1930. There she'd embarked on a four-year affair with Bertrand de Jouvenel, the elegant, well-connected journalist stepson (and also, briefly and scandalously, the lover) of the legendary Colette. The romance introduced Martha to the salons of *le Tout-Paris* where politics, culture, society, and fashion mingled; soon she was wearing Schiaparelli suits, hobnobbing with highly placed government ministers, and working in the Paris office of *Vogue*.

But there were problems: Bertrand was married, his wife wouldn't give him a divorce, his emotional neediness made Martha claustrophobic, and the relationship caused a painful rift with her parents, in particular with her father, an otherwise free-thinking gynecologist, who acidly told her that "there are two kinds of women, and you're the other kind." In 1934 she and Bertrand called it quits; Martha returned to the United States, where she went to work for the Federal Emergency Relief Administration, reporting from rural counties and small towns all across America on the desolate conditions of people trying to survive the Depression. Appalled by the poverty, disease, and privation she found in a country where nearly a quarter of the nation was still out of work, she took her distress to the White House dinner table—"Franklin, talk to that girl," fluted Mrs. Roosevelt to her husband; "she says all the unemployed have pellagra and syphilis"—and managed to get herself fired for inciting a riot by a group of Idaho laborers whose sufferings she was chronicling.

In the meantime she'd also published a novel, a quasi-autobiographical chick-lit bildungsroman about three college girls looking for sex and the meaning of life but instead finding disillusion and the clap. Originally she'd intended to call it *Nothing Ever Happens*, with a nod to a line from Ernest Hemingway's *A Farewell to Arms*—"nothing ever happens to the brave"; but by the time it was published she'd settled on *What Mad Pursuit*, swapping Hemingway for Keats. The novel wasn't well reviewed, nor did it sell, and her father hated it. Martha was crushed, to her own surprise.

"It has meant more to me than I would have believed, that my book is a failure," she wrote to de Jouvenel. Determined to get it right—to "write great heavy swooping things [that] throw terror and glory into the mind"— she'd begun another project, a linked series of fictional portraits of the Depression's victims, among them a labor organizer, a preteen child prostitute, and a grandmother on relief, called *The Trouble I've Seen*. It was this book for which Wells had procured her an English publisher, and its appearance, first in London and later in New York and Paris, was greeted with admiring press, including several mentions in Eleanor Roosevelt's widely read syndicated column, "My Day." Even her father approved; unfortunately, soon after reading the manuscript he died suddenly, of heart failure following surgery, in January 1936.

Martha had been living in New York, trying to get a staff job at *Time* magazine, submitting ideas for pieces about Europe to *The New Yorker*, and carrying on an affair with a *Time* writer named Allen Grover, who like de Jouvenal was married and showed no inclination to leave his wife. When her father died, and neither *Time* nor *The New Yorker* offered her employment, she decided to cut her losses and run. During her romance with Bertrand she'd toyed with the outlines of a novel about the French and German pacifists they knew—the young internationalists in both countries who were determined not to repeat the holocaust of World War I, no matter the provocation; maybe now was a good time to return to Europe to make a start on it.

In London she cadged an invitation to stay in Wells's beautiful house in Regent's Park, which she intended to use as a base in between her evenings out with the young men she seemed to collect on her travels. Fortunately, whatever his amorous fantasies about her, Wells was safely enmeshed in a long affair with Moura Budberg, Maxim Gorky's former mistress, and during her visit seemed content to behave more like a mentor than a paramour. He told her he believed in her talent but felt it needed discipline, and he surprised her by insisting not only that she rise at eight to breakfast with him, but that she buckle down to work for several hours afterward, as he did.

Martha was annoyed—that kind of regimen wasn't for *her*, she sniffed, "not then or ever"—so she decided to get back at him by beating him at his own game. One morning, after the breakfast table had been cleared, she went out into the garden with her little portable typewriter and started tapping away. Before lunchtime she had dashed off a short, pungent piece called "Justice at Night," an account of what happened when she and a companion (Bertrand de Jouvenel, although she called him "Joe" in the piece) were witnesses to the lynching of a seventeen-year-old black share-cropper outside of Columbia, Mississippi, not far from the Louisiana border. Like *The Trouble I've Seen*, "Justice at Night" displayed the sharp eye for precise detail and the clear, cool, seemingly neutral reportorial voice Gellhorn had developed in her short journalistic career, a voice that made the lurid narrative all the more shocking by contrast. Wells loved the piece and thought it should be published immediately, so Martha sent it to her London agent, who in turn sold it to *The Spectator* for fifty dollars; in the United States, *Reader's Digest* bought the rights and it would later be reprinted by another U.S. periodical, *The Living Age*. She'd certainly shown Wells what she could do if she set her mind to it.

There was only one thing wrong with this success story, however: Martha hadn't actually seen the atrocity she wrote about so vividly. She hadn't heard the victim "making a terrible sound, like a dog whimpering"; she hadn't smelled the kerosene with which the onlookers doused the body of the hanged man, nor the sizzling flames nor the burning flesh. In fact, although she and Bertrand had indeed taken a road trip through the Cotton Belt on their way to California in 1931, they'd never come within miles of a lynching. But Martha *had* spent time in the poor backcountry South; she'd driven those dusty roads, talked to those angry white farmers and downtrodden black sharecroppers; in North Carolina, when she was working for FERA, she'd once got a lift from a truck driver who said he was on his way home from "a necktie party"—the slang term for stringing up a black man without benefit of the law. Sometime later she'd met a man whose son had been lynched. It was just a *little* step, wasn't it, from there to writing about this fictional incident as if it had really happened? In any case, Martha didn't give the matter a second thought: once she had the *Spectator's* check, she left for Paris to begin research for her proposed pacifist novel.

She arrived on a continent much changed from the place she'd left two years before. Germany had become an increasingly bellicose and anti-Semitic dictatorship whose ruler, Adolf Hitler, had illegally sent troops in March to occupy the Rhineland, the buffer area along France's north-eastern border that had been set aside as a demilitarized zone by postwar treaty. Some of the idealistic pacifists who had formed part of her and Bertrand's set, such as the novelist Pierre Drieu de la Rochelle, had now veered politically to the right, saying that the only real enemies of peace were the Communists and the Jews. Even Bertrand himself managed to look like an apologist for the Nazis when, trying to promote the *rapprochement* with Germany that he felt might ensure peace, he published an interview with Hitler in which the Führer said that he *loved* France, despite what he'd written in *Mein Kampf* about its being "the mortal enemy of our nation."

In the meantime, the Depression had caught up to France in earnest; the streets of Paris were full of the unemployed and the homeless; and armed fascist hooligans, some in uniform, were increasingly preying on anyone whose politics, ethnicity, or appearance they didn't like. In fact, they had nearly killed the Socialist leader Léon Blum—a professorial-looking former theater critic, and a Jew—in the days before the general elections, dragging him from his car and beating him half to death. In the end, however, Blum's Popular Front coalition had been victorious, and the new government proceeded to give workers the right to organize, the right to strike, and the right to a forty-hour workweek with two weeks of paid vacation every year. The right-wing daily *Le Temps* complained that Blum had ushered in "the dictatorship of the proletariat" but the very best, most expensive restaurants were still so full they had to turn people away; although the newly legitimized strikes disrupted the collections at most of the couture houses, Martha's beloved Schiaparelli had a triumphant season, accessorizing many of her ensembles with a Phrygian cap modeled on the one worn by the Revolutionaries of the 1790s.

Martha herself wasted no time in buying a smart new wardrobe and a paletteful of fashionable face paint; but she found the atmosphere in Paris "vile." There were too many "gloomy rich" people complaining that guests at the strike-torn Hotel Crillon, or the Ritz or the George-V, had to make their own beds. Weary of privileged self-pity, she decamped for Germany, where she began research for her novel in archives in Stuttgart and Munich. Germany, however, seemed more poisonous than Paris, "a foreign caricature of itself," full of uniforms and salutes. Signs everywhere announced "*Juden verboten*"—a slap in the face to Martha, both of whose parents were half Jewish; in Stuttgart she saw uniformed Nazis jeering at an elderly (probably Jewish) couple who had been forced to scrub paving stones and watched the mousy librarian cringe in terror before the boorish young "brownshirt" who had recently been appointed her superior. The newspapers were full of belligerent hate speech, which reached a crescendo with the first bulletins about fighting in Spain—the result, the papers said, of mob rule by "Red Swine Dogs." Disgusted, Martha decided she couldn't stay in Germany any longer, or even in Europe.

"Europe is finished for me," she would write to Allen Grover. "A lot of things are finished"—her old life among *le Tout-Paris*; the casual affairs with men who gave her "company, laughter, movement" but not passion; even, maybe, her pacifism, and her pacifist novel. She had intended to spend time touring the Great War killing fields in France and Flanders, but now she would go home to St. Louis, where she'd spend the long, dark winter keeping her widowed mother company. St. Louis was a good place for waiting. She wasn't sure what would happen next, but she was confident something would. For despite all the strangeness and anxiety she'd encountered in France and Germany—the feeling that the War to End War might be followed by the War to End Europe—the trip had done her good, she felt. It had given her a chance to exhale and relax. Now, she told Grover, she was ready to "start all over."

July 1936: Paris

On Sunday, July 12, a young man with a camera hanging from his shoulder got off the train from Paris in Verdun, on the Meuse River 130 miles northeast of the capital. Of medium height, with a shock of dark hair, black eyebrows, and the face of a gypsy, he was somewhat shabbily dressed, in an old leather jacket and much-worn shoes. His French was fluent, but his accent hinted at somewhere in Middle Europe—not surprisingly, since he'd been born in Budapest twenty-two years before, as Endre Erno Friedmann. That wasn't the name on the press card he carried in the pocket of the weather-beaten jacket, though; there he was listed as André Friedmann. But for the past few months he'd been calling himself Robert Capa.

Luckily, Capa's camera wasn't in the pawnshop, as it often was when he needed cash, because today he had an assignment from one of the smaller Paris agencies to photograph an event that all the European newspapers and magazines would want to cover: the peace demonstration taking place outside Verdun, where for eleven months in 1916 German and French troops had fought the longest and costliest battles of the Great War. Nearly 300,000 men had died there: 13,000 of them were buried beneath the white crosses that dotted the green grass of the French military cemetery, with the remains of a further 130,000, all unidentifiable, contained in an ossuary nearby. Now, on a gray, chilly July day twenty years after the battle, more than seventy thousand "Peace Pilgrims," veterans and noncombatants from fourteen countries—including a phalanx of Germans marching under a flag bearing a huge swastika and throwing the Nazi salute—were gathering to honor the dead and to pledge that their sacrifice would not be repeated.

There were occasional spatters of rain as an honor guard of three wounded veterans carried the ceremonial torch, which had been lit in Paris from the eternal flame beneath the Arc de Triomphe, to the Douaumont ossuary. Capa caught them with his Leica: three unsmiling middle-aged men in carefully brushed dark suits, each wearing a beret against the chill, two of them blinded, gripping their canes, their free hands touching the torchbearer's shoulders for guidance. They had been Capa's age when they lost their sight.

As dusk began to fall, Capa followed the crowd of Peace Pilgrims into the floodlit cemetery, where each former combatant took his place behind one of the white crosses that marked the graves. *Click, click, click* went Capa's camera as each veteran laid a single flower on the mound before him. A trumpet called from the ossuary, and was answered by the boom of a cannon. Then silence, followed by a second cannon salute. From the loudspeakers at the corners of the cemetery came the order to cease fire, doubly poignant on this occasion. Into the echoing stillness a child's voice spoke: *For the peace of the world.* And the assembled thousands swore aloud, each in their own language, to ensure the peace for which the dead had made the ultimate sacrifice.

When Capa at last headed back to Paris he knew he had some good pictures in his camera; he knew, too, that the odds were stacked against the promises the Peace Pilgrims had just made so solemnly. He'd seen enough of the world to figure out what was coming: he might be only twenty-two, but he was already a political refugee twice over. As a teenager in Budapest—son of a spendthrift carriage-trade dressmaker and his hardworking wife—he'd gotten involved in avant-garde and antifascist circles, joining in demonstrations against Admiral Miklós Horthy's iron-fisted and anti-Semitic regime; shortly before he passed his final examinations he'd made the mistake of being seen talking to a known Communist Party recruiter. That night Horthy's secret police picked him up and took him for "questioning" to headquarters, where his interrogator, an officer with a taste for Beethoven, whistled the Fifth Symphony while beating him up in time to the music. In an act of teenage bravado he'd laughed at his tormentor, after which two thugs knocked him senseless and threw him into a cell; the next morning, since there was no hard evidence against him, they'd turned him loose with orders to leave the country as soon as possible.

So he'd gone to Berlin, whose Weimar-era adventurousness had only just begun to be tainted by encroaching Nazi brutality, and enrolled in journalism classes at the Hochschule für Politik, where all the young bohemians went; but hard times put an end to the allowance he'd been receiving from his parents, and he had to drop out of school. Hungry, homeless, desperate for money, he talked himself into a job as a darkroom assistant at Dephot, one of the agencies that had sprung up to supply the new illustrated magazines and newspaper supplements that suddenly seemed to be everywhere. His good eye and his eagerness earned him a few small assignments, and then came a big break: Sent to cover a Copenhagen speech by the exiled Russian leader Leon Trotsky, he smuggled his flash-less little Leica into the lecture hall, where bulky box cameras, which might have concealed a gun, were prohibited, and captured Trotsky at the podium at point-blank range. *Der Welt Spiegel* gave his dramatic pictures a full page—*with* a credit—but his triumph was short-lived. Three months later, Adolf Hitler, riding a tide of anti-Semitic nationalism, was appointed chancellor of Germany; a month after that, the new government suspended all civil liberties, banned publications "unfriendly" to the National Socialists—the Nazis—and started rounding up Communists, Social Democrats, liberals, and Jews. Berlin, already unsettled, was now unsafe, and André Friedmann was on the run again.

Like many other refugees from Nazism, he ended up in Paris; despite the French economic downturn, it was still the place where everything was happening—art, theater, literature, philosophy, fashion, *le jazz hot.* As an émigré, however, he couldn't get a regular job when so many Frenchmen were out of work, so he subsisted on a variety of short-term, low-paying gigs, cadging meals or money or cigarettes from acquaintances, shoplifting the occasional loaf of bread or tin of sardines, or making do with sugar dissolved in water, a trick he'd learned in his lean times in Berlin. That was when the Crédit Municipal pawnshop came in handy—he used to say he'd left his camera "chez ma tante"; when the money from his "aunt," the pawnbroker, ran out he'd simply slip out of whatever cheap Left Bank hotel room he'd been calling home for the past few months (chronically behind on the rent, but with such charming excuses to the proprietor) and leave his few belongings behind, never to return.

Despite his poverty, he was proud; even if he had to ask for a handout he did it as if it didn't matter whether he got it or not. "Why work at little things that bring no money?" he'd say, scornfully. "Wait for the big things, the big moment you can sell." When he *did* make money there would be drinks for everyone at the Dôme, at the crossroads of the Boulevard Montparnasse and the Boulevard Raspail—La Coupole, just down the street, was too expensive; or dinner at La Diamenterie, the Middle Eastern restaurant on the rue Lafayette. For by this time he had a group of pals, *copains*, that included the refugee Pole David Szymin, a chess-playing staff photographer for the Communist weekly paper *Regards*, whom everyone called Chim; his own boyhood friend from Budapest, Geza Korvin Karpathi; and Henri Cartier-Bresson, the son of a prosperous Normandy textile merchant, who'd started out to be a painter before being seduced by photography.

Then, one day, there was Gerda, or Gerta, as she spelled it then: a petite green-eyed girl with artfully arched eyebrows and hennaed hair cut short like a boy's and a sharp little face—"like a fox that is going to play a trick on you," said a friend of his later. He'd met her through her roommate, a German secretary named Ruth Cerf, whom he'd asked to pose for some advertising photos he was shooting. Cerf, put off by his scruffy appearance—*I'm not going anywhere alone with this guy*, she told herself; *he looks like a tramp*—had brought Gerda with her as a chaperone; to Cerf's surprise, the chaperone and the scruffy photographer hit it off immediately.

They had nothing, and everything, in common. Like him, she was Jewish—but her father, a Pole named Heinrich Pohorylle, was a prosperous egg merchant in Stuttgart, not an improvident Hungarian dressmaker. She'd been expensively educated, following *gymnasium* with a fancy Swiss finishing school, where she learned French, English, and the art of making influential friends; then business college, where she took Spanish and typing. Smart, vivacious, ambitious, and chic—as a teenager she'd always worn high heels to her classes, even when on a field trip to Lake Constance— she was already skilled at keeping several men on a string simultaneously. While still in school she'd become engaged to a wealthy thirty-five-year-old cotton trader, then disengaged when she got involved with a charismatic Marxist medical student, Georg Kuritzkes, a member of the German Socialist Workers' Party, or SAP (Sozialistische Arbeiterpartei). Kuritzkes introduced her to his crowd of committed young SAP activists, among them a strong-jawed youth named Herbert Frahm, who would later change his name to Willy Brandt; and one of the SAP boys—another medical student, Willi Chardack—also fell for her. "I just have to wiggle my little finger to have five or six guys after me," she wrote to a friend, amusedly. "I'm continually amazed that it's possible to be in love with two men at the same time—but I'd be an idiot to wonder why."

She and André Friedmann had both had brushes with the fascist police, too; and like him she'd refused to be cowed by the experience. Held in prison for two weeks after helping to write, edit, and distribute anti-Nazi leaflets before the 1933 German parliamentary elections, she'd shared smuggled cigarettes with the other women inmates, taught them American popular songs, and showed them how to communicate with each other during lockdown by tapping on the walls of their cells—all the while telling her captors she was just a silly girl who didn't know anything about politics. When an outraged letter from the Polish consul at last secured her release (technically, she was a Polish citizen) she fled to Paris, but the city was hardly more hospitable to her than it had been to the young Hungarian photographer. Even though she found friends from Germany such as Ruth Cerf and Willi Chardack, she couldn't get a residency permit, so she had to work off the books as a secretary for starvation wages. The room she shared with Ruth was so cold, and they had so little money for food, that on winter weekends they'd stay in bed all day to keep warm and conserve energy before venturing out to their favorite haunt, the café La Capoulade on the corner of the Boulevard Saint-Michel and the rue Soufflot, where they could huddle next to one of the huge charcoal braziers to talk politics and philosophy.

Maybe because Gerta preferred the company of the Sorbonne students, political theorists, and exiled SAP members at the Capoulade, while André liked the more freewheeling artistic atmosphere at the Dôme, they saw little of each other in the months after their first meeting, although Gerta did give him story ideas and big-sisterly advice about what clothes to wear or what to read. (Left to himself, he'd read detective stories; she was more inclined to books like John Dos Passos's epic modernist novels *Manhattan Transfer* and *1919*, the story of John Reed, "the last of the great race of war correspondents who ducked under censorship and risked their skins for a story.") By this time she was in a liaison with Willi Chardack—her old flame Georg Kuritzkes had gone to study medicine in Italy—while André was having a desultory affair with a striking redhaired German fashion photographer named Regina Langquarz, who called herself Relang and sometimes let André use her darkroom. But in the spring of 1935, while he was in Spain shooting two assignments for his old Dephot boss, he'd written Gerta a letter in which, after describing the Holy Week celebrations in Seville where "half [the people] are drunk [and] the crowd is so thick that one can get away with fondling the breasts of all the señoritas," he confessed that "sometimes . . . I'm completely in love with you."

Gerta kept him at arm's length until that summer; but then she invited him to accompany her and Willi Chardack—with whom she was no longer romantically involved—and another male friend to the tiny island of Ste. Marguérite in the south of France, a half-hour's ferry ride from Cannes. For almost three months the four young people lived on tinned sardines and slept in tents under the umbrella pines near the fortress where the Man in the Iron Mask had been imprisoned; during the long sunlit days they rambled over the island's *garrigue* or swam in the sea, and André taught Gerta how to use his camera. Soon the two of them had become lovers. When they returned to Paris in the fall, suntanned and inseparable, André told the Hungarian photographer André Kertesz, who had become a mentor, "Never before in my whole life have I been so happy!"

Gerta took him in hand, as if he were a school project. "It's impossible how you live," she told him. Together they found a modern one-room apartment in the Seventh Arrondissement with a view of the Eiffel Tower; although its divan bed was so narrow they couldn't both sleep on their backs at the same time, it had a tiny kitchen where they could prepare meals ("I do the washing up and break all the glasses," he wrote to his mother), so they spent less time (and money) in cafés. They began working together, André shooting photographs and Gerta typing up accompanying stories to submit to magazines, or Gerta taking photographs and André making enlargements; soon he got her a full-time job as a sales representative for the photo agent Maria Eisner, his friend from Berlin days. "Because Gerta is so pretty, the editors buy from her," he boasted; and it didn't hurt that she spoke three languages and could negotiate with foreign clients. She'd already persuaded André to start wearing a necktie and have his hair cut—"It has a part in it, and I am shaved to hell," he half-complained; now she spent one of her early paychecks to buy him a winter coat.

Gerta wasn't like any girl he'd ever had before; she was sensual and direct, with no sense of *pudeur*. She'd entertain friends while she was half-naked, bathing or dressing; and her enjoyment of their lovemaking seemed uncomplicated by anxiety that she might get pregnant—probably because she had a clever gynecologist who made such fears irrelevant. André was devastated when their relationship hit a bad patch in December—maybe, some of their friends thought, he was upset that Gerta slept with other men if she felt like it. Others thought she was pressuring him to be more committed politically, and he jokingly resisted: *ugh, those Party girls are too ugly for me*. In any case Gerta moved out; André, desolate, ill, and in despair over a temporary lack of work, considered abandoning photography altogether. By the spring, though, they'd made up—if you loved Gerta, you forgave her, no matter what—and they were living, and working, together again, in a room at the Hôtel de Blois in the rue Vavin. André had scored a contract with Maria Eisner's Alliance Photo agency that paid him a thousand francs a month for shooting enough material for three *reportages* a week.

But he and Gerta wanted more, and faster; and in April they cooked up a brilliant plan. They would reinvent themselves as "Robert Capa," a rich, famous (and imaginary) American photographer, whose pictures would actually be taken by André, with Gerta, in her job at Alliance, cutting deals for their publication with magazines and newspapers. "What, you don't know who he is?" she'd ask derisively; and then, because "Capa" was so famous, demand that editors pay three times the prevailing rate for his photographs. If anyone wanted to actually meet the elusive lensman, she'd put them off by saying, "That bastard has run off to the Côte d'Azur again with an actress."

At the same time as this pseudonym made its debut, Gerta also decided to give *herself* a new name: Gerda Taro. Like "Robert Capa," it was short, glamorous, of indeterminate ethnicity, the sort of name that makes you think you must already have heard of it. *Oh, of course, Gerda Taro. Isn't she a movie star? A poet? A photographer?* Writing to his mother about his own transformation, Capa said, "It is like being born again (but this time without hurting anybody!)." He might have been writing about Gerda as well. From this time on each acquired a secondary self, a cosmopolitan, successful doppelgänger that was all they had each strived to be, and were now becoming.

For things were looking up: the strikes and Popular Front demonstrations of the spring were full of opportunities for the kind of vivid, visceral pictures that were becoming the young photographer's trademark. Then, in June, just before he went to Verdun to cover the peace demonstrations, the newly born Robert Capa had his first scoop. Italy had just invaded Abyssinia, and the country's deposed emperor, Haile Selassie, was appearing before the League of Nations to ask for sanctions against the invaders, something the League, in the end, declined to do. In Geneva to photograph the proceedings, Capa witnessed a much more compelling drama than the staid images of delegates the other news photographers focused on: the arrest of a protester, who was thrown into an open police car and bound and gagged right in front of Capa's camera. The resulting pictures, more than anyone else's, told you what was *really* going on in Geneva: that the League of Nations, designed to be a peaceful forum to settle international grievances, had become nothing but a place to silence them.

Not surprisingly, Lucien Vogel, editor of the weekly newsmagazine *Vu*, was eager to publish Capa's Geneva photos, but he wasn't fooled by Gerda's assertions about the man who'd taken them. "This is all very interesting about Robert Capa," he said dismissively—and then ordered her to send "that ridiculous boy Friedmann who goes around shooting pictures in a dirty leather jacket" to see him immediately. In the Paris magazine world this command was like a royal summons. Vogel, a balding, Proustian figure who favored stiff collars and waistcoats, was married to Cosette de Brunhoff, the editor of *Vogue*; before founding *Vu* he'd cut a swathe in the media world as an editor and art director of *Art et décoration* and *La Gazette du bon ton*. *Vu*, whose documentary images and dynamic

layouts gave the printed page the immediacy of a newsreel, had a circulation of almost half a million readers; under the art direction of the
Constructivist-influenced Alexander Liberman, it published all the best
photographers: Man Ray, Brassaï, Capa's mentor Kertesz, his friend Cartier-
Bresson, and others.

So the newly minted Robert Capa anxiously presented himself at
Vogel's sixteenth-century chateau, La Faisanderie, for one of the Sunday-
afternoon "at homes" to which all the *gratin* of the political and media
worlds were invited. And Vogel, who claimed that all he had to do was
stroll the length of his vast lawn with you before he knew whether you
belonged, took the young man by the arm for a chat. By the time they returned to the house, Capa had passed the lawn test: *Vu* published Capa's
pictures from Geneva, with a byline (by no means a usual occurrence), as
well as the photos he took of the raucous Popular Front celebrations in
Paris on Bastille Day, July 14.

Then, a week after he'd gone to Verdun to photograph the Peace
Pilgrims' demonstration, the first news came from Spain of an uprising by
the army against the government. At first, the reports were dismissive:
leftist papers claimed the rebellion was being "crushed," while more conservative ones said the situation was "confused." By the end of the week,
though, it was obvious that something very big was happening in Spain,
and both Capa and Taro—who had been shooting pictures herself and
developing them in a darkroom she shared with Capa and his friend
and colleague Chim in the rue Daguerre—felt the adrenaline rush of a
scoop in the making. Chim, in fact, had been in Spain all summer, and
was still there, working on a series of features about the political and
social situation—much as they loved him, why should he have a monopoly on this story?

Fortunately, Vogel seemed to agree. He immediately plunged into planning for a special issue of *Vu* devoted to the unfolding events in Spain,
which would call on the talents of a fleet of journalists, among them
Robert Capa and the as-yet-unpublished Gerda Taro. Vogel would give
them accreditation and charter a plane to fly them to Barcelona, after
which they'd fan out across the country to chronicle what was happening
there. On the strength of Vogel's offer, Gerda quit her job at Alliance, and
she and Capa set about getting the necessary papers for their trip. Here
was a chance to document the struggle between fascism and socialism

that was already consuming their homelands and might soon spread to all of Europe. It would all be a most extraordinary adventure, and it would make them famous. Together. They could hardly wait.

July 1936: Brno

Ilse Kulcsar had been underground for almost two years when she heard the news about Spain. Well, not underground *exactly*; she and Poldi—her husband, Leopold Kulcsar—went by their own names in this Czechoslovak university city, where they edited a leftist newspaper and met with the other Austrian political exiles who gathered in the coffeehouses near Masaryk University, smoking and talking about the precarious state of the world. But when they'd crossed the frontier into Czechoslovakia in November 1934, they'd done so with false passports; they knew that if either of them ever set foot in Austria again they'd be arrested and possibly executed—even though, or maybe because, Ilse's uncle by marriage, Johann Schober, a former chancellor of Austria, was currently president of police.

Living dangerously, however, is what they did: Ilse's father, a mild-mannered school headmaster and government councilor, described his daughter's existence as *a powder keg*. Always gifted and forthright—the words her father used were *passionate* and *turbulent*—Ilse had turned her back on the conventions of her Viennese childhood, the strolls in the Belvedere gardens, the afternoons at the opera, *kaffee mit schlag* at Sacher: instead of pursuing a degree in medicine or science, as her father hoped, or in music, her mother's choice, she'd enrolled in the new field of political science at the University of Vienna. Convinced that capitalism was doomed, she had joined the fledgling Communist Party of Austria. Because she was a persuasive speaker, the Party sent her to make presentations to workers' groups in Scandinavia (where she'd spent time as an exchange student as a child) and England. It was through the Party that she'd met Leopold Kulcsar, a blond working-class youth whose ice-blue eyes burned with a fierce intelligence that belied his lack of formal education. They were married with her parents' reluctant consent (they would only have lived together anyway, her father realized) and almost immediately got into trouble trying to smuggle Party funds across the Hungarian border to a Romanian opposition leader. Something had gone wrong, wrong enough that they were picked up by Horthy's secret police and thrown into jail in Budapest for four months. But the Party never lifted a finger to help them—it was Ilse's parents who scraped together money for lawyers to get them out of Hungary—so they'd quit in disgust.

That wasn't the end of their political involvement, however. Joining the more moderate Social Democratic Workers' Party, they'd dedicated themselves to writing and speaking against the efforts by Austria's chancellor, Engelbert Dolfuss, to break the power of the socialists—whose policies favoring worker housing, free clinics, and children's day care made them popular in Vienna and distrusted in the conservative, Catholic countryside. Then, in February 1934, fighting broke out in Vienna between armed militias of the conservatives (the *Heimwehr*, or Home Guard) and the socialists (the *Republikanischer Schutzbund*, or Republican Protection Association), and Dolfuss sent the army to fire on the socialists. Hundreds of people were killed and thousands more arrested; the Social Democratic Party was outlawed and its members hunted down; and the conservatives replaced Austria's constitutional democracy with an authoritarian regime modeled on Mussolini's. Kulcsar was briefly imprisoned, but he was released when he argued that he wasn't *involved* in the fighting, just covering it as a journalist. At that point he and Ilse made a fateful decision.

Using their apartment on the Herrengasse as a headquarters, they started a resistance cell that they called Der Funke, "The Spark," a translation of the name of Lenin's original revolutionary unit, *Iskra*. The idea was to get medical aid to victims of the fighting—many of whom had been hiding out in Vienna's sewers for weeks—and spirit them and others out of the country with false papers. Der Funke would also stay in illicit contact with the exiled Social Democratic leaders and bring in underground literature from abroad. All of this would cost money, more money than two impecunious journalists could scrounge up, so they were glad to recruit as a member a young American heiress named Muriel Gardiner, who had come to Vienna to study psychoanalysis with Sigmund Freud and would become a valuable colleague of theirs. Another member was an English economics student, Hugh Gaitskell, later head of Britain's Labour Party; not officially *in* the cell, but in contact with it, were two other Englishmen, one a tall, blond, pink-faced poet, Stephen Spender, who (somewhat surprisingly, since his previous relationships had all been with men) was having an affair with

Muriel Gardiner, the other a dark, extremely charming aspiring journalist, recently married to an Austrian girl who, like him, was a Communist. His name was Harold Adrian Russell Philby, but everyone called him Kim.

The Spark was successful at first, using contacts in England to channel aid from British trade unions, and getting the word out about what had really happened in Vienna. But then the unthinkable happened. The Austrian police arrested a courier that the group used to carry money, messages, and illegal documents between Vienna and their exiled leadership in Brno, and through the courier—who was having a romance with the Kulcsars' maid—Ilse and Poldi's cover was blown. It would be only a matter of hours before they were picked up and imprisoned, or worse. Fleeing to a little inn in the mountains two hours south of Vienna, where Ilse had spent carefree summers as a child, they waited for terrifying days until Muriel Gardiner could bring them the false papers they needed to escape. Finally, near midnight on a stormy evening, she appeared—soaked to the skin, having traveled by bus and on foot up the icy road in the rain to deliver the precious documents; the next day, with their photographs neatly inserted into two strangers' passports, Ilse and Poldi crossed the Czech border and made their way to Brno.

That was in November 1934, and nearly two years of life in exile had been hard. Ilse missed her family, and Brno's medieval alleyways and sleek new Bauhaus apartment buildings made her homesick for her beloved Baroque Vienna. She and Poldi were working together to launch a new, multinational socialist review for which she planned to write, and that was exciting; but the rootlessness and petty infighting in their circle of émigrés were wearing Ilse down. Developments in Germany, where Hitler had just occupied the Rhineland and was making noises about annexing northern Czechoslovakia, were far from reassuring; things were worse at home, where Dolfuss (having eliminated the leftist opposition) had been assassinated by Austrian Nazis and, Muriel Gardiner reported, many of their former associates were being arrested.

But the real trouble, for Ilse, was with her husband. There was the business of the money: back in Vienna, Poldi had been the bookkeeper for the Spark, and before they left he'd apparently started skimming off some of its funds into a special account he had—for what? There was his domineering streak, his need to tell her what to do, what to think. Then there were his contacts with a shadowy network of operatives in Germany and elsewhere, in which he used the code-name "Maresch." Most ominous of all was the new hardness he'd begun to demonstrate: speaking of a comrade he suspected might be a turncoat, he'd said, with a look that blended pleasure and cruelty, "If it is true, we shall have to put him out of the way."

Into the anxious fog that surrounded her, the bulletins from Spain—the army's attempted coup, the government's resistance, and even more the revolutionary changes that were taking place in the wake of the rebellion—came like a ray of clear light. In Spain fascism was being openly confronted, not accepted, or appeased, or explained, or ignored; people were *acting* on their convictions, instead of endlessly talking about them, as her and Poldi's friends seemed to do. Perhaps, she thought, she could find a way to get to Madrid, where she could volunteer as a writer, an editor, a translator—there must be some use for the six languages she spoke—and start fresh, doing work that mattered. A new life! It seemed just barely possible.

July 1936: Key West

On July 17, the cruiser *Pilar*, thirty-eight feet long with a black hull, green roof, and mahogany cockpit, tied up in Key West harbor after a six-week fishing trip to Bimini; and its captain, Ernest Hemingway—burly, dark, unshaven, in his usual Key West getup of dirty shorts and torn T-shirt—made his way home to the big house on Whitehead Street that he shared with his second wife, Pauline, and their two sons, Patrick and Gregory. The Bimini trip had been a fine one. To begin with, Hemingway had hooked a 514-pound, eleven-foot-long tuna off Gun Cay, and after a seven-hour battle—Hemingway had sweated away more than a pound an hour hauling on the lines—he'd managed to land it, still full of fight, thirty miles away from where he'd started; by the time he got back to port he'd drunk so much beer and whiskey he could hardly stand, but somehow he pulled the fish up on stays on the dock and proceeded to use it for a punching bag. Almost as good as the fishing were the couple of meetings he'd had with an editor from *Esquire* magazine, Arnold Gingrich, who suggested he make a novel out of a couple of short stories he'd written about a renegade Caribbean rumrunner called Harry Morgan—a book that, both men felt, would put Hemingway back on top of the literary world where he belonged.

In the early 1920s, in Paris, when he had lived in the cramped flat above the sawmill in the rue Notre Dame des Champs with his first wife, Hadley, and their baby son, John, nicknamed Bumby, and his first collection of short prose sketches (with its bravely uncapitalized title), *in our time*, had been published by one of the little presses, no one had been more innovative, more exciting, or more admired among the Lost Generation literati than Hemingway. And when *The Sun Also Rises*, his novel about angst-ridden expatriates in Paris and Pamplona, appeared in 1926, followed three years later by the tersely elegiac Great War love story *A Farewell to Arms*, no writer had seemed so successful. His spare, clean prose and his clear-eyed presentation of unvarnished subject matter that he knew from personal experience—"All you have to do is write one true sentence," he would say; "write the truest sentence that you know"— seemed to set him apart from all who had come before him; in consequence he'd been rewarded with critical praise, robust book sales, and record-setting magazine fees. For the past three years *Esquire*, for which he'd been writing articles about such far-flung places as the Caribbean and Kenya, had been giving him an audience of half a million readers a month. And when *A Farewell to Arms* was made into a movie starring Gary Cooper and Helen Hayes, Hemingway became even more of a celebrity than before.

With fame had come fortune: and not just, or even principally, from his earnings as a writer. Pauline Hemingway, née Pfeiffer—dark, *gamine*, quick-witted, tart-tongued—was the wealthy daughter of one of the richest landowners in the state of Arkansas, and the niece of a childless pharmaceutical czar whose greatest pleasure was to give her (and her husband) presents. The green-shuttered stone house on Whitehead Street ($12,500)? Out came Uncle Gus's checkbook. A big-game safari in Africa, complete with guides and private planes ($25,000)? Uncle Gus was happy to foot the bill. The days were long gone when Hemingway had had to write in cafés to escape the noise of the downstairs sawmill, or take the train to the races at Auteuil because it was cheap, and bring along a packed lunch so as not to spend money in the racecourse restaurant. Now he worked in a spacious second-story study in the Whitehead Street carriage house; cruised to Cuba and the Bahamas on his own boat to fish; and spent the late summer and fall on a Wyoming ranch where he and Pauline could hunt and he could write in a cabin among the trees.

Despite all these signs of success, however, something had gone wrong for Hemingway in the years since the publication of A Farewell to Arms. The old friends, the writers and painters with whom he'd talked about art and life on the terrasse at the Closerie des Lilas or the Dôme, had been largely displaced by the sportsmen he hunted and fished with, or the rich men and their wives who frequented his new haunts: places like Bimini, which one of the old friends, who'd come for a visit, described as "a crazy mixture of luxury, indigence, good liquor, bad food, heat, flies, land apathy and sea magnificence, social snoot, money, sport, big fish, big fishermen, and competitive passion." Hemingway was living large, and conscious that he was often paying for it with others' money (whether Pauline's or Uncle Gus's or Esquire's or his publisher's). Sometimes he confessed to feeling like a peasant in this luxe milieu; and in his letters to his editor at Scribner's, Maxwell Perkins, he fretted over advances the publisher had made him that had not earned out—though Perkins, soothingly, told him that any money in the debit column was Scribner's problem, not his, so he shouldn't worry about it.

What did worry Hemingway, though, was the nagging feeling that all this success might have blunted the sharp implement of his craft, that he might have sold out his talent. The books that had followed A Farewell to Arms—a romantic paean to bullfighting, Death in the Afternoon; a collection of stories, Winner Take Nothing; a self-aggrandizing account of his 1934 Kenyan safari, The Green Hills of Africa—had been greeted with disappointing sales and mixed reviews. ("Bull in the Afternoon" was the headline for one, which compared his macho literary style to "wearing false hair on the chest.") Hoping for his author to return to form, even Maxwell Perkins permitted himself to say, "You must finish a novel before long."

But what kind of novel? In 1936, after six years of world economic depression, with fascism on the rise in Europe (and in America, if you counted Father Coughlin's anti-Semitic right-wing radio rants), Hemingway's usual subject matter—expatriate life, bullfighting, game hunting, deep-sea fishing—seemed exotic, if not trivial; and the pose of his protagonists, which veered between stoicism and cynicism, didn't satisfy an audience that increasingly wanted its artists to be engagé, like John

Steinbeck or John Dos Passos. Why didn't he write about a strike? one critic suggested. Although he *had* written an article for the left-wing magazine *New Masses* excoriating the U.S. government for neglecting victims of the 1935 Florida hurricane, Hemingway derided such ideas as "so much horseshit." He wasn't going to become a cheerleader for communism, or "a Marxian viewpoint," he said, because "I believe in only one thing: liberty."

The other thing he'd believed in, the thing that had inspired his most completely realized fiction, was love—love lost, love denied, but still love. Lately, however, he'd seemed soured on the whole idea: the only love he wanted to write about was love gone bad. Waiting for him on his antique Spanish writing table at Whitehead Street were the edited manuscript of one story about an adulterous woman who hates her husband so much that she plugs him in the back of the head with a shotgun, and the advance copies of the August issue of *Esquire* magazine containing another story, this one about a has-been writer dying of gangrene in Africa, literally corrupted by his relationship with his rich wife. As good as these stories were—and they were among the best he had ever written—they dealt with themes that didn't bear exploring too deeply without risk to the marriage he'd built with Pauline.

Maybe that's why he'd fastened—the way that Bimini tuna had on his hook—on to Gingrich's suggestion that he make a novel by combining two published Harry Morgan stories with a third, which he'd started working on early in the year. Soon after his return from Bimini he sat down in his second-story writing room; there, looking out at the tree-shaded garden where the tame peacocks and flamingoes roamed, he began outlining the book he and Gingrich had discussed: a book that Hemingway intended to be a condensed, twentieth-century *War and Peace*. Set in a shabby, corrupt Key West and an even more corrupt and revolution-torn Cuba, full of rich people and poor people—many of them versions of individuals Hemingway knew, or wanted to settle a score with—and featuring smuggling, storms at sea, and plenty of violence, it would document the decline and fall of the rugged individualist, Morgan, betrayed by the forces of wealth and privilege. It would also resurrect the fortunes of that other individualist, Hemingway. That this resurrection was essential became all too clear as he read a letter Gingrich had written him about the new project: "What I like to feel," Gingrich told him, "is a resurgence . . . of confidence in your stuff. I want to be able to shut my eyes and count ten and be sure that *A Farewell* was no fluke."

With the same mail that contained Gingrich's letter came a pile of newspapers and magazines telling of trouble in Spain—and for a fleeting moment Hemingway wondered if there was enough juice in that story to make him want to go to Europe to cover it. He'd had romantic feelings for Spain ever since his first trip there, and the accounts of the storming of the Montaña Barracks sounded like just the sort of action he was hungry to write about. But he decided the fighting was an insignificant mutiny that would peter out before he could even get there: not worth the trouble. Besides, Pauline was already packing their Ford for the long trip to Wyoming, where they would fish for trout and shoot elk and antelope, and he would listen to the wind in the pines and the murmur of the Yellowstone River below their cabin and write the novel that would revive his reputation. *That* would give him the fresh start he was looking for. It had to.

August 1936: Paris/Barcelona/Madrid

Shortly before he and Gerda were supposed to leave for Barcelona, Capa had a surprise: his mother, Julia Friedmann, arrived in Paris, accompanied by his younger brother, Kornel, who had just graduated from high school with vague hopes of becoming a medical student. Convinced that another world war was on the way, Julia had left her husband, Deszö, behind in Budapest and was planning to emigrate to New York, where her sisters worked in the garment business, as soon as she could obtain the necessary visas for herself and Kornel. She also hoped to persuade her adored elder son to emigrate with them; and she was horrified by his plan to cover the fighting in Spain.

She was even more horrified by Gerda; and the feeling was mutual. Julia had always had an intensely close relationship with Capa: he called her "Julia"—never *anyuci*, "mother"—and teased her by saying "Do you want me to treat you like I treat my girlfriends?" Over the winter Capa had written to her, "Don't scold me on account of Gerda. When you meet her you'll like her better than me"; and as long as Gerda was just a name in a letter Julia could bear the thought of her—just barely. Now here she was in the flesh. Once Julia had taken in the cropped hennaed hair, the plucked eyebrows, the assurance with which this girl handled her body and the way Capa looked at her, *like* wasn't the word she would have used.

Gerda wasn't much happier. She hadn't escaped her own family to run afoul of Capa's; she didn't want to share him with them, and she certainly didn't want Julia sabotaging their Spanish trip. Anxious to keep peace between the two women in his life, Capa found an accommodation that would make everybody happy (or equally unhappy): he installed Julia and Kornel—temporarily, it was to be hoped—in their own quarters in the Hotel de Blois, where he and Gerda were living, and quickly taught his brother how to make photographic prints in a darkroom he'd improvised in a bathroom across the hall. He was taking a Leica with him to Spain, and Gerda had a somewhat larger Rolleiflex; now both of them could send Kornel their film from Spain, and Kornel would print it.

On August 5, Gerda and Capa took the train to Toulouse, where Lucien Vogel had acquired an airplane to carry himself and his party of journalists from France to Spain. The plane took off, headed south, crossed the Pyrenees, still white-crested even at this season, and had started its descent for Barcelona when a siren in the cockpit started wailing: the pilot announced that something was wrong with one of the engines and he would have to make an emergency landing. The plane dropped out of the sky and crashed, wheels first, in an open field. Farmers and militiamen came running to the scene, but miraculously no one had been injured except for Vogel and one of the journalists, both of whom had suffered broken arms. Vogel and the journalist were taken to the hospital—where Vogel, learning that the aircraft would take weeks to repair, grandly decided to give it away to the Catalonian government for use as a warplane—and Capa and Gerda hurried on to Barcelona.

On the road, they passed gun-toting countrymen, some of them sporting military helmets or cartridge belts over their farmers' trousers, who were marching to the city to join the defense forces. But when Capa and Gerda arrived there themselves they discovered that in the three weeks since the generals' revolt Barcelona had come to resemble a kind of anarchic carnival more than it did a battlefield. On July 20, after barely more than a day of street fighting, the rebel garrisons in the city's two army barracks had surrendered, not to government forces, but to anarchist militiamen from the FAI (Iberian Anarchist Federation) and the CNT (National Workers' Confederation); whereupon the president of the Catalan

Generalitat, Luís Companys, had forged an antifascist coalition with the victors that also included members of the Socialist UGT and the Communist PSUC. Overnight, businesses and industries had been either turned into workers' collectives or closed; banks had been taken over; lipstick factories had started making munitions; and churches had been closed or even—*too many of those old black beetles*—burned.

Now armed workers in civilian clothes carried rifles as they walked along the Ramblas, and newly requisitioned cars marked with militia and party signs—UGT (Unión General de Trabadores), CNT-FAI (Confederación Nacional de Trabajo–Federación Anarquista Ibérica), PSUC (Partido Socialista Unificado de Cataluña), and the like—sped up and down the wide tree-lined boulevards that ran between blocks of elegant *modernismo* apartment buildings. Male pedestrians were wearing open-collared shirts, women were in coveralls or trousers; hats (except for proletarian berets), jackets, ties (unless they were militia insignia), or dresses marked you as dangerously bourgeois. At Gerda and Capa's hotel, humble men and women who would previously never have dreamed of crossing the threshold ate in the dining room as if in a workingman's canteen, their elbows on the crumb-strewn table.

Gerda was exhilarated by what she saw. Wearing workers' overalls and rope-soled shoes—*alpargatas*—instead of the tight skirts and high heels she sported in Paris, armed with the Rolleiflex, a camera you held at your waist, with the shot you wanted in a viewfinder you looked down at, she went about the streets capturing the spirit of this revolutionary moment in photographs as artfully composed as the ones she'd admired as a girl in Weimar Germany, in the *Berliner Illustrierte Zeitung* or *Die Dame*. The Rollei's square film format tightened her already rigorous focus, and its low shooting angle intensified the drama of her images: knobby-kneed little boys wearing FAI militia caps, playing on the sandbags and stone barricades that had been hastily thrown up across the streets; militiamen and children with their arms around each other; three handsome young men grinning flirtatiously at her from the windows of the Socialist Party headquarters at the Hotel Colón; and women, women everywhere—in blue uniform jumpsuits, carrying guns (or reading fashion magazines with their rifles propped beside them), training for battle—an army of ardent young Amazons who symbolized the extent to which the world in Spain had turned upside down.

She and Capa went to the bullfights—Gerda took no pictures of the bull being worked and killed, though Capa did—and were startled to see (and photograph) a woman matador, Juanita Cruz, who faced the bull not in a suit of lights but in a sober tailored jacket and skirt. Capa was just as diverted by the collective fiesta atmosphere that so enchanted Gerda: the troop trains bedizened with painted slogans, that left for the front with grinning militiamen at each window waving their fists in the antifascist salute, and girlfriends, wives, and musicians serenading the departing heroes. But traveling around the city, he saw an uglier side of things as well. Here a row of religious statues, some missing their heads, others falling over as if in a swoon; there a group of men swinging their pickaxes at figures of the Madonna and child; there a pile of shattered timbers from a ruined church, with the broken statue of a dimpled baby Jesus placed atop it as on a funeral pyre. The pictures he took of such things probably wouldn't make the pages of *Vu*; but some impulse—for a powerful image? for the truth?—made him go on clicking his shutter.

During those heady first days in Barcelona, if he picked up a copy of *La Vanguardia* or *La Humanitat*, or the new *Treball* or *La Veu de Catalunya*—newspapers filled with pictures taken by the Spanish photographers of the events following the generals' insurrection—he couldn't have missed seeing Agustí Centelles's images of the conflict he and Gerda had missed. Shot with a fast, portable Leica like his own, they showed a woman in black keening over the body of a man lying on the pavement; a group of Assault Guards, *asaltos*, firing from behind the contorted bodies of their dead horses; a trio of the same *asaltos*, guns drawn, surrounding a man in a tweed cap, as if all of them were partners in a grim dance—powerful, emblematic photographs that were simultaneously composed and immediate. And he'd have recognized in Centelles a kindred impulse for rushing into the thick of what was happening and photographing it; only in this case the subject wasn't speeches or demonstrations, it was life and death. By now, the opportunity to get such pictures was over in Barcelona; the drama was elsewhere. In the weeks since the rising, the rebels, or the Nationalists as they called themselves, had gained control of the northwestern third of Spain, and a tiny wedge of the southernmost part; the government forces, the Loyalists, were pushing back along a line that extended from Huesca in the north through Aragon before looping back to the Guadarrama, northwest of Madrid. That was where the closest fighting was. And so Capa and Gerda packed up their gear, exchanged their French press credentials for Spanish ones, and moved on.

The road to the front—one of the fronts—led west along the valley of the Ebro toward the cathedral city of Saragossa, then north to Huesca through the dry, dusty hills. Traveling in a press car provided by the Generalitat, along with an armed driver and an armed bodyguard, they made their way slowly, stopped at almost every village by residents brandishing ancient shotguns and demanding to see their papers. Near Barcelona these guards were anarchists from the CNT-FAI; but closer to the front they were members of the anti-Stalinist Marxist party called the POUM (Partido Obrera de Unificación Marxista), which was allied with Gerda's old group from Leipzig, the German SAP. No matter their party affiliation, though, they seemed unsure of where the fighting was. "It may be the front begins there," a gaunt, bearded man in a bandana told the photographers. "We aren't sure." *Nobody's sure of anything*, Capa thought.

At Santa Eulalia, northeast of Huesca, one of several villages of that name, they found a company of militia—including at least one woman—trading occasional volleys with a rebel force so far away across the valley that they were barely possible to see, let alone shoot at; in the hills above Lecineña, where the POUM were headquartered, soldiers—shirtless in the hot sun—struggled to place their field guns to protect against an attack that didn't come. Everywhere, it seemed, both sides were at a standoff. To compensate for the lack of real action, Capa and Gerda did what virtually all other news photographers did: they persuaded the soldiers to simulate it, running down grassy hillsides brandishing their rifles, taking aim at imaginary enemies. But although Gerda did take one extraordinary photo of a hillside gun emplacement in which the lines of the terraced fields, shot from above, have the vertiginous quality of Breughel's *Fall of Icarus*, most of these pictures lacked tension and excitement. So the photographers turned to symbolic, poster-like images that would humanize the war for audiences in the rest of Europe: a genial militiaman flanked by a line of smiling boys; another squirting wine into his mouth from a wineskin; four soldiers, each in a different uniform, but all squinting heroically into the sunlight; another soldier in a helmet with "POUM" stenciled on it, his rifle at his side, delicately petting a dove.

Hoping to get closer to the story they'd come to Spain to find, they drove south and west over the flat Aragonese plateau toward Madrid. It was harvesttime, but the landowners who had formerly owned the grain fields were gone—fled or killed—and peasants in wide-brimmed straw hats were harvesting the wheat for themselves with the help of a detachment of militia. For the first time, they told Capa, there would be enough bread for all the villagers, and for their defenders as well. Both Capa and Gerda were entranced by the sight of the men with their rakes and winnowing sieves, who had the immemorial look of farmers from a Millet painting—and then there were the little girls riding the mules that turned the well wheel, and the soldier feeding a baby lamb from a nursing bottle while a cigarette dangled from his other hand. Peasants and soldiers proudly lined up for Capa's camera in front of a threshing machine that bore the legend "Appropriated by the Authorities" and held their left fists aloft in salute. In Barcelona and Aragon, at least, it looked as if the enemy was invisible, and a revolution had triumphed. But maybe it would be different in Madrid.

Madrid was baking in the summer heat, the trees in the Paseo del Prado barely stirring in the nonexistent breeze, the smell of dust and yesterday's frying mixing with the aroma of the coffee roaster's cart in the Plaza Anton Martin. Work in the patent office in the Calle de Alcalá had ground to a standstill, and Barea was spending most of his days—except for the afternoon tête-à-têtes Maria still insisted on—drilling men who had signed up for the Clerical Workers' Battalion, which they called La Pluma, "The Pen." Turning clerical workers into an organized fighting force was exasperating labor—"I haven't come here to play at soldiers," whined one of the pasty-faced clerks, who just wanted to be taught how to fire his rifle so he could "get on with it"—but Barea knew that the government needed all the help it could get. The rebels were pressing south toward Madrid from the Guadarrama, and north from Andalusia through Extremadura; although Hitler was assuring other European governments that no war materials would *ever* be sent to Spain, the Führer had already provided ships and planes to help ferry Franco's Army of Africa across the Strait of Gibraltar to Andalusia, as well as bombers to attack government targets. Meanwhile, Britain and France—France, with its own Popular Front government!—had agreed to a nonintervention agreement, eventually signed by all the European powers (nominally including Germany and

Italy), under which each country promised neither to send military or other aid to the Spanish republic nor to sell it armaments of any kind. No one wanted to upset Hitler and provoke another terrible war, everyone agreed, particularly since this was surely just an internal, civil conflict—a conflict in which, senior British diplomats murmured, *We really have to stand by our class.*

While the diplomats looked the other way, the war was transforming the capital. Streets were blocked with barricades made from dug-up paving stones; shop windows were crisscrossed with lattices of tape to prevent breakage in case of a bombardment. The whole city was tensed, waiting. Then one morning a bomb fell into the Calle Jesus y Maria, a block from Barea's house, where new and expectant mothers had lined up to receive their daily ration of milk: running to the scene, Barea found the street covered with debris and blood and body parts, and the air full of the sound of screaming. That night, still shaken but determined to do something to stop this from happening again, he ignored Aurelia's cloying pleas that he stay at home and instead joined a blackout squad that was going from block to block until daybreak, painting the bulbs on the streetlamps with a mixture of plaster and blue aniline dye that plunged the streets into a ghostly crepuscule. In the shadows the taillights of the troop trucks glowed red: *like the eyes of nightmare monsters*, Barea thought, summoning Goya.

Monsters prowled in the daylight, too: the vigilantes brought into be-ing by a toxic combination of zealotry and fear. You saw their work at the old slaughterhouses in Mataderos, where the bodies of those who'd been executed the day before were laid out on display before being buried, and hordes of gawkers came to peer and jeer at them. Or you saw it in the in-terrogation cells and holding pens of the CNT *checa* at the Circulo de Bellas Artes, the former cultural center where suspected fascists were detained; in the peoples' courts held in commandeered churches, where those who'd been denounced were pronounced guilty or—rarely—not guilty, and either freed (again rarely) or imprisoned, or condemned to death. Barea tried fighting with the monsters: searching for a friend's son in the wilderness of detention; protesting the arrest of a colleague, a frail old Catholic of considerable wealth but incorruptible principles; cursing an acquaintance who boasted about how many fascists he'd shot. But then, in Extremadura, the Army of Africa overran the walled city of Badajoz, Barea's birthplace, and machine-gunned 1,800 of its defenders—men and women—in the bullring there. The bloodstains, it was said, were palm-deep on the walls. After that it wasn't so easy to intercede for anyone suspected of fascist sympathies without risking your own neck.

Barea had always been (as he put it) *an emotional socialist*, not a doctrinaire one; and in the last weeks he'd felt as uncomfortable with the cautious old-line Republicans who'd been ready to make a deal with the rebels as he did with the anarchic Jacobins who were behind the popular tribunals and executions that so sickened him. He was damned if he'd go in for the kind of reflexive saluting and sloganeering that passed for patriotism among many of his fellow Madrileños, but he was frustrated at not being actively and positively involved in the war effort.

Remembering a patent application that had crossed his desk in the days before the insurrection—the design for a simple hand grenade that would be easy and cheap to make—he had an idea. The Republic needed cheap, available weapons; he was an engineer. Why didn't he start producing those grenades? He located the inventor, an old mechanic named Fausto; and the two of them went to a friend of Barea's, the Communist leader Antonio Mije García, who had enlisted him for the blackout squad. Barea wasn't a Communist, just a union man; and he knew that—with a membership of approximately 130,000 and only seventeen members in the Popular Front Cortes—the Communists were an insignificant force in Spanish political life. But recently they'd seemed like the only people with a sense of organization, the only ones who understood what it would take to actually defeat the fascist insurrection. Barea was particularly impressed with their new enterprise, the Fifth Regiment—a strike force modeled on the regiments of the Red Army during the Russian Civil War, in which each company had its own political commissar, an officer whose job was to explain to the untrained, often uneducated, even illiterate troops what they were fighting for. So he was encouraged when Mije told him to get the cooperation of the Fifth Regiment's leader, a charismatic professional revolutionary who went by the name of Carlos Contreras, or "Comandante Carlos."

Barea found his quarry—a burly, thick-necked man, by turns impatient and charming—in a requisitioned nobleman's palace in the Salamanca barrio where he was overseeing the training of recruits. Contreras wasn't his real name: he'd been born Vittorio Vidali, in Istria, near Trieste, thirty-six years earlier. Since then, under a variety of aliases, he'd been a founder of the Italian Communist Party; an agent of Stalin's secret police, the NKVD; a steelworker in Chicago; and a hit man involved in the assassination, in Mexico, of a dissident Communist who was the lover of the photographer Tina Modotti; afterward, Modotti had become *his* mistress, and they'd come to Spain together in 1934. Now, in addition to leading the Fifth Regiment, he was acting as a general strategic advisor to the government, and unofficially he was one of the most powerful men in Madrid. But this morning he was shaking his head over the intransigence of the Asturian miners who were making their own grenades—from pipe segments filled with dynamite—in a workroom in the palace. The place was littered with open boxes of explosives and to Barea's horror the miners insisted on smoking there, tossing their spent cigarette ends onto the floor. When he pointed out the danger, Contreras just nodded glumly. "Nobody will ever persuade them that they're crazy, because they've been handling dynamite all their lives," he said. Barea's proposal cheered him, though; and he was glad to authorize it. Shortly afterward, Barea left the palace with the necessary papers in his pocket—and half an hour later the palace workroom blew up.

Things didn't go much better for Barea and Fausto. The factory where they proposed to start grenade production was in the old medieval capital of Toledo, perched on a rock over the Tajo River forty-five miles away. The city had been in government hands since the outbreak of the war but a garrison of rebel soldiers had managed to hold out in the Alcázar, the fortified palace on the city's heights; they had taken about a hundred hostages into the building with them and the fortress was now under siege. The atmosphere in the city was understandably tense; and the workers at the munitions factory were suspicious. Although they were all set up to produce screws and pins and other external parts of the grenade Fausto had designed, they explained that they couldn't manufacture the explosive charge itself because their explosives expert was unavailable. Actually, he was dead—executed. By them. He'd refused to give them the makings of rifle cartridges; so they'd appropriated his stock of dynamite and simply packed the loose gunpowder into the barrels of the rifles they were making. They were astonished when the rifles exploded when they were fired. "It was sabotage," they said; "so we had to shoot him." Fausto and Barea just looked at each other and left.

"I don't know whether to laugh or cry," Fausto said, as they got into their official car to drive back to Madrid. "We're going to lose the war if this is a symbol." The road was crowded with military vehicles, and militiamen and women, as well as a handful of photographers, were clustered in the main square, watching as soldiers and Assault Guards vainly peppered the massive stone walls of the Alcázar with rifle fire. Barea and Fausto threaded their way through the bystanders until they came to the bridge over the Tajo, where they had to pull over to let a garbage truck go by. It was one of the vehicles used to take the bodies of the executed to the cemetery, and Barea held his breath as the driver hit a pothole that banged the truck's rear doors open. The hold, thankfully, was empty.

Milling about with the crowd in front of the Alcázar, Gerda and Capa could be forgiven for feeling frustrated. They'd arrived in Madrid at the end of August to find a city girding for war, not celebrating a revolution: a far cry from the "show-off city" Capa had discovered on his first trip only a year ago. They'd taken pictures of cobblestone street barricades, of slogan-plastered cars crammed with waving *milicianos*, of the protective brick cocoon being constructed around the Fountain of Cibeles, the beloved landmark at the junction of the Paseo del Prado and the Calle de Alcalá; and Gerda had gone to the barracks of the recently formed Fifth Regiment, where she photographed a military barber cutting the hair of some of the new recruits. But this was all just background to what they were looking for: real fighting. There was plenty of it in the Guadarrama and at Talavera de la Reina, seventy-six miles southwest of Madrid, where government troops were vainly struggling to hold off the Nationalist army advancing on the capital: the rebels were causing heavy losses for the Loyalists, whose militiamen refused to dig trenches because they thought that was cowardly. But the combat zone had been declared off-limits and the photographers' passes were no good to them. So they'd doubled back eastward to Toledo, hoping to shoot the breaking of the Alcázar siege, which would be an important symbolic victory for the government. Unfortunately, they learned, it would probably be days, if not weeks, before that happened, because the attackers were waiting for a team of Asturian *dinamiteros* to lay tunnels beneath the ramparts and blow holes in the walls.

It looked like there was nothing for it but to head to the Córdoba front, several days' journey to the south. The Nationalist rebels had taken control of Córdoba itself at the beginning of the war, but the Loyalist Third Brigade, under the command of General José Miaja, had dug in to the east and north of the city and were planning an assault that would retake it; if Capa and Gerda could arrive in time, perhaps they could at last get the pictures they had come to Spain for. Certainly they hoped so: their money was running out and they couldn't stay much longer—Gerda, at least, wanted to be back in Paris by the second week in September. Throwing their cameras into their official car, they set off.

September 1936: Paris

Really, it was a strange sort of coincidence—if it *was* a coincidence. Ilse had been hoping to go work for the Spanish government's war effort, and by doing so to put some distance between herself and Poldi, whose secretiveness and strange moods were making her more and more uncomfortable. But she'd had only vague ideas for how to make this happen: until Poldi told her that for the past several months, using the alias "Maresch," he had been working as an undercover agent for the Spanish Republic, traveling around Germany and central Europe to find out what kinds of material resources (principally guns, ammunition, and airplanes) the Nazis were sending to the Spanish rebels; and he'd been forwarding this information, or some of it, to his Spanish handler, a Socialist minister named Julio Álvarez del Vayo.

Now Álvarez had been promoted to minister of foreign affairs in a new "Victory Government" headed by another Socialist, Francisco Largo Caballero, and he was handing off control of Poldi to the new ambassador to France, Luís Araquistáin, who would also be in charge of the government's Arms Purchase Commission in Paris—or would be if the French ever suspended the arms blockade that was denying the government the sort of help the Nationalists were getting from both Italy and Germany. And so, just like that, Poldi and Ilse left Brno for Paris; and Ilse discovered that the Spanish visas and safe-conducts that had seemed almost unattainable to her in Czechoslovakia were not so hard to get after all.

And thank heaven for that, because the situation in Spain seemed increasingly critical. On September 3, after days of bombing and street fighting, the Nationalists had taken the city of Irun, on the Bay of Biscay near the French border, thus cutting off the Loyalist Basque provinces from contact with France; and while the French blockade continued in effect the rebels had just taken delivery of a dozen new warplanes from Germany. The French press was covering it all with gusto, but although the French workers were striking and demonstrating, in huge numbers, in support of the Republic and against the blockade, the people who mattered, the people in France and Britain and the rest of the world who could decide to help Spain's government defeat the rebels, were hanging back. They needed to be persuaded to commit themselves, which Ilse was sure would happen if they just knew the truth of what was going on; and *this* was something she could help with. She could write for European papers in their own languages—in fact, she had already gotten assignments from some of the Norwegian and Czech papers she'd written for in the past. And since Álvarez del Vayo's portfolio as foreign minister also included the Propaganda Ministry, he would surely help her with access to stories that needed covering.

There remained, however, the problem of physically getting Ilse to Spain. She didn't have the money for train fare, still less for an airplane ticket—and she apparently didn't know her husband was being handsomely paid by the Spanish government for his intelligence work. But then fate intervened in the person of the Stendhalian novelist/adventurer André Malraux, whose résumé included stints as an editor of artistic dirty books (limited editions of Sade's *Le Bordel de Venise* and *Les amis du crime*), smuggler of Khmer bas-reliefs from Indochina, and anticolonial propagandist. A nervous man with a furrowed brow, dark slicked-down hair, and a cigarette seemingly permanently affixed to the corner of his mouth, Malraux had recently conceived the notion of forming a kind of airborne Foreign Legion, the Escuadrilla España, to aid the Spanish Republic. He'd managed to hire a handful of pilots, most of them out-of-work rumrunners and bushwhackers, and scrounge together some outdated aircraft, mainly Dewoitine D372 fighters and poky Potez 54 bombers, in which he himself occasionally flew as copilot and tail gunner, wearing a uniform designed for him by the couturier Jeanne Lanvin. Although the Escuadrilla was based in Madrid, Malraux continually shuttled between there and Paris, where he came to raise money for more planes.

And on one of these trips he found out about Ilse. Perhaps, it was suggested, she would like to fly down to Spain with him?

   She would.

September 1936: Madrid

It was one of the many ironies of the war that the headquarters of the
Communist Party in Madrid were now located in the Palacio de Liria,
the grand residence of the Duke of Alba on the Calle de la Princesa, a
place which under normal circumstances Arturo Barea would never have
been privileged to visit. But today he had an urgent message from his
friend Antonio Mije, whose office was—naturally enough—in Party headquarters; so he presented himself at the Palacio, where he found the
formal gardens and their baroque fountains guarded by young militiamen
and women, while inside the boiserie-encrusted rooms soldiers were
polishing the parquet floors, dusting the stuffed crocodiles and suits of
antique armor, and taking inventory of the palace's collection of Goyas,
Titians, and other old masters before packing them away for safekeeping.

   Mije had a proposition for him. The inclusion of Communists in the
government had given him some patronage power, and he might be able
to suggest Barea for a post at the Foreign Ministry—that is, if he had any
fluency in English. Although Barea's other language was French, he could
read English well enough, and translate it; so within minutes he was
being hustled off to the Foreign Ministry, where a harried young assistant
ushered him into the crepuscular office of Luis Rubio Hidalgo, the newly
appointed chief of the ministry's Press and Propaganda Department. Pale,
bald as an egg, with a thin mustache on his upper lip and lashless eyes
peering from behind round tinted lenses, Rubio sat impassively in the
cone of light cast by his solitary desk lamp, his white hands folded in front
of him, while Barea described his qualifications. Then he asked Barea if
he would like to join the Propaganda Department as a nighttime censor
for the foreign press—an important job, since most journalists wrote and
wired their stories from Madrid at night in order to catch the morning
editions of their newspapers in Europe and America.

   The moment the words were out of Rubio's mouth, Barea knew they
were what he'd been waiting weeks to hear. Although he was personally

repelled by his prospective chief, the work the man was describing was essential and interesting; unlike his frustrated efforts at the Toledo grenade factory, it might allow him to actually make a difference in the struggle for the Republic's survival. It involved working with words and writers, something he had always longed to do. And the hours, far from being a disincentive for him, represented an opportunity for him to escape the twin demands of Maria and Aurelia. He accepted the job with alacrity; and broke the news to each of the women, separately, the next day. Aurelia, predictably, was vocally dismayed when he told her: *why did he have to get mixed up in these things?* Maria, on the other hand, was overjoyed: If duty kept Barea out of Aurelia's bed, wouldn't this be *her* chance at last? Barea didn't have the courage to tell her how wrong she was.

That evening, just before midnight, he was driven through the dark, silent streets in a ministry car, pausing at checkpoints while the sentries shone their flashlights at his papers, until he reached the Telefónica, the white New York–style skyscraper that towered fourteen stories over the Gran Via. Built in the late 1920s as the headquarters for the Spanish subsidiary of the International Telephone and Telegraph Company, the Telefónica housed telegraph transmitters and connectors to underwater cables, as well as the main switching terminus of the Spanish telephone system, and was thus the nerve center for communications coming into or out of Spain. ITT technicians still worked in the building, but with the onset of war the Press and Propaganda Department had established an outpost there as well, with a newsroom for correspondents on the fourth floor (along with camp beds for those who had long waits for transmitting their stories) and censorship offices on the fifth.

After handing his credentials to the guard at the security desk in the entrance hall, Barea went up in one of the building's five clanking elevators to the fifth floor, where he found the censors' office at the end of a maze of passages. It was a narrow room, lit only by the purplish glow of a single desk lamp around which a sheet of carbon paper had been taped to form an improvised blackout shade. The wax on the paper, heated by the bare bulb, made the room smell like a church.

Barea introduced himself to the other censor on duty, a man named Perea, and they started dividing up their workload. In the first days of the war there had been no foreign-language censors—journalists had to translate their dispatches into Spanish before they could be approved;

and the censors themselves were ITT employees with little idea of, and no direction about, what details constituted permissible news and what were breaches of security. Their standards varied wildly and randomly: sometimes a correspondent would send a story to his newspaper with no interference and a colleague, transmitting the same information a few minutes later, would find his report struck through with red pencil; no one was happy. But with the arrival of Rubio Hidalgo, a former journalist himself, things were going to be different: the censors would now be able to read the stories in the language they were written in, and there would be consistent standards for what to approve.

That, at any rate, was the way it was *supposed* to work. In practice, problems persisted. The big agencies—United Press International, Associated Press, Reuters, Havas—had teams of reporters filing almost around the clock; the major foreign newspapers all had their special correspondents; material poured out of them all. And the word from on high, to Barea and Perea, was that nothing, *nothing* should be passed that hinted at anything other than success for the Republican forces. Given what was going on from day to day, this seemed a near-impossibility: the rebels took San Sebastián, the country's summer capital on the Bay of Biscay, extending their hold over the north; in the south they rolled, seemingly inexorably, toward Málaga; at Madrid's threshold, they continued to press south from the Guadarrama and east from Talavera de la Reina. And the journalists, who often made daily trips to the front, knew what was happening and wanted to report it.

But when Barea went to the Foreign Ministry for his daily meetings with Rubio, his chief would complain about correspondents sneaking negative stories out in the diplomatic pouches of their embassies, or extremists who threatened him for letting through too much bad news. Not that he was frightened, of course. Opening his desk drawer, he showed Barea the pistol he kept inside it. "Before they get me, I'll get one of them!" he said. He didn't seem to be joking. "Take care, and don't let anything pass!"

September 1936: Córdoba Front

In the first days of September, Robert Capa and Gerda Taro worked their way south from Toledo across the tawny plain of La Mancha, passing white stucco windmills Don Quixote might have battled against, toward the mountains of the Sierra Morena. Sometimes they stopped to stretch their legs and refill their canteens, and Capa snapped pictures of Gerda, in her worker's coveralls, bending over a mountain stream and grinning flirtatiously back at him, or curled up like a sleepy child with her head resting on a stone boundary marker engraved with the letters *P.C.*—which meant *partido communal*, but which could just as easily stand for "Partido Comunista." On the Sierra's northern slopes, in the village of Almadén, they paused to photograph a mercury mine that had once been the property of the Rothschild banking family but had been—like so much else since the beginning of the war—taken over by a workers' committee. Because mercury was an important element for munitions production the mine was good material for reportage; and the brutalist machinery and heroic laborers, the lead amphorae packed with mercury standing like so many soldiers in regimented lines, provided striking, resonant images for their cameras. But it still wasn't enough, wasn't *combat*. So they headed over the mountains, to Andalusia.

There, shortly after sunrise on the morning of Saturday, September 5, Nationalist Breguet bombers began attacking government troops encamped in the hills near the copper-mining village of Cerro Muriano, just north of Córdoba. By midmorning the rebel forces, which had launched their attack from Córdoba, had brought in artillery and were shelling both the village and the Loyalist encampment. By midafternoon, when the Nationalist infantry arrived with their machine guns, the place was in pandemonium. Men, women, and children were fleeing the village on foot, on horseback or on mules, in cars or trucks; the women sobbing, cradling their infants or leading mules or cattle; the men clutching forlorn bundles of clothing or household objects or valises. Nor were they the only fugitives: behind them came scores of the Loyalist *milicianos*—terrified volunteers whose previous experience of firearms probably involved no more than shooting small birds on their farms. Now, crying out that rifles were no use against shells and bombs, they fled on foot or in commandeered automobiles, in some cases threatening to use their weapons on anyone who got in their way. Others, however, remained at their posts, and they and the few regular infantrymen managed to hold position until evening. At that point the rebels—planes, artillery, infantrymen—retired to Córdoba for the night; but they would return the next day to finish what they started and send the remnants of the government detachment back to its base camp at Montoro, twenty-seven miles to the east.

It wasn't supposed to happen this way. After spending a month vainly firing at the rebel garrison in Córdoba along a line just east of the city, the Loyalist general, José Miaja, had planned a bold flanking maneuver in which a detachment from his Third Brigade would go to Cerro Muriano and stage a surprise attack, planned for September 5, on the rebels from the north. Miaja must have been very sure of success, because a handful of journalists—the photographers Hans Namuth and Georg Reisner, the Austrian writer Franz Borkenau, Clemente Cimorra from the Madrid daily *La Voz*, and Robert Capa and Gerda Taro—had been permitted to witness the action. In the event, what they saw was a table-turning rout.

The journalists were billeted in a 1920s country estate called La Malagueña, on a hill of the same name just south of the village; and Capa and Taro probably didn't get there until early afternoon, when the two-hour lunch break that combatants on both sides customarily observed would have given them the all-clear. By that time the refugees from the village were in full flight, and Capa, who always remembered that behind his images were actual people with actual emotions, trained his camera on the straggling families on the road—on the barefooted children in their cotton dresses and shorts, and their exhausted, terrified parents. *This is what war does.* In the late afternoon, the fighting started up again in earnest; but it seems as if the only photographs he and Gerda were able to make of the combat were of government soldiers carrying machine guns on their shoulders, or unspooling telephone wire to hook up field communications devices—all taken behind the lines, on the wooded slopes around La Malagueña.

That was more than Namuth and Reisner were able to get, despite being in the thick of fighting with Borkenau in Cerro Muriano itself, where the journalists had to hide in a railroad tunnel from bombs and insurgent machine-gun fire. But Taro and Capa were still hungry for action, and seemingly exhilarated by what they'd tasted so far. "They were like young eagles," their friend Chim said of them later, "soaring in this new brilliant clean air of Spain." Coming upon them at La Malagueña that afternoon, Clemente Cimorra—a dashing playwright-journalist in his mid-thirties with a flair for the dramatic—was enchanted as much by this eagerness, the "naïve courage" of this couple in love, as by their youth. *Just kids*, he thought when he saw them, armed with their cameras and nothing else, running out fearlessly to look at a spiraling enemy plane, and when he heard their excited talk about how they wanted to capture on film what was happening in Spain, no matter the danger to them. *Brave, generous kids who are searching for the truth*, he wrote, in a dispatch he filed with his paper the next day.

Before Capa and Taro left the Córdoba front they also stopped at a Loyalist camp—possibly the Third Brigade headquarters in Montoro, east of Córdoba: there Capa photographed an officer in grimy coveralls standing on a barrel to talk to his men while Gerda stood to one side, listening; then he walked around the little group to catch their upturned faces: one bored, one inspired, one downhearted, one frowning in concentration. And either at this camp, or another, during the siesta hour, he wandered among the sleeping *milicianos*, sprawled on the bare ground like bodies on the field of battle, one of them cuddling one of the dogs the troops kept as mascots: in sleep even the older men looked innocent and defenseless, and all seemed to prefigure the grim destiny that awaited so many of them. But as poignant as these images were, they didn't have the drama Capa was looking for—the drama he'd been unable to capture at Cerro Muriano.

So one morning he and Gerda drove thirty miles southwest of Montoro, across the Guadalquivir and through rolling hills covered by wheat fields, bare now after the harvest, until they reached the camp of a small detachment of CNT militia just outside the farming village of Espejo. The journey wasn't without danger: just a few days earlier another journalist, Renée Lafont, had been fatally shot in an insurgent ambush nearby; but they reached their destination without incident. It was still early when they got there, and the sun made long, sharp shadows on the dry ground. The *milicianos*, men from the Murcian village of Alcoy, were happy to pose for the two young photographers, the dark, tousle-haired boy with the ready laugh and the pretty blond girl: they ran up one of the bare hills in a combat crouch, with their officer beckoning them on; knelt on the grass to aim their rifles at a distant target on the next hill; stood at the edge of a dusty trench and brandished their guns in a show of *macho* bravado. Then Taro and Capa squatted in the trench as the soldiers ran down the hill toward it and leaped across before taking up firing positions on its farther lip: the photographers closed in on them with both the Rolleiflex and the

Leica as the men fired their guns into the empty air. The brightness of the sun, still low in the sky, lit the soldiers like a klieg light and threw every detail, from lumps of soil to the stitching on the men's caps, into crisp relief.

Finally—it seems it must have been finally, given what happened next—either Capa or Taro asked if some of the *milicianos* would simulate being hit by gunfire. One, a dark mustached man in a khaki *mono* or boiler suit, ran down the hill toward Capa; then, pretending he'd been shot, he threw himself on the ground, hanging on to his rifle and breaking his fall with his left hand before coming to rest on his back, his gun across his body. Two others simulated corpses, lying on their sides in the stubble. Perhaps Capa wasn't sure he'd got what he wanted, though; or maybe one of the other men wanted a turn in the limelight. However it was, another soldier, with a lean, creased face and heavy black brows, his shirt white under the straps of his leather cartridge boxes, came down the sunlit slope, his rifle in his right hand, the rope soles of his shoes crunching in the dry grass. And then—what? Was there a report, the sharp crack of rifle fire? Because suddenly the man's legs went slack, his hands limp; with his rifle flying away from his loosened fingers, he too dropped to the ground, just where his comrades had been moments previously. And in the seconds before the soldier fell Capa squeezed the shutter of his Leica and took what would become one of the most famous photographs in the world.

What really happened on that hillside? Capa himself maintained almost total silence about it; although a year later a friend, acting as his interpreter for an interview with a New York newspaper, would give a highly colored account that places Capa and the white-shirted soldier alone on a hilltop, hiding in a trench from enemy gunfire until the *miliciano* attempts to break away to rejoin his detachment and is felled by the blast of a machine gun. A thrilling story—but one belied by the presence of Gerda, and of the other soldiers, by the other militiamen lying on the grass, by the difficulty of machine-gun bullets pinpointing a single target more than a hundred yards away across the mown fields. Ten years later, in a radio interview, Capa embroidered the *Telegram* story slightly: there had been twenty *milicianos* in the trench with him, he said, facing machine-gun fire from a neighboring hill; one by one the soldiers had surged out of the trench, only to be felled by enemy bullets, and Capa had got the last lucky shot by holding the camera above his head, never actually seeing the image in the frame. This narrative, too, is hard to square with the details of the actual photographs he took.

Sometime in the 1940s, however, Capa would privately tell another friend, a fellow photographer from Stuttgart, Gerda's hometown, that he and Gerda and the soldiers had all been actors in a tragedy of coincidence. They'd been fooling around, he said, running, firing their weapons, acting crazy, laughing—*this is how we'll shoot those fascist bastards*—and he'd been taking pictures; he didn't hear any shots, "not at first." But as the soldiers played at combat for the benefit of his camera, a real bullet, fired perhaps from a fascist sniper's high-powered hunting rifle, or by one of the rebel Guardia Civil active in those hills, had pierced a real man's heart.

Confiding this story all those years later, Capa—his friend would say—seemed stricken: "dejected and defensive, like a beaten puppy." No wonder. *I do not wish to hurt,* a woman he knew recalled him saying; even at twenty-two, he was tender and compassionate, and he had never seen death, especially not a death of his own making. Although he might have been an indifferent bar mitzvah student, never bothering to remember all the stories and rituals his family's rabbi had tried to teach him at thirteen, he'd surely learned that when he became a man he took on responsibility for all his sins—and this would have been a heavy one.

But what if the man in the photograph simply got up from the ground after the shutter clicked, dusted himself off, and went on his way, alive and well? Questioned about this possibility six decades after the fact, a homicide detective and forensics expert was dismissive: the slackened limbs and fingers looked like death to him, not mimicry. The other men lying on the ground might have been playacting; but this, the detective maintained, was the real thing.

Whether it was or not, however, a conundrum remained: Capa had come to Spain to capture the *truth*—to take the truest, best pictures, pictures that would show how the Spanish people were fighting for their ideals, pictures he would pursue without regard for personal risk. If the photographs from Espejo were staged, even though one of them might have been transformed by dreadful irony into reality, then the only one who had been at risk when they were taken was the man who had stopped a bullet. After Espejo neither Capa nor Taro let that happen again.

Shortly after the two photographers left Espejo they gave their rolls of film to a pilot who carried them from a nearby airfield and thence by stages to Paris, where they were developed and the strips of images cut up for easier submission to newspaper and magazine editors. On September 23 *Vu* ran a spread of six of Capa's photos from the Córdoba front—along with one of Georg Reisner's—and gave pride of place to the picture of the white-shirted *miliciano*. The caption had the cadence of an epic: "With lively step, their breasts to the wind, their rifles in their fists, they ran down the slope . . . Suddenly . . . a bullet whistled—a fratricidal bullet—and their native soil drank their blood." Other magazines, in other countries, would publish other photographs from the sequence; and in July 1937, *Life* magazine would transform the image of the "Falling Soldier" into a symbol of the Spanish conflict by making it a visual epigraph to its editorial summary of the war. As Capa himself would describe it in his radio interview, "the prize picture is born in the imagination of the editors and the public."

In that sense, then, the picture more than fulfilled the intentions its photographer had had when he went to Spain: it had become a symbol, even *the* symbol, of Loyalist sacrifice. For now, though, it was just one frame on a strip of film Capa had sent off to Paris without seeing the results; and he and Gerda were on the road to Toledo.

September 1936: Toledo/Madrid

By September 18, when the Asturian *dinamiteros* finished mining its two eastern towers, the Alcázar at Toledo, the ancient citadel dating back to Roman times, had been under siege for a month, with the Nationalist commander refusing any terms for the surrender of the garrison, or for the release of the more than two hundred women and children who were their hostages. Despite the fortress's lack of strategic importance the government had spent an enormous amount of energy and ammunition trying to capture it, and it had become an emblem of Nationalist resistance and an object of obsession to Prime Minister Largo Caballero. So as the *dinamiteros* prepared to ignite the fuse that would topple the two towers, the government had invited every war correspondent in Madrid to watch the event.

Capa and Gerda were among them; but if they'd counted on getting dramatic photographs of the Alcázar's liberation, they were disappointed. Although the northeast tower fell, the southeast one was undamaged by the blast and the wall still stood; the defenders, meanwhile, who had used stethoscopes to pinpoint the placement of the land mines, had escaped harm by gathering at the far side of the building, away from the explosion. No Loyalist troops were going to enter the Alcázar that day; worse, with the Nationalists grinding toward Madrid, it seemed unsettlingly possible that the capital's survival—maybe even the republic's—was in doubt. Suddenly Toledo, and Madrid, didn't seem like safe places for two socialist photographers from France. So Capa and Taro left for Barcelona, and then Paris, not knowing if the cause in which they'd invested their hopes and energies in the past weeks would in fact survive.

The other correspondents, meanwhile, were converging on Barea's office in the Telefónica with stories reporting the rebel advance, and the failure of the Alcázar attack; and Barea was torn between his duty, his conscience, and his feelings. He knew what was happening and believed it was futile to deny it: on the road between Toledo and Madrid he'd seen the fleeing villagers and retreating *milicianos*, the ditches full of discarded weapons, equipment, blankets, clothing; he'd heard the sounds of rebel bombardment. But in their daily conferences Rubio continued to insist that no news be approved that didn't parrot the official line: *the Alcázar will surely fall tomorrow, the rebel troops have been stopped in their tracks, a few milicianos have stampeded, but all is well.* And the correspondents, who also knew what was going on, were so certain the rebels were winning, and so eager to find sensational details to confirm it, that Barea perversely found himself hating them, hating their cynicism, the way they treated his country's fight to the death as just another story. Alone in his blackout-shaded room—his colleague Perea, unable to stand the stress, had quit in panic—he slashed through their copy in a fury; and when one of the journalists, a snotty young Frenchman from *Le Petit Parisien*, tried to sneak an uncut dispatch through, Barea lost his temper. *I'll have you arrested*, he shouted, waving his newly issued Star Modelo A pistol in the man's face. The correspondent rewrote the story—just. The transmitted version led with the words: "A certain mystery persists on the subject of Toledo."

Denials, however, could only go so far. On September 26, making a detour from its advance on the capital, Franco's army cut the main Madrid–Toledo road; by the next evening the rebels had entered Toledo's medieval gates. They took no prisoners—even pregnant women were loaded onto trucks at the maternity hospital to be driven to the cemetery and shot—and the cobbled main street that ran downhill to the city gates flowed with blood. For the Nationalist forces, this was a major symbolic victory: Toledo, the religious capital of Spain, had been the first important Muslim-occupied city to be captured by the forces of Their Catholic Majesties Ferdinand and Isabella during the Reconquest of Spain in the fifteenth century, and by taking it from the Republican government Franco was equating himself with the Catholic heroes of the medieval struggle against the infidel.

To underscore the point, the day after his troops entered the city, the general staged a reenactment of its "liberation" for the benefit of newsreel cameras, a gesture that undercut the grumblings of those who thought he should have pushed on to take Madrid and let the Loyalists abandon Toledo themselves. And on the last day of September, the rebels proclaimed Francisco Franco Bahamonde supreme commander of all the Nationalist armies, and—although the elected Republican government, inconveniently, still survived—*caudillo*, or head of government, of the Spanish state.

September 1936: L Bar T Ranch, Wyoming

In the three summers that he'd been hunting and fishing at the L Bar T, the Wyoming dude ranch owned by Lawrence and Olive Nordquist, Ernest Hemingway had never bagged a grizzly bear; but this year, he vowed, would be different. One of his new fishing buddies from Bimini, a wealthy young sportsman named Tom Shevlin, had come out to L Bar T with his wife, Lorraine, and to show them a good time, and maybe display his own prowess, Hemingway planned to take the couple grizzly-hunting. "I want to shoot one in the belly to see if I can make him come," he wrote to Arnold Gingrich. So on September 10, to guarantee some sport for the new guests, the ranch's owner, Lawrence Nordquist, killed a couple of mules and set out their carcasses to ripen on the slopes above the ranch, where they'd bring the bears to the hunters' guns.

While the would-be grizzly-slayers waited for the baits to acquire the requisite attractive pong, Hemingway busied himself with his novel. He'd written more than thirty thousand words since arriving at the ranch, despite taking time off for a couple of fishing and hunting expeditions, and he was pleased with the results—so pleased, in fact, that he offered to let Tom Shevlin have a look at the manuscript. Although he didn't say so, it was important to Hemingway that Shevlin like what he read.

Because just a few weeks ago the ranch mailbag had delivered a surprise: the August 10 issue of *Time* magazine, with a cover story devoted to Hemingway's sometime friend, the writer John Dos Passos. Since their first meeting in a regimental mess hall in Italy during the Great War, the two men had argued over the future of fiction in Paris cafés, partied at the Gerald Murphys' at Antibes, skiied in the Vorarlberg, gone to the bullfights in Pamplona, and fished in the Caribbean; and in their relationship, Dos (as everybody called him) had always been the beta male to Hemingway's alpha. Shy, balding, nearsighted, with a rheumatic heart, Dos Passos was the illegitimate son of a distinguished Portuguese-American lawyer: he'd spent his childhood in European spas and hotels, not fishing camps in northern Michigan; he'd been educated at Choate and Harvard, not Oak Park High School and the newsroom of the *Kansas City Star* (Hemingway had declined to apply to college); and he'd married Hemingway's boyhood girlfriend, Katy Smith, after Hemingway introduced them in Key West.

For years their friendship had been held in balance by Hemingway's success and Dos's admiration; but lately, as Dos Passos had labored on the third installment of an epic trio of novels about social and political upheavals in twentieth-century America, that balance had shifted imperceptibly. The first two volumes of the trilogy garnered admiring reviews, although they still didn't sell well, and Hemingway's *amour propre* was unsettled. He sneered when "poor Dos," who needed the money, wrote a screenplay for Marlene Dietrich, and he complained that a man who had defended Sacco and Vanzetti and supported striking Kentucky coal miners shouldn't be "living on a yacht in the Mediterranean while he attacks the capitalist system." That the yacht belonged to their mutual friends the Murphys, and that Dos Passos was there recuperating from a serious bout of rheumatic fever, made no difference to Hemingway. And as he often did when he had some private score to settle with someone, he put Dos Passos into the novel he was writing—as a sexually impotent phony-radical novelist named Richard Gordon who lives off loans from his wealthy friends.

Now Dos was squinting out at him from the cover of *Time*, wearing a macho open-necked shirt and drawing deeply on a little cigar; and inside the magazine was an article, occasioned by the publication of *The Big Money*, the last novel in Dos Passos's U.S.A. trilogy, calling the whole sequence "one of the most ambitious projects that any U.S. novelist has undertaken" and saying that to find its equal "one must look abroad, to Tolstoy's *War and Peace*, to Balzac's *Comédie Humaine*, to James Joyce's *Ulysses*." For someone with Hemingway's overdeveloped sense of competition, this was a barb guaranteed to go straight to the heart. Damn it, *he* was the one who was supposed to write a new *War and Peace*; not poor, awkward, myopic Dos.

So the stakes were high when he gave his work-in-progress to Tom Shevlin to read; and unfortunately Shevlin wasn't impressed by what he saw. He liked the parts about the rumrunner Harry Morgan all right, he said, but not the portrait of the pseudo-*engagé* writer Richard Gordon, the character based on Dos Passos. And although he was hesitant to say so directly, Shevlin hinted that the disparate strands of the novel made for "lousy" reading. When he heard this, Hemingway erupted in a fury: grabbing the manuscript from Shevlin's hands, he chucked it out the window of the cabin into a patch of early snow, and for three days neither man spoke to the other.

But then the baits ripened, and Hemingway apologized for his outburst, and the Shevlins and the Hemingways rode their horses up to a camp near the timberline to find grizzlies. It was chilly, early fall on the mountain, and the days were drawing in. Late in the afternoon they arrived, Hemingway and Lorraine Shevlin were investigating one of the baited carcasses when three bears, attracted by the smell of meat, trotted out of the forest, their coats shining in the setting sun. As the largest bear approached the bait Hemingway stood up out of cover to shoot, and the bear, surprised, also reared up, its forepaws outstretched, claws extended. It was a magnificent and terrifying sight. Aiming his Springfield rifle at the bear's chest, Hemingway fired; the grizzly fell to the ground, wounded, as the other two bears turned and ran for cover. Hemingway went after them and killed one, then returned and finished off the first bear with a shot to the neck. He was exhilarated—and seemed only a little disappointed when Shevlin killed another bear, bigger than either of Hemingway's, two days later.

After the hunting party returned to the L Bar T, Hemingway wrote to both Maxwell Perkins and his old friend from Paris days, the poet Archibald MacLeish, to boast about the expedition; and by then he'd arranged the facts more comfortably. He'd been up on the mountain, he wrote, and just "ran into" the grizzlies while looking for elk. He'd shot two of them—he could have killed all three, he told Perkins, if he hadn't been deterred by how beautiful they were. Shevlin had bagged a third one two days later, he added; but, he said dismissively, using the same wording in both letters, the younger man "got his on a bait."

He'd been working very hard on his book, he reported; and he told Perkins that when he was finished with it he wanted to go to Spain if he wasn't too late to get in on the action. Which is also what he said when—ignoring whatever bad feelings he'd had over the past months, and neglecting to mention the reception for *The Big Money*—he wrote a cheery letter to Dos Passos to say he was three-quarters finished with his new novel, and planned on going to Spain as soon as he was done, as long as there was still fighting. If not, they would have each missed the best novelistic material there ever was—material they, or at least he, was uniquely equipped to handle. But he doubted the war would be over that quickly, because the Spaniards, and the Moors, could really fight. If the battle was carried to Madrid, he hoped they'd spare the pictures in the Prado and elsewhere—though he didn't care about the buildings themselves. "Anything looks better after being shelled," he quipped.

October 1936: Madrid/Cartagena/Moscow

On October 13 Barea heard enemy guns for the first time.

The rebel commander General Emilio Mola had announced that he would be drinking coffee on the Gran Via on the twelfth, and he seemed only a little behind schedule. His troops were pressing ever closer to Madrid, while rebel planes continued to bomb it. The city swarmed with refugees: on the broad tree-lined avenues of Castellana and Recoletos, where the wealthy had lived in spacious stone *palacios*, they slept outdoors and did their cooking on open fires; the lucky ones were given quarters in deserted private houses where they camped with their dogs and goats in formerly grand salons hung with tattered tapestries.

The government had imposed a strict curfew and no one was permitted on the streets after eleven o'clock at night. Barea, who had to work into the small hours to censor reports going out to night desks at newspapers the world over, found himself confined to the Telefónica. He sent food, when he could get it, and money to Aurelia and the children, but going home was out of the question. Occasionally Maria called, pestering him for a rendezvous, and he found himself unable even to be civil to her on the telephone. His world had narrowed to one purple-shrouded cone of light in the censors' office; soon, he felt, the darkness would engulf it altogether. Yet still the journalists came to him with their copy every night, trying to find ways to tell the truth of what they saw and heard on the streets; and still, despite the nagging feeling that it was wrong to do so, he had to cut that copy to order, until it was just a bloodless recital of old military news.

Under the circumstances, then, it was just as well that neither he nor the reporters knew about the coded cable that had arrived at the Soviet embassy on October 12. Marked "Absolutely Secret" and ostensibly sent by Nicolai Yezhov, people's commissar for internal affairs and overseer of the NKVD in Moscow, to General Alexander Orlov, the recently appointed NKVD station chief in Madrid, the cable was in fact signed "Ivan Vasilievich"—the code name of General Secretary Joseph Vissarionovich Stalin himself. And it ordered Orlov to make immediate and covert arrangements to ship to Russia all of Spain's most valuable treasure, her gold and silver reserves, which were the fourth largest in the world: a huge store of ingots, Louis d'or, dollars, sovereigns, and other coins that had been accumulating since the days of the *conquistadores* and had hitherto been the guarantee of the nation's currency.

Until a few weeks ago this hoard had lain undisturbed in moated vaults under the Banco de España on the Paseo del Prado—vaults that were designed to flood in the event of a robbery. But a far greater danger than mere robbers had now appeared in the form of the rebel armies that were drawing ever closer to Madrid; and in mid-September the government had decided to move the reserves to a safer, more defensible place. The coins and ingots were crated and transported by truck to Cartagena, on the Mediterranean coast in Murcia, where they were hidden in the caves that the Spanish Navy used to store munitions; but this was only a temporary stopgap. For there were threats to the treasure's security not only from the Nationalist insurgents but also from the anarchist leader Buenaventura Durruti, who (it was feared) wanted to hijack it and take it to Barcelona.

The likeliest refuges would have appeared to be France or Britain; and indeed, some withdrawals from the reserves had been sent to France around the time of the insurrection in July. But both of these countries, for different reasons, seemed to have turned their backs on the Republic in the name of nonintervention. What if they decided that letting the Spanish government draw on its own gold reserves was as much off-limits as selling it arms? Meanwhile, as every day brought another insurgent victory, Fascist Italy and Nazi Germany were sending money, men, and matériel to the Nationalists—motivated not just by ideological kinship, but by Hitler's belief that a Spanish war distracted the world's attention from his own rearmament and gave him a laboratory to test its products, and by Mussolini's desire for a stage on which he might be seen as an important actor.

As disturbing as this state of affairs was to President Azaña, Prime Minister Largo Caballero, and Spain's finance minister, Juan Negrín, it was equally unsettling to Stalin, for it threatened the balance of power on his own geopolitical chessboard. On the one hand, a Nationalist victory in Spain, which would surround France with three potentially hostile countries and free Hitler to attack Russia, had to be avoided at all costs. But on the other hand, an outright triumph for the Republicans would allow Germany to redirect its aggression eastward, and would also alarm the right in Britain and France. A continuation of the conflict, however, would deflect attention from Stalin's own ongoing purge of old Bolsheviks; and it might even make possible a world war that would consume Germany, Italy, France, and Britain, leaving Russia unscathed and dominant.

So: help must be forthcoming for the Spanish Republic—food, tanks, planes, guns, cars and trucks, as well as field officers, pilots, technicians, and political advisors. But how would this aid be compensated, Stalin wondered. Fortunately, Prime Minister Largo Caballero and Finance Minister Negrín had a suggestion: For helping the Republic, for being the only government to stand beside it in its hour of greatest need, *Russia* could become the guardian of Spain's gold reserves. They would be shipped to safety in Moscow, where they could form the basis of a drawing account from which the Soviet Union could deduct for the Republic's purchases of Russian arms, oil, and foodstuffs. And if, or when, the government defeated the rebels, Spain's good friend would *of course* return its treasure intact.

The cable to Orlov was Stalin's answer; and within days of receiving it Orlov met with Negrín, to hammer out the details of the transfer. The crates of gold and silver would have to be loaded onto Soviet ships at Cartagena for transport through the Mediterranean to the Bosporus and thence to the Black Sea and the Russian port of Odessa—a journey fraught with danger. German and Italian warships patrolled the Mediterranean and could seize the precious cargo if they knew anything about it; and there might be an outraged reaction among the non-Communist majority of the left at the removal of their country's reserves to Communist Russia. So Orlov and Negrín cooked up a cover story in which Orlov was given false credentials as the representative of the Bank of America in order to claim, if the need arose, that the gold was going to the United States and not the Soviet Union. And the arrangements for the transfer were kept secret from anyone without a specific need to know about it— which included, to his later fury, the president of the Republic, Manuel Azaña.

On October 22, the first crates containing the reserves, which weighed 145 pounds apiece, were loaded onto trucks holding 100 boxes each and driven from the caves to the docks at Cartagena under cover of darkness; after two nights more the trucks made their final trip, and a flotilla of Soviet steamers sailed off with more than $500 million in gold— worth more than 8.5 billion in today's dollars—in its holds. At the same time Spain took delivery of approximately one hundred T-26 Russian tanks and the same number of aircraft, including I-15 and I-16 fighters— "Chatos" (snubnoses) and "Moscas" (flies)—which were the fastest in Europe. And Azaña and Largo Caballero endorsed a proposal by the Comintern—the Moscow-directed organization devoted to advancing the cause of communism internationally—to form a volunteer force made up of foreign antifascists to aid in the defense of the Republic, "the common cause of progressive humanity," as Stalin put it in an open letter to *Mundo Obrero*, Madrid's Communist newspaper.

In his blacked-out room at the Telefónica, Arturo Barea knew that that cause was also desperate. General Mola had four columns of soldiers massed on the outskirts of Madrid and was claiming to reporters on the Nationalist side that the city would soon fall to his *fifth* column, "men now in hiding who will rise and support us." The bombing grew more intense every night: Barea's sister's house in the western suburbs had been reduced to rubble and she and her children were now staying with his brother in Lavapiés. Others weren't so lucky. On October 30, in an attack on the neighborhood around the airport at Getafe, just outside the city, fifty children were killed: Barea saw the photographs taken in the morgue afterward, the children lying in neat rows, their eyes closed and their lips parted as if in sleep, numbers on their chests for identification. They might have been his, or his brother's or his sister's. He couldn't get them out of his mind.

Meanwhile, far away in Odessa, a gray ship with no markings, flying no flag, tied up in the harbor, and an armored train ferried its cargo to Moscow. To celebrate its safe arrival, and that of other, similar ships with similar cargo, General Secretary Stalin threw one of the loud, lavish, and vaguely threatening Kremlin dinner parties for which he was famous—the kind where even the seating has political implications. As the evening drew to a climax Stalin raised his vodka glass for a toast. The company fell silent. To the Spanish gold, their host said, which for the Spanish people would be like the ears on their heads: they would know it was there, but they would never see it again.

November 1936: New York

It really was a most unpleasant surprise. Just when she was about to have a little taste of celebrity as one of a starry roster of speakers—along with the poet Edgar Lee Masters, the actor Burgess Meredith, the lawyer and free-speech advocate Morris Ernst, and the Pulitzer Prize–winning novelist and playwright Margaret Ayer Barnes—at the first-ever New York Book Fair, Martha Gellhorn found herself in an embarrassing predicament. Things had started off so promisingly, too: she'd returned from Europe to a fanfare of admiring reviews for *The Trouble I've Seen*, and she'd learned that her *Spectator* piece about lynching, "Justice at Night," had been reprinted by a transatlantic magazine called *Living Age* and in the States by *Reader's Digest*, whose circulation numbered in the hundreds of thousands. It was the most natural thing in the world for her to mention this to Eleanor Roosevelt over lunch at the presidential retreat at Hyde Park on November 1; and just as natural for the First Lady, who liked the article very much, to pass it along to Walter Francis White, the director of the National Association for the Advancement of Colored People, which had been trying for several years to get Congress to pass an antilynching bill. But that's where the trouble started. White was hoping to spur congressional hearings on the bill, and now he'd written Martha a lengthy and complimentary letter asking her, since she'd been a firsthand witness to this dreadful miscarriage of justice, to testify about it before a Senate committee.

Unfortunately, no matter how much she might have wanted to, there was no way in the world that Martha could do that. If she did, she would have to raise her slender hand and swear that the testimony she was about to give was the truth, the whole truth, and nothing but the truth, so help her God—and she couldn't. Because it wasn't. And now, somehow, she was going to have to turn White down. Worse, she was going to have to explain to Mrs. Roosevelt, as well as to White, what had happened: that she'd written a terrifyingly plausible piece of sensational, finger-pointing journalism that just happened to be fiction.

Trying both to brazen things out and to apologize to the woman she regarded as a "pillar" of her "cosmos," she wrote ER a chipper little note whose tone veered back and forth between swagger and shame. She confessed that the story was just that—a story: "apparently I am a very realistic writer (or liar), because everyone assumed I'd been an eye-witness to a lynching whereas I just made it up." But, she rationalized, she really couldn't be blamed for its publication: all those magazines had simply helped themselves to her piece—she (or her agents) had had nothing to do with placing it. (She didn't explain how it was that she'd been paid for the piece.) Now, although she was bewildered by finding herself "on something of a spot" for her creativity, and although her first instinct had been to ask Mrs. Roosevelt to intervene with White on her behalf, she said she'd be "a big brave girl and tidy it all up myself."

Whether or not she hoped Mrs. Roosevelt would take the hint and defend her, and whether or not she felt any queasiness about being publicly caught out as what she herself would later call an "apocryphier," Martha wasted no more time on self-recrimination. On the evening of November 17, with an unseasonably cold wind whipping the flags along Fifth Avenue, she made her way to the most recently opened of the monumental palaces of Rockefeller Center, the International Building. Passing the huge bronze statue of Atlas, effortlessly hefting his earthly burden in the building's forecourt, she joined the thousands of people packing the streamlined escalators and pushing past glass cases full of first editions of Dickens, Joyce, and Whitman to the crowded auditorium.

Martha had little experience of public speaking and it didn't help that she was slated to go on near the end of the evening's program: she was trembling like a racehorse in the starting gate by the time it was her turn, and gripped the shaky lectern for support. The subject of the evening's program was "Listening to America," and although her predecessors had talked about their American readers, or about the state of literature, or drama, in the United States, Martha decided to widen her focus. Writers, particularly American writers, she said, needed to develop their social consciousness. They needed to "dramatize, advertise, and sell democracy" to their readers—and if they didn't, she warned, they risked having what was happening in Germany happen to them. Despite her initial nervousness, she appeared unfazed, at one week past her twenty-sixth birthday, to be playing Cassandra to a capacity crowd of her elders. "It seemed to make some sense to some people," she said of her speech afterward.

Describing the proceedings later to Mrs. Roosevelt, Martha was disdainful of her fellow speakers, who made her "mad" or "miserable" by mumbling or producing platitudes. She had particular scorn for Margaret Ayer Barnes, who had spoken of asking her husband for background about bank failures so she could describe one in her fiction. How pathetic, Martha thought, to "go feminine publicly" in this way, when writing was really "as practical as plumbing." But Barnes was no fluttery lady writer; she was a professional who wanted to be sure of her facts—as Martha might have realized if she'd heard Barnes earlier that day, in another session, talking about the importance of checking the truth of details when writing about the past. It was much harder to do this than anyone would suppose, Barnes said; "but if the author makes such a mistake, a thousand people will detect it."

November 1936: Madrid

It had turned colder in Madrid, and in the mornings when you looked out the windows of the Telefónica toward the Guadarrama the mountains were mantled with white. The soldiers, going out to the front, wore heavy scarves with their overcoats, and were glad of the extra warmth of the blanket rolls strapped over their shoulders.

On November 6, Barea arrived at Rubio Hidalgo's office for his usual briefing to find the place in turmoil: drawers open, papers stacked on the desk, other papers burning in the grate. Rubio told him to shut the door and sit down. With the Nationalist armies poised on the west bank of the Manzanares, it was obvious that Madrid was doomed, Rubio said; President Azaña had already fled to Barcelona, and now the rest of the government was relocating to Valencia, on the coast. The press office was going with it. Or rather, the permanent staff was going, as well as any foreign journalists whose lives would be at risk when Franco entered the city, as he would surely do either tomorrow or the next day. As for Barea: Rubio would have liked to move him to safety, too, but really there was nothing he could do about it. He was sorry.

"I hope—the government hopes, I should say—that you will remain at your post up to the last moment," he said. And waited for an answer. What could Barea say? *Of course, sir.*

Over the distant *obbligato* of munitions fire from the west, Rubio told him that General José Miaja, who had been in charge of the government's ill-fated assault on the Córdoba front, would take over political as well as military control of the capital, with instructions to negotiate a surrender with the least amount of blood spilled. He, Barea, should issue a bulletin saying that the press services were being evacuated, but that was all; then he should just close the censorship office, go home, and try to save his own neck.

Rubio handed him a packet containing two months' salary for himself and the wages for his orderly, Luis, and for the couriers; then he rose, came around the desk, and shook Barea's hand solemnly. *Like a funeral*, thought Barea. He glanced at Rubio's desk, saw the photographs of the murdered children of Getafe spread out on the surface. "What are you going to do with these photographs?" he asked. Burn them, of course, Rubio answered; they were obvious propaganda and anyone found with them would be shot on the spot. "Let me take them," Barea said. He didn't know what he was going to do with them, but he couldn't abandon these children to die a second time. Rubio shrugged and handed over the prints and a box of negatives, and Barea put them under his arm and left.

It was raining when he came out of the Foreign Ministry, a cold, dank drizzle that went through your clothes into your bones. Making his way through the rain-slick streets, he went to Calle del Ave Maria to tell Aurelia to pack bags for herself and the children in case they, too, would have to flee; then he headed back to the Telefónica to issue Rubio's bulletin and try to keep the reporters from writing nonsense about it. In the hours just after midnight, news came that the fascists had crossed the Manzanares and that there was fighting in the Model Prison, less than a mile away; one of the American correspondents, a big man named Louis Fischer who wrote for *The Nation* and had been knocking back whiskey all night while waiting for a free telephone line, wanted to send the story that the capital had fallen. When Barea refused, Fischer grabbed him by the collar and shook him, and Barea had to call guards to throw the correspondent onto one of the emergency beds, where he promptly sank into a sodden sleep.

In the morning, although the Nationalists were still at the city's western boundary, they had got no farther. The convoys of journalists and diplomats and government employees left, and Barea paid off the couriers and Luis, as he'd been told to do; he was about to leave the Telefónica himself and go home when one of the switch censors—who listened in to the correspondents' calls and switched off the line if anything forbidden was mentioned—asked him who was going to take over now. No one had given orders not to let the journalists' calls go through, the man said; but now who would censor their stories? Barea started to repeat what Rubio had told him—*We're done for, just get out while you can and leave the journalists to General Miaja*—and found he couldn't do it. He'd started working as a censor not because it was just another job, but because he wanted to make a stand against fascism, and believed that the story of the government's fight had to be told to the world. If he walked out now, he risked allowing lies or fabrications to be published, or having the stories silenced altogether by military censors.

Just months ago he'd been wrapped in a fog of professional ambivalence, political alienation, marital exhaustion, and sexual ennui; but today the fog had rolled away and was replaced with a strange clarity. "We can't let things go," Barea said to the switch censor. Rubio and the others could run, but he had work to do.

How much work was confirmed that evening, when Henry Buckley, the slight, sandy-haired, soft-spoken correspondent of London's *Daily Telegraph*, telephoned his editor to report that despite Franco's attack on suburban districts across the Manzanares, Madrid itself was calm and unvanquished.

"I say, Buckley," the young man in London said, "do you know your copy does not tally with the other information we have? We have it quite definitely that Franco's forces are now fighting in the center of Madrid." Buckley, generally the politest of men, hung up on him.

Over the next two days, Barea stepped into the vacuum left by the departure of his chief and became a leader. He pulled the remnants of the censorship staff together and ordered them to start vetting all journalists' reports for accuracy and confidentiality before allowing them to be transmitted; then he went to the Foreign Ministry, rounded up a few left-behind office employees to form a "Popular Front Committee," and got an authorization from them (really just a piece of paper with an impressive-looking stamp on it) to assume the duties of head of the Press Office; finally he found someone at the newly established defense committee, the Junta de Defensa, to make the whole process official. He thought it entirely possible he'd be shot for insubordination, but he was too tired to care.

While Barea was knocking on doors in nearly empty ministries, however, something surprising was taking place. On Saturday, the day that the government convoys had set out for Valencia, they passed the first detachments of foreign soldiers from the recently formed International Brigades that had mustered at Albacete, 140 miles southeast of Madrid; by Sunday morning, November 8, a battalion of Germans, another of French and Belgians, and still another made up of Polish miners, as well as a section of British machine-gunners and two squadrons of French cavalry, were marching down the Gran Via toward the front. And incredulous Madrileños—who believed these multinational *dei ex machina* had been sent by their new Soviet allies—were cheering "*Viven los Rusos!*" and waving their handkerchiefs from the balconies along the avenue. By that evening the international battalions had joined the civilian volunteers and Loyalist troops in the Casa de Campo; by the next day the rebels' advance there had been halted, and suddenly it seemed as if Madrid might not fall after all.

Barea had been sleeping in an armchair in one of the gilded reception rooms at the Foreign Ministry when just after dawn he was jolted awake by the scream of shells from enemy guns and the sound of explosions: first in the Puerta del Sol, then, even closer by, in the Plaza Mayor. Suddenly the walls of the ministry, the old Hapsburg Palacio de Santa Cruz, shuddered, and Barea braced himself for a crash. But none came: all he heard were shouts and running footsteps. Hurrying downstairs into the building's courtyard, he found half-dressed staffers and a handful of Assault Guards standing in front of an unexploded shell the size of a large dog. An artillery technician was sent for to defuse the ordnance, and when he pulled out the fuse cap he found a piece of paper in the unexploded bomb. "Comrades," it read, in German, "do not be afraid. The shells I charge do not explode.—A German worker." *They're paying attention to us after all.* Absurdly heartened, Barea fetched Rubio's discarded photographs of the slaughtered children of Getafe and took them to his friend Antonio Mije to be turned into propaganda posters.

But any thoughts he might have had about patting himself on the back for his enterprise were dispelled by an unexpected visit from a stranger, a Russian journalist named Mikhail Koltsov. The chairman of the Soviet Writers' Union's foreign committee and correspondent for the official Soviet newspaper, *Pravda*, Koltsov had arrived in Madrid in August, but although he was staying in the Hotel Florida, in the Plaza de Callao just down the street from the Telefónica, his stories must have been filed through some back channel to Moscow, because Barea had never met him. Now he was confronted with a pale, shortish man with small soft hands, wearing round wire-rimmed spectacles that gave him the look of a barn owl. An angry barn owl, in this case: smacking a sheaf of press dispatches against the desk, Koltsov began haranguing him in bad Spanish, demanding to know who had been responsible for letting these reports through. He'd been at the War Commissariat, he said, when the Foreign Ministry had sent the dispatches over for forwarding to Valencia—and whoever had let the journalists who wrote them get away with such sensationalist sabotage deserved to be shot.

After his initial shock at Koltsov's attack had subsided, Barea was less defensive than pleased that someone—anyone—actually *cared* about the foreign press coverage. He pointed out that the dispatches Koltsov was brandishing had all been sent the day the government left Madrid, before he himself had taken charge of things, while unsubstantiated rumors were flying all around the city. No wonder some of the reports declared that white flags had been seen fluttering from government buildings, or that Nationalist armies were marching down the Gran Via. Since then he'd been keeping such misinformation from being printed; but, he added, he didn't have anyone's authority to do so except that of his own ad hoc "committee."

Koltsov's response to this was to hustle Barea into his official car and take him along to the War Ministry, where after a series of conversations with various officials—more bad but emphatic Spanish, more insistence—a truly official document was produced that placed the press office in Madrid under the direct jurisdiction of Álvarez del Vayo, now "war commissar" as well as foreign minister, and definitively appointed Barea its head. If Barea found it at all peculiar that a mere foreign journalist could make Spanish government ministries do his bidding, he said nothing. For the word on the street was that Koltsov was far more than a *Pravda* correspondent: he was Stalin's personal agent, his eyes and ears (some said) in Madrid, with a special line of communication direct to the secretary general. He was supposed to have attempted to shoot Republican *milicianos* to stop their retreat from Talavera back in September; and just days ago, it was whispered, he'd also been involved in—had even been responsible for—the removal and subsequent gunpoint execution of more than a thousand prisoners with Nationalist affiliations from the Carcel Modelo. So if he wanted something done, it would, in most cases, *get* done.

Within days Barea found out to what extent this was true: for Rubio Hidalgo hastily arranged to make a flying visit from Valencia to pass the baton of authority to his erstwhile deputy. Barea received him, awkwardly, in his own old office—really, where else could they have such a meeting?— and they agreed that while Rubio remained the head of the Foreign Ministry's press department, and would continue to receive copies of outgoing dispatches, since he was now located in Valencia it made sense for Barea to be in charge of the Madrid foreign press office, and for day-to-day supervision of that office to pass to the Madrid War Commissariat. For safety and convenience, Barea would relocate their headquarters from the Foreign Ministry to the Telefónica; and Rubio would send him a new deputy from Valencia. No mention was made of Koltsov.

When their business was finished Barea came around the desk to shake Rubio's hand in farewell. *You hate me more than I could ever hate you*, Barea thought; and Rubio turned on his heel and left.

It was nearly midnight. Ilse Kulcsar had just spent the better part of two days wedged into a hired car with three journalists—a large, rumpled, blustery Englishman named Sefton Delmer, who wrote for the *Daily Express*; a slender, sallow, impeccably groomed Frenchman, Louis Delaprée, correspondent for *Paris-Soir*; and Andreas Vinding, a rotund Dane from *Politiken*—and she was bone-weary, hungry, and aching with cold. At the roadblocks on their way from Valencia sentries wearing red-and-black Anarchist scarves had come out of their posts to stare at the crazy foreigners who wanted to drive to Madrid when everyone else was going the other way; now, as they got out of the car in front of the Telefónica, a fleet of motorcycles equipped with sirens were screaming off into the night to sound an air-raid alert. Soon Nationalist planes would be flying over, and the bombs would fall. But despite these ominous signals, and despite her discomfort, Ilse felt absurdly elated to be back in Madrid.

She'd first arrived there in October and had just been learning her way around when the government relocated to Valencia and Rubio Hidalgo insisted that—as an unattached woman correspondent with no embassy to seek refuge in—she be evacuated along with it. But she hadn't wanted to be in Valencia among the bureaucrats and the orange groves; that wasn't why she'd come to Spain. As a socialist journalist she wanted to *bear witness*, wanted to be where the fight was going on, and that was in Madrid. So as soon as it seemed as if the city might withstand Franco's onslaught, she scrambled to get herself back. Delmer, Delaprée, and Vinding, whom she'd met when she'd first come to Spain, and who saw in the beleaguered city the journalistic scoop of a lifetime, had decided to return themselves, and they offered her typing and translating work if she wanted to go with them. All she needed were credentials and a place to stay. When she asked Rubio if he could arrange those for her, he'd replied sourly that the person she'd have to talk to was a man named Barea, one of the self-appointed heroes who'd stayed on when the government left. "He's the master there now," he said.

When Ilse and the journalists arrived at the Telefónica they discovered that conditions in Madrid were far more dangerous than they had realized. Yes, the *milicianos* and the International Brigades had stopped the Insurgent advance through the scrublands of the Casa de Campo; but in compensation the rebel forces had stepped up their bombing attacks on the city. And they'd added incendiary bombs, whose sheets of white fire gutted buildings and spread panic among the population, to their arsenal of destruction. So tonight, as the sirens wailed in the darkened streets, Ilse and the others had to make way for a crowd of women and children from the neighborhood who'd come to take shelter from the air-raid in the skyscraper's deep basements. In silence they shuffled down the stairs, which were illuminated only by blue-painted blackout bulbs; the journalists got into the elevator, standing shoulder to shoulder in the cramped space. As the lift groaned upward Ilse found herself wondering what would happen if a bomb hit while they were in it—and looking at Vinding, the Dane, who'd begun to perspire profusely despite the cold, she knew he was thinking the same thing.

On the fifth floor they groped their way along the dark passages until they came to a windowless vestibule where the censor had taken refuge from the possibility of flying glass in the outside offices and was reading reports by the uncertain beam of his flashlight. Ilse saw a tall man with a long sallow face, sculpted cheekbones, arched brows, a full but sardonic mouth. His thin frame was wrapped in a shabby tweed overcoat against the cold, and he was wearing a black workingman's beret with a five-pointed Russian star on it. He looked up at the journalists with impatience. *Couldn't they keep quiet while a raid was going on?*

Eventually the bombs stopped falling and the censor ushered the little group into his office. They all identified themselves and shook hands— *Andreas Vinding, Tom Delmer, Louis Delaprée, Ilse Kulcsar, Arturo Barea Ogazón.* Barea looked the newcomers over in the dim violet glow of his lamp. The men he knew by sight or reputation; the woman, whose name he couldn't pronounce, was a stranger. Too round for his taste, he thought: big green eyes, like a cat's, pointed chin—*stubborn*—lots of dark curly hair, broad shoulders. He dismissed her as no beauty, and unfashionably dressed to boot. *Why the hell did they send me a woman?* She'd have to wait to be assigned a billet, he said in his fluent but badly accented French, the only common language between him and the journalists;

first he had to look over reports of the raid just past and clear them for transmission.

The men left and Ilsa sat down on the other side of his table, watching in silence as he struggled to translate the unfamiliar words for the horrors the war was causing. He almost forgot she was there until he heard her husky voice: "Can I help you with anything, *camarade*?" she asked in French. He surprised himself by handing her the dispatch he was working on—he told himself it was to see what she'd do with it—and surprised himself again by taking her advice about some of the language in it. Then he endorsed her papers, gave her a room assignment at the Gran Via Hotel, just across the street, and rose to shake her hand. But he addressed her formally as *señorita*, and when he did so her face broke into a mischievous, little-girl grin. He shouldn't call anyone *señorita*, she said: "We're all comrades here." And marched off down the hall, her shoulders squared in her severely cut coat.

She came back the next morning to get her safe-conduct, which would allow her to go freely about the city as long as she gave the password of the day to the sentries, and Barea asked her a little about herself. She told him of her hatred of fascism, her work in Vienna, her flight to Brno with Poldi, her university background, her travels, the eight languages she knew; and Barea felt both dismissive and resentful of her erudition and her passion. *Who needs a bluestocking like this in a war zone?* Ilse, however, had a proposition for him: wouldn't it be useful to have someone working in his office who could read the correspondents' reports in their native languages and talk to them about what cuts or changes were needed? Wouldn't it save time? Wouldn't it serve the cause better to have a spokesperson who could speak directly to journalists?

Somewhat unwillingly—after all, who did she think she was, barging in with all these suggestions?—Barea called Rubio in Valencia to ask him what he thought of the idea. To his surprise the normally cautious Rubio enthusiastically endorsed it. "Ask her to join the censorship," he said. "Ask her today." And by that evening Barea and Ilse—whose name he Hispanicized to "Ilsa"—were working across from each other at the big desk in his office. He began explaining the rules: that anything negative had to be suppressed, that no mention could be made of defeats, setbacks, catastrophes, shortages, or anything that would give a picture of what life was really like in a besieged city where aircraft rained destruction every night.

And Ilsa, who wasn't used to being coy or deferential to male colleagues if she disagreed with them, told him flat-out that such a strategy was wrong—"catastrophically wrong," she said. It made the government's losses inexplicable. What they should be giving the foreign press was *more* information, not less: if a bomb falls, tell them the make and give them the factory identification number, if possible. Put as much into the dispatches as you can, so people understand what is really happening here. Make them see the true collective spirit in Madrid's struggle; make a propaganda for the new out of the dirt and blood.

Instead of resenting her insubordination—her assumption, which a Spanish woman would never have made, that she had as much right to speak as he did—Barea was perversely exhilarated. What she was saying was what he'd felt all along, and had so often repressed: and now, it seemed, he might have an ally, and a coworker, agreeing with him. Excitedly, they pushed the idea this way and that: perhaps, together, they might have a chance to persuade their superiors to change their tactics. They could try, anyway.

Ilsa didn't go back to the Gran Via Hotel that night. She'd hated lying in bed listening for the sound of the Junkers and Capronis in the sky overhead, and watching her window light up with the glare of incendiary bombs; so Barea offered her the third camp bed in the office (Luis, the young orderly who ran the censors' errands, was snoring in the other one), and she and he took turns sleeping and censoring until morning. They spent all day working and listening to the rumble of firing from the trenches, only a tram ride away at the northwest of the city; after midnight they dozed on the camp beds. Suddenly, during what was normally a quiet time between three and five, they heard the insidious purr of a bomber directly overhead. Ilsa sat up. "What are we going to do?" she whispered. Luis wasn't there; probably he'd gone down to the shelter. "Nothing," Barea replied. Seconds ticked by.

The explosion seemed to take place within the room itself: the furniture jumped, the floor swayed, and there was a sucking roar, then a tinkling arpeggio as the windows shattered and the blackout curtains were blown inward by the draft. The bomb had fallen on a building twenty yards away, in the Calle de Hortaleza, and completely demolished it; outside, in the street, there was a flurry of cries, and the sound of bricks and plaster falling. Neither Barea nor Ilsa could speak for a moment; then Ilsa came and sat on Barea's bed and they began talking, talking about anything, as if by doing so they could prove to themselves that they were still alive.

The next day they moved their desks and camp beds to an office on the fourth floor. To Barea's intense discomfort, both Aurelia and Maria came looking for him and were openly curious, and jealous, to find him with Ilsa. There were scenes with each of them: Where had he been? Who was this foreign woman? What was she to him? Any response seemed inadequate, self-serving; he felt ashamed, in front of Ilsa, of the evident mess he'd made of his personal life, and defensive that he should feel that way at all. In fact, he *didn't* know what Ilsa was to him. A colleague, certainly; a woman he could really talk to, which was something he had never known. But she was married. And she wasn't at all the sort of woman he'd usually been attracted to.

For the next day and a half, like an automaton, he censored reports, dealt with journalists' questions, fell into exhausted slumber, rose and worked again, all the while watching himself and his interactions with this mysterious foreigner, trying to explain them to himself. Day wore on into night, and finally the last reports had been checked and sent out; Luis was already curled up in his corner of the room, and Barea and Ilsa stretched out exhausted on their own camp beds. Perhaps emboldened by the darkness, they talked softly of her life, his life, their marriages, their hopes and fears. At length, and at last, they fell silent. Barea got up, carefully and noiselessly moved his own cot close to hers, lay down, and reached out for her hand. And like that they slipped into sleep.

In the morning, when Luis was out of the room, he kissed her for the first time, and they both started laughing. But then Barea brought himself up short—what was he getting himself into? This wasn't a feeling like any he'd ever known. Exasperated and confused, he barked to Ilsa, "*Mais, je ne t'aime pas!*" But she just smiled back at him. "No, my dear," she replied.

She had her own puzzle to work out: She was in a war zone, in a country where she didn't speak the language, in a culture unlike any she'd ever known. She had only just met this man, and it was obvious that he was already entangled, disastrously, with two other women. She couldn't fall in love with him, when his relationships with women were everything she hated and had worked against. She tried to make herself think about Poldi: once he'd been comrade, lover, and husband to her, but now he seemed like a character in a book, distant and unreal. Nothing was right in her marriage anymore, she thought. But somehow *this* felt right, and real. Looking at Barea, she felt she knew already exactly how things would unfold between them. As Barea himself would write, much later: "It did not seem worthwhile to pretend; there were so few things that mattered."

November 1936: Paris/Madrid

Capa's and Gerda's photographs from Spain were all over the European— and even the American—press: in *Vu*, in the Communist-backed news-weekly *Regards*, in the Dutch *Katholieke Illustratie*, the German *BIZ*, the *Illustrated London News*, *Time*, and elsewhere. Suddenly there was money in their pockets for food and drinks and cigarettes and clothes; and there were, for Gerda at least, bragging rights in the Spanish conflict, which for her SAP friends at the Dôme and the Capoulade was the greatest thing to happen to the left since the October Revolution. But when they'd left Madrid the government's prospects had seemed dim; and in the intervening weeks Capa had gone to cover regional political events in France rather than seek another Spanish assignment, while Gerda had planned a trip to Italy to see her old beau Georg Kuritzkes, now studying medicine in Naples.

After November 8, however, things seemed to change overnight. The headlines in *L'Humanité* told the story: "MADRID HOLDS!" "MADRID RESISTS FIERCELY!" and—over one of Barea's rescued images of the murdered children of Getafe—"'NO PASARAN'—MADRID, LIBER-TY'S VERDUN." Madrid was still a big, big story, bigger than ever; and if you wanted photos of actual combat all you had to do was take a tram to University City or the Parque del Oeste and get off right at the front.

Gerda didn't change her Italian plans. She had, after all, just bought herself a new travel wardrobe, including a very pretty lacy brassiere that she gaily modeled for Capa and the Hungarian photographer Kati Deutsch—Capa's first teenage crush in their Budapest days—who'd dropped by the Hotel de Blois to reminisce and talk shop. But Capa immediately set about trying to get assigned to go to Madrid on his own. He'd just cut his ties to *Vu*, which had been losing advertisements because of its outspoken support of the Spanish government, and had been sold to a rightist businessman who promptly fired Lucien Vogel. Now Capa had a contract with *Regards*, whose stance on the Spanish war was made clear by the cover of the October 26 issue, showing a French soldier in a gas mask against the backdrop of a spookily realistic air-raid simulation: "PARIS BOMBED: SPAIN DEFENDS OUR LIBERTY," it said.

On Saturday the fourteenth *Regards* gave him a letter to take over to the Spanish Embassy in the Avenue George-V, asking that Capa be fast-tracked for a visa; by Monday, visa in hand, he was packed and ready to go. He picked up a letter of introduction from his editors that stated he was their exclusive correspondent in Madrid and took the night train to Toulouse, where he stopped only long enough to send Gerda a postcard before boarding a flight to Valencia and getting a ride to Madrid. If he was anxious about Gerda's trip to Italy, or jealous of Kuritzkes, he apparently knew better than to say so.

In Madrid he was assigned quarters at the Hotel Florida. At its opening a dozen years before, the Florida had been a posh hostelry in a swank location—a ten-story marble-clad jewel box with centrally heated, opulently furnished rooms surrounding a glass-roofed atrium, around the corner from the smart shops of the Gran Via, face to face with the modern picture palaces of the Plaza de Callao, and just down the street from the Telefónica. Now it was a target for the same shells and bombs that were aimed at its neighbor; and it had become a haven—not for successful business travelers or wealthy tourists, but for a polyglot collection of journalists, French and Russian pilots, and opportunistic ladies of the evening. The pilots and the tarts (and some of the journalists) spent their evenings getting roaring drunk in the little bar, and when shells weren't whistling over the building the night was punctuated by shrieks and slamming doors and running feet.

Such antics would certainly help keep his mind off whatever Gerda was up to in Italy; but Capa had barely slung his bag into his room before he had to go get his papers from the foreign-press censors in the Telefónica—which is probably where, on November 19, he met Gustav Regler. Blond, fine-featured, and pale from nerves and lack of sleep, Regler was a German Communist writer, a refugee from the Reich, who'd originally come to Spain bringing a printing press, film projector, and propaganda films as gifts from the International Union of Authors to the Loyalists, and had then stayed on to become the political commissar of the Twelfth International Brigade. He had known Ilsa Kulcsar "from before," as Barea put it, from their years in European leftist journalism, and since his regiment was stationed on Madrid's northwest perimeter he liked to come to the Telefónica when there was a lull in the fighting, to talk about old times and flirt mildly with her, to Barea's concealed fury. So it would have been natural for Ilsa to pass the eager young photographer from *Regards* along to Regler—particularly given that Regler's commander, a chunky, jovial, mustached former Red Army officer whose *nom de guerre* was General Pavol Lukács, was a compatriot of Capa's, a Hungarian novelist named Máté Zalka.

Regler was instantly charmed by Capa, describing him as "this small beautiful boy whom everybody loved." He immediately whisked his new acquaintance off to Lukács's headquarters in the outlying suburb of Fuencarral, where the general was trying to plot maneuvers with the inadequate help of a map torn out of an old Baedeker guidebook. Introductions took place in German; then Lukács broke into Hungarian. "What do you really want?" he asked Capa. "To see the enemy," Capa said. "We haven't found him yet," Lukács responded tersely. Turning to his political commissar he muttered, "How do you know he's not a spy?" Capa overheard him and was indignant. "Are you discussing my reliability?" he asked. He extended his Leica toward the general. "Here's my passport."

Disarmed, Lukács agreed to let him go out on a patrol with Regler and another officer: word had come that some of Franco's Moors were bivouacked in the barns of an old estate, the Palacita de Moncloa, on the Manzanares, and Lukács wanted confirmation. The patrol should try to determine the enemy's positions, he said, but on no account should they fire at them. Capa was perfectly amenable. "If shooting can be avoided, I don't mind," he confided to Regler.

The three men set out for the river and were soon making their way cautiously along its eastern bank. Suddenly firing broke out, and Capa, Regler, and the other officer threw themselves down in the frost-rimed underbrush and waited for it to be over. Finally the guns fell silent; but when the men rose to continue their reconnaissance, Capa said he needed a minute to change his trousers: "My guts aren't as brave as my camera," he explained.

He made himself tough to do his job, however, Regler said later. In the next few days Capa went out with other patrols from the Twelfth International Brigade's Thaelmann Battalion, a force mostly made up of German Communists with a smattering of English and Scandinavians, as they set up machine-gun positions in farm buildings along the western perimeter, or by the North Station, where they pulled suitcases out of the left-luggage office to form makeshift barricades. Another time, he followed Asturian *dinamiteros* as they used slingshots to lob grenades over the city's former slaughterhouses and into the insurgent lines. And he and Louis Delaprée both went to cover the battle that had been playing out in the recently completed Bauhaus-style buildings of Madrid's university.

To get there you rode the streetcar—not the metro, which might take you too far, into enemy territory—to the end of the line; then you had to run, bent double, through a hail of machine-gun bullets and shell debris that Delaprée called "a good approximation of hell" until you reached the shelter of the buildings. Once there, you found yourself in a world of surreal shadows, where (said Capa) "the abnormal . . . had become normal": makeshift gunners' nests, built from piles of textbooks, cross-hatched with diagonal stripes of shade from venetian blinds; a cannon positioned on a library table; soldiers seated at a classroom piano, singing lustily, while behind them a disused blackboard still showed a bygone professor's scribbles and students' old papers littered the floor. The air echoed with commands shouted in a Babel of languages, because the fighters were German (the Thaelmann Battalion) or French (André Marty Battalion) or Polish (Dombrovsky Battalion). Fighting was at close quarters, and ugly: Thaelmann Battalion soldiers put grenades in the elevators in the Clinical Hospital building, then sent them to the next floor to explode in the faces of the Nationalists' Moroccan troops.

Capa witnessed only a fraction of this activity, but his photographs captured University City's atmosphere of chiaroscuro chaos; and he soon found an even more powerful if less obviously dramatic story, whose heroes were ordinary men and women, suddenly thrust into front lines they hadn't known were there. For when Franco had found the prize of Madrid withheld from him by the unexpected strength of the International Brigades and the *milicianos*, he'd announced that he would rather destroy the city than cede it to the "Marxists," and invited Germany's new Condor Legion to test how a civilian population would react to methodical quarter-by-quarter firebombing. Now, night after night, the Junkers swept over Madrid as they would one day sweep over London, and Glasgow, and Coventry—and as American B-17s would sweep over Dresden and Berlin; in their wake they left a landscape like none anyone had ever seen before. And as Capa walked the streets of the city in those November days, he passed the tumbled carcasses of burnt-out automobiles, lampposts transformed into Giacometti sculptures by the heat of incendiary bombs, vacant lots strewn with shattered masonry and charred timbers. On block after block, buildings whose facades had been sheared away by bombs or shellfire gaped open like oversize dollhouses.

What had happened to the people who had lived there? Were they the elegant young couple—she in a fur wrap, he in a beautifully tailored camel's hair coat—standing next to a pile of their belongings on the sidewalk of what had once been a graceful street and was now a wasteland? The haggard woman, cloaked in a blanket, her lined face a mask of sorrow, whose children had just been killed? Her black-clad sisters, somehow finding the strength to smile at the camera as they stood in line waiting for bread? The two little girls sitting on a curbstone chatting, seemingly oblivious to the pockmarked wall behind them or the fallen bricks at their feet? The mother and son staring with vacant, haunted eyes out of the gloom of the subway tunnel that was their air-raid shelter? There were no answers here, only questions. But Capa kept on taking pictures because, as he said, "Into the future one dares not look."

When he wanted to think, sometimes Barea took the elevator up, past the partially gutted and deserted rooms of the Telefónica's upper stories, to the terrace that ran around the clock tower at the top. "I don't like coming up here," said the girl who ran the lift. "It's so lonely. I always think the lift is going to shoot out of the tower into thin air." But Barea liked the silence and the solitude.

He and Ilsa had got the censors' office working well now, he thought. After the German government recognized Franco's Nationalists and closed its Madrid embassy, the two of them had taken a huge gamble by allowing journalists to report on a police raid of the vacated premises that turned up links to the pro-insurgent Fifth Column. The day the news broke Koltsov had called them up in a fury, threatening to have them both court-martialed for leaking sensitive information, but he'd reversed himself when international reaction to the stories had been positive, and the journalists had practically cheered. Lester Ziffren, the reporter for the American agency United Press International, was going around saying that the Madrid press office had "the most reasonable war censorship that can be expected"—a backhanded compliment, maybe, but still a compliment.

Then, because Ilsa said "you must feed the animals in the zoo," she and Barea—at Gustav Regler's suggestion—had arranged for some of the correspondents to visit the Eleventh International Brigade. They had also persuaded its commander, General Emilio Kléber, another of the Brigades' Red Army officers (real name: Manfred Stern), to talk to the journalists and be available for photographs. Up until now it had been forbidden to mention the participation of the International Brigades in press reports; but now Barea and Ilsa were pledging to provide the information *and* make sure that it would go out uncensored.

The maneuver had succeeded beyond their expectations. Capa, Delmer, Delaprée, Barbro Alving of Sweden's *Dagens Nyheter*, a woman with the gender-neutral pseudonym of "Bang," and others had all made the trip to Kléber's headquarters; Capa photographed the touchingly youthful infantrymen, idealists from far-off countries, as well as the grizzled, charismatic Kléber, an icon of unglamorous toughness in his worn uniform and woolen sweater and two-day growth of beard, while the others wrote enthusiastic reports of the Brigades' activities, their polyglot energy ("the Babel front," Delaprée called it), their optimism.

So, Barea wondered, looking out over Madrid from his perch, why wasn't he happier about his success? On the other side of the silver loop of the Manzanares he could see puffs of smoke from the big guns, and tiny, ant-like soldiers running this way and that, as if the war were a movie on a distant screen. This was the stuff the journalists down on the sixth floor were clamoring after: the guns, the tanks, the line of fire. But the glowing press accorded to the Brigades—press that he and Ilsa had arranged—ignored, even obscured the courage of the people of Madrid, and of the *milicianos* who had borne the brunt of the fighting in the beginning. Who would tell *their* stories to the world outside Spain?

Already some of those who could were leaving. Capa had to return to Paris because his visa would expire at the beginning of December; he was eager to be reunited with Gerda and wanted to supervise the layouts of his photo-essays for *Regards*. Louis Delaprée, who had come to Madrid intending to be an impartial witness, but whose reportage had become increasingly filled with Bosch-like images of murdered women and children, was sickened because his editors at the conservative, celebrity-oriented *Paris-Soir* had spiked his pieces about bombing victims so they could run gossipy drivel about Edward VIII's romance with the American divorcée Wallis Simpson. So he'd decided to leave as well. He'd hoped he might write a book that would make it impossible for a war such as this ever to happen again, but he wondered now if it would have an audience. He brought Barea a final dispatch for *Paris-Soir*: "You have not published half my articles," it began. "That is your right. But . . . for three weeks I have been getting up at 5 a.m. to give you the news for your first editions. You have made me work for the wastepaper basket . . . I am sending nothing more. It is not worth the trouble. The massacre of a hundred Spanish kids is less interesting than a sigh from Mrs. Simpson, the royal whore."

Barea read through the pages and stamped them with his official seal, while Delaprée perched himself on Barea's camp bed, looking like a large bird incongruously wearing an overcoat and red scarf against the cold. "I hate politics, as you know," he said; "but I'm a liberal and a humanist." When he got back to Paris, he said, he would try to protest France's non-intervention policy with friends of his in the government; but he couldn't promise anything.

Neither of them knew that at that very moment, in London, the novelist Virginia Woolf was staring at the photographs Barea had rescued of the dead children of Getafe, at Capa's images of the bombed buildings of Madrid, and reading some of Delaprée's dispatches; nor did they suspect that the photographs and dispatches would help crystallize the argument in her long essay entitled "Three Guineas" which attacked, in the name of preventing war, the patriarchal society that produced it. And if they had known it might have made no difference. For Barea was feeling increasingly cynical. When a former associate of Ilsa's from Vienna and Brno, the Austrian Social Democratic leader Julius Deutsch, came to tour the front, his guide—a Spaniard suspicious of German-speakers—had taken Barea aside. "Tell me, *compañero*," the guide had asked him, cocking his head in the direction of the two foreigners, "what do they seek in Spain? It can't be anything decent." And Barea had laughed, bitterly, because the thought so closely mirrored his own worst ones. Deutsch, Koltsov, Delmer, Capa, Delaprée, all of them—what was this war to them, beyond an opportunity?

Even Ilsa, he feared, was no different: just another foreigner who had no real stake in what happened in Spain, for whom the politics mattered more than the people. He couldn't know, however, what she told the other journalists when he wasn't there. "*We* are here for the story," she would say. "But they—" meaning the Spanish, the Madrileños—"are here for their lives."

November 1936: Key West

At the big stucco house on Whitehead Street, Ernest Hemingway was playing host to a reporter from the Key West *Citizen*. Pauline wasn't there that day; she'd gone to New York for a couple of weeks of Christmas shopping and theater and big-city good times after her three months in the mountains. But Key West's most famous resident, newly back from Wyoming and a visit with his wealthy in-laws in Piggott, Arkansas—and looking, his old friend John Peale Bishop wrote in *The New Republic*, like "the legendary Hemingway," sunburned and swaggering—proudly led the *Citizen*'s reporter around, pointing out where he planned to build a trophy room for his African kudu heads and where the new saltwater swimming pool, the first ever on the island, would go. When the reporter left, Hemingway went back to his second-floor writing room to work on his new novel, because trophy rooms and swimming pools are expensive, no matter how much money your wife's family has; and a lot more than money was riding on this manuscript.

Despite his confident-sounding pronouncements to Max Perkins and Arnold Gingrich, he was having trouble weaving the disparate strands of the Harry Morgan stories into one satisfactory web. Morgan was going to die, of course: shot in the guts in the course of a bank robbery gone wrong, gasping to the Coast Guard officers who have picked him up, "A man alone ain't got no bloody fucking chance." But Hemingway was still groping for "the old miracle you have to finish with" (as he described it to Gingrich). He believed he *might* be close to nailing it: one of his wealthy characters, the millionaire sportsman Tommy Bradley, would become a convert to the Cuban revolutionary cause, and would ferry a load of dynamite to Cuba so as to blow up a bridge and stop the counterrevolutionaries from winning a critical battle. But the logistics of the thing were fuzzy: he was thinking he'd have to make a trip of his own to Havana, where he frequently stayed in the Hotel Ambos Mundos, to check the geography.

In the meantime, here was a letter from John Wheeler, general manager of a journalistic consortium called the North American Newspaper Alliance, which commissioned and syndicated articles to a number of the leading American and Canadian papers. After mentioning their "many mutual friends," from the prizefighter Gene Tunney to the writer Ring Lardner, Wheeler got down to business: apparently Walter Winchell—a commentator who'd parlayed a gift for weaponized media and political gossip into a widely circulated column in the tabloid *New York Mirror*, a hugely popular radio show on NBC, and a regular table at New York's most celebrated nightspot, the Stork Club—was reporting that Hemingway was going to Spain to cover the war there. If this was true, Wheeler said, NANA wondered if Hemingway would do it for *them*.

As the conflict in Spain had persisted and deepened, Hemingway had indeed been talking of his interest in it, but in a theoretical way, as one might say to an acquaintance, "We really must have lunch." Now Winchell and Wheeler were all but calling his bluff—or were they presenting him with an opportunity? Despite the pleasure he took in the life he and Pauline had constructed in Key West, he was restless. "I've got this nice boat and house," he told a friend, "but they're both really Pauline's. I could stay on here forever, but it's a soft life. Nothing's really happening to me here and I've got to get out . . . In Spain maybe it's the big parade starting again." His work had always fed on his own experience, and now he found himself desperately needing new material: the fishing trips and safaris were pretty much used up, and for the new novel he'd had to ask a Havana-based journalist friend, Dick Armstrong, to dig up stuff about Cuban revolutionaries because he had no firsthand knowledge to draw on. If he went to Spain with an assignment to report on the war, he'd get the makings of any number of novels.

But still he hesitated, putting Wheeler's letter under a pile of paper on his writing table, leaving it unanswered. For there remained the question of Pauline, whose anxiety for Hemingway's safety set her against the whole idea of his going to a war zone, and whose fervent Catholicism made her leery of the Loyalists, with whom Hemingway's own natural sympathies lay. He would have to find a way to deal with her. Meanwhile there was the Harry Morgan novel, which he had to finish before he could even think about what would come next.

He'd been using its pages as a shooting gallery, taking aim at one person after another from his real life, as if to destroy whatever hold they had over him: his former lover, Jane Mason, and her husband, Grant, thinly disguised as rich Tommy and nymphomaniac Helene Bradley; Dos Passos, as Richard Gordon; even Pauline, one of several sources for Helen Gordon, who tells her husband, "You were a genius and I was your whole life. I was your partner and your little black flower. Slop. Love is just another dirty lie . . . Love is all the dirty little tricks you taught me that you probably got out of some book . . . You writer."

Of course, for Hemingway, the dirty little trick—one he'd employed in more than one book—was to make a real person's fictional avatar do something, or say something, that he could legitimately despise that person for, thus leaving himself free to treat that person badly. Like a papal indulgence purchased in advance of the sin, it was an insurance against blame, or self-recrimination. And now he was using it on Pauline. *You writer.*

November 1936: Naples

Gerda arrived in Naples toward the end of November to find Georg Kuritzkes sharing a large room with two other students in a house in the old town. The last time she had seen Georg she was still Gerta Pohorylle, an unknown ingénue activist in Leipzig; in the three years since, she'd become Gerda Taro, a published combat photographer who had been under fire in Spain. Then, she'd been Georg's lover and political follower; now she had a highly visible liaison with Robert Capa, a man even more well-known than she—and certainly more so than Georg, who was still after all this time a medical student. For any other woman their reunion might have been difficult, full of questions about the past, the present, the future; but Gerda was different. She slipped into and out of encounters as she would a pretty negligée; they meant something while they were on, nothing when they were off. Guilt and regret were not in her repertoire. When she had gone to Paris, and Georg to Italy, their sexual relationship had ceased, but she still wrote him warm, newsy letters. Just because she wasn't sleeping with him didn't mean they weren't still friends; on the other hand, just because they were friends didn't mean they couldn't sleep together.

The shared room in the old town wasn't the best place for that, though;

and anyway Gerda wanted to spend some time sightseeing, and visiting with Georg's sister Jenny, who had followed her brother to Italy and was now working as a governess for the children of an American diplomat, Douglas MacArthur (nephew and namesake of the more famous general). But then they all went to stay with the third Kuritzkes in Italy, Georg's younger brother, Soma, who was studying at the university in Naples but living an hour's boat ride away on Capri, in rooms rented from a winegrower. Who would pay attention there if, just for a while, Gerda and Georg resumed their old intimacy?

Gerda loved the steep green terraced hills and the views of the sea, and the companionship of other young people who lodged nearby. But she couldn't give herself over to the holiday spirit wholeheartedly. Because across the water, in Spain, people were dying for the principles she believed in, that Georg had taught her to believe in. She had brought with her some of the photos she and Capa had taken there, and now she took them out and spoke of her experiences, and Capa's; told Georg and Soma and the rest of them about the International Brigades, and how they were the first line of defense against the tide of fascism.

When she left Naples a few weeks later her commitment to *la causa*, or his feelings for her, or both, had persuaded Georg to leave his studies and join the Brigades, where his medical training would be of real use. By the time he arrived in Paris to sign up Gerda was on the point of going back to Spain; so she didn't know that when he got to the border his Marxist bona fides were questioned by the special agent of the NKVD who was supervising the intake of foreign volunteers. Nor did she hear how he was denounced, and sentenced to be shot as an Italian spy; nor that he was saved at the last minute by the intervention of a Polish doctor, and made his way to the front. For by then she was in Madrid with Capa, and she never saw Georg Kuritzkes again.

December 1936: Madrid

As winter closed in on Madrid the city settled into a state of siege. Many Madrileños had left, heeding the posters showing a stylized woman and her daughter dancing in front of a shell-battered building: "So your family doesn't have to be a part of the drama of war," the legend ran, "EVAC-

UATE MADRID and help us to final victory." For those who stayed, food and fuel were harder and harder to obtain: shivering women lined up every morning with pails or baskets hoping to buy just enough coal or wood to cook the handful of rice they were able to purchase, and even the shells and bombs didn't scare them away from their places. The rebel armies were massed to the west, trying to bomb or starve or freeze the Madrileños into submission, but could make no headway; both sides seemed locked into a face-off, looking for some means to break out.

Aiming to cut Madrid off from the government's forces in the Guadarrama, the rebels began planning an offensive to the north of the city, on the Corunna Road leading to Philip II's palace at El Escorial; the Loyalists, on the other hand, directed their energies at their own organization, hoping that changes, even divisive, painful ones, might alter the direction of the war. With the influx of aid and personnel from the Soviet Union came pressure from Stalin to centralize political and military decision-making and dampen the revolutionary fervor that might frighten the Western democracies. The old militias had already been ordered dissolved, to be absorbed into or replaced by regular army units; and the anarchists of the CNT and FAI had been almost forcibly included in the government, with any contrary ideas they might have had about the direction of government policy smothered in the name of the "three virtues" of the Communists: "Discipline, Hierarchy, and Organization." Meanwhile, wrote Louis Delaprée, the self-described "accountant of horror," scores of people were being killed by enemy bombardments every day on the streets of Madrid.

It was raining, a cold December drizzle, when Barea said goodbye to his family. After weeks of arguing, Aurelia had finally agreed it would be best if she and the children relocated to Valencia; and this morning a convoy of cars from the Foreign Ministry was waiting to take them and other staff dependents to safety. Aurelia had put on her best coat and hat and her most fashionable shoes—she looked as if she were going to a dinner party, not an evacuation center—and as Barea embraced Carmen, Adolfina (whom he called Fina), Arturo, and Enrique, she started haranguing him: Why wasn't he coming with them to Valencia? Did he want to stay in Madrid so he could romance other women? Explanations of duty and responsibility were no use to her: *You have brains but no heart*, she flung at him. *Or you have a heart, but only for other people. Not for me.*

Things were no better in the censors' office: Rubio had begun telephoning him daily, telling him he should transfer the office to Valencia (in
the name of *Discipline, Hierarchy, and Organization*); also daily, General
Miaja, the chief of the Junta de Defensa, Madrid's Defense Council, told
him to stay. Koltsov would call with a set of instructions that contradicted
what Rubio had ordered the day before. Whiplashed by conflicting orders,
Barea was at his wit's end, snappish, inconsistent. When Maria called to
importune him (had she heard that Aurelia had left?), he dressed her
down on the phone; then—ashamed of his bad temper—took her out for
a drink he didn't really want to have, especially with her. As he left the
office Ilsa looked up (with reproach? disdain?) but said nothing.

Determined to resolve at least his professional situation, he decided he
must go to Valencia and settle things with Rubio once and for all. Miaja,
however, refused to give him a safe-conduct for what the Junta considered desertion of his post. Providentially, an anarchist friend, recently
appointed to a government post, offered him a lift as well as the necessary passes and papers. So on December 6, feeling like a traitor, or maybe
just a fool, Barea left Madrid. He wondered if he would be coming
back.

December 1936: New York

As 1936 drew to a close, John Dos Passos should have been in a celebratory mood—*The Big Money* had turned into a bestseller and was due to
be translated into French, Italian, Hungarian, and German—but he was
too anxious about the course of the war in Spain to enjoy himself. One of
his best friends, his Spanish translator, José Robles Pazos, was actually in
Spain at this moment, accompanied by his wife and children; Dos Passos
hadn't heard from Robles for some time and was worried for the family's
welfare. On a larger scale, he was dismayed by the biased, polemical, and
inaccurate coverage of the war in the United States, where (as one reporter put it) the Catholic Church had all but instructed newspaper ad-
vertisers "not [to] imperil their immortal souls or their pocket-books by
dealing with supporters of leftists, pinkos, and radicals." Dos Passos had
only to look at *The New York Times*'s front page on December 7, where the
headline "MADRID SITUATION REVEALED" was followed by the sub-

head: "All Semblance of Democratic Forms of Government in Spain Disappears—25,000 Put to Death by Radicals—Priests, Nuns Slain." No wonder the U.S. Congress was rushing through an extension of the 1935 Neutrality Act that would embargo any arms sales to either side in the Spanish conflict, and ban all travel to Spain by U.S. passport holders.

Dos Passos wasn't content to just wring his hands on the sidelines—a decade ago he'd been arrested along with his fellow writer Dorothy Parker for marching in protest against the execution of the anarchists Sacco and Vanzetti—and he wanted to *do* something to dispel this cloud of misinformation. So it must have seemed a fortunate coincidence when he met the very person who might help him accomplish this.

Joris Ivens was a thirty-eight-year-old Dutchman, a director of artistically aspirational documentary films about railroad bridges, dyke-building on the Zuyder Zee, workers in a radio factory, miners in Belgium, and the like. He'd spent the previous two years in Moscow, drinking vodka and eating black bread with all the right people: the Hungarian revolutionary Béla Kun, the journalist Mikhail Koltsov, the directors Erwin Piscator, Sergei Eisenstein, and Vsevelod Meyerhold, the German writer Gustav Regler. He'd even worked with Regler on a short picture about the political struggle between Nazis and antifascists in Germany's Saar Valley. "Simplicity is what works," he'd told Regler, whose screenplay he thought was too nuanced. "Listen: 'The Nazis lie, the Russians tell the truth.' That's what we have to say, nothing else!"

Although Ivens was employed by the Soviet film company Mezhrabpom, founded by the ubiquitous propagandist Willi Münzenberg as part of the Comintern's image-making apparat, and was also a member of the Dutch Communist Party, he hadn't yet been deemed qualified for membership in the party's Soviet Union division, and during the past two years he'd been frustrated when plum projects at Mezhrabpom went to more established party men. He'd also become unsettled by the increasingly dangerous atmosphere in Moscow, as Stalin carried out a murderous campaign against old Bolsheviks who might have mounted a threat to his absolute dominance; Meyerhold and Eisenstein, for example, were already in trouble with the regime, and Regler had left for Paris so he wouldn't be.

Luckily, Ivens managed to get leave (or was ordered) to go to America for a "creative vacation" in January 1936, and after traveling to Hollywood and back, lecturing and making contacts, he and his lover, a film editor named Helene Van Dongen, had quickly established themselves among the progressive intelligentsia in Greenwich Village, where Dos Passos met him at a screening of his Zuyder Zee film, *New Earth*. Tall, lean, with a shock of wavy dark hair, cleft chin, and deep-set blue eyes under strong black brows, Ivens had the kind of rugged but puckish sex appeal that speaks to both women *and* men—Dos Passos described him as looking "like a high-school boy playing hookey." Soon after the two of them met they'd begun talking about collaborating on a documentary about the American film industry that would be, Ivens said gleefully, "scathing and one-hundred percent anti-Hollywood"; but somehow the Hollywood exposé never got off the ground.

Now, however, Ivens had a better, more important idea, something that was sure to stir Dos Passos's blood: Helene Van Dongen had been asked to put together some existing newsreel footage in a documentary about the background to the Spanish Civil War that would be given a commercial release early in 1937. The film's producers needed money, of course; and someone would have to write voice-over commentary for it. Dos Passos had done a successful adaptation of Pierre Louÿs's novel *La femme et le pantin,* called *The Devil Is a Woman,* for Paramount; would he like to be involved? Of course he would; and he would also bring in his old friend the poet Archibald MacLeish. MacLeish might be working as an editor at Henry Luce's elegant and intellectually stimulating business magazine, *Fortune* (for which Dos also wrote), but his antifascist politics were considerably to the left of his boss's, and he was just then composing a radio play about fascism, *The Fall of a City,* for Orson Welles. So he'd be helpful with script advice, planning, and contacts.

The tweedy, sandy-haired MacLeish was captivated by Ivens: he was "a communist who [would] never let communism get in the way of his work," he declared, and unlike some radical writers, he wouldn't "set out . . . to discover his preconceptions." The poet was less enthusiastic about the Van Dongen documentary—an opinion with which Ivens rather surprisingly agreed. Even with the addition of excerpts from a Russian-made film about the war, and a lurid new title, *Spain in Flames,* the whole thing just seemed like a mash-up. "It would be cheaper and more satisfactory to make such a documentary film on the spot," he said, instead of cobbling it together from preexisting material.

So MacLeish came up with a new plan: put *Spain in Flames* together as quickly, painlessly, and cheaply as possible, and then send Ivens to Spain with a dedicated camera unit to produce an entirely new film there. They'd have to form a production company for it, of course—they gave it a worthy and neutral-sounding name, Contemporary Historians, Inc.— and they'd want to recruit other members for its board, people with the right amount of political passion whose celebrity would help them raise the funds they needed. They'd ask the playwrights Lillian Hellman and Clifford Odets, the theater producer Herman Shumlin, the philanthropist and civil liberties activist Margaret De Silver, and perhaps Dos Passos's picket-line pal Dorothy Parker. Anyone else, someone who could help *write* it? Oh, yes—what about Dos and MacLeish's great friend Ernest Hemingway?

December 1936: Valencia

Barea's trip to Valencia was a disaster. In the car on the way from Madrid, exhausted by stress and the conflicting pressures of work, he'd run off his mouth to his Anarchist companions about his difficulties with Rubio, and was alarmed when one of them, a tough named García, offered to take care of things for him: "People sometimes disappear overnight here in Valencia," he said. "They're taken to Malvarrosa, or Grau, or the Albuféra, get a bullet in the neck, and the sea carries them away." Barea hastily assured García that such dark doings wouldn't be necessary: things weren't as bad as all that, he said, Rubio was really a patriot. "All right," said García. "But one day you'll be sorry . . . I know that type. We're going to lose the war because of them. Or do you believe we don't know about the many things the censors let through?" Not for the first time, Barea felt he was walking on a tightrope.

He went to see Rubio in the shabby but still grand palace the Press and Propaganda Department had taken over on the Calle del Mar; but when he got there his chief waved him off. He was far too busy to talk to Barea today. Maybe tomorrow. Barea emerged into the sunlit streets in a daze. He passed food stalls overflowing with fruits and vegetables, poultry, flowers, all the kinds of things no one in Madrid had seen for months; well-dressed people were hurrying along the pavement or laughing on the terraces of cafés. A band was playing in the middle of the Plaza de

Emilio Castelar, in front of the Ayuntamiento; on the other side was a gigantic billboard showing photographs of the murdered children of Getafe superimposed with the silhouetted images of bombs. It all seemed unreal.

In the afternoon he took a poky little train to the outlying village where Aurelia and the children had been assigned space in a rambling old farmhouse with several other displaced families. The children were touchingly happy to see him; and Aurelia was glad to be able to show off the husband who "was something in the Foreign Ministry" to the other women. She wanted him to spend the night and he resisted. She wept, the children pled; and he ended up sharing Aurelia's bed with the children nearby, unable to sleep because he felt like a liar—to the children, to Aurelia, to Ilsa, and to himself, for pretending to an intimacy he could no longer feel, would never feel again.

The next morning he returned to Valencia, only to be rebuffed again by Rubio; then came back to the village to visit his children, only to reject their mother and return to Valencia. It went on like that for more than a week—lying, being lied to. Hanging around the office in town, he heard unsettling and conflicting rumors: he was going to be punished for staying in Madrid (*playing the hero*, they called it); he was going to be sidelined as a postal censor in Valencia; Ilsa was going to be given his job; she was going to be fired for being too friendly with foreign journalists. Terrible news came: Louis Delaprée, flying back to France in an Air France plane, had been shot down—possibly by a Russian fighter—and had died of his wounds three days later; then Luis, Barea's orderly, driving to Valencia from Madrid with a letter from Ilsa, was mortally wounded in a car accident. Barea managed to get to the hospital to see him before he died: his spine had been shattered and peritonitis had set in, but he knew Barea, and gave him a heartbreaking smile when he walked into the room. "Don Arturo," he said, with difficulty, "don't let that woman get lost. She's a great woman. She's in love with you, and you're in love with her. Don't let her go."

When Ilsa arrived in Valencia on the day after Christmas, the pain of losing Delaprée and then Luis lifted a little: for a moment it seemed as if the jumbled pieces of Barea's world had fallen into place. But then, the day after her arrival, she disappeared: a friend of hers, an Austrian journalist, told Barea that an agent of the Political Police had come to her hotel and taken her away. Frantic, Barea called Rubio Hidalgo; and this time he not only took Barea's call but also came around to Ilsa's hotel at once and started telephoning government ministries to see who could help. Barea barely paid him any attention: instead, he reached into his pocket for his pistol and laid it on the table in front of him. When he was told to calm down, he just took two filled cartridge frames and put them on the table next to the gun. "It doesn't matter if she appears tonight or not," he said. "Other people will die in Valencia, that's all."

Two hours later Ilsa returned to the hotel, laughing at her experience. It had all been a stupid mistake—a ridiculous little man, an Eastern European journalist, had denounced her as a Trotskyist spy. At first the police had seemed to believe him, but after all the telephone calls from government ministries they had changed their minds. Wasn't it ridiculous? Everyone except Barea agreed that it was; they all had a good chuckle over it. All Barea could think of were the corpses he'd seen in Madrid in the early days, the *checas* and tribunals, the stories he'd heard from García about what might happen to you when they came for you. But he had her back now, and he wouldn't leave her again. Ever.

That night they became lovers. *The most natural thing in the world*, thought Ilsa, as he lay in the crook of her arm; and her knowledge of him, his openness to her, made her feel like crying. In the morning they took the tram to the seaside district of El Cabanyal and walked past the tiled and whitewashed houses to the beach. They told each other they wanted to be together forever. But: "You know," Barea said to her, "it will be a lot of pain for the others, and pain for ourselves as well as happiness. One's got to pay, always."

"I know," she replied.

December 1936: Key West

It was Martha's mother who saw the sign—"Sloppy Joe's Bar," painted on the white stucco wall—and suggested the three of them go in out of the sun for a drink. Having an afternoon cocktail in a conch bar was the furthest thing imaginable from the way they'd always spent the Christmas holidays back in St. Louis; but on this Christmas, the first since Martha's father had died, they *wanted* to do something different. And sleepy, shabby

Key West, as far south as you could get in the continental United States, was certainly different.

The café was dim and cool, with sawdust on the floor and a long, curving bar presided over by a 300-pound African American barkeep, "Big Jimmy" Skinner. At one end of the bar, reading his mail, was a burly dark-haired man in a T-shirt and dirty white shorts held up by a length of rope. He looked up as the trio came in: the earnest young man, Martha's brother, Alfred, on vacation from medical school; the silver-haired, still-beautiful Edna Gellhorn; and Martha, tanned and tawny-maned in a little black sundress that showed off her racehorse figure to advantage. Later he would say he'd figured that Alfred and Martha were a couple, and that given three days he could win the beautiful blonde away from "the young punk"; but that turned out not to be necessary.

Because the blonde came over to him, hand outstretched, and introduced herself and her companions to Ernest Hemingway. He had been her writing lodestar forever, her "glorious idol"—hadn't she kept his photo tacked to her dorm room wall at Bryn Mawr? Hadn't she taken her epigraph for *What Mad Pursuit* ("Nothing ever happens to the brave") from *A Farewell to Arms*? And hadn't her clear, taut prose in *The Trouble I've Seen* been compared with his? So imagine how thrilled she was to just walk into a bar in Key West and stumble over him this way.

The social preliminaries were quickly dispensed with. Hemingway charmingly pointed out that his wives had both gone to school in St. Louis, and he'd spent considerable time there himself in his youth; he would be delighted to show these St. Louisans around Key West, and make sure they found all the best beaches and watering holes. Drinks came as they talked, then more drinks and more talk. At length a friend of Hemingway's, Charles Thompson, appeared in the bar, sent by Pauline, who had laid on a splendid crayfish dinner for the Thompsons at the house on Whitehead Street and was wondering why her husband hadn't shown up for it. He'd have to skip dinner, Hemingway said; Thompson should just tell Pauline to meet up with him later, at Pena's Garden of Roses, a beer garden and former speakeasy in the Old Town. Thompson looked around Hemingway's table, took in the blond hair and the black dress, and did as he was told.

Over the next weeks Hemingway made good on his offer to the Gellhorns; and, when Alfred's medical school vacation ended and mother and son returned to St. Louis, Martha remained at the Colonial Hotel on Duval Street for nearly a fortnight and became, as she herself described it in a thank-you note to Pauline, "a fixture, like a kudu head," in the Hemingways' house. Hemingway took her swimming and barhopping, but mostly they just talked: about her writing (she was too careful and cautious, he said—she should just *write* her novel and if it didn't turn out the way she wanted she could tear it up), about *his* writing (he was a great craftsman, she said, and he knew more about writing dialogue than anyone), about the conflict in Spain ("the Balkans of 1912") and the situation in Europe ("war is nearer than even the pessimists thought"), and about the nature of storytelling ("In a writer this is imagination," Martha asserted; "in anyone else it's lying. That's where the genius comes in"). She began calling him "Ernestino"; he called her "Daughter," a moniker he frequently bestowed on women even slightly younger than himself, and one that seemed more than usually apt for Martha, who with her long blond bob and coltish limbs looked even less than twenty-eight.

The two of them cut a striking figure around the sleepy little fishing town, she in her Riviera resort clothes and he in his scruffy shorts and rope-soled shoes; and the effect wasn't lost on Pauline Hemingway—or "Pauline cutie," as Martha addressed her in her thank-you note, a salutation that must have set Mrs. Hemingway's teeth on edge. "I suppose Ernest is busy again helping Miss Gellhorn with her writing," Pauline said drily to a friend who had remarked on Hemingway's absence from some occasion. Once, Hemingway was driving Martha around the island and, seeing Pauline walking along the sidewalk, pulled over and told her to get into the car. "She was very grumpy," Martha noticed, and affected not to know why.

But Pauline knew what had come into her and Hemingway's perfectly constructed life. Later Hemingway himself described it: "the oldest trick there is . . . [A]n unmarried young woman becomes the temporary best friend of another young woman who is married . . . and then unknowingly, innocently and unrelentingly sets out to marry the husband." *Pauline cutie*. Martha Gellhorn was the literary girl of the moment, with her sharp new book whose style was being compared with Hemingway's; she was pretty, well educated, well connected (those White House overnights, those dinners with Colette, those sojourns *chez* H. G. Wells); and she was conversant, in a way no one else in their circle was, with the European political situation that Hemingway was more and more obsessed with. When the two of them started talking about the Spanish war, which Martha said she was "desperate" to experience at first hand, the possibility that Hemingway would actually go over to cover it—something Pauline was both politically and personally opposed to—became worryingly acute. Worse, the probability was extreme that he would act, perhaps was already acting, on his evident attraction for this new girl. "I'm a fool with women," he confessed sheepishly to a friend in a conversation of which Martha was the subtext; "I always feel I have to marry 'em."

And Martha? Martha herself was dangerously entranced. Hemingway's attentions were so flattering that she couldn't help boasting about them just a little in her letters to Mrs. Roosevelt. He had let her read his manuscript, and she'd been "smart" about it! Unlike the cerebral, even effete men she'd previously been involved with, he was a paradigm of machismo: seeing battle in Italy, steering his boat through hurricanes, running with the bulls in Pamplona, shooting sharks with machine guns. He didn't just talk about his antifascist principles: he'd already put his money where his mouth was, paying the passage for two volunteers who were going to Spain to join the International Brigades, and borrowing $1,500 to buy ambulances for the Medical Bureau of the American Friends for Spanish Democracy. And now, when they discussed the news from Europe, he agreed with her (she told the First Lady, who must have wondered what to do with these confidences) that suddenly "there seemed terribly little time to do anything," that they had to "work all day and all night and live too . . . and love as many people as one can find . . . and do all this terribly fast, because the time is getting shorter and shorter every day."

When Martha finally left Key West for St. Louis, Hemingway—having somewhat hastily arranged a business trip to New York to talk to John Wheeler of NANA and also John Dos Passos and Archibald MacLeish, who had a Spanish film project they wanted to involve him in—followed her. They met up in Miami, where he took her out for a steak dinner and they boarded the northbound sleeper together. Although Martha changed trains along the route to go west, they stayed in close touch by mail and telephone: Hemingway, lonely for her and excited about the adventures he wanted them to have together, called her from

New York, often several times a day. He'd decided to accept NANA's offer to do reportage from Spain, and he thought he could help her get an assignment there too. Of course, there might be problems obtaining visas because of the non-intervention pact, which forbade civilian travel to Spain, but they could find ways around *that*.

Martha had finally found the fresh start she'd been yearning for, and she entered into these plans with gusto. "This is very private," she said to Hemingway in a letter about their arrangements: "We are conspirators and I have personally got myself a beard and a pair of dark glasses. We will both say nothing and look strong." Her pacifist novel was finished but on rereading it she was unhappy with the result and buried the manuscript in a desk drawer. She didn't care about it, anyway—she had other things to do now. "Me, I am going to Spain with the boys," she wrote to a friend. "I don't know who the boys are, but I am going with them."

PART II

"YOU NEVER HEAR THE ONE THAT HITS YOU"

January 1937: Madrid

A lot can change in a month. When Barea left the new capital of Valencia to come back to Madrid in mid-January, it wasn't as a suspect, renegade temporary appointee of an emergency junta, but as the newly designated and official head of foreign press censorship, with Ilsa as his deputy. He and she—their liaison seemingly stamped with government approval— were to be given quarters in the Hotel Gran Via (no more camp beds in the press office), a raise in pay, and a living allowance; and they were whisked from Valencia in an official car with all safe-conducts and fuel vouchers laid on. Barea was mystified by this alteration in his circumstances; but apparently Rubio Hidalgo, fearful of potential competition from unknown Foreign Ministry appointees, had decided to back the devil he knew, and that was Barea.

Leaving the coast and driving north and west through the suddenly wintry hills, Barea found even the road transformed. The ragtag pickets and patrols that used to stand outside each village had disappeared, to be replaced by uniformed detachments of Assault Guards at the major crossroads; and as they neared Madrid their car passed convoys of trucks and tanks rolling toward the capital. In the Telefónica there were other differences: under Ilsa's temporary tenure the journalists, and some of the foreign brigades, had begun to treat the censors' office as a kind of clubhouse where they could exchange information, get letters mailed, and hear gossip, as well as receive hotel assignments, fuel vouchers, and passes for restricted areas of the front. Now, as Barea and Ilsa had dared to hope in the first hours of their meeting, the censorship seemed less an emergency news blackout than a machine for getting out information.

Everywhere, in fact, the impromptu crisis arrangements of the first months of siege had been superseded by more professional organization: instead of a city surprised by war, Madrid had become a city *at* war. The courtyard of the former Finance Ministry had been swept clean of the litter of old loan certificates and economic reports that had been dumped there when the government fled in November; now trucks and Russian tanks and official cars were parked on the paving stones, and in his office in the building's underground bunker General Miaja, the Defense Junta chief, was less and less involved in the administration of the city because he had been made commander of a reorganized regular army corps charged with attacking the rebels on the city's northwest front.

The paunchy, red-faced general still sped around Madrid in an armored motorcade, luxuriating in the adulation of the (mostly female) crowd—"*¡Soy la vedette de Madrid!*" ("I'm the star of Madrid!"), he told a visiting President Largo Caballero—but more and more the real power in the city seemed wielded by Vladimir Gorev, the Soviets' special military attaché and Madrid station chief of the GRU, Russian military intelligence. Forty years old—he was the youngest general in the Red Army—tall, lean, with high cheekbones, thin lips, and pale blue eyes, Gorev took a dim view of the Spanish army's commanders, and a dimmer one of Largo Caballero. The Loyalist prime minister, complained Gorev in the secret dispatches he sent, under his code name of SANCHO, to the GRU's directorate, was "playing a complicated and dangerous political game, pandering to the anarchists" to "avoid strengthening the Communists." If Moscow wanted to defeat the rebels, or just hold them indefinitely at bay, Gorev thought that he and his fellow advisors should break off *official* contact with the Red Army, which would free them to take greater control of the war effort since they wouldn't be hindered by fear that their foreign military status might "dirty [their] laundry."

During the time that Barea had been away in Valencia, Gorev had begun to show great interest in the work of the censorship office, and in the unflappable Austrian woman who was in temporary charge of it. He'd started sending for Ilsa in the early hours of the morning, after the correspondents' dispatches had been vetted and sent; he'd fill his pipe and settle back to talk with her about theories of propaganda, and about certain press coverage of the war in particular. Now that Barea was back in Madrid and in command, he started accompanying her to these late-night sessions, whether he was invited or not, and listening while Ilsa and Gorev talked—mostly in French, for Barea's benefit, although the general spoke fluent English, the fruit of three years' residence as an undercover operative in New York. Sometimes the Russian had explicit advice for the two censors, which he expected them to follow even though, strictly speaking, they didn't work for him; but mostly he seemed to focus less on the content of the dispatches they had passed than on the question of Ilsa's political allegiance. On the one hand he was puzzled that she'd renounced her Party membership ("I could not live without my Party membership card," he told her); on the other, he was diverted by her feistiness and lack of orthodoxy. Barea he dismissed as a romantic, not worth bothering about. And Barea, on his side, was unsettled by the general's watchfulness and air of steely determination. *Not a man to cross.*

He'd have felt more at ease with the general's former aide José Robles Pazos, a Spaniard who for the past few years had been teaching in America, at Johns Hopkins University in Baltimore. The Republican black sheep of a well-connected conservative family, Robles had returned to Spain to offer his services to the Republic when war had broken out, and because he had a reading knowledge of Russian—and both he and the general spoke fluent English—he had seemed a useful temporary interpreter for Gorev, who spoke no Spanish, until an official replacement could be trained and sent from Moscow. Robles was both literate and literary, and before the war he'd been an initiate in the *tertulias*, the writers' café discussions, around whose fringes Barea had hovered as a starstruck boy; one of his best friends in Spain, in fact, was Barea's idol, the white-bearded novelist and playwright Ramón del Valle-Inclán. So the two of them would have had much to talk about; but although Robles had been working for Gorev when Barea took over the censorship, he'd been reassigned to Valencia by the time Barea returned to Madrid.

Despite Barea's vague discomfort about Gorev, not everything was bleak. The Nationalist attempt to cut the Corunna road between Madrid and El Escorial had been halted after much fighting and heavy losses; the resulting standoff outside the city limits felt almost like a victory. Madrid's continued defiance of the fascist juggernaut seemed to promise an even greater triumph: the Defense Junta had recently plastered the city with a poster that showed Madrid's symbol, the bear, devouring a swastika over the legend *"El Oso de Madrid Destrozara al Fascismo."* ("The Madrid Bear Will Destroy Fascism.") Some journalists who had left Madrid returned: Robert Capa was at the Hotel Florida and prowling the streets with his camera, and Claud Cockburn, a lanky Englishman with long, slightly receding dark hair—who was a cousin of the Catholic and conservative novelist Evelyn Waugh but wrote (as Frank Pitcairn) for London's *Daily Worker* and for his own scrappy and incisive review, *The Week*— had returned from several months' service as a private soldier with Commandante Carlos's Fifth Regiment. The *New York Post* had sent the muckraker George Seldes, who had been thrown out of Italy for speaking out against Mussolini. A new correspondent had come from *The New York Times*: Herbert L. Matthews, a patient, careful reporter with a sure grasp of the stakes in the conflict, which he was already referring to as "the little world war." And there was a new medium for coverage of the war, an organization Cockburn was working for in addition to his other jobs: a Paris-based press service called Agence Espagne.

Agence Espagne was the brainchild of a multilingual Sudeten German named Otto Katz. A smooth, dark, ingratiating man with multiple aliases, at least as many passports, and an eye for the ladies, Katz was a kind of Paganini of propaganda: someone for whom the truth was simply the departure point for magnificent invention. He claimed to have been Marlene Dietrich's first husband (though probably he was only one of her numerous lovers in Berlin in the 1920s); he'd been a director of the Soviet film company Mezhrabpom and the principal author of *The Brown Book of Hitler Terror*, a creative exposé of the plots that helped bring Hitler to power; and even Cockburn admitted he fabricated news stories to serve his cause. That cause, currently, was the Loyalist resistance; and with the approval of his boss, the Comintern's Willi Münzenberg, and the blessing of Álvarez del Vayo, he'd founded the Agence Espagne to disseminate— and report, or if necessary invent—stories that would tell the government's side of what was going on in Spain. After all, the rebels were issuing exaggerated, often fictitious accounts of "Red" atrocities, illustrated with faked photographs of mutilated bodies, to inflame feelings against the government; why should they have a monopoly on such propaganda?

Katz had worked with Gustav Regler in the Saar and in writing *The Brown Book*, and in the early '30s, in Paris, he had met with Ilsa's Vienna associate Kim Philby; if he didn't know Ilsa already, they certainly had friends in common. Now he'd turned up in Madrid, using the name of André Simone. He was, he said, looking for stories about war-battered

Madrid from a Spanish perspective, and he had the idea of asking Ilsa's Spanish lover, a man who had once had dreams of being a writer, if he could provide them.

The request was enough to stir the nearly dormant embers of Barea's ambition. Long ago, when the teenaged Barea had dared to speak to his hero Valle-Inclán at the Café Granja in the Calle de Alcalá, the great man had told him not to waste his time trying to gate-crash the *tertulias*; instead, he'd said, the young man should study the best authors and stick to his work, whatever it was; "then you may begin to write, perhaps . . ." In his prickly boyish diffidence Barea had taken Valle-Inclán's words for a brush-off; was it possible that they had really been sage advice, advice that was at last bearing fruit? Could his literary aspirations become reality?

Before Barea could feel pleasure in this unexpected turn of events, however, something else unexpected happened: a telephone call came for Ilsa from Paris. It was Leopold Kulcsar, announcing that he was transferring his operations to the Spanish Legation in Prague, where he'd be doing vague "propaganda work" for Spain in Czechoslovakia, Hungary, and Poland, and demanding to know what Ilsa's plans were. Was she returning to Paris? Would she be coming with him to Prague?

To her horror, Ilsa realized he must never have received the letter she'd written him, from Valencia, telling him that their marriage was definitively over and that she had fallen in love with someone else; now she had to explain all this to him through the static of a bad connection and in the hearing of her colleagues. *Like something in a novel*, thought the young censor on duty, who didn't even pretend not to stare. At length she hung up the telephone, pale and shaking. When she could speak at last, she told Barea she would have to fly to Paris to sort things out.

Barea was stricken. Had she only been playacting when she said she loved him? Would Kulcsar win her back in Paris? Would she decide to stay no matter what, somewhere far from the cold and hunger and daily bombardments that were life in Madrid? Would she even make the journey safely? He had no right to beg her to stay, he thought, miserably. No right, even, to worry about her.

She left the next day in a small car, bound for the airfield at Alicante on the coast, where she would get the plane to France. Barea had never felt so alone.

January 1937: Valencia

By the first winter of the Civil War, Valencia—formerly a sleepy if elegant, historic, and cosmopolitan city, the third largest in Spain—had become a kind of caravanserai, its population tripled by refugees, transplanted
government officials, hangers-on, and journalists, its palm-shaded streets
full of people in uniform, its once-sacrosanct siesta hours superseded by
wartime bustle. It was a place where you might meet anybody, at any time
of day; where the war, and the business of the war, was on everybody's
lips; and at that moment it must have seemed like a good place for Gerda
Taro to be.

She'd returned from Italy for a brief stopover in Paris; now she and
Capa were both in Spain again. He'd gone to Madrid, although nothing
seemed to be happening there just now, and she'd stayed on in Valencia.
One day she sat in the corner of the Hotel Victoria's lobby—"a nest of
newspaper correspondents, governmental agents, spies, munitions sales-
men and mystery women," as an American writer put it—chatting over a
glass of wine with the exiled German composer Hanns Eisler, a collabo-
rator of Bertholt Brecht, who'd come to Valencia for a benefit concert in
which his songs would be sung both for and by the soldiers of the International Brigades. On a couple of other occasions she met up with Alfred
Kantorowicz, another German émigré, who'd been an associate of Gustav
Regler and Willi Münzenberg in Paris and now edited the French and
German editions of the battlefront newspaper *Volunteer for Liberty* from
an office in Valencia. Both Kantorowicz and Eisler were well-traveled,
German-speaking, like-minded antifascist intellectuals, and they could
give Gerda a sense that she was participating in an enterprise greater
than photojournalism, and had an identity beyond that of the unknown
half of "Robert Capa."

For her ingenious creation of this professional persona had succeeded
almost too well. "Capa" had indeed become a famous photographer, but
that byline was being associated mainly with the man who was her lover
and partner; "Gerda Taro" was an also-ran. She told Ruth Cerf that she
felt "insulted" by such treatment. And Capa's most recent reportages, from
Madrid, had cemented his reputation as a photographer of risk and action: "He shared the perils and the heroism of the antifascist volunteers,"
Regards had boasted in their accompanying text. Gerda had photographs

on the cover of two magazines this month, *Einheit* and *Unité*, but in each case they were images of children—touching human-interest photos, not visceral combat pictures. If she wanted to take such photographs, though, she'd have to get another camera. The Rollei was too boxy and cumbersome, its presentation too formal. What she really needed, in addition to her own byline, was a Leica. Like Capa's.

January 1937: New York

Hemingway got off the Florida Special in Pennsylvania Station and took a taxi to the Barclay Hotel, the Waldorf-Astoria's smaller, more intimate, but no less elegant neighbor. He had a lot to do. His first stop was his publisher's office, three blocks away on Fifth Avenue, where he had to tell Maxwell Perkins that the Key West novel wasn't done yet. Yes, he knew he'd wired Perkins that the manuscript was finished; but Arnold Gingrich, who would be serializing part of it in *Esquire*, had asked a lot of pesky questions—some of them about the resemblance of characters in the novel to actual people (Dos Passos among them) who might get litigious if it were published in its present form. Hemingway could take care of Gingrich's queries, he told Perkins, but not before June, because he had to honor his commitment to go to Spain, no matter what Perkins thought about it. (Perkins had confessed he believed "this Rightist general must be good" and had repeatedly urged his famous author to "give up" the idea of covering the war.) In the meantime, Hemingway said, Perkins should read a story called "Exile" by a remarkable young writer named Martha Gellhorn—it might be something for *Scribner's Magazine*.

From Scribner's Hemingway went to the offices of the North American Newspaper Alliance, where he signed a contract that would give him $1,000 per story—or $500 if it was cabled and had to be deciphered from shorthand "cablese" into prose—for dispatches sent from Spain, an extraordinary sum, but then, he was a very famous writer. He stopped at the Medical Bureau of the American Friends of Spanish Democracy, where he agreed to serve as chairman of their ambulance fund-raising drive. He visited his sister-in-law, Virginia Pfeiffer, at her new apartment, where the two of them got into an argument about Hemingway's wandering eye, his disregard of Pauline's feelings, and his decision to go to Spain.

But much of his trip to New York was spent on an unexpected writing assignment: the voice-over for the second half of *Spain in Flames*, the documentary pastiche that John Dos Passos, Archibald MacLeish, and Joris Ivens were putting together. Dos Passos was at work on the script for the historical first half, but wouldn't be able to complete the second, which dealt with the first months of fighting, in time for the film's release at the end of the month. Since Hemingway was actually here, in New York— and with his NANA and ambulance-drive credentials, so publicly committed to the cause—couldn't *he* undertake the job? He'd have an assistant, a twenty-four-year-old Cuban-American writer, Prudencio de Pereda, whom they'd engaged to do a first draft; in fact, Hemingway already knew him. The boy had been sending him reverential fan letters for two years and finally, this past December, Hemingway had offered to loan him the money to go fight against Franco. "If you didn't get killed you would get wonderful material," Hemingway had told him, "and if you did get killed it would be in a good cause."

De Pereda hadn't taken him up on the offer; among other things, it would mean he might not get a chance to actually meet the writer he idolized. And now, for a brief two days in January, he came to the Barclay and fed Hemingway the raw material he could hammer into the commentary for *Spain in Flames*. Encouraged by proximity, de Pereda gave a manuscript of his short stories to his hero to read, and shyly suggested he might accompany Hemingway to Spain; but to his dismay Hemingway didn't like the stories and was even more negative about de Pereda's potential as a companion in arms. You aren't a fighter, Hemingway said dismissively; "not even a good behind-the-lines man."

Fortunately, however, de Pereda bore these snubs with good grace, claiming his time with Hemingway was "the highlight of my writing career"; and Dos Passos and MacLeish were so happy with the *Spain in Flames* script that they asked Hemingway the question they'd had on their minds since December. Would he like to be involved—really involved—in the original documentary they planned, the one Joris Ivens was going to direct? Ivens had already left for Spain to start preliminary work on it, but Hemingway was headed there himself shortly and could link up with Ivens then. What about it?

Hemingway said yes.

Before he could return to Florida to prepare for his Spanish assignments, however, he had another, sadder errand to perform. On January 16 he drove with Jinny Pfeiffer and Sidney Franklin, a Brooklyn-born matador who was one of his cronies, to Saranac Lake, a sanitarium resort in the Adirondacks, where Gerald and Sara Murphy were keeping a death-watch over their youngest child, Patrick. He and the Murphys had had a complicated relationship over the years: they had been among the first people to take him up, in the days when they were the center of artistic expatriate society in postwar Paris and he was a struggling writer; and he had always been attracted to Sara's beauty and charm, always been a little in love with her, and always mistrustful and uneasy around Gerald, scorning him for his bisexuality and his dandyism and perhaps envying him for the mysterious paintings he produced, as terse and clean as any of Hemingway's own writing. But however he thought of the Murphys, he ached for their agony as they saw their son, whose name his *own* son bore, losing his seven-and-a-half-year struggle with tuberculosis, just two years after the sudden death of the boy's brother, Baoth, from meningitis. And he knew if he went to Spain he might not have another chance to say goodbye— not just to Patrick, but to the life all of them had shared in the days when, as Sara put it, life was like "a great fair, and everybody was so young."

He arrived at the huge half-timbered Adirondack lodge the Murphys had rented in Saranac to discover things were even worse than he expected: emaciated, bedridden, and on oxygen, Patrick was barely clinging to life. Going in to see him for a few moments that evening, Hemingway found himself promising the boy a splendid Christmas gift, one he knew would never be received: a skin from a bear he had shot himself. *It's not ready yet, but it will be,* he said. Patrick was tremulously excited; and Hemingway, coming out of the room, broke down in tears, weeping perhaps as much for the lie he had told as for the boy's fate.

He and Sidney Franklin left Saranac the next day; Jinny, with whom he'd been sparring more or less continuously since their argument at her apartment, stayed behind with the Murphys. When he got back to New York Hemingway had a fitting at the bespoke tailors Gray and Lampel, on East Fifty-third Street, which Gerald Murphy had recommended to him as a "very good reliable old N.Y. house, no chi-chi"; for despite his oft-expressed feeling that he "couldn't stand" his old friend and sometime benefactor, no one could say that Murphy wasn't always impeccably and elegantly dressed. And because he wasn't the kind of man who would spend his wife's money on another woman, he stopped at his bank to set up a special account, to be funded by his writing income, which he intended to use for any expenses associated with his relationship to Martha Gellhorn.

February 1937: Málaga Front

Although the Nationalist armies, professionally trained, augmented by Italian troops and outfitted with German and Italian munitions, had rolled over a huge swath of Spain during the autumn of 1936, the months of November and December had seen them halted by the government's motley assemblage of trade-union militias, loyal soldiers, and International Brigaders. In the first months of the new year the front around Madrid, drenched by cold rain and swept by the bitter wind from the sierra, froze into deadlock; but fighting continued in the south. Republican forces attempted an offensive around Córdoba in the weeks after Christmas, but were beaten back (a number of British Brigaders, among them the poet John Cornford, were killed in that attack). And farther south, the Nationalists began eyeing the twenty-mile-wide strip of coastline to the east of Gibraltar—including the important port of Málaga—which had remained in Loyalist hands since the beginning of the war.

Sometime between February 3 and February 8, Robert Capa and Gerda Taro arrived in Cartagena, home port of the Spanish Navy, 391 kilometers to the east of Málaga, to take pictures of the Republican battle cruiser *Jaime I.* Christened after the great Aragonese king who had wrested Catalonia back from the French in the thirteenth century, *Jaime I* these days had a new nickname: the Spanish *Potemkin*—in homage to the vessel made legendary by Sergei Eisenstein's film *The Battleship Potemkin*—because at the beginning of the war her Republican crew had mutinied against their rebel officers and commandeered her for *la causa.* The ship was a potent emblem, and indeed Capa's friend and colleague Chim had published one reportage about her back in October; but perhaps because February 2 was the historic King Jaime's birthday, or because February 5 was the ship's twenty-fifth anniversary, she could be thought of as back in the news again.

So on a bright, balmy day Gerda and Capa clambered all over, from the bridge to the decks to the stygian engine room, shooting frame after frame; and Gerda's photographs in particular had the heroic grandeur of Eisenstein's cinematic epic. Here were the smiling sailors with their arms flung around each other—*click*; cannon mouths making a perfect line of O's—*click*; brawny stokers shoveling coal in their undershirts—*click*. There was an atmosphere of fiesta on board and the crew had got up an impromptu band, with an accordion and a guitar and a Galician bagpipe; behind the players, the crew stood on bollards and risers, grinning and clapping for the music and for the pretty blond girl and her companion.

El cañón ruje, tiembla la tierra
Pero a Madrid . . . ¡NO PASARÁN!

[The cannon roars, the earth trembles—
But at Madrid . . . THEY SHALL NOT PASS!]

You could almost have forgotten there was a war going on, until Málaga was attacked.

The assault, by Nationalist troops joined by Italian Black Shirts, had begun on February 3; on February 5, rebel warships had started to bombard the city from the sea. Those who could flee began to do so, streaming eastward toward Almería, 130 miles away; by the time Málaga fell on February 8, and between two and four thousand people were rounded up and shot by the conquerors, the ribbon of coast road between the mountains and the sea had become packed with refugees—"seventy miles of people desperate with hunger and exhaustion," as a British volunteer ambulance driver described it. A handful of them, mostly the city's Republican high command, had automobiles; most were on foot, some leading mules or donkeys laden with their pitiful possessions. Many were children. All suffered from exposure to the sun by day and the cold by night; but worse was to come: Nationalist tanks followed them from Málaga and ran them down, Nationalist planes strafed them from the air, and Nationalist ships fired on them from the sea. Their only defense came from the now mostly decimated Escuadrilla España, André Malraux's tatterdemalion air squadron; the effort brought most of his remaining planes down in flames, and marked the end of the squadron as an independent unit.

As soon as the two photographers heard what had happened they scrambled to get to Almería to document it, but by the time they arrived the Nationalist tanks and airplanes had finished their work. There would be no dramatic pictures here. Capa and Gerda were directed to a modest brick building with a sign over the door—"Refugio Lenin"; inside was a large bare room with tattered grimy mattresses and bedrolls pushed up against the walls. There the men, women, and children of Málaga sat, their faces showing the devastation of those who have seen the unimaginable: the father clasping a baby with a bandaged head, the toddler with her fat little legs swathed in bloody gauze, the family clustered like a modern *pietà* against the whitewashed plaster. Outside, isolated refugees were still trickling into the city, and on the outskirts some had found makeshift shelter in a roadside cavern.

The Nationalists had withdrawn westward to Málaga after their pursuit of the refugees, but there was still scattered fighting along the unstable front to the north of the coast: units of Loyalist militia, along with soldiers from the Polish Chapaiev Battalion, were pushing back against the rebels in the vicinity of Motril and Calahonda, and Capa and Gerda joined them. They found Calahonda a whitewashed shell, seemingly empty except for the corpse of a soldier curled up as if in sleep next to a bullet-pocked wall, and a live sentry sitting surreally at the entrance to the lifeless village, peering through binoculars at nothing; in the plaza, however, a heroic-looking young woman was preparing to ride her white horse up into the hills with provisions for the *milicianos*, and they followed her. It was wild country, strewn with boulders and prickly pears, and punctuated by massive limestone crags that dwarfed the soldiers they photographed; but although it made for striking pictures, the landscape wasn't enough to keep them if they couldn't find a story. So they made plans to return to Madrid, where there was disturbing news about a Nationalist drive to cut the road that lay between the city and Valencia.

Before they left, however, Capa had a surprise for Gerda. On a flying trip to Paris he'd bought himself a new camera, a 35mm Contax, so he could give her his speedy compact Leica—the camera she had coveted for so long—in place of her boxy Rollei. And there was something else. He'd had a new stamp made for the back of their prints. Up to that point their photographs had run with the credits "PHOTO CAPA" or "PHOTO TARO"—but now, even before they were sent out to magazines and newspapers for submission, their pictures could be stamped "REPORTAGE CAPA & TARO."

February 1937: Madrid

Ilsa had returned to Madrid from Paris at the end of January, after brow-beating the military governor at Alicante into giving her an official car for the journey, and telling the guards at all the filling stations along the road that she was the daughter of the Soviet ambassador so they'd sell her fuel. In Paris, she'd extracted a promise from Leopold Kulcsar that he would give her a divorce as soon as the war was over, and for now she and Barea would have to be content with that. At least Barea could stop drugging himself with brandy every night to get to sleep.

Having Ilsa back was almost the only comfort he could find in this bleak midwinter, however. The news of Málaga's fall came just as the Nationalists began a new offensive in the Jarama Valley, southeast of Madrid, just west of the main road to Valencia; the journalists in the pressroom were taking bets on how soon Madrid would surrender once the rebels cut its lifeline to Valencia. Food and fuel, already scarce, were becoming almost unobtainable; the metro stations and the Telefonica's cellars were crowded with a permanent population of the newly homeless. Although the air raids had slackened, the shelling kept up; all day and night the horizon to the east, south, and west was lit by artillery flares.

And as if Barea didn't have his hands full trying to handle the news-papermen while all this was going on, he and Ilsa would now have to deal with two filmmakers—armed with safe-conducts from the Socialists, the Anarchists, *and* the Communists—who'd arrived from Valencia to make a documentary about the war for an American group of Loyalist sympa-thizers. Joris Ivens and his cameraman and compatriot John Ferno, along with 450 pounds of baggage that included three movie cameras, had checked into the Hotel Florida on January 22.

In addition to his equipment, Ivens had with him a short scenario that he and Archibald MacLeish had concocted for the project now called *The Spanish Earth*—a title MacLeish, with his poet's instinct for the telling metaphor, had come up with. As sketched in its pages, the film would tell the story of a fictional village whose citizens—landowners, military officers, priests, doctors, shopkeepers, laborers, and peasants—witness the flight of King Alfonso XIII in 1931 and must grapple in their different ways with the tensions and possibilities of the Republic, then with the struggle to preserve it: "a great struggle which has shape and purpose." It had sounded fine and noble in New York, and maybe it had still sounded all right on board the S.S. *Normandie*, when Ivens and Lillian Hellman, who was supposed to be working on the film script with him, conferred about it as they sailed across the Atlantic. But Hellman, who was still smarting from the failure of her latest play, a labor-union drama entitled *Days to Come*, caught pneumonia in Paris and decided not to go on to Spain. And as soon as Ivens got to Madrid he could see the treatment they'd outlined wasn't going to work. There was no way he was going to be able to stage dramatic reenactments of recent history when current events were playing themselves out, under fire, everywhere, and—as he put it—"the direction is in the hands of life and death."

In Madrid he and Ferno set up an office in the building on Calle de Velázquez where the International Brigades and "Commandante Carlos's" Fifth Regiment were headquartered, and Ivens sought out Carlos and Mikhail Koltsov, whom he had known during his time in Moscow with Mezhrabpom, to ask for help in revising his shooting script. Both his new advisors thought he should focus on the ordinary lives of common people, with Carlos also lobbying for glimpses of parliamentary democracy at work in the new Spanish society. But with the government relocated to Valencia, the closest they could come to democracy at work was a rally announcing the final abolition of the various party militias and their absorption into the new Popular Army. The participants included Enrique Líster, the twenty-nine-year-old Soviet-trained commander of the army's 11th Division, the Spanish Communist Party's general secretary, José Díaz; and Dolores Ibárruri, the legislator and ideologue known as "La Pasionaria"—none of them exactly *common people*, but Ivens would identify them as a Galician stonemason who'd risen from the ranks to become an officer, a typesetter turned parliamentary delegate, and "the wife of a poor miner from Asturias."

For the next few days they filmed the extraordinary things that were part of everyday life in Madrid: men carrying the doors of ruined houses to use as reinforcements for the trenches, soldiers getting a shave inside a truck painted with the whimsical legend *"Brigada Mixta Jefe 'Líster'— Peluqueria"* (Chief "Líster" Mixed Brigade—Barbershop), coffins being carried through crowds of shoppers, people running in terror as the shells rained down, the limp forms of those who didn't make it safely across the street. Then came the word that insurgent troops had started an all-out drive toward the main road from Madrid to Valencia, which lay to the east of the Manzanares and Jarama rivers. If Ivens and Ferno wanted footage of real combat, that was where they would get it; but they were prevented from setting out immediately by several days of steady drenching rain that would make filming impossible. And when the deluge let up on the morning of February 11, the Nationalists were claiming to have taken the bridge at Arganda, near the junction of the Jarama and the Manzanares, and to control the road to Valencia.

But *The New York Times*'s correspondent, Herbert Matthews, thought the Nationalists were bluffing; and to find out, he commandeered a car and set off south between the sodden, olive-clad hills, with Ivens and Ferno in his wake. They discovered that the government's troops had managed to check the insurgents' advance, but the insurgents had redirected their efforts farther south and west, to Pindoque, where a railway bridge— guarded by French International Brigaders—spanned the Jarama. There, the night before, a Nationalist contingent of Moroccan troops had crept over the fields and knifed the French sentries, enabling two Nationalist brigades to cross the river and launch an attack on another International Brigades unit, the Italian volunteers of the Garibaldi Battalion, who were dug in at Pajares, just north of Pindoque. As Matthews, Ivens, and Ferno drove over the Arganda bridge they heard the sound of mortars and machine guns; Matthews, who wanted to learn whether the Valencia road was still open, proceeded down the highway into Arganda itself, to the southeast, but Ivens and Ferno went due south, toward Pajares, right into the line of fire.

They found the Garibaldi Battalion on the road, where soldiers were leaping out of their transport trucks and forming ranks for the assault, as their dashing commander, Randalfo Pacciardi, roared from position to position on the back of a motorcycle. Holding their cameras in front of their faces, as much as a shield against gunfire as to focus their shots, Ivens and Ferno followed the soldiers into the field. A grenade exploded five yards from them and they threw themselves on the ground, then got up and ran forward as a shell slammed into the earth, raising a geyser of clods and broken rock. At one point Pacciardi fell, his face struck by a bullet or a fragment of flying debris. From the bit of cover behind which he was crouching, Ivens tossed him a handkerchief to use as a makeshift bandage; and the bespectacled, professorial-looking Pietro Nenni, who had cofounded the Garibaldi Battalion with Pacciardi and was its political commissar, knelt beside him and tenderly dressed the wound. Then the two of them got to their feet and Pacciardi strode forward, calling out "*Avanti!*" as he beckoned his troops forward. Eventually the Garibaldis secured their stretch of the road, and it seemed safe enough for Ivens and Ferno to drive on to the village of Morata de Tajuña, where they witnessed something even more harrowing than the battle they had just been in—though to the citizens of Madrid, or the refugees of Almería, it was horribly familiar.

Morata was a farming village that had become a mustering point and operational headquarters for some of the various International Brigades coming to the Jarama front from their main base at Albacete. When Ivens and Ferno got there, however, the streets were nearly empty of soldiers: the rebels had managed to capture another Jarama bridge, due west of Morata at San Martin de la Vega, and any remaining Brigaders had been rushed to the battle lines. The fighting was elsewhere; so the first hum of aircraft might not have warned Morata's villagers that they themselves were about to become collateral damage.

Then the bombs came, a steady rain of ordnance that pounded the village "to smithereens," as one of the soldiers left behind put it. Buildings crumbled, and those who'd been unable to get to shelter were slaughtered. At length the shuddering roar of explosives stopped, and all was still. "You should hear the silence of five hundred people after the crash of bombs," Ivens remembered later. Cautiously, he and Ferno ventured out into the ruined streets—"not realizing we were being brutal but feeling we had to get those pictures"—and filmed the dazed women, "their hands over their bellies in the agony of shock," the crumpled dead, the children already playing in the rubble. They didn't shoot any film of the Brigades headquarters that might have been the bombers' real target, though; or if they did, they didn't identify it as such. *Simplicity is what works.*

Down the east-west road, toward Pingarrón, the International Brigades were being shot to pieces trying to hold the line against the advancing rebels, and it was by no means certain they'd be able to do so. Ivens and Ferno packed up their gear and drove back to Madrid while they still could.

•

As the filmmakers were driving back to Madrid, Gustav Regler—the political commissar of the Twelfth International Brigade who had been Capa's guide to the Casa de Campo front—was at the Palace Hotel, opposite the Prado, looking for Mikhail Koltsov. The Nationalists' offensive along the Jarama, in particular the slaughter of the French troops who were a part of his brigade, had shaken Regler badly and he wanted to be rescued from his visions. *Koltsov will distract me*, he kept telling himself. And up to a point, Koltsov did. "I know all about it," the Russian said to Regler reassuringly; even though the attack had been a surprise, Regler was already second-guessing himself, blaming himself for something he couldn't have foreseen. But he shouldn't. Koltsov paused, took off his glasses to polish them, and put them back on. "Without glasses everything looks black to me," he remarked. "If they ever shoot me I'll have to ask them not to take my glasses off first." He laughed, a short sharp bark, and stood up. "I'm going to take you to a party."

They went to one of the private rooms in the hotel where a farewell fete was being given for an engineer about to go home to Moscow. The engineer, Gorkin, showed off the presents he was taking to his wife and children, toasts were drunk, and the head of the Russian delegation, whom Regler called Maximovich, gave a moving speech, wiping away tears at the end of it. Regler's spirits lifted—what important work they were doing, and what a bond of comradeship it created! The next day he spoke of this to Koltsov, and was brought up short when Koltsov said, "Gorkin will be arrested when he reaches Odessa."

"How do you know?" Regler demanded, incredulous. "Is it something political?"

"Yes," Koltsov replied. "Why are you so surprised? Because of the farewell party? We all knew. That's why we gave him the party. It's why Maximovich came." Seeing Regler's expression, he continued, "The French give a man rum before leading him out to the guillotine. In these days we give him champagne."

The Battle of Jarama lasted most of February, in part because of infighting between Generals Pozas and Miaja—*"la vedette de Madrid"*—over who was *really* in command. Both sides suffered heavy losses, with the International Brigades hit especially hard; more than half of their combatants, and most of their officers, were killed or—like the twenty-eight-year-old commander of the Abraham Lincoln Battalion, Robert Merriman—wounded. In Madrid, Ilsa Kulcsar learned with sorrow that two of her English friends, an archaeologist from Cambridge, and a promising young poet, Christopher St. John Sprigg, who wrote under the name Christopher Caudwell, had died in battle. They had all paid, Barea said, "a terrible price" to contain the Nationalists along the banks of the Jarama, to the east of the Valencia road; but they had done it—they and the Russian *Chatos*, the aircraft that had harried the German Junkers out of the sky, and the Russian tanks, the light-infantry T-26s.

By the time Capa and Gerda arrived in Madrid in the third week in February the front had subsided into stalemate, and it was too late, as seemed to happen so often, to get any dramatic shots of the fighting. But they had no time for disappointment, for they'd scored a career double coup: each of them had contract offers from *Ce Soir*, a fledgling Parisian daily—Communist-run, politically left, but independent—that would be edited by the poet Louis Aragon. And although their primary allegiance would now be to *Ce Soir*, they were also free to sell photographs to other periodicals. With the prospect of an ever-widening demand for their work, they were talking about leaving Maria Eisner's Alliance Photo agency and setting up their own studio, submitting directly to photo editors and avoiding having to pay a commission on their sales.

In Madrid they found a room in the Hotel Florida, which was still being pummeled by Nationalists' shells at irregular intervals; the spacious front rooms, which overlooked the Plaza de Callao and faced the incoming barrage, were now much less expensive than the dark back rooms whose only view was an alleyway. But the Florida was one of the few places in Madrid that still had abundant hot water for the long soaking baths Capa liked to take after a rough day; and at least one of the resident journalists, Sefton Delmer, held festive court there in the evenings, offering his guests bottles looted from the cellars of the Palacio Real, which he'd picked up in an Anarchist bar in the Puerta del Sol.

Despite the daily bombardments that sent pedestrians scurrying for the shelter of overhanging buildings, some things seemed disconcertingly unaffected: shop windows still displayed furs and French perfume and beautiful handmade shoes, Lionel Barrymore was appearing in *David Copperfield* at the Genova movie palace in the Plaza de Callao, yellow trams whizzed about the streets. Gerda and Capa headed to the Telefónica to pick up Gerda's new *Ce Soir* Madrid press pass; and almost incredibly, they happened to meet Capa's boyhood friend Geza Korvin Karpathi. He and Capa had last seen each other during their days of bohemian poverty in Paris, when they'd perfected an ingenious tactic for borrowing money from better-off acquaintances: they'd position themselves on opposite sides of the street and if the mark crossed over to avoid meeting one of them, the other would be waiting on the other side. Now Karpathi was making a documentary film about a Canadian blood transfusion unit that was working with the Loyalist army, while Capa had become a journalistic sensation; so their meeting called for a celebration—at the very least lunch, or what passed for it, in the journalists' unofficial canteen at the Hotel Gran Via across the street. The restaurant was in the Gran Via's basement, and the entrance was heavily guarded; you couldn't enter without a pass, and once there, correspondents and aid workers generally ate at the long table in the middle of the room, with visiting dignitaries and soldiers at smaller tables tucked into the alcoves. The menu seemed limited to beans, potatoes, and the occasional odoriferous fish, salami, or mysterious meat dish that was usually mule, donkey, or horsemeat; but there was wine, and whiskey, and you could buy contraband American cigarettes from one of the waiters for ten or fifteen pesetas a packet.

The little group went down the stairs into the crowded, clattering, smoke-filled room, where the talk was all about new concentrations of fascist Italian troops to the north and east of Madrid, near Guadalajara; and where one of Karpathi's new acquaintances, a young Canadian named Ted Allan, looked up from the unidentifiable *plat du jour* and saw Gerda, and Capa, for the first time. Allan was twenty-one, a dark, curly-headed youth who had volunteered for the International Brigades but had been drafted away from combat to be the political commissar of the mobile blood transfusion unit whose work Geza Karpathi was filming. He was also a romantic and deeply impressionable young man, and his first sight of the two photographers, their cameras around their necks, still dusty from their drive to Madrid, struck him forcibly. Capa, "black eyed, handsome," and "already famous," seemed impossibly glamorous to Allan, who was also an aspiring journalist, writing for Canadian leftist newspapers and broadcasting over the Madrid radio; but it was Gerda, with her short blond hair and bewitching smile, who took his breath away.

Karpathi made the introductions—to Allan, and to his commanding officer, the Canadian doctor Norman Bethune, who was also lunching at the canteen. Allan held on to Gerda's hand a fraction too long, then dropped it in confusion. Capa "couldn't say shit or sheets" in English, he discovered, but French served as a common language for the few pleasantries they exchanged before Karpathi, Gerda, and Capa moved away. Allan turned to Bethune. "Isn't she beautiful?" he asked, cocking his head in Gerda's direction. "A delicious thoracic creation," commented Bethune; to which Allan replied, "Yum yum."

If Gerda saw the glance that passed between them—she rarely failed to notice the effect she had on men—she nonetheless had more important things on her mind just at the moment. She had yet to try out her new Leica, and Arturo Barea and Ilsa Kulcsar had arranged for her and Capa to be shown around the new warren of trenches, fortifications, and tunnels that the Loyalists had built in the Parque del Oeste south of University City—just across the river from the four thousand wild acres of the Casa de Campo. Before they even got there, however, they passed a little parade of reinforcements marching through the streets toward the defenses, led by a ragtag band of drums and bugles, while their officers took the clenched-fist salute. She and Capa each photographed the scene, but Gerda hadn't quite got used to framing her pictures in the Leica's viewfinder, and although her compositions were strong she cut most of her images off at the bottom.

Madrid's front-line trenches were the pride and joy of their commandant, Colonel Antonio Ortega, who in addition to his military duties was also president of the Madrid Club de Fútbol (the team had dropped the monarchist "Real" from its name at the beginning of the Republic, and continued to play occasional matches in Chamartin Stadium). When Capa and Gerda had been ushered through the tunnel from Ortega's headquarters to the fortifications they found that their host kept his fiefdom neater than a locker room: the ground was swept, the damp earth was held back by walls made out of doors salvaged from the ruined houses along the Paseo de Rosales just behind the line, and some of the fortified areas were furnished with wicker porch furniture in which the soldiers sat and read, or played chess, or even shaved when they weren't busy returning fire to the other side. There didn't seem to be much action: just riflemen jamming their guns into position between sandbags so they could be fired more quickly, officers squinting through gun slits and relaying information on enemy movements over field telephones, engineers hacking out new tunnels with their pickaxes, men standing around blowing on their hands to keep warm, waiting for something to happen. The photographers shot their pictures anyway. Years later, Capa would explain that such quotidian images "showed how dreary and unspectacular fighting actually is"; what he hoped was that if one of the soldiers saw them ten years later he'd be able to say, "That's how it was."

And then he and Gerda saw the bear. Enormous, black, with rounded haunches and small neat ears set close to its furry head, it was crouched on a slab of rock just behind the shoulder of one of the soldiers, rifling through the soldier's rucksack. Had it come from the wilderness of the Casa de Campo across the river? Was it wild? A half-tamed mascot, an embodiment of the Junta's antifascist *Oso de Madrid* poster? Or some darker omen? The soldiers seemed oblivious to its presence, but both Capa and Gerda, who were facing it, clicked their shutters almost involuntarily; if they hadn't they might have wondered if it had been an apparition. Because in the next second it was gone.

Barea and Ilsa went to see the trenches, too—if they were going to send foreign journalists there, Barea reasoned, they should know what they'd be looking at. Ortega treated them to a fancy lunch with lots of drinking and singing, then to a tour of the earthworks. It was a sunny day with the promise of spring: buds on the ravaged trees, warmth implicit in the breeze from the river, and only the occasional *pfft* of a stray bullet to remind you of where you were. The soldiers, mostly broad-shouldered Basques and Asturians, were jokey and confident. The war seemed like just something to laugh at; what could go wrong with the sun on your back and these big, easygoing men between you and the enemy?

Then Ortega wanted to show off his new mortar, a kind of catapult that silently hurled its payload into the rebel lines. When the first shell detonated with a roar, the front erupted in rifle and machine-gun fire. The jokes were over.

February–March 1937: New York

There was no sign outside the "21" Club, a former speakeasy on East Fifty-second Street wedged in between the jazz joints that punctuated the block, but it was set off by the spiky wrought-iron fence that ran the length of its brownstone façade, and by the tiny statue of a jockey, dressed in the racing colors of one of the restaurant's patrons, Jay Van Urk, that stood by its door. If you knew what you were looking for, you could find it. And on this February afternoon Archibald MacLeish, John Dos Passos, Ernest Hemingway, and other members of the Contemporary Historians filmmaking corporation made their way without difficulty to 21 East Fifty-second Street, past the plainclothes doorman (another relic of "21's" speakeasy days), and into the dim, wood-paneled lobby bar. They didn't stop there, though, or go on into the dining room, where the regulars sat on red leather banquettes under a ceiling hung with big boys' toys—model airplanes, model ships, model cars; instead they headed upstairs, to a long table in one of the private rooms, to talk about their new film, *The Spanish Earth*.

MacLeish, the corporation's president, had good news for them all: the Spanish double bill *Spain in Flames*, which had opened at the end of January, was bringing in revenue, and donations for the new film were running ahead of expectations. Gerald Murphy, the Broadway producer Herman Shumlin, the philanthropist Margaret De Silver, several anonymous donors, and a number of organizations had all given more than $500 apiece. Joris Ivens was already in Spain filming, and would have preliminary reels ready to screen by the end of the month. And Hemingway and Dos Passos would each be going to Spain shortly to work with him. Hemingway had just arrived from Key West and would be sailing at the end of the month; and as an editor for *Fortune*, MacLeish had arranged to commission a series of articles about Spain from Dos Passos that would pay for *him* to travel there as well.

Now the Historians could talk about exactly what shape they wanted this new film to take—and that's when the first hints of discord crept in. Dos Passos, who had spent long periods living in and traveling through Spain starting in 1916, had written widely on Spanish literature and culture, and had been contracted for a book on Spain's Second Republic, wanted it to be a portrait of Spain in transition—to make clear what the aims and stakes of the people were, and how the war affected them. Hemingway's experiences of Spain had centered on the bullring, which he celebrated as the locus of "one of the simplest things of all, and the most fundamental": "violent death." What he called the "tragedy" of the *corrida* was for him the mirror of, and in a world at peace a substitute for, death in war. So it was only natural that *his* interest in this film was to make it about war and death, full of scenes of battle and destruction. *That's* what would galvanize the American public.

Before this disagreement could get ugly—because when Hemingway was crossed things could sometimes get very ugly indeed—the meeting was adjourned. Some of the participants, Dos Passos and Hemingway among them, went downstairs for dinner, where they were joined by Katy Dos Passos and, to everyone's surprise but Hemingway's, Martha Gellhorn, elegantly got up in an orange dress that brought out the reddish lights in her tawny hair. Hemingway told everyone that Martha had just arrived in New York and was going to Spain as a correspondent for *Collier's* as soon as she got all her papers in order. Dos Passos and Katy, who were devoted to Pauline Hemingway and could see exactly what was going on, were not impressed. During dinner Martha revealed that since *Collier's* wasn't actually *sending* her to Spain (they were just writing her a letter she could use for accreditation), she was paying for her trip with the proceeds of an assignment from *Vogue* that involved her trying out a skin-exfoliation treatment for older women—pretty funny, since she was only twenty-eight! Hemingway recited stories about his African safari: everyone at the table except Martha had heard them before, but she was the one Hemingway was telling them for, and she was "goggle-eyed," Dos Passos noticed. The party broke up early.

On the twenty-seventh, Hemingway boarded the American Line's steamer *Paris*, bound for Le Havre. He was accompanied by Sidney Franklin, looking even paler and more hollow-eyed than usual, who was going to Spain to act as Hemingway's go-between and factotum, and the writer Evan Shipman, a friend from Hemingway's expat Paris days, who had volunteered to deliver one of the ambulances Hemingway had donated to the Loyalists. Martha was not in evidence. A swarm of newspapermen streamed into Hemingway's stateroom to take down his thoughts on his impending journey, and he was happy to oblige: he was going to Spain, he said, to cover the "new style war" being fought there, a war "where there is no such thing as a non-combatant," a war that "come[s] right smack into everybody's home and drip[s] blood all over the carpet." He hoped that if his dispatches gave American audiences "fear-knots tied into their guts," it would keep America out of "the next war." Not that he'd be concentrating only on military matters: he also wanted to write about "the little people, the waiters and taxi drivers and the fellow who fixes your shoes." And he and Sidney Franklin would find time for their favorite Spanish pastime: Franklin would be facing the bulls in Madrid, Barcelona, Valencia, and a few other cities, and Hemingway would be cheering him from the stands. "A little thing like a war isn't going to stop bullfighting in Spain," Franklin opined. If any fascist bombers *did* threaten the *corrida*, added Hemingway, he and Franklin had a strategy all figured out: "We're going to take along a bottle of Scotch and drink plenty."

The *Paris*'s whistle blew—*all ashore that's going ashore!*—and the newsmen snapped their notebooks shut and departed; shortly afterward the liner slipped out of her berth and steamed down the Hudson River into New York Harbor. In his stateroom, surrounded by telegrams and bon voyage baskets, Hemingway, too, had pulled up anchor. A few weeks before, writing to his conservative Catholic in-laws to justify his forthcoming trip, he'd scribbled a postscript down the right margin of the letter. "I'm very grateful to you both," it said, "for providing Pauline who's made me happier than I've ever been." The past tense sounded valedictory in more ways than one.

As Hemingway was steaming across the Atlantic, John Dos Passos—having convinced the State Department that he and Hemingway were not, contrary to a persistent press rumor, traveling to Spain as combatants—was getting his passport renewed. He was now free to sail with Katy on the *Berengaria* on March 18. Dos Passos had an additional purpose, beyond the Spanish film and his *Fortune* articles, for making the trip. His friend and translator, José Robles Pazos, whom he'd first met traveling in Spain in 1916, had apparently been arrested in Valencia and had disappeared into the political prison system. Robles had been working in Madrid as an interpreter for the Russian general Gorev, and then in Valencia for the War Ministry, when the extralegal police picked him up; Dos Passos hoped he might find out what had happened to him, and if necessary intervene to get him freed.

Just before he and Katy were due to depart, they went to dinner in

Brooklyn Heights with Dos's fellow Contemporary Historians board member Margaret De Silver and her lover, the Italian anarchist journalist Carlo Tresca. When they arrived Tresca was teaching De Silver's African American cook how to make scaloppine like his mother used to; but he paused in his ministrations to admonish Dos Passos. He should leave Katy behind in Paris, Tresca said, and he should be very, very careful in Spain—not just about what he did but about whom he saw and what he believed of what they told him. "They gonna make a monkey out of you, a *beeg* monkey," he warned. "If the communists don't like a man in Spain, right away, they shoot him."

March 1937: Paris/Pyrenees

It was a cold, wet spring in Paris, with late snow and heavy rain that swelled the Seine to overflowing. The weather matched the city's prevailing mood: Premier Léon Blum's Popular Front government, plagued by deficits, had placed promised reforms on hold—"a phase of prudent consolidation," is how the premier put it—and both the haves and the have-nots were surly and disillusioned. The left was outraged by the book of the moment, André Gide's *Retour de l'U.R.S.S.*, in which the high priest of French Marxism recounted how he'd gone to Russia and had been shocked to discover bad food, ugly consumer products, public ignorance and inertia, artistic repression, and a Stalinist cult of personality in a place where, he'd previously believed, "Utopia was in process of becoming reality." The right was stung by a new production of Shakespeare's *Julius Caesar* at the Théâtre de l'Atelier that had the title character made up to look like Colonel François de la Rocque, head of the proto-fascist Croix de Feu organization. The bipartisan sourness was only slightly mitigated by the spectacle of Josephine Baker, still shaking her naked bottom at the Folies-Bergère, and by Maurice Chevalier's show at the Casino de Paris, in which the straw-hatted entertainer cheerfully proclaimed, night after night, "Y'a d'la joie!"

Arriving in Paris in the first rainy week of March, however, Robert Capa had reason to feel as joyful as Chevalier sounded. He had money and *Ce Soir*'s new contract in his pocket, and he was shopping for space for the studio he and Gerda wanted to set up. On the rue Froidevaux, just opposite the Cimetière de Montparnasse, he found what he was looking for: a 600-square-foot third-floor *atelier* in a recently remodeled five-story building at number 37. It had double-height windows all along one side of its lofty main room, and a spiral staircase leading to a narrow balcony, off of which was a little kitchen, so you could live in the studio as well as work. There were famous neighbors, past and present: Kertesz had lived in the building, as had Amedeo Modigliani, and Marcel Duchamp, and Hemingway had stayed in Gerald Murphy's loft a few doors away at number 69 before his marriage to Pauline. The studio was even perfectly situated for access to Capa's preferred watering holes—all you had to do was cross the street and walk along the tree-lined avenue that bisected the cemetery and you'd soon find yourself at Le Dôme or La Coupole.

He took a lease on it, hired Imre Weisz—a childhood friend from Budapest whom everyone called Csiki—to be the darkroom manager and another Hungarian émigré, Taci Czigany, to assist him, put in a telephone, and had stationery and a stamp made for his prints: "Atelier Robert Capa." And he permitted himself to dream, just a little, of the life he and Gerda could make here as partners—in every sense of the word. He wanted very much to persuade her to marry him; but he wasn't sure she would accept. Unfortunately, he wouldn't be able to see her until she returned to Paris, or he got a formal assignment that would send him to Spain. Unlike Gerda, who had a passport, he was a stateless person; he could get special clearance to travel, but only with sponsorship. Infuriatingly, *Ce Soir* didn't seem overeager to assign him a Spanish story—maybe they thought one photographer in Spain was enough—and instead they sent him to shoot the opening of the Salon des Indépendents, a costume ball at the Cirque d'Hiver, an agricultural fair, a parade of the Laurel and Hardy fan club. All Capa could do was collect his paycheck and hope something would come up that would allow him back across the border again.

On the other side of the Montparnasse cemetery, at the posh Hotel Dinard in the Sixth Arrondissement, Ernest Hemingway was assembling his forces for Spain. His friend the Associated Press reporter Lester Ziffren, who'd been in Madrid all the autumn and was now in Chicago nursing a case of whooping cough, had told him to bring plenty of canned goods with him (Ziff's guts had suffered mightily from the alkaline diet of potatoes and beans) as well as warm clothes and as much currency as he could carry. So Hemingway had sent Sidney Franklin—who was staying in more modest lodgings in the rue St. Benoit—to buy tinned hams, prawns, pâté, bouillon cubes, and Nescafé, which Evan Shipman would transport to Spain in one of the ambulances he was delivering. Meanwhile, he himself telephoned everyone from the American ambassador to the State Department in Washington to the Spanish ambassador to France, Luis Araquistáin, trying to persuade them that Franklin, who still needed a visa to enter Spain, was "a bona-fide newsman" and not a would-be combatant in a war America had pledged to stay out of. When time hung heavy on their hands, Franklin would get out his bullfighting gear—the stockings, breeches, cape, sword, and embroidered "suit of lights"—and Hemingway would pretend to be a bull, waggling his hands over his ears and charging at Franklin as the matador called out "Toro—huh—toro" and practiced passes with his cape.

From the Hotel Dinard, Hemingway filed his first NANA dispatch, a jokey tongue-in-cheek story about the difficulties over Franklin's visa, and got down to more serious business: a rendezvous with his new filmmaking colleague Joris Ivens. Ivens had arrived in Paris late in February for a brief visit to screen early footage of the Contemporary Historians film for an invited audience of Popular Front journalists and filmmakers, including the Russian émigré and spy Vladimir Pozner and the director Jean Renoir; and perhaps the warm reaction to his rushes had gone to his head. For, over copious drinks at the Deux Magots, Ivens came on a little patronizingly to his scenarist. Hemingway probably didn't understand what the stakes were in Spain, he implied—how important it was to make a stand against fascism there, using whatever means were necessary and not worrying, the way a journalist might, about the strict accuracy of one's reporting. Usually quick to flare up at any suggestion that he didn't know exactly what was what, Hemingway let Ivens talk; something about this magnetic Dutchman with the deep-set blue eyes mesmerized him. He even found himself trying to impress Ivens by boasting about the "beautiful girlfriend" who would be coming to join him in Spain. "She has legs that begin at her shoulders," Hemingway said.

A few days after their drinks at the Deux Magots, leaving Sidney Franklin—still awaiting the final resolution of his visa problems—to finish shopping for their provisions, Hemingway and Ivens took the night train to Toulouse, where they'd get a flight across the Pyrenees into Spain.

A major Nationalist offensive, which included 35,000 Italian troops, was taking place near Guadalajara, northeast of Madrid; and although at first it had seemed the rebel forces would prevail, the Republicans were now fighting back tenaciously. This was news in the making, and NANA would want it covered.

Hemingway didn't leave France immediately, however; first he wanted to see his old friend the Spanish painter and muralist Luis Quintanilla. Not just for old times' sake, but for background: Quintanilla was an *engagé* artist who'd been jailed for his support of the Asturian miners' revolt in 1934, had taken part in the attack on the Montaña Barracks at the outbreak of the war, and had fought in the Madrid outskirts and in the Guadarrama. And since the previous November he'd been director of the Spanish government's intelligence services in southwest France, gathering information about the various refugee groups seeking shelter there.

As they generally did when they met after a long separation, the two men went out for an evening of dedicated drinking (*la gran borrachera*, Quintanilla called it). How was it in Madrid, Hemingway wanted to know; and Quintanilla told him it was pretty bad. His studio had been bombed; and his monumental frescoes at University City and in the Casa del Pueblo had all been smashed to bits. "Let's not talk about it, Ernesto," he said. "When a man loses his life's work . . . it is much better not to talk about it." They had more drinks and still more; and then someone had the idea of driving to the frontier to see what the border security was actually like. How serious were they about this visa business?

Very serious, it turned out. Twenty miles from the French border control point at Le Perthus two armed guards with bayonets stopped Hemingway's car. Only when he and Quintanilla produced their impeccable papers were they allowed to proceed, up and up a winding road through the budding almond orchards that hugged the lower slopes of the Pyrenees, until at last they reached the guardhouse at the frontier, where a police officer told them that since February 20, when the new visa rules had been put into effect, no one had crossed the border here except for a few diplomats. "Even you," the officer admonished Hemingway, "no matter what papers you have with you, you could not pass that line without the new visa." On the other hand, Quintanilla told Hemingway on the drive back to Toulouse, there were now 88,000 Italian troops in Spain—

including 12,000 who had just landed in Málaga and Cadiz—and between 16,000 and 20,000 Germans; in Germany recruitment posters were offering bonuses of a thousand reichsmarks to volunteers who would fight for Franco's rebels.

"No matter on which side of the Spanish war people may be on," Hemingway sarcastically cabled back to NANA, "they all agree on one thing—the Spanish border is closed up and airtight."

A week later, two other journalists tried to gauge the airtightness of the border: Capa and the reporter Charles Réber from *Ce Soir* drove the length of the frontier from the Mediterranean to the mountains near the Andorran border to the fascist "embassies" in the posh precincts of Biarritz and Hendaye on the Atlantic coast. Capa wore a *miliciano's* jacket against the mountain cold, and had brought with him a box of flashbulbs that looked awfully like tiny bombs; his appearance was so suspicious that the pair were repeatedly hauled in for questioning by guards who were certain they were arms smugglers, or at the very least illegal volunteers trying to cross the border to enlist. It took all of Capa's charm to keep them out of jail.

Unfortunately he didn't get very interesting pictures for his trouble, unless you counted the one of the Basque refugee children the French border patrols had arrested. In a circle on a windswept beach, they were all holding hands and dancing.

March 1937: Madrid/Valencia/Madrid

The Casa de Alianza de Escritores Antifascistas—the Madrid headquarters of the antifascist writers' union—was a grand brick mansion, formerly the palace of the Marques del Duero, on a quiet street near the Parque del Retiro. Although it had been taken over by the government when its aristocratic owners fled the city, its walls were still hung with tapestries and Old Master paintings, its windows draped in purple velvet, and the antifascist intellectuals ate their beans and rice off the Marques's ancestral silver, crystal, and china while being waited on by his self-effacing servants, all of whom had stayed on in the house. The secretary of the Alianza, the vivacious, well-connected writer Maria Teresa Léon, and her husband, the distinguished poet Rafael Alberti, ran the place like a twenty-four-hour salon: putting up visiting intellectuals, staging readings, plays, and cultural events, and publishing a journal, *El mono azul*, featuring work by José Bergamín (the Alianza's president), Antonio Machado, Ramón J. Sender, and foreigners such as André Malraux, Pablo Neruda, and John Dos Passos. And when Gerda Taro was left on her own in Madrid after Capa went back to Paris, the Albertis asked her to come and stay there.

The Casa de Alianza could not have been more unlike the raffish quarters she'd shared with Capa at the Hotel Florida. Instead of shells whistling over the roof you heard birds chirping in the spacious garden; the people you passed in the halls were writers and artists—including Ilsa Kulcsar's former connection from her Viennese cell, the English poet Stephen Spender—not newsmen, soldiers, and prostitutes. Of course Gerda accepted the invitation, especially when Alberti and Maria Teresa offered to help her set up a darkroom on the ground floor, where she could develop and enlarge her own prints and teach Alberti, an aspiring photographer, to do the same.

She'd been taking pictures almost nonstop all month. Before Capa left, she and he had chronicled the forlorn, often bizarre detritus left behind by the rebel bombers: empty facades through whose windows sunlight streamed as if from a lighted interior; a dining table—suddenly visible in an apartment without walls—set for a meal to which no one would come; the burned, battered shell of the residence of the Chilean consul, Pablo Neruda, in the once-leafy suburb of Argüelles; the rubble-filled courtyard of a convent children's shelter; a little girl gathering firewood that was evidently the remains of someone's house. "*Le bombardement de Madrid*," wrote Gerda on a page in one of the notebooks where she pasted contact prints—and then, in parentheses: "*Surréalisme*." On a trip to Valencia she'd shot a roll of film in the *plaza de toros* where a group of men and women, citizen volunteers, were being drilled by Loyalist soldiers: lyrical photographs, in which the idealistic young trainees were lit like dancers in a ballet as the sun moved across the bullfighting arena. Someone would buy them—the young people looked so fervent and committed, and it made a nice message. *Citizens learn to defend their own hearths and homes.* (A few weeks later *Regards* did indeed run a page of those photos.) But with so much happening all around her in Madrid, she wanted to shoot *breaking* news. Herself. Over her own byline, not one she shared with Capa.

For Gerda had begun to feel ever more sharply the professional limitations, not to mention the personal ones, of her relationship with her now-famous lover, and she was looking for ways to proclaim her independence. She wasn't sure she saw a future with Capa, she confided to Ruth Cerf; and despite what some people might think, she wasn't his property, especially if he wasn't around. If anyone asked, she started saying that they were really just *"copains"*—buddies—not lovers.

Certainly she said that to Ted Allan, the young Canadian she called "the kid," who'd been following her around like a puppy since her arrival in Madrid. Of course she loved Capa, she told him, but she wasn't *in* love with him—she didn't *want* to be in love, not ever again. She'd been in love once, desperately, with a boy in Prague who was killed by the Nazis. But no more. "It's too painful," she said. Allan believed this invented romantic fable, but her protestations of unavailability made him more eager to be with her rather than less. And he offered to drive her to the still unsettled Jarama front, where she could take pictures of battle sites and maybe, even, of combat. He was going there with Geza Karpathi and the screenwriter Herbert Kline to scout locations for their film on Bethune's blood transfusion unit, and he hoped to be able to find some of his old International Brigades mates, whom he hadn't heard from since the bloody fighting of the previous month. Why didn't Gerda come along?

The German photographer Walter Reuter saw her setting out for her trip to the front and couldn't help noticing she was wearing stockings and high heels more appropriate to the Ritz than the battlefield. When he teased her about her outfit, Gerda just laughed. Wouldn't it make those boys happy to see a *woman?* she wanted to know. Well, that's what they were going to get.

The sun was shining as the little group drove south toward Morata de Tajuña, where the Brigades headquarters were. She and Allan were lighthearted; they sang Brigade songs, and she taught him the words to *"Freiheit"* ("Freedom") and *"Los Cuatros Generales,"* which ridiculed the four rebel commanders:

Los cuatros generales,
Mamita mia,
Se han alzado . . .

Para la Nochebuena,
Mamita mia,
Seran ahorcados.

The four generals,
Dear little mother,
They tried to betray us.

By Christmas,
Dear little mother,
They'll all be strung up.

When they crossed the Jarama north of Arganda, Gerda got out and photographed the bridge that the Nationalists had claimed they took, and—for good measure—the road sign that pointed to Madrid one way and Valencia the other. *The road's still open! See?* Near Morata, although the front seemed quiet, the officers in charge were reluctant to allow "the lady comrade" to go into the trenches; but Gerda talked her way past the authorities, and the soldiers smilingly posed for her, their arms draped loosely around one another's shoulders, cigarettes—a quantity of which she and Allan had had the foresight to bring along—dangling from their mouths. They showed her their bivouacs, and pointed out "Suicide Hill," the heights of Pingarrón, where half the British battalion had fallen in February. Then, suddenly, just as thick gray clouds rolled in over the ruined olive groves, there was firing from the Nationalist lines to the west, and Gerda—seemingly impervious to the idea she might be in danger—darted from cover like a gazelle so she could photograph the brigade artillery being brought into position to fire back. There was no further action, however; the front settled back into that state of armed deadlock it had been in since the end of February, and eventually Gerda and Allan, and Karpathi and Kline, headed back to Madrid. In her camera bag Gerda had two rolls of what she thought would be good and saleable pictures. But Allan had nothing but sadness: in Morata he'd learned that twenty of his comrades, the boys he'd shipped across the Atlantic with and left behind when he went to take his political commissar's job in Madrid, had been killed in the assault on Pingarrón.

•

The springlike weather that had smiled on Gerda's trip to the Jarama front didn't last. In its place came freezing rain—in the midst of which, at dawn on March 8, the Black Flames, a motorized division of Italian troops fighting under the rebels' flag, broke through government lines northeast of the provincial capital of Guadalajara, on the road from Saragossa to Madrid. Over the next two days, despite the fog and sleet that reduced visibility to as little as a hundred yards in some places, the Nationalists, including another Italian division, the Black Arrows, continued the on-slaught in an effort to encircle, and perhaps capture, Madrid before the winter's end. The poor visibility produced one *opera buffa* moment, when the Black Flames cried out to another group of Italian speakers, telling them to stop firing on their own countrymen. *"Noi siamo italiani di Gari-baldi!"* ("We're *Garibaldi* Italians!," Loyalist supporters), their supposed allies yelled back. But the rebels' strategy otherwise appeared to be devastatingly successful: by the evening of the tenth, the rebel forces had overwhelmed the old walled town of Brihuega and were advancing toward Madrid.

On the fifth floor of the Telefónica, where the sleet rattled at the win-dows, the reporters were queuing up for the available telephone lines. "Better announce a retreat for tonight," Ilsa told them all, grimly. "Prepare for the worst." At dinner at the Gran Via restaurant, she found her Vienna colleague Stephen Spender, who'd recently joined the British Communist Party and had come to Spain as a journalist. How had Madrid's Republi-can defenders done today, he asked anxiously; and was shocked when Ilsa gave him the unvarnished truth: *"Sie läuften wie Hasen!"*—they ran like hares. When she and Barea had their nightly briefing with General Gorev at the War Ministry, he was cool and unruffled—*as if we had all the space of the Russian steppes to maneuver*, Barea thought; but back in the press room *The New York Times*'s Herbert Matthews was more pessimistic. He'd seen what the Italians had done in Abyssinia, he told his comrades. And now they were here in Spain, in open violation of the Non-Intervention Agreement, and probably on the verge of entering Madrid. Sitting at the telephone, with a line censor listening in, he tried to send that story to the *Times*'s Paris office. *Hold it*, the man on the other end kept saying; *stop saying these are Italians. You and the Commies are the only people who use that kind of propaganda tag.* Normally a calm, patient man with the mournful features of Erasmus in a drypoint etching, Matthews exploded in a fury; then, pinching his lips into a severe line, sat down and typed out a cable: If the *Times* had no confidence in his reporting, they could have his resignation instead.

The *Times* tried to cool Matthews down—they weren't accusing him of *propagandizing*, they said; they just worried that he was parroting one of Barea's press releases; and by the twelfth, as a heavy storm system moved slowly over the Castilian *meseta*, the winds of fortune miraculously changed direction. Republican bombers, taking off from permanent concrete runways at Albacete, were able to pummel the Italians, whose tanks were bogged down in the mud, and government and International Brigade troops began pushing back along the road to Brihuega. There were many casualties—very nearly including Ted Allan and Geza Karpathi, who'd been in a station wagon with Norman Bethune, attempting to get blood to the front lines, when enemy bullets shattered their windshield. But they, and the blood they carried, were saved by a Loyalist tank; and the enemy began to fall back, leaving incriminating evidence behind. Mikhail Koltsov, rushing to the front, found abandoned Fiat tractors and Lancia trucks jamming the highway, which would make interesting reading in his next communication to Moscow (how was Mussolini going to deny helping the rebels now?); and Pietro Nenni, the Garibaldis' soft-spoken political commissar, showed up in the censors' office with a mailbag his men had seized from one of the Nationalist battalions. It was crammed with mail and postal orders with Italian addresses and bloodstained diaries, handwritten in Italian, which Ilsa and Barea could give to any reporters who needed proof of the travesty these documents made of the Non-Intervention Agreement.

Then, a few freezing, sodden days later, the weather cleared; and the Republicans, who had managed to nearly encircle the Italians under cover of the wintry brume, went on the attack in earnest. At that point, machinegunned from the air by Russian Chatos, overrun with T-26 tanks, freezing in the tropical uniforms they hadn't had time to exchange for winter battle dress, the Italians turned and ran. Eight months into the civil war the government finally had a decisive victory, and in the streets of Madrid people were buying newspapers, with their red banner headlines that screamed ¡Victoria a Guadalajara!, and throwing them into the air in celebration.

In the days leading up to the battle Gerda had been frantic to get to the field, and Allan's and Karpathi's tales of their narrow escape can only have sharpened her desperation. Finally, she was able to commandeer a car with the *Humanité* correspondent Georges Soria, who at twenty-three had been covering the war, alongside Chim and Capa, since the beginning; and together the two journalists scrambled over the muddy fields where machine guns still chattered erratically, Soria with his notebook, Gerda with her Leica. Everywhere you looked there were the trucks, mortars, rifles, machine guns, and boxes of ammunition the Italians had left behind in their flight; and among them, strewn like broken toys in the rain-filled craters and the ditches beside the rutted roads, were the bodies of the dead, hundreds of them, their faces gray under the pallid sun. It was the first time Gerda had seen slaughter on this scale. When she returned to Madrid that evening, at dinner with Ted Allan and Herbert Matthews and others in the restaurant at the Gran Via, she seemed exhausted and pale; the sight of so much carnage had shaken her. "It was terrible," she kept repeating. "A hand here. A head there . . . They were so young. Young Italian boys." But she had taken "wonderful pictures," she was sure of it: pictures that would help establish her as a combat photographer in her own right. Eager to get them into the hands of editors in Paris, she headed for Valencia the next morning.

Valencia was in full battle dress. Although the streets were still thronged with people and the grocers' shops overflowed with produce, everywhere gigantic posters proclaimed the Valencianos' fighting spirit. On the wall of one building was an enormous map of Spain—with a big dot for Valencia and an arrow pointing to the Nationalists' positions at Teruel, in the Aragonese mountains—under the legend, "VALENCIANOS! The front lines are *150 kilometers* from Valencia! Don't forget!" You could try to forget by ducking into a movie theater—*Give Me Your Heart*, a Warner Brothers weeper starring Kay Francis and George Brent was playing in one—but when you came out what met your eyes was the stern, uncompromising hulk of the "Tribuna de Propaganda," a massive ziggurat painted with patriotic slogans, adorned with a sculpted fist clutching a rifle, and crowned with the word "VENCEREMOS," which dominated the center of the Plaza de Emilio Castelar.

Not that Gerda was spending much time at the movies. Instead she was photographing the unveiling of a unit of the new Popular Army, the Ejercito Popular, a centralized, top-down, made-for-efficiency fighting machine modeled on the Red Army that was being phased in at the urging of the government's Russian allies and its Communist members. After the disaster at Málaga the process was being accelerated, apparently to Prime Minster Largo Caballero's chagrin—"he fears the exceptional influence that the Party has in a significant part of the army and strives to limit this," is how the Soviet advisor General Jan Berzin (code name "DONI-ZETTI") reported things to Moscow. Caballero was increasingly on the defensive, and he and his foreign minister, Álvarez del Vayo, who had begun siding with the PCE (Partido Comunista de España—the Moscow-oriented Communists) on most issues, were barely speaking. In the PCE's congress in Valencia early in the month, the party's secretary general, José Diaz, had pushed strongly for the unified army; and his associates were privately saying Caballero was a handicap to victory. "To win the war"— the French Communist André Marty, supreme commander of the International Brigades, told his Comintern associates—"the [popular] front demands radical rapid changes," such as a government "without Caballero . . . And on this issue the public opinion of the front is being prepared."

The publication of photo essays like Gerda's on the Popular Army might have seemed like a subtle part of this preparation. But although Gerda had moved closer to Communist orthodoxy since her SAP days in Germany—it would have been hard not to, working for *Ce Soir* and staying with Alberti and Maria Teresa Léon at the Casa de Alianza, where Mikhail Koltsov was a frequent visitor—if she'd come to share the PCE's belief in regimentation, it was more an emotional reaction to the devastation of war than a political one. She wasn't an ideologue. She did, however, recognize a potent visual symbol when she saw one. The new armed force marching in lockstep, standing in unwavering lines, its soldiers forming human chains as each grasped the shoulders of the man in front of him (and with women now excluded from the military they were *all* men)— these images had the heroic, and monolithic, grandeur of a Soviet poster. And Gerda celebrated them as she'd once celebrated the anarchic spirit in Barcelona at the beginning of the war. Gerda *evolved*, is how Koltsov described it: *When she came here she was a child-woman playing at war; she became an antifascist warrior.* And the warrior in her seemed to have decided that this was what it would take to win the fight with fascism. If that meant abandoning the social revolution—well, so be it.

Hemingway arrived in Madrid on the evening of the day Gerda Taro left it.

When he and Joris Ivens had reached Valencia on March 16, he'd sent NANA a dispatch, full of the sort of scene-setting local color he could do in his sleep, describing their journey and his impressions of the conditions in Spain. And the New York office had fired back, in terse cablese: "WE UNWANT DAILY RUNNING NARRATIVE [YOUR] EXPERIENCES." What they *did* want, the cable continued, was "CONSIDERED APPRAISAL SITUATION." In other words, *get to where the fighting is and report on it—that's why we're paying you the big bucks.*

The fighting was over at Guadalajara, but maybe he could catch the tail end of things if he was lucky. Visiting the press office to discuss travel arrangements to Madrid, he met Stephen Spender, who'd just come from the beleaguered city and seemed relieved to get away. Something about the fair-haired, fair-skinned English poet seemed to rub Hemingway the wrong way: he told Spender he couldn't wait to get *to* Madrid: he wanted to see if he had lost his nerve since he'd been under fire in Italy. And fortunately, Rubio Hidalgo's new deputy, a very tall, dark, aristocratic woman named Constancia de la Mora, who was married to the Republicans' air force chief, Ignacio Hidalgo de Cisneros, was able to help him.

Constancia, nicknamed Connie, spoke English fluently—the result of three years in a convent school in Cambridge—and her girlhood in the drawing rooms of Madrid society had given her the sort of natural authority that gets things done. In addition, she and her husband had become members of the PCE, so Joris Ivens's party credentials were as impressive to her as Hemingway's literary ones. Very quickly she produced a car, ration slips for gasoline, and a driver, Tomás, a tiny man whose nearly toothless mouth made him look like one of Velázquez's dwarves; and on the morning of March 20, Ivens and Hemingway were on their way to their destination, up through the coastal mountains and across the high plain of La Mancha. Although Valencia was warm and springlike, here it was bitterly cold; there was no heat in the car, so Hemingway—not neglecting

Tomás—passed around his silver flask, engraved "E.H. from E.H." and full of scotch. By the time they discerned Madrid rising like a citadel on the horizon, everyone was a little the worse for drink, and Tomás was moved to whiskey-fueled tears by the sight.

"Long live Madrid, the capital of my soul!" he cried.

"And of my heart," Hemingway responded—adding, as Tomás's emotions caused them to narrowly miss colliding with an army staff car, "Just try to watch where you're driving."

Soon they were pulling up in front of the Hotel Florida, where John Ferno was also staying; and the next day all three of them went to the battlefield beyond Guadalajara with Colonel Hans Kahle, a burly Prussian Communist who had commanded the first International Brigades battalion to relieve Madrid the previous November. With Tomás at the wheel, they drove out the Guadalajara road through freezing drizzle mixed with flakes of wet snow. Beyond the provincial capital, on the muddy hillsides around Brihuega and Trijueque, they saw, and filmed, the abandoned tanks and weapons, the corpses surrounded by the scattered contents of their rucksacks; and although Hemingway wasn't the first journalist on the scene—Matthews, Sefton Delmer, Georges Soria, and others had all filed stories already—he saw details they hadn't, or hadn't been interested in describing: the weather, the terrain, the "waxy gray faces" of the fallen.

Over the next few days, he accompanied the two filmmakers to various sites in the vicinity of Guadalajara. At Valdesaz, a hamlet outside Brihuega, he met the temporary commander of the Garibaldi Battalion (Pacciardi had been slightly wounded and was temporarily out of action); and later they were taken in hand by the German novelist Ludwig Renn, the Thaelmann Battalion's commander. The tall, balding Renn looked every inch the professional soldier in his natty uniform, complete with puttees and Sam Browne belt; and as he talked about how Franco had been foiled in his quest to encircle Madrid, and how, because of its natural position, the city would now be nearly impregnable to assault, Hemingway felt the seductive pull of what he would come to call "the true gen"—the real lowdown, the inside dope. He might be a former ambulance driver, not a military man; but when he walked the battlefield talking with Renn (a fellow novelist, after all) he felt like one of the brass hats from headquarters. Back in his room at the Hotel Florida, typing the dispatches he would send to London and thence to New York, he wrote, sweepingly, that Guadalajara was "the biggest Italian defeat since Caporetto," the retreat he had so memorably chronicled in A Farewell to Arms; more than that, it was "a complicatedly planned and perfectly organized military operation comparable to the finest in the Great War," and one that "will take its place in military history with other decisive battles of the world." If that wasn't CONSIDERED APPRAISAL SITUATION, he didn't know what was.

He got an even stronger whiff of the true gen when Joris Ivens took him to a gathering in Mikhail Koltsov's rooms at Gaylord's Hotel, where most of the Russian advisors had moved when the Palace was taken over for use as a military hospital. Ivens knew how important it was to Hemingway to feel he had privileged access to the real movers and shakers in Madrid, "an edge," as the filmmaker put it, that "other correspondents did not have." He'd resisted Hemingway's first entreaties to be included in the Gaylord's set, waiting until he judged Hemingway was "ready"; so this evening had almost the feeling of a debut about it. Hemingway had brought two bottles of whiskey from his well-stocked armoire as gifts, and set them on a table next to the wine and vodka and the huge ham that were already there. The smoky rooms were full of people who made things happen: There was Gustav Regler and General Lukácz; and Alexander Orlov, who was spending most of his time in Valencia overseeing a new network of guerrilla fighters. There was Koltsov himself, whom Hemingway liked immediately for his intelligence and sardonic humor, and even his way of spitting when he talked because of his bad teeth. And there was the Izvestia correspondent Ilya Ehrenburg, who almost started a fight with Hemingway by asking him, in French, if he sent nouvelles—news—to the United States by cable. Hemingway thought he meant novelas—novels— and was so insulted that his reportage should be considered fiction that he swung at Ehrenburg with the bottle he was pouring a drink from. Fortunately, the misunderstanding was cleared up, they all had a good laugh over it, and Ehrenburg saw to it that Hemingway met someone who might give him material for a dozen nouvelles or novelas: a dark, hawk-faced man calling himself Colonel Xanthé. No one was sure of his real name—it might have been Hajji Mourat Mamsourov, or Mamsurov Haji-Umar—but what was certain was that he was a guerrilla from the Caucasus who had come to direct some of Orlov's aktivi, sabotage groups working behind the lines in Nationalist territory. Tough, fearless, his skin tanned mahogany from exposure to sun and wind, Colonel Xanthé was the genuine article, a real freedom fighter; what a subject he would make! Unfortunately, Hemingway wasn't able—or wasn't encouraged—to talk to him at length just then; but, Regler promised him, that time would come.

March 1937: Barcelona/Valencia/Madrid

Martha Gellhorn got out of her second-class railroad compartment at the Catalan border town of Puigcerdá on the morning of March 23 and stretched her long legs. She'd sat up all night and she was stiff, and cold—for although the fruit trees were blooming on the slopes of the Pyrenees it had snowed as they climbed to Puigcerdá, and the fields were as white as the trees. Alone on the platform, she watched the train reverse and chug back into France—because French and Spanish railroad tracks have different gauges, French trains couldn't continue across the border; then, picking up the backpack and duffel bag which were the only luggage she'd brought with her from Paris, she crossed the track to the *aduana*, where they stamped her passport and nonintervention papers, and waved her on to the waiting Barcelona train.

Paris had annoyed her. The *fonctionnaires* she had to get papers from were bureaucratic and rude, and she was put out by having to deal with Sidney Franklin—a pet of Pauline's, and therefore a potential enemy—over the matter of getting her baggage to Spain. In order to maintain deniability about her relationship with Hemingway she had to make the border crossing alone; she'd wanted to travel light, so she'd handed off her suitcases to Franklin in his role as Hemingway's majordomo before getting on the train for Toulouse and the border.

The ride to Barcelona, however, restored her sense of adventure. At one stop a group of young recruits, scarcely more than boys, got on, bound for the front; they were singing and joking like prep school boys going home for the holidays until their leader, who told Martha he was the regional Communist Party commissar, made them quiet down. The cause needed discipline, he explained to her, and the Party would provide it; those Anarchists in Barcelona, for example—they wanted too much, too soon, and they'd have to be paddled to make them behave. Certainly Barcelona, when she got there, didn't seem very disciplined: the streets were festooned with political posters and red banners, and crowded with red-and-black Anarchist taxis whose drivers refused tips, and everywhere there was a spirit of joyous camaraderie that she later described as "the greatest atmosphere going." A great contrast, in fact, to Valencia, to which she was transported by government car, along with three other passengers, also journalists, two days later; Valencia seemed full of profiteers living high off the hog and loving it. She was warmly received by Rubio Hidalgo, though, who welcomed her as if he'd been expecting her and had got her a room at the Victoria; and in the morning Constancia de la Mora came by to tell her the press department had made arrangements for her and Sidney Franklin, who had just arrived from Paris, to be driven to Madrid early the next day with another journalist.

That turned out to be Ted Allan, on whom Martha's charms—her smile, her golden bob, her racy figure—had the effect they usually did on impressionable young (and not-so-young) men. When a big Citroën pulled up in front of the hotel, with Sid Franklin in the front seat beside the driver, Allan made sure—once all the luggage, including a couple of typewriters, was arranged inside the car and Martha's duffel was tied to the front fender—that *he* sat in the back with her, the better to bring her up to date on "policy matters." Franklin, whose brief now included acting as Martha's chaperone, seemed none too pleased.

It was a long, cold drive and the packed car made it hard to get comfortable; perhaps that's why Martha ended up half in Allan's lap, with her legs draped over the seat. He flirted with her, she flirted back, but nothing much could happen with Franklin in the front of the car, turning back every now and then to glare at Allan—mystifyingly, since Allan had no idea what the connection between this glamorous girl and the surly American matador might be. The rest of the time Martha gazed out the window at the treeless, ocher-colored hills and endless fields of La Mancha. Eventually the road became crowded with military and official traffic, and a sentry stopped the car to ask for their papers. They got out and stood in the grass by the side of the road, looking north and west to where the peaks of the Guadarrama were catching the last rays of the sun. There was a rumbling like thunder in the distance. "Guns?" asked Martha. "Yes," said Ted Allan. The day before, Good Friday, there had been so little fighting that soldiers in the trenches near University City had left their shelter to play football in the street without attracting a single bullet from the rebels a hundred yards away; but today, apparently, firing had resumed.

Suddenly they were in the city. At the bullring another sentry stopped them for their papers and the daily password; then they went on, through the rutted and darkened streets, past the shattered buildings and papered shop fronts that told Martha she was in a war zone, until they reached the Hotel Florida.

Ted Allan, who had to report to duty at the transfusion unit's head-quarters, parted with Martha reluctantly, but not before saying he wanted to see her again. By now it was dinnertime, and the Florida's soaring lobby was deserted except for the reception clerk, Don Cristóbal, who was studying his stamp collection behind the desk and barely looked up to tell the new arrivals that Señor Hemingway was not here; he had gone to eat at the Gran Via. To which Martha duly went, shadowed by Franklin; and found it full of smoke and loud laughter. Hemingway, wearing his wire-rimmed glasses, was sitting at the long table with an American airman who flew for the Republican air force under the name Hernando Diaz Evans, but whom everyone called Whitey because of his pale blond hair and eye-brows; both of them looked up when Martha came in. Hemingway's face broke into a broad smile and he got up from the table to put his arm around her. "I knew you'd get here, daughter," he said, proud and proprietary, "because I fixed it up so you could."

Martha, who prized her independence and self-sufficiency, and thought she'd done a pretty good job of getting to Spain alone, looked at him in-credulously. *You fixed it up?* She was fuming. That he'd had Sidney Frank-lin get her luggage to Valencia, that he might have put in a word with Álvarez del Vayo and Constancia de la Mora to provide her transport to Madrid, cut no ice with her at all.

So it must have amused her that later that evening, as she was sitting alone in one of the two rooms Hemingway had taken at the Florida—numbers 108 and 109 at the back of the third floor—Ted Allan came looking for her, imagining he might take up where they had left off a few hours before. He had just sat down beside her on the bed when there was a brief knock, and the door opened to admit a burly dark man with wire-rimmed glasses and a mustache. It took Allan a few seconds to realize it was Ernest Hemingway.

)

"Oh, come in," said Martha redundantly. "This is, uh, Ted."

"Hi," said Allan awkwardly, scrambling to his feet. Hemingway stared at him.

"I'll see you later, okay?" Martha prompted.

"Okay. Yeah," said Allan, and left. Outside in the hall he discovered Sidney Franklin, who seemed much bigger at the Hotel Florida than he had in the car. Franklin made it clear that if Allan tried to see Martha again, he would be sorry; and Allan, who knew what Franklin could do to a bull weighing more than a thousand pounds, swore to keep his distance. He left the hotel in a hurry.

That night—really in the small hours of the next morning—Martha was awakened by a bombardment. She was alone in the bed, alone in the room. Feeling forsaken and uncharacteristically terrified, she went to the door and found it locked from the outside. She hammered on it and shouted for help, but no one came; at last, after the shelling had stopped, someone—a hotel employee—arrived with a key. Wondering what had happened to Hemingway, Martha ventured out into the hall and, following the sound of men's voices, went into one of the neighboring rooms. There was Hemingway, playing poker with a bunch of International Brigaders on leave. He was sorry if she'd been frightened, he said; he'd locked her into the room so no one would bother her while he was gone.

The next day was taken up with arranging passes and getting oriented, with a quick trip to the by-now-obligatory University City front—like a walk in Central Park, thought Martha, until she heard the ping of bullets on the other side of the wall she was standing against. At midnight Hemingway came in—covered with mud from the Guadalajara battlefield, where he'd been all day—in company with Gustav Regler and the Twelfth Brigade's medical officer, a German named Werner Heilbrun, and the four of them sat up talking until three. The next morning she was brushing her teeth when she heard the sickening whine of a shell approaching, then a noise "like granite thunder" as it hit just outside the hotel. At first she stood rooted to the still-shuddering floor; then, going downstairs to find out what had happened, she discovered that the shell had decapitated a man standing on the corner. Ivens and Ferno went out to film the corpse: it would make effective footage in the documentary. *Breathe in but don't inhale*, Martha told herself, because there were lyddite explosive fumes and granite dust everywhere. *Now breathe out. Breathe in, breathe out.* As Hemingway reminded her, "The dead man wasn't you or anyone you know." That was one way to see it, certainly—to think of the conflict as something separate from yourself.

After breakfast the two of them drove, in one of the two cars the Propaganda Ministry had assigned to Hemingway, to the Jarama front, where the opposing armies had gone to earth in lines of trenches from which they fired intermittently at each other and staged brief, sometimes bloody sorties in an attempt to break through somewhere. If you weren't in the line of fire, however, it was quite peaceful, and Hemingway and Martha picnicked by a stream before going on to Morata. There, at the hospital run by the Friends of Spanish Democracy, one of the patients, a Lincoln Brigader named Robert Raven, asked to speak to Hemingway. He was a social worker from Pittsburgh who'd been blinded during the fighting a month ago when a grenade exploded directly in front of him. Hemingway could hardly bring himself to look at the burned, ruined face, which "looked like some hill that had been fought over in muddy weather and then baked in the sun"; but Raven bore the injury with fortitude. He claimed only to regret that he might not be able to be useful to the cause he'd come to fight for.

"Listen, Old Timer," Hemingway told him heartily, "you're going to be fine. You'll be a lot of good, you know. You can talk on the radio."

"Maybe," said Raven. As Hemingway rose to go, he asked, "You'll be back?"

"Absolutely," Hemingway assured him, and perhaps even meant it. For with his soft voice and his ravaged face, the Pittsburgh social worker had suddenly brought the war close in a way that even the shells slamming into the Hotel Florida had not done. "It still isn't you that gets hit," Hemingway would write later that day, in a kind of twentieth-century iteration of John Donne's famous meditation beginning "No man is an island"—"but it is your countryman now."

April 1937: Madrid

In the weeks after Guadalajara, Barea thought, the atmosphere in Madrid had begun to change. There were still artillery barrages, and bombings, and the correspondents still queued anxiously for the two long-distance phone lines if something important seemed to be brewing; but suddenly there were more correspondents, some of them barely more than day-trippers popping in with a prewritten story they wanted to file in the Tele-fónica just to get the now-coveted Madrid dateline, others coming as if on a pilgrimage to a shrine. Spain was still news, and now it seemed safe to cover it; nobody was talking about "the fall of Madrid" anymore. Antoine de Saint-Exupéry, the debonair French writer-aviator, came to write a series of articles on the war for *Paris-Soir*. Virginia Cowles, a darkly glamorous, well-connected twenty-seven-year-old who (she herself admitted) "had no qualifications for a war correspondent except curiosity" arrived— with "three wool dresses and a fur jacket"—to cover both sides of the conflict for the Hearst newspapers in the United States. The decidedly *un*glamorous Iowa novelist Josephine Herbst, armed with little more than her Communist sympathies and some vague letters of interest from magazines, wanted to cover what was happening to the man—or the woman—on the street. The swashbuckling Hollywood actor Errol Flynn, star of *Captain Blood* and *The Charge of the Light Brigade*, appeared on some kind of vague fact-finding trip. And of course now there was Heming-way, who blew in to the Telefónica press room one day with a beautifully groomed blonde on his arm.

"That's Marty—be nice to her," Hemingway said. "She writes for *Collier's*—you know, a million circulation." Or maybe, thought Barea, dazed by Martha Gellhorn's aura, it was half a million, or two million—the numbers were unimaginable.

The new correspondents, along with the aid workers and off-duty In-ternational Brigaders, made a kind of expatriate colony that drifted from watering hole to watering hole along the Gran Via and the Calle de Alcalá—from the Miami Bar, with its collection of American jazz records and its frescoed murals of Bright Young Things disporting themselves on the beach, to the Café Molineros, or the Aquarium, or Chicote's, Heming-way's favorite, where an American girl who worked in the press office performed a striptease she called "The Widow of General Mola," and an inebriated *miliciano* got himself shot dead for spraying guests with a Flit gun filled with lavender water. "We were a jokey bunch," Martha would recall later.

Barea and Ilsa, however, didn't join in any of these hijinks. Perhaps the jokes didn't seem very funny to either of them. Instead, Barea took Ilsa back to his old neighborhood, to the narrow lanes of Lavapiés and Serafín's bar on Calle Ave Maria, past the streets and squares he'd known as a boy and a young man, the landmarks of his life. Aurelia had agreed to a divorce and he had filed the papers necessary to begin the process; a future with Ilsa now seemed not only possible but attainable, and he wanted to share with her not only his present but his past. He pointed out where his mother had laundered shirts in the Manzanares, or where he had waited for the stagecoach to take him to Brunete to stay with his father's family, and Ilsa's curiosity and enjoyment nourished him. Under her eager gaze he became a storyteller, weaving a tale of another Madrid, as different from the one they traversed—or from the one in Hemingway's dispatches—as Goya's pictures were from Capa's. And for the first time, but not the last, Barea knew what it was to have an audience hang on his every word.

Although she'd originally thought this trip was going to be a great adventure, Martha was having a hard time in Madrid.

To begin with there was the noise: the rifles and machine guns that yammered all night in metallic bursts—*tacrong, crong, cararong,* as Hemingway, who liked sound effects, put it; the shells; the loudspeakers on the Casa de Campo through which each side bombarded the other with music ("Kitten on the Keys" was a bipartisan favorite) and propaganda. She was cold at night, despite hot-water bottles and an electric heater that blew the fuses at the Florida; hungry all the time or disgusted by what food was available ("horrible" was a frequent note in her diary); and disdainful of most of the people she met. George Seldes and his wife were "unpleasant," Koltsov's mistress, the German journalist Maria Osten, "ominous," Ehrenburg and Georges Soria self-important, Errol Flynn both "dumb" and a "shit," Virginia Cowles (for coming to Madrid with only high-heeled shoes) frivolous, and Josie Herbst—an old friend of Hemingway's, to make matters worse—was "ugly and vulgar and has a voice like scratching one's fingernail on a blackboard."

Finally, despite their shared quarters and pet names—he called her "Mookie" as well as "Rabbit" and "Daughter," she called him "Scrooby" (for "screwball") or "Bug" or "Rabby"—Martha was confused and ambivalent about her relationship with Hemingway. She'd run off to Spain to be with him, but he was hardly ever around. Most days he was away playing grip for Joris Ivens and Johnny Ferno, kitted out like them in a black workman's beret and ratty old cardigan; in the evenings, he was drinking or talking— either in their suite at the Florida, or down the hall in Tom Delmer's rooms, or at Chicote's or Gaylord's—with the circle of cronies he'd acquired since coming to Madrid. Many were military men: Hans Kahle; Pavol Lukács; the scarred, thin-lipped, shaven-headed Pole who went by the name "General Walter"; the handsome Spanish composer-turned-soldier Lieutenant Colonel Gustavo Durán, his acquaintance from Paris days; the charismatic colonel Juan Modesto, who liked to flirt with Martha; or the police commander José "Pepe" Quintanilla, the brother of the painter Luis Quintanilla. Others—Koltsov, Regler, or Ehrenburg—were Communist intellectuals; or, like Matthews, Delmer, or Cockburn, journalists. And again there was Ivens, in his self-appointed role as Hemingway's tutor, helping him "to understand the anti-fascist cause." Hemingway, Martha was learning, "was able to sit with a bunch of men for most of a day or most of a night, or most of both day and night though perhaps with different men, wherever he happened to have started sitting, all of them fortified by a continuous supply of drink, the while he roared with laughter at reminiscences and anecdotes." And unless she wanted to sit with them, too, she wouldn't see much of him.

It was almost worse when he *wasn't* surrounded by his mates. Then she had to endure Sidney Franklin's disapproving eye, or Hemingway's caresses, which she dealt with awkwardly. Despite her coolly flirtatious manner and seductive appearance, Martha had never found sex easy, not even during her long *liaison* with Bertrand de Jouvenel; with Hemingway, most of the time, she found herself wishing "that it would soon be over." But—and this was the damnable thing—she also found herself falling in love with him, in a way she never had with anyone before. Part of it was his paradoxical vulnerability: his need for approval, coexisting, in what he called his "skyzophrenia," with his need for dominance, and his childish anxiety about sleeping alone. And then he seemed so heroically, romantically wrapped up in Spain's struggle. "I think it was the only time in his life," she would say afterward, "when he was not the most important thing there was. He really cared about . . . that war. I believe I never would've gotten hooked otherwise."

Stopping by the Telefónica one evening, when the sandbagged windows and shaded lights of the censor's office made the place seem to her like "a dugout or a watchtower . . . a place for conspirators," Martha unburdened herself to Ilsa—who, after all, had left her husband and her old life and come to Spain and was now living with Barea as his wife, and working alongside him. How *old* are you, my dear? Ilsa wanted to know; and when Martha told her twenty-eight, asked—not unkindly—if she thought she was perhaps spoiled. "Folk are odd," Martha commented to her journal afterward.

Paradoxically, given that Ilsa was superficially so unlike herself, she was drawn to this "small, dark, square-faced" Austrian—to her courage under fire, her calm authority in a job so often handled by men ("note the role of women in this mess," Martha reminded herself), and especially her journalist's understanding of and respect for accurate and thorough reporting. "She demanded facts," Martha noted, "[and] she understood that the Loyalist cause did not need propaganda, it could stand on truth."

Ilsa had assigned her a guide and interpreter, Kajsa Rothman, a tall Swedish Valkyrie with red-gold hair cut in a Greta Garbo bob, who dressed in men's clothes, spoke seven languages fluently, and had been first a nurse for and then the lover of Norman Bethune. Martha wasn't sure she liked Kajsa, with her "conceit of a beautiful woman" and her pride in her contacts and sources of confidential information (sins Martha herself could be equally guilty of). But Kajsa took her, not only to the usual war-tourist sights but also to others less celebrated but more revealing: the grand hotels, the Ritz and the Palace, which had become hospitals, with stretchers being carried up and down the grand staircases and people giving blood under the chandeliers in what had been the dining room; a shoe store where the girls trying on strappy sandals were urged by the salesman to move to seats farther back in the store, lest they be cut by flying glass from a shell; a coiffeur ("dirty as only places that deal with hair can be," Martha noted) where she queried the proprietor in detail about the economics of his business in a besieged city where permanent-wave fluid and hair dye had become precious commodities, and peroxide was requisitioned for surgical disinfectant.

Kajsa also introduced her to Bethune, and to the recently arrived Cambridge biologist J. B. S. Haldane, with both of whom she went to Morata on April 5. There had been a skirmish—shelling and inconclusive infantry attacks—on the Jarama front and a number of wounded had been brought in to the first-aid station there; Bethune was taking blood for transfusions and asked if she wanted to come along. Bouncing along the rutted road she was excited—at last she really *was* going to war with the boys. But when they got to the old mill where the field hospital was she was taken aback by the suffering she found, even as she found herself noting its particulars: how peroxide foamed in a wound, for example, or the way the hospital smelled.

Back in Madrid, she tried to draw on some of what she had seen for the first writing she had done in months: a radio talk about her impressions of Madrid and the war. With powerful transmitters in Madrid and in rebel territory sending out news and propaganda that could be picked up by foreign relay stations as well as by radio sets in Spain, radio was playing a bigger and bigger part in the national, and international, conversation about the war. In the south, in Seville, the Nationalist general Gonzalo Queipo de Llano broadcast a nightly rant against targets such as France's premier, "the Jew Blum," and gleefully detailed (among other things) what Moorish mercenaries might do to Republican women in the cities they captured; in Madrid, station EAQ, officially under the control of the Loyalist government, transmitted pro-Republican dispatches by different speakers in different languages, among them Bethune and Haldane. And someone—possibly her sometime confidant Ilsa Kulcsar, whose job it was to arrange for press coverage of the war—suggested that Martha try her hand at one. As it turned out, she was not only game but also, thanks to her and Hemingway's press connections, able to get a tentative commitment from America's National Broadcasting Company to transmit her talk over their network as well.

On a borrowed typewriter in her room at the Hotel Florida, she began. "Living here is not like anything you ever knew before," she wrote; and gradually a portrait of Madrid as she experienced it came into focus, full of the kind of detail and sharp-edged irony that animated her best work. Although she'd been making careful notes each day of everything she saw and heard in Madrid, Martha felt a wave of relief at simply *writing* again. And she was thrilled when, after she showed it to Hemingway, he said, "Daughter, you're lovely," because he thought it was good.

Although he liked to talk about strategy and tactics with the military men who had become his friends, Hemingway's only combat experience had been in the last year of the Great War, when as a fresh-faced eighteen-year-old Red Cross driver, delivering chocolate, cigarettes, and postcards to the trenches, he'd been wounded by an exploding shell, then shot in the knee, but had refused evacuation until soldiers hurt in the same attack were tended to. Despite this grim memory, and despite his promises to Pauline to keep himself out of danger, he desperately wanted—or he told himself he wanted—to see action in Spain. But Joris Ivens and Johnny Ferno had already filmed most of the combat sequences for their documentary by the time he arrived in Madrid. He accompanied them back to the area around Morata around the time of the April 5 sortie, but the closest Hemingway got to actual combat was the evacuation point where the injured men were being picked up for transport to Bethune's hospital. The rest of the footage they shot that day was of tanks lumbering around the dusty hills.

A few days later, though, it seemed like he might get a real taste of battle. Since the beginning of November, Franco's soldiers had been lodged in the Casa de Campo, where from the heights of Cerro Garabitas they lobbed shells with impunity into the heart of Madrid and protected the rear flank of the Nationalist contingent still dug in at University City. But the Republican command hoped to drive the rebels from their position, and perhaps also distract them from a planned offensive in the Basque country, as an anniversary present to the government, which had been elected on April 14 a year earlier. They were planning a concerted attack on Garabitas for April 9, and Joris Ivens and his crew—including Hemingway, and a ringer in the form of the United Press correspondent Hank Gorrell—were going to be allowed to take long-range cameras to the Parque del Oeste to film the action.

Hemingway was excited, as much at the prospects for the government's forces as for his own reportage. The night before, in celebration, he'd given expensive small leather goods to Martha and Sid Franklin and Ivens and Ferno and had drunk an awful lot of whiskey. And his head and guts were paying the price as he and the others hiked down the Gran Via in the chilly dawn to set up. At first they tried filming on a knoll in the park, from which they were rewarded by a near-diorama of the assault— the guns firing puffs of smoke, the infantrymen charging forward like the soldiers in *War and Peace*—as they peered through field glasses or the cameras, shielding the lenses so they wouldn't catch the sun and betray their hiding place to any sharpshooters. But the threat of stray bullets drove them back across the Paseo del Pintor Rosales, a battered but still elegant avenue that ran along one side of the park, where they took shelter in one of the ruined houses.

By now the spring day had turned warm and they were sweating as they lugged their equipment up three flights of stairs to a deserted apartment with a balcony facing the park. Shielding the camera with old clothes they found in the abandoned armoires, they trained the lens on the action and filmed all through the afternoon: the tanks darting back and forth like beetles, and the tiny infantrymen looking like children's toys as they ran and dropped to their stomachs and then ran again. Except for the daily (and sometimes nightly) shelling at the Hotel Florida, it was the closest Hemingway had come to battle since he'd arrived in Spain, and he was exhilarated: it had been "marvelous," he thought, as they packed up their equipment. Then, as they walked up the Gran Via in the dusk, disillusionment set in. They'd been too far away, he told himself; worse, "any fool could see the offensive was a failure." And when he got home to the Florida he found that Martha had spent the afternoon with the British biologist, Haldane, watching the very same action from another house on the periphery of the Casa de Campo—"like college kids on an outing," she said.

But a college outing to a failed offensive wasn't the sort of thing NANA was paying him $500 a dispatch ($1,000 if he mailed a manuscript copy) to write about; it wasn't what he and Joris Ivens were making their movie about; and it wasn't what he himself could bear to admit he'd been a party to, even in private. Never mind that, just by being in Madrid, he was running a risk of being killed every time he went outside his hotel. Never mind that men had died during the afternoon's fighting. Never mind that Nationalist shells hit buildings on the Paseo del Pintor Rosales regularly and might have landed in the building they'd been filming in. Readers in New York, and Chicago, St. Louis, and San Francisco, would never believe you could be in a war zone where there were bars and functioning movie theaters and shops selling perfume; they needed to smell cordite and hear guns. So in chronicling the past few days' events, Hemingway made them into a *better* story, as he'd done with his account of the bear hunt at the L Bar T. The attack in the Casa de Campo wasn't a futile effort that he and his companions had observed from a distance, but the beginning of a "most important battle," the launch of "a long-awaited

Government offensive," which they'd been in the thick of. The hours he and Ivens and Ferno had spent shooting at Morata weren't an exercise in cold and gritty monotony, but a dramatic attack by tanks and infantry, in which, "as you flopped at a close one and heard the fragments sing over you on the rocky, dusty hillside, your mouth was full of dust."

He wrote the dispatch out in longhand before typing it in "cablese"— the journalists' patois he'd been using since his days as a Paris correspondent for the *Toronto Star*—in which, to reduce expensive word count, articles were left out, modifiers run in to the words they modified, "do not want" was rendered as "unwant," "from Madrid" was "exmadrid." Then he gave the manuscript to Martha to proofread; afterward Sidney Franklin would take it to the Telefónica for Barea or Ilsa to vet before telephoning it to the NANA bureau in London, from which it would be cabled to New York. His last dispatch, about his visit to the blind soldier Raven at Morata, had been sent by mail—albeit through a diplomatic pouch—and it still hadn't reached NANA; this one would hit U.S. newspapers in two days, at most.

The following morning, at the Telefónica, there was a cable for Martha from NBC; they had scheduled a broadcast time for her talk on Madrid, but now they were changing it—and, by the way, they wanted her to concentrate on the "human interest" angle, not on the war. Was this because she was a woman, and "human interest" was a woman's bailiwick, or did NBC want to soft-pedal the war itself? Furious, Martha told the broadcasters to forget it—they would get no report from *her*. Storming out of the building, she went to buy perfume in one of the shops on the Gran Via. That afternoon, as a kind of consolation prize, Hemingway took her to the building he'd been filming in the previous day, which he'd begun calling the "Old Homestead," after his grandfather's house in Oak Park. Martha tiptoed through the ruined rooms, peering into the medicine cabinet— she found a douche and hair curlers and bottles of peroxide—and looking at the former owners' wedding pictures. Hemingway called to her to come pay attention to the fighting across the river in the Casa de Campo, so she went to his balcony observation post: but the tiny soldiers, and the miniature tanks spurting little tongues of flame, all seemed unreal to her. The only reality, she felt, was in the house behind her, with its detritus of interrupted lives; the only beauty in the white peaks of the Guadarrama shining coldly, unchangeably in the distance.

•

When they returned from their visit to the Old Homestead that evening, Hemingway and Martha noticed a pile of suitcases on the pavement in front of Hotel Florida, next to a gleaming Hispano-Suiza whose chauffeur was listening uneasily to the still-crackling gunfire from the Casa de Campo and looking as if he would rather be anywhere else than where he was. Walking past him into the hotel lobby, they ran straight into John Dos Passos and two Frenchmen with whom he'd driven up from Valencia in the fancy car outside: Lucien Vogel, the editor of *Vu*, and Philippe Lamour, an antifascist lawyer and journalist who was a close friend of Bertrand de Jouvenel—the man to whom, until very recently, Martha had been all but married.

The encounter could have been a scene from a boulevard comedy: raised eyebrows, a flurry of greetings—swift *bisou-bisous*, first on one cheek, then on the other—then awkward introductions, during which the inevitable conclusions could be drawn, and comparisons made between Hemingway, in his beret and grimy trousers and shabby tweed jacket, and the invariably soigné and elegant Bertrand. Tongues would certainly wag in Paris.

At last Martha and Hemingway were able to break away; and while Sid Franklin—who had magically appeared in the lobby—took care of getting Dos Passos's bags up to his room, Dos followed the two of them to their suite. The old comrades' reunion left something to be desired. Not only had Dos brought insufficient contributions to the Hemingway larder—a few measly bars of chocolate and four oranges—he also seemed less interested in the progress of *The Spanish Earth*, the project that after all had brought him to Spain, than in the disappearance of his translator and friend José Robles Pazos. It was all he wanted to talk about.

No one in Valencia had been able to tell him anything, Dos complained; not Robles's wife, Márgara, nor his teenaged son, Francisco (nicknamed Coco), who was working part-time as a translator in Rubio Hidalgo's propaganda office, nor even Álvarez del Vayo, to whom he'd appealed for information. All Dos knew was that one night in December Robles had been taken away by a group of men in civilian clothes, shut up in the Foreigners' Prison on the Turia River, and charged with treason against the Republic.

When Márgara had visited him in prison he'd reassured her that it was all a misunderstanding and everything would be cleared up—but in January he'd simply vanished, and no one seemed to want to say where or why. At the end of February, or maybe the beginning of March, Liston Oak—an American Communist working in the propaganda office—had apparently told Coco that his father was dead. But there was no confirmation, and Robles's family hoped that the news of his death might just be a false rumor. Especially when Álvarez de Vayo—who should know, shouldn't he?—told Dos Passos that Robles was "quite all right."

Dos showed all the signs of being ready to take his inquiries to anyone in Madrid who might know something, and the idea of his blundering like a bull into Hemingway's carefully assembled china shop of connections caused immediate alarm. "Don't put your mouth to this Robles business," Hemingway told him brusquely. "People disappear every day." Certainly Dos could not be allowed to start making trouble with Ivens, or the army men, or Pepe Quintanilla, or the Russians. It would make Hemingway look bad, and screw up his access to them for sure. Not only that, but Dos's questions made it seem he didn't trust the government he was supposed to be making a propaganda film for, which wouldn't go down well with donors to the cause. Hemingway went on the offensive, like a boxer, the better to upset Dos's equilibrium. "Just suppose," he said, "your professor took a powder and joined the other side?"

"That could not be," Dos Passos protested. "I've known the man for years. He's absolutely straight."

His insistence irritated Martha, who was already suspicious of him because of his affection for Pauline. Didn't he understand the situation in Spain? His questions, she told him pointedly, "have already caused us embarrassment." *Us.* Suddenly it seemed as if there were two sides, and she and Hemingway were on one, Dos Passos on the other.

After an uncomfortable drink in Hemingway's suite they all went to dinner at the Gran Via, where by a potentially uncomfortable coincidence they found Pepe Quintanilla already dining. But he greeted Dos Passos effusively—*Dos, que tal?*; apparently they'd known each other in their student days, had even gone mountain-climbing in the Guadarrama together. And when dinner was over Quintanilla invited Dos to the Telefónica, where his office was. He showed his old climbing buddy around the building, stopping on the fifth floor to introduce him to Barea ("underfed and underslept," thought Dos Passos) and Ilsa, and afterward the two men sat down for a conversation. Dos Passos wasted no time in bringing up Robles; but alas, it was the same old story: Quintanilla was unable to shed any light on Robles's disappearance. He would find out, though; he promised. But Dos Passos should remember: there were dangerous people out there, anarchists, Trotskyists, "uncontrollables"—who knows what they might have done or might do to such as Robles. Or what would happen to Robles if it turned out that he was one of them.

There was really nothing more Dos Passos could do. He might, if circumstances had been otherwise, have gone to see Robles's former boss, General Vladimir Gorev, to ask *his* help in finding out what had happened to his friend; but in a move some saw as a power play by the NKVD against the military-intelligence GRU, Moscow had just removed Gorev from his post in Madrid and sent him north to the Basque country, ostensibly to help mobilize resistance to a major new Nationalist offensive. There really were no more doors in Madrid to knock on.

Meanwhile, back at the Hotel Florida, Hemingway and Martha were having a conversation of a different kind. In the weeks since he had been in Madrid, Hemingway had sent Pauline a few cables, and only one letter; none gave her any hint of what was now public knowledge to everyone in town—his relationship with Martha Gellhorn. In the alternate reality of the war it had been possible for Hemingway, and Martha too, to pretend that their former lives existed in some other universe; but suddenly here was Dos Passos, who had known Hemingway for decades, who was married to Hemingway's old girlfriend, and who was friends with Hemingway's wife. And here were those Frenchmen, Vogel and Lamour, friends of Bertrand de Jouvenel, "to whom," Martha reminded herself, "God knows how many memories attach." The outside world was about to make demands on Hemingway, and on Martha.

Whatever drove him—and perhaps it was only the rumble of Time's chariot wheels in Madrid's daily bombardments—Hemingway chose this moment to ask Martha to marry him. He wasn't really free to court her, which Martha, having been in this situation before, with Bertrand, knew all too well. But she gave him an answer, of a sort. "Note to H.," she wrote in her diary before going to bed that night: "I love you very much indeed."

Perhaps she meant it. Perhaps she *wanted* to mean it. But left to herself she knew that (as she'd written in that same diary only a few days previously) she'd never found *anyone* who didn't ultimately exhaust her, anyone of whom she could say that she could "go away and if I never see them again it will not matter." People palled for her, she was discovering; only writing did not. A few days after Dos Passos's arrival her amended radio report finally aired, and she felt encouraged to start a magazine piece for *Collier's* about life in the besieged city. She wasn't sure how she felt about the story itself, but the process of composing it was, she said, "the only thing which does not bore or dismay me, or fill me with doubt." It was even a cure for the terror that still gripped her when the shells screamed overhead. Although she continued to visit hospitals to cheer up sick or wounded soldiers (unlike Hemingway, who seemed uncomfortable when confronted with them), and shopped for clothing and handmade shoes and those alluring silver foxes, although she flirted with correspondents and soldiers and shared Hemingway's bed, none of these things was as important as what happened between her and her typewriter. Writing, she found, gave her a sharp, hard focus, a cocaine-like rush, that made everything else in her life seem beside the point.

April 1937: Moscow

On April 2, Mikhail Koltsov crossed the border from Spain to France, on his way to Moscow for what he hoped was a brief visit. He was apprehensive about the trip, not without reason. The previous month, Genrikh Yagoda, formerly people's commissar for internal affairs (and thus supervisor of the NKVD), had been arrested by his successor in the post, Nikolai Yezhov, a diminutive, swarthy, and sadistic man whom Stalin nicknamed "the blackberry." The charges were corruption, diamond smuggling (Yagoda was a Jew, son of a jeweler from Nizhniy Novgorod—*obviously* he had connections with those thieving Antwerp diamond brokers), and espionage; it was alleged that he'd been spying for the Germans since he'd joined the Communist Party in 1907. His real offense, which no one would mention but everyone knew, was that he'd told Stalin that arresting, trying, and executing his old associates, men such as Grigori Zinoviev and Lev Kamenev, and moving to purge the Red Army's commander in chief, Marshal Mikhail Tukaschevsky, was bad for business; that both within and without the Soviet Union public reaction to show trials was unfavorable. To Stalin this was insubordination, even opposition, and Yagoda must pay for it with his life. As Yezhov put it, "We are launching a major attack on the Enemy; let there be no resentment if we bump someone with an elbow. Better that ten innocent people should suffer than that one spy get away. When you chop wood, chips fly." And lest anyone doubt who was doing the chopping, he added, "I may be small in stature but my hands are strong—Stalin's hands."

The atmosphere in Moscow was dangerous, but Koltsov believed he had an ally in the "poison dwarf," Yezhov—or at least some kind of relationship. He was, in fact, sleeping with the new security chief's wife, Yevgenya Feigenberg—she might put in a good word for him with her husband. And he had written warmly of Yezhov in *Pravda*, calling him "a wonderful unyielding Bolshevik." Surely that should count for something.

Nonetheless he cannot have been comfortable when he was summoned to the Kremlin on April 15 for two hours of cross-examination by Yezhov, Defense Minister Voroshilov, Prime Minister Molotov, and Stalin himself about the progress of the war in Spain. Fortunately, when Koltsov had answered all their questions, the general secretary proclaimed himself pleased with the performance of the Soviet mission to the Republic— such a comfort in these grim times, he said, when he was beset by traitors lurking in the Party's bosom.

Thinking himself dismissed, Koltsov rose to take his leave; but Stalin wasn't finished with him yet. *Not so fast, Comrade Koltsov.* "What are you called in Spanish?" he asked. "Miguel?" Incredibly, he bowed to Koltsov in what he must have believed was the Spanish fashion, right arm across his chest. (The left, withered in a childhood accident, hung uselessly by his side.)

"Miguel, Comrade Stalin," Koltsov said.

"Very well, Don Miguel. We, noble Spaniards, thank you cordially for your most interesting report. We'll see you soon, Comrade Koltsov. Good luck, Don Miguel."

"I am entirely at the service of the Soviet Union, Comrade Stalin," murmured Koltsov; and as that seemed the end of the conversation, he started for the door. But Stalin called him back.

"Do you possess a revolver, Comrade Koltsov?"

Koltsov wasn't sure what to say. "Yes, Comrade Stalin," he replied.

"You aren't thinking of committing suicide, are you?"

"Of course not," Koltsov said. *Was that the right answer?* "It has never occurred to me."

"Excellent. Excellent," said Stalin. "Thank you again, Comrade Koltsov. We'll see you soon, Don Miguel."

April 1937: Madrid

April had brought a change in the air, Barea thought. Not just the sudden warmth, which brought the leaves out on the trees along the Paseo del Prado and beckoned the news vendors and shoeshine boys and the old women selling shoelaces to set up their stands on the streets, never mind the shells. No, the bureaucrats in Valencia—Álvarez del Vayo, and Rubio, and Rubio's new deputy, Constancia de la Mora—were paying Madrid increased attention, scrutinizing requests, asking questions. An unspoken and unbroken tension had crept into relations between the temporary capital and the besieged city. And now, here was the Comintern's smooth propagandist, the wily Otto Katz, this time using the alias André Simone and acting as *cicerone* for a gathering of Englishwomen, including three members of Parliament, Ellen Wilkinson, Eleanor Rathbone, and Katharine Stewart-Murray, Duchess of Atholl, who had come on a fact-finding mission to Spain. It was to be hoped that the facts they found would help them persuade Parliament to abandon the Non-Intervention Agreement, so it was of the utmost importance that they be handled expertly; and apparently Rubio and de la Mora felt this task was beyond the talents of Barea and Ilsa.

Barea arranged the ladies' itinerary—bomb ruins, a hospital, a visit to an artillery post in a relatively safe part of the front, tea with Miaja—Ilsa translated, and Katz/Simone hovered over their every footstep. After a morning of sightseeing, thinking it would be more pleasant than the raucous, smoky depths of the Gran Via canteen, Ilsa and Barea invited the Duchess and her companions to lunch in their quarters upstairs; but the visitors insisted on joining the crowd in the basement. They didn't want any special treatment, they protested. So they shared beans and watery soup and desiccated sausage with the correspondents and International Brigaders in the canteen, where the bursts of lunchtime shellfire were drowned out by the buzz of conversation and the clatter of crockery.

They had just finished their coffee and followed Barea to the lobby when the hotel manager appeared. Could Barea come upstairs, please? There had been a fire in his and Ilsa's room. With the Englishwomen at their heels, Barea and Ilsa followed the manager upstairs to find their quarters a sodden wreck. A shell fragment had burst through the window, setting fire to the curtains and immolating Ilsa's shoes, which had been arranged on a shelf under the sill; it had then landed on the table, smashing the dishes laid out for Ilsa and Barea's lunch, and now lay there, still smoldering, as firemen coiled up the hoses they'd used to spray the room. Ilsa bent over the shoes, mourning her favorite blue pair—brand new, too!—and the Englishwomen clustered around her, patting and cooing. Just think, if she and Barea had come upstairs to lunch instead of going to the canteen with them, she or he might have been killed! Or if they'd all come to the Bareas' room, they might have been killed as well! Not a bit of it, Ilsa maintained stoutly; it wasn't as serious as all that. Just a little piece of metal. Look, there were some eggs, sitting unbroken in a bowl on a side table! And now they really *must* get going, they were scheduled to visit Ortega's artillery observation post.

Going outside to round up the party's cars, Barea found the street littered with debris from the shelling. Then he caught sight of something else, on the glass expanse of a ground-floor shop window full of records and Victrolas: a pulsating gray lump about the size of an apricot, veined with red, surrounded by gray spatters. It took him a minute to understand that it was a fragment of someone's brain. Time seemed suddenly suspended, like music at a fermata. As if in a dream he put out his hand to stop one of the Englishwomen from going closer to look at it, turning her instead toward where he thought the car must be; but he himself couldn't move. He heard Ilsa's voice nearby, hoarse, insistent: "Arturo! Come away from here!" But he still stood motionless. His feet, he realized, were stuck in a puddle of blood.

With effort he tore himself away, allowed Ilsa to push him into one of the cars, wiped his feet on the matting on the floor. In silence he rode with the group to Ortega's artillery lookout, where the Englishwomen peeped excitedly through the lens of a rangefinder at the University City trenches and the puffs of smoke issuing from the mouths of government artillery. When it was Barea's turn he looked into the rangefinder at the target Ortega's forces were shelling: it was the chapel of the cemetery whose office Barea's uncle had been in charge of, and where as a boy he'd played, chasing butterflies and lizards through the sunlit alleys of cypresses, waiting for his uncle to finish his business and go home. Now, he saw, the cypresses and rose trees were gone and the thick brick walls of the chapel were pocked with shells.

Martha and Hemingway missed the noontime appearance of the British delegation at the journalists' canteen and the carnage that followed the shelling on the Gran Via because they had been invited to lunch with Luis Quintanilla's brother, the man some called "The Executioner of Madrid"—Pepe Quintanilla, chief of Madrid's secret police.

Quintanilla lived in an opulently furnished flat—crystal chandeliers, *savonnerie* carpet—in a new apartment building on the north side of the city, with broad terraces commanding a view of the Casa de Campo; and the luncheon party, which included his wife and small son, seemed to take place in a very different Madrid than the one Martha had come to know. With his impeccable dove-gray suiting, his high forehead, slender hands, and bright brown eyes framed by horn-rimmed glasses, Quintanilla looked less like an executioner than an intellectual or an aristocrat; his manner was all graciousness, his voice like silk. But Martha was naggingly conscious of the steel beneath the smooth exterior, the gap between this elegant luncheon party and what Quintanilla actually *did*.

Somewhere between when the butler served the soup and when he poured the coffee, either Hemingway or Quintanilla brought up the matter of José Robles and Dos Passos's inquiries about him. Dos should really stop asking awkward questions, Quintanilla said; it could only lead to trouble. Whatever Robles's situation was, whatever had happened to him, he would get a fair trial. Hemingway should tell Dos that. And *that*—he fixed his interlocutors with his bright nutmeg-brown stare—should be the end of it. There was, or there should have been, no mistaking what Quintanilla meant.

As Hemingway and Martha prepared to go, Quintanilla asked if he might be permitted to bestow a small gift upon Martha, as a token of esteem and admiration, something to remind her of her time in Madrid. He held it out to her in his long fingers: an exquisite little cup of antique Limoges glass, as fragile as a bird's egg. She should treat it carefully, Quintanilla said. Such a shame if it were broken.

•

It was balmy, almost hot, when Hemingway and Martha left the Quinta-
nillas' flat. Unless they wanted to watch the Englishwomen watch the
shelling at the artillery post, there was nothing to do; so Martha went
shopping with Ginny Cowles, whom she had decided to like. First they
priced some pretty silver fox furs—such a bargain in Madrid just now—
then they stopped at a linen shop, where Martha bought handkerchiefs
for Hemingway, and went to the coiffeur to get their hair washed.
("Come what may," she wrote in her journal, "one washes one's hair, has
one's nails tended, sends out the laundry." Edna Gellhorn had schooled
her well.)

Returning to the hotel, they found the usual evening drinks party in
full swing in Hemingway's room: Norman Bethune had turned up,
sweaty and dirty from a day at the front, to take advantage of Hemingway's bathtub and the Florida's plentiful hot water, and Dos Passos and
Hemingway were working on Hemingway's whiskey. None of them were
feeling any pain when they went on to the Gran Via, where they found to
their fury that the Duchess of Atholl's party had eaten all the spinach
(and, depending on who you talked to, had been given a *chicken* for dinner as well). Heated things were said about class distinction and Anglo-
American relations, but in the end some aged whitings were produced by
the kitchen, and the Americans washed them down with more drinks
before going out into the moonlit night.

Upstairs in the Gran Via, Barea and Ilsa had come back from work at
the Telefónica to discover that their belongings had been moved to new
rooms. They were both exhausted from the events of the day, and all Ilsa
wanted to do was crawl into bed; but Barea couldn't bear to be alone with
silence or his thoughts. André Simone was having a party on another floor
of the hotel, and Barea went in search of distraction: what he found was
bad liquor and worse gramophone music, and a smoky room full of International Brigade officers and American correspondents. In one corner
Hemingway's Guadalajara battlefield guide, Colonel Hans Kahle, was holding forth to an American film critic; in another Simone was fondling one
of the censorship employees, a white-blond Canadian girl called Pat who
had very fair skin, like a child's, and a moll's hard mouth. Everyone there
seemed to be posing—*look at us, how tough and jaded we are*—and suddenly

something inside Barea snapped. All of these people—the ones here, the ones downstairs in the restaurant, the ones in Chicote's and the Miami Bar—were behaving as if *they* were the main actors in the war; none of them understood that this was *Spain's* war, Spain's agony.

He began shouting at them over the din of the dance music: they were all self-satisfied posers, playing at helping the war effort; they didn't really care what happened to Spain, they were just here for themselves. But no one except the film critic paid him any attention. Disgusted and dispirited, he left and went back to his and Ilsa's room.

When the bombardment started again the next morning, he crept out of bed carefully so as not to wake Ilsa. He wanted a bath, a shave, a fresh start; but he'd left his soap and shaving things in their old room, and went to get them. Although the room still smelled of smoke the sun was streaming in the windows, and he paused a moment to look out at the Gran Via, where a few people had started on their morning rounds. One of them, a woman in a green suit, looked uncannily like Ilsa from behind. Had she suddenly got dressed and gone out?

Suddenly there was a sound like ripping fabric, then the explosion as a shell hit a theater down the block; the woman in green crumpled to the pavement. In an unreasoning panic Barea raced down the hall to the room he'd left minutes ago. But Ilsa was there, awake, looking out the window. Seeing his face, she asked, worriedly, "What's the matter with you?" and he just had time to say "Nothing" when another shell struck the Telefónica just across the street. Pale and shaking, he sank to his knees. The smell of the dead he remembered from his army service in Melilla, so many years ago now, filled his nostrils, and a wave of nausea passed over him. Ilsa managed to get him downstairs, where he drank a couple of brandies, and somehow he got through the day until the afternoon. But then, as he and Ilsa were putting books into shelves beside the window, they saw two more women killed on the Gran Via—one of them had been carrying a parcel wrapped in pink paper, and after the police came to take away the bodies the parcel lay forgotten in the street. Looking at it, Barea felt the bile rise in his throat, the sweat break out on his forehead and upper lip.

He couldn't work that afternoon, or that evening. Instead he scrolled a piece of paper into the typewriter and almost automatically began to write. What emerged was a phantasmagoric story full of images: the pulsating brain matter on the shop window, the black discs of the phonograph records in the shop display behind it, the frisky little RCA terrier, cocking his head to listen for a command that never came—and a woman, dressed in green, lying on the shop floor with a hole in the middle of her forehead. As he typed, Ilsa came into the room and almost automatically he handed the pages to her to look at; her response cut through the fog surrounding him. "But that's *me* you've killed here," she said in alarm. He took the pages back and tore them to shreds.

Fuentidueña de Tajo lay forty miles southeast of Madrid, just off the main road to Valencia: a village of 1,500, with unpaved streets running between the tile-roofed cracked stucco houses that seemed to spring organically from the parched fields surrounding it. Some of the houses had been bombed by Nationalist aircraft and now many villagers preferred to live in the cave dwellings carved into the terraced hillsides along the river—dwellings whose cone-shaped chimneys, seen from afar, looked as if they'd been built by elves in some children's story. But to Martha Gellhorn, arriving there on the sunny April morning after the shelling on the Gran Via, Fuentidueña was "only picturesque because it is not Bearcreek, Kansas."

Possibly Martha was in a bad mood because she and Hemingway had driven to the village with Josie Herbst, whose gentle frumpiness and harsh Midwestern vowels grated on her; or because Dos Passos was with them, since they'd all come to Fuentidueña to shoot footage for *The Spanish Earth*. It was Dos who had argued loudest and hardest for the documentary to portray the social background to the war, and now he'd got his way. As recently as the beginning of April, Joris Ivens had been lobbying for *two* films, one a compendium of the battle footage he and Ferno had completed at that point and sent to New York, which he thought could be readied for release by midmonth, the other a human-interest documentary focusing on village life, which would take longer to shoot and could be released sometime in the summer, perhaps. But when Archibald MacLeish screened the combat footage Ivens had sent to New York, he'd cabled that it was too good to be chopped up and presented as a short film. With both Hemingway and Dos Passos to help frame the story, MacLeish said, Ivens could surely combine the two narratives in such a way as to make a compelling feature. And here they all were, with two cars and a lot of camera equipment—Martha and Hemingway, Josie Herbst, Sid Franklin, Dos Passos, and Joris Ivens and Johnny Ferno.

Ivens and Ferno had discovered Fuentidueña during their explorations of the Jarama Valley, and it turned out to suit their purpose better than they could ever have hoped. Poor and feudal, the village had been controlled for centuries by a handful of landowners—descendants of the hidalgos whose shields still adorned the houses clustered around the main square—who'd taken all the proceeds from the surrounding vineyards and forbade the villagers to plant gardens of their own. But the landlords had been killed or had fled at the start of the war, the villagers had collectivized the vineyards, and had invested the income from them in a pump to bring water from the Tajo to irrigate the fields, so that for the first time they would be able to grow their own food, and maybe even to provide some for hungry Madrid. This was perfect material for Ivens, the man who had made such social-realist documentaries as *Saarland* and *Zuyderzee*. And Dos Passos, by interviewing the village elders, discovered a young man he called Julián (it might even have been his real name) who had been serving with the army outside Madrid and might serve as a link between Fuentidueña and the front.

Dos Passos discovered more than Julián, as it turned out: Walking down a little dirt track to the new pumping station with the village mayor, a socialist UGT member, he noticed men and boys sitting on the bank, fishing. All anarchists, CNT men, said the mayor: you wouldn't see *socialists* loafing around when there was spring plowing to do. "We've cleaned out the fascists and the priests," said one of the other UGT men. "Now we must clean out the loafers."

"Yes," the mayor responded. "One of these days it will come to a fight." By the time Dos Passos got back to the United States and published an account of this conversation, other events would lend it an unsettling resonance; but for Hemingway and Ivens the mayor's comments, and Dos's interest in them, were at best an irritant, at worst malign. For Ivens, the only fight he wanted to cover was that between the villagers, united with Loyalist soldiers under a common banner, and the forces of fascism; for Hemingway, Fuentidueña and its politics held little interest. If he thought about them at all, observed Josie Herbst, he "naively" adopted whatever the simplest party line was—especially if "at the very moment Dos Passos was urgently questioning" it.

That kind of *aperçu* wasn't going to endear Josie to her old friend Hemingway, however. And not surprisingly, when the day's filming was over, he and Martha somehow managed to forget Josie was with them, and drove back to Madrid leaving her behind.

Capa had been trying to get back to Spain for almost a month, begging magazines for an assignment that would justify a visa, until at last, at the beginning of April, he'd gotten *two*: one from *Ce Soir* and one from Metro-Goldwyn-Mayer News, for whom he was supposed to shoot newsreel footage even though his experience with a film camera was next to nonexistent. Unfortunately, before his visa came through, *Ce Soir* had sent him on an infuriating trip to Brussels to cover a parliamentary by-election between a fascist and a liberal candidate; but finally, in the middle of the month, he and Gerda were able to travel to Madrid.

By the time they arrived, though, the Casa de Campo offensive had all but petered out; and except for the daily ordeal by artillery shell there seemed nothing new to report from the beleaguered capital. The important action was all in the north, where rebel forces were moving to encircle the isolated Loyalist enclave in the Basque country and in Asturias, whose iron and coal, respectively, were vital resources for either side. But since Nationalist territory lay between the northern provinces and the government-held center of the country, there was no way to get there except by sea or air; and in any case Capa's travel documents were only good for Madrid and Valencia. To get new ones meant going back to Paris and starting all over again.

While he and Gerda were trying to figure out a way around this problem they came across Geza Korvin, who was still in Madrid working on his film about Norman Bethune. And Korvin, it turned out, had just discovered someone else with a Budapest connection, the Dutchman John Ferno, who was married to Capa's childhood friend Eva Besnyö, and was working with Joris Ivens on a documentary with two renowned American writers, Ernest Hemingway and John Dos Passos. Why didn't they all get together?

Capa, who would always seize any excuse for a party, immediately made a plan. He and Gerda and Korvin and Ivens and Ferno, and the Americans, would have a festive meal together. They would go to Botín, a very old, very famous, very good restaurant near the Plaza Mayor where the specialty was suckling pig. Maybe, because of the war, there would be no suckling pig; but there would be something, and Botín's cellar was reputed to be excellent. Hemingway had written about Botín's *rioja alta* in *The Sun Also Rises*, and he would certainly be happy to revisit it.

Which he was; although, depending on who told the story later, they didn't eat suckling pig but paella—and Hemingway (probably with most of a bottle of *rioja alta* inside him) insisted on going into the kitchen to help prepare it. *Less skillful in the kitchen than at the typewriter*, said the *padrone*, Emilio Gonzales, tactfully. Although Capa's English was rudimentary at best, he and Hemingway could communicate in French, and he immediately recognized in the older man an appetite for life, what Josie Herbst called "a splurging magnificence," that he found irresistible. And Hemingway liked this impetuous young photographer, who ran after combat the way a child would chase butterflies, and annexed him as a kind of adopted son.

He was less enchanted with Gerda, despite her charm and her crop of dark-gold, sunburnt hair. Maybe it was her knowing, foxy little face that irritated him; or her ability to jump effortlessly from German to French to Spanish to English; or her cool familiarity with the Spanish generals and battlefields Hemingway wanted to think of as *his* property. Maybe it was her fondness for the work of John Dos Passos, whose novels he'd just been dismissing to Martha as bogus and unreadable. Or maybe it was the way Capa looked at her, as if she were some magnificent present that he didn't deserve. Whatever it was, Hemingway disliked Gerda on sight: enough to tell Ted Allan later that she was a "whore."

Fortunately, however, Capa had no inkling of Hemingway's dislike that day; and later it wouldn't matter. For now they were just having a marvelous party, as if they were sitting at the Dôme or the Deux Magots instead of less than two miles from the front lines in Madrid.

Just before dawn on April 22, two artillery shells smashed into the stone walls of the Hotel Florida. The hotel had been accidentally hit before by artillery fire aimed at the Telefónica, but this barrage was different. After the initial impact, blast after blast shuddered directly into the roof tiles and masonry, shattering skylights and windows, as if this morning the rebel battery on Garabitas was trying to send a message to the foreigners in the Florida—*we can exterminate you.* From inside the walls came the mad skittering of rats trying to escape; and from the back of the hotel, an ululation, as from a flock of birds, as the *whores de combat* (as Hemingway called them) awoke in terror.

Doors were flying open around the Florida's atrium. John Dos Passos, in bare feet and a plaid bathrobe, peered myopically into the hallway, then withdrew into his room like a snail into its shell. Hemingway, John Ferno, and Virginia Cowles, all fully dressed because they'd been planning to go to Fuentidueña to film, emerged into the corridor and headed for the stairs, Hemingway followed by Martha, who was wearing a coat over her pajamas, her blond hair still mussed from sleep like a child's. As they passed Josie Herbst's door she darted out from it, her face in a rictus of panic, her dressing gown askew. "How are you?" Hemingway asked her, but when she opened her mouth to reply no sound came out. She took a deep breath and went back into her room, emerging a few minutes later with her clothes on, if not much more composed.

The shells kept coming—first that tearing sound, then a shattering primal roar—as the guests continued to stream down the stairs and congregate in the relative safety of the ground-floor lobby. There was Dos Passos, bathed and shaved now, but still wearing his plaid bathrobe; Claud Cockburn, pale as marble, holding a coffeepot in his hands as if it were a votive offering; and Antoine de Saint-Exupéry, in a vibrantly blue silk dressing gown, standing at the foot of the stairs with a box of grapefruit, asking, "*Voudriez-vous une pamplemousse, madame?*" to each woman who passed him. Someone brought coffee to put in Cockburn's pot, and bread to toast on someone else's hot plate; still another someone found chocolate to share around. Hemingway looked about and pronounced, "I have great confidence in the Hotel Florida," and it turned out to be prophetic, because the shelling slowed, then stopped altogether, and the walls were still intact.

By seven the sun was well up in the sky and the hotel staff began sweeping up broken glass and crumbled stone and plaster. Capa appeared—where had he been during the bombardment?—and photographed the clean-up effort. Hemingway went out to investigate the damage to the neighborhood and returned to report cheerfully that the Paramount Theatre across the plaza had taken a hit—including its giant sign advertising

Charlie Chaplin's *Modern Times*. Martha, wrung out, announced she was going back to bed to sleep. And Josie Herbst sat on one of the wicker chairs in the lobby, looking angry and unhappy, like a wet owl, until Hemingway sympathetically offered to pour her a snifter of brandy before he went off to Fuentidueña for the day.

It soon became apparent that Hemingway had more in mind than a drink, however. He and Josie and Dos had all been friends since their Paris days, had spent time fishing in Key West together, and so he felt he could tell her that he was getting fed up with Dos and his questions about Robles. Dos was going to get all of them in trouble. This was war, and you didn't question the motives of the government, or the fate of anyone who might be suspected of wrongdoing. Couldn't Josie talk to Dos and tell him to shut up?

For a moment Josie seemed to be struggling with some decision. Then she put down her drink. "The man is already dead," she said. "Quintanilla should have told Dos."

It turned out that Josie had been given the news, in confidence, in Valencia; her informant was someone official, and *that* person had supposedly been sworn to secrecy by someone else higher up. Maybe the official had been Constancia de la Mora, who—having been given the word by Álvarez del Vayo—had taken Josie aside for a little woman-to-woman chat. Maybe it was someone else. Josie named no names. She seemed not to question that she—a journalist almost without portfolio, a B-list novelist, a woman of no influence—had been entrusted with this sensitive secret; nor did she wonder if her informant had *meant* her to tell someone. Had counted on it, in fact: because what would a decent, kind woman, an old friend of both Dos Passos and Hemingway, do if she were confronted with Dos's questions? She would spill the beans, of course; maybe not to Dos himself, which would be a direct betrayal of her confidant's trust, but to Hemingway, their great mutual friend, and ask *him* to break the news to Dos Passos. That way both of them would know, and Hemingway would be bound to speak to Dos about the matter. And by now, after several weeks of patient handling by Joris Ivens, Gustav Regler, and others, Hemingway would certainly press the government's case to his friend.

They didn't have the conversation that day, though: there was filming in Fuentidueña to attend to, and in the evening they all went to Chicote's for drinks. The next day, and the one after that, were a blur of official events: There was a ceremony marking the integration of the International Brigades' Martinez Barrio Battalion into the new Popular Army, and a fiesta to celebrate the four-month anniversary of the Fourteenth International Brigade, which was largely made up of soldiers from France and Belgium. Miaja, a stout figure in breeches and boots and a Sam Browne belt, spoke at both events; at the Fourteenth Brigade celebration its commander, Karol Swierczewski, otherwise known as General Walter, began his own speech in halting Spanish but switched to Russian (which an aide translated sentence-by-sentence for the crowd). And there was a lunch for the American journalists given by some of the Soviet military advisors at Aldovea, the former castle of the Dukes of Tovar, just east of the city near Alcalá de Henares, a get-together that had been arranged by Maria Teresa Léon and Rafael Alberti.

When Dos Passos wrote about these events later that year he would conflate them all into one and call it "the fiesta at the Fifteenth Brigade"—the brigade that included the American fighters of the Abraham Lincoln Battalion. He would place the flamenco singer Niña de los Peines and the dancer Pastora Imperio at the festivities, although surely he was remembering their participation at a benefit gala the previous week. He would say that General Walter was replacing a French officer at the head of the brigade, which was wrong on two counts: if he was indeed talking about the *Fifteenth* Brigade, it had always been led (and continued to be) by a Yugoslav Communist, Colonel Vladimir Copic; as for the Fourteenth, Walter had been its commander from the beginning. Dos Passos wasn't a sloppy journalist; maybe he was combining several events into one for simplicity, or to safeguard a source. Or perhaps his memory was clouded, or his reporting slanted, by what he had just learned—for at some point during those few April days Pepe Quintanilla told him that José Robles Pazos *wasn't* waiting for a fair trial, or indeed for any trial. He had been shot. No reason was given. "These are terrible times," Quintanilla said, by way of excuse. "To overcome them we have to be terrible ourselves."

Accusations would swirl around Robles for decades: he had been a Fifth Columnist, he'd been helping his fascist brother escape from the Loyalist zone into Nationalist territory, he'd been blabbing about military secrets in the literary cafés, he'd been seen—this last, physically impossible suggestion came from Joris Ivens—"using a concealed light to flash signals to the fascist lines" that were eighty-seven miles away. Maybe Ivens was conflating Robles's fate with what had happened in Madrid a few months earlier, when an inadvertent chink of light glimpsed through a faulty blackout shade touched off an armed assault on the offices of the newspaper *El Socialista*. But the probable truth about Robles was that, as Vladimir Gorev's aide and sometime translator, he knew too much about the Soviet Union's plans for its Spanish protégés, and had too many well-connected and crucially important friends to whom he might reveal them; or he had become collateral damage in a strike against the GRU and its representative, Gorev, by Russia's civilian spy agency, the NKVD, just then extending its influence in Spain. Gorev had already been sent to Bilbao on a doomed mission to shore up Loyalist defenses there; and his former aide had become a very inconvenient person indeed.

However much of this Dos Passos could have known or guessed (and it would have been very little), he was almost literally sickened by Quintanilla's news. He kept imagining his friend's last moments and replaying them in his mind: "They shove a cigarette into your hand and you walk out into the courtyard to face six men you have never seen before. They take aim. They wait for the order. They fire." It didn't help when, in the middle of the Russian lunch at Aldea, Hemingway—unaware of what Dos already knew—delivered the blow afresh. Watching the two men from the other side of the table, Josie Herbst saw Dos Passos's face go slack; she thought it was from shock, but more likely it was bewilderment, and then suspicion. *How the hell did Hem know?*—and, looking around at the Russian advisors and their Spanish counterparts, with all of whom Hemingway seemed on intimate terms, *Did they tell him? Were they all in on it?* Dos's feelings weren't soothed by Hemingway's implication that Robles was probably a traitor and had got what he deserved—and that even if he wasn't and hadn't, this was war, and you had to fall in line with whatever the leadership told you.

By the evening of April 24, Dos Passos was clearly a man in turmoil. Although, he'd say later, he "felt a heartbroken admiration for the ordinary people of Madrid," he now believed their cause had been taken over by Moscow-influenced hard-liners; that "the Party ha[d] climbed into the shell of the Republic and [was] eating it up the way a starfish eats an oyster." Although he'd previously agreed to take part in a live radio broadcast to the United States that night—along with Josie Herbst, Hemingway, Joris

Ivens, a Loyalist Catholic priest named Leocadio Lobo, the wounded commander of the Lincoln Battalion, Robert Merriman, and, improbably, Sidney Franklin—he was having second thoughts about it. What could he say? *These are terrible times—we have to be terrible ourselves?* That wouldn't go down well with the Loyalist sympathizers in Washington and New York who were attending fund-raisers to listen in. No wonder that, as the Hotel Florida contingent gathered in Hemingway's room for prebroadcast cocktails, Robert Merriman's wife found Dos Passos "wishy-washy" and "scared," while the cocky, confident Hemingway, holding forth in his corner of the room, "knew what the war was about" and "let you know by his presence . . . exactly where he stood." Where he stood was with the men of action, which the tall, strong-jawed, handsome Merriman—the son of a lumberjack, with a degree in economics from the University of Nevada and a shoulder wound from the Battle of Jarama—emphatically was.

Dos Passos managed to get through the cocktail hour, and the broadcast, which was moderated by Hemingway and the somewhat clueless Franklin; but by its end it was clear that, as Marion Merriman noticed, "he wanted out." The very next day, after stopping in at the Telefónica to sign copies of the Tauchnitz paperback editions of his books for Barea, he drove out of Madrid, past the Sunday strollers on the Paseo de la Castellana and the now-shuttered café opposite the Post Office where he used to sit "late in the summer evenings, chatting with friends, some of whom are only very recently dead."

Joris Ivens left the same day, in a different car; and when he got to Valencia he sent Hemingway a carefully worded letter. Dos Passos, he reported, "is running here for the same cause as he did in Madrid—it is difficult. Del Vayo spoke to him about it. Hope that Dos will see what a man and comrade has to do in these difficult and serious wartimes." Certainly Hemingway did, Ivens implied, so he wanted *him*, not Dos, to be responsible for writing the voice-over narrative for *The Spanish Earth*, to which Dos, apparently, had agreed. ("Aha!" Ivens added.) In addition, Ivens wondered if Hemingway would write "one of your articles about the great and human function of the political commissar on the front." As a reward for such dedicated work, Ivens promised, "You will go to the front, comrade."

•

Martha wasn't at the fund-raising broadcast on April 24, or at the brigade fiesta with the other journalists. She was leaving Madrid two days later, and she spent the morning and afternoon making the rounds of tailors and furriers to pick up clothing she'd ordered (including that coveted fox wrap), dropping by the hospital to say goodbye to some of the wounded soldiers she'd befriended, and having Quintanilla's little glass cup carefully packed for traveling. In the evening she went to dinner with Randalfo Pacciardi, the handsome commander of the Garibaldi Battalion, who had already singled her out for attention, flirting with her at a brigade party, squiring her around the front lines at "his" front, and generally making her feel like the belle of the ball at an Ivy League college weekend. Tonight he was gay and gallant during their meal—greasy lamb and potatoes in a tomato-scented sauce, rough cold red wine that tasted of the tin cups they drank out of—but afterward, hoping to make love to her, he insisted on taking her for a walk during which they got lost and nearly wandered into enemy lines. Then in the car coming back to the city he tried to put her hand on the front of his trousers. Furious and repelled, she pulled away—in silence because of the driver and orderly in the front seat; flirting was one thing, she thought, but seduction, and vulgarity, another. Pacciardi just laughed: *So brave under fire, and so terrified of sex!* When he dropped her off at the Hotel Florida, she raced up to the room she shared with Hemingway—but to her irritation Hemingway, who'd been at the broadcast until the small hours of the morning, seemed barely to realize she'd been away. "I hope this war lasts long enough for him to say something," she thought, and almost immediately reproved herself: "What an awful thing to think! Maybe I've been here too long."

In the morning she was finishing her packing at the Hotel Florida when a correspondent for the *Manchester Guardian*, Frederick Voigt, approached her for a favor. Voigt was something of a bad joke to the Americans, a tall, balding man with small childish features and a graying comb-over, who imagined leftist vigilantes around every street corner. "There is a terror here," he'd told Hemingway when he'd arrived a few days previously. "Thousands of bodies are being found; you see them every morning." Voigt produced no evidence for his sensational claim, and Hemingway had given him a hard time. "You haven't even been out in the town and you tell those of us who are living here and working here that there is a terror," he'd sneered, just barely restraining himself from throwing a left hook to Voigt's jaw. And now here was that same Voigt, asking if Martha would take a sealed envelope across the border for him into France and mail it. *There's nothing to worry about. It's just a carbon of a dispatch—it's already been through the censor.* She didn't know how to say no—she hardly knew the man—so she accepted the envelope. But Claud Cockburn thought the whole thing seemed suspicious; she should steam the envelope open, he told her, and make sure it was what Voigt said it was. She and Hemingway put a kettle to boil on the hot plate in their room and, with her heart hammering in her chest, Martha held the envelope over the spout. The flap lifted to reveal, not a carbon, but a typed uncensored dispatch which began, "There is a terror here in Madrid." Hemingway was furious. If it had been found in Martha's papers as she tried to cross the border, he said, she could have been shot as a spy.

That night, after Martha had left for Valencia, Hemingway stalked into the Gran Via restaurant and proceeded to tell anyone who would listen what Voigt had done. Maybe, he suggested, the man should get a taste of his own medicine. Voigt had previously been posted to Germany and was reputed to have had a £20,000 bounty placed on his head by the Nazis—why didn't the journalists in the Gran Via shoot *him* and send his head to Berlin packed in dry ice? One of the reporters went over to discuss the matter with Voigt, and Hemingway was pleased to note that the man turned ghastly white. The reporter came back to Hemingway. "There isn't any reward for his head," he said. "That was just something his editor made up." They got a good laugh out of that one.

Voigt was nowhere to be seen the next day at lunch at the Gran Via, which was a pity, for he might have found the conversation instructive. Hemingway was just finishing his coffee at the correspondents' table, in between Virginia Cowles, in one of her little tailored suits, and Josie Herbst, in her well-worn shapeless tweeds; outside, in the street, the noontime bombardment had started. There wasn't much point in trying to leave just yet. Hemingway glanced over to the other side of the restaurant and saw Pepe Quintanilla seated alone at a table for two. "That," Hemingway said to the two women, cocking his head in Quintanilla's direction, "is the chief executioner of Madrid."

He invited Quintanilla to join their little party, which the police chief said he would be honored to do, so long as he might be permitted to buy them a carafe of wine. The four of them sat for a time, talking about the

Spanish artists that Quintanilla—and Hemingway, too—had known in
the old days in Paris, men who hung around the Rotonde and painted
fake El Grecos for newly minted South American millionaires. A shell
whistled and crashed to the street outside and Quintanilla, still spinning
charming stories, began counting them as he talked. By the time he reached
ten the other patrons, and most of the waiters, had left the restaurant;
and Quintanilla had moved on from talking about Paris in the old days to
the war—the first months of fighting, the crazy, quixotic soldiers who refused to believe Franco would take Madrid and so had saved it. *Fifteen.*
Now he was talking about what had to be done to guard against Fifth
Columnists and other traitors. There were, regrettably, executions. *Sixteen.* "I know how men die, all right," said Quintanilla, lighting a cigarette
with his long, tapering fingers and putting it to his lips. "It's worse if it has
to be a woman, of course. *Seventeen.* One officer shat in his pants, had to
be carried out, to be shot like a dog. *Eighteen.*"

"Have many people died in Madrid?" Hemingway asked.

"A revolution is always hasty," murmured Quintanilla.

"Have there been many mistakes?"

"Mistakes?" Raising an eyebrow. "It is only human to err." *Nineteen.*

"And the . . . mistakes—how did they die?" Hemingway wanted to
know.

"On the whole, considering they were mistakes, very well indeed."
Quintanilla reached out for the carafe and poured a crimson stream of
wine into Ginny Cowles's glass. He smiled. "In fact, *magnifico!*"

Hemingway looked at his watch, started to get to his feet. It was late,
he had to go.

"Nonsense," Quintanilla said, in the tone of one who was rarely contradicted. "No one goes." *Twenty-two.*

"I must work," Hemingway protested.

Quintanilla looked at him. "There is no work once you get hit," he
said. He turned and fixed Ginny Cowles with his bright marble-brown
stare. "We will all go to my house," he said, patting her knee, "and I will
divorce my wife and marry you. My wife can be the cook. I have lived
with her so long that it is just like mailing a letter, and my only worry is
will the stamp get on."

"I'm afraid when you get tired of me you'll make me be the cook," said
Ginny.

Their laughter echoed hollowly in the empty basement.

After a little while the *Americanos* decided to risk escape. As they emerged into the glare of the Gran Via, Hemingway grabbed Ginny Cowles's arm. "A *chic type*, eh?" he asked. "Now remember, he's mine."

At the very end of the month, just before Hemingway was due to leave Spain, he and Ginny Cowles were given clearance to go to the front in the Guadarrama, where Loyalist troops had been keeping the rebels at bay from a series of positions on the forested slopes, from time to time launching desperate surprise attacks in the hope of dislodging them or beating them back. The two journalists set out from Madrid in the morning and a few hours later their car was climbing through pines and meadows of wildflowers to brigade headquarters. Except for his day filming tank maneuvers in the Jarama, and his several visits to watch the abortive Casa de Campo offensive, it was the first time Hemingway had been to an active combat zone in Spain; and his soldier hosts, wanting to ensure that he and the lady comrade would have something dramatic to write about, put the two correspondents into an armored car and drove them to a forward position along a road that was under enemy fire. The car lurched and rattled over the rutted paving and bullets pinged against the steel plates on the sides, but its occupants arrived unharmed at the top of a hill to find that the soldiers they'd come to see were playing the guitar and singing while machine guns chattered in the distance.

As the soldiers finished their song their commander appeared, a lean, battle-hardened man in boots, breeches, a green turtleneck pullover, and a forage cap worn atilt over one eye, who called himself El Guerrero. He'd been a truck driver in Madrid before the war, but when the generals had risen against the Republic he'd volunteered for the militia. He told the correspondents that he'd been in the mountains all winter, and seen his battalion shot to pieces on more than one occasion; his wife had fought alongside him, he said, until she got pregnant. Then he had to send her back to Madrid.

Poorly fed, inadequately clothed, their feet shod in rope-soled canvas *alpargatas* instead of sturdy boots, El Guerrero's fighters had proved their toughness throughout a grueling winter; but paradoxically most of them seemed touchingly young and enthusiastic: one picked a bouquet for Ginny

Cowles; another showed her a poem he'd written about the woods and mountains; all of them were eager to demonstrate what would happen if they fired a trench mortar at the farmhouse down the hill, which was an enemy position. When the rebels fired back they mistook the direction of the assault, and instead of aiming at El Guerrero's position they shot at another house in the distance, which apparently belonged to the brigade's colonel. The soldiers couldn't stop laughing. But they knew the war wasn't a joke; they'd lost too many comrades for that. And they believed, passionately and optimistically, that the Republic would prevail. *You'll see—by Christmas our flag will be flying in every village in Spain.*

That night, back at the Hotel Florida, Hemingway wrote what he knew would be his last dispatch from Madrid. El Guerrero didn't make it into this story; nor did his wife, or his men, or Ginny Cowles—although Hemingway did mention how well-disciplined and smart he thought the troops in the Sierra were, and described the armored car he'd ridden in and the machine guns that had fired at him. Instead, Hemingway treated his readers to a lesson on strategy and geography: although the insurgents were mounting a determined offensive against Bilbao in the north, he maintained, "Madrid is the key position on a front 800 miles long," and because of its impregnable position its defenders had "a huge advantage"—even if the government decided to "allow Bilbao to fall." To justify his credentials for making this sort of pronouncement, he said he'd "spent a hard ten days visiting four central fronts, including . . . climbing to important positions 4,800 feet high in the Guadarrama Mountains"; the implication that he'd just taken an arduous ten-day circuit ride around Spain, instead of making ten separate day trips over the course of the month, was both inescapable and (if necessary) deniable. Two days later, after a riotous farewell party at the Twelfth Brigade base hospital attended by Lukacs, Werner Heilbrun, Gustav Regler, Sid Franklin, Josie Herbst, and a host of others that ended with Hemingway passed out on Heilbrun's operating table, he left Madrid for Paris. Standing in the courtyard at the Foreign Ministry as he waited for his car, he indulged in a little man-talk with Barea. "His jokes told me how near he was to understanding Castilian double meanings," Barea said later—"and how far."

When Hemingway wrote his last Madrid dispatch, one of the most horrific stories of the war had been unfolding in Guernica, the ancient spiritual capital of the Basques near Bilbao. The rebel drive on the Basque front wasn't going as quickly as its commander, General Mola, wanted; and on Sunday, April 25, he broadcast the following warning over the Nationalist radio: "Franco is about to deliver a mighty blow against which all resistance is useless. Basques! Surrender now and your lives will be spared!" The next day, at 4:30 in the afternoon—market day in Guernica—a German Heinkel 111 bomber from the Condor Legion's "experimental squadron" flew over the town center, dropped a load of bombs, and flew away. When the all-clear signal sounded people emerged from their shelters to help the wounded—at which point the sky suddenly filled with planes. First the full squadron, which dropped more bombs; then wave after wave of Heinkel 51 fighters, sweeping low to strafe and hurl grenades at men, women, children, farmers, nuns, even livestock. Finally, at 5:15, three squadrons of lumbering Junkers 52 bombers carpet-bombed the town—a technique the Condor Legion had implemented for the first time a few weeks before on Republican positions around Oviedo, two hundred miles to the west—with antipersonnel twenty-pounders and incendiaries. Cows and sheep, crazed and burning, ran in panic through the streets; whole families perished as their houses crumbled in upon them; people covered in third-degree burns lurched between the blazing buildings. By morning Guernica was a charred carapace.

Although the London *Times*'s correspondent, George Steer, arrived on the scene before dawn on the twenty-seventh and was able to take down eyewitness accounts of the destruction, his own paper refused to publish (as its editor said) "anything that might hurt [German] sensibilities"— leaving it to *The New York Times* to pick up the entirety of Steer's story. The paper counterbalanced Steer almost immediately, though, with a report by their pro-rebel correspondent, William P. Carney: Guernica, he said—parroting the line of Luis Bolín, who'd arranged Franco's escape from the Canary Islands and was now the insurgent propaganda chief— had been burned by the *Basques*, with help from Asturian *dinamiteros*; no insurgent planes had come near the town. That last, at least, was true— the planes themselves were German, and the order to bomb Guernica, a target of limited strategic significance, came from the German air minister, Colonel Hermann Goering, who wanted to demonstrate to the German general staff what the results of such an exercise would be.

In one sense, they were everything the rebel high command and their Nazi allies could have hoped: Guernica fell to the insurgents two days later, opening the way for their offensive against Bilbao, and two years later the Luftwaffe would employ the same tactics to conquer Poland. But despite the official denials of the Nationalist authorities, or perhaps because of them, the destruction of Guernica would inspire headlines for weeks afterward, and go on to become a central symbol of the civil war—especially after Pablo Picasso made it the subject of his eponymous painting for the Spanish Pavilion at the International Exposition in Paris, which opened that summer.

Why didn't Hemingway cover what happened at Guernica? The story would have been a huge scoop for him, and for NANA—and neither Matthews nor Delmer could get it, because they'd both gone on leave ten days earlier. Traveling to the devastated town would certainly have been difficult, since it was on the northern coast, separated from Madrid by a huge swathe of rebel territory; but he didn't even mention the bombing in his last dispatch from Spain. Perhaps Guernica didn't seem important to the men he talked to—Durán, Walter, Lukacs, Hans Kahle, and the others in Madrid. Certainly the moderate and conservative French newspapers, such as Le Temps and Le Figaro, ignored it at first.

For some reason, though, it seemed to matter to Virginia Cowles, who despite her gold bracelets and high-heeled shoes was a very determined reporter; and when she left Madrid she headed to the Nationalist zone and visited Guernica, "a lonely chaos of timber and brick, like an ancient civilization in the process of being excavated." When she asked what had happened there, a Nationalist staff officer told her, "We bombed it and bombed it and bombed it and *bueno*, why not?" At which her official escort interrupted, saying grimly, "I don't think I would write about that if I were you." She ignored the suggestion.

May 1937: Paris

It was May Day and Paris was *en fête*. The chestnut trees were blooming in the Bois and along the boulevards, the sun was shining, and the whole city was on holiday. Shortly after noon an enormous crowd—estimated by some as more than a million people—gathered in the Place de la République to march "for bread, peace, and liberty," as *L'Humanité*, which suspended publication for the day, put it. Planned as a celebration of the achievements the French Popular Front had made in promoting workers' welfare, the demonstration had taken on a darker tinge with the recent news from Spain, particularly the reports of what *L'Humanité* called "the horrible Fascist crime of Guernica." As a light breeze fluttered the placards and banners of the demonstrators and the parade coursed down the broad avenues toward the Place de la Nation like a mighty river, an airplane traced the word *Bilbao* with its vapor trail in the pearly blue sky overhead and then flew low to scatter pamphlets urging aid for the Basque victims of the war. And on the speakers' platform in the Place de la Nation the Spanish Republican flag flew alongside the *tricolore* and the banner of the CGT, the Confédération Général des Travailleurs.

Capa and Gerda moved along the margins of the crowd. Capa was snapping pictures of the demonstration for *Ce Soir*, but when they came to a street-corner flower stall they stopped in front of a display of *muguet*. It was Charles IX who in the sixteenth century first bestowed the lily-of-the-valley as a May Day talisman on the ladies of his court; now it was a traditional token of luck, love, and renewal—the *de rigueur* offering from any man to his sweetheart on this day. As the flower seller looked on indulgently, Gerda hovered over the flowers, a chic beret perched on her dark-gold hair, a long scarf knotted at her throat, posing prettily for Capa's camera as she sought out the freshest and most fragrant bouquet. *This one, please.* Clasping the flowers to her, she pulled out a sprig and carefully pinned it to the lapel of his jacket.

May 1937: Barcelona

John Dos Passos left Barcelona's Hotel Continental at dawn on the first day of May in a Hispano-Suiza supplied by the Catalan Generalitat. On the seat beside him, masquerading as his secretary until they had passed the guards at the French border, was Liston Oak, the American propaganda worker who had originally told Coco Robles that his father was dead.

Oak had appeared at Dos Passos's hotel room door after midnight the night before, white-faced and stammering; he was on the run, he said, because he'd been denounced as a Trotskyist to the security services and was certain that what had happened to Robles would happen to him, too.

This wasn't necessarily paranoia. Earlier in the spring Oak had been transferred to Barcelona for the purpose of setting up a new English-language press office, and soon after his arrival he'd had lunch in a hole-in-the-wall off the Ramblas with Andrés Nin, the charismatic former teacher and journalist who was head of the POUM, the Catalan anti-Stalinist Marxist revolutionaries. Oak had been deeply impressed by Nin, and based on their conversation had written an article, which was now about to be published by London's *New Statesman and Nation*, supporting Nin's argument that the government could never win the war with Franco if in the name of solidarity it crushed the revolutionary spirit of 1936. When he'd first interviewed Nin this position might have seemed defensible; but the Communist Party's congress in Valencia in March had demonized the POUM and urged that it be dissolved, and by now any article taking the POUM point of view would be viewed as subversive by many in the government, certainly his employers, Constancia de la Mora and the increasingly Communist-leaning Álvarez del Vayo. What would really get him in trouble, though, was his assertion that the anarchists and the POUM believed there was "a plot to eliminate them from the Spanish scene" and that Stalinists in the government had "organized a GPU [secret service] in Spain controlled from Moscow."

Already nervous about the article's publication, Oak had been sent into a real funk when, strolling along the Ramblas, he'd run into a Russian agent he'd known in New York who went by the name of George Mink. Mink had invited him for cocktails at his hotel, an invitation Oak had warily accepted, and over their scotch the agent had told him, as one warrior to another, that the Communists had finally persuaded the government to strike against the POUM and its sympathizers. People would die, and other people would be arrested and jailed, if they were lucky, or shot, if not. And after that things would certainly be different in Barcelona. All this was unsettling enough, but what made Mink's warning (was it a warning?) particularly terrifying to Oak was that Mink—not his real name, of course—was a political assassin.

Dos Passos had his own reasons for believing Oak's story. Since his arrival in Spain he'd been struck by the government's increasing desire for central control; in Barcelona he'd seen at once that this was putting Valencia at odds with willfully independent, revolutionary Catalonia, where different factions—the anarchist CNT, the socialist UGT, the anti-

Stalinist, Marxist POUM, the Communist PSUC, all suspicious of one another—had been arming themselves. What was it the mayor of Fuenti-dueña had said? *One of these days it will come to a fight.* Dos Passos had gone to interview Nin himself, late at night in a large bare office full of cast-off furniture; and at first Nin, who'd spent nine years in the Soviet Union, in the process becoming close to Lenin as well as Trotsky, seemed to make light of what was going on in Barcelona, the growing violence and lawlessness and the sense of foreboding that had replaced the fiesta spirit Robert Capa and Gerda Taro had rejoiced in less than a year ago. Yes, things are different, Nin said: people are wearing collars and ties on the streets again. And he laughed, flashing his white teeth. But then he spoke with concern about the way the Valencia government was taking over police services, and about the barricades being erected in the streets of the suburbs, as if in preparation for some kind of armed action. "Take a car and drive through the suburbs," he suggested, then laughed again. "But maybe you had better not."

In the corridor outside Nin's office a thin, dark-haired militiaman in a baggy khaki jumpsuit was sitting on a bench, and jumped up when Dos Passos emerged. He was an Englishman named Eric Blair, a young writer who published under the pseudonym of George Orwell; he was desperate to meet the great American leftist novelist, and he'd begged his wife's boss, who was arranging Dos Passos's stay in Barcelona, to get him even a minute's interview. This was the best the go-between could manage; but fortunately for Blair, Dos Passos was flattered and sat down for a chat.

Blair had enlisted in the POUM militia some months ago but was back in Barcelona on sick leave; now he was trying to arrange a transfer to a more active front, and he agreed with Dos Passos that there was an ominous change in the city, maybe in the whole country. "It's this bloody Non-Intervention Committee that is the root of all evil," he said: with Britain, France, and the United States refusing to support the govern-ment, the only friend Spain had was the Soviet Union, and Stalin was using that friendship as leverage. And now that the Russians were ob-sessed with purging Trotskyites at home, "they have to find Trotskyites to purge in Spain. Since they don't happen to have any Trotskyites they pick on the independent working-class parties."

"A perfect recipe for a Fascist victory," Dos Passos had remarked.

"A Fascist victory," Blair echoed, "and it won't be the last."

These two conversations, with Nin and Blair, had made Dos Passos think, if he didn't already, that there might be some justification for Oak's paranoia; so after allowing Oak to spend the night on the sofa in his hotel room he'd agreed to help get him out of the country the next morning. By then Dos Passos himself had begun to feel jumpy—no one would try to stop *him* leaving, would they?—and it was a relief to both of them when, on the afternoon of the first, the Generalitat's Hispano-Suiza rolled up to the *douane* at Cerbère, where the border guards gave their documents a few thwacks with an official stamp and let them through. At Perpignan, they parted: Dos Passos was going to meet his wife, Katy, in Antibes for a few days, and Oak was headed to Paris and thence to the United States. Dos never saw Oak again.

Two days later Barcelona exploded.

The trouble started when Barcelona's police chief decided to take over the telephone exchange in the Plaza de Cataluña, which until then had been operated by the anarchist union CNT. Arriving at the telephone building with several truckloads of Assault Guards armed with rifles, the police chief was met by machine-gun fire from the entrenched workers within; then, as if at a signal, all the political organizations in the city pulled out the arms they'd cached away, and barricades went up all over town. Shopkeepers pulled down their shutters and unarmed citizens bolted the doors on their houses. For nearly a week the streets of Barcelona echoed with gunfire—"like a tropical rainstorm," said Eric Blair, who spent much of that time standing guard on the roof of the Poliorama, a movie theater across the street from the POUM headquarters—as Assault Guards, who had been taken away from the Jarama front for the purpose, fired on the CNT and the POUM, and the CNT and POUM fired back. The commandant of the air force, Inigo Hidalgo de Cisneros, brought four squadrons of planes to a nearby airfield in case they were needed to reimpose order. By the time the government forces prevailed, five hundred people had been killed and a thousand wounded.

Within days the Communists, prompted by Alexander Orlov's NKVD officers, were blaming the events of the May Days on "Trotskyist-Fascist" *agents provocateurs*, with whom, it was charged, the POUM was riddled. The POUM was outlawed and its leaders arrested; and Prime Minister Largo Caballero, who resisted this step vigorously—how could you outlaw a working-class party without any proof of wrongdoing?—was forced to resign. Juan Negrín, the multilingual socialist finance minister who had negotiated the transfer of the Spanish gold reserves to Moscow (and whom the Communists, seeking a friendly but nonpartisan candidate, had already approached about taking on the job), became prime minister. And Andrés Nin was spirited out of Barcelona by the NKVD—some said by order of Alexander Orlov, still others that the directive came from Stalin himself—and taken to an interrogation center at Alcalá de Henares, where he was pressured to confess that he'd passed military secrets to the Nationalists. He refused. So he was removed to a nearby country house owned by Hidalgo de Cisneros, the air force chief who was married to Liston Oak's Propaganda Ministry supervisor, Constancia de la Mora, and tortured to death.

Like many of the "disappeared" on both sides of the war, Nin was buried, secretly, in an unmarked grave. But not before a grotesque pantomime was staged at the house where he died: a "rescue" by costumed soldiers carrying fake Nationalist and German documents and insignia which were left behind as "clues." *Mundo Obrero*, the PCE's newspaper, soon reported that Nin had been freed by Falangists and was in Burgos, now the Nationalist capital; and thereafter, when POUM sympathizers scrawled graffiti on walls demanding, "Where is Nin?" someone else would scribble slanderously underneath: "In Salamanca [the former rebel capital] or Berlin."

May 1937: Paris

Hemingway got to Paris the day the shooting started in Barcelona, his passage from Spain smoothed by a chartered plane laid on by Álvarez del Vayo. Although he hoped to rendezvous with Martha before they each went home to the United States, they had to do it clandestinely—*we will both wear long beards and look strong*—because in Paris Hemingway was in the public eye again, the kind of public eye that saw things and reported them to Pauline.

When he arrived he gave an interview to a gaggle of newspapermen—he hadn't expected the war would last this long, he told them, he was going home to finish a novel, he would return to Spain when the "big war of movement" began in the summer—and on the ninth he delivered a speech about Spain to the Anglo-American Press Club. He had a meeting with the Spanish ambassador, Luis Araquistáin, about the Loyalist army's medical needs. And in the time before he was to sail for New York he turned out two more dispatches for NANA. One, a charming series of portraits of the various chauffeurs he and Martha had had in Madrid, read almost like one of his short stories—closely observed, tightly constructed, funny in the way the best of his letters were funny, as if he were telling the story to *you*, to amuse and touch you. It was also (as another writer would one day point out) a not-so-subtle allegory of the Republic's change of leadership, from common-man Tomás to the quixotic anarchist David to the solid "union man" Hipolito. The other dispatch was an armchair analysis of the military situation in Spain as he saw it, with a preamble comparing the civil war there to civil wars in the United States and Russia, and prognostications about where new fronts would develop and when. Hemingway's money was on renewed fighting in the Jarama Valley, or maybe along the Guadalajara road; Franco, he said, "must attack and he must attack Madrid"—but, warned Hemingway, "Madrid is a death-trap to any attacking force."

He sent the typed story by pouch to NANA on May 9, and can't have been happy to get a return cable from NANA's London office manager, H. J. J. Sargint, saying that the New York editors "ASK YOU UNSEND ADDITIONAL STORIES." Whether NANA was considering the expense—this piece, which was mailed in typescript, would earn Hemingway $1,000 instead of the $500 he got for cabled dispatches, bringing his total for his Spanish reportage to $7,500, or just under $120,000 in 2012 dollars—or whether they were reluctant to publish another lecture on military strategy, they ended by spiking the story. It was just one more reason for Hemingway to dislike and distrust them.

Meanwhile, with one article about Spain accepted by *Collier's* for publication and another under consideration at *The New Yorker*, Martha was writing to John Gunther, the bestselling author of *Inside Europe*, with whom she'd indulged in a mild flirtation before her Spanish trip: "There are practically no words to describe Madrid, it was heaven, far and away the best thing I have ever seen or lived through . . . I want to do a book on Spain fast and I want to go back." Neither she nor Hemingway mentioned, or seemed to notice, what was going on in Barcelona while they were in Paris. Apparently they both thought, as Martha would say years later, that the POUM and what happened to it were "irrelevant to the great drama of the war."

On May 11, Hemingway went to the Gare St. Lazare, where John and Katy Dos Passos were watching a porter load their luggage onto the boat train for Cherbourg, where they'd board the *Berengaria*, a Cunard liner that had seen better days, bound for Southampton and New York. They looked up as Hemingway came down the platform toward them, and if either of them felt pleased to see him—if they thought he'd just come to bid his good old friends *bon voyage*—the pleasure evaporated with the first words out of his mouth. "What are you going to do about this Robles business?" Hemingway asked Dos, sharply.

"I'll tell the truth as I see it," Dos replied, in that soft-spoken way that made Hemingway angrier than shouting would have. "Right now I've got to straighten out my ideas. The question I keep putting to myself is, what's the use of fighting a war for civil liberties, if you destroy civil liberties in the process?"

"Civil liberties shit," growled Hemingway. "Are you with us or against us?" Dos Passos shrugged at this, and Hemingway balled up his fist as if he were going to punch his friend in the face.

A whistle blew and the trainman came down the platform, calling out "*En voiture, messieurs-dames!*" Hemingway took a breath and let his arms fall to his sides. "I'll tell you one thing," he said to Dos Passos in a cold, hard voice. "These people"—he meant New York book reviewers—"these people know how to turn you into a back number. I've seen them do it. And what they did once they can do again."

"Why, Ernest," said his old girlfriend, now Dos's wife, "I've never heard anything so despicably opportunistic in my life." Hemingway said nothing, but turned and headed out of the station without looking back.

The next evening he returned to his and Dos's old haunt from a decade ago, Sylvia Beach's English-language bookshop, Shakespeare and Company, where he and Stephen Spender, also newly returned from Spain, were to give a joint reading. Spender was in the process of being purged from the Communist Party for speaking out against the severe treatment meted out by the Loyalists to party "deviants," among them his own lover, Tony Hyndman, who had deserted from the International Brigades; and some of the poems he read that evening sounded a note of disillusion with *la causa*, or at least with the idea of the war. Hemingway, who didn't know anything about Spender's romance and would have despised him if he had, read from his as-yet-unfinished Harry Morgan novel, in which Morgan, the narrator, breaks the neck of the Chinese refugee-smuggler, Mr. Sing, and drops him overboard in the Gulf. "What did you kill him for?" a companion asks, and Morgan answers, "To keep from killing twelve other chinks."

After the reading Hemingway went to the Select, in Montparnasse, with a handful of journalist friends including George and Helen Seldes. Over the *boudin noir* he groused to Seldes, "I had to go to Spain before you liberal bastards would believe I was on your side."

The following morning, alone, he left for New York on the *Normandie*.

May 1937: Bilbao

Because of the Nationalist blockade, the safest way to get to Bilbao was to fly in from Biarritz, to the east across the French border. Even that wasn't foolproof; the rebels said they would shoot at French planes, and the consulate in St. Jean de Luz took them at their word. But there didn't seem to be any alternatives, so when Capa at last got his assignments from *Ce Soir* and *Regards* to cover the Basque front, and the passes and reentry papers that came with them, he went to Biarritz and found a plane whose pilot said he could get him to Sondika, the airfield just outside Bilbao.

By now the Nationalist lines had moved westward along the coast from San Sebastian almost as far as the postcard-pretty fishing village of Bermeo, just twenty-two miles from Bilbao, so the pilot set his course over the Bay of Biscay to avoid their guns, then banked south and flew high over the bare, scrub-covered hills—who knew where the front was today?—before dropping down onto the field at Sondika. Capa clambered out of the plane carrying an Eyemo movie camera, a rugged 35-millimeter that carried 100 feet of film, in addition to his still cameras. Maybe on the Basque front he'd be able to shoot some usable footage for MGM News, as he hadn't been able to in Madrid in April.

Bilbao—its residents affectionately if scatalogically nicknamed it *el botxo*, the hole—turned out to be a grimy industrial city, sprawling across the banks of the Rio Nervión where it flowed into the Bay of Biscay, surrounded by the chemical and steel works that brought it wealth as well as clouds of smog and soot. In peacetime the docks that lined the estuary had bustled with stevedores heaving ingots and crates onto the ships in Spain's largest and busiest port; but today the cargo waiting to be boarded was children. As Nationalist troops came closer to the optimistically named "iron ring" of fortifications around Bilbao (whose blueprints had been smuggled to them in March by a disaffected Basque officer) and German bombers swept over the city as well as the Basque villages in the surrounding hills, British and French rescue organizations were arranging the evacuation of 22,000 children from the war zone; and today, May 5, a handful of rusty ships, the French freighter *Carimare*, the Spanish liner *Habana*, and others, were preparing to receive a number of them.

In a tree-shaded square near the port a group of men, most in uniform, clustered around a notice detailing when and how the evacuations would be carried out; closer to the quays a line of women and children, dressed in somber black as if in mourning for what the war had done to them, waited to be told which group of evacuees they belonged in. Capa raised his camera, shot: as he did so, a solemn little girl, a white-clad apparition in the black line, tuned around and regarded him gravely from under her dark bangs, sucking her thumb. He went on. At the dock was an enormous crowd—men, women, and children—waiting to board tenders for the ships, or to kiss their loved ones goodbye. The *Bilbainos* were prosperous—one woman sported a luxurious fur collar, while the little girl next to her at the barrier was clutching a fur scarf as well as her proper English-style coat—and orderly; there were tears, but they were bitten back, dignified. In Madrid, Regler had said, Capa *made himself tough to do his job*; the job here was different, but it required just as much toughness.

The next day Capa headed out of Bilbao to Mount Solluve, twenty miles to the northeast, where Basque Loyalists were dug in on the heights above Bermeo. German aircraft had been pounding the mountain since dawn, and the Nationalists' general, Emilio Mola, had just brought in North African troops, the first ever deployed in the Basque country, to break through the Loyalist line. The North Africans were finding the spiky gorse bushes that covered the slopes made for hard going, and Mola had ordered a unit of Italian tanks to spearhead the attack, but the Basques had rolled logs across the road to stop them.

Capa attached himself to a group of Loyalist infantrymen and *dinamiteros* defending positions on the mountain, some in stone farm-houses they had turned into improvised fortresses, some out in the open. It was cold for early May, and the soldiers were wearing gloves and woolen caps or leather helmets as they waited in the piney scrub for the tanks and trucks to come. At intervals they had to dive for cover as the German Heinkels and Junkers swooped low over the mountain, spraying machine-gun bullets at the trenches. Then came the grinding of gears as a staff car and a battered pickup truck rumbled along the road and stopped at the improvised barricade. From their hiding place by the side of the road the *dinamiteros* hurled grenades at the car, and the other soldiers opened fire. Capa got no shot of the attack, but he did get photographs of the soldiers walking out of cover to inspect their handiwork, and remove any useful supplies from the truck.

Elsewhere other *dinamiteros*, with the help of an antiaircraft gun trucked in from Bilbao, were able to destroy a number of tanks, so that by nightfall the mountain—and its commanding position on the route to Bilbao—remained in Basque hands. But not all its defenders were lucky. Capa photographed one of the unfortunate ones, lying facedown in the coarse grass, and then, with his borrowed Eyemo, filmed a nearly identical shot. The only difference between the two was the contrast in the film footage between the motionless form of the dead man and the stalks of grass waving gently above him in the dusk.

As darkness drew in, Capa left Mount Solluve in a big black Packard, the driver riding the accelerator all along the pitted road to the airfield at Sondika. There, a French plane like the one Capa had come in on— maybe even the very same one—was disgorging another load of passen-gers, one of them the tall, black-haired American newsman Jay Allen. Allen took in Capa's grimy raincoat, the cameras dangling around his neck, and he saw the photographer thrust a package containing his film into the pilot's hand. He heard the words *Regards* and *urgent*; then the plane roared off into the night. And Allen and the others got into the Packard with Capa and rode back into Bilbao.

It wasn't until a few days later, though, that Allen and Capa formally introduced themselves. Allen was an intrepid journalist, an old friend of Hemingway's from prewar Madrid, the first man to interview Franco af-ter the mutiny, the man who'd been smuggled in on the floor of a car to report the massacre at Badajoz at the beginning of the war; and for his pains he'd been fired by his pro-Nationalist employer, Colonel Robert R. McCormick of the *Chicago Tribune*. He'd been freelancing since then, but had just been engaged by David Smart, the editor of *Esquire*, to help create a new "insider's" newsmagazine, called *Ken*, for which he was gathering material in Bilbao. Like most reporters, he was wary of cameramen: they were grandstanders, he thought, who didn't do the same kind of work *real* journalists did. Or he thought so until he found himself standing next to Capa on a busy street when the air raid sirens sent out the four short blasts that meant *aircraft approaching*. The crowds dispersed in panic, women clutching the hands of their children as they ran toward the nearest shelters. Capa stayed in the open, his camera trained on the figures and faces of the terrified civilians, chronicling what happens when ordinary men and women and children know they are in the enemy's crosshairs. Only when a policeman with a rifle forced him into a bunker did he leave the street. And Allen recognized a kindred spirit.

Over the next week Capa photographed more air raids, including one that turned the city's petrol depot into a holocaust of flame and smoke; he shadowed the women sifting through the city's refuse heaps in search of fuel; he watched the children and their mothers resting on sandbags in between enemy sorties, the black-clad grandmothers sitting on a bench and weeping at the news contained in the paper one of them held in her hand. It was grim but to him necessary work.

On May 15 the journalists remaining in the city were told to evacuate: the airfield had to be closed, and only one more plane would leave for Biarritz. The correspondents flocked to Sondika to get on board—all except Capa, who wanted to stay behind and document the fall of the city. Keeping only one Leica, he gave the rest of his equipment and all his exposed film to the Yiddish journalist S. L. Schneiderman, Chim's brother-in-law, asking him to get it to Paris safely.

But although the enemy was just outside the Iron Ring, and the Loyalist forces were all withdrawing within it, Bilbao didn't fall. In fact, feelers were being extended to the Catholic Basques by the Pope, who hoped to arrange a separate peace between them and Franco. Without waiting to see what the result of such negotiations might be, Capa decided to run the blockade in a fishing boat. The little vessel put out to sea on the night of the seventeenth and safely skirted both the mines at the mouth of

Bilbao's harbor and the waiting ships, arriving in Bayonne on the eighteenth. Within days, Capa was back at the rue Froidevaux—but except for Csiki Weisz and a telegram from Gerda, the studio was empty. Gerda was in Valencia.

May 1937: Madrid

On May 1, the Madrid Foreign Press and Censorship Department moved from the Telefónica to the Foreign Ministry in the Palacio de Santa Cruz, near the Plaza Mayor, a massive stone-and-brick pile whose iron-barred windows made the building seem like a fortress. The Telefónica had become untenable—the correspondents had already insisted on moving the transmission room from its upper floors to the basement—and for Barea, now overcome with terror at every loud noise, it was torture. In the days before the move he'd been feverish, racked with convulsive nausea, and unable to cross the shell-racked Gran Via to the censorship; silent and shaking, he'd sat in a darkened corner of the hotel doing office busywork, leaving the transfer of all the censorship papers and files to Ilsa.

The day after the move, a shell sailed through the windows of the deserted office and exploded in front of Ilsa's old desk.

The nightmare of what might have been tormented Barea. Unable to work, eat, or sleep, he went to see the ministry doctor, who prescribed an opiate that knocked him out but gave him hallucinations, horrifying visions of disintegrating bodies accompanied by the sensations of falling and being torn apart. When he awoke at last, trembling and drenched with sweat, he resolved to stay away from drugs: but that single dose, or maybe the experience of the past few weeks, had changed him. He felt both clearer about and more removed from the work he had been doing. And as he'd done in the aftermath of the Gran Via shelling a week earlier, he began to write. Instead of a phantasmagoria of apocalyptic images, however, what came out of his typewriter was a simple, unvarnished tale, told in the colloquial voice of Barea's Lavapiés barrio, of a trench-bound *miliciano* who stays at his post for increasingly absurd reasons. Although Ilsa had been horrified by that earlier effort at fiction, she was moved by this one, and something at last clicked into place for him: he could exorcise his inchoate feelings by writing them down, giving form to them in fiction.

Certainly he had to find *some* outlet for them, and the safer, the better. For now came the news of the events in the streets of Barcelona—
and, Barea thought, *All of us who stood at the barricades in November had
better keep our thoughts to ourselves.* Especially when those thoughts took
the turn his were now taking. Dos Passos, who'd sat and talked with him
in his office in the Telefónica, had understood what gnawed at the corners of his and Ilsa's minds: it wasn't just the shelling, Dos Passos said, it
was "a fear that tortured every man or woman who was doing responsible
work . . . They were being watched." And the watchers didn't like men
like him to have doubts.

But Barea had begun to doubt. Yes, he thought, the war had been
started by a cabal of stiff-necked generals who'd joined forces with a reac-
tionary elite to put the brakes on any progressive developments in the
country; and yes, he and others like him had joined the fight against the
generals to defend their dreams of a true republic of the people. But when
outside aid started coming in, from Germany and Italy on one side and
Russia on the other, this civil conflict between the forces of change and
the forces of reaction had been transmogrified into something else. Suddenly Spain's war had become an experimental exercise—which will prevail, fascism or socialism? Whose weapons are stronger, Germany's or
Russia's?—that the rest of the world was watching with interest. Or worse:
for although the powers-that-be in Europe and America hoped militant
fascism might be weakened by the war, they actively *didn't* want the Russian Communists and their *de facto* protégées, the Spanish government,
to win it—that would make communism too powerful.

We're condemned in advance, Barea thought. *We can't win, but we have
to fight. Maybe we'll be saved if an antifascist war starts in Europe; maybe all
we can do is carry on and give the other countries time to arm themselves.
Either way, we pay in blood.*

It was a bleak and terrible epiphany. And it made him, and Ilsa, vulnerable in ways he could not then begin to imagine.

Sometimes, during this strange spring, Barea's old friend Angel would
come to visit during his furloughs from military duty, bringing with him
some of the awkward, illiterate boys who fought alongside him in the
trenches at Carabanchel. Holding out a threadbare, mud-spattered copy

of the poems of the martyred Federico García Lorca, he would ask Barea, who had loved the poetry of Lorca since his youth, to read to them. And Barea would repeat Lorca's chilling lines about the officers of the Guardia Civil, dark-cloaked specters on iron-shod black horses, or his poem about the Andalusian olive orchard that was alive with birdsong. "That's right," cried a boy from Jaén, who'd worked in the olive groves before he'd run away to join the militia. "The olive trees are full of cries and calls. The thrushes come in flocks and eat the olives and make a great noise . . . Go on." Eagerly he waited for Barea to continue.

That boy, thought Barea, had starved working in those orchards, orchards that belonged to someone else; now he was fighting for them. And Lorca, by the power of his words, had given those gray-green, bird-thronged olive trees to him. Forever.

May 1937: Valencia

When Capa left Paris for Bilbao, Gerda intended to travel to Catalonia, where one of her old SAP friends from Germany, Herbert Frahm, who'd been living in exile in Norway under the name Willy Brandt, was working as a liaison between the SAP and the POUM. Possibly he'd hoped to get her to do a photo session with Andrés Nin; maybe he had no agenda other than a meeting with a former comrade. On her side, she might have been looking forward to a chance to commiserate about what was going on in Germany, where her family, having lost both their business and their home, had been forced to emigrate to Yugoslavia. But by the time Gerda crossed the border the May Days had erupted and Brandt was on the run after trying to mediate between the government and the POUM. In hiding he ran across Eric Blair, the POUM militiaman who'd been so eager to talk to John Dos Passos; and Blair tried to persuade him to flee to England. But Brandt thought he'd be better able to fight fascism from Norway; he went back to Oslo.

And Gerda, who might have found Barcelona hostile territory herself these days, went south, first to the wide, wildflower-spattered fields around Los Blazquez, northeast of Córdoba, where Alfred Kantorowicz, whom she'd met in February in Valencia, had been sent as information officer of the Chapaiev Battalion. Finding no action there, however, she retraced her steps to Valencia—and there the war caught up with her.

General Francisco Franco, leader of the Nationalist rebellion: "There can be no compromise, no truce."

"I'm no use as a capitalist," Arturo Barea said, but sometimes he had to pass as one.

Loyalist militiamen (and women), photographed by Robert Capa in Madrid, August–September 1936

Gerda Taro: "Like a fox that is going to play a trick on you"

Capa's photograph of World War I veterans carrying the eternal flame to Verdun's military cemetery, July 1936

Gerda Taro and Robert Capa—wearing a necktie and "shaved to hell," as he wrote his mother—in Paris, autumn 1936

Ilse Kulcsar, around the time of her marriage, looking deceptively demure

To have and have not: Pauline (*left*) and Ernest Hemingway (*right*) fishing in the Gulf of Mexico

John Dos Passos and his wife, Katy, on Gerald and Sara Murphy's yacht in the Mediterranean

"I suppose Ernest is busy again helping Miss Gellhorn with her writing," Pauline told a friend after Martha met Hemingway in Key West.

Gerda Taro's photograph of harvesttime in Aragon could have been painted by Millet; a careless developer (possibly Kornel Capa) left a shadow on one side of the print.

Loyalist volunteers leave for the front, Barcelona, 1936. "They could not have known what was in store for them," said Capa.

The new order: Gerda Taro's photograph of the Popular Army training in Valencia, May 1937

Milicianos leap across a gully for Capa in September 1936. Seconds later he will take one of the most famous images of his career.

After an air raid, Madrid, February 1937. "Into the future one dares not look," said Capa.

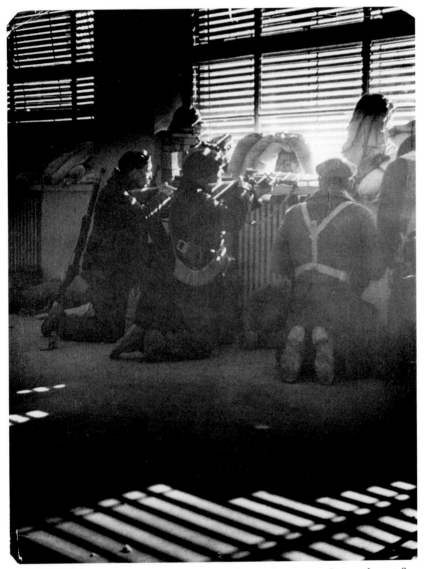
With Capa behind them, International Brigaders in University City exchange fire with Nationalists in the next building, November–December 1936.

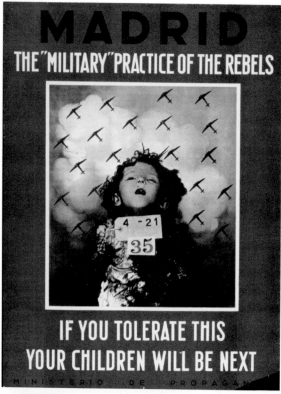

One of the children of Getafe, whose photographs Barea saved from destruction, immortalized in a Propaganda Ministry poster

The three ambulances Hemingway donated to the Spanish Republic

Gerda with her Leica at Guadalajara, captured by an unknown photographer, July 1937

Taro by Capa—an image the photographer kept among his possessions

Ted Allan, from the tattered dust jacket of his autobiographical novel, *This Time a Better Earth*

Capa by Taro, Segovia front, May–June 1937

Gerda Taro's photograph of air-raid victims in the Valencia morgue, May 1937 (*top*), and of a burning supply truck at Brunete two months later (*above*). "You get an absurd feeling that somehow it's unfair still to be alive," she said.

Capa's photograph of one of the casualties of Teruel. "Dead men have indeed died in vain," wrote *Life* magazine, "if live men refuse to look at them."

Hemingway wore tweeds, and Martha her silver fox coat, for Hemingway's Carnegie Hall speech.

Hemingway (left) and Joris Ivens filming *The Spanish Earth* in the Jarama Valley

(Left to right) On November 7, 1937, Langston Hughes, Mikhail Koltsov, Ernest Hemingway, and Nicolás Guillén celebrate the anniversary of the October Revolution and the arrival in Madrid of the International Brigades.

Father Leocadio Lobo (left) and Barea. "Write down what you think you know . . . tell it honestly and speak the truth," said the priest.

Joseph Stalin (right) plays cards with Hitler's foreign minister, Joachim von Ribbentrop. "Stalin never tricks anyone," said a Spanish official. "At least not Communists."

(Clockwise from left) Hemingway, Capa, Vincent Sheean, Herbert Matthews, and Hans Kahle take a break from covering the Loyalist retreat, April 1937.

Near Fraga, on the Rio Segre, November 1938. Capa kept moving forward, using the camera like a weapon.

After an air attack on the Tarragona–Barcelona road, January 1939

"*¡Salud, hermanos!*": At
Montblanch (*above*), the
International Brigades
give their last salute; in
Barcelona (*left*), they
march under a flurry
of confetti made from
folded notes of thanks.
Capa wore a suit and tie
to chronicle the solemn
occasion.

A young girl in a refugee transit center in Barcelona, January 1939. "I have seen hundreds of thousands flee thus," Capa wrote. "It is not always easy to stand aside and be unable to do anything except record the sufferings around one."

Part of the "Mexican Suitcase": a collection of film shot during the Spanish Civil War by Capa, Gerda Taro, and Chim, lost during the German invasion of France in 1940 and rediscovered in 2007

At dusk on May 14, a wave of Nationalist planes rolled in from the sea and dipped low over the city, spraying it with bombs; the attack continued through the night and into the next day. A number of buildings were destroyed or damaged, including the British Embassy, and men, women, and children were killed and injured. By morning the toll stood at thirty dead and at least fifty wounded; and Gerda Taro, not content to photograph the wreckage-strewn streets and eviscerated apartment houses she'd taken too many pictures of in her short career, took her camera to the city morgue.

Somehow she argued her way past the guards at the gates; once through she stopped, turned back, and photographed the crowd pressed against the iron railings, sweeping her camera back and forth to capture the panorama of anxiety and grief she saw there. Then she went inside. There, on marble slabs, on the tiled floor, or laid out on makeshift beds of wooden stools placed next to one another, were the bloodied, broken bodies of the dead. A man in his business suit, blood pooling under his bald head; a black-clad woman, one arm flung up as if in sleep; a little girl with her bare legs akimbo. She and Capa had both come to Spain searching for—what? Romance? Excitement? Pathos? Danger? This is what she had found. Walking up and down between the rows of corpses, stepping carefully to avoid the puddled blood and stained sheets and tangled limbs, Gerda looked into the face of death; quietly, unsensationally, almost lovingly, she documented it. "If your pictures aren't good enough, you're not close enough," Capa used to say; that day Gerda was very close indeed.

Afterward she went to the hospital where the survivors of the attack were being cared for. There she took pictures of the injured—despite his wounds, one young man, flanked pietà-like by his mother and his wife or sweetheart, glanced up at the pretty blond photographer and managed a faint smile for her—but after what she'd seen at the morgue she seemed barely able to click her shutter.

Later she encountered a Danish reporter she knew from Madrid, Ole Vinding, the son of *Politiken*'s Andreas Vinding. The younger Vinding, whom the other journalists rather meanly referred to as the "Trembling Dane," had been traumatized in Madrid, first by seeing a child killed in a bombardment and then, when Kajsa Rothman took him to Chicote's to restore his morale with whiskey, by watching one soldier shoot another at point-blank range in a bar fight. Barea, as a fellow sufferer from combat nerves, had tried giving Vinding a pep talk; but finally he'd given up, and

Vinding had left Madrid, hitching a ride to Valencia with Virginia Cowles and Sidney Franklin. Now he was flying back to Paris, couldn't wait to get on the plane, actually; so Gerda gave her exposed film to him, and asked him to take it to Capa at the rue Froidevaux studio. She sent Capa a telegram: She wanted the Valencia and Córdoba photos she'd given to Vinding printed on ExtraDur Kodak photo paper, and would Capa please bring floodlights and reflectors for the movie camera when he came to Valencia? Also coffee and chocolate. Apparently the horrors she'd witnessed had only made her ready for more.

June 1937: New York

On the night of June 4, Carnegie Hall's pillared galleries were packed with 3,500 people—another 1,000 had been turned away at the door—for the opening of the second congress of the League of American Writers, an earnest politico-cultural powwow about "the writer and fascism" that had been transformed into a must-see event by its headline attraction, the screening of footage from Joris Ivens and Ernest Hemingway's new film, *The Spanish Earth*, and by a promised address from Hemingway himself.

Hemingway had returned from Spain on May 18; and when Pauline had received the wire announcing his arrival date she'd thrown an impromptu dinner party on the patio in Key West from which the last guest left at 4 a.m. "Now I am cold sober," she'd written to her husband the next day, "and missing you as much as ever." He'd gone directly from the French Line dock to Key West, and thence, in the *Pilar*, to Bimini (Pauline and the boys flew from Miami); and Pauline hoped he'd settle back into his old routines—writing, fishing in the Gulf Stream in the summer, hunting in Wyoming in the early fall, then home to Key West. "I am sick and tired of all this," she'd told him when he was in Spain; "I wish you were here sleeping in my bed and using my bathroom and drinking my whiskey." But Hemingway had other plans.

There was *The Spanish Earth*, for which Ivens had sent him a mission statement to edit; Hemingway cut it by half, although he kept its polemical tone: "We fight for the right to irrigate and cultivate this Spanish Earth which the nobles kept idle for their own amusement." As soon as they had a rough cut of the film Ivens would want him to come to New York and work on the voice-over script; certainly neither of them had any intention of letting Dos Passos reinvolve himself in it, despite MacLeish's rather timid request that they do so.

There was Martha, who had sailed from France on the *Lafayette* and announced bracingly to the reporters who met her at dockside on May 23, "The Loyalists will win in Spain simply because they have an apparently unlimited supply of guts." She'd seemingly waltzed from the pier straight to the publishing offices of William Morrow and Company, because on the basis of her month in Madrid she'd already negotiated a contract for a book on Spain, to be published in the fall, in which—said *The New York Times*—she'd use "the same technique" she'd employed in *The Trouble I've Seen* to "show what the millions of common men and women are thinking and doing in Spain." When not writing she'd been working with Ivens on the film in New York, and peppering Hemingway with anodyne notes, addressed to "Hemingstein" and signed "Gellhauser," that were designed to pass inspection if they fell into Pauline's hands.

And finally there was the congress of the League of American Writers, which he'd rashly agreed to address. An organization of left-leaning intellectuals whose members ranged from socially conscious liberals such as Archibald MacLeish, William Carlos Williams, and John Steinbeck to more committed leftists such as Josephine Herbst, Lillian Hellman, and even Earl Browder, the general secretary of the American Communist Party, the League was one of a number of Popular Front initiatives that sought to promote the cause of democracy against fascism. Its actual membership—you were supposed to actually be a writer to join—wasn't large, but its appeal was broad. And a speech about the situation in Spain at its opening session would bring the issue of Spanish self-determination the kind of visibility no money could buy. Hemingway hated public speaking—he'd choked up just reading to the gang at Shakespeare and Company—but he said he'd go.

New York was experiencing a day of premature summer heat when he landed at Newark Airport. For some reason he'd chosen to wear a tweed suit—perhaps to coordinate with Martha, whom he picked up on his way to the theater, and who was wrapped in her silver foxes—and as he stood in the wings the combination of the heavy fabric and whatever alcohol he'd consumed beforehand made him sweat heavily. Out in the audience and on the stage a throng of New York intellectuals waited, like seals at feeding time: Archie MacLeish, Gerald and Sara Murphy, the journalists John Gunther, Walter Duranty, Joseph North, and Vincent Sheean, the critics Van Wyck Brooks and Carl Van Doren, the playwrights and screenwriters Marc Connelly, Thornton Wilder, and Donald Ogden Stewart, the novelist Dawn Powell. John Dos Passos wasn't among them; nor was the former secretary of the League of American Writers, Liston Oak, who had resigned from the organization on his return from Spain.

The evening had opened with speeches by Earl Browder (brief, serious) and Donald Ogden Stewart (longer, funnier) about the role of writers in the struggle against fascism. Then Ivens stepped forward to introduce the clips from *The Spanish Earth.* "Maybe it is a little strange," he said, in his slightly awkward English, "to have at a writers' congress a moving picture, but . . . this picture is made on the same front where I think every honest author ought to be." The clips were run without sound, so as footage of the Morata air raid and shelling in University City flickered on the screen, Ivens kept up a running commentary—"At this point you would hear machine guns"—to fill in what was missing.

Shortly after 10 p.m. came the main event, when, as Dawn Powell somewhat acidly described it to Dos Passos later, "all the foreign correspondents marched on, each one with his private blonde, led by Ernest and Miss Gellhorn, who had been through hell in Spain and came shivering on in a silver fox cape chin-up." Hemingway's face was shining with sweat, his glasses were fogged, and he kept tugging at his tie as if it were choking him; but when Archie MacLeish, the master of ceremonies, introduced him, he bounded to the podium like a prizefighter. The hall thundered with applause. Without waiting for it to die down, Hemingway launched into his speech.

He began by framing what he said was "the writer's problem": "how to write truly and having found what is true, to project it in such a way that it becomes part of the experience of the person who reads it." This kind of writing, this kind of truth, was impossible under fascism, he said, because "fascism is a lie told by bullies. A writer who will not lie cannot live under fascism."

Part of what they were all fighting for in Spain was the truth, he said, and to do that, to "quell" the bullies, they had to "thrash . . . the bully of fascism." And by God, they were doing it. "In this war, since the middle of

November," Hemingway said, in the cadences of a politician or a revival preacher, the fascists "have been beaten at the Parque del Oeste, they have been beaten at the Pardo, they have been beaten at Carabanchel, they have been beaten at Jarama, they have been beaten at Brihuega, and at Córdoba, and they are being fought to a standstill at Bilbao." That most of these victories were in fact failures seemed not to occur to him, or at least not to trouble him. Because what he was here for, regardless of all the fine talk about truth, was to dare the writers sitting in Carnegie Hall to rally to his cause.

"It is very dangerous to write the truth in war," he warned, "and whether the truth is worth some risk to come by, the writers must decide for themselves. Certainly it is more comfortable to spend their time disputing learnedly on points of doctrine." Such ivory-tower esthetes, he sneered, could sit on the sidelines if they liked; "but there is now and there will be from now on for a long time, war for any writer who wants to study it . . . When men fight for the freedom of their country against a foreign invasion, and when those men are your friends . . . you learn, watching them live and fight and die, that there are worse things than war."

By the time Hemingway finished, the audience was on its feet in the stifling hall, whistling and stamping. One of those beating his hands together was Prudencio de Pereda, standing in a balcony to watch his hero "lap up the warm acceptance." It was, de Pereda thought, "the speech of the meeting. The audience had come for Ernest; he was there for them." Instead of basking in the acclaim, however, Hemingway turned and dashed into the wings and then (noted Dawn Powell) "went over to the Stork Club followed by a pack of foxes."

The following afternoon Martha had her turn on the podium, at a closed session of the congress at the New School for Social Research, where she, too, played the truth card. "A writer must be a man of action now," she declared. "If you should survive such action, what you have to say about it afterwards is the truth, is necessary and real, it will last." She added, apparently without irony: "the writers who are now in Spain . . . were just brave, intelligent people doing an essential job in war . . . completely unaware of *themselves*."

After Martha's speech Hemingway flew back to Bimini; but he managed to find time beforehand to see Scott Fitzgerald, newly sober, who had just taken a job as a screenwriter for MGM and was making a stopover in

New York on his way to Los Angeles. "I wish we could meet more often," said the man who had introduced Hemingway to his publisher and suggested the ending for his most successful novel: "I don't feel I know you at all."

In truth, Fitzgerald's old friend was changing. Down at Cat Cay, where he planned to finish the promised draft of his new book, Hemingway had come to the conclusion that perhaps this new novel shouldn't appear on its own. Plaiting its disparate strands together had already been proving almost impossible, and now his other commitments would leave him little time to accomplish its ambitious design. What if he scaled it way back, to novella size almost, cutting out the Cuban revolution, most of the literary gossip, and some of the innuendos about real people that Arnold Gingrich had so many problems with? And what if he made this streamlined version the centerpiece of a collection? He'd include the two long stories "The Short Happy Life of Francis Macomber" and "The Snows of Kilimanjaro," his *New Masses* piece about the drowned veterans, excerpts from his NANA dispatches, the story "Horns of the Bull," about a poor Madrid waiter who dreams of being a matador, and the speech he had just given in Carnegie Hall. That's what the crowds that had cheered him were waiting for: a book that would speak to his position as a public intellectual, a man of action who knew there were worse things than war. In keeping with his new *engagé* persona, he could call it *The Various Arms,* or *Return to the Wars.* Or maybe *To Have and Have Not.*

Back in New York, Martha Gellhorn and Joris Ivens were busy. "I am now Joris's finger-woman and secretary," Martha wrote Hemingway in mid-June, appropriating gangster lingo (finger man) for someone who targets unreliables for mob hits. New footage had come from John Ferno, and Ivens was editing it; she, meanwhile, was trying to set up benefit showings of *The Spanish Earth* in New York and Hollywood and talking to RKO about distribution. She'd pulled the biggest string she had by going to lunch at the White House and asking Mrs. Roosevelt to invite her, Hemingway, and Ivens to screen *The Spanish Earth* for the president. And, the finger-woman added gleefully, "Joris has had a dandy meeting with our pals Archie and Dos and it must have been something. These Communists are sinister folk and very very canny. The upshot is that he

[Ivens] is President of the affair, and Dos has poison ivy." Or, as she put it in a cable confirming the news, "Rotfront [red front] working like mad."

MacLeish did indeed tell Hemingway that he'd been persuaded Ivens was the "real" president of Contemporary Historians, so he was ceding the group's leadership to him and resigning forthwith, taking the role of vice president instead. And Ivens, eager to press his advantage, asked Hemingway, as an influential board member, to "send back that sheet of paper about Cont. Historians, that you agree that I am the president." But this was one move that Hemingway, who had lent—not contributed—$1,000 of his own money to the organization and was eager to have it repaid promptly, seemed reluctant to make. Ivens's lack of legal and business experience might be a problem, he cabled MacLeish, not to mention his foreign citizenship, and it would be "unwise" for him to take over the running of an American charitable organization. Without Hemingway's support, Ivens's attempted *putsch* failed.

Undaunted by this, however, Ivens was working almost round the clock on *The Spanish Earth*. In a CBS screening room and sound studio at the Preview Theatre, in the Studebaker Building at the north end of Times Square, he and Helene Van Dongen were editing the film with the help of Martha and Prudencio de Pereda, who had volunteered to write a draft screenplay for nothing. Ivens and Van Dongen cut and spliced the footage shot in Spain into a rough narrative that set the viewer down into the Spanish landscape and then into the village of Fuentidueña, establishing the viewer's identification with its proud, tough, honest citizens. Only then was the war introduced, literally as a kind of distant thunder, a rumbling on the soundtrack, followed by voice-over: *The villagers say, "Our guns."*

Although there was considerable coverage of air raids and the fighting in University City, and the complicity of Italian and German troops in the Nationalist cause was acknowledged, the filmmakers portrayed the war less as a complex political, social, and military struggle than as an effort by the common folk to prevent the rebels from taking the road that ran through Fuentidueña from Valencia to Madrid. *Simplicity*, Ivens always said, *is what works*. So the bloody, weeks-long, deadlocked battle of the Jarama was condensed into a quick victorious fight for "the Arganda bridge," which seemingly concluded just as the villagers finished their irrigation project: the film's final moments would alternate footage of triumphant

Loyalist soldiers, waving their fists from trucks bearing them down the newly secured road, and images of water gushing forth into the parched Spanish earth—an image that had immediate and poignant resonance for an America still struggling with the devastation of the Dust Bowl.

The filmmakers used a variety of devices to make the war seem direct and simple. Maps of the conflict were repeatedly flashed on the screen, but they didn't show all of Spain, where the rebel zone now comprised two-thirds of the country—they focused only on the Loyalist-controlled area around Madrid, and Fuentidueña and Arganda were highlighted. To connect the conflict at the front with the village, a fictional letter from "Julián," the young *miliciano* from Fuentidueña whom Dos Passos had discovered, was shown onscreen right after footage of fighting at University City. *Dear Papa*, the letter read. *We're taking advantage of a few days of calm; soon I can spend a few days in the village. Tell Mama.* The same shot was repeated, a reel later, just before a scene in which a soldier returned to the bosom of his family in the village. They'd never been able to find "Julián" at the front, but it didn't matter: the made-up letter made it seem as if he'd been there, and was now coming home.

Actual chronology and context also didn't matter: film was cut and pasted into the narrative Ivens and Van Dongen wanted to tell, no matter when it was shot, who had shot it (some material came from preexisting documentaries by other filmmakers), or when the events it depicted had happened. Ivens and Ferno had got extraordinary footage during the bombing at Morata, the sniping at University City, and the fighting at the Jarama front, but not all the film had the same drama. Sometimes sound was needed to enhance it, or to make it "show" something other than what was actually on the film. Martha (as she wrote to Eleanor Roosevelt) helped the filmmakers produce the rattle of bullets with her fingernails on a screen, and the whine of incoming shells with "a football bladder and an air hose"; the roar of bombs was achieved with a recording of earthquake sounds from a film called *San Francisco*, which they ran backward. Once they'd recorded these sound effects, all they had to do was add a hailstorm of "machine-guns" to a shot of soldiers walking unmolested across a field, or the crash of "shells" and "bombs" to footage of tanks maneuvering on a hillside and presto!: you had soldiers and tanks under fire in the midst of battle.

While the filmmakers were busy with this work, bad news came from the actual war zone. On June 11, the Twelfth International Brigade's

General Lukács had been killed, and Gustav Regler almost fatally wounded, near Huesca, in Aragon, during a government offensive meant to draw Nationalist fire away from Bilbao; and the next day Werner Heilbrun, the Twelfth Brigade's medical officer, had been machine-gunned by a Nationalist plane near the Pyrenees. Although Ivens and Martha had both been pressuring Hemingway to come to New York and get busy on the text for the voice-over narration, he'd stayed in Bimini trying to keep Pauline happy, work on his novel, and fish; but now two men he admired were dead, and another was clinging to life in a Spanish hospital. *When men fight for the freedom of their country and those men are your friends . . .* On June 20, to Pauline's irritation, he flew from Bimini to New York and came straight to the editing room.

Prudencio de Pereda had already written a Hemingwayesque first draft of a considerable portion of the narration script, but Ivens was finding it too metaphorical; Hemingway himself went at it with a pencil and tightened and toughened it. Ivens still wasn't happy—"don't write about what you see, don't repeat the image," he said; and at first his editorial markings stung Hemingway's always touchy sense of *amour-propre*. "You Goddamned Dutchman," he shouted, "how dare you correct my text?" But he quickly climbed down and produced what was required. He had to—they were on an insanely tight deadline.

Archie MacLeish had arranged to have the narration recorded by Orson Welles, the *wunderkind* actor-director who'd just defied a government lockout to stage a production of Marc Blitzstein's Brechtian prolabor operetta, *The Cradle Will Rock*; but Hemingway wasn't thrilled by the idea, especially when the twenty-two-year-old Welles arrived at the screening room on June 22 with his own script suggestions. "You effeminate boys of the theatre, what do you know about real war?" Hemingway sneered. The six-foot, nearly 200-pound Welles rose to the bait: "Mister Hemingway, how strong you are and how big you are," he fluted sarcastically (and incongruously), all but flapping his wrists. Hemingway picked up a chair and swung it at him, and in a flash the two of them were squaring off before the screen. "It was something marvelous," Welles would remember later, his account possibly heightened by hindsight: "two guys like us in front of these images representing people in the act of struggling and dying . . . !" The confrontation ended with the two of them sharing a bottle of whiskey, and Welles recorded the voice-over.

June 1937: Segovia Front/Madrid

The Navacerrada Pass lies about 6,200 feet above sea level in the Sierra de Guadarrama, forty miles or so from Madrid, on the road to Segovia. It is high country, and even in June the air is cool during the long daytimes and cold at night. Although positions on the peaks give a clear view of the valley, the mountains are thickly forested with pines and holm oaks that provide excellent cover for your opponents, so it can be a difficult place to fight. But at the end of May, in an effort to pull the Nationalists away from the Bilbao front by making a drive on Segovia, government troops under the pseudonymous General Walter—the Pole Karol Swieczerski— were trying to do just that. On May 30 they had started an attack on La Granja de San Ildefonso, the old summer palace of the Spanish kings, in the valley on the other side of the pass; despite being mistakenly bombed by their own aircraft and ordered into battle without proper support, they'd still managed to get positions on the mountain called Cabeza Grande, over-looking the Segovia road, and now they were struggling to hold on to them. Which is where they were when Robert Capa and Gerda Taro ar-rived from Madrid to cover the offensive.

In the short layover he'd had in Paris after Bilbao, Capa had maneu-vered a significant career change. Fed up with *Ce Soir*'s assignments and restrictions, he'd gone after a much bigger prospect, Time Inc., the American-based media empire of Henry Luce, which had recently started a *Vu*-style large-format weekly called *Life,* as well as a series of newsreels, to be screened before the feature in movie theaters, under the title "The March of Time." These films—which always ended with the orotund voice-over pronouncement "Time marches on"—combined actual news footage with reenactments or dramatizations, sometimes using professional ac-tors rather than the real participants, in a process Luce himself called "fakery in allegiance to the truth." True or fake, the series had won an Academy Award earlier in the spring for having "revolutionized" the news-reel medium, while *Life* had surged from an opening circulation of 380,000 copies to more than a million. Clearly, Time Inc. was the place to be if you had ambitions in photojournalism. And Capa had persuaded Richard de Rochemont, Time Inc.'s man in Europe, to send him to Spain both to film footage for "The March of Time" and to take pictures for *Life.* He still had to give *Ce Soir* first look at his work for the French market, but what was that compared with the American audience these new arrangements would open for him?

Within days of getting his safe-conduct from the Spanish Embassy on May 26 he'd flown to meet Gerda in Valencia, and the two of them had gone on to Madrid, where Gerda used her connections to get them to the Segovia front. Polish by birth herself, she'd made friends with General Walter and his Polish adjutant, Alexander Szurek, the last time she'd been in Madrid; Walter in particular was charmed by her unexpected combination of youth, beauty, and bravery, and seemingly couldn't refuse her anything. It was easy for her to wangle an invitation for her and her "husband" (as Walter and Szurek considered them) to join the troops at Walter's headquarters.

The two photographers arrived as the men were making camp—lashing logs to the trees to make canopies, covering them with bracken for shelter and camouflage, building a cookfire to heat their rations—and Gerda photographed them while Capa circled around with Time Inc.'s Eyemo, trying to film the scene for "The March of Time." The general insisted that Capa and Gerda eat their meal with him, and demanded that a tablecloth be brought for his visitors even though they had no forks and knives, and had to pull apart the chicken they were eating with their fingers. After dinner Capa and Gerda handed out cigarettes, which were hard to get in Spain since tobacco imports to the country had been halted, and everybody lit up. A soldier wrapped in a blanket against the chill sadly cradled a puppy in his arms, one of the pets the men kept with them as mascots; the little dog had died, and the men dug a grave for it and hid the place with branches. Then they all curled up in their sleeping bags for the night.

The next morning, June 1, the rebel commander, José Varela, launched a counterattack against the government forces, seeking to dislodge them from the sierra and drive them back toward Madrid. The detachment Gerda and Capa were with broke camp and scrambled into position, seeking cover behind boulders and under thickets; the two photographers were close behind them, Gerda with the Leica and Capa with the Eyemo, both of them shooting as they ran through the woods, unable to take the time to focus. Enemy fire ricocheted off Gerda's camera: "better there than in my heart," she cracked, and hurried on. Soon the forest stillness was shattered by the rumble of tanks, the whine of bullets and artillery shells, and the roar of orderlies' motorcycles; and as Nationalist bombers and fighter planes screamed over the hillsides the Loyalist lines broke. In a matter of hours they were on the run, but not before an infuriated Walter—who suspected any laggards of being fifth columnists—ordered "the machine-gunning of all who pull back . . . and the beating of stragglers." Gerda and Capa, now shooting still photos with his Contax, were left to capture images of wounded men, bloody stretchers, and lifeless bodies left behind in the agony of retreat. By the next day it was clear that the offensive had failed; and the Nationalists resumed their assault on Bilbao.

Discouraged, their camera bags full of film bearing witness to chaos and defeat, Capa and Gerda fell back to Madrid. There the shelling was worse than ever, but what good did it do to photograph that? They'd already taken rolls and rolls of blasted buildings and weeping women, and after a while magazines and their readers are numbed to images of destruction. Instead they took pictures and shot footage of workers at a munitions factory, soldiers (many of whom were illiterate) being taught to read and write, *dinamiteros* lobbing grenades from slingshots at fascist street fighters in Carabanchel, defensive workers sandbagging the "French Bridge" across the Manzanares—which had inspired a verse of the antifascist song "Los Cuatros Generales"—and General Miaja strolling in the Alianza garden. Then came word of the offensive at Huesca, another effort to distract the rebels from Bilbao; and almost immediately afterward the report of Lukács's death and Regler's injury. Heartsick at the loss of their friends, Gerda and Capa packed up their gear and headed for Valencia, where Lukács would receive a state funeral on June 16.

A week later Bilbao fell to the rebels.

Barea heard the news about Bilbao from the correspondents at the press office, who'd been told by their home offices that the city had fallen; they'd been ordered to find out what people in Madrid were saying about it, but the censors wouldn't allow any reports about Bilbao to be transmitted. As frustrating as Barea found the situation, it wasn't his problem anymore—Ilsa and the blond Canadian censor, Pat, who had been sent from Valencia by Constancia de la Mora, were handling the day-to-day business of the press office, and Barea had been sidelined, in part by

Connie de la Mora's mistrust, in part by his own recent mental and physical fragility.

Some days previously, however, he'd discovered that no one was in charge of the government's short-wave station EAQ—*Who cares about foreign propaganda broadcasts*, the bureaucrats said, and refused to pay the broadcasters—and he'd seen an opportunity like the one he'd seized at the censorship in November. He'd persuaded General Miaja, who seemed more than usually distracted just now, to fund the station, and (since nobody else wanted to do it) to appoint him commissioner of broadcasting as well as chief radio censor. And now, when foreign correspondents were telling him news that his own government refused to release, he decided to use his new office for the purpose.

We can't continue to be silent about Bilbao, he told Miaja; silence will hurt us more than defeat. It was the same message he'd been repeating since the beginning of the war: they had to tell the truth. He begged Miaja to let him report the story on the radio that night; grudgingly, Miaja assented. And late that same night, identified by the announcer only as *La Voz Incógnita de Madrid* (The Unknown Voice of Madrid), Barea sat down in front of a microphone for the first time in his life and read what he'd written: an open letter to one of the British blockade-runners who had been keeping Bilbao alive for the past months, a man nicknamed "Potato" Jones (his real first name was David) because he hid guns in his cargo of potatoes. Despite such heroic efforts, Barea told Captain Jones, Bilbao had fallen to the rebels; and although Spaniards would never forget the city and what it had meant to them, there was no time to weep for their loss, for they had to fight on. The engineers and security guards were wiping away tears when he finished, and it was decided that Barea would keep broadcasting every night, still using the sobriquet of the Unknown Voice and speaking directly to listeners in Europe and the Americas about what was going on in Madrid.

As the shelling on the city intensified, the idea of the broadcast became a lifeline for Barea, a means of speaking out and a way to channel his fears. He didn't want to be like the Trembling Dane, Ole Vinding, whose paralysis had made him useless to himself and others; and he didn't want to play games like the German Communist journalist he knew as "George Gordon," a hard-liner from Otto Katz's Agence Espagne, who'd been complaining to his bosses in Valencia and Paris—and maybe

Moscow—about Barea's and Ilsa's lack of *political discipline.* Instead Barea went around the city, collecting the stories told by the many voices of Madrid: the telephone girl who didn't desert her post in the bombardments; the street cleaners on the Gran Via who mopped up the blood after the shelling stopped; his friend the saloon-keeper Serafín, who was sleeping in an improvised bed on the top shelf in a pawnbroker's cellar, and banged his head every time an explosion startled him from his slumbers, and every time he roused himself to go patrol his neighborhood. "His fear and his courage both gave him bruises," Barea wrote.

Listening to these voices, and trying to reproduce their rough street *argot* in his own telling, carried him out of himself. Now, night after night, he was driven through the empty, silent streets from the ministry to the broadcasting studio in the Calle de Alcalá; the upper floors were bombed out and empty but the transmission center had been relocated to a tiny dank room in the basement, next to an evil-smelling lavatory. There Barea sat in front of the microphone and read, in the accents of his native barrio, the stories of the Unknown Voice of Madrid; and there he and his station manager read his fan mail—for to Barea's and really everyone's surprise, the Unknown Voice had begun to attract a following, and that following wasn't limited to Spain, or even Europe. One letter came from a miner in the United States:

> When I was thirteen [the miner wrote] I went underground to dig coal in Peñarroya. Now I am sixty-three, and I am still digging coal in Pennsylvania. I am sorry I cannot write better, but the Marquis and the priest of our village did not grant us any schooling. I bless you who are fighting for a better life, and I curse those who do not want our people to rise.

June 1937: Córdoba Front

Valencia had given General Lukács a hero's farewell, with muffled drums, lowered bayonets, black-plumed horses, parading ranks of khaki-uniformed soldiers, and grim-faced onlookers giving clenched-fist salutes, and Capa and Gerda covered it exhaustively, from the flag-covered bier to the solemn procession. It must have been a relief to get out of the funereal city and into the rolling country north of Córdoba, where they had first come at the beginning of their Spanish adventures a year ago, and where the Chapaiev Battalion of the Thirteenth Brigade, with Gerda's friend Alfred Kantorowicz as political commissar, had been carrying on a long-running struggle with the Nationalists for control of the mining area around Peñarroya.

When Gerda had been there earlier in the spring, the Chapaiev soldiers had just managed to retake the abandoned villages of Los Blazquez and Valsequillo; but since then the Córdoba front had dropped out of the headlines, and the Chapaiev soldiers had begun thinking of themselves as "the forgotten brigade." Now Capa had come up with an idea that could cure that memory loss, and give him and Gerda a chance to shoot some film for "The March of Time": they would use the deserted villages as stage sets for a dramatic re-creation of the earlier fighting, which he would film and Gerda would photograph; the results could put Capa and Taro on front pages, and the Chapaiev Battalion back in the public eye.

When the two photographers arrived at the old farmhouse that served as battalion headquarters they found themselves instantly among friends— not just Kantorowicz but also Hans Schaul, a lawyer from Paris whom Capa had once instructed in how to use a camera. Schaul, Kantorowicz, and the battalion commander, Otto Brunner, brought out bottles of wine, plans were discussed, and Brunner insisted on sending a messenger immediately to outlying companies, telling them to be camera-ready by the following morning.

The men took the order seriously: at dawn they were lined up by the nearest well or fountain, scrubbing like mad, and—Kantorowicz would remember—"You never saw so many neatly shaved faces." It wasn't Capa they were trying to impress: it was Gerda, who was looking particularly fetching on this trip, with her cropped gold hair under a black beret, the sleeves of her *mono* rolled up, and a neat little revolver tucked into her belt. One of the soldiers, Hans Quaeck, did a drawing of her for the cover of the battalion newspaper—a svelte and seductive blond movie director, her hands in the pockets of her jumpsuit and surrounded by eager soldiers in various stages of their *toilette*, all under the caption "Warning! Filming in progress." (*Achtung! Aufnahme.*)

The filming was going to take place in a deserted hamlet called La

Granjuela, a collection of stone and stucco buildings surrounded by walled fields, that the battalion had successfully taken in the spring. Capa enthusiastically set up his forces: the soldiers, kitted out in helmets and rifles, were to storm supposed fascist positions in the village, while he filmed them and Gerda photographed. At his direction the men crouched in an overgrown field, burst out through the gate, and ran along the dirt road into the village, hurling grenades, firing their rifles, and shouting with blood lust as they came; then he made them repeat the whole thing. Finally Capa was satisfied with the result: "a *real* attack," he confided to Kantorowicz, "wouldn't have seemed as authentic as this." Henry Luce, the man who wanted *fakery in allegiance to the truth*, would have been proud of him.

While Capa was filming, Gerda had been photographing the same action with her Leica—the precisely choreographed running and shooting, the men's cigarette break; but the next day she wanted to get pictures of actual fighting, so she and Capa went to visit her compatriots in a company named after the Polish nationalist poet Adam Mickiewicz, which was dug in close to the Nationalist lines. They arrived at lunchtime, when the noontime cease-fire was in force, and she merrily joked with the soldiers in Polish while she and Capa worked. But soon enough the shooting started again, and Gerda wanted to rush out of cover to get better pictures of what was happening. Hunkering down in a dugout next to one of the infantrymen, she squinted across at the enemy positions as if judging whether to run toward them; the soldiers had to forcibly restrain her and Capa until sunset, when it was safe for them to go back to the crossroads where they'd left their car.

It wasn't all fighting on the Córdoba front, however. In the abandoned village of Valsequillo some Anarchist refugees from another part of the province had settled and—as Loyalist propaganda was urging them and others to do—planted grain for a "Sacred Harvest," the first since the collectivization of 1936, to help feed the defenders of the Republic. And for a short, blissful interlude, Capa and Gerda joined them. They spent the still, hot days filming and photographing the straw-hatted farmers, whose ranks had been swelled by wounded and recovering soldiers, as they drove long-eared mules to and fro in the golden fields, tossed pitchforks of hay into heaps, lofted shovelfuls of grain to separate the wheat and chaff. Gerda admired a litter of snuffling pink piglets; Capa let a little boy look through the viewfinder of his Eyemo. At night they tumbled exhausted into sleep.

Although Capa was leaving soon for Paris, while Gerda would stay behind in Spain to cover a writers' conference in Valencia, during this trip they had been as close as they ever had been. No more talk of being just *copains*; both Szurek and Kantorowicz had assumed from their manner that they were married, as Capa still hoped they might be. So perhaps it was in Valsequillo, not in Paris, or Madrid, that—waking early while Gerda still slept—Capa photographed her, lying on her side, her legs kicked free of the sheets and bent like a runner's, her cropped hair mussed from the pillow, her lips parted like a child's. She was wearing his too-big, rolled-up pajamas, and her face, artless and bare of makeup, was pure and beautiful.

As Capa's shutter clicked Gerda stirred slightly, nestled her head more deeply into the pillow, like a kitten; and he took one more picture. He would keep it with him to remember these good times, to remember her, while they were apart.

July 1937: New York/Washington/Los Angeles

Hemingway had been back in Bimini for hardly more than a week before coming north again, like a homing pigeon. Martha's string-pulling at the White House had had extraordinary results: an invitation to screen *The Spanish Earth* for the president and first lady after a small VIP dinner on July 8; and Hemingway wanted to see the finished version of the film—with all the added vocal tracks and sound effects, and the music, arranged by Virgil Thompson and Marc Blitzstein from Spanish recordings lent by Gerald Murphy—beforehand. He flew up from Bimini on the sixth, and two days later he, Ivens, and Martha went to Newark Airport to get a plane for Washington. As the three "trench buddies" (Martha's term) waited for their flight, he and Ivens watched in astonishment as Martha went to the airport buffet and ordered—and ate—three sandwiches. Dinner was bound to be inedible, she told them, between bites; she'd stayed at the White House before and she should know. As it turned out, she was right; it was "the worst I've ever eaten," Hemingway said—"rainwater soup followed by rubber squab, a nice wilted salad, and a cake some admirer had sent in."

The screening, for an audience of about thirty in the White House movie theater, pleased him better. Both Roosevelts seemed to feel that in some respects the film hadn't gone far *enough* in underlining the causes of the Spanish conflict: the president in particular wanted more emphasis on the fight to cultivate fields that had been forcibly left barren by the *latifundistas*. But although he was sympathetic to the aims and needs of the Republic, he told the filmmakers, he couldn't single-handedly lift the arms embargo enforced by the expanded Neutrality Act passed by Congress in May.

From Washington, Ivens and Hemingway went on to Hollywood, along with Pauline, who had flown up from Bimini for the occasion; Martha (whom Hemingway had described to his in-laws as "the girl who fixed it for Joris Ivens and I to go [to the White House]") tactfully stayed behind in New York, ostensibly to start work on her Spanish book for William Morrow. But she felt that what emerged from her typewriter was "lousier and lousier," and was discouraged when people told her that it sounded just like Hemingway; perhaps, she began to suspect, it was too soon, and she didn't have enough background, to write about *what the millions of common men and women are thinking and doing in Spain.*

Martha's "trench buddies," though, were having a triumph in Hollywood. Lillian Hellman had helped to arrange an A-list screening at the home of the actor Fredric March and his wife, Florence Eldridge, with herself, Robert Montgomery, Errol Flynn, Luise Rainer, Fritz Lang, Joan Bennett, Dorothy Parker, King Vidor, Dashiell Hammett, and others in attendance, at which the organizers raised funds enough to buy and equip seventeen ambulances for the Spanish government. (Flynn, afraid he would be asked for money, hid in the bathroom and escaped through an open window.) Joan Crawford (and her then-husband Franchot Tone), John Ford, and Darryl Zanuck also hosted private screenings, and there was a sold-out showing at the 3,500-seat Paramount Theatre, with speeches by both Hemingway—wearing a dark blue suit and an expression of extreme anxiety—and Ivens. Reaction to the film was almost overwhelmingly positive; the only thing wrong with it, some people said, was that Orson Welles's delivery of the narrative track was too mellifluous, too aristocratic-sounding, for the populist subject matter. There wasn't much time, and there was certainly no money, to pay for a substitute narration; so with some persuading from Ivens, Helen Van Dongen, Lillian Hellman, and others, Hemingway himself recorded a new track at Paramount's Hollywood recording room.

"THE PICTURE WAS BEYOND PRAISE AND SO WAS YOUR ATTITUDE," wired Scott Fitzgerald after the screening he saw, at which Hemingway had spoken about *la causa* and the loss of Lukács and Heilbrun. Fitzgerald sensed in his old and now distant friend an attachment to the film project, and to the war in Spain itself, that had "something almost religious about it." As so often, he saw Hemingway more clearly than Hemingway saw himself.

July 1937: Valencia/Madrid

On July 4, the second International Congress of Writers for the Defense of Culture—the first had been held in Paris two years previously—convened in Valencia's Ayuntamiento, the grand town hall on the Plaza de Emilio Castelar. Prime Minister Juan Negrín and Álvarez del Vayo, until recently the foreign minister, gave the welcome speeches, and among the delegates were André Malraux, Stephen Spender, Ilya Ehrenburg, José Bergamín, Anna Seghers, Malcolm Cowley, Pablo Neruda, Tristan Tzara, Alexis Tolstoi, and more—two hundred writers from twenty-six countries. (Ernest Hemingway cabled his regrets from New York, where he was completing work on *The Spanish Earth*; he planned to return to Spain in August and in the meantime sent "comradely greetings.") Some of the attendees, unable to meet the visa requirements of the non-intervention pact, had entered the country with forged passports or by smugglers' routes over the Pyrenees; but they had all come together to show their solidarity with the Spanish Republic, to speak out against fascism, and to discuss what the role of a writer should be in these dangerous and difficult times.

Some of them had another purpose, too, although this wasn't openly advertised: to blacklist André Gide for his "treacherous" book, *Retour de l'U.R.S.S.*, which had dared to point out that all wasn't perfect in the Workers' Paradise that was the Soviet Union, and to denounce "Trotskyism," or any deviation from Stalin's party line, at a time when some on the left were beginning to ask questions about the purges and show trials that had been taking place in Moscow, not to mention the liquidation of the POUM in Catalonia.

The keynote speech on this touchy question was given by Mikhail Koltsov, who'd returned from Russia, and his meetings with Stalin, in June, and now denounced Gide's book as "a filthy slander." He went further:

> There are some people who are wondering why we, the Soviet Union, support the vigorous and pitiless measures of our government against traitors, spies, and enemies of the people . . . why we do not interfere and simply keep quiet about it, not drawing attention to it in the pages of our publications. No, colleagues and comrades, for us this is a matter of honor. The honor of the Soviet writer consists precisely in being at the forefront of the battle against treachery . . . We support our government because . . . its hand does not shake when punishing the enemy.

Robert Capa and Gerda Taro, just arrived in Valencia from Valsequillo, circled the hall of the Ayuntamiento with their cameras in hand, Gerda svelte and cool in an embroidered cream blouse and skirt, Capa darker than ever from the Andalusian sun, his hair long again. During a break in the proceedings they struck up a conversation with Elena Garro, the novelist wife of the Mexican writer Octavio Paz, who was entranced equally by Gerda's musical voice and Capa's black hair and violet eyes. There were more famous people at the conference, but Capa and Taro were the ones she would remember later—"wrapped in the tragic, romantic aura of adventurers who were young, beautiful, and very much in love."

Capa left that afternoon for Paris to sell their pictures of the opening ceremony, as well as those from Segovia and Córdoba, and to take the "March of Time" film to Richard de Rochemont; Gerda was staying behind to cover the conference for *Ce Soir*. As he left Capa told Ted Allan, who had come to Valencia on one of his frequent errands, "I leave Gerda in your charge, Teddie. Take good care of her." He must have noticed that a number of the conference delegates, from the Prussian journalist Bodo Uhse to the French writers Claude Aveline and André Chamson, were already giving her the eye. And Gerda was never one to discourage a little masculine attention.

The conference moved *en masse* to Madrid on July 5—stopping en route, to the discomfiture of some of the conferees, to be fêted and fed in an impoverished village that could ill afford such generosity; in Madrid they were welcomed with a banquet featuring flamenco singers and a recitation by Rafael Alberti of a ballad he'd composed about Franco. The evening broke up when the Nationalists on Garabitas started firing shells over the city and most of the delegates scurried for cover to their hotel. André Chamson, in fact, was so alarmed that he wanted to leave Madrid directly, saying that if he were killed by a bombardment France would have no choice but to declare war on Franco at once. "I am the only one here who *feels* all this!" he proclaimed histrionically.

He was persuaded to stay, however, and the next morning the conference went on as scheduled. The proceedings had a more military tone than the session in Valencia, with a guard of honor stationed at the front of the hall, and a military band playing the "Internationale" and the jaunty Republican anthem, "The Hymn of Riego"—"Soldiers, our country calls us to fight: swear we will give her victory or death!" Unbeknownst to most of the attendees, however, a real military drama was about to take place not twenty miles away.

For days there had been rumors of a new offensive against the Nationalist forces along the Manzanares; trucks were moving troops north and west, and men and matériel were coming in daily from the coast. But though every journalist in the Gran Via basement suspected something was up, nothing could be written about, by order of Rubio Hidalgo and Constancia de la Mora, and suddenly no passes could be issued to sensitive areas to the west of the city. Then, on the morning of July 6, in an attempt to cut off the Nationalist salient protruding into Madrid's boundaries, government troops attacked the hamlet of Villanueva la Cañada and started moving on the nearby village of Brunete, accompanied by Loyalist bombers. The offensive met fierce resistance, however, and General Miaja gave orders to place artillery behind the infantrymen to *make* them go forward. That afternoon, as the congress delegates were just applauding yet another speech, three government soldiers—in an extraordinary piece of political theater—burst into the conference hall, still wearing their battle helmets. "The town of Brunete," they announced, "is now in our power." Then, like Roman centurions displaying an enemy's trophies, they held aloft two captured Nationalist battle flags on the points of their bayonets, and the crowd went wild.

To Gerda, who'd been snapping photographs in the front row, the appearance of the flags was like a signal. She *had* to get to the front, *had* to get pictures of the action while it was happening, before anyone else had them. Racing out of the auditorium with her colleague, *Ce Soir*'s Marc Ribécourt, and the film critic Léon Moussinac scrambling after her, she tried in vain to get passes and transportation from the censorship: but Barea and Ilsa had their orders from Valencia: *absolutely no journalists at the front.*

This didn't stop Gerda. She commandeered a car, told the chauffeur where to go, talked her way through roadblocks; she was, by now, a familiar figure to the *brigadistas*, who called her *la pequeña rubia*, the little blonde. Ribécourt and Moussinac could only follow where she led. Dodging tanks and trucks, they managed to get to Brunete itself, and Gerda, knowing it was important to document that the village had been won and she had been there to witness it, photographed three government soldiers in front of a doorway bearing an enameled plaque with the village's name on it. Another of her photographs showed a soldier painting over Falangist graffiti, replacing the beribboned bundle of arrows that was a Nationalist symbol with the hammer and sickle and the words *Viva Rusia*. What a message to send the world, one year into the war!

In the late afternoon they began to make their way back to Madrid along a road now lined with the dead and wounded. Toward sunset they came upon a column of French, Belgian, and Italian volunteers who invited them to share their rations, and—when it came time for them to drive on—serenaded them with the "Internationale." Gerda joined in, raising her voice in song and her clenched fist to the sky, *la causa*'s own Marianne. Moussinac, watching, found his eyes wet with tears.

Over the next two days—except for a junket to Guadalajara, where she photographed the culture defenders gawking at the battle site and touring ruined villages with the ever-present Hans Kahle—Gerda virtually ignored the congress. The real story, for her, was in the parched brown hills west of Madrid, where the Loyalist armies were trying to hold the ground they had gained and press forward; and to get to the front she hijacked congress cars and brought along any of her admirers who dared go with her, braving the heat and dust and danger—even briefly breaching enemy lines when one bewildered chauffeur didn't know where he was going and drove them into Nationalist territory. Gone were the high heels and the tailored skirt she'd worn in Valencia; she was in her combat uniform of khaki overalls and *alpargatas*, her cameras around her neck, dust in her hair. And she came back with pictures no one else had, pictures whose dynamism—learned perhaps in her film work over the past few months—set them apart from the elegant but sometimes stagy photographs she'd made up to now. On July 8, Jay Allen, Capa's Bilbao acquaintance who was now in Madrid, came into the basement canteen at the Gran Via and saw her sitting in the corner with Ribécourt, Georges Soria, and other French correspondents. *Look*, someone said with awe, *that's Gerda Taro*. Allen, a renowned journalist himself, was too shy to approach her. "She had become legend to me already" is how he put it.

July 9 was the last day of the Madrid portion of the congress, and the delegates were moving on to Barcelona; but Gerda didn't want to go with them. A year ago she might have been inspired by the speeches and by scenes like the presentation of the captured battle flags, but she'd gone beyond such pageantry now. She had seen too much death and destruction, felt too personally the stakes Spain was fighting for. She wired her editors at *Ce Soir* and asked to be taken off the conference coverage and assigned to Brunete instead. She was a war correspondent, and she needed to cover the *battle*—not (as Stephen Spender had described it) "a circus of intellectuals."

But the offensive stalled; the Loyalists needed to regroup, bring up supplies and reinforcements; and Gerda seized the opportunity to make a flying visit to Paris and celebrate July 14, Bastille Day, with Capa.

Barea and Ilsa weren't sorry to see the congress delegates go; *a lot of posturing intellectuals, using Madrid as a backdrop for arguments about the politics of André Gide*, Barea grumbled. They had enough to do dealing with the correspondents who wanted to send out real news, not just official bulletins about the fighting at Brunete, and were resorting to oddly worded "personal" telegrams about sick aunts and travel plans that were obviously coded reports of what they'd been able to find out. It was like the bad old days of November: Why couldn't the press cover the truth? Finally, Barea went directly to the war secretary, Indalecio Prieto, who had come to Madrid to be close to operations, and begged him to lift the prohibitions on journalists' copy. Grudgingly, Prieto agreed. But by then the Nationalists had brought up reinforcements and were fighting fiercely back, and caught in the middle of the field of fire, Brunete—where

Barea had spent his childhood summers in his aunt and uncle's big whitewashed house—was being pounded to ruins.

Every day the Messerschmitts and Chatos flew over Madrid on their way to drop bombs on the battlefield; the smoke and the dust clouds from the fighting could be seen in the city, and in his bunker in the Palacio de Santa Cruz, where the Foreign Ministry was, Barea could hear the din of battle, like summer thunder. Finally he could hold off no longer, and climbed the stairway to the westernmost of the Palacio's towers. In the distance, over the dun-colored *meseta*, hovered a dark, almost biblical cloud from which a column of smoke rose into the hot bright sky. In the magic lantern of his memory flashed images of Brunete, its pond and its dry plowed fields, and of himself as a boy, walking between his uncles down the hard, dusty street. His stomach turned and he tasted bile at the back of his throat. Brunete's unforgiving soil was where his roots were—"the roots of my blood and my rebellion," he would say—and the war was turning it into a wasteland.

That night, when the car had taken him to the broadcasting station on the Calle de Alcalá, he sat before the microphone to read what he had written about Brunete, and he wept.

July 1937: Paris

Coming out of the Gare d'Austerlitz into the cool gray evening drizzle, Gerda found that the copies of *Ce Soir* in the news kiosks around the Place Valhubert were full of her pictures of Brunete. *Ce Soir* had been featuring her all week, in fact: her very first Brunete photos on the eighth, as well as images from the Writers' Congress on the ninth and the eleventh. At the studio on the rue Froidevaux there was more good news: Capa's photograph of the falling militiaman had been reprinted as the sole accompaniment to an editorial in *Life* magazine marking the first anniversary of Franco's uprising: "DEATH IN SPAIN: THE CIVIL WAR HAS TAKEN 500,000 LIVES IN ONE YEAR"; her stills of the Granjuela reenactment would be in *Ce Soir* (presented as a real-life attack on an unnamed village), and *Regards*—which had already given her photos of the Valencia bombing victims a prominent spread—would be including her photos and Capa's in its own anniversary issue, due to appear on Bastille

Day. What a contrast to their situation a year ago! Then they had been poor and unknown, refugees ekeing out an existence on the margins; now they had become the person they had invented, the famous international photographer—no, *two* famous international photographers, each with a name to conjure with. Even Gerda's anxieties about her family appeared on their way to a solution: they had applied for clearance to emigrate from Yugoslavia, where they were living with her mother's parents, to Palestine.

As if all this good fortune weren't enough, Capa had had another of his ideas, this time about something even more ambitious than their original expedition to Spain. On July 7, just days ago, the Empire of Japan—an ally of Nazi Germany and Fascist Italy, hungry for territory and historically opposed to Russia—had declared war on China; this war was going to be a big story, he knew it, and no European or American journalists were on the spot yet. He'd had gone to see Richard de Rochemont of *Life* and had asked him to send the two of them to cover it. De Rochemont had promised him an answer soon. It would mean a long sea voyage to a place unlike any they'd ever been to; it would be just the two of them, far from home; but they would be working together, on *Life*'s masthead alongside Alfred Eisenstadt and Margaret Bourke-White; *Life* paid well, and their photographs would be seen by millions of readers. Would Gerda do it?

If Capa had worried about Gerda's diffidence, her self-protectiveness, her need to put personal and professional distance between them, he need not have. She couldn't *wait* to go. She just had to return to Spain to see the Loyalists win at Brunete and get those pictures; but she'd only stay ten days. Then she'd come straight back to Paris; by then Capa should have good news from *Life* and they'd start packing for China. She didn't promise more than that; and perhaps he was wise enough not to ask.

On July 14, Bastille Day, a crowd numbering in the hundreds of thousands marched through the streets of Paris, which were hung with tricolors and red bunting. Everywhere there were banners calling for aid to the Spanish republic, or dissolution of the fascist leagues; everybody sang the "Marseillaise" and the "Internationale." In the morning the gray skies had seemed to promise rain, but by evening the clouds were blowing away, and Capa and Gerda went dancing up in Montmartre, on the Place du Tertre, just beneath the white domes of Sacre-Coeur, with an acquaintance from Spain, a young American wire-service correspondent who had quit to join the International Brigades, and his Viennese girlfriend.

The four young people were gay: it had been an exhilarating after-noon, and Capa and Gerda, at least, had much to celebrate. They had money in their pockets, their work was everywhere, and they were on the brink of a great adventure on the other side of the world. At the back of all their minds was the possibility that there was danger ahead for each of them; but tonight there was music—"Parlez-moi d'amour" was big that year—and their bodies moving together as they danced, and the smell of the soft breeze, and the sky over Sacre-Coeur, pierced by a thousand stars.

July 1937: Valencia/Madrid

Constancia de la Mora was at the end of her rope: with the fighting at Bru-nete every correspondent in Spain wanted to get to Madrid, and she just didn't have enough cars and drivers and fuel to go around. So when Gerda Taro showed up, fresh from her holiday in Paris, and asked for transport to the combat zone, she couldn't help her. Maybe she snapped at the girl just a little—it was hot and the phone kept ringing and she was tired; but Gerda didn't pout, or leave the Propaganda Ministry in a huff. Instead she went out and bought Connie de la Mora a bunch of flowers, and left them on her desk with a polite little note, apologizing for giving her trouble when she was so busy. And she hitched a ride in another correspondent's car.

When she got to the Alianza in Madrid she learned that things weren't going well at Brunete. Stretched to their utmost in the attempt to advance against the Nationalists in the blistering July weather, the Republican forces were short of food, water, ammunition, bandages, stretcher bear-ers, ambulances, everything. The government's Chatos and Moscas had been outnumbered and outgunned by the Condor Legion's new Messer-schmitt bombers, and the bare baked earth of the Castilian plain offered the Loyalist forces no cover. Losses were mounting: 3,000 men had fallen between the tenth and the sixteenth, among them the hugely popular George Nathan, operations chief of the British and American Fifteenth Brigade. On the eighteenth, the anniversary of the outbreak of the war, the Nationalists launched a counteroffensive whose casualties included Virginia Woolf's nephew, the ambulance driver Julian Bell. Both sides seemed locked in a grim dance of death. At dinner with Claud Cockburn, who'd moved into the Alianza to be closer to her, Gerda remarked, "When you think of all the fine people we both know who have been killed even in this one offensive, you get an absurd feeling that somehow it's unfair still to be alive."

For the next few days she drove herself mercilessly, rising early and taking her cameras—her Leica and the "March of Time" Eyemo that Capa had given her—to the front. Once she had to lug the Eyemo eight miles in order to reach the sector where she thought she'd get the best footage, and she still wasn't satisfied. "Tomorrow I'll get up at six so I can get better shots," she sighed. Sometimes Cockburn went with her; sometimes Ted Allan did. Allan had resumed his puppylike attendance on her, had even brought her his short stories to read; and she'd been encouraging about them: *They're good, Teddie, very good.* He was, however, anxious about going with her to the front lines, although—or because—he'd promised Capa to take care of her. Maybe, he suggested, they shouldn't go too close to the action. "How do you want me to take pictures?" she asked, laughing. "Long distance?"

Through days of scorching heat, she photographed officers in the field and soldiers in the trenches—one of them a heartbreakingly young boy, too young to shave, in a too-large adult's uniform; she photographed the bombers in the sky and the shattering impact of their payloads, the smoke and flying clods of dirt. "In case we do somehow get out of this," she told Cockburn, who'd come along with her that day and was crouching beside her as she focused on the Messerschmitts above them, "we'll have something to show the Non-Intervention Committee." She photographed the wounded, even riding in the ambulance with them. She photographed the dead. The pictures had none of the careful structure and artful composition of her early work; they were jittery, sometimes out of focus or overexposed, but vital, immediate, even terrifying. One day she and Cockburn were visiting the British Battalion when enemy aircraft bombed the supply vehicles, and as Gerda rushed to the scene one of the trucks burst into flames. Black smoke filled her viewfinder. Soldiers ran, panic-stricken, to extinguish the fire; one of them was hit and fell to the ground. And Gerda stood in the middle of this apocalypse, clicking her shutter.

It was odd to come back from the inferno of Brunete every evening and sit in the garden of the Alianza, where Alberti wanted to talk about Faulkner's *As I Lay Dying* and everyone would listen to the news on the radio and then sing along with whatever popular songs were playing. Odder still to find Ted Allan waiting for her, hoping to romance her, as if this were Leipzig in 1933 and she were still the girl who just had to wiggle her little finger to have five or six guys running after her. Not that she didn't like the attention, and even enjoy teasing him a little: stripping to her lacy underthings in front of him after her day at the front, lying down on the bed beside him, touching him lightly and suggestively, then watching him—*like a fox that is going to play a trick on you*—to see how he reacted. But this was July 1937, and she had more important things to do than flirt with a lovesick twenty-one-year-old.

She did, however, want his company in the field, especially if she was taking two cameras with her. On Saturday, July 24, the rebels had smashed their way back into Brunete, only to be driven out of it again by nightfall in fierce house-to-house fighting. Journalists hadn't been permitted to go to the front to report on the battle, so it wasn't clear exactly what was happening; but any prohibition was just one more challenge to Gerda, and on Sunday she asked Allan to come with her to the front lines. Her ten days in Madrid were up, she said, and tomorrow she was leaving to join Capa in Paris; this would be her last chance to get photos and footage of what was already the biggest and costliest engagement of the war.

Allan met her outside the Alianza. She'd found a car, and a chauffeur who kept trying his American slang on them—"Okey-dokey," he would say, whenever Gerda gave him directions—and they drove north along the Paseo de Recoletos to the road for El Escorial, then turned south to Brunete. The sun made the car feel like an oven; to keep their minds off the heat Gerda suggested they sing.

When they reached the front Gerda managed to talk her way as far as General Walter's position before they had to stop. She got out of the car, sure of her welcome from the officer who had been so taken with her just a month ago in the Sierra; but the shaven-headed Walter was the opposite of welcoming. The line ahead of them had broken, he told them, and it was no longer safe where they were. "You must go away immediately," he said; and, turning to Allan, "Get her away from here." Gerda protested: it was her last day, she needed the pictures. *Please.* Walter lost his temper. "Go immediately," he ordered. "In five minutes there will be hell."

Allan wanted to leave, but Gerda refused to move. "*You* can go," she told him; "I'm staying." In the distance they could hear the low drone of approaching aircraft. There was no time to get out now. Gerda pulled Allan into a shallow foxhole on the hard, tawny-colored hillside and they tried to hide themselves in its insufficient cover as a formation of Condor

Legion bombers, pursued by a tiny cloud of Loyalist Chatos, flew over the field. Then bombs began falling all around them: the earth around their foxhole heaved, spewing clods and rocks everywhere; the roar of the explosions was deafening, the acrid smoke suffocating. Allan burrowed deeper into the dirt, but Gerda stayed standing up in the foxhole, filming the assault. When fighter planes followed the bombers, flying low so their gunners could strafe the field with automatic fire, Gerda switched to her Leica. By the time the artillery shells started, she'd finished the roll; pausing only long enough to put in fresh film, she kept on shooting.

The assault seemed to go on for hours until, unnerved by the unremitting barrage of bombs, guns, and shells, some of the infantrymen that had been dug in along the slope in front of them abandoned their trenches and began to run. Out in the open, they were easy prey for the enemy tailgunners, who blew them into the air like chaff. Other soldiers tried to stop them, with one officer threatening to shoot anyone who ran; at this Gerda leaped from the dugout to join him, calling on the retreating soldiers to halt and reform their lines. Faced with the apparition of *la pequeña rubia*, this slight blond girl with her camera around her neck and her khaki overalls streaked with dirt, they complied, and at the same time the bombers passed on, leaving the hillside eerily quiet.

Suddenly, like a child that has been too long without a nap, Gerda had had enough. She wanted to go. Their chauffeur had long since disappeared, so when Allan had climbed out of their foxhole they trudged on foot across the fields toward Villanueva de la Cañada and the road for Madrid. Villanueva was pandemonium: cars, trucks, transports, and soldiers on foot, going this way and that, some withdrawing from the front, others advancing to cover positions. On the road they saw a big black touring car, which Gerda recognized as belonging to General Walter. She flagged it down. The general wasn't in it; instead there were three wounded men in the backseat who were being taken to the hospital at El Escorial. After a brief conversation the chauffeur agreed to give her and Allan a lift as far as El Escorial; they could find a ride there back to Madrid. But they'd have to stand on the running board—there wasn't room inside the car.

Okey-dokey. Gerda tossed her cameras into the front seat next to the driver and she and Allan jumped on the running board and held on to the sides of the car, just like Bonnie Parker and Clyde Barrow making a getaway in the American newsreels. Gerda was tired but exhilarated: she'd got wonderful pictures, she said, and now they could go back to Madrid and drink the Champagne she'd bought for her farewell party.

Neither of them saw the tanks until it was too late. Fleeing from airborne machine-gun fire and careering along the road in the opposite direction, a convoy of Loyalist T-36s was bearing down on the touring car like a herd of clumsy prehistoric animals. The chauffeur swerved left, hoping to avoid a collision, but the first tank clipped the car and sent it rolling into a ditch. The next thing Allan knew, he was lying in the road, covered in blood, with no feeling in his legs. And Gerda was underneath the wreckage, her lower body crushed and her belly slit open by the tank's treads.

Someone managed to get her, and Allan, to the hospital at El Escorial, where she was given a transfusion, and a surgeon tried to repair what the tank had done to her. It was clear, however, that her case was next to hopeless. "Keep her comfortable," the doctor told her nurse, Irene Goldin— meaning, *Give her fluids and as much morphine as you can, because there's nothing else we can do.* Gerda was still conscious, and her only concern was for her cameras: "Did someone take care of my cameras?" she asked, before the blessed morphine dulled her pain. "Please take care of my cameras. They're brand new."

During the night, after the surgeons had set his broken femur and put it in a plaster cast, Allan kept asking to see her, but the nurse told him to wait until morning. Gerda needed to rest, she said. It was around 6:30 or 7:00 that the doctor came to his bedside with the news: Gerda had died a few minutes earlier.

July 1937: Paris

Richard de Rochemont's telephone call was everything Capa had been hoping for: *Life* was indeed going to send him, and Gerda, to China to cover the war with Japan. He was so excited by the offer that he wanted to book a plane ticket to fly to Spain right away and tell Gerda in person, but he was persuaded to wait and surprise her with the news when she got to Paris.

By evening on the twenty-sixth, though, she hadn't arrived, and she hadn't wired to say her plans had changed. Capa was concerned enough to put through a call to the Alianza in Madrid, but no one he talked to there seemed to know where she was.

The next morning he got up early and went to an appointment at the dentist. On the way he picked up a copy of *L'Humanité*. The front-page story was almost entirely devoted to war news—the Japanese had attacked Peking, and the rebels appeared to have retaken the town of Brunete. "The war photographer's most fervent wish is for unemployment," Capa would say later; but on this evidence it didn't look like he, or Gerda, was going to be out of work anytime soon. Sitting in the dentist's waiting room, he turned to the newspaper's third page, where the international news was. Air raids in China, the Non-Intervention Committee voicing platitudes in London, the British offering a partition plan for Palestine; in Spain, the Republicans trying to hold on at Brunete, the Cortes planning to convene a session in August, and so on and so on. Then, at the very end of the column, a subheading:

A FRENCH JOURNALIST,
MLLE. TAROT,
IS REPORTED TO HAVE BEEN KILLED IN THE
COURSE OF A BATTLE, NEAR BRUNETE

Maybe it was a mistake: the lines underneath said only that there were rumors of Mlle. Tarot's death on the twenty-sixth, but that they could not be confirmed. It was Louis Aragon—having spoken by telephone to Gerda's colleagues Georges Soria and Marc Ribécourt in Madrid—who had to tell him the terrible truth. When the reality sank in Capa collapsed in despair; nothing Aragon said could stop his tears.

His first, nearly obsessive thought was that he had to retrieve Gerda's body; but almost as soon as she died others were trying to lay claim to it for their own purposes. First Maria Teresa León and Rafael Alberti had taken it to the Alianza in Madrid, where her coffin was displayed, a stream of artists, journalists, politicians, and soldiers (including the divisional commander Enrique Líster) passing before it. Then it had been transported to Valencia, where Constancia de la Mora placed on the flag-draped bier the faded bouquet of flowers Gerda had brought her ten days earlier. And then Louis Aragon, saying that Gerda was "a daughter of Paris" who should be buried in that city, prevailed on the Spanish Republic to relinquish what was left of her. Although Gerda was not in fact a Party member, the French Communist Party bought a hundred-year lease on a burial plot near the wall commemorating the executed Communards of 1870 at Père-Lachaise cemetery, the resting place of Paris's *gratin intellectuel,* and started planning a funeral for her like that given to a head of state. And *Ce Soir* and other journals began a days-long barrage of tributes and reminiscences—illustrated sometimes with Gerda's photographs, sometimes with Capa's, but credited to her—by a Who's Who of antifascist intellectuals: Mikhail Koltsov, Claud Cockburn, André Chamson, José Bergamín, Gustavo Durán, and more.

Desperate to reclaim Gerda for himself, and hearing that Louis Aragon had arranged for Gerda's remains to be flown from Valencia to Toulouse, Capa insisted on traveling there immediately; and since he was in no state to make the trip by himself, Ruth Cerf, Gerda's old friend and flatmate, and the novelist Paul Nizan, who was *Ce Soir's* foreign affairs specialist, went with him. But when they got to Toulouse they discovered that international law forbade the air transport of the dead across an international border; so Capa had to return with Ruth to Paris, while Nizan met the casket, which had been driven to Port Bou, and accompanied it on the train northward.

When the locomotive pulled in to the echoing glass train shed of the Gare d'Austerlitz at 8:39 on the morning of July 30, a crowd of more than a hundred people was waiting outside the station, alerted by a notice of the arrival time in *Ce Soir.* Six uniformed employees of the Societé National des Chemins de Fer carried Gerda's coffin, still blanketed in the flowers placed on it in Valencia, onto the platform; waiting to receive it were Capa, Louis Aragon and his wife, Elsa Triolet, Capa's Japanese friend Seichi Inouye—and Gerda's father, Heinrich, and one of her brothers, who had managed to make the journey from Belgrade. They had never met Capa, and now, when they were introduced, Gerda's brother turned on him. It was Capa's fault Gerda was dead, he shouted; he'd introduced her to photography, taken her to Spain, and then he'd left her there to be killed. Wild with grief and anger, he punched Capa in the face. Capa, for whom Pohorylle's accusations were nothing he hadn't reproached himself with, was too numb to fight back, and Aragon, Elsa Triolet, and Inouye had to step between the two men. Heinrich Pohorylle, meanwhile, hardly noticed what was happening. Instead he wrapped himself in his *tallis*, approached the coffin, and standing before it began to recite the words of the mourner's kaddish: *May His great name be magnified and sanctified in the world that He created . . . May His kingdom come in your lives and in your days and in the lives of all the house of Israel, swiftly and soon . . . .* Hearing this prayer, in the Hebrew of his childhood, Capa broke down completely; and Aragon signaled to his wife and Inouye to take him home. For the next two days he remained in seclusion, refusing to eat or drink, only emerging, red-eyed, for the funeral two days later.

By then Gerda had become a symbol, a Joan of Arc of the left, an anti-fascist martyr, and enormous floral tributes from "young athletes" or "the seamstresses of Paris" banked her coffin at the PCF's black-draped Maison de la Culture in the rue d'Anjou, where an exhibition of her photographs—her first—included Capa's now eerily prescient portrait of her with her head resting on the stone marked *P.C.* There were still more flowers in the funeral procession, which set out for Père-Lachaise accompanied by an honor guard that included Pablo Neruda, Lucien Vogel, Tristan Tzara—founder of Dada, but also correspondent for *Ce Soir*—André Chamson, and the leaders of the Young Communist Women of France. Down the rue d'Anjou they went, past the Opéra, the offices of *Ce Soir* in the rue du Quatre-Septembre, the Bourse, the Place de la République, preceded by a band playing Chopin's funeral march and trailed by a crowd numbering in the tens of thousands; it took hours to reach their destination. Almost unnoticed amid the spectacle were Heinrich Pohorylle, accompanied by Ruth Cerf, and Capa, who wept uncontrollably and hid his face in Louis Aragon's shoulder whenever the cortège came to a stop. "He was just a great boy, crazy with courage and overflowing with life," Aragon said of the twenty-four-year-old Capa; "now war had murdered his youth."

At Père-Lachaise there were speeches and more speeches; finally the coffin was lowered into the grave. Afterward, Capa went back to the rue Froidevaux, barricaded himself in his studio, and proceeded to drink himself into oblivion. "Now Gerda is dead," he told his old friend Eva Besnyö, John Ferno's wife, "it is finished for me." It was Sunday, August 1, Gerda Taro's twenty-seventh birthday.

August 1937: Madrid/Valencia

With the coming of August the light and heat made Madrid close to un-
bearable. A strange lassitude had settled on the city in the aftermath of
Brunete. Although government communiqués and the news accounts of
the pro-Loyalist correspondents like Herbert Matthews tried to maintain
that the nineteen-days-long engagement had ended in a victory for the
Republic, the government had had 20,000 casualties (4,300 of them International Brigaders), lost a hundred aircraft, and—despite pushing a
dent into the rebel line—had failed in the attempt to encircle and cut off
the force threatening Madrid's western boundary. In fact, the only thing
preventing the Nationalists' general, Varela, from pushing forward and
taking Madrid itself was Franco's order to hold off until the war in the
north was won.

Relations between the press on the one hand and Ilsa and Barea on
the other seemed to fray in the August sun. The journalists blamed them
for the restrictions imposed by Valencia, and—ironically—complained
about them to the press office there; even more ironically, the Valencia
office, encouraged by the insinuations of the oily Agence Espagne agent
"George Gordon," took the complaints as evidence that Barea and Ilsa
weren't up to their jobs. Barea especially came under suspicion: his divorce from Aurelia was in its final stages, and suddenly people who hardly
knew him were raising their eyebrows at his wanting to put aside his
Spanish wife to marry a foreign woman. It was all of a piece with the rest
of his peculiar recent behavior, they said—his nerves, his short temper,
the problems in the censorship.

Barea was almost past caring about any of it, but for Ilsa's sake he tried
to pull himself together. And then Constancia de la Mora came to Madrid on a formal tour of inspection.

Tall, full-figured, with strong black brows over deep-set eyes and a
flashing smile, Constancia de la Mora y Maura was, like Barea, Madrid-
born; but there the resemblance ended. The granddaughter of a renowned
prime minister, Antonio Maura, and daughter of the managing director of
one of Madrid's electrical companies, she had been educated by govern-
esses and at St. Mary's Convent in Cambridge, England, not at the Escuela
Pía; while Barea was chasing rats through the attics in Lavapiés or swimming naked in the Manzanares, she was promenading with her nursemaid

on the Castellana, where—she recalled—"no middle-class child ever walked." And when she spoke to Barea he was uncomfortably aware of the gulf between them. "She grated on me," he said, "as I must have grated on her."

It wasn't just their class difference that made relations difficult: Constancia was used to running things and it nettled her to have a satellite press office making its own rules, lobbying government ministers directly for exceptions to policy, giving journalists so much leeway, when *she* should be in charge. "She does things *this* way," the war minister, Indalecio Prieto, said, emphatically thrusting his arm from side to side: "Bah, bah, bah." And he added, "She is a Maura"—referring to her wealthy, well-connected family—"and she is brusque." She was also, as a recent convert to communism, a zealot to whom Barea's socialist agnosticism—and worse, Ilsa's connection to the Social Democrats—was deeply suspicious. Her commitment to the Party, and to control of the press, had recently got her in trouble: In June, in an effort to depoliticize the armed forces, Prieto had ordered all political commissars to stop recruiting members for the Communist Party, and his decree had been published in all the Spanish papers. Constancia, however, had forbidden foreign journalists to mention it: "I had to suppress it," she said; "it would have created a bad impression." Furious, Prieto had demanded her resignation—who was she working for anyway, Spain or Stalin?—but a number of correspondents, including Louis Fischer, Herbert Matthews, and Ernest Hemingway, petitioned to have her reinstated. And here she was, in Madrid, in Rubio's empty office, now used only for ceremonial occasions, sizing up her subordinates.

They sat across the desk from each other: Constancia sleek and perfectly groomed, Barea and Ilsa threadbare and anxious. Like the well-brought-up woman she was, Constancia tried to put them at their ease. Such hard work they'd been doing! And for such a long time, too. Surely they deserved a little holiday. Things were slow now in Madrid, they could go away for a while and let others take care of things. Yes?

Exhausted as much emotionally as physically, Barea wanted to agree with her, to believe in her; it was Ilsa who was skeptical. We're dinosaurs, she told Barea later, when they were alone—our way of doing things, our independence, they don't want them anymore. They think we're dangerous, you because you don't think like they do, and me because I'm a foreigner. They want us out of here.

Nonsense, Barea reassured her. Constancia might be a hard-liner but she was a woman of honor, and they could trust her. They would take their vacation. After all, they had been at their posts since November. They'd drive to Valencia, where Barea could see to the last details in his divorce proceedings; after that they'd go to Altea, on the Costa Blanca, and rest. And then they'd come back and pick up where they left off.

Valencia was muggy, but it was cool and dark in the café near their hotel; Barea could barely make out the features of the big man sitting with Ilsa at the table in the back. He'd just come from seeing his children and signing divorce papers at the local magistrate's, and he wasn't in the mood to socialize with strangers; however, when he got closer he recognized the policeman who'd arrested Ilsa when they had last been in Valencia, in January. His stomach gave a sudden lurch. But the big man signaled to him to sit down—this was a friendly visit.

It was not, however, a welcome one. The big man had friends in high places, and they'd let him know that Barea and Ilsa were being investigated. People had said things about them—Ilsa, in particular, was being spoken of as a possible Trotskyite, which these days was a dangerous thing to be—and they might not be allowed to return to Madrid. In his opinion, they should just get out of town. Now.

Barea and Ilsa looked at each other. What could they do? They couldn't fight an enemy they couldn't name, or deny charges that hadn't been made. Stopping only to leave word with friends who might do something if they never made it to their destination, they took the car Miaja had given them and went to Altea. They spent a week, two weeks, in a tiny whitewashed inn by the sea, where they ate fresh-caught fish and slept through cool nights disturbed only by the susurration of the waves. And then came the letter from Rubio Hidalgo, registered: Barea and Ilsa were being granted indefinite leave, effective immediately; when (if?) they returned to work, it would be in Valencia, not Madrid. As for the car they'd taken to get to Altea, that belonged to the government and had been taken without a permit; it was to be returned to Valencia at once. Beneath the formal, neutral words, there was a vague sense of threat.

In response, Barea fired off his own letter: he and Ilsa refused to be put on leave, and instead were resigning from their censorship posts. They were returning to Madrid, to report to General Miaja. And they were taking the car—which Miaja, not the Foreign Ministry, had given them—with them. It was a challenge, Barea knew it; but he knew also that it was time, finally, to make some kind of stand against the reflexive, truth-smothering conformity that more and more seemed official policy. What he couldn't know was where that challenge would lead.

August 1937: New York

On the afternoon of August 11 Ernest Hemingway paid a visit to Maxwell Perkins's office in the Scribner building on Fifth Avenue. After dithering about the form his Harry Morgan book should take, he'd finally decided *not* to make it part of an omnibus, but to publish it—with the cuts he'd proposed in June—as a stand-alone novel; and Perkins, not waiting for him to change his mind again, had rushed the manuscript of what was now officially called *To Have and Have Not* to the printer in July. The galleys had been corrected and the book was scheduled for publication in October, but there were still a few details that needed tending to; surely Max wouldn't mind his dropping in unannounced to take care of them.

It was a hot day, and the fans were stirring the heavy air without making it seem any cooler. As Hemingway walked through Perkins's door, Perkins rose from his desk chair, a slight frown of anxiety on his face. "Here's a friend of yours, Max," Hemingway heard him say. He realized that there was already someone else in Perkins's office, and that that person was Max Eastman.

Eastman had indeed been a friend of his, once: a Greenwich Village radical, comrade of John Reed, and editor of *New Masses*, he had tried to help the ten-years-younger Hemingway get published when he was still unknown. But then he'd written that review in *The New Republic* of Hemingway's bullfighting book, headlined "Bull in the Afternoon"—the one in which he referred to the Hemingway prose style as "wearing false hair on the chest"—and recently he'd been associating with none other than that renegade Communist Leon Trotsky, translating him and acting as his unofficial agent. So Hemingway was *not* pleased to see him.

But he smiled—just a little too broadly—and shook hands; and Perkins settled down in his chair again, relieved. At which point, still wearing that dangerous ear-to-ear grin, Hemingway started to unbutton his shirt. There was his suntanned barrel chest, covered with a thick mat of black hair. *Look at this, Max—does this look like false hair to you?* Eastman laughed nervously. Still showing his teeth, Hemingway asked Eastman to open *his* shirt; which Eastman did, revealing a chest as hairless and smooth as a baby's bottom. Now it was Perkins's turn to laugh. Would he be next? Suddenly the hot blood rushed into Hemingway's face and he started shouting. "What do you mean," he bellowed at Eastman, "accusing me of impotence?"

With Perkins looking on helplessly, Eastman gestured toward a book lying open on Perkins's desk, which happened to be a collection of his essays in which "Bull in the Afternoon" was reprinted. Why didn't Hemingway read what he'd actually *said*—he'd see there was nothing about impotence in it. Hemingway snatched the volume up and flipped angrily through its pages until he found the passage he wanted, then read it, grunting like a bull. Finally he whirled around and slapped Eastman across the face with the open book. That did it. Eastman launched himself out of his chair and grappled with the younger man, and the two of them fell heavily to the floor; Perkins, terrified that Hemingway would hurt his opponent, raced around his desk to pull them apart. But it was Eastman on top, not Hemingway, and when Perkins dragged Eastman off him the younger man burst out laughing. *Just kidding!*

Three days later, surrounded by reporters and photographers, Hemingway stood on the French Line pier at Forty-eighth Street, waiting to board the S.S. *Champlain*, bound for Le Havre and Paris. He was on his way to Spain with a new contract from NANA, which wanted "straight, unbiased, colorful reporting"—and, John Wheeler had reminded him at a bon voyage lunch at the Stork Club, *exclusives*—and he was also going to write for the glossy new current-events magazine, *Ken*, that *Esquire*'s publisher David Smart had started. Even without those assignments, however, he couldn't stay away from the war, much as Pauline entreated him to. "I promised them I would be back," he told his mother-in-law, and through her, the wife he had once sworn to love and cherish till death did them part: "and while we cannot keep all our promises I do not see how not to keep that one."

The reporters clustered around him on the pier, however, weren't interested in what he had promised to whom, or why he was going to Spain.

All they wanted to talk about was his tussle with Eastman in Perkins's office, which had already made all the gossip columns. Hemingway obligingly gave them a recap: Eastman, he said, "jumped at me like a woman, clawing . . . with his open hands. I just held him off. I didn't want to hurt him. He's ten years older than I am." At which point he bounded up the gangplank to the ship.

"He is living in a world so entirely his own," wrote Scott Fitzgerald to Max Perkins when he heard of the Eastman episode, "that it is impossible to help him, even if I felt close to him at the moment, which I don't."

September 1937: Paris

The other promise Hemingway had to keep, one he certainly did not mention to his mother-in-law or to Pauline, was to Martha—with whom his feelings about Spain were inextricably tangled. It was with her, maybe even because of her, that he had gone there; it was, to a considerable degree, to be with her that he wanted to return. Throughout the past month, since they had parted after the White House screening, they had been trying "steadily and in vain to be discreet," communicating by carefully phrased letters and stolen, secret telephone calls; and the day after Hemingway's departure she, too, sailed for Le Havre, on the *Normandie*.

If she'd been hoping for a solitary and low-profile crossing, Martha was disappointed: for also on board the luxurious liner were Lillian Hellman and Dorothy Parker and Parker's husband, the actor and screenwriter Alan Campbell, all of whom were connected both to Hemingway and to *The Spanish Earth*. Hellman wasn't in good spirits. Recently reunited with her on-again, off-again lover, the alcoholic novelist Dashiell Hammett, she'd been overjoyed to find herself pregnant until she'd come home one evening from the Hollywood studio she was working in to discover Hammett in bed with a starlet. Now she was on her way to Europe, ostensibly to attend a theater festival in Moscow, but possibly also to get an abortion where they were easier to come by than in the United States. Dottie Parker and Alan Campbell had a more cheerful mission: they were headed for the International Exposition in Paris, and were delighted to think they'd be able to meet up with Hemingway and other old friends while they were there.

From the start, Martha didn't like Hellman—didn't like her flat, lidless-seeming eyes, her thin upper lip, or her bad teeth, didn't like her "expression of polite spite." Really, thought Martha, Hellman shouldn't "hate all women simply because one man left her." Hellman didn't seem much taken with Martha, either. She commented acidly on the amount of time the younger woman spent in the *Normandie's* lavishly appointed gymnasium—perhaps she was beginning her "basic training" for life with Hemingway? But Dottie Parker admired Martha's "looks and her spirit and her courage and her decency" and despite Hellman's digs asked the younger woman to drinks in First Class. Martha reported to her mother that Parker was "nice."

The *Normandie* docked at Le Havre on August 23 and Martha left for a few days of sea and sun in Le Lavandou, on the Côte d'Azur, where she and Bertrand used to spend their holidays; on her return to Paris she lay low. Too many of Hemingway's—and Pauline's—friends were there, including Gerald and Sara Murphy, who had been spending the summer in Europe trying to recover from the loss of their son Patrick earlier that year. Hemingway had drinks or dinner with them, and the Campbells, and Hellman at the Meurice, at the Deux Magots, at the Closerie des Lilas, and Sara Murphy fussed over him as she might have done over her dead sons, offering to store luggage he didn't want to take to Spain with him, and arranging for mammoth food packages to be sent to him in care of the press office in Valencia.

Hemingway fled from the warm embrace of his and Pauline's friends with the alacrity of "a horse that has escaped from a burning stable," observed Martha, to rejoin her and Herbert Matthews, who was preparing to return to Spain himself after a four-week holiday. Sitting at a café table with them in the late-summer sun, Hemingway was dismayed by the news he found in the newspapers—not just *The New York Times* but even the dull, responsible *Le Temps*. A map in the *Times* told the story: the rebels had by now occupied an enormous mushroom-shaped swath of territory, from the south coast through the mining districts of Peñarroya to the coal-rich industrial north, and with the exception of a tiny Loyalist enclave around Gijón on the Bay of Biscay the government was being squeezed into an ever-smaller triangle whose points were Barcelona in the north, Madrid in the west, and Almería in the south. After Brunete, the Nationalists had turned their undiminished attention to the northern front, taking Santander and drawing ever closer to Gijón. The Loyalist forces there, advised by General Gorev, seemed to have little hope of holding out against the onslaught; but the government wanted to divert the rebels, and score a decisive victory, by moving against Saragossa, to the east in Aragon, which had been in Nationalist hands since the beginning of the war the previous summer. On August 24, with troops under the commanders Líster, Kléber, Modesto, and Walter, the offensive had begun; but now, like the action at Brunete, it appeared to have run out of steam. And the Loyalist armies, fighting in appalling heat in which the stench of rotting corpses forced anyone who had a gas mask to wear it, were reported to have been surrounded by the rebels and decimated.

Hemingway, Martha, and Matthews were shaken. It wasn't just that, as Martha said, "your friends got killed"; it was that with each Loyalist defeat the legend of Nationalist invincibility, even inevitability, grew. Even more dismaying, much of what newspaper readers saw was being written by pro-Nationalist journalists (like the *Times*'s William P. Carney) whose stories were essentially transcriptions of rebel communiqués, sent from the safe vantage point of Hendaye or Biarritz, over the border in France. This wasn't news, they all agreed—and Hemingway went further. It was "criminal lying." If stories like that made Franco and his generals seem on their way to certain victory, why would anyone in Washington or London or New York or Paris support the government? Yes, it looked as if the north was lost, but what about the rest of the country? Over the coffee and croissants Hemingway mapped out an itinerary for himself, Martha, and Matthews. They'd investigate fronts in Aragon and around the two places where the next offensives seemed likely—Teruel and the Castilian plateau. And with luck they'd be able to show their readers that as "precarious" as things were in the north, in Asturias, the government's position elsewhere was, as Hemingway put it, "strong" and "solid."

On the morning of September 6, *Le Matin* carried, on the front page, the story of a grisly murder: a man's body had been found, his chest riddled with machine-gun bullets and his temple pierced with some kind of projectile, by the side of the road bordering Lac Léman, near Lausanne, in Switzerland. Papers on the body indicated that the dead man was a Czech, a salesman named Eberhardt; he carried a wallet full of French and Swiss francs that also held an unused railway ticket from Lausanne to Paris; and clutched in his now stiffened fingers was a lock of someone's— presumably his assailant's—hair. The police had no further clues, but they were presuming from the victim's nationality that the crime might be an act of "political vengeance."

Reading *Le Matin* with his morning coffee, Walter Krivitsky, the GRU's northern European *rezident*, or chief—normally stationed in the Hague, but currently sojourning in Paris—noticed a particularly alarming detail. He recognized the murdered man's surname as one of the aliases of Ignaz Reiss, the GRU's man in Belgium, one of his subordinates, with whom he'd discussed their shared disillusionment with Stalin's search for "traitors" within the ranks of government. And he knew that Reiss had recently been recalled to Moscow, but instead of obeying the summons had fled to Switzerland, where he was planning to defect—something Krivitsky was also contemplating. The NKVD's Mobile Group, which included Liston Oak's nemesis, the ubiquitous George Mink, had been too quick for him. Now Krivitsky had to wonder how long it would be before they came after *him*. He didn't have long to wait: within days he, too, received orders to return to Moscow.

But Krivitsky was luckier, and perhaps more skillful than his late friend Reiss in avoiding the long reach of the Mobile Group. He made good his own escape, and soon was telling the French Sûreté, and later Britain's MI5, most of what he knew. And one of the things he knew—and the NKVD knew that he knew—was that Generalissimo Francisco Franco's inner circle had been breached by a Soviet agent: a British journalist, masquerading as a fascist sympathizer, who was a former associate of Ilse Kulcsar's in her Viennese cell, the Spark. His name was Kim Philby.

September 1937: Madrid

Barea and Ilsa felt very small as they drove over the flat plain of La Mancha in their borrowed official car: on either side stretched endless rolling fields scored with grapevines, the ripened fruit powdered with white dust, and above them soared the infinite blue sky. They felt even smaller when they arrived in Madrid to discover that they had indeed been pushed to the margins of the world they had known. The chief of the foreign press censorship was now a young woman named Rosario, who'd been recommended for the post by Maria Teresa Léon; and General Miaja, though still a military commander, had been replaced as an administrator by a new civil governor. Barea was still radio censor and commissioner of the EAQ radio station—that is, unless and until the new civil governor decided he wanted someone else in the job—and Ilsa was his deputy, in charge of transmissions in languages Barea didn't know; but they had to move their few possessions out of the Gran Via and into another hotel, the Reina Victoria, a turreted building on the Plaza Santa Ana south of the Puerta del Sol. They were allowed to keep the car, and Hilario the driver—they would need them for late-night journeys to the broadcasting station. And because no one could find an office for them to use for their radio censorship work, they had to camp out—to the girl Rosario's irritated discomfort—in an empty room at the Foreign Ministry.

This situation bore awkward fruit: because they were *there*, in the building, just down the hall from where they'd been before, the foreign journalists continued to ask them for advice, or dropped by to gossip with them. Trying to be helpful—or maybe trying to force the issue—Rosario invited Barea to a banquet given by the civil governor; surely he could talk to his new superior, play the good civil servant, make the case for separate quarters for the radio censors, which would get them out of the Foreign Ministry for good. But Barea was in no mood to play the courtier. All the benefits of his holiday had vanished with the sound of the first shells over Madrid, leaving him shaky and nauseated. The day before the banquet he'd gone to the front at Carabanchel, where soldiers were dug into the same stinking rat-infested trenches they'd been in for a year, ever since he and Ilsa and their comrades had insisted on staying at their posts to defend the city and what it stood for. And now, as he and Ilsa entered the room, full of well-groomed bureaucrats, newly arrived from Valencia to get things back on a *professional* footing, he felt the old rage rise within him. He tossed off two glasses of wine, then confronted the civil governor. *There are people—kind, ignorant people, who think this war is being fought for them, for their happiness, their future. Do you care about them? Do you care about the soldiers in those trenches? Or do you just care about the well-fed, the well-behaved, the complacent—the people who won't rock the boat?* Even Ilsa's agonized expression couldn't make him stop.

It was as if he were daring the government, Negrín's new, regulated government—which the new premier had once described as "a dictatorship under democratic rules"—to regulate *him* out of existence. At first it seemed as if he wasn't important enough for them to worry about. He was allowed to go on broadcasting, and the Unknown Voice spoke about those stinking trenches, and the rough, irreverent Madrileños who somehow made a life amid the shattered stones of their city. He spoke about these things in the unbeautiful *argot* of Lavapiés, with the directness, the immediacy, of one of Robert Capa's photographs; and hundreds of letters poured in from listeners all over the world who had been touched, and sometimes shocked, by what he said. He even wrote a story, about a *miliciano* who makes a pet of the fly who buzzes around in his trench, which Tom Delmer helped to get published in London's *Daily Express*.

But then came the hints: regrets from friends that Barea and Ilsa hadn't joined the PCE, that they weren't card-carrying civil servants; warnings that something dangerous might be brewing. Former associates crossed the street to avoid speaking to them. Soon there were more than hints: the German Communist George Gordon told Barea his days at the radio were probably numbered, and claimed to the other journalists that Ilsa was being investigated as a Trotskyist. *Better steer clear of her.* A friend in the Assault Guards sent Barea and Ilsa a message: the SIM, the new secret police force modeled on the NKVD, was interested in Ilsa, and might want to interrogate her. The friend offered her a bodyguard, one of his own officers—he'd watch her and make sure no one tried to pull her into one of the black SIM cars and take her away.

Barea went to Miaja, who told him his troubles would be over if he got rid of Ilsa; he went to Antonio Mije, who'd got him his censorship job in the first place and was now very high in the PCE organization. Mije repeated what Miaja had said, and went further: why had Barea gone overboard and asked for a divorce? Why couldn't he just sleep with the foreign woman? She would bring him nothing but trouble. She was definitely some kind of Trotskyist but was too smart to have been caught at it—so far. Barea should save his own neck and get rid of her. Barea stared at him in astonishment. Was this the Party's position? he asked; but Mije denied it. Just his own opinion, he said. Barea told him to go to hell.

Back at the Hotel Reina Victoria, in the long afternoons, Ilsa sat at the piano in the dining room and played Schubert *lieder* for the waiters and Barea, singing in her husky contralto the songs of her Viennese girlhood. It was eerily appropriate music for the situation they found themselves in—a situation straight out of one of the Goethe poems Schubert had set:

Wer reitet so spät durch Nacht und Wind?
Es ist der Vater mit seinem Kind;
Er hat den Knaben wohl in dem Arm,
Er faßt ihn sicher, er hält ihn warm.

"Mein Sohn, was birgst du so bang dein Gesicht?" –
"Siehst, Vater, du den Erlkönig nicht?
Den Erlenkönig mit Kron und Schweif?" –
"Mein Sohn, es ist ein Nebelstreif."

Who's riding so late, in the night and the wind?
It's the father with his child.
He has the boy in the crook of his arm,
He holds him safe, he keeps him warm.

"My son, why are you hiding your face so fearfully?"
"Father, don't you see the Elf-King,
The king of the elves, with his crown and his tail?"
"My son, it's only a wisp of fog."

Perhaps the hints and rumors that bedeviled them were only a wisp of fog. But in Schubert's song the danger was real, and at its end the boy was dead.

September 1937: Aragon/Valencia/Teruel Front

Flying down from Barcelona to Valencia on September 6, Hemingway, Matthews, and Martha Gellhorn looked out the window of the plane and saw, in the blue Mediterranean, the black stain of a spreading oil slick where a blockading Italian submarine had sunk the British tanker *Woodford*—sailing under the Spanish flag—four days earlier. It was the kind of thing that made Martha (as she wrote to Eleanor Roosevelt) "sick with anger . . . against two men whom I firmly believe to be dangerous criminals, Hitler and Mussolini, and against the international diplomacy which humbly begs for the 'continued cooperation' of the Fascists." In Valencia, however, the traveling companions had good news: the Loyalist forces in Aragon had *not* been surrounded and defeated, as *The New York Times*'s William Carney had claimed; they had actually advanced, taking two villages, Quinto and Codo, and the fortified town of Belchite, although they hadn't managed to win the prize of Saragossa. And a parallel initiative in the mountains of the Sierra Palomera, in southern Aragon west of Teruel, had put government troops in position over the highway that led to Saragossa from Madrid. That they might have done even more if the Russian tank commander at Belchite hadn't insisted on giving orders to his Spanish troops in Russian, or if the Anarchist CNT *milicianos* hadn't been denied proper weapons by the Communists, who were determined to be the lead players in the war effort, wasn't mentioned.

Leaving Valencia almost as soon as they arrived, Hemingway, Matthews, and Martha managed to get to Belchite three days after the surrender to find it little more than a smashed, smoking ruin, uninhabitable and deserted except for the stinking bodies of humans and animals that littered its ruined streets. About three miles outside what was left of the walls, camped in a streambed only slightly sheltered from the windblown yellow dust of Aragon, they came upon some old friends: soldiers of the Fifteenth Brigade, along with their chief of staff, the former Lincoln Battalion commander Robert Merriman, who had recovered from the wounds that had taken him out of action at Jarama. Tall, unshaven, with dust on his glasses and in his dark hair, he managed to look like the college professor he once had been as he diagrammed the battle with a stick on the dirt floor of his lean-to, showing the correspondents how he'd led his men through heavy house-to-house fighting to take Belchite's domed sandstone cathedral. Both Martha and Hemingway were impressed, as much by Merriman's quiet strength as by the victory. And Martha felt "proud as a goat," she said, at the performance of the American *brigadistas*: "you can tell a brigade is fine," she boasted, "when they move it from front to front, fast, to wherever the danger is."

But the International Brigades, and the ragtag *milicianos* who had volunteered to defend the Republic in 1936, weren't what the higher-ups at the Propaganda Ministry wanted to feature now. The big story, the story Hemingway and Matthews were encouraged to focus on, was the new, reorganized, Communist-dominated Army of the Levante; and on their return from Belchite, Constancia de la Mora's office was only too happy to arrange a three-day tour of that army's positions around Teruel for them.

There wouldn't be any inns to stay in, or even troop billets, because soldiers were occupying every bed; they'd have to bring their own food and provide for their own lodging for the two nights they would be on the road. They got hold of an open truck, equipped it with mattresses and blankets for sleeping, and packed enough food for the three of them and their drivers—Sara Murphy had sent lots of tinned salmon, not to mention ham, *poulet roti en gelée*, bouillon, coffee, and malted milk powder. They planned to park the truck under the overhanging roofs of farm courtyards for shelter, and cook their meals over villagers' open fires.

They were still in Valencia, waiting for their safe-conducts to come through, when Hemingway got a call from Alexander Orlov, the NKVD's Spanish station chief, who ran the government's guerrilla warfare program from his headquarters at the Hotel Metropole on Calle Xátiva, just opposite the bullring. Ever since the previous spring, when Hemingway had met the guerrilla fighter Colonel Xanthé with Orlov at Gaylord's Hotel in Madrid, he'd wanted to find out more about the *aktivi*, irregulars who worked behind the enemy lines, blowing up bridges and trains and carrying out other kinds of dangerous clandestine work; but despite his renown, he hadn't then passed the tests that would make him *de confianza*, trustworthy. Now, though, he had made *The Spanish Earth* with Ivens, spoken out for the Republic at Carnegie Hall, raised thousands of dollars for ambulances; and he'd shown himself to have none of the skepticism, or apostasy, of a Dos Passos or an Orwell. From the rehabilitation hospital where he was recovering, Gustav Regler had begged Orlov to give Hemingway the access he craved. And now Orlov was inviting him to visit the training camp for *aktivi* at Benimamet, just outside Valencia.

At Benimamet Hemingway was met by Orlov's lieutenant, Leonid Eitingon, who went by the name of Kotov. Three years later Kotov would direct the assassination of Leon Trotsky, in exile in Mexico; but today he was all welcoming smiles. He took Hemingway around the camp, gave him a lavish lunch, even allowed him to shoot target practice with one of the Russian-made Nagant sniper rifles the guerrillas were being equipped with, and sent him off with a bottle of rare Baczewski vodka, distilled from potatoes instead of grain. Everything was calculated to appeal to Hemingway's love of being on the inside track, of knowing and having things that others don't, and that he could never, ever talk about. Nor *did*

Hemingway speak of his visit to Benimamet. But a few days later it would have an interesting sequel.

Hemingway, Matthews, and Martha set off from Valencia early on the morning of September 20, driving up the coast and inland to Sagunto, with its Roman walls that Hannibal had breached, before beginning the long climb through the Sierra Calderona. Coastal plain gave way to rolling pastures punctuated with pine and scrub, and the air grew noticeably cooler. They stopped at Segorbe to buy vegetables in the farmers' market, loaded them in the truck, and kept driving, up and over the pass at Puerto Ragudo to Barracas, where they stopped for lunch. At Sarrión they turned north into the jagged limestone outcrops of the Sierra de Gúdar, where the tallest peaks were already streaked with white, and began a circuit of the high country that lay just to the east of the provincial capital of Teruel, passing stone villages that clung to the sides of the mountains. The roads here were rough, but they made good time: the late-model Dodge Hemingway had been given by the Propaganda Ministry was up to the job, built—and geared—like a bulldozer, and it was only midafternoon when they reached Mezquita de Jarque, a tiny village where the 1st Battalion of the newly formed Army of the Levante was encamped. Along the way they'd picked up the divisional commander, Colonel Juan Hernández Saravia, and now they paused long enough for him to review the battalion; then, following the route that Saravia's troops had taken just weeks before, they pressed on to Alfambra, on the heights above Teruel.

Alfambra was the headquarters of a band of guerrillas commanded by a Pole named Antoni Chrost, whose job—one of whose jobs—was to blow up trains, such as the one that ran from Calatayud, north of Teruel, to Saragossa. And many years after the fighting in Spain was over, Chrost would remember coming in to his headquarters one afternoon and finding a stranger sitting at the table, chatting with one of the other officers. "*Me cago en la leche de la madre que te parió* [I shit in the milk of the mother who bore you]," Chrost overheard him saying. Who was this self-confident foreigner? Chrost wondered; introducing himself, he asked for the man's documents ("revolutionary vigilance required it"). The stranger's safe-conduct bore the name "Ernesto Hemingway."

As Chrost would remember it, Hemingway was both fascinated by and knowledgeable about the activities of the guerrillas: he knew what weapons they used and how they used them, but he wanted to find out how they got to their targets (using relay teams of local guides, Chrost told him) and what happened when they got there. And Chrost, though initially cautious, was happy to tell him, in great detail. Later he would also swear that Hemingway not only questioned him but also ate and drank with him, talked about women with him, even went on a mission with him some days afterward. These romantic details never made it into Martha's diary, nor into Hemingway's dispatches. Did Chrost make them up? Was a purely speculative conversation—*What would you do if you had to blow up that section of railway track?*—transformed into reality? Did Hemingway even meet the guerrilla commander? Certainly he *was* in Alfambra on the afternoon of September 20; Martha, always careful about such details in her personal journals, noted it in her diary. That much, at least, was true, even if he and Chrost didn't meet, even if he never promised (as Chrost recalled it) to write about the guerrilla captain, even if he didn't say, when Chrost told him he was a Pole and not a Russian: "In my book, you'll be an American."

The correspondents spent their first night on the road back in Barracas—an unlovely town whose name means "The Shacks"—and early the next morning set out for a lookout post over Teruel, which the rebels had been occupying since the beginning of the war. Teruel was an unlikely target for an offensive: the mountain-rimmed capital of a poor province, it had no mineral or agricultural wealth and no important industry. But, located at the apex of a salient driven deep into government territory, it provided a perch from which the Nationalists could pounce down on Valencia and cut the Republican zone in two. On a map, it looked like a threat, and Hemingway wanted to check it out.

Leaving their cars, the scouting party walked uphill to a dugout and crawled the last few yards on their hands and knees over the straw on its earthen floor until they could peer in safety at Teruel, perched on its rock in the valley below them. The early morning sunlight slanted across the sugar-beet fields, picking out the five brick Mudéjar towers rising from the city walls and throwing into strong relief the prow-shaped mass of the Mansueto, a rock formation enhanced with Nationalist fortifications that dominated the approaches to the town like a natural bulwark. "You see it?" their guide asked, meaning the Mansueto. "That's why we haven't taken Teruel."

It didn't help, he added contemptuously, that the Anarchists who used to patrol this sector thought that contact with the enemy was playing football with them. As Martha peered down through the field glasses and saw "a few soldiers, very leisurely, loading up their donkeys with blankets from the empty houses, for the winter," Hemingway scanned the scene, noting the tactical problems it presented. Yes, it was impossible to take Teruel from any direction but the northwest, but once winter filled the mountain passes behind the town with snow, that wouldn't matter. The rebels would be stuck up here. They wouldn't try anything. The Teruel front would be out of bounds until the spring.

The journey after Teruel was rougher, through wild upland where villages were few and far between, and small and primitive when they found them; the roads were rougher, too, some of them newly cut by the army, in places where no roads had been before—indication, if you were looking for it, that the government had plans for this part of the world. The journalists spent the night parked in a farmer's courtyard in a tiny hamlet called Salvacañete, in Cuenca province, where the braying of the donkeys woke them at dawn; the next day, abandoning the car and truck, they got a cavalry escort and went on horseback up to mountain positions on Monte San Lazaro before coming down toward Cuenca, in a steep ravine between two rivers, the Júcar and Huécar. Hot and dusty from the ride, Hemingway went swimming in one of the streams that fed the Júcar, near rebel lines; there were fat trout in the clear, cold water, and Hemingway threw them grasshoppers, the bait Nick Adams had used in his story "Big Two-Hearted River," watching as they lunged for the insects and made deep swirls in the current. It was, he thought, "a river worth fighting for."

That night he and Martha slept in Madrid, at the Hotel Florida.

September 1937: New York

In the lounge of the Bedford Hotel, a modest establishment on East Fortieth Street in Manhattan, a reporter from the *New York World-Telegram* took out his pad and pencil and prepared to interview Robert Capa.

Capa had had a harrowing few months. After the macabre carnival of Gerda's funeral he'd begun drinking heavily and talking wildly: what had happened to Gerda was all his fault, he should have stayed with her, he didn't deserve to live and without her he didn't want to. One day he disappeared—stopped answering his telephone or his doorbell—and his friends were afraid he'd killed himself; but he had only left Paris, where Gerda's ghost haunted every street corner and café, and taken refuge with old Berlin comrades in Amsterdam.

When he felt stable enough he'd ventured back to Paris, planning to stay a short while and then sail to New York to see his mother and Kornel, who had finally emigrated in June; but sometime in August he had an unexpected visitor: Ted Allan, patched up by the doctors in Madrid, standing on his threshold in dark glasses and on crutches. He'd been released from duty in Spain and had come to Paris to see Capa, to tell him he had tried to take care of Gerda, that he wasn't to blame for her death; but Capa seemed not to pay any attention to his protestations—only took his hand and asked about his leg. Allan didn't want to let the subject of Gerda alone. "Don't you realize I loved her?" he asked, to which Capa replied, "So what? How could you help it?" It was just as well he didn't know what Allan had thought when the doctor brought him the news that Gerda was dead: *Capa won't get her now.*

Capa insisted that Allan stay with him; the Canadian was, after all, one of his only remaining contacts with Gerda, one of the last people to see her alive. And when Capa was getting ready to leave for New York, Allan impulsively decided to come with him; the two of them sailed on the *Lafayette* on August 20. It turned out to be a good arrangement. *Capa couldn't say shit or sheets in English*—what Allan had observed when he first met him was still true, and this way Allan could be his interpreter. When the man from the *Telegram* showed up, therefore, it was Allan who played go-between.

Capa's photo of the falling militiaman, the one he'd taken at Espejo, had recently been republished in *Life*, splashed like an emblem across the editorial page to mark the anniversary of the war in Spain; and that was what the interviewer wanted to talk about with the "handsome" and "bashful" young Hungarian. Who was the soldier, and how had Capa managed to capture him just at the moment he fell? The reporter asked the questions in English, but Ted Allan translated them—into German, the reporter thought, though it could as easily have been French.

To answer, Capa would have to relive that hillside in Espejo: the men laughing and running, the hot sun in their faces, Gerda in the trench beside him, frowning into the viewfinder on her Rolleiflex. Remembering it would hurt. And what kind of a story would those memories make for this eager reporter, scribbling earnestly on his notepad? *My girlfriend and I were fooling around with the soldiers and they were shooting guns, and I asked one of the guys to pretend he got shot, and then he was, for real.*

He said something, in German—or French, it was all foreign to the reporter—to Allan, and Allan told the man from the *Telegram* that the picture had been taken when Capa and a soldier had been stranded, just the two of them, in a trench; and that after waiting an interminable time the *miliciano* had got up to make a run for it and was shot, with Capa "automatically" snapping his shutter to capture the image. "No tricks are necessary to take pictures in Spain," Capa said—or Allan *said* he said. "You don't have to pose your camera. The pictures are there and you just take them. The truth is the best picture, the best propaganda."

They spoke of other things as well: Capa's youth in Budapest; his coming of age on his own in Berlin; his arrival in Paris, where—he, or Allan, said—he had married Gerda Taro, who accompanied him to Spain. But then Capa excused himself, and after he left it was Allan who told the interviewer about Gerda's death, which he said happened while he and Capa were both riding in a car with her. It was "a thing Capa did not talk about," Allan murmured, sotto voce.

In the days after the *Telegram* interview, Capa took care of business. Unhappy with the efforts his previous agency had made to place his work in American periodicals, he negotiated a deal for U.S. representation with Léon Daniel of Pix, who wanted to sign Capa badly enough that he also agreed to hire Kornel (now going by the all-American name of Cornell) as a darkroom assistant. It was Daniel who did the translating when, later in the week, Capa met with the editors at *Life*, who offered him a contract that would pay him a regular advance against a guaranteed monthly minimum of pages in the magazine. It was a life-changing deal, the sort of thing he and Gerda could only dream of when they were making the rounds of Paris photo editors two short years ago. Now, whatever happened, Capa had an income to count on, and the backing of what was becoming one of the most powerful news media franchises in the world.

But he had something closer to his heart to accomplish in New York: to arrange for the publication of a book of his and Gerda's Spanish photographs—something that would give permanence to Gerda's work as well as his own, and be a kind of memorial to her. He persuaded the publisher Pascal (Pat) Covici, who had already made a name for himself by championing the writers Nathanael West and John Steinbeck, to take the book on at his imprint, Covici-Friede, and then enlisted his Bilbao acquaintance Jay Allen to write a brief introduction and translate the captions, and his onetime mentor André Kertesz, who had moved to New York, to do the layouts. Although both Gerda and Capa would be credited with the photographs, there was no distinction made between his pictures and Gerda's in the images he handed over to Kertesz, any more than there had been in those the pair of them had made in the early days in Spain and sent to Maria Eisner under the byline "Robert Capa." (In fact, it would later turn out that some of the photographs in the book were by neither of them, but had been taken by Chim.) When he'd signed the contract, selected the images, and written the captions, Capa went back, alone, to Paris.

The book would be published after the new year, under the title *Death in the Making*. On the dedication page was one of the pictures Capa had taken of Gerda—smiling, chic, and insouciant—hovering over her bouquet of *muguet* on their last May Day together; and underneath it was the legend: "For Gerda Taro, who spent one year at the Spanish front—and who stayed on."

October–November 1937: Madrid

They had patched up the shell holes at the Hotel Florida, refurbished the lobby, and Don Cristóbal had moved his reception desk from the front, where flying glass from broken windows might hit him when the hotel was shelled, to the back. But otherwise things were much the same. True, Herbert Matthews and Tom Delmer had moved out, to a penthouse apartment overlooking the Parque del Retiro, a more prudent distance from the guns on Garabitas—Delmer's quarters at the Florida had been destroyed during one of the attacks last spring, but fortunately he'd been on leave in London at the time. Incoming fire didn't deter Hemingway; the rooms he and Martha now checked in to, numbers 113 and 114, were at the corner of the hotel, in what he was convinced was a "dead angle" impervious to Nationalist shells. Besides, he joked, "you never hear the one that hits you."

The new, professional order—the "strict disciplinary basis" Hemingway had noticed, and praised, in the troops he'd just been visiting—was also evident at the Censura, where he and Martha discovered that Barea and Ilsa were no longer at their old posts. Stopping to talk to them despite their pariah status, Hemingway professed to be bewildered by the change. "I don't understand the whole thing," he told Barea, frowning, "but I'm very sorry. It seems a lousy mess."

The air had turned cool and crisp, with sun shining on the shattered buildings and barricaded streets; the shops, astonishingly, were full of clothes and pictures and antiques and cameras; and although food was scarce, beer hard to find, and imported hard liquor virtually unobtainable, the bars and restaurants were crowded. Hemingway and Martha made the circuit of their old haunts, eating at the Gran Via and drinking at Chicote's; afterward, in the evenings, the salon Hemingway had held in his room at the Florida the previous spring resumed. There were some new faces, among them Evan Shipman, who after delivering Hemingway's ambulances in April had enlisted in the International Brigades and was now recovering from war wounds; Alvah Bessie, another fighter from the Lincoln Battalion, who called Hemingway "the Great Adolescent" and Martha "his long-legged moll"; and Bessie's fellow Lincolns, Marty Hourihan, Freddy Keller, Phil Detro, and Milton Wolff. They and the old rotating cast of regulars—correspondents, army officers, Russian advisors—all drank Hemingway's whiskey and ate whatever was left of Sara Murphy's delicacies. When the shelling started they'd open the windows so the glass wouldn't shatter in the blast, and play Hemingway's Chopin records— the opus 33 mazurka, number 4, and the opus 47 A-flat minor ballade were favorites—at top volume on the Victrola to drown out the sound of the bombardment.

The gossip during these gatherings was that, as Hemingway repeated in his NANA dispatches, "sooner or later [Franco] must risk everything in a major offensive on the Castilian Plateau." To get a feel for the territory, Martha and Hemingway went to Brunete one day with Delmer and Matthews, driving in Delmer's Ford with American and British flags flying on its hood in a mistaken attempt to demonstrate neutrality—mistaken, because the Nationalists watching with binoculars mistook it for a high-ranking staff car and lobbed a few shells at the road. Hemingway was philosophical: "If they don't hit you, there's no story," he said afterward; "if they do, you won't have to write it." But the correspondents switched to a camouflaged military vehicle for their trip to the battlefield. All four of them gazed solemnly at the treeless fawn-colored plain; Hemingway analyzing the terrain, Martha noticing—in addition to the open field of fire with "no cover anywhere"—the ruined houses, one with an empty bird-cage hanging from what was left of a window, and a pink petticoat left to dry, forever, on the stone rim of a well. Like the ruined apartments on the Paseo Rosales, it was a place out of time; and Hemingway found himself thinking, "If Franco's going to take the offensive, let's have it soon and get it over with."

Certainly precious little was going on in Madrid. It was calm enough that Dorothy Parker, persuaded by journalist friends in Paris that as a good leftist she was *obligated* to make a pilgrimage to Spain, had showed up in Madrid with Alan Campbell and a lot of canned goods, as well as a shocking-pink hat that she wore even while eating lunch at the Hotel Reina Victoria, to the puzzlement of the dining-room staff. She and Martha renewed their acquaintance at dinner at Herbert Matthews's—Martha still thought she was nice—before she and her husband left for Valencia.

The lack of anything to report had left Hemingway and Martha enervated, sniping at each other for no good reason. Martha tried to turn an expedition to the Morata front into an outing, with lunch at an inn at Aranjuez for themselves, Matthews, and Delmer; Hemingway derided her plans, and then the action they'd all hoped to cover turned out to be a failure, which meant more recriminations, more quarreling. They went to the Censura, but the girl Rosario had no news for them, and Barea and Ilsa weren't supposed to talk to them—all very tedious, thought Martha. Nor was she pleased to encounter Lillian Hellman, who'd been talked into coming to Madrid by the ubiquitous propagandist Otto Katz. She'd just arrived and was planning to visit the usual war-tourist sites; tonight she would be giving a radio talk that would be broadcast in the United States by Columbia Broadcasting Service, and she'd come to the Censura to have her remarks cleared by the censor. Although Martha eyed her with distaste, Hemingway asked her to dinner that very evening at Delmer and Matthews's penthouse; he had got some beef from the bullring, he said, and she'd better come because she wouldn't see any more beef during her stay in Spain.

"Dinner," said Martha later, "was a meal like scratching your fingernail over the blackboard." Hellman arrived at the apartment bearing two cans of sardines and two cans of pâté as gifts, and proceeded to stare critically at Martha's "well-tailored pants and good boots." She wasn't impressed by

the "overknowing" Delmer, either, nor by the athletic beef, although she
seemed to find the wine tolerable; over dinner she quizzed Martha about
the series of lectures she was planning to give on her return from Spain,
and when Hemingway turned mocking about the project she egged him
on until he was telling Martha he thought she was "moneygrubbing" at
the Republic's expense. It was, Martha reflected, "the kind of show usually reserved for enemies."

Suddenly a bombardment started, and everyone rushed out onto the
terrace to watch the shells bursting over the Telefónica—all except Hellman, who sat on the sofa with her head down and her eyes shut in terror.
Then the phone rang: it was one of Barea's people at the radio station, calling to say that their building on the Gran Via had taken a hit and Hellman
should tell the station chauffeur, who was on his way to pick her up, that
the broadcast was canceled because the street wasn't safe. But when the
chauffeur arrived Hellman started going downstairs to get in the car anyway. Hemingway tried to stop her, but she insisted: it might be her only
chance. "So," Hellman would remember him saying, as he watched her
go, "you have *cojones* after all."

Martha and Hemingway left, too; walking angrily back to the Hotel
Florida "with plenty of street between us." The quarrel that had begun at
dinner continued in their room, and it got physical: at its climax Hemingway swung at her, but his hand caught the lamp on the bedside table and
it crashed to the floor and shattered. There was a pause in which they
looked at the lamp and each other, and then they started laughing. Afterward, on his way to bed to make love with Martha, Hemingway cut his
bare feet on the broken glass. But once again he was "Mr. Scrooby, as
friendly as a puppy and as warm as fur."

To Have and Have Not was published on October 15; and if Hemingway
still truly believed it was the triumphant achievement he had counted on,
he had to be disappointed. "It would be pleasant," wrote J. Donald Adams
on the second page of *The New York Times Book Review* the following
Sunday, to say that Hemingway "is a writer who has grown steadily in
stature as well as in reputation. But that, unfortunately, would not be the
truth. His skill has strengthened but his stature has shrunk . . . [His] record as a creative writer would be stronger if [this book] had never been

published." Other critics took up the theme: Hemingway was perhaps unrivaled as a prose stylist, but the novel suffered from structural problems, awkward transitions—the result of hasty cutting—unrealistic dialogue, two-dimensional characterization, moral ambiguity, and (said one of America's leading novelists, Sinclair Lewis) a combination of "puerile slaughter" with "senile weariness." Still others, however, praised what they saw as Hemingway's awakened social consciousness, even while they were unsure of his political savvy. And *Time*, extoling his new "maturity of outlook," gave him the big cover story he'd been longing for ever since he saw the one on Dos Passos—even though it hinted that his writing method was becoming dated.

Predictably, Hemingway was infuriated and hurt by the negative press, refused to be comforted by the positive, and cabled Max Perkins frequently for sales reports. Here, fortunately, there was good news: the critical controversy—along with Hemingway's heightened public profile and the fact that this was his first full-length work of fiction in eight years—meant that sales were brisk. At least he didn't have to worry about that. As for the critics, he would remember the names of the ones who had ganged up on him, he promised. Meanwhile he wanted to get to work on something else.

Not dispatches for NANA: there wasn't enough news for that. And not, after the hard birth and uncertain welcome of *To Have and Have Not*, a new novel, or even the long short story about Spain he'd fleetingly considered over the summer. Instead he'd begun to write a play—a play about war correspondents and soldiers in Madrid that could draw on the material that *hadn't* gone into NANA stories, the rich cache of characters, incident, and emotion that he had built up in his time in Spain. Its main character, Philip Rawlings, is a kind of idealized self-projection: a man as cynical as Jake Barnes, as sensitive as Frederic Henry, as tough as Harry Morgan; a man who, like Hemingway, enjoys raw onions and corned beef and Chopin records. A dedicated Communist who says, "My time is the Party's time," Rawlings uses his profession as a journalist as a cover for his real work as a counterspy for the Loyalists. Directed by his political commissar, Max, a man with teeth as bad as Koltsov's, and by the secret police chief, Antonio, whose dove-gray wardrobe might have been filched from Pepe Quintanilla's closet, Rawlings spends much of the play finding and questioning, and executing, suspected fifth columnists, committing what

W. H. Auden, in a poem he'd written after his trip to Spain the previous spring, called "the necessary murder." Rawlings believes that what he does is always justified. "Were there ever any mistakes?" he asks Antonio; but Hemingway knew the answer, which had already been spoken, at lunch with Virginia Cowles and Josie Herbst half a year before, by Pepe Quintanilla:

ANTONIO: Oh, yes. Certainly. Mistakes. Oh, yes. Mistakes. Yes.
     Yes. Very regrettable mistakes. A very few.
PHILIP: And how did the mistakes die?
ANTONIO: All very well.

In the play Rawlings and Max make a "mistake" of their own: the execution of a man who resists being brought to headquarters for questioning. "He would never have talked," says Max, by way of excuse; at which the man's comrade, whom they are about to interrogate, and who Rawlings believes is a weakling who *will* talk, cries accusingly, "You *murdered* him!" Perhaps John Dos Passos said the same thing when he learned what had happened to José Robles.

When he's not doing undercover work for the Republic, Rawlings is carrying on a love affair with a blond Vassar graduate named Dorothy Bridges, who writes—"quite well, too, when she's not too lazy," he says—for *Cosmopolitan* and other magazines; Rawlings tells Antonio that he would like to marry her "because she's got the longest, smoothest, straightest legs in the world." Although she has hung a sign on the door of her room at the Hotel Florida that says, "Working. Do Not Disturb," Dorothy actually doesn't seem to do much other than sleep, or buy silver fox furs that, Rawlings witheringly points out, cost the equivalent of four months' pay for a member of the International Brigades. ("I don't believe I know anyone who's been out four months without getting hit—or killed," he says.)

Lone wolf though Rawlings is, Dorothy is attracted to him: in her dreams they will "work hard and have a fine life," as well as two children who will roll hoops in the Jardin du Luxembourg. And he asks her "to marry me or stay with me all the time or go wherever I go, and be my girl." But their relationship founders: by the play's end Rawlings feels it truly is the "colossal mistake" he says it *will* be at the beginning. At one point Hemingway had wanted to blame its failure on Dorothy's desire for marriage: if she'd just been content with being a mistress, Rawlings could have gone happily home to his wife once the affair was out of his system. Perhaps this scenario seemed altogether too close to Hemingway's own triangulated situation for comfort, so he discarded it; instead, Rawlings concludes that Dorothy is a social parasite, a money-grubber, "uneducated," "useless," and "lazy"; she isn't pure enough for a dedicated warrior like himself, and sex, the only thing she has to offer him, is only "a commodity." In fact, the only things separating her from the *whores de combat*—one of whom says, pointing at the notice outside Dorothy's door, "I'll get me a sign like that too"—are her Vassar diploma and American passport. He breaks with her; and in parting she lands the one punch Hemingway allowed her: "Don't be kind," she admonishes him. "Only kind people should try being kind."

At the end of October, Hemingway wrote Pauline that he had finished the play, which he variously called *Working: Do Not Disturb* and *But Not for Love* (he would eventually settle on a more topical, less personal title: *The Fifth Column*), and he seemed confident enough in his achievement to talk it up among his circle in Madrid: Mikhail Koltsov mentioned it in his diary, although he was under the impression that it was a comedy. And Martha? She maintained to friends later that she thought Dorothy an affectionately parodic portrait of herself; but the play can't have made easy reading for her.

She was finding this autumn in Madrid difficult in many respects. She was working on a long story for *Collier's* about the American *brigadistas*, a story that began with her observations of Belchite and the Brunete battlefield, but that devolved into an elegiac meditation on "the handsome land" that was being punished by the war, and the young men, some from very far away, "who came all this distance, neither for glory nor money and perhaps to die." They "knew why they came," Martha concluded, "and what they thought about living and dying, both. But it is nothing you can ask about or talk about. It belongs to them."

She was proud of the article, which she sent to her mother in St. Louis to read, and *Collier's* liked it and wanted to publish it, the second piece of hers they'd taken; but she was suffering from "bad weather, bad tummy, cold feet and weltschmerz." During the bitter nights she lay awake, thinking about the boys she'd interviewed for the *Collier's* piece; after tossing and turning for an hour or so she'd take a sleeping pill at 4:30 and then couldn't rouse herself before lunchtime. Hemingway wasn't sympathetic: years afterward he would tell a friend that he hated to watch Martha when she was sleeping, because "no ambitious woman looks lovely when asleep." Looking out the window of her room at the Florida, Martha saw a girl in the gutted house across the street chopping up her furniture to use for firewood. It made her think of herself and Hemingway. "So now the long winter starts," Martha wrote in her journal: "So no doubt he and I will wear each other out, as millions have done so well before us, chipping a little each day, with just a little dig or a minor scratch, until it ends in fatigue and disgust, and years later we will be able to think of all this as a brief infatuation. Oh, God, either make it work or make it end now."

Although Herbert Matthews was reporting to *The New York Times* that the reorganized Loyalist army was becoming "stronger and stronger with the passing of time"—indeed, had to be considered "a powerful fighting force by any standard, especially if it came to a question of mere defensive warfare"—his confidence, and Hemingway's, wasn't completely shared by the Spanish government. Its former prime ministers, Azaña and Giral, and the current war minister, Prieto, were weary and pessimistic, afraid of what would happen if the Nationalists won the war, as it now appeared they might. (Prieto, in fact, had tried to resign, and had contemplated suicide, after the fall of Bilbao.) On October 21 the rebel army entered Gijón, completing the Nationalist conquest of the north, and initiating a bloody purge of thousands of government soldiers and sympathizers; days earlier, the Loyalist commanders and most of the Russian advisors had fled by plane, except for General Gorev, who had insisted on staying behind and who was now reported to be in hiding somewhere in the Asturian hills. What was next—Catalonia? Before that happened, wouldn't it be better to negotiate peace with the rebels now and protect those who had stuck by the Republic? The wavering Loyalist ministers couldn't know that Hitler had recently alarmed his inner circle by declaring, "We are most interested in the continuance of the war"—and that Spain's nominal supporter, Stalin, had just said much the same thing. Or that Franco, in a memorandum to the Italian ambassador, had committed himself to the painful ritual purification of what he considered a contaminated country:

> I will occupy Spain town by town, village by village . . . [T]his civil war could still last another year or two, perhaps three. Dear am-

bassador, I can assure you that I am not interested in territory, but in inhabitants. The reconquest of the territory is the means, the redemption of the inhabitants the end. I cannot shorten the war by even one day . . .

Prime Minister Negrín—whom Martha Gellhorn described to Eleanor Roosevelt as "a brilliant gay lazy man with strong beliefs and perhaps too much sense of humor . . . who surely never wanted to be prime minister"—was as much in the dark as Prieto and Giral, but more optimistic. He felt if he could just turn the tide of public opinion abroad in the government's favor, he could negotiate for peace from a position of strength. In the meantime he was pursuing his vision of a democratic dictatorship "which would prepare the people for the future," ruling more by decree than by consensus. And when he unilaterally decided to move the seat of government from Valencia to Barcelona—ostensibly to shore up Catalonia and ensure its supplies of manufactured goods for the Republic, but also to strengthen his control over it—it must have seemed more like dictatorship and less like democracy, at least to the dismayed Catalan authorities and the dissenters in his own government.

Negrín had done something more ominous than move the government to Barcelona, though. Although he claimed to feel uneasy about the political purges that were convulsing Moscow ("This will do us a lot of harm," he told his frequent confidant, the American journalist Louis Fischer), Negrín had created a purge instrument of his own: a powerful central security and counterespionage organization, the Servicio de Información Militar, or SIM. Established during the summer, the new service already had a network of thousands of agents, a payroll in the millions of pesetas, and a system of secret prisons and interrogation centers that would have been familiar to anyone who had any experience with the Soviet NKVD. In fact, it was partly staffed by NKVD officers. And one of them, sent from Prague to Barcelona in September with orders to "discover the possible ramifications of an international ring of spies and *agents provocateurs*," was Leopold Kulcsar.

There was a man waiting to see Barea when he arrived at his office—a young, raw-boned Prussian Communist who called himself Felix Albin.

Years later, under his real name, Kurt Hager, he would become the chief propagandist, or *chefideologe,* of the East German Politburo; today he carried an official letter informing Barea that he was relieved of his duties as radio commissioner and censor, effective immediately. These duties, the letter went on, would now be performed by Comrade Albin, who would also preapprove the texts of any and all broadcasts by the Unknown Voice of Madrid.

Barea was only partly surprised when, within days of Albin's arrival, the Unknown Voice's radio talks were canceled. But he was both shocked and alarmed when, early one morning while Ilsa was still in bed, two police agents came to search her and Barea's room at the Reina Victoria. Manuscripts, letters, photographs, Barea's pistol and gun permit, and his autographed copy of Dos Passos's *42nd Parallel*—the work of a known Trotskyist, the agents muttered—all were dumped out onto the carpet and confiscated. The agents hinted that someone had denounced Ilsa; but in the end nothing could be found among their papers to make any accusation stick. She and Barea were free, for now at least; but they were under no illusions that things would ever return to normal, whatever that was. If there was a list of those under suspicion, they were on it—why, they didn't know. Friends told them to get out of Madrid while they still could, go somewhere, anywhere, and lay low; but Barea couldn't bring himself to take that step. Madrid was his *home*, it was what he knew and loved. It was also the source of his thinking and writing, the stories he had only just begun to tell and wanted to keep on telling. How could he leave? And yet, seeing the fear and pain in Ilsa's eyes every day, how could he stay?

Improbably, he sought counsel from a priest—but not just any priest, and not in a church. Strong-featured, with prematurely white hair, bright black eyes beneath dark brows, and a grizzled walrus mustache, Leocadio Lobo didn't wear a cassock, or even a dog collar, but went about in an old, somewhat shiny dark suit and a tie. In the days before the war he had been a pastor to the poor, and after the rebellion broke out he had chosen to stay loyal to the government and to minister—even when it was dangerous to be a priest—to anyone who wanted to receive the Sacraments. He'd risked his life in the trenches alongside the *milicianos*; now, when the government had renewed the licenses of loyal priests, he was working for the Ministry of Justice to investigate cases of hardship among the clergy.

He lived in the Victoria, and soon after Ilsa and Barea had moved in there he'd begun joining their table at lunch or dinner. Although Barea had made a point of telling him he was no longer a practicing Catholic, and was divorced and living with a woman not his wife, Father Lobo had been unimpressed; Barea and Ilsa were his friends, and that was that. Now he listened patiently over cups of weak ersatz coffee as Barea poured out his conflicted feelings. Only when the torrent of words stopped did he say anything at all, and then he was both tough and compassionate. What was Barea whining about? he asked. He wanted everyone to be as good and idealistic as he was, so things would be easy for him. Well, they weren't, and if he wanted to stand up for his ideals, he'd better get used to it. As for Barea's relationship with Ilsa, it had hurt people, and Barea was right to regret this; but their love was also an example to others of what was possible, and he should rejoice in *that*. And yes, the war was brutal and painful and destructive; but it had taught people what they could do if they tried—it had shaken them out of paralysis and into action. Even in this evil there was good. So. "We all have our work to do, so do yours instead of talking about the world which doesn't follow you," he said. "Talk and write down what you think you know, what you have seen and thought, tell it honestly and speak the truth. Let the others hear and read you, so that they are driven to tell their truth, too. And then you'll lose that pain of yours."

Then he turned to Ilsa. She was a fish out of water in Madrid, he told her; she was too intelligent, she knew and talked to too many people, in Spain and abroad, for anyone in Spain to trust her. "We aren't used to intelligent women yet," he said. "You can't help being what you are, so you must go away with Arturo because he needs you and you belong together. You will want to work. So go away."

She looked at him out of her big green eyes. "Yes, I know," she responded.

On November 7, the anniversary of the International Brigades' arrival in Madrid—and also, according to Russia's Gregorian calendar, of the October Revolution—the weather was raw and blustery, the sky an even dove gray. At the old mill at Ambite, which was the Fifteenth Brigade headquarters, an hour's drive southeast of Madrid, a festive lunch had been laid on for officers and visiting dignitaries: Robert Merriman, James Benet, nephew of the

American poet Stephen Vincent Benet, the African American poet Langston Hughes, Herbert Matthews, Ernest Hemingway, Martha Gellhorn.

Despite the abundance of red wine and the fire blazing in the mill's ornate tiled hearth, Martha was glad of her long woolen underwear as she sat through the toasts and speeches, and particularly afterward when they all had to line up in the courtyard for photographs to mark the occasion. On his way outdoors Hemingway stopped to comb his hair and remove his glasses, then stood, smiling, with the others as shutters snapped and someone filmed the proceedings with a movie camera. When all the posing was done, he and Martha walked to one of the waiting automobiles—Hemingway pausing to put his glasses on again—and then drove back to town.

Things were merrier in Madrid, where the buildings were draped with banners and the trams and automobiles sported the Republican and Soviet colors. There was a big parade through the streets of the city, featuring a float on which rode the bear of Madrid, sitting on a model of Franco's head, with the inscription, "Long live Madrid, the capital of the world." That evening the Russians gave a party at Gaylord's, where the Pravda correspondent, Boleslavskaya, a plump, maternal woman whose sharp eyes missed little, and Werner Heilbrun's widow, Ailmuth, were dressed up in national costumes and the Bulgarian general Petrov, Soviet advisor to the Twelfth Brigade, was dancing with another man. Koltsov, and the Spanish commanders Modesto and Durán, flirted with Martha, to Hemingway's annoyance, and everyone drank a lot of vodka. Then Koltsov changed into a traditional Russian overblouse and breeches, and they all went on to the Alianza, where Maria Teresa Léon and Rafael Alberti, not to be outdone, went upstairs and put on their own Russian costumes. Everyone drank a lot more, and sang, and danced *sardanas*, and it was three in the morning before the guests went home.

The next day was Martha's twenty-ninth birthday, and after she woke, somewhat the worse for wear, at one in the afternoon, Matthews gave her a huge basket of flowers and pulled together a lavish feast of caviar, pâté en croûte, Christmas pudding, and ham, to which Hemingway added bottles of Champagne and Chateau d'Yquem. She didn't feel very celebratory, however; she'd just heard that the word was out in the United States about her relationship with Hemingway, and she dreaded the consequences for Pauline, for Hemingway, and for her own mother. Once again, it seemed, she'd found herself being *the other kind* of woman, just as her father had said.

Anomie enveloped her like the November damp. With nothing happening she filled her days with shopping—ordering clothes from the dressmaker and tailor and furrier—and trips to the hairdresser, where hairs in the sink and used wads of varnish-stained cotton filled her with revulsion. "I am wasting everything and I am only twenty-nine," she lamented to her journal. Going to the Victoria with the script for a radio broadcast that had to be approved by Albin, the new radio censor, she learned that Barea and Ilsa had made plans to leave Madrid, something that saddened and surprised her. When she'd first come to the city Ilsa had been "the power here," the one who had showed her the ropes; now, although nothing had been proved against her, she was running away for reasons Martha didn't want to guess at.

Martha brought her a book as a parting present, and the two women, so seemingly unalike, sat and talked. Ilsa, Martha sensed, was "exhausted, nervous, and still immeasurably proud and dangerous in some way." Where will you go, Martha asked her; what will you do? Ilsa said they would go to Alicante, on the coast; the mother of their friend Father Lobo had a place for them. There they would write, and wait. "Wait for what?" Martha didn't say aloud, but thought; "and will Arturo stay and what does she hold him with except terror." *Make it work or make it end now.*

Ilsa wanted some practical literary advice, which Martha happily gave her, both of them solemnly pretending this was a normal conversation that professional women anywhere might have about editors and submissions and contracts. And then they said goodbye.

The next evening, it was time for another farewell. Koltsov, who had been so high-spirited and flirtatious at the anniversary party, told her and Hemingway that the day before the party he'd received notice from Moscow: he was being recalled, effective immediately. Although his articles for *Pravda*, including one claiming that Andrés Nin was not dead, but had been spirited away by friendly Gestapo agents, had all hewed to the Party line, he knew how little protection that was these days. He'd got his mistress, Maria Osten, a job as the correspondent for the *Deutsche Zentral Zeitung* in Paris so that she wouldn't be tempted to join him in Moscow. He didn't want to risk it. On the eleventh, he came to dinner with Hemingway and Martha and was in his usual sardonic good form, regaling them with stories of the days of the siege of Madrid. Let me tell you about the two wounded Russian tank officers who were being treated at the Palace Hotel, he said. When it looked as if the fascists would take the city I was ordered to poison them before the rebels took them prisoner so their nationality wouldn't be discovered. Wasn't that difficult? Hemingway wanted to know; but Koltsov just laughed. Not when you always have the cyanide with you, he said, showing them the little vial tucked into his cigarette case. And laughed again.

After that, the days all ran into each other and Martha began pulling back, her diary entries sketchily scribbled in pencil, noting little, as if she didn't want to commit even her attention to people and places she would soon abandon. "And now the leaving, the dreadfulness of leaving," she wrote.

December 1937: Playa de San Juan

The tiny village where Father Lobo's mother lived was on a white swath of beach between the blue hills and the sea. The priest had told his mother that Barea and Ilsa were a married couple—why bewilder her, he'd said, when this was the essential truth; and she found them lodging with a cook who was famous in the region for his paella. In addition to renting them a room in his cottage by the shore he taught Barea how to make his signature dish, and Ilsa gave lessons to his little girls. During the still-warm days they swam in the Mediterranean, and tried to catch fish and the tiny crabs that burrowed into the sand when the waves receded; and at night Barea took the first steps toward writing.

When they left Madrid he'd asked Sefton Delmer if he might have the journalist's old broken typewriter, which Delmer had been on the point of throwing away; and now he disassembled the battered machine, carefully taking out all the type bars and laying them in order on the pine kitchen table, detaching the keys and the carriage, and cleaning every last part before putting it back together. It was slow work, but it calmed him. He told himself he was building his instrument, the way his uncle used to cut quills for pens. The night after he finally reassembled the typewriter, an Italian air strike hit Alicante, down the coast, but the only thing killed by it was a frog in someone's back garden. Imagine, said the other boarder in the cottage the next day, laughing: all they could hit was a frog! It wasn't a laughing matter to Barea, though. Even a frog's death diminished him. And he sat down and started typing: "The frog lay on the edge of the crater, its upturned belly a white stain against the wet black earth." *Tap tap tappety tap.* In the end he had four pages: the story of a ruined garden, a little Eden destroyed by war. Maybe he was becoming a writer after all.

Then it happened, the thing they had been half expecting for months. In the darkness just before the dawn, a hammering on the door, two men brandishing fistfuls of paper, demanding to see Ilsa. Outside. Now. Hearts hammering, Ilsa and Barea threw on clothes and went out of the cottage. The sky and sea were gray and sullen. It was cold.

"Have you a husband in Barcelona?" the agents asked Ilsa, and when she denied it, they waved the papers at her again. They had orders to take her to her husband, Leopold Kulcsar, in Barcelona, they told her; if she didn't come voluntarily they would arrest her.

Well, she *did* have a husband named Leopold Kulcsar, Ilsa said, but she was separated from him, and the last time she'd heard, he was in Prague; if he was in Barcelona the only way she was going there was if Barea went with her. And who was *he?* the agents wanted to know. Barea went back in the house, produced his own papers; the two strangers looked them over, then decided they might as well take him as well. Maybe he should be arrested, too. They gave Barea and Ilsa only enough time to pack a small suitcase before shoving them into the black car parked outside.

"Don't worry so much," Ilsa said, as they bumped off down the dirt track toward the highway. It was just some stupid misunderstanding, she went on; Poldi would soon set it right. She seemed ready to treat the whole thing like an outing. But Barea, sitting silently beside her, knew better. He put his hand in his coat pocket to feel for the gun his friend Agustín had given him as a parting present when they left Madrid. For he'd looked at the papers the agents had handed him, even if Ilsa hadn't. They were stamped SIM, Servicio de Información Militar.

December 1937: The North Atlantic

During the night of December 19 two ships, going in opposite directions, passed each other in the dark waters of the North Atlantic. One was the *Normandie*, the French Line's luxury flagship, which had sailed from Le Havre the day before, its first-class cabins filled with celebrity passengers, including the film star Charles Boyer and the composer Richard Rodgers. Also on board were Joris Ivens and Martha Gellhorn. Martha had traveled to Paris in early December with Rubio Hidalgo, who had filled her full of political gossip; and on her arrival she'd got a royalty check from *The Trouble I've Seen*, which she promptly endorsed over to Hemingway to cover her share of expenses for the past few months—happy, as she wrote to him in a note, that "this book, which is the best thing I ever wrote, paid for Spain, which is the best thing I ever did." She'd booked passage on the *Aquitania*, which was to sail on December 15, so she could be home in St. Louis in plenty of time for Christmas; but she'd had to make new, more expensive, and less satisfactory arrangements when Ivens, her intended traveling companion, didn't turn up in Paris on time.

Ivens had been in Europe trying to raise money for a new film about the Sino-Japanese War that had all the earmarks of a Willi Münzenberg propaganda project. Originally, while Mao Tse-tung's Communists were still fighting with Chiang Kai-shek's Kuomintang, it had been planned as a celebration of Communist achievements in rural China, but as Japan encroached ever farther into the country and the Communists and Kuomintang closed ranks, the Party had decreed that the film's theme would be Chinese unity against Japanese aggression. And although Ivens had intended to go back to Spain and was initially unhappy about what he called a "sudden change in assignment," he'd thrown himself into fundraising and preproduction, forming a new American production company, History Today, that excluded John Dos Passos, whom he now considered an "enemy." When contributions were slow to materialize he'd gone to Europe, where he also met with Münzenberg to talk about the film's content; and he'd made a flying visit to Amsterdam, where he participated in a shadowy Party "cleansing action"—a purge of "people who were once good friends," which he said was "hard work." It was these murky doings that had made him late for his rendezvous with Martha.

Did they talk about them as they tramped around on the *Normandie's* deck or sat in each other's cabin, with Martha acting as "Joris's secretary again," as she'd done in *Spanish Earth* days? Did they brainstorm about fund-raising or writing a treatment for the Chinese film, or strategize how Ivens might preemptively strike at his "enemy" Dos Passos? Whatever they discussed, Martha was fully aware of, even complicit in, Ivens's Party commitments. Writing to Hemingway from the boat, she urged him not to encourage their friend Gustav Regler, still convalescing from his wounds, to embark on anything so ambitious as a U.S. speaking tour. Ivens believed it would be a mistake, she reported, and if Hemingway wanted "the good old Party" to forbid it, he should wire Ivens. "Yes, Hem," Ivens scribbled in the margin of Martha's note, and added a precautionary comment: "You must *not* have any connection with his . . . political appearances in public." Was he worried that association with the political commissar wouldn't go down well with Hemingway's American contacts? Ivens had sent his own letter to Hemingway: he regretted not being able to see his friend before he left Europe, because there were "many things that cannot be written" that they needed to talk over—among them the growing internal friction in the Loyalist government. "Prieto is trying to make a deal with the republicans," he said, "and Negrín with us [i.e., the Communists] . . . With us he knows he has the help of a great country." If Hem needed guidance, Maurice Thorez and Marcel Cachin, two Communist founders of the French Popular Front, would give him "the right inside picture." And, he promised Hemingway, "one thing is good, that you . . . will be in an action on the front now."

As the *Normandie* steamed westward, carrying Ivens and Martha to New York, the Hapag Lloyd Line's ship *Europa*, twinkling with Christmas lights and garlanded with evergreens, plowed east through heavy seas with Pauline Hemingway aboard. "Very cute and nervy," as Katy Dos Passos had found her during a visit to the Dosses in Provincetown a month earlier, Pauline had dyed her dark hair blond and let it grow long into a bob like Martha's, and (she wrote to Sara Murphy from the boat) she was "not stuffing my face, and seeing *nobody* but my masseuse, Mrs. Tiffany, and the Duchess of Westminster." After spending months ignoring gossip and suppressing suspicion, she'd finally recognized that her husband was in the grip of a powerful obsession, one whose measure she had to take. She would go to him, and they would spend Christmas together in Paris, the city where they had first become lovers. She would patch things up, just as she had after Hemingway's affair with Jane Mason, and all would go on as before.

She arrived on December 21 to find snow mantling the buildings along the boulevards—but, at the Hotel Elysée Park, no Hemingway. Despite two cables from Barcelona in which he'd assured her he would be with her by the twenty-second, he failed to appear.

December 1937: Teruel

At 7:10 on the morning of December 15, with a blizzard whistling through the passes of the Montes Universales, the Loyalist Army of the Levante launched a surprise attack on Teruel, the bleak walled Aragonese town that Hemingway, Herbert Matthews, and Martha Gellhorn had squinted at through their binoculars in September. The offensive began before sunrise, without preliminary shelling or bombing, which would have softened resistance but would also have tipped off the rebels that something was afoot; as a result, by the end of the day the Loyalists had cut the road from Teruel to Saragossa and were preparing to strike at the town itself.

The Nationalists were caught completely unaware. They hadn't been planning to swoop down on Valencia during the winter—Hemingway had been right about that—and they *had* been preparing an assault on Guadalajara, and then Madrid, the plans for which were fortuitously betrayed, with days to spare, by a Loyalist spy. By moving so suddenly and swiftly on Teruel, the government hoped to abort the Nationalists' Guadalajara plans and knock them off their threatening perch before snow closed the mountain passes for the winter. And a victory here—especially after the bitter losses in the north during the summer and autumn—might turn popular opinion abroad and the tide of the war at home. At the very least it might make it possible to negotiate with Franco from a position of strength.

When the news of the offensive reached Hemingway in Barcelona, where he had been on the point of leaving for Christmas in Paris, he was as surprised as the Nationalists. He'd been so sure that the Teruel front would be dead after the first snowfall, so sure that the only action, if it came, would be on the Castilian plain. But no matter where it was happening, it *was* action, and if he moved fast he could at last be a part of it. He turned around and headed for Valencia, from which Teruel was only a few hours' drive. *You will be in an action on the front now*—that's what Joris Ivens had promised him, and that's what he was going to do.

For three days, waiting for the government troops to break through the Nationalist defenses, he, Matthews, and Tom Delmer shuttled back and forth from Valencia to the command post that Colonel Hernández Saravia had established in a railroad train sheltered in a tunnel under the mountains near Teruel. It was bitterly cold—"cold as a steel engraving" was how Hemingway put it: so cold that putting binoculars to your face was an act of masochism; so cold that soldiers froze to death in the front lines, and casualties from frostbite numbered in the thousands. But by December 21, as the three men drove up the Sagunto road in a car with *Ce Soir*'s correspondent Mathieu Corman, a thaw had set in. It was a good day to go into battle.

At Saravia's dugout the word was that the Loyalist troops would try to fight their way past the Mansueto, Teruel's heavily fortified natural rock bulwark; and Corman, a good-looking young Belgian who claimed to have contacts in the field command, proposed heading forward with them, so the four correspondents continued on toward Teruel behind a mass of troops and armored cars. Nine kilometers from the town they had to get out and leave the car. They made an odd quartet: the dashing Corman, the tall, schoolmasterish Matthews, the lumbering Delmer, and the unkempt Hemingway, in his shabby tweed jacket and wire-rimmed spectacles. The sun was warm as they walked along, the snow of the past few days had melted, and although the Loyalist artillery was keeping up a constant barrage on the Mansueto they heard no answering gunfire. Then suddenly a khaki-clad wave of Loyalist soldiers surged over the hill on their left, aiming for the Mansueto and shooting as they came.

Hemingway and his companions scrambled up a rise to the right, just behind a line of shallow trenches from which more Loyalists were firing on the Mansueto. Answering machine-gun volleys raked the ridge and the correspondents, who didn't have the advantage of trench cover, threw themselves flat, pressing their faces close to the earth as bullets struck around them with a whispery *pfft*. Gradually the rebels fell back. One of the Loyalist riflemen was cursing at his weapon, which kept jamming after every shot; and Hemingway, a man who knew his way around a rifle, was happy to show him how to bash the bolt open with a piece of rock.

As the day wore on, the Loyalists pressed forward, the journalists following behind the first wave of the attack, being shot at when the soldiers were shot at, resting when they rested. But it didn't seem like they were going to make it into Teruel today after all: the December sun was touching the horizon and they were still two kilometers away from the prize. Then two trucks drew up, unloading a squad of *dinamiteros*, their faces and hands grimy, grenades dangling from their belts, who ran down the road toward the front line. Soon the air was full of the sound and smell of explosives, and bursts of flame punctuated the gathering twilight. The phalanx of troops started moving forward again, and an armored car passed the journalists, the driver leaning out, shouting, "You can get up to the Plaza de Toros," then driving away with a grinding of gears. Hemingway, Delmer, and Matthews—Corman had slipped off on his own—looked at each other in the dusk. Why not? Attaching themselves to two Loyalist officers so they wouldn't be mistaken for rebel sympathizers and shot by the invaders, they walked unopposed into the outskirts of Teruel.

Capa hadn't been planning on coming back to a battlefield so soon. With his *Life* deal and the arrangements for *Death in the Making* completed, he'd returned to Paris, and the studio on the rue Froidevaux, in November; and he had started a casual, no-strings affair with a beautiful North African woman who was, according to some of his friends, both a sometime prostitute and bisexual. She teased him and made him laugh, and once she tried to strangle him at a café when he teased her back; but neither of them expected anything from the other. It was better that way.

Before leaving New York he'd agreed to make a short film for the North American Committee to Aid Spanish Democracy, a documentary about the committee's services for children—schools, hospitals, and suchlike—in Spain; and the committee had paid him an advance of $100 and lent him a movie camera for the purpose. Hoping to get some additional photo income, Capa had asked *Ce Soir* to underwrite the trip as well; but it was taking them a long time to decide about it. In the meantime, Joris Ivens, in Paris to raise money for his upcoming China film, made him a proposition. Why didn't Capa come to China with him and John Ferno? He could take still photos for their movie, and his connection with *Life* would help them get publicity for it. Capa said yes immediately. It was the trip he had meant to make with Gerda, and now he could make it *for* her. He'd learn more about filmmaking, which he was eager to do. And since Ferno, with whom he planned to travel, wasn't sailing until late January, he would still have time to go to Spain—if *Ce Soir*'s sponsorship, and his papers, came through.

They did, in mid-December. He had a new press card from the Préfecture, for "M. Cappa" of *Ce Soir*, showing his new face: thinner, unsmiling, older; the hair slicked down and brushed to the side the way Gerda had liked it; the eyes, under their black brows, smudged with deep shadows. He had a ticket for Barcelona, too; but as soon as he arrived there and heard that the government had attacked Teruel, he knew where he had to be.

He left Barcelona immediately. He might not have had the high-level contacts Hemingway did, but he'd spent enough time in the field to have friends in uniform who could tell him where things were likely to happen, and make sure he got there. While Hemingway and his comrades were waiting on the Sagunto road in the wintry dusk for the signal to move ahead, Capa, and his camera, were in the very front of the assault, with the first T-26 tanks that rumbled past the bullring, and with the *dinamiteros*, as they opened the way for the Army of the Levante to enter Teruel.

Late that night—after Hemingway, Delmer, and Matthews had received a hero's welcome from a family of villagers who mistook them for high-ranking officers, perhaps Russians, and after Capa had shot a roll of photographs to send off to *Ce Soir*—they all met, like characters in a French bedroom farce, at the same hotel in Valencia. Instead of celebrating their joint scoop in the hotel bar, however, Matthews and Hemingway went to their rooms, where they stayed up past dawn writing their stories of the Teruel attack in order to send them by courier to Madrid. Hemingway, even more than Matthews, was so excited he couldn't have slept anyway. At last he'd been not just a witness to but a part of an important assault, one of the most important in the war so far, one that he told himself he had been predicting *all along*; and (as he put it in the dispatch he was writing) he had "received the surrender of [the] town" as if he had been a Loyalist general. The experience was, he said, "very fine." He thought enough of his account of it not to send it in cablese: because, he wired, in addition to "COLOUR YOU ALSO BUYING STYLE." And he planned on sticking around to file at least one more dispatch, so he asked NANA to send correspondents' credentials to Pauline, care of Guaranty Trust in Paris, so she could join him in Barcelona for Christmas.

As soon as everyone had had a few hours rest they all piled into Matthews's battered old Ford and went back up into the mountains to Teruel. Although the walls had been breached the evening before, the Loyalist troops hadn't tried to enter the city in the dark, and today Hemingway and his comrades could move in with them, Capa photographing the first

wave of soldiers, wrapped in their greatcoats against the cold, marching
up the steep street and peering warily about for resistance. They were
right to be careful. There were six thousand Nationalist troops—many
with civilian hostages, including women and children—holed up behind
the pockmarked walls of Teruel's houses and municipal and ecclesiastical
buildings, and the town was riddled with underground passages through
which the defenders could retreat and regroup. If they felt threatened in
one building, the Nationalists would just blast a hole through its walls
into the house next door so they could move about without exposing
themselves to enemy fire. The Loyalist invaders fanned out through the
rubble-filled streets, trying to clean up these knots of resistance; but it
was drawn-out and dangerous work—as the journalists found out when
they followed a tank towing a 6-inch gun to fire on the seminary, where
Nationalist machine-gunners were barricaded and shooting from the windows. To get to cover you had to sprint across the street, doubled over to
present as small a target as possible; Hemingway dropped to his knees to
crawl, but Delmer, whose bulk didn't lend itself to such an activity, was
reluctant. "Do we *have* to crawl?" he asked. "I run faster when I'm standing." They all laughed; but while they were watching, three of the men
trying to get the gun into position were killed. And then the gun did its
work on the seminary walls, and the façade crumbled like a sandcastle.

That day and the next, as the government troops tried to establish their
hold over Teruel, Capa, Hemingway, Matthews, and Delmer shuttled
back and forth between there and Valencia, Hemingway glorying in the
rot-pop-pop (as he described it) of machine-gun fire, the dangerous chaos
of the "godwonderful housetohouse fighting," the back-slapping camaraderie with the Loyalist officers, the sense of being in on a Big Thing.
Capa photographed him in a stocking cap and muffler, a huge grin festooned across his unshaven face, sharing American cigarettes with Loyalist officers, and elsewhere in the city, inspecting tanks, talking to soldiers
who were digging graves for their fallen comrades. But "taking pictures of
victory," Capa would say later, "is like taking pictures of a church wedding
ten minutes after the departure of the newlyweds." He sought out other
images in Teruel: the central plaza, its prosperous *modernista* houses shattered and the Doric column at its center stripped of the bronze statue of
the *torico*, the little bull, that was the emblem of the city; the pitiful
streams of refugees, many of them children, lugging their belongings in

shapeless bundles as they boarded evacuation trucks or stumbled across the frozen fields; three bodies, now just crumpled heaps of clothing, lying on a flat terrace behind which the shadowed clefts of the Montes Universales loomed like a theatrical backdrop. And in a tree on the outskirts of the town, something that looked at first like someone's coat that had been blown into the branches by the blizzard winds.

Capa knew what it was. He took one shot, then another, walking closer and circling the tree, pointing his camera up into the branches to frame his subject perfectly: a soldier, his tasseled cap still on his head, his hand still grasping the field-telephone wire he'd been stringing when a fascist bullet took him, his eyes staring, his face twisted in a grimace straight out of one of Goya's antiwar engravings. Capa's photos, and Hemingway's and Matthews's and Delmer's stories, would soon be in all the world's newspapers and magazines, proclaiming the news of victory in Teruel. And that would be, as Hemingway would say, *very fine*. But this is what such a victory came down to: just a body in a tree that could be anyone—fear in a handful of dust.

December 1937: Barcelona

Barea and Ilsa's journey from San Juan de la Playa had been a kind of torture. The SIM agents had taken their time getting to Valencia, driving the long way around the lagoon of Albuféra—the dumping ground for bodies of those executed in the chaos of 1936—and Barea found himself slipping the safety catch off the gun in his pocket, ready to fire through his coat if he and Ilsa were ordered out of the car. Arriving in Valencia after dark, they'd been held briefly at the SIM office; then, in the small hours of the morning, transferred to another car for transport to Barcelona. In the shuffle—by accident or by design—the attaché case holding all the records of their work in Madrid, as well as Barea's manuscripts, disappeared.

Unfed, sleep-deprived, anxious about their missing papers, they reached Barcelona just after sunrise, and were taken to a large stone mansion with modern stained-glass windows on the Calle de la Diputación, in the fashionable Ensanche district. The official who would question them wasn't there, so they were put in a guarded room to wait, and passed the time wondering what sort of building this was. It was too big for a bourgeois Catalan's house, they thought, but not quite a palace. It was just as well they didn't know it was the former Seminario Conciliar, the Catholic seminary, now notorious as an SIM prison and interrogation center.

At length the door of the room banged open to admit a man of medium height, balding, with thinning light-brown hair, dark-smudged eyes, a tight-lipped mouth. The guard threw the newcomer a smart salute, spun on his heel, and left.

"Poldi!" cried Ilsa, flying to him. The man bent over her hand with exaggerated courtliness, and she broke into German: "Why did you have me arrested?"

He recoiled as if she had slapped him.

Barea struggled to his feet, and, in French, Ilsa introduced her estranged husband to her lover. Kulcsar bowed, like a figure in a comic opera, from the hips; Barea nodded curtly. Kulcsar took Ilsa's elbow and led her to a velvet-covered bench where they could talk; Barea went to the stained-glass window and stared out at the porticoed courtyard. What was this all about? What was going to happen? Would this stranger take Ilsa away, have him imprisoned—or have *her* imprisoned, and brutally questioned? How could he protect her, here, where he knew no one, had no papers to prove anything? He still had the gun in his pocket—somehow no one had bothered to search him—but using it wouldn't get him very far with guards outside and downstairs. Behind him he heard, but couldn't understand, the buzz of German, first quiet, then agitated and angry, then quiet again, with Ilsa's voice firm, Kulcsar's muted.

Suddenly Ilsa was beside him, telling him to come with her. They were going to Poldi's hotel, she said. She would explain everything later. Barea followed her out into the street, where they walked, three abreast, himself, Ilsa, and Kulcsar; Kulcsar tried to start a conversation with Ilsa in German, but when she insisted they all speak French together, there was silence. Along the Paseo de Gracia they went, under the plane trees and past the surrealistic stone façade of Gaudi's Casa Batllo, to the Hotel Majestic, on the Calle Aragón; and there, in the lobby, Barea saw a clutch of journalists they knew. But, like a ghost, he couldn't speak to them; and they didn't speak to him. He followed Kulcsar and Ilsa into a waiting elevator, and the gate slammed shut.

•

Hemingway didn't notice Barea and Ilsa in the lobby of the Majestic when he arrived from Teruel on Christmas Eve, along with Capa, Delmer, and Matthews. Instead he was buttonholed—almost the minute he walked in—by Jay Allen, just in from Paris, where he'd found a very distressed Pauline Hemingway. She'd been expecting her husband to turn up for Christmas, Allen said, and when he didn't she'd tried to wangle a visa for Spain, begging Allen to help her. Hemingway seemed both stunned and flattered that Pauline had gone to such efforts, and blamed Allen for not making things work out. Certainly *he* had done all he could, asking NANA to get correspondents' credentials for her; but, as in so many other things, NANA had disappointed him.

So Hemingway spent Christmas in Barcelona with Matthews, Capa, and *Izvestia*'s Ilya Ehrenburg, who was also in the Majestic on his way back to Moscow. On Christmas Day he went to the Ritz Hotel to serve, along with the government's Interior minister, Julián Zagazagoitia, as host and commentator, *amistoso comentarista*, for the opening of an exhibit of war drawings by his friend Luis Quintanilla. It was a gala occasion—Prime Minister Negrín and the Catalan president, Luís Companys, were there, as well as other government and literary and artistic luminaries, some of them wearing frock coats and top hats—and the walls of the Ritz's salon had been hung, either for symbolic or aesthetic reasons, with red fabric. But the subject matter of the drawings themselves seemed at odds not only with their sumptuous background and well-heeled audience, but also with the artist's presentation: wrecked buildings, uniformed soldiers, corpses with distended bellies, all were limned with the lightest and most delicate of pencil strokes, and the result was both sculptural and surreally calm.

Since he was already late getting to Paris, Hemingway stayed around to celebrate what was being trumpeted as the great (if as yet incomplete) victory of Teruel with a parade and speeches by Negrín and Companys and the newly promoted General Hernández Saravia. It wasn't until the morning of December 28 that, neatly barbered and wearing a dark shirt and sober striped tie, he dropped in at Ehrenburg's room at the Majestic to say goodbye. "But we'll be seeing each other again soon," the Russian protested. "You'll be here in June, won't you?" Hemingway wasn't so sure: NANA had been unhappy with his reporting from Teruel, which it said duplicated

Matthews's, and had canceled any further stories; he himself wasn't feeling too well, what with the aftereffects of a grippe he'd had in Madrid and a painful liver from too much drinking; and then there was the question of what he would say to the wife who was waiting for him in Paris if he decided to return to Spain. He left Barcelona without making any promises.

His companions went back to Teruel.

December 1937: Teruel

As Matthews, Delmer, and Capa drove up the Sagunto road on December 28 they saw a ragged column of men trudging toward them, wrapped in blankets against the cold and chivvied along by government soldiers on shaggy-coated mules. The men were in the uniform of the Guardia Civil, and they were lugging suitcases, their eyes downcast. Their barracks had fallen to the Loyalists the night before, and now they were prisoners.

Inside the town the journalists found a crowd surrounding the Guardia barracks, where the real prizes, the officers, were being taken out. Capa pushed as close as he dared to the column, aiming his camera right into their determinedly vacant faces; the lieutenant colonel, whom Matthews would describe as a "heavy, flat-faced, brutish man," tramped by impassively, but one of his lieutenants turned to look behind him and his face filled Capa's viewfinder like an El Greco portrait, his brow creased, his mouth set in a bitter curl of defeat. He knew what was waiting for him: as Matthews thought of it, *in war you can shoot the people who deserve to be shot.*

But even as Capa was photographing this sign of victory, the Nationalists—who still held a number of buildings in Teruel, including the Palace of the Civil Governor and the Santa Clara Convent—were beginning a counterattack. Franco had ordered an army to be put together to retake the city, and the Condor Legion was sent in to begin bombing the area in preparation. As usual the bombs fell on combatants and civilians alike. On a road on the outskirts of town, where pastures sloped steeply down to the river valley, Capa saw the results. A man came running toward him, cradling his young son, a boy of about eleven, whose trouser leg had been cut away and whose thigh was wrapped in a bloody bandage. Near them soldiers were helping other wounded, both military and civilians, to safety; and off the road, down a steep hill, a group of peasants, evacuees who had been leaving their homes in the battle zone, were stooping over something in the rock-strewn field. Capa didn't have a tele-photo lens, so he ran down the hill toward them. He found them bent over an injured man, loading him into a makeshift stretcher; and when they'd got him in it and started uphill, Capa started climbing with them. The crowd on the hillside were paying no attention to the rescue mission, however. They were scanning the sky in anxiety—and suddenly Capa, standing with the peasants in the open field, heard what they heard: the buzz of approaching aircraft. Looking up, he could see bombers, specks against the sky like so many malevolent wasps. Without even thinking he himself might be a target, he aimed his camera skyward.

December 1937: Barcelona

Neither Barea nor Ilsa had any papers entitling them to be in Barcelona at all; but for Kulcsar this was not a problem. He settled them among the tarts and war profiteers at the Ritz, on the Gran Via, in a room with a balcony overlooking the garden—*where I can find you*, he explained—and took them to lunch.

The story he had told Ilsa was that he'd heard she was living with a dangerous and dissolute man and had got herself into trouble with the authorities, and he'd planned to take her out of Spain—forcibly, if necessary—and get rid of Barea. He had ways of making people disappear for good. But now he'd seen, and she had told him, how happy she was; and he would try to help them. He said. Barea was still suspicious.

Over lunch he learned more, and not all of it made him feel better. He could see that Kulcsar really did seem to love Ilsa, and want to protect her even if he could no longer possess her; and he began to wonder if Kulcsar's imperious brusqueness didn't compensate for a sort of vulnerability. He didn't, for example, know how to ask their waiter nicely to go and find them some hard-to-come-by cigarettes: instead he was rude and peremptory, and the waiter just shrugged at him. But when Barea interceded, and made soothing small talk with the waiter, who then conjured up not only ciga-rettes but also a really first-class lunch and a bottle of wine, Kulcsar was chagrined: *I wish I knew how to do that.* He looked almost like a shamefaced small boy. It would have been touching, if he hadn't seemed to offset the vulnerability with ruthlessness.

Kulcsar was also insistent, now that he could see Ilsa would never leave Barea, that the two of them had to get out of Spain. *Why?* thought Barea. It was his home, it was where his family was, it was where the war was being fought—leaving all this was crazy and wrong. And as an adult male of fighting age he couldn't leave without an exit permit. Kulcsar, however, seemed to think they were both in danger here, whereas if they left they might be able to work against fascism in the bigger war that was almost certainly coming. He told them he would try to get them safe-conducts from the SIM that would allow them to stay in Barcelona unmolested until Barea could arrange for an exit permit. As for a divorce, he was willing to give Ilsa one; but since they were both fugitives from Austria, where the marriage was registered, it might be difficult.

For the next ten days Kulcsar hustled Barea and Ilsa in and out of government offices all over Barcelona, trying to pull the right strings to free them from their entanglement with the SIM. He seemed almost obsessed with this mission; and at last he appeared to have accomplished it. They just needed to come to the SIM headquarters in Paseo San Juan and submit to a few questions from the chief officer, a youngish man with a humorless smile named Ordoñez. Under his watchful guidance they went over old ground—who they had worked for in Madrid, what they had done, how long they had done it—expecting at any moment for some trap to be sprung at them; but in the end Ordoñez scribbled his signature on their documents, and they should have been free to go. Except that Kulcsar wanted them to see something first.

They had barely seated themselves in his office when a deep, rumbling vibration shook the building—bombs were falling on Barcelona. The lights flickered and went out, and Barea felt a cold wave of nausea, an echo of the terror that had gripped him in Madrid. Someone lit candles, throwing the room into deep chiaroscuro; and guards brought in a tiny, dark-haired woman whose wide black eyes darted back and forth like those of a cornered animal before taking in Kulcsar's two visitors.

"You're Ilse," she said, in recognition. "Don't you remember me? Twelve years ago in Vienna?" Tentatively, Ilsa rose to shake her hand. The woman's name was Katia Landau, and a dozen years earlier she and her husband, Kurt, had been members of Ilsa and Leopold Kulcsar's underground Social Democratic group, the Spark. What was going on here? Was Kulcsar trying to use Ilsa as a tool to frighten information out of the Landau woman, or was it something else?

Kulcsar was speaking in his prosecutor's voice—cold, hard, insistent. The NKVD had sent him to Spain on a special, historic mission, he began: to prove that out of twenty Trotskyists in Spain, eighteen were fascists, agents of Hitler and Franco. "Perhaps subjectively you are a good revolutionary, but you are convinced that the victory of Franco would be more favorable to the realization of your Trotskyist ideas than the victory of Stalinism." He had proof of her activities, he said, waving pieces of paper at her that he said contained "plans" that she had drawn and was planning to send to the French. She'd been spying for the Austrian fascists, also, he continued. And he knew that she and her husband, Kurt, who had been arrested in Barcelona on September 23 and had subsequently disappeared, had been in contact with the British intelligence service. Kurt should be careful, wherever he was, warned Kulcsar: "If he falls into my hands one day, I will make him pay dearly for it."

Ilsa was sitting rigid in her chair, as if she could not bear to listen; whatever game Kulcsar was up to, Barea didn't want any part of it. He managed to make their apologies and get them both out of the room as fast as he could. He thought Ilsa must be as horrified as he was by the pleasure Kulcsar was taking in his show of power—and certainly this demonstration of his instinct for domination, which had destroyed her marriage, was distasteful to her. But was that all? Or was she wondering why Kulcsar, or his superiors at the NKVD, were so interested in the former members of the Spark? And why Kulcsar should have wanted to make that interest, and its consequences, so clear to her? Was there something about their old group, or the people who had belonged to it, or Ilsa's knowledge of them, that was mortally dangerous to her? Barea had no idea that the GRU's renegade former *rezident*, Walter Krivitsky, was—or was about to be—telling all his secrets to the Sûreté, MI5, and the FBI. And he probably had never heard Ilsa mention the name of her and Katia Landau's former colleague from Vienna, the undercover Soviet agent Kim Philby, whose history with the Spark, if revealed, would have threatened his cover as a pro-fascist journalist covering Generalísimo Francisco Franco. If Barea had known either of these things he would have been a great deal more anxious than he already was, for such knowledge was dangerous, possibly even fatal.

A few days after the scene in the SIM headquarters, Kulcsar came to bid Barea and Ilsa goodbye: his work in Barcelona was done, at least for the time being, he told them, and he was summoned back to Prague. Not a moment too soon—he hadn't been feeling at all well and the hours he'd been keeping didn't help—but he found himself short of cash and wondered if they could lend him some. He'd leave the repayment in an account in Ilsa's name in Perpignan; when they left Spain, as he urged them to, it would be waiting for them. He hoped they would all meet again. Despite his and Ilsa's philosophical differences—her belief in the individual, and his in ideology, meant they were "spiritually divorced"—he would always love her, and, he said, "if it weren't for Ilsa, blast her, you and I would have been friends." Barea was dubious about that; but for Ilsa's sake he was happy to pretend.

December 1937: Moscow

On December 25, Georges Luciani, a French journalist who had been covering Moscow for both the sobersided *Le Temps* and the slightly racier *Le Petit Parisien* for the last six years, made his way across a wintry Dzerzhinsky Square. Passing the red stone walls of the Lubyanka Prison, the NKVD's headquarters, he entered a ramshackle building next door, the Commissariat for Foreign Affairs, where he had been summoned to an interview with the Soviet foreign minister, Maxim Litvinov.

For some time, Litvinov, a portly former arms smuggler with a staunch belief in the power of collective security—the theory that the security of one state is the concern of all—had been troubled by the spineless response of France and Britain to Germany's increasingly bellicose behavior. He'd watched in dismay as Hitler marched into the Rhineland, and engineered a Nazi putsch in Austria, without raising so much as an eyebrow in Paris or London. He'd listened in disgust to French and British hand-wringing about nonintervention in Spain while Germany and Italy shipped arms and men to the insurgents. Now Nazi provocateurs were starting riots in Czechoslovakia, in the Sudetenland, close to Germany's border, and Hitler was wondering aloud if he would have to intervene to "protect" the German minority there. And Litvinov (and, it might be inferred, Stalin) had had enough. He wanted to make a few things clear to Luciani—not the kind of things that could be said, formally, by the people's commissar for foreign affairs to the French ambassador; that might create difficulties. But if M. Luciani wished to share them with the French ambassador, Robert Coulondre, no objection would be raised. M. Luciani could even take notes, if he wished.

He did.

Litvinov was brusque, even testy, about the extent to which he felt his concerns had been ignored by Russia's supposed allies in Paris. They had allowed the balance of power in Central Europe to be unsettled, and Russia could not countenance that, he said.

Where was this conversation going? Luciani tried conciliation: surely something could be done to remedy the situation, he murmured. After all, their countries' long shared history . . .

Litvinov interrupted him. "Other arrangements are possible," he said, elliptically. Luciani thought for a moment.

"With *Germany?*" he asked.

"Why not?" Litvinov responded. Hitler, he reminded Luciani, had renewed the old 1926 Soviet-German Non-Aggression Pact in 1931; by its terms, Hitler and Stalin were each bound to come to the other's aid in the event of attack by a third party. And of course, since Russia hadn't signed the Versailles Treaty ending the Great War in 1919, Stalin wasn't obligated to maintain *French* security. Recently the Kremlin had "established contacts" to initiate a German-Russian *rapprochement*. M. Luciani surely understood what this meant.

Luciani understood it all too clearly, and communicated as much to his ambassador. Two days later Ambassador Coulondre sent the journalist's notes to the French foreign minister, Yvon Delbos, along with a dispatch: "It is improbable," he wrote, "that M. Litvinov would have dared upon such a point without having been authorized from on high, and his declaration appears to me as a sort of warning that the Soviet government wished to give in a roundabout way . . . If the Western powers should permit the strangulation of Czechoslovakia, the Soviet government would then break with [them] and turn to Germany, giving it a free hand in Europe."

What Coulondre didn't spell out for Delbos was that in that case—having used the war to keep Germany, Italy, and everyone else occupied, and having secured the contents of the Spanish treasury in his own vaults—Stalin would cut the Spanish Republic loose and leave it for Franco to finish off. But Coulondre's warning went unheeded, maybe even ignored, by Delbos and his premier, Édouard Daladier: the ambassador's letter, and Luciani's notes, were buried in the Foreign Ministry archives for decades. And Spain, as Arturo Barea had foreseen, had given gold, and would now pay in blood.

PART III

"LA DESPEDIDA"

January 1938: Teruel

At the stroke of midnight on New Year's Eve, the city of Teruel—as the Republican Interior Minister, Júlian Zugazagoitia, would say later—"belonged to nobody." A Nationalist counterattack over the past few days had retaken the fortified crest of La Muela, across the Turia south of the city, and Teruel's new Loyalist commandant had panicked and ordered his troops to abandon their positions. By the next day the Republican army's chief of staff, General Vicente Rojo, had countermanded the order and summoned reinforcements; but not before newspapers around the world were proclaiming Teruel recaptured by the Nationalists. And then a blizzard enveloped the mountains of southern Aragon, sending flakes slantwise across the whitened fields, crippling communications and making movement almost impossible.

On January 2, Robert Capa and Herbert Matthews—dismayed by the news about Teruel and desperate to find out what was *really* happening there—were sitting in Matthews's ancient Ford, forty-five miles north of Sagunto and 4,000 feet above sea level. In front of them snaked a ten-mile-long column of trucks, tanks, and cars, all carrying men and matériel bound for Teruel, that had been stuck in the snowbound pass for two days. Workmen were trying to break through two feet of ice pack on the road with pickaxes, and a tractor had been brought in to haul vehicles up the steepest stretch at the top of the pass; in the meantime, Capa and Matthews tried alternately driving and pushing their fishtailing car uphill, cursing as they slipped and fell on the slick surface. After eight hours of this punishment, bruised and freezing, they reached the top and let the car roll downhill toward Barracas, where they bunked for the night with a group of officers, sharing their meal of salt cod, bread, wine, and coffee in a peasant's hut, and sleeping in bedrolls by the fire.

Although the approach to Teruel was littered with burnt-out vehicles and dead mules, they found the city itself still nominally in Loyalist hands. But the Palace of the Civil Governor remained full of rebel soldiers and their hostages, and in an effort to clear them out the government sappers had mined the outside wall facing the Turia, planning to blast their way in. Capa and Matthews arrived there just as the wall collapsed into a heap of charred timbers and crumbled stone and cement, and when soldiers started swarming up the heap of wreckage to enter the palace, Capa unthinkingly scrambled up after them. He seemed, probably was, heedless of his own safety. *Now Gerda is dead it is finished for me.* Matthews followed him.

The noise inside was deafening and chaotic: shouts and explosions, pistol shots and rifle fire, all coming from every direction. Keeping his camera going constantly, Capa made his way through a warren of bombed-out rooms, with no idea whether the footsteps he was straining to hear belonged to a friend or an enemy—or whether, around the next corner, he would find armed men or the hostages that had been imprisoned in the dungeons of the building. "The war correspondent has his stake—his life—in his own hands," he would say later, "and he can put it on this horse or that horse, or he can put it back in his pocket at the last minute." Capa wasn't the back-in-the-pocket type, certainly not now. So he followed a group of government soldiers down a bombed staircase, where he and Matthews found the shell of a room in which a rifleman was aiming his weapon through a hole in the floor. "Here's one for you and one for Franco!" the rifleman cried, and fired. The journalists could hear moans and the sound of weeping; looking through the hole, they saw a Nationalist on the floor below with a grenade in his hand—but before he could throw it the Loyalist fired four more bullets into him and finished him off. "Rather terrible, isn't it?" murmured Matthews to the captain standing beside them. The officer shot him a look: "But he was right!" he replied.

After a while, things seemed to quiet down, as if the building had indeed been cleared out, and Capa and Matthews crept cautiously down a wrecked stairway behind a group of helmeted soldiers until they reached the courtyard, where a group of prisoners was being brought out under guard. Then a door opened and the first of fifty hostages, mostly women and children, groped their way into the wintry sun. They were blinded by the light, their faces filthy and streaked with blood, their bodies emaciated from a weeks-long diet of table scraps. Some were so weak they had to be helped to hobble out of the dank cellars. Capa, who had negotiated the terrors of the palace's shooting gallery without a second thought, broke down in tears at the sight.

Then it was dusk, and there was only one more photograph to take: the spire of the cathedral, with the flag of the Republic flying from the lantern tower to its right, showing that the Loyalists had indeed conquered the city. With that in his camera, Capa headed back to Barcelona with Matthews; the next day he was in Paris, and on January 21, along with John Ferno, he left for China.

January–February 1938: Key West

At the house on Whitehead Street there was a new brick wall around the property to keep out the celebrity hunters, and the lawn had been dug up for the new saltwater swimming pool; there were piles of unanswered mail and children clamoring for Hemingway's attention, and he was in no mood to deal with any of it.

He'd arrived in Paris—bilious from his liver complaint and suffering from insomnia—to find Pauline on the edge of hysteria. Anything seemed to set her off: she even became jealous when he went off to spend afternoons in a café with Malraux, Capa, and Gustav Regler, talking about Spain. But what really fed her fury were her suspicions about Martha. In their suite at the Elysée, Pauline raged, remonstrated, wept, even threatened to jump off the balcony. It was almost a relief when their ship, the *Gripsholm*, encountered fierce storms in the Atlantic that kept her seasick and confined to their cabin. She'd booked the tickets for convenience, because the ship docked first at Nassau before going on to New York, enabling them to disembark there and fly to Miami; but in the event it was good not to have to meet throngs of reporters at the pier in New York. *Mr. Hemingway, is there any truth to the rumors about you and Martha Gellhorn?*

Pauline's agitation subsided when she reached Key West, but Hemingway was more and more unhappy. Still seething over the fact that NANA hadn't wanted him to write more about Teruel (a subject he called "the best thing I've ever had I think"), he became enraged by a story in *Time* that seemed to imply that Herbert Matthews had been the only American reporter to cover that battle. What the hell, he fumed in a letter to his first wife, Hadley, he'd made it *possible* for Matthews to even be there. He'd engineered the passes from Constancia de la Mora, and persuaded her to let Matthews file more than just a rehash of the government's communiqué, *and* he'd scooped Matthews by ten whole hours. "Matthews is a wonderful guy and I'm glad I could be of any use to him," he said, with dubious sincerity. "But when you wait three months for something that you absolutely know is going to happen and then have your work absolutely and completely sabotaged . . . maybe I'd better change my name and start over." He was only slightly mollified by the memory of the reverence with which he'd been treated by *Ce Soir*, which had interviewed him on his arrival in Paris and given the results (in which he'd boasted several times of having "fought in Europe" in the last war) front-page treatment: "Hemingway, the great American writer, tells of the victory at Teruel."

He continued to fret over the reviews of *To Have and Have Not*; disappointed that after its initial flurry of activity it had failed to become a major seller, he wondered aloud to Max Perkins whether Scribner's had any plans for promoting it more aggressively. Then there was his connection to *Ken*. He'd gone along with advance publicity for the political glossy that named him one of the editors, but now he was waffling. He wired Arnold Gingrich a self-important disclaimer that he insisted the magazine run in its first issue: "Ernest Hemingway has been in Spain since *Ken* was first projected. Although announced as an editor, he has taken no part in the editing of the magazine or in the formation of its policies. If he sees eye to eye with us on *Ken* we would like to have him as an editor. If not he will remain as a contributor until he is fired or quits." Gingrich and the publisher, David Smart, accepted the qualification; but Hemingway kept pestering them about *Ken*'s commitment to antifascism and how far it went. "I don't think it necessarily follows," Gingrich finally responded, "if *Ken* praises, as it should, the Communists in Spain, that it must equally laud the Communists in this country. Because *Ken* is avowedly anti-totalitarian it is against the seizure of the government by a dictatorship of either the left or the right."

Hemingway's anxiety about *Ken*'s political stance wasn't alleviated, and may have been stoked, by a long letter he got from Joris Ivens, in Honolulu on the first stage of his journey across the Pacific to start work on his Sino-Japanese war documentary. Ivens was unhappy with Smart and Gingrich for publishing (in *Esquire*) "dirty" articles by the "enemy" Dos Passos—the most recent of which had expressed some ambivalence about the way Spain was being led—and he wanted Hemingway to use his "influence" on Smart to rectify the situation. "He should print now some decent articles about Spain." Maybe Hemingway should be the one to write them ("You know you are the propagandist!" Ivens joked), or maybe he should write another book or another play, like *The Fifth Column*, to "help us in [our] fight for Spain."

Despite its bracing, occasionally jocular tone, there was a certain heavy-handedness about Ivens's letter. Although he praised Hemingway for being such a good "Commissar" to Herbert Matthews ("I could read it all the time in his dispatches!") he wanted to make sure Hemingway understood the fine points of the "party and individual fights in Barcelona," and urged him to be in touch with "our leading people" in New York for clarification. And Ivens had an agenda for him: writing projects, a campaign against Dos Passos, financial oversight of the complicated revenue streams connected with Contemporary Historians and *The Spanish Earth*.

Hemingway *was* trying to get started on some short stories about Madrid—but they simply wouldn't assemble themselves on the page. He wondered if he was too close to the material. It didn't help that both Patrick and Gigi (Gregory) came down with measles and upset all the household routines; that Gustav Regler, newly arrived in the United States, would be coming to stay with the Hemingways on Whitehead Street on February 7, or that in the mail awaiting his attention was a clipping from the *St. Louis Post-Dispatch*: Capa's photograph of him at Teruel, wearing his glasses and a stocking cap and a windbreaker over his shabby tweed jacket. On the clipping was written, "Just picked up the paper my dearest and there you were, stocking cap and all, listening so hard to the man. It will hurt me forever that I did not do Teruel with you." The handwriting was Martha Gellhorn's.

"I am delighted to be back in Key West," Hemingway told a reporter from the local paper, the *Citizen*, who came to interview him on the last day of January. "It is my home, and where my family is." To Maxwell Perkins he was more honest. "I did not want to leave Spain," he wrote, "and all I want to do now is get back."

January–February 1938: Post Agency lecture circuit, United States

Good afternoon, ladies and gentlemen. We are fortunate to have with us this afternoon Miss Martha Gellhorn, correspondent for Collier's Magazine and author of The Trouble I've Seen, who will be speaking on "Both Sides of the World."

Martha Gellhorn was barnstorming. From Minneapolis, Milwaukee, Des Moines, and Chicago to St. Louis, Louisville, Montclair, Newark, and places in between—twenty-two cities in less than two months, trying (as she wrote to H. G. Wells) "to save the damned in one hour." At the University of Minnesota she told three thousand people that Spain was "a single cell where the body's illness [spreading fascism] could be fought and arrested"; at the Sheldon Concert Hall in St. Louis, where she'd been invited by the League for Industrial Democracy, she "called Franco a butcher." And instead of bridling at being lectured to (or at) by a twenty-nine-year-old bareheaded blonde in a short black dress, the overflow audiences at every whistle stop seemed to agree with the reporter for the *Louisville Courier-Journal*, who said she had "the voice, the culture, the art of pose, the poise, gesture, diction which succeed upon the stage at its best." On the basis of one article in *The New Yorker* and two in *Collier's*—her piece about the *brigadistas*, "Men Without Medals," had just been published in *Collier's* January 15 issue, for the handy sum of $1,000—Martha had become a certifiable Expert, and a star.

She wasn't gratified. She felt disdain for her audiences: "idiotic lazy cowardly half baked flabby folk" who wondered why she didn't wear a hat and whether she thought women should marry, and asked her, "Now which are the Loyalists, Miss Gellhorn, I just can't keep them all straight." She was depressed by the isolationism she encountered in her country, and by the inability of its leaders, including her revered Eleanor Roosevelt, to do anything to counter it. The travel and irregular meals had worn her out: she'd lost fourteen pounds in three weeks and was (she told Mrs. Roosevelt) "shaking with exhaustion." And despite her considerable ambition, she was discovering that fame could be a relentless and consuming thing. "I cannot tell you how I loathe lecturing," she complained to the First Lady: "the listening faces—I want people to talk back—the awful 'celebrity' angle which I have never met before and which makes me sick . . . I see these rows on rows of faces, often women and sometimes men, and think, 'I have one hour to tell them everything I have painfully learned and to shout at them if they go on sleeping they are lost.'"

Saying that her doctor had told her "either stop it or you will crack up," she canceled the last stops on her lecture tour and went home to St. Louis to be fussed over by her mother and receive telegraphed expressions of concern from the White House. "If one is a writer, one should be a writer, and not a lecturer," Martha wrote to Mrs. Roosevelt. "That's about all I do know now."

January–February 1938: Barcelona

Writing, Barea thought, was the only thing that was keeping him from going mad. The air raids were a constant threat now: the Italian Savoia bombers, based in Mallorca, had taken to cutting their engines while they were over the sea so they could glide silently in over Barcelona and release their cargoes of bombs without warning. Only then did the sirens, activated by sound sensors, start wailing. For Barea it was torture. Any loud noise made him panicked and nauseated, so that he had to concentrate to keep himself from vomiting; he couldn't sleep, and he was drinking and smoking too much.

Fortunately, he'd been able to bring Delmer's old typewriter with him from Playa de San Juan, and he'd started taking it down to an unused room behind the bar in the Ritz's basement, where he could work all day, and often all night, turning the radio talks of the Unknown Voice of Madrid into a series of stories—vignettes, really, or portraits, more like photographs than narratives—that recaptured the Madrid he had left behind. Sometimes he ventured out, to one ministry or another, hoping to find some other work he could do to help with the war effort; but he met with nothing but discouragement, from friends and acquaintances, or— from the younger, ambitious Party members—hostility. *It's my own fault*, he thought; *if I'd been more accommodating, I might still be working in Madrid.* But he didn't see how he could put aside his dreams of equality and social justice even to fight Franco, still less to get ahead with government higher-ups. Maybe Kulcsar was right; he would never fit in with these people. Better just to write.

He had nearly finished his manuscript when, on a Saturday evening at the end of January, the bar waiter at the Ritz told him that two agents of the SIM had come to talk to Ilsa. They were in the lobby, he said. Barea ran up the stairs.

Ilsa was sitting next to one of the agents, her face ashen, a piece of paper in her hand. Wordlessly, she handed it to Barea. A telegram: "POLDI DIED SUDDENLY FRIDAY. LETTER FOLLOWS."

Ilsa was overcome with guilt. All that night she berated herself: He had looked so ill when he'd left Barcelona, she said—he hadn't been taking care of his health, and if she had given him a chance, stayed with him, he might have rallied, gotten better. It was her fault he was dead. Barea could do nothing but sit beside her and hold her hand.

The letter, when it came, seemed to exonerate her: it was from her mother, who had been summoned by Kulcsar to Prague when he was hospitalized with what was diagnosed as kidney failure. Kulcsar had been entirely reconciled to Ilsa's relationship with Barea, her mother wrote; he thought the Spaniard a fine man with whom Ilsa would be happy. And that made *him* happy. However, her mother went on, Kulcsar had been adamant that Ilsa and Barea *must* get out of Spain and go to Paris. At once.

This insistence, and the manner of Kulcsar's death, might easily have made Ilsa more anxious, if less guilty, than before. What if Kulcsar's kidney failure wasn't the natural consequence of overwork, but the result of intentional poisoning by agents of his own organization, the NKVD? What if he'd been targeted for liquidation because he, like the other "Trotskyists" he'd been hunting, had been a member of the Spark—and had given his former wife, also a member of the group, a safe-conduct from the SIM? What if the NKVD was trying to eliminate people with potentially damaging information about one of its assets—specifically, the supposed fascist journalist Kim Philby? Father Lobo had put the problem succinctly to Ilsa back in Madrid: *You know too much, and too many people.*

If she wondered about these things, Ilsa said nothing, although her face was drawn and anxious and her green eyes more watchful than ever. And whatever her fears, Barea still didn't want to leave Spain. Things would resolve themselves, surely, he felt; he would finish his book of Madrid stories; he and Ilsa could get married; he would find war work to do. On the day after the telegram arrived, he was going over the final typescript of his book when the air-raid sirens started up. Ilsa was out, acting

as interpreter for a British peace activist friend of hers, Henry Brinton; and
Barea was terrified for her safety. Then the ground began shaking,
and Barea began to envision what could happen if the hotel were struck
by one of the deadly fuse bombs, designed not to detonate on impact but
to burrow deep into a tall building before blowing up and out and destroy-
ing the entire structure. Gagging as he crouched in the dark basement, he
heard a sucking sound and then a deafening explosion that seemed to
come from next door. The whole building rocked. Someone, somewhere,
began screaming.

When at last the all-clear sounded and he could leave the basement,
Barea found the houses next door to the hotel and behind it reduced to
rubble, the garden a surreal tangle of Venetian blinds, and Ilsa, safely returned from her duties, practically weeping with relief to discover him
alive after a raid that had killed hundreds of people. It was all unreal to
him; he felt as if, at last, some spring had snapped deep within him, so that
the mechanism kept working, but he had no control over it. He realized
he couldn't stay in Barcelona, or in Spain, any longer. He felt he would
certainly go insane.

Somehow, over the course of the next few weeks, the rights to his book,
which he was calling *Valor y miedo* ("Courage and Fear"), were sold to a
small press, Publicaciones Antifascistas de Cataluña, for just enough money
to pay their hotel bill; and with the help of friends he was granted the papers that would exempt him, on account of his broken nerves and ill-health,
from the most recent military draft of older men and boys, and allow him
to leave the country. And on a bright chill day smelling of spring, he and
Ilsa were married by a sardonic Catalan judge. "One of you is a widow,
the other divorced. What could I say to you that you don't know?" the
judge remarked dourly. "You're aware of what you're doing. Good luck."

On February 22, the day Barea's exit permit was due to expire, he and
Ilsa set out for the border crossing at La Junquera in a borrowed British
diplomatic car. The news that day was bad: after months of back and forth
battle in the bitter cold, and the loss of 60,000 men, Teruel had fallen finally and definitively to the Nationalists, causing an orgy of finger-pointing
and blame among the Loyalist commanders that targeted Indalecio Prieto,
the socialist defense minister. Now it seemed that the government's bad
luck was following Barea and Ilsa, for thirty miles from the border their
borrowed car broke down. The roadside garage couldn't repair it; they'd

have to go back to Barcelona, which would mean that Barea would have to reapply for an exit visa. Barea was in despair: it had taken all his strength to get this far, and he knew he could never go through it all again.

The garage owner looked at the threadbare couple with their three suitcases and their battered typewriter, took in the British flag on the car's bonnet and Ilsa's foreign accent. And he made a phone call to the police station: could someone come and drive these people to the border before it closed for the night?

In the end they made it to the *aduana* just as the church clock was striking twelve. The customs official barely glanced at them before he stamped their passports, and they crossed over into France.

March 1938: The North Atlantic

On March 18, bareheaded and without an overcoat, Ernest Hemingway dashed up the gangplank of the *Ile de France*, en route from New York to Le Havre, Paris, and Barcelona. Three days before, in Key West, he'd read in the newspapers that Nationalist troops, aiming to cut the Loyalist zone in two, had rolled through Aragon, encircling an American brigade base and advancing to within forty-five miles of the Mediterranean; "the fate of Spain," Herbert Matthews had intoned in *The New York Times*, "hangs in the balance at the front."

It was all the excuse Hemingway needed. Wiring Max Perkins to book him a stateroom at once on whatever ship was leaving soonest, he'd thrown clothes into a suitcase and got the clipper from Miami to Newark on the seventeenth. Either because he couldn't stop her or because, in an effort to assuage his feelings of guilt, he didn't want to, he'd allowed Pauline to accompany him to the dock. But although he'd been affectionate in the plane, calling her by his old pet name for her, "Poor Old Mama," they both knew he was about to put more than the Atlantic between them. "Where I go now I go alone," his alter ego, Philip Rawlings, had said at the end of *The Fifth Column*, "or with others who go there for the same reason I go." For Hemingway, now, that other was Martha.

He'd been busy in the days before he left. Despite Joris Ivens's recommendation that he distance himself from Gustav Regler, he'd written an introduction to be read before each of Regler's scheduled speaking engagements ("Gustav Regler has no right to be here; he should be in a cemetery in the outskirts of Valencia"). He'd dashed off a prefatory note for the catalog of Luis Quintanilla's war drawings, which were being shown at the Museum of Modern Art. He'd churned out a piece for *Ken*, "The Time Now, the Place Spain," which argued that fascist countries were moving boldly while democratic ones "talk, vacillate, connive, and betray," and the only way to counter an inevitable fascist-led war was to attack Italy, "fascism's weakest link," in Spain "and beat her now." Whatever reservations he, and Ivens, had had about *Ken*, he'd satisfied himself that it was sufficiently "leftwing anti-fascist" (as George Seldes, now acting as one of its editors, told him); they'd made him an offer of $200 every two weeks for a series of biweekly articles, and it seemed like the magazine would provide him with a platform for the kind of opinion pieces Ivens had urged him to produce and which, in his new role as public intellectual, he was eager to do. Certainly NANA wouldn't want them. He'd managed to get a new six-week contract from them, saying he wanted to gather additional material for a book, but Jack Wheeler hadn't been enthusiastic about it; they'd reduced his pay rate to $500 for every typed dispatch and $250 for every cabled one, and Wheeler told Hemingway he shouldn't expect much in the way of compensation unless the war spread to the rest of Europe.

Hemingway had another article due for *Ken*, and he'd stuffed his briefcase with the manuscripts of stories Max Perkins had agreed to publish in a collected edition in the autumn; but he didn't make any headway writing the one or organizing the other on shipboard. Instead, sitting down one day to flip through the February issue of *Redbook* magazine that he'd brought for deck-chair reading, he found, somewhere between an article about "Guest-Proof Houses" and a short story called "An Instinct for Love," an article by John Dos Passos entitled "Interlude in Spain." It was Dos's compressed, semifictionalized account of what he referred to as "The Fiesta at the Fifteenth Brigade"; and on its face there was nothing very upsetting about it: just the account of a military celebration in Spain. But the fact that Dos Passos, the "enemy" Ivens had warned him about, had identified the brigade in question as the Fifteenth, home of the Abraham Lincoln Battalion, and that he had underlined the presence at the fiesta of the "Russians," among them the Polish-born, Soviet-trained Colonel Walter— for some reason these things goaded Hemingway into a fury. He sent Dos Passos an angry, nearly incoherent cable which accused him of "ratting" on the Loyalists "for money" and getting the story wrong. Then, not satisfied that he'd attacked Dos Passos aggressively enough, he sent him a follow-up letter as soon as the *Ile de France* landed.

"I'm sorry I sent you that cable from the boat," he began; then moved swiftly from apology to aggression. "A war is still being fought in Spain between the people whose side you used to be on and the fascists. If with your hatred of communists you feel justified in attacking, for money, the people who are still fighting that war I think you should at least try to get the facts right." Dos, Hemingway said, had implied in his article that Communists were running the war in Spain, and "you name a Russian General you met. The only trouble about this, Dos, is that Walter is a pole. Just as Lucacz was a Hungarian, Petrov a Bulgarian, Hans a German, Copic a Yugo-Slav and so on." Ignoring the fact, which he well knew, that all these officers had been trained at the Soviet war college and had been sent by Stalin to help replace Franco's mutinous commanders, Hemingway mendaciously declared, "I'm sorry, Dos, but you didn't meet any Russian generals."

Nor, he continued, was this the only thing Dos Passos had gotten wrong. He'd also, in an earlier piece, for *Esquire*, written sympathetically about Andrés Nin. "Do you know where Nin is now?" asked Hemingway belligerently, parroting the NKVD slander that the murdered Nin had fled to Berlin. "You ought to find that out before you write about his death. But what the hell."

By now, having been alone with his own thoughts for too long ("I know the way your mind works round and round . . . like a dog in cover going over and over the same track," Archie MacLeish had once written him), Hemingway was in the claustrophobic grip of something close to paranoia. He began to wonder whether, if he was attacking Dos Passos this way, "the enemy" wouldn't also attack *him*. "Now I am very easy to attack and if you want, instead of trying to get straight on Spain you can simply attack me too. But that won't help you on the road you're going." Because, he said, the road his old friend was traveling was the road of betrayal. "Good old friends," Hemingway wrote, and it sounded like he'd been drinking: "Always happy with the good old friends. Got them will knife you in the back for a dime. Regular price two for a quarter. Two for a quarter, hell. Honest Jack Passos'll knife you three times in the back for fifteen cents and sing Giovanezza [the Italian black-shirt anthem] free."

For not repeating—as Hemingway himself was willing to—whatever the propagandists told him, Dos Passos was now (in Hemingway's eyes) not only a liar but a fascist. *It is very dangerous to write the truth in war,* Hemingway had said at the Writers' Congress, *and the truth is very dangerous to come by.* Honest Jack Passos could certainly tell you that.

As Hemingway was leafing through *Redbook* on the *Ile de France*, Martha Gellhorn was following him on the *Queen Mary*. She'd booked passage as soon as Hemingway told her his plans; as she wrote Eleanor Roosevelt, "The news has been terrible, too terrible, and I felt I had to get back . . . I don't believe anything any of us does now is useful. We just have to do it . . . I have gone angry to the bone, and hating what I see, and knowing how it is in Spain, I can see it so clearly everywhere else. I think now the only place for us all is in the front lines, where you don't have to think, and can simply (and uselessly) put your body up against what you hate."

Before leaving port on March 22, she'd cabled Hemingway to expect her in Cherbourg on the twenty-eighth; she'd also arranged to ship a car for them to use in Spain, which was traveling separately, on the *Aquitania*. And she'd got *Collier's* to sponsor her trip. "IF ANYTHING EVER STOPS OUR WORKING TOGETHER," the cable concluded, "THEN FUTURE NIX." Was it a commitment or an ultimatum? No wonder Hemingway had told Perkins, in a letter in February, that he was in "such an unchristly jam of every bloody kind . . . that it's practically comic."

March 1938: Paris

It was just another narrow, grimy building on a narrow street lined with similarly grimy buildings near the Gare Montparnasse, the hallways smelling of old cooked food, the floorboards creaking. The hotelkeeper's wife, a thin-lipped woman with jet-black eyes who still carried herself like the good-looker she'd been in her youth, told Barea and Ilsa that she could let them have the third-floor bedroom for less if they paid for a whole month in advance; so they gave her almost all the money they had, leaving only enough to buy meals for a few days. They could always pawn Barea's watch, or Ilsa's paisley shawl, they told themselves, as they followed Madame's swaying bottom up the three flights of stairs to the bedroom with its stained cabbage-rose wallpaper. Later, while Ilsa was trying to put their few clothes away in the battered armoire, Barea tried to cheer her up. The Hotel Delambre, on the rue Delambre—if you said it in Spanish, it was *Hotel del Hambre* on the *rue del Hambre*, the Hunger Hotel on Hunger Street.

They'd arrived in Perpignan to discover that, despite his assurances, Kulcsar had left no funds on deposit at the bank in Ilsa's name. Maybe he'd forgotten; maybe he'd never intended to repay their loan. With only four hundred francs between them they had been lucky to get a lift to Paris from a friend of Sefton Delmer's; the car wasn't heated, and the drive had taken all night, with a predawn rest stop somewhere near Clermont-Ferrand, where a factory whistle set Barea's stomach lurching. Now, in Paris, they looked for work—translating, writing, anything they could find—but it was 1938; the tide of émigrés from fascism was swelling; and there was little work to be had. A commercial translation agency threw a few jobs their way, and Barea managed to sell a handful of sketches from *Valor y miedo* to some leftist papers in France and abroad; but the sums involved were negligible and although the acceptance letters bought them some time from their landlady, soon they were behind on their rent. On some days they might be able to afford the seven francs for the set menu in one of the *bistrots du quartier*; more often they went hungry, fueled only by bread and black coffee. Meanwhile the stress of the past year had finally caught up with Ilsa, and she was suffering from rheumatic pains and exhaustion; but she dragged herself out of bed and went in search of work, or just friends from whom she could borrow a little money for food.

They wrote to Ilsa's parents, the Pollaks, in Vienna, saying that they were married, and had gone to Paris—as Kulcsar had urged them to—and were working, but their economic situation was "precarious"; Barea included a photograph of himself, and an attempt at self-explanation or self-justification, telling his new parents-in-law of his love and deep respect for their daughter. But they heard nothing. And then, on March 13, they found out why.

Two days before, after a month of escalating threats and ultimatums that gave the Nazi Party greater and greater power in Austria, Hitler—

claiming the alternative was to turn the country into "another Spain"—
had forced the resignation of his nominal ally, the Austrian prime minister
Kurt von Schuschnigg. On the night of the eleventh, 200,000 German
troops had crossed the border, and on the twelfth, the dreaded head of
the SS, Heinrich Himmler, arrived in Vienna, followed—in a triumphal
motorcade—by Hitler himself. No longer a sovereign nation, Austria was
now only another part of Hitler's Thousand Year Reich; the streets of
Vienna, Barea and Ilsa read in *L'Humanité*, echoed with cries of "One
People! One Reich! One Führer!" Within days the anti-Jewish laws of
Germany were being enforced in Vienna, the city of Mahler, Schnitzler,
and Freud; Jewish shops and homes were looted; Jewish factories, stores,
and restaurants were designated by signs forbidding Aryans to patronize
them; and Jews were forbidden to own property, to employ or be employed
by others, or to practice their professions.

What this meant to the Jewish headmaster Valentin Pollak and to his
Gentile wife Alice, Barea and Ilsa could only guess.

Martha landed at Cherbourg on March 28. For her, and for Hemingway,
it had been a long separation—more than three months. One day she
would write a story about lovers who have been apart for a long time:
"You've been gone so long I don't know how to treat you." They figured it
out. *Mr. Scrooby, as friendly as a puppy and as warm as fur.*

They had more than endearments to share: they were, as she'd declared at the beginning, members of the same union, and just now they
were needed on the front lines. The situation in Spain was as terrible as
Martha had envisioned: in the past week or so the insurgent juggernaut
had swept across Aragon and the Loyalist defense line had "crumpled like
paper," as Herbert Matthews would say later. In Barcelona, horrific air
raids were killing more than a thousand people a day in sorties that lasted
for hours and were being used to test yet one more obscene weapon in the
bombardier's arsenal: antipersonnel bombs that exploded horizontally on
impact, shearing trees off below the branch line and vaporizing any or-
ganism within range. Between the allies' anti-intervention policy and the
fact that the French government had sealed the border, Spain couldn't
acquire the ammunition or antiaircraft guns to defend itself against the
weapons and planes sent by Germany and Italy; and factional fighting

was immobilizing the government. It looked entirely possible that the Republic would collapse within a matter of weeks.

John Wheeler at NANA had cabled Hemingway in Paris, asking him to report the developing news from the fascist side instead of returning to his comfortable berth among the Loyalists; but Hemingway wasn't enthusiastic about following up the request. He had a *Ken* article to write—in which he excoriated the Catholic archbishop of New York, Patrick Cardinal Hayes, for supposed complicity in the Saint Patrick's Day bombing of Barcelona that killed 118 children—and he was much more concerned about what would happen to the more than 500 wounded American brigaders in Loyalist hospitals in Spain if the Fascists won. On March 29, goaded by Martha to "see . . . the top people and yell at them," he made a flying visit to the American ambassador to Spain, Claude Bowers, in the border town of St. Jean de Luz, where he extracted from the ambassador a promise to evacuate the wounded and the medical personnel looking after them.

He was only gone for half a day, but by the time he returned there was better news: the French government had unsealed the border and promised to ship forty-five planes and some heavy artillery to Spain; and Prime Minister Negrín, pledging that his government would "resist, resist, resist," had made a radio broadcast asking for 100,000 new volunteers for the army. By the time Hemingway boarded the night train to Perpignan on the thirty-first—Martha was traveling separately with the car that had come on the *Aquitania*—he was feeling a good deal more cheerful. He had company on the train, the *Herald-Tribune's* Vincent Sheean, whom everyone called Jimmy, and Sheean's younger *Trib* colleague, Ring Lardner's son James, a gangly bespectacled twenty-three-year-old who'd become a reporter immediately after graduating from Harvard and, despite his age and inexperience, knew far more about the war and its leading characters than the veteran Sheean did. The three of them sat up much of the night in Sheean's *wagon-lit*, talking and lubricating themselves with swigs from Hemingway's capacious silver flask. "I don't know why you're going to Spain, anyhow," grumbled Hemingway to Sheean, at one point. "The only story you could get would be to get killed, and that'll do you no good. I'll write that."

"Not half as good a story as if *you* get killed," responded Sheean, "and I'll write that." Lardner, a kid allowed to sit with the grown-ups, laughed and laughed.

April 1938: Barcelona

The Hotel Majestic was, Jimmy Sheean thought, maybe the worst hotel in Europe. The food was bad, and there wasn't much of it. The rooms were frequently dark because of power outages, and Barcelona had run out of soap, so the chambermaids stripped the dirty sheets off the beds, ironed them, and put them back on, grimy but freshly pressed. But in the lounge or the big dining room, where the mirrored walls were x-ed with paper strips to protect against air raids, you could nearly always find a group of journalists or furloughed International Brigaders talking or drinking: Sheean, Hemingway, Martha Gellhorn, Tom Delmer, Herbert Matthews, young Jim Lardner, Evan Shipman, Marty Hourihan. (An exception was André Malraux, who stayed with the profiteers and their floozies at the Ritz: "I prefer whores to bores," he said.) They needed to talk and drink together in the evening, because the daytime was always full of bad news.

By the beginning of April, the rebel army, augmented by Italian troops and German and Italian aircraft, had pushed eastward from Saragossa; and the Loyalists had fallen back, down the valley of the Ebro toward the Mediterranean. On April 3, Lérida, the stronghold of the POUM militia in the days when Capa and Gerda visited it at the beginning of the war, was lost to the Nationalists; the nearby mountain reservoirs and their hydroelectric plants, which supplied much of the power for Barcelona, went with it. Next was Gandesa, where the American and British battalions had both been surrounded, with many killed and more missing. But still the rebels came on, and the beleaguered Loyalist army and International Brigades retreated, trying to preserve men and matériel, regroup, and fight on.

Before dawn most mornings Hemingway and Martha would leave Barcelona, generally with Delmer and Matthews accompanying them, and drive long hours along bomb-pitted roads choked with refugees, soldiers, tanks and artillery, to where the story was today. Sometimes there was fighting along their route and they had to detour; sometimes the Italian Savoias or German Heinkels bombed the road, or the Fiat fighters swooped dangerously low over it, and they had to get out of the car and huddle behind stone walls for shelter. They made an odd sight speeding along in their fancy open car: Hemingway in his ratty wool stocking cap and battered tweeds, Martha with a bandanna tied around her blond bob to keep away the dust from the road, Delmer in a too-small leather aviator's cap, and Matthews puffing away on his ever-present cigar. People wondered if they were Russians. The weather was unsettlingly balmy and springlike, and the palisaded bluffs along the Ebro, the slopes of the coastal sierra, frothy with almond blossom, and the glassy, foam-edged sea looked like plaster scenery. Even the spring sun, Martha thought, seemed made of "translucent paper." Except that the thunder of the big guns, the rumble of the tanks, and the *bung-bung-bung* of the bombs dropping from the silver Heinkels and Savoias were real, and territory was being lost and people were dying. The destruction everywhere was the worst she could remember, and her spirits were very low. Although she could still muster fury when writing to Eleanor Roosevelt, privately she felt despair. "It was hard to believe the war is almost over and almost lost," she wrote in her diary.

On April 4, in the hills behind Rasquera, on the east bank of the Ebro, they found Milton Wolff, Freddy Keller, Alvah Bessie, and several other members of the Washington-Lincoln Battalion, who had had to cut their way through enemy lines and swim naked across the Ebro to safety after being surrounded in the night by Nationalist infantry. Keller had been wounded in the hip, but at least he was alive and accounted for. Many of those who'd tried to swim across had drowned or been shot by the insurgents, and the battalion commissar, Dave Doran, and chief of staff Robert Merriman, whose exploits at Belchite had made Martha "proud as a goat," were still missing. But these bleak reverses didn't seem to unsettle Hemingway. From his earliest days hunting and fishing in Michigan, he had always found strength in the company of men, in being a man among men; to be back among the Loyalist commanders he admired seemed to stiffen his spine. And he had Martha beside him, with her long legs and her smart mouth, and that helped. On the tenth, they lunched on mutton chops with tomatoes and onions and drank red wine out of a tin can with Lieutenant Colonel Juan Modesto, the tough, handsome, sarcastic thirty-two-year-old Andalusian Communist, at his headquarters in the middle of a vineyard. Although Modesto seemed weary and grubby in his worn uniform and *alpargatas*, he stated confidently that the Nationalists would never get to the sea. Just then a shell landed a hundred yards away. "They're shooting at the map," he said, dismissively. "That sort of shooting isn't serious." It was the kind of talk Hemingway loved, and he took on some of Modesto's cockiness. "Franco's forces are absolutely held up in their attempt to come down the Ebro," he told the American readers of his NANA dispatches.

A little more than a week later, though, a midnight bulletin issued by Constancia de la Mora's office indicated that there was trouble on the coast road south of the river, and the next day, Good Friday, April 15, Hemingway and Martha joined Matthews and Delmer to see for themselves what was happening. It was four in the morning when they left Barcelona, the silver moon dimming the blue glow of the blackout. Delmer drove. Near Tarragona the sun came up, illuminating clusters of refugees traveling north; they weren't carrying very much, which meant they'd left their homes in a hurry. At Tortosa, at the head of the Ebro delta, a once-picturesque town now laid waste by daily aerial bombardments, the journalists crossed the swollen yellow flood of the river on the great, three-spanned steel bridge and turned left onto the Valencia highway, wondering where the fighting had got to and what they would find around the next bend.

They soon found out. First bombers, then fighter planes roared over the road, and they all dove out of the car to take shelter. Bombs were falling on Tortosa, behind them, and on the Loyalist lines in front of them, and the fighters were strafing Ulldecona, where they were headed. Meanwhile, motorcycle couriers were racing up and down the highway, but not even they seemed to know what was going on. On the outskirts of Ulldecona a group of Loyalist staff officers, huddled over a map, filled the journalists in: the Nationalists had broken through the government lines and were now fighting their way toward Vinaroz, on the coast; two more rebel columns were headed north. Afraid of being trapped by the advancing Nationalists, Hemingway told Delmer to turn around and began retracing their route.

They had been driving for almost eight hours by now and they were dusty and hungry, so they stopped for lunch in an olive grove, where they found Jimmy Sheean, the *Daily Worker*'s Joe North, and two other colleagues, on their way to Ulldecona. As they all ate their sandwiches more bombers flew over, headed for Tortosa, and soon a cloud of smoke and dirt mushroomed on the horizon, accompanied by the continuous thunder of explosive. Finally the bombing stopped, and Hemingway tried to talk

Sheean out of continuing toward the front, but Sheean (who suspected Hemingway of trying to keep a scoop to himself) insisted on pressing on.

It was dangerous no matter where you went. As Delmer navigated the fresh bomb craters on the road just outside Tortosa, a guard came running over to the car, waving his arms: the bridge they'd driven over in the morning, the great steel structure that Hemingway had declared as impervious to bombs as "a bottle on a string at a French fair," had been demolished little more than an hour ago, and the only way across the swollen Ebro was on a rickety footbridge, itself severely battered by the bombardment. Soldiers were hastily laying boards along its length to reinforce it and cover the holes; trucks probably couldn't cross it, but their car might be able to. The journalists decided to take the risk: the Nationalists' Savoias could return at any minute, and the car was an easy target. Hemingway and Matthews got out and walked to lighten the load, and Delmer let in the clutch and rolled onto the bridge just behind a mule cart whose iron wheels made the boards rattle alarmingly. There was a gaping hole halfway across and they all averted their eyes so as not to see where they'd end up if the bridge gave way.

Finally they reached the other side, and found themselves in an inferno. Tortosa was still ablaze from the morning's attacks and Delmer had to speed through streets full of burning debris to the Barcelona highway. There they had to slow down, because the road was clogged with military vehicles and fleeing civilians. Nobody found very much to say. Suddenly exhausted, Martha leaned against the car window and stared at the people they passed: an old woman cradling a chicken, a young woman clutching a canary, a mother incongruously making up her face in a small mirror. "A retreat," Martha told herself, fighting despair, "can be braver than an attack."

It was dark when Hemingway and his companions drew up in front of the Majestic. Although they'd been working for fourteen hours with barely a letup, they still had dispatches to file; and Hemingway's—which was accompanied by a request that NANA wire Pauline to tell her he was all right—marked the first glimmer of doubt in the hopeful story he had been trying to frame for so long. Good Friday, he said, marked "a bad night for the west bank of the Ebro."

Exactly how bad he had yet to find out. For that afternoon, as he and his companions had been inching their way across the bridge at Tortosa, soldiers of the insurgent general Alonso Vega's 4th Navarrese Division had waded, delirious with joy, into the Mediterranean at Vinaroz, while their commander dipped his fingers in the salt water as if into a baptismal font and crossed himself. "The victorious sword of Franco," as one newspaper in insurgent Seville would put it, "had cut in two the Spain occupied by the reds."

On April 24, after playing all over Europe, an edited version of *The Spanish Earth* opened in Barcelona with Spanish dubbed narration, new music, and different, less realistic sound effects. For weeks Barcelona had been papered with advertising posters for the film that carried a comment from Franklin Roosevelt (one of the remarks he'd made informally to Hemingway and Ivens at the White House screening), and the theater was crowded. But five minutes after the titles ran, just at the point where the narrator was asserting that, to win the war, the rebels *had* to cut the Madrid-Valencia road, the screen suddenly went dark. An announcement came from the back of the theater: "Gentlemen, there is an air raid alarm." Instead of the clumsy sound effects, the audience could hear the real-life thudding of the ack-ack guns as bombs fell on the outskirts of the city. No one moved. After a while the manager played "The Hymn of Riego" and the Catalan anthem "Els Segadors" (*"Drive out these people, so conceited, so arrogant!"*) on the theater's loudspeakers and everybody sang along and applauded; after about an hour the all-clear sounded, and the projectionist started up again.

At the picture's end the lights went on and someone pointed out Hemingway in the audience, seated with Martha and his journalist buddies; he got a five-minute ovation. Then Jim Lardner, who had also been in the audience, came up to say goodbye: he was going from the theater to the International Brigades headquarters to enlist as a gun layer, the man who calculates the angle and trajectory of a gun, in the artillery corps. He'd talked about doing this before, and both Hemingway and Jimmy Sheean had tried to dissuade him. It was too late to enlist, they told him; there were rumors the brigades were going to be disbanded. Anyway his eyesight was bad, and he was a journalist, not a soldier. Why didn't he go to Madrid, Hemingway wanted to know, and stay there until it fell to the Nationalists, and write about *that*? That was a story no one else would have. But Lardner was adamant. As the junior *Trib* correspondent in Spain he felt redundant, he said; he wanted to make a *real* contribution to the

Loyalist cause, in which he'd come to believe "absolutely" and confidently, and action, not writing, was the way to accomplish that. Going to Madrid and waiting for it to be taken over so he could write about it seemed "defeatist" to him.

Hemingway—paradoxically for a man for whom action had always been a byword, and who had been so desperate to be a part of the Great War that he'd become a Red Cross ambulance driver when the army rejected him for his poor eyesight—seemed exasperated rather than sympathetic. Although he sent a short human-interest story about the new volunteer to NANA the next day, it was perfunctory and impersonal, and somehow managed to make its subject seem like a coddled Ivy Leaguer with an unrealistic idea of his own abilities. Privately, Hemingway was even more dismissive: Lardner, he said, was "pig-headed" and "a superior little snot."

Something was eating at him. It wasn't just anxiety over the course of the war: it was deeper than that, something that went to his essence, to the part of him that craved only to "write one true sentence." For the past year, except for *The Fifth Column* and the stories he'd been unable to make progress on down in Key West, he had written nothing but propaganda. The *Spanish Earth* narration, the Carnegie Hall speech, the fund-raising talks, the articles for *Ken*, the preface to the book of Luis Quintanilla's drawings, even the purportedly journalistic, highly compensated NANA dispatches, which he'd been churning out almost daily since he returned to Spain—they were all eloquent, vivid, often heartfelt. But they were in the service of something other than his own vision, and though he would loudly proclaim otherwise, he knew not all of them were truthful. *You are the propagandist*, Ivens had told him; but that wasn't who he really was, who he wanted to be. *Just write one true sentence.* Sitting in the theater, he'd heard the real bombs and guns interrupt their filmed, manipulated avatars in *The Spanish Earth*; saying goodbye to Lardner, he'd been face to face with his younger, eager self. And the contrast must have unsettled him.

A week earlier, on Easter Sunday, he'd gone with Martha and Matthews to Amposta, in the Ebro delta below Tortosa, to see how far the rebel tide had reached: on the way they saw more cars, more carts, more refugees, a Breughel landscape of dispossession. A pontoon bridge had been put in place where the permanent one had been bombed by the Nationalists; and as Hemingway's car went over the bridge, the journalists passed an old man in dust-covered clothes and steel-rimmed glasses like Hemingway's, sitting on the ground. When they returned several hours later, having made certain that the rebel armies hadn't yet made it to the banks of the Ebro, the retreat had passed on but the old man was still there. They stopped the car and Hemingway got out. He took one of the pieces of paper he used for note-taking out of his pocket—a letter-size sheet, folded in quarters marked 1, 2, 3, and 4, so he could write on it easily, unfolding and refolding it as he filled each numbered quarter. He'd already noted the gray sky and now-empty road, the detritus of flight, scattered corn kernels from a chicken coop tied to the back of a peasant's cart; now he wanted to know something about the old man in glasses. The old man said he'd come from San Carlos, on the coast. He'd been taking care of a couple of goats, some cats, four pairs of pigeons, and hadn't wanted to leave them; but the army captain told him the artillery was coming, so he'd walked, twelve kilometers since daylight. He was worried about the animals; and he was tired, too tired to go on. He could get a ride on a truck, Hemingway suggested; but the truck would take the old man to Barcelona, and he had no wish to go there, he said. He would stay by the bridge.

Hemingway wrote down enough to remember things: the sky, the road, the old man, the animals. And then, because he and Matthews had deadlines, and were still six hours from Barcelona, they left.

Back at the Majestic, Hemingway mulled over what to do with his notes from the trip to the delta. He could file a NANA dispatch about the Nationalist advance (imperceptible) and the Loyalist retreat (orderly), which would end up covering the same ground as Matthews, and run the risk of the *Times* spiking his story because of duplication. Or he could write something about the old man who had caught his fancy. It wouldn't be something for NANA; but it would do for *Ken*, and he owed them a piece this week. He set to work.

What emerged wasn't a polemic, like the other articles he had done for *Ken*, nor larded with military exegesis, like so many of his NANA dispatches. It was short, barely more than two pages long; and it was sharp and tight, the way his best fiction was—simply an account of his conversation with the old peasant at Amposta, a man claiming to be "without politics," who has walked so far he doesn't think he can go farther, who has had to abandon what was left in his care, and who in turn is abandoned by the narrator to the advancing fascists. The story's last image is of the old man, sitting on the ground by the bridge, on an overcast day whose clouds has kept Nationalist bombers back at their bases: "That and the fact that cats know how to look after themselves," the narrator explains, "was all the good luck that old man would ever have." *That* was a true sentence; maybe the truest Hemingway had written in Spain.

Unlike Hemingway's journalism pieces, but like his fiction, this story (as he would later write to Arnold Gingrich) "took charge of itself very quickly"; by 11:10 that evening he was cabling the finished version to *Ken*. And the next day Gingrich wired him that it was "marvelous," adding: "THESE SHORT PUNCHES HAVE DONE MORE GOOD FOR LOYALIST CAUSE THAN VOLUMES ORDINARY REPORTING."

Although she made copious notes as she and Hemingway and their companions chased the front along the Ebro, Martha wasn't writing much for publication during this trip to Spain. She'd wanted to do a piece for *Collier's* about the plight of the refugees she'd seen on the road and described in her journal; it would be like an account of "the last days of Pompeii," she told her editors. But *Collier's* wasn't interested. "Stale by the time we publish," they cabled back. The attention of the world had moved on to an increasingly probable European conflict, and the magazine wanted her to go to France, and England, and—now that Hitler was eyeing it so greedily— Czechoslovakia, and find out what was going on there. Rumors had begun to circulate that a German invasion—like the incursion into Austria in March—was imminent. If that happened a European war wouldn't be far behind.

Martha was torn. On the one hand, as she wrote to Eleanor Roosevelt, "What goes on here seems to be the affair of all of us who do not want a world whose bible is *Mein Kampf.*" Spain, she believed, was "fighting our battle"; and it should be "saved for decent people"—not fascists—because "it's far too beautiful to waste." But she sensed, even as Hemingway struggled *not* to, that the fight was over, that writing any more about Spain wouldn't save it, that her work was elsewhere now. She begged off an excursion to the American brigade's headquarters at Darmos for May Day celebrations because she couldn't bear to listen to the hopeful and hortatory speeches that would be a part of it; and although Hemingway and Herbert Matthews were planning to travel to Madrid to report on conditions there she declined to accompany them, exasperated by the amount of red tape she'd have to cut through to get clearance.

"Maybe," she wrote in her diary, making herself feel better about her choices, "history is just a big stinking mess and a big injustice anyhow, and the victory is always wrong. But one thing is sure: good men are as absolute as the mountains and as fine, and as long as there are any good men then it is worth while to live and be with them And one cannot feel utterly hopeless about the future knowing that such people exist, whether they win or not."

At the beginning of May she went with Matthews and Hemingway to Marseille, from which they planned to fly into the Loyalists' southern zone; then, by leisurely stages, she drove north to Paris. And on May 1, Prime Minister Negrín, one of her "good men," released a thirteen-point peace manifesto, outlining the sort of government—a much-watered-down version of the Popular Front, with accommodation for private capital and an amnesty for the rebels—he envisioned for a postwar Spain, if the back-channel negotiations he'd been making to Franco through the Vatican and other parties resulted in an armistice. All he had to do was keep fighting until Franco said yes. He didn't seem to understand that the only thing Franco was interested in was unconditional surrender.

May 1938: Madrid

Hemingway and Matthews arrived at the Hotel Florida on May 9. They'd flown down the coast the day before, the only two passengers in a twenty-two-seat plane, gazing out the windows at the brown hills—"like a dinosaur come to drink," Hemingway said—that were all that stood between the Nationalist lines and Castellón and Valencia; and their visit to the front at Castellón had reassured them that the Nationalists' steamroller advance seemed to have stalled, at least momentarily. Madrid cheered them up even more. Dropping in on their old haunts in the trenches in University City and talking to the soldiers, they'd concluded that Fortress Madrid was, as Hemingway described it, "unchanged and more solid than ever." If Hemingway had had a crisis of confidence in Barcelona, two days of high-level military briefings were enough to cure it: they had plenty of guns and ammunition, the commanders told him, all they needed was more artillery, more planes, more automatic weapons, and they could *win* this thing. He wanted to believe them; "certainly there will be bitter fighting," he cabled to NANA, "but there is a year of war clearly ahead where European diplomats are trying to say it will be over in a month."

The Hotel Florida, Hemingway and Matthews found, was outwardly the same as they remembered it, if slightly more shell-battered, with Don Cristóbal still tending his stamp collection at the reception desk; but the pilots and correspondents and *whores de combat* had for the most part moved on, and the raucous sense of life that had pervaded the place in the first year and a half of the war seemed to have ebbed away. In the lobby Hemingway ran into *The Daily Worker*'s Joe North, who had also come to check the situation in Madrid. As editor at *The New Masses*, North had been responsible for commissioning Hemingway's "Who Killed the Vets" piece in 1935; and he'd watched the formerly apolitical Hemingway's evolution into an engagé writer and antifascist spokesman with interest and some skepticism. Did he now try to probe the depth and nature of Hemingway's commitment to antifascism? Whatever it was, Hemingway—beginning to chafe at the propagandist's harness, and probably several drinks beyond rationality—turned swiftly pugnacious. "I like the Communists when they're soldiers," he said to North, doubtless thinking of Líster, Modesto, even the irascible Walter; "but when they're priests I hate them." North must have looked puzzled, because Hemingway went on to explain: "Yes, priests, the commissars who hand down the papal bulls."

Nonsense, North replied; the generals were good soldiers *because* of their political conviction, not in spite of it. He didn't add, although he could have, *What about your friend Gustav Regler, the political commissar? Or the Lincoln Brigade's Marty Hourihan?* Because by now Hemingway was dancing around the room on the balls of his feet, shadowboxing. "I keep fit that way," he said, swiping at North. Then, sneering: "I suppose *you* keep fit reading *Das Kapital*."

Suddenly, as quickly as it had appeared, the black cloud of hostility blew away. Hemingway dropped his fists and started laughing. "Hell," he told North, "I believe you're one of the goddamn bishops." Sketching a sacerdotal little bow, he held out the whiskey bottle. "Here, *mi padre*, a libation."

May 1938: Paris

Martha had been zigzagging north, from Marseille up through the French Alps to the Napoleonic fortress town of Briançon, then across the vineyards and wheatfields of *la France profonde*, gathering material for a *Collier's* article on the state of the country; and she reached Paris in the last week of May, just before Hemingway sailed for New York on the *Normandie* on May 25. "Am going home to see Pauline and the kids and take them wherever they want to go," he'd written to a friend. "Have neglected my family very badly this year and would like to make it up." Whether he'd be *able* to make it up was an open question: Pauline had already warned him not to come home and sulk, like last time. "If you are happy over there don't come back here to be unhappy," she'd told him. But he seemed reluctant to take responsibility for his happiness, or anyone else's.

As for Martha, once again watching her lover leave her behind: she was, as she wrote to her mother, "not exactly happy, but . . . being what the French call 'reasonable.' There isn't anything left to be, I have tried everything else. I believe he loves me, and he believes he loves me, but I do not believe very much in the way one's personal destiny works out, and I do not believe I can do anything about this."

What she *could* do was throw herself into her work. On the trip north she'd talked to postmen and metalworkers and border guards, noticed the new tanks rolling along the roads of Burgundy and the new fortifications in the high passes of Quercy. Now, in Paris she had meetings with the fascist Jacques Doriot and the Communist Maurice Thorez; and to fill out what she called "the bright or social end" of her article, she went to lunch with the Aga Khan, to the races at Longchamp, to cocktails among the *gratin*—the upper crust. As her mother's well-connected, socially conscious daughter, Martha had always moved easily between the picket line and the receiving line; her years with Bertrand de Jouvenel had given her entrée to the most exalted salons of Paris, and her time with Hemingway in Spain had put her on easy footing with the soldiers, politicians, and journalists in whose male-dominated club she enjoyed being the smart, sassy, good-looking "It" girl. She'd tested her own courage and perseverance in the back country and under fire, and—in her work on *The Spanish Earth*—her ability to pull strings. And her writing had taken on an authority and toughness that came from her increased self-assurance. Although she'd been sincere in her passion for *la causa*, now Spain had become just another thing to be angry about in a growing list of bigger things. She had moved on.

"The war in Spain was one kind of war," she wrote to Eleanor Roosevelt, already using the past tense; "the next world war will be the stupidest, *lyingest*, cruelest sell-out in our time."

Behind on the rent again. Ilsa just couldn't bear meeting Madame's boot-button stare when she went past the desk in the hotel lobby; so it was Barea who sneaked down the stairs, waiting until the landlady's back was turned before he darted out into the street. Hoping to find a friend from Spain who could lend him a little money, or at least give him a cigarette, he headed for the Dôme, on the corner where the rue Delambre intersected with the Boulevard Montparnasse. He scanned the crowd enjoying the spring evening on the *terrasse* under the black iron marquee: nobody he knew. So then, inside, where the din of conversation bounced off the tile floor and the smell of food made him light-headed. Still no one. But, at his customary seat at one end of the horseshoe-shaped bar, there was a little man Barea had noticed before, whose shiny suit and pencil mustache gave him a forlorn kind of respectability. The little man never spoke, just nursed a glass of Pernod and water from which he occasionally looked up, pointed at some unsuspecting person, and began gesticulating wildly and wordlessly at him before falling motionless again over his drink. This evening Barea caught a glimpse of his face, the eyes empty and dead, like the windows of one of the bombed apartment buildings in Madrid, and realized the man was mad.

With that realization came another, a revelation, really: despite the fears that had haunted him for months, he himself was *not* going mad. Yes, he'd been weakened and traumatized; but the thing that had tormented him, that had both goaded him into action and destroyed his ability to act effectively, wasn't terror, and wasn't lunacy: it was the conflict within himself. He'd wanted to win his own war with society, but he'd refused to make any compromises to do it. He'd wanted to change, but he didn't want to turn his back on who he was. Trying to avoid these contradictions had led him into a fog of denial and deprived him of the will to go forward. Suddenly he could see this, as the little man with his Pernod *couldn't* see what was preying on *him*. And, he thought, he could fight his way out of it if he faced it and explored it.

Even more important, exploring his own conflicts might help him explain, to himself, and maybe to others, the crisis of his generation in Spain. *That* was what he should be writing about, not propaganda, not human-interest reportage. He should tell his own story, the story of his childhood and coming of age in a world that was changing beyond recognition. He might not be a Hemingway, or a Dos Passos, but he could, he must, write the truth about what had happened to him and to his country. *A writer who will not lie cannot live under fascism.* He hadn't been at Carnegie Hall to hear Hemingway say that, but he knew, perhaps better than Hemingway did, that it was true.

For the first time in months, though he was still starving and penniless, he felt as if a weight had rolled off his shoulders.

On May 29, as a watery sun at last broke through the rain clouds that had hung like bunting over Paris for two days, two very different commemorative events were taking place.

In the Avenue George V, at the American Cathedral, the U.S. ambassador, William Bullitt, the Duke and Duchess of Windsor, and France's Marshal Pétain, hero of Verdun, among a multitude of others, attended a memorial service for the fallen soldiers of the Great War. Hymns were sung, "Taps" was played, and at the ceremony's end the flags of Britain, the United States, and France, which had been carried into the sanctuary, were dipped in tribute. Afterward, a detachment of the Garde Républicaine and the 24th Colonial Regiment accompanied Ambassador Bullitt to the Arc de Triomphe, where he solemnly laid a wreath on the Tomb of the Unknown Soldier.

At the other end of Paris, a crowd numbering in the thousands—factory workers, officials of the French Communist Party, young women, old men, Spanish war orphans—converged on Père-Lachaise cemetery, at whose wall 147 holdouts of the Paris Commune had been gunned down and shoveled into a mass grave fifty-eight years before. The crowd's banners and placards fluttered in the spring breeze: *Unity!* they cried; *Jobs for the Young, Retirement for the Old!* And also, *Down with Fascism! Help the Spanish Republic! End the Embargo!* As the marchers approached the sacred wall, whose stones were still riddled with bullet holes from the volleys that had killed the Communard martyrs, some noticed a new installation: the grave of Gerda Taro, which lay nearby, had finally been marked by a stone.

And not just any stone. On the gray slab that had been placed over the grave the Italian sculptor Alberto Giacometti had erected a kind of bier made from granite blocks, in the center of which rose a rectangular stele bearing Gerda's name, her birth and death dates (the former a year later than her actual date of birth), and the inscription: KILLED IN JULY, 1937, ON THE FRONT AT BRUNETE SPAIN IN THE EXERCISE OF HER PROFESSION. In front of the stele, at one corner of the stone bier, was an empty stone bowl, like a ritual vessel; to the side of the plinth was the carved, elementally simple figure of a bird—whether dove or falcon, or something else, it was difficult to say.

Giacometti was already famous as a sculptor, and getting him to make a monument for Gerda was no small undertaking, although as a leftist he was sympathetic to the cause for which she died. The editors at *Ce Soir*, among them Louis Aragon, Giacometti's friend, took responsibility for persuading him to accept the commission; but then there was the matter of his fee. The person who paid that was Capa.

June–July 1938: Key West

Hemingway's homecoming had not, so far, been a success. Stopping briefly in New York after he landed, he'd gone to dinner with Jay Allen and his wife in Washington Square, pumping them with questions about Pauline's probable state of mind, and blaming his sister-in-law, Jinny Pfeiffer, for telling Pauline lies about him. Martha was never mentioned. He flew to Miami the next day, then on to Key West, where Pauline met his plane, having protected herself with company—their sons, Patrick and Gigi, and a family friend, Toby Bruce—for the drive back to Whitehead Street. Martha was still not mentioned. But the atmosphere in the car was strained; and five minutes after they started out, at the intersection of Simonton and United streets, Hemingway drove his Ford convertible into the ancient car of a WPA worker named Samuel Smart. Smart's car rolled over and landed on the sidewalk, but fortunately Smart wasn't hurt. He was angry, though, and he and Hemingway leaped from their cars and started shouting at each other in the middle of the street; even the arrival of a police officer didn't stop them, so the policeman arrested them both and took them to Police Court.

Although the judge ended up dismissing the case as trivial, things were off to a bad start. Back at Whitehead Street there were raised voices and wounded feelings, and again Martha's name wasn't uttered. But Hemingway, defensive about his own behavior, now went on the offensive against friends and business associates he claimed were trying to stiff him or slight him. In the process he used his activities in Spain as a weapon, indulging in a kind of grandiose chest-thumping that made him sound almost like a caricature of himself.

He accused Jack Wheeler, at NANA, of holding back payments for articles and expenses and not appreciating the pains and risks he'd taken to report his stories: covering the fronts at Castellón and Madrid, he complained, had required him "to come out from Toulouse, go to Marseilles, wait there for a plane to fly, for visa, non-intervention and Spanish. The Italians shot down this sort of plane when running between Santander and France and if they had known I was aboard you can be sure they would have tried for it."

He attacked Archie MacLeish for not repaying him money he'd put into Contemporary Historians for *The Spanish Earth*, and for maintaining that those funds should be used to help Spain—which after all was the Historians' stated objective. He listed, with rhetorical flourishes and some exaggeration, the engagements he'd been in (or just missed being in) in Spain, making it sound like he'd been a combatant and not a reporter, then sneered: "When you write that the only effect of paying a certain amount which was promised to be re-paid to me of a very large amount I had furnished 'would be to make less money available for ambulances etc' I laugh at you . . . What did you ever give, my boy?" After telling MacLeish to "keep your long Scotch mouth shut," he fired one Parthian shot: "Much love to your wife and children—and you know what I think of you because I told you one time."

He fought with the people—he referred to them as "the jews"—trying to produce *The Fifth Column* on Broadway, who were having trouble raising capitalization for the show; he wrangled with Max Perkins about the edition of his collected stories, because Perkins wanted him to cut explicitly sexual language from "Up in Michigan," and seemed dubious about including the script of *The Fifth Column* as the lead-in to the story collection, as Hemingway was proposing.

Even his writing became a battleground. The first piece he sent to *Ken* on his return from Spain was entitled "Treachery in Aragon," and it laid the blame for the government's recent retreat not on insufficient matériel or the Nationalists' superior strength, but on the betrayals of fifth columnists (supporting details, he claimed, were too sensitive to be included in the article). As corollary evidence of widespread perfidy Hemingway cited the case of the American writer, "a very good friend of mine," who'd refused to believe that a Spanish associate of his could possibly have been a traitor. "I happened to know," asserted Hemingway, "this man had been shot as a spy after a long and careful trial in which all the charges against him had been proven." The references to Dos Passos, and to Robles, were obvious.

They were less obvious but also present in a short story he'd begun in Paris and completed soon after his return to Key West: "The Denunciation," set in Chicote's Bar in Madrid, in which the narrator tells a waiter how to denounce a man he knows to the secret police. "I would never denounce him myself," he says, although to protect the waiter he later claims to have been involved in doing so. "I am a foreigner and it is your war and your problem." Betrayal and responsibility—other people's if not his own—were almost all he could think about now.

When he wasn't writing he was traveling to New York for the Joe Louis–Max Schmeling fight at Madison Square Garden, which he reported on, jokingly, for *Ken*; or refereeing semipro boxing matches at Key West's Blue Goose arena; or sparring with a young, unsuccessful boxer named Mario Perez; or telling a gullible journalist from the Key West *Citizen* that in his youth he'd been an amateur boxing champion. Or he was fishing in the Gulf Stream, on the *Pilar*.

He returned from one such trip, at the beginning of July, to discover Pauline, dressed as a hula dancer, grass skirt and all, preparing for a costume party at the Havana Madrid nightclub to celebrate the opening of the Overseas Highway to the mainland. Refusing, angrily, to go with her, he stomped off to his locked writing room—but he couldn't find the key. Before Pauline knew what he was doing, he'd pulled out a pistol and was waving it around: *God damn it, I'll shoot it open*. Pauline tried to reason with him—*let's just* look *for the key*—but he couldn't be talked to. Instead he fired the gun, first at the ceiling, then at the door, breaking the lock; finally he barricaded himself inside the room.

Pauline sent the children to stay with the neighbors, but went on to the nightclub as planned. A few hours later Hemingway showed up there—the black mood seemingly dissipated—but soon started a fight with one of the guests. Punches were thrown, furniture was broken. Pauline was furious.

Shortly afterward, they celebrated, if that was the right word for it, their joint birthdays—his thirty-ninth, on July 21, her forty-third, on the twenty-second—and started packing for another family trip to the L Bar T Ranch. They'd missed going last year; perhaps Pauline thought that some time in the mountains would restore their equilibrium. For his part, Hemingway wrote to his mother-in-law from the ranch, if he'd hired someone to run his life badly, he could hardly have made a more thorough mess of it.

June–July 1938: Paris

Ilsa had had a windfall: 180 francs for a bit of business translation; and with these unimaginable riches she and Barea bought a little spirit stove and a frying pan, and some forks and spoons and knives and plates, so they could cook and eat in their room at the Hotel Delambre. The purchase did more than provide them with food: for Barea, it became a way to recapture the world he was trying to portray in the book he had started, haltingly, to write.

Every day he'd go to the *marché du quartier*, the market at the top of their street, looking for fresh sardines and potatoes to sauté in oil the way his mother had done in their attic in Lavapiés, or squid—the cheapest thing at the fishmonger—to serve in a sauce of squid ink, fragrant with garlic and bay leaves and brightened with vinegar; and hovering over the spirit stove, in front of the cold black hearth, he would keep up a running commentary for Ilsa as he cooked. The alleys and parks of Madrid, the fields around his grandparents' house at Brunete, all were summoned with the hiss of the sardines in the hot oil and the scent of garlic, returning to him the Spain he had lost. And when he and Ilsa had finished eating and had washed their dishes in the tiny sink, the images and tastes and sounds and smells of his old life formed themselves into words almost as soon as he sat down at Tom Delmer's old typewriter.

It was doubly painful, after an afternoon immersing himself in his past, to pass the news kiosk on the corner and read today's headlines about Spain, where—after retreating and regrouping and resting from the fascist onslaught of April—the government's army was now making a desperate new offensive. Since his tentative peace overtures to the Nationalists in the spring had failed, Prime Minister Negrín, who was also minister of war, had decided to throw the army, now rested and enhanced by the addition of new conscripts, as young as sixteen and as old as thirty-five, into a three-pronged surprise attack back across the Ebro. If it was successful, he hoped, it would give him leverage to make a deal with Franco. And even if it wasn't, if he could just keep the fighting going on long enough, the crisis in Czechoslovakia, where Hitler was now warning he might have to "march to the rescue" of the country's German minority, would bring about the long-feared European war—and Britain and France, desperate to keep Spain from being taken over by Hitler's allies, would at last intervene in the Republic's behalf. Or so Negrín believed.

On the moonless night of July 25, Republican troops began crossing the river on hastily constructed pontoon bridges, followed by rafts and assault boats. At first a salient was pushed into Nationalist territory; but almost as soon as the offensive began Franco threw all his resources into crushing it. Divisions were brought back from the area around Castellón to join the counterattack; dams in the high Pyrenees were destroyed, sending floodwaters rushing down the Ebro to sweep away bridges; and three hundred aircraft from the Condor Legion, the Italian Legionary Air Force, and the Nationalists' own air squadrons pounded the infantry positions, and the vastly outnumbered Republican air force, with impunity. As July turned into August the two armies were locked into a bloody, seemingly hopeless struggle near Gandesa, and optimism was hard to come by.

At the corner *bistrot*, Barea listened to the workers arguing: Why should they fight for their country when Spain showed you what happened if you risked your life for freedom? When they turned to him, a Spaniard, and asked what he thought, he couldn't answer.

July 1938: Hankow

If Capa had not had a bad case of dysentery he might have gone to the races on July 14: the Race Club was still one of the centers of social life in Hankow, the treaty port on the mile-wide Yangtse River that, after the fall of Nanking in March, had become the wartime capital of China. The club grounds, which looked as if they belonged on the Berkshire Downs instead of in the middle of the steaming green Hupei plain, were located at the outskirts of the tile-roofed Chinese city that had grown up around the European-style buildings of the waterfront Bund; and on a good afternoon the grandstand boxes were crowded with everyone who was anyone in Hankow society: Madame Chiang Kai-shek, the American leftist journalist and aid worker Agnes Smedley, the British ambassador, Sir Archibald Kerr, General Chou En-lai, or any one of the number of émigré Russian princes or princesses who had drifted eastward to Hankow in the years since the October Revolution.

Today, Capa was not among them. In addition to the dysentery he was suffering from Hankow's 100-degree summer heat and humidity: "if it's not the runs, it's the sweats," he wrote to his friend Peter Koester, his contact in Léon Daniel's photo agency in New York, "and I can hardly stand up." A year earlier he had been in Paris, dancing with Gerda in the streets of Montmartre; he wished desperately that he were back there now. His heart still ached for her: he'd brought a small valise full of prints of the photo he'd taken of her with her May Day bunch of *muguet*, and in China he gave them to nearly everyone he met, telling them she'd been his wife. Beyond that, however, he never spoke of her; it was important for his own self-preservation to seal off the part of himself that could be hurt, and to enjoy—or to seem to enjoy—friends, women, money, life itself. His new acquaintances, such as the English poets W. H. Auden and Christopher Isherwood, with whom he and John Ferno had become friendly on the long sea voyage from Marseille, were enchanted by his merriment, his cries of "*Eh, quoi, salop!*" when he met them on deck, his "drooping black comedian's eyes"; but they didn't realize what lay behind the ribald tough-guy disguise.

He'd been in China since the end of February, following and assisting Joris Ivens and Ferno as they shot the film that would become *The Four Hundred Million*. Although Peter Koester told him that the pictures he'd been able to send back to New York—including shots of a Chinese victory at the walled town of Taierhchwang, unprecedented coverage of one of Chiang Kai-shek's cabinet meetings, and a series showing peasants fleeing the defensive flooding of the Yellow River—were "first class . . . technically, reportagewise, better than your Spanish work," Capa was having a difficult time of it. Part of the problem was financial: *Ce Soir*, which had originally promised to underwrite his China trip, had reneged (although they did give him a token advance against payment for photos they bought); Ivens likewise balked at paying for his passage out, although he did agree to cover his expenses in China; and his *Life* retainer wasn't enough to make much of a difference, particularly since he was sending back money to pay for Gerda's gravestone and to support her brother and her father, Heinrich. In addition, in the time since he'd originally proposed the project to Richard de Rochemont, other photographers had arrived to cover the war, among them a former Dephot man named Walter Bosshard, working for the Black Star agency but competing with Capa for space in *Life*.

But the truly painful thing for Capa was that Ivens, and the Chinese, were treating him like the director's hireling. He wasn't allowed to pursue independent reportages but had to stay with Ivens and Ferno; and Ivens forbade him to take still photos of material that was to be featured in the film. "I am the 'poor relation' of the expedition," he wrote to Peter Koester. "They are fine fellows, but the movie is their private affair (and they let me feel that), and the still pictures are completely secondary." There was also trouble with Chiang's Chinese censors, who wanted to prevent any coverage of "backward" peasant life or of the Communist leadership of their Eighth Route Army; waiting for clearance to cover what he and the filmmakers were *allowed* to photograph, Capa spent too much time kicking his heels in the flyblown White Russian bars along Dump Street—the Navy Bar, or Mary's, or the Last Chance—wishing he could go back to Europe, or looking forward to the day when Ivens and Ferno finished shooting and left him alone in China to take the pictures he wanted.

And then the Japanese, advancing ever farther into the Chinese interior, began bombing Hankow. First they attacked strategic targets: the airfield, and the railroad tracks, and the godowns on the waterfront; but then—as had happened in Spain, as would happen in Poland, and France, and Britain, and Germany—it was the civilians' turn. On July 19, Imperial Japanese Air Force bombers pummeled theaters, temples, churches, and houses with incendiary bombs, killing hundreds in one strike. The next day, Capa went to photograph the smoking aftermath, capturing images of firefighters and rescue workers searching through the wreckage for bodies; but the filmmakers had a prior engagement elsewhere and he had to stop work and go with them. "Unfortunately," Capa wrote Koester, "the story is incomplete. I wanted to finish it the next day (they now come over daily), but on the 20th there was only an alarm, no bombing."

He had no sooner typed these words than he seemed to hear them—hear the sound of the journalist so hungry for a story he forgets that real people are dying to make it happen. And he was horrified, wanted to take them back. "Slowly I am feeling more and more like a hyena," he admitted to Koester, and he hated to "make money at the expense of other people's skins." If you were a combat photographer, he told Koester, the thing you should want more than anything in the world was to be out of a job. Even his work seemed to hold no joy for him just now.

But in addition to the "first-class" pictures he was taking—one of which, a portrait of a child soldier in the People's Army, became one of only two *Life* covers in his career—he was getting something else out of his China sojourn. He was learning English, the lingua franca of Ivens and Ferno's film crew, and of most of the expatriate community of Hankow. Although he would later say, mockingly, that he'd "won his English in a crap game in Shanghai," he actually worked hard trying to master the alien grammar and idioms. Usually he wrote in French in the work notebooks he kept, but in China he began trying to do so in English, for practice. And on one piece of foolscap, along with notes on some of his pictures, he typed a misspelled but revealing sentence: "He was best [beset?] b[y] per[s]onal troubles with his co-workers and missed his Europe grievously."

September 1938: Prague

On September 12, after months of threats and demands about the "self-determination" of ethnic Germans living in Czechoslovakia's Sudetenland, Adolf Hitler delivered an ultimatum: unless the Czech president, Eduard Benes, put an end to what Hitler called the "oppression" of the Sudeten Germans, steps would be taken.

Benes had already offered the Sudetens regional self-government as well as a massive loan to stimulate Sudeten industry; but this wasn't enough for the Führer. He wanted that mountainous slice of Czechoslovakia for himself. And once he got it, as should have been obvious to anyone not bent on self-deception, he would want more.

France, tied by treaty to defend Czechoslovakia in case of invasion, began a limited mobilization. But the British prime minister, Neville Chamberlain, hoped to avoid a conflict by appeasing Hitler; and the French, realizing they couldn't stand alone against Germany, agreed to negotiate instead of fight. By September 20, Chamberlain and the French premier, Édouard Daladier, had worked out a plan whereby Czechoslovakia would be urged to cede all German-speaking areas of the country to the Reich, in return for a vague guarantee of sovereignty for what was left over. And Hitler asked Daladier, Chamberlain, and Italy's Mussolini to come to Munich to formalize the agreement. The Czechs were not invited to discuss the dismemberment of their country. At his residence in Prague, the medieval Hradçany Castle, Eduard Benes went into seclusion.

Martha Gellhorn, who had just been reunited with Hemingway and was enjoying a brief holiday with him on the Côte d'Azur, heard this news with dismay. She'd declined to return to the United States with him in May—there was no point, she'd decided, being "within telephoning distance of something you can't telephone to"; instead she'd remained in Europe all summer, continuing to work on her article about France and finishing two intensively reported, increasingly indignant pieces for Collier's about the public mood in Britain and in Czechoslovakia. At the beginning of September, Hemingway had arrived in Paris with a contract from NANA to cover what his editors were sure was the impending European war. Before leaving the L Bar T, he'd somehow smoothed Pauline's ruffled feathers, enough that she'd taken a short-term lease on a New York apartment whose "golden key" she promised to send him, believing that he'd return from Europe soon and rejoin her. But in Paris he'd promptly reset his compass; anyone watching him and Martha as they sat in the sun on the terrasse at Café Weber, on the rue Royale, or holding hands as he walked with her down the street, would have thought Martha the only woman in his life.

With Europe hovering on the brink of war, however, Collier's wanted Martha in Czechoslovakia, not Paris or the Riviera, and she had to cut short their reunion and fly to Prague. Hemingway, despite his brief from NANA to cover a wider European conflict, didn't go with her. Was he reluctant to blow his alibi by filing dispatches from Czechoslovakia when Martha was also reporting from the same place? Or honoring his promise to Pauline to stay away from potential combat? Or was he angry with Martha for paying more attention to an assignment than to him? In the preface to his soon-to-be-published collection of stories he'd set forth a kind of manifesto: "In going where you have to go, and doing what you have to do, and seeing what you have to see, you dull and blunt the instrument you write with. But I would rather have it bent and dulled . . . and know that I had something to write about, than to have it bright and shining and nothing to say, or smooth and well oiled in the closet, but unused." Now, however, he took his instrument and went pheasant shooting in the Sologne, then headed back to Paris to work on two Spanish war stories for *Esquire*.

Prague, thought Claud Cockburn, was just like Madrid in '36—all the same people seemed to be turning up (himself included). *Next thing you know, we'll have shells falling on the hotel.* In his dual capacity as correspondent for both *The Week* and *The Daily Worker*, he'd gone to see the Soviet ambassador, anxious to find out what Russia's position in the Czech crisis would be: for Russia was also a party to the Franco-Czech mutual defense treaty and could step in to defend Czechoslovakia with its formidable air force if France agreed to do its part. Almost the first person he saw at the embassy was Mikhail Koltsov, from whom little had been heard since he'd been recalled to Moscow from Spain almost a year previously. It was a relief to know he was not only alive, seemingly unscathed by Stalin's purges, but still writing for *Pravda*; and excerpts from his "Spanish Diary" had been running in the magazine *Novyi Mir* to considerable acclaim. Perhaps not coincidentally, *Pravda* had also just published an article by his friend Ernest Hemingway on "the barbarism of Fascist interventionists in Spain"; if Koltsov had helped to snare this big-name American author for *Pravda*'s pages, surely that would help keep him in Stalin's good graces?

Koltsov, his teeth as bad as ever and his humor as dark, was cynical about his standing with the general secretary. Stalin had by now arrested, tried, and executed all the members of Lenin's original Politburo, and the man who had helped him to do this, the "poison dwarf" Nikolai Yezhov,

seemed himself on the verge of being ousted (or worse) by his own lieutenant, Lavrenti Beria. Koltsov made jokes even about this. *Everyone gets
his turn—why not me?* Over lunch with Cockburn, Koltsov acted out the
scene of his own imagined trial: the implacable prosecutor hammering
away at him, his fatally clownish responses, the inevitable verdict. *Guilty
of telling bad jokes in the people's tribunal!* And laughed, as he had when
showing Hemingway and Martha his hidden supply of cyanide. Then,
serious, he told Cockburn that Russian planes were already at the airfield
outside Prague; if Benes wanted them, if he would fight, they were his.
Of course, this would mean that the Red Army, or at least the Soviet air
force, would have to occupy Czechoslovakia in order to defend it, a situation not without a certain dark humor of its own. Benes would have to
decide whether to embrace it.

Which was why, shortly after his lunch with Cockburn, Koltsov was
sitting on a wooden bench in a dimly lit hallway at Hradčany Castle waiting to talk to the Czech president. Suddenly he heard the tapping of high
heels and looked up to find Martha Gellhorn, her blond bob bright, clutching her silver fox fur around her against the autumnal chill.

She, too, wanted to talk to Benes, it seemed, and like Koltsov she also
had an offer for him—to use *Collier's* as a platform from which to "win
the public opinion of America"; but despite lobbying the president's secretary and his chief of protocol, she was getting nowhere with her requests.
Sitting down on the bench beside Koltsov, she chattered away in French—
their only common language—telling him of what she'd been doing in
Spain, how pitiful the refugees were, particularly the children, how bad
the bombing was. Koltsov seemed not to be attending. After a while he
stood up. He'd been waiting to talk to Benes for four days, he said; but it
didn't seem worthwhile to wait any longer. He took Martha to dinner in a
workingman's restaurant in the old quarter, not the sort of place he would
have frequented in Madrid; they spoke, each despairingly, of the situation
in Europe, and afterward, on a street corner, they shook hands goodbye.

On September 29, Neville Chamberlain and Édouard Daladier flew to
Munich to meet with Hitler; twenty-four hours later, a protocol giving
Hitler what he wanted in Czechoslovakia had been signed, and Chamberlain had a goodwill memorandum from the Reichschancellor that would,
he told his fellow Britons, ensure "peace with honor." Martha, after making several more vain attempts to contact Benes, returned to Paris; and

Koltsov—his mission unaccomplished—went back to an uncertain future in Moscow. Before he left, he saw Cockburn one last time. They both had to know what was going to happen now, and it was worse than a victory for Hitler in Central Europe. Stalin had finally lost patience—*faith* was not a word you would apply to him—with the democracies; to protect himself, and Russia, he would act on the threat hinted at by Foreign Minister Litvinov almost a year ago. He would begin taking his chess pieces off the board and make common cause with his former enemy, Germany.

The most obvious victim of this decision was Czechoslovakia; almost unnoticed, in the din that had been emanating from Munich and Prague, was Spain. For at the height of the Czech crisis Stalin had agreed that Prime Minister Negrín, in a bid for the sympathies of Britain, France, the United States, and other governments nominally opposed to "foreign intervention" in Spain, could announce the unconditional withdrawal of the International Brigades. This the Spanish premier did in a speech to the League of Nations on September 21, the day that the terms of the Sudeten handover were also made public. In practical terms the gesture meant little—there were only about seven thousand *brigadistas* still in Spain—but it was invested with a wealth of symbolism.

None of which was lost on Koltsov. "The only thing to say," he told Cockburn, "is that in the little moment that remains to us between the crisis and the catastrophe, we may as well drink a glass of champagne."

September 1938: Paris

On the day the Munich pact was signed, Barea and Ilsa moved out of the Hotel Delambre. When the mobilization posters went up all over Paris the manager of the hotel had demanded they pay their back rent immediately: he and his wife wanted to close the hotel and go to the country to escape the war they were sure was coming, he said, and in any case they didn't want foreigners—the words *sales metèques*, "dirty wogs," weren't used but implied—sponging on them anymore. "I've spoken about you to the police anyhow," the manager growled.

Hoping a glass of wine would help him figure out what to do, Barea had gone to the Dôme; and there, by some miracle, he encountered a prosperous Cuban he and Ilsa had befriended in Madrid and hadn't seen since. Horrified to hear of the fix Barea and Ilsa were in, he insisted on lending them the money they owed their landlord; and a Norwegian journalist, one of Ilsa's contacts from the old days, said he could rent them a room in his airy, modern flat. They could hardly believe their good fortune.

Soon after they moved in, Barea received a parcel of books from Barcelona: the first copies of *Valor y miedo*, the book of stories he'd written before leaving Spain. Paging through them, Barea allowed himself a little flicker of pride that he'd been able to make something simple out of something so tumultuous: *Maybe a little lightweight*, he thought, *but not so bad*.

It was the only good news from Spain. After some initial success the Ebro campaign had turned sour, with the Nationalist armies pushing the government's forces back again toward the Ebro and the Rio Segre. Then Negrín had announced the dissolution of the Brigades, and Britain and France had made a deal with Hitler for the corpse of Czechoslovakia. *This is the end of Spain's last, best hope*, Barea told himself. Now Russia would withdraw her aid to Spain. Even worse, people like himself and Ilsa would be considered troublemakers, Reds who wanted to drag all of Europe into their conflict.

But as the trees turned bronze and yellow along the boulevards and the banks of the Seine, and peace—however spurious—seemed to have been at least temporarily bought, he and Ilsa allowed themselves a tiny sigh of relief. They had a comfortable place to stay; they were working. Perhaps it was foolish to always imagine the worst that could happen, instead of the best. Strolling one late golden afternoon along the gravel paths in the Jardin du Luxembourg, where Hemingway had liked to walk when he was young and unknown in Paris in the twenties, they saw an old couple, he bearded and erect, carrying a silver-handled cane, she petite, lively, elegantly dressed in black. "When we're as old as they, we might be rather like them," Ilsa murmured. "We'll take walks, and tell each other about old times, and smile at the dreadful things that happened to us when we were younger." They were just enjoying the idea—themselves, old, at peace, together—when the old gentleman bowed, kissed the lady's hand, and strode away, leaving her alone; and Ilsa's eyes suddenly filled with tears.

October 1938: Barcelona

Early in the second week of October Robert Capa returned to Spain. He'd done all he could in China, including shooting a Bosch-like series of color photographs for *Life*—the first he'd ever taken, and the first color prints *Life* had ever published—of the aftermath of a bombing raid on Hankow; but, as he'd written in his English-language practice sentences, *he missed his Europe grievously.* It was time to come back.

Walking into the Majestic bar, he was greeted with a chorus of welcome from all the journalists: Jesus, it was about time. Where the hell had he been? He dumped his camera bag on the floor and sat down and almost immediately had a circle around him: Matthews, and Georges Soria from *L'Humanité*, and André Malraux, who was in Barcelona trying to shoot a movie of his Spanish war novel, *L'Espoir*, and Sheean, and Sheean's English wife, Diana Forbes-Robertson (whom everybody called Dinah). The couple had recently come in from Prague, where Sheean had been covering the Munich crisis; and Dinah was feeling very much like the new girl in school who doesn't know anyone. Telling stories and joking in French and his newly acquired English, Capa soon made her feel as much a part of the group as the old hands were. And the next day, when he discovered her sitting forlornly in the lobby because no one had arranged transport or passes for her, he grabbed her arm. "I take you," he announced; and dragged her along to Constancia de la Mora's office. "Connie," he called out to the propaganda chief, "Diana would like to do something about Spain. Speak or write or whatever you want. Find something." And he left.

On the sixteenth he went to Falset, a hamlet ninety miles south and west of Barcelona, where the International Brigades were to have a final muster. He'd been with these soldiers—and some who had not made it this far—in Aragon, in the Guadarrama, in Madrid, at Peñarroya; shared meals and cigarettes and jokes with them; come under fire with them. And he wanted to be with them today.

It was hazy, but the autumn sun was still warm on the terraced hills. Near the village of Falset a makeshift reviewing stand had been set up by the side of the dusty road; flags were clustered around it, including the flag of the Spanish Republic, the hammer and sickle, and a mordantly funny hand-lettered banner with the words *"J'Aime Berlin"*—Chamberlain—drawn under a swastika with an interdict symbol. A meager band struck up, just a couple of slide trombones, trumpets, some clarinets, and a tuba, and the Brigade columns, including a detachment of cavalry, began to march past the reviewing stand: the men of the Lincoln Battalion (now formally the Lincoln-Washington Battalion), 300 out of the 4,000 who had originally sailed to Spain, with their lanky twenty-three-year-old newly created major, Milton Wolff, striding along at their head; Canadian Mac-Paps (the Mackenzie-Papineau Battalion); Polish Dombrowskis; Yugoslavs, Britons, Czechs, Austrians—and the 150 survivors of the Thaelmann Column, the heroes of Madrid, all of them refugees from Germany who were now without a homeland, marching to their anthem, "Freiheit." The men had already given up their weapons, so their arms swung loosely by their sides until it came time for them to throw the clenched-fist salute; their numbers appeared pitifully small, and as they stood at ease listening to the speeches of their commanders, they were dwarfed by the hills of the foreign country they had come to defend.

Eight days later came the official dissolution of the Brigades, at a mill at Montblanch that had been converted into a hospital for the wounded. Capa got there early, while soldiers were still sweeping the courtyard with leafy branches (even brooms were hard to find in wartime) and flags and garlands were being hung on the balcony where the dignitaries would stand. The Brigaders trickled in, some still in their tattered uniforms but most in mufti, since all government-issued equipment and clothing had to be left behind; as the ceremony began they formed themselves into columns, filling the courtyard, and Capa clambered up onto the balcony to shoot the crowd: a sea of upturned faces, some lined and coarse with stubble, others youthful, under berets or caps or visored officers' hats. Some of the soldiers had their dogs with them, curled at their feet or cradled in their arms. The band played, the speeches began: Colonel Modesto, dark and romantic-looking in his uniform, his voice breaking as he spoke of their "shared experiences" and "common suffering"; then Prime Minister Negrín, in riding breeches and puttees, offering "profound and eternal gratitude" for their help. "¡Salud, hermanos!" he cried, raising his fist to the side of his head; with tears streaming down their faces, they saluted him back—and the commissar for the Army of the Ebro read them, for the last time, the order to dismiss.

After that the gigantic parade in Barcelona should have been an anticlimax: but it wasn't. "La Despedida," the farewell, took place on the twenty-eighth, and until twenty minutes before it began there was no official announcement for fear the Nationalists would bomb the parade route. Incredibly, three hundred thousand people turned out on short notice, lining the broad Avenida Diagonal in the crisp autumn sunlight, waving from office windows and balconies, pelting the parading soldiers with flowers or scraps of paper covered with scribbled notes of thanks, and darting from the barricades to embrace them as they marched past. Capa, who had dressed carefully in a suit and tie in honor of the occasion, scrambled along beside the procession, sometimes shinnying up lampposts to get a better shot; across the avenue, the Spanish photographer Augustí Centelles was doing the same thing, and the two photographers played a little game, trying to catch each other in the backgrounds of their pictures. On either side of the Diagonal, at each intersection, were plaques bearing the names of the Brigades—Abraham Lincoln, Louise Michel, Hans Beimler—or of notable Brigade heroes; billboards were emblazoned with the names of the battles they had fought in: Las Rozas, Madrid, Teruel, Guadalajara, Belchite, Brunete.

On a dais, Negrín—looking formal today in topcoat and homburg—Luís Companys, General Rojo, and former president Azaña saluted the Brigades; behind them stood Constancia de la Mora, tears filling her eyes; in the bright blue sky her husband's air force fighters darted to and fro to ward off any Nationalist bombers.

At the parade's end, Republican troops, the only ones to carry arms, presented them under a giant portrait of Stalin and there were more speeches: Negrín, misty-eyed, promising Spanish citizenship to any of the men who returned to Spain after the war, and Dolores Ibárruri, La Pasionaria, in a flowered scarf and a torrent of rhetoric. "You are history!" she cried. "You are legend. You are the heroic example of democracy's solidarity and universality. We shall not forget you, and when the olive tree of peace puts forth its leaves again, mingled with the laurels of the Spanish Republic's victory—come back!" Capa's camera whirred, capturing the flurry of applauding hands, the storm of confetti. Everyone sang the "Hymn of Riego," and then, leaving behind 9,934 dead and 7,686 missing, most of whom were already dead or soon would be, the seven thousand remaining men of the International Brigades shipped out to miserable, lice-ridden, unheated barracks in Catalan villages, where they would wait—some for months—for authentication and exit permits from the League of Nations commissioners sent to examine them before they were allowed to go home.

October 1938: Paris

Martha Gellhorn wasn't in Barcelona for "La Despedida," although in the story she wrote for *Collier's* about that autumn in Spain she described the parade, with its marchers looking "very dirty and weary and young," in such a way that it sounded as if she had been there. In fact, she and Hemingway were ensconced in Paris, where he'd just finished his two Madrid stories for *Esquire*, one an account of filming the failed offensive in the Casa de Campo, the other a version of the anecdote he'd put into *The Fifth Column* about the *miliciano* who'd been beaten and then shot to death in Chicote's, back in the spring of 1937, for spraying patrons with a Flit gun full of lavender water. Except in his story he said it was eau de cologne, and the *miliciano* a civilian, and he made the whole thing a kind of parable of what happens to gaiety in the exigencies of war.

Hemingway was in a sour mood. *The Fifth Column and the First Forty-nine Stories* had been published on October 14, and the reception for the collection he'd thought was "unbeatable" had been disappointing, with the stories coming in for praise while most critics had disparaged the play as melodrama or agitprop. Although seeing his collected short fiction gathered together between two covers had made him feel "I was alright as a sort of lasting business if I kicked off tomorrow," the fact that "those guys" had just ganged up on him again took away all his pleasure in his achievement. It didn't help that the book had sold 6,000 copies in two weeks; it would have sold *more*, he grumbled to Maxwell Perkins, if Scribner's had taken out bigger ads, or given the book more space in its Fifth Avenue bookshop window.

He was, therefore, already seething with resentment when he and Martha read the news accounts, or saw the newsreels, about the disbanding of the International Brigades. To Hemingway, in this frame of mind, Negrín might as well have called off the war: he felt personally betrayed. And then he and Martha, entering their hotel lobby one evening, came face to face with Randalfo Pacciardi, the former commander of the Garibaldi

Battalion, whom neither had seen since their first spring in Madrid. Pacciardi had left his command, and Spain, in August 1937, unhappy at the consolidation of his battalion into a Communist-controlled brigade, and furious at the government's use of his troops in their campaign against the anarchists; since then he'd been living in penurious exile in Paris, where he'd founded an antifascist magazine, *La Giovine Italia*. Though he was dressed in civilian clothes instead of his khakis and jaunty cap, he was as charismatic a figure as ever; his abandonment of his command now seemed almost prescient, and his refusal to blame anyone for his predicament heroic. And Hemingway began to wonder if the war had not devolved into what he called "a carnival of treachery and rotten-ness" on both sides.

Leaving Pacciardi, he and Martha had started to climb the stairs to their room when Hemingway suddenly faltered and leaned against the wall, weeping. "They can't do it," he cried. "They can't treat a brave man that way!" And Martha, seeing his tears for Pacciardi, and for the loss of what he had fought for in Spain, felt her heart melt at his "generosity & compassion."

"I really did love E. then," she wrote later.

November 1938: Barcelona

Two days after Barcelona bade goodbye to the remnants of the International Brigades, Nationalist troops began a fierce counteroffensive along the Ebro, bombing Republican positions in the Sierra de Caballos east of Gandesa, then advancing to take possession of the only high point left in government hands, at Pandols. The Ebro Valley now lay open to Nationalist attack; but although it was clear that there was no way the war would now end well for the Republic, no one—not the journalists, or the photographers, or the soldiers, or the members of the government, least of all Prime Minister Negrín—would acknowledge the fact. "In a war," Hemingway would write later, speaking of this time, "you can never admit, even to yourself, that it is lost. Because when you will admit it is lost you will be beaten."

Hemingway arrived in Barcelona for what he knew was the last time on November 4. At the Majestic, he had a reunion of sorts with Herbert

Matthews, Tom Delmer, Jimmy Sheean, Hans Kahle—who as a divisional commander in the Popular Army had taken him around the battlefield at Guadalajara—and Capa. Sheean had some bad news for him: young Jim Lardner had disappeared on September 21, the day of the dissolution order, and was presumed killed, almost certainly one of the last International Brigade casualties. Did Hemingway remember then what he had said to Prudencio de Pereda at the beginning of the war? *If you didn't get killed you would get wonderful material, and if you did get killed it would be in a good cause.*

The others filled Hemingway in on the military situation: Enrique Líster, whose troops he, Matthews, and Delmer had followed in triumph into Teruel, had been holding a bridgehead on the far side of the Ebro, but the Nationalists were pressing his position and it was clear he would have to fall back. Kahle, who as an army officer had papers to get past any roadblock, was offering to accompany some of the journalists to Líster's headquarters; so very early the next morning they set out in two cars— Kahle, Hemingway, and the *Daily Telegraph*'s Henry Buckley in one, and Matthews, Capa, and Sheean in the other. Stopping for breakfast along the way, they learned that the bridge over the Ebro at Mora, which they'd meant to use, was gone—first bombed and then swept away when the rebels reopened the Ebro floodgates upstream. It might be possible to get across by boat, though—they'd have to see when they got there.

Matthews's car, a lumbering Belgian Minerva with a faulty clutch that had replaced the broken-down Ford he'd had at Teruel, had trouble navigating the rutted road and was soon lagging far behind Kahle's official automobile. The fields on either side of the dirt road were empty in the November sunlight, and as they drew nearer to the front the sound of bombs and cannonades made the road seem even more exposed. When the Minerva reached Mora la Nueve, on the left bank of the river, the journalists found a deserted village filled with wrecked houses, and Kahle's car and its occupants were nowhere to be seen. Shells were coming over the shattered streets, and a couple of sentries tried to wave the journalists away. *"Muy peligroso!"* they shouted. Matthews found a ruined stable near a crossroads and drove the car into it, figuring it was as good as anywhere else to stow it in case they *were* able to get across the river and back.

For a while the four men stood by the stable trying to see if there were any signs of Kahle, Hemingway, and Buckley; but the shells started landing closer and closer, whistling over their heads and exploding about fifty yards up the road, sending them diving for cover in the debris-filled stable yard. As they were picking themselves up from the ground, Sheean remarked to Capa that it was a bad day for photographers, but Capa shot him a withering look. "This is the only kind of day that is *any* good for photographers," he said scornfully, picking a wisp of straw from his tweed jacket.

Just then they saw Hemingway coming up the street looking for them: He and the others had been waiting down by the river, where Kahle had found some soldiers willing to row them across in exchange for cigarettes from Hemingway's supply. They all trooped down and climbed into the soldiers' boat, a big flat-bottomed tub, and shoved off into the fast-flowing ocher-colored water; the opening of the floodgates had created a strong current and the oarsmen had to pull hard to keep from being swept downstream. Once on the opposite bank the journalists walked uphill from Mora de Ebro along a dusty road to Líster's headquarters, a white farmhouse on a rise with a view of the river valley and the sierra beyond; from the wooded slopes they could hear the rattle of machine-gun fire that meant the enemy was advancing. It was hot in the sun, and the men stripped off their coats and pullovers and neckties. Líster came out of his headquarters to chat with them, and Capa photographed him and Hemingway sitting on a stone parapet on the farmhouse terrace. Líster looked tired, although he was cheerful and cordial; and Hemingway had lost the jaunty confidence he'd radiated at Teruel. Instead he seemed tentative and wary. Líster excused himself several times to take telephone calls inside the house, finally coming back to tell them they would all have to leave, and quickly, because he was giving orders for a retreat.

Walking back to Mora they passed a handful of battered tanks on the road, and the soldiers riding on them shook their fists in the air: a photo opportunity. Buckley and Matthews took out their cameras and clicked away but Capa, unimpressed, left his dangling on its strap. "This kind of thing is no good to me," he complained. "These are not pictures of action. I can't take good photographs unless I'm in the front lines." When they reached the river they piled into the boat for the return crossing; but the vagaries of the current made rowing in this direction more difficult, and when they were in the middle of the river a burst of shellfire made the soldiers drop their oars and duck for cover beneath the gunwales. Suddenly the small craft started drifting dangerously downstream toward the blackened spars of the bombed-out bridge. Kahle, sure they would founder on the wreckage and have to swim for it, began pulling off his boots; Capa started shooting pictures; but Hemingway, who'd learned a thing or two about rowing guide boats up in Michigan as a boy, seized the oars and began to pull against the current as if his life depended on it. And gradually the boat's prow turned away from the remnants of the bridge and they reached the other side safely.

The next day, November 6, Matthews drove Hemingway from Barcelona to Ripoll, near the French border, where the remnants of the Lincoln Battalion were waiting for evacuation, shivering in their filthy quarters. On a street in the village they found Alvah Bessie, hobbling along with the aid of a stick, so crippled with rheumatic pain that he'd been unable to march in the Brigades' parade. Hemingway had first met Bessie in Madrid, at the Hotel Florida, and had last seen him in April after he and his companions had escaped from the Nationalists during the Great Retreats along the Ebro. Then Hemingway had still felt full of zeal and confidence; but the past weeks had unsettled him, and he was like a boxer who has taken a punch and doesn't know how it happened.

"I'm glad to see you got out of this alive," Hemingway said to Bessie.

"I am, too," Bessie responded.

"Because," Hemingway went on, as if Bessie had not spoken, "I always felt responsible for your being here."

Bessie must have looked perplexed, because Hemingway continued: "You heard the speech I made at the Writers' Congress?" Bessie nodded. "I know that speech was responsible for a lot of guys coming over," Hemingway said, as if he had been a one-man recruiting office for the International Brigades. Bessie just stared at him.

On the night of November 6, "Bola" Boleslavskaya, Mikhail Koltsov's old *Pravda* colleague, had a party in her rooms at the Majestic to celebrate the anniversary of the October Revolution and the relief of Madrid by the International Brigades in 1936. It was a fête like the ones they'd all had in Madrid in what seemed increasingly like the good old days: the Sheeans were there, and Matthews, and Capa, and Hemingway, and André Malraux, and Georges Soria, and Dinah Sheean's brother, Arthur Forbes, a right-wing *Daily Express* correspondent, and many others besides. Capa organized provisions, sending people to get ham, beans, *bacalao*, and wine, and dragooning Forbes into lugging all the foodstuffs back to the Majestic under a bright full moon. "It's a bomber's moon," Capa helpfully told him—and indeed there were air raids early in the evening, which they all watched from the hotel roof: bombs and antiaircraft fire thundering in the distance, red tracer bullets streaking across the sky, and searchlights illuminating the silver bodies of the Italian Savoias as they flew overhead.

When the raids stopped, everyone came back to Bola's rooms and they put Strauss waltzes on the Victrola, and Capa and Georges Soria pinned flowers in their hair and danced to "Rustle of Spring," Capa tossing flowers to all the girls. Then Agrippina, the Asturian singer famous for her appearances on the front lines, led them in "Viva la Quince Brigada"; and at midnight somebody suggested they should make speeches to mark the occasion. But Bola's chauffeur, a tall, taciturn Madrileño, raised his hand to shush them. Instead, he said, they should all stand and observe a moment of silence for those who had died in defense of Madrid.

Those who weren't already standing struggled to their feet. The names of the dead—from Madrid, from Brunete, from Aragon and the Sierra and the Ebro—were too numerous to utter aloud. But they all bowed their heads for a moment and remembered.

The next morning, eager to rejoin Martha in Paris, Hemingway got Matthews to drive him to Perpignan. For him the war was over.

While the Italians were bombing Barcelona and Bola's guests were singing and dancing at the Majestic, Loyalist troops were splashing across a tributary of the Ebro, the Segre, near the town of Fraga, forty miles west of Barcelona. Spreading themselves out along a six-mile stretch of riverbank, they prepared to launch an attack on the highlands to the west that would—it was hoped—distract the Nationalists from their drive on the Ebro at Mora. The attack was meant to be a secret, so there was no preliminary artillery barrage or bombing of enemy positions; but somehow the news leaked out in Barcelona, and as Capa was leaving Bola's party he heard about it. Within hours he was at the front.

When he arrived, pontoon bridges had just been built to bring in supplies to the attackers and carry out the wounded, and there were already stretchers lined up along the bank. Next to one of them a soldier draped in a blanket against the morning chill was bent over, painstakingly writing down the muttered words of his comrade on the stretcher; from the man's glazed expression and the bloody bandage wrapped around his head Capa guessed they would be the last he spoke.

Among the troops mustered on the riverbank was a company of marineros, seafarers from Asturias, whom Capa had encountered at Teruel. He attached himself to their unit and when they moved out he went with them, huffing up the slope from the river, through the olive orchards and scrub to the rocky hills above. The company commander, a former lawyer in incongruous horn-rimmed glasses, hunkered down with his officers and a map under an overhanging ledge, getting his final orders over a hastily strung field telephone; and the political commissar spoke to the men, telling them where they were going and how much was at stake. Then, after daubing mud all over their helmets for camouflage, they all picked up their weapons and blanket rolls—some of them strapping grenades to their chests—and headed for the hilltop.

It wasn't long before the incoming fire started: first rifles and machine guns, then artillery shells. Capa kept moving forward, using his camera like a weapon. He didn't stop to think. A man in front of him was running uphill with a cigarette in his mouth when he was hit and doubled over, the cigarette still clenched in his teeth. Another was shot in the leg: one of his comrades picked him up, slung him over his shoulder, and carried him toward the stretcher bearers who'd been following the assault. All around men were stumbling forward and firing and ducking for cover; the air was hazy with explosives and alive with bullets. At the top of the first hill a small roofless farmhouse looked like it might provide shelter, and Capa started toward it behind a handful of soldiers; just then a shell landed squarely on it, a cloud of dust and smoke filling Capa's viewfinder. When the smoke cleared, the house and the soldiers hiding in it were gone.

The fighting went on all day. Eventually Capa's company managed to secure a small hamlet on one of the windswept hills, where they paused to regroup and gather their wounded for evacuation, and Capa made his way back to Barcelona. In his camera were pictures that were nothing like what he had taken when he first came to Spain; they weren't even like what he had *thought* he would take back then. Blurry, chaotic, choppily framed, immediate, and terrifying—these were pictures of what war really was like. And when he sent them on to Paris, they created a sensation. *Life* gave them two pages, *Regards* five pages and the back cover, *Match* seven pages; and the British magazine *Picture Post* ran them in an eleven-page spread prefaced by a huge portrait of Capa over the caption: "The Greatest War-Photographer in the World: Robert Capa."

The Segre offensive, however, was a failure. The Nationalists rallied, and pushed the Republicans back again across both the Segre and the Ebro. On November 15, leaving between ten and fifteen thousand dead and an enormous amount of precious war matériel behind, the remnants of the government's army crossed the iron bridge over the Ebro at Flix and blew it up behind them.

After seeing Hemingway off for New York on the *Normandie*, Martha Gellhorn arrived in Barcelona on November 21, intending to write the story about the sufferings of the civilian population that she'd tried to interest *Collier's* in the previous April. Perhaps she felt that, having delivered three tough analytical reportages about Europe to her editors, they owed her this; perhaps, too, she knew this would be her last chance to write about Spain.

She went to hospitals, reporting on the children lying in the wards, staring with huge dark eyes; to food lines, where tiny pieces of salt cod and little packets of rice or dried peas were doled out to housewives who would have to feed their families on these starvation rations; to munitions factories, where shells were made out of fabric that in peacetime would have been turned into women's summer dresses. Sometimes she was with Herbert Matthews, who was still besotted with her—"underneath she's a lot softer than she seems," he wrote defensively to his wife, Nancie—sometimes with Capa, whom she had unaccountably not met in Madrid with Hemingway, and whom she took to immediately. "He was my brother, my real brother," she would later say; and although he made her laugh (always an important touchstone for her) they also fought, loudly and passionately, about almost anything. How could she write about suffering and injustice and expect it to end? he would ask. *You are more stupid than a herd of mules.* And she would shout at him that he was a self-involved cynic. *Do you think taking pictures of wars and refugees is any way to help people?* At its best, though, her journalism was very like his: short, sharp vignettes that put you into the frame with her subjects; at its worst, when in her zeal to make a point she made up facts to go with it, it fell into traps that he had learned to avoid.

One night he held her hand during an air raid, and she teased him about the camel's hair coat he was wearing, a coat with wide lapels and enormous mother-of-pearl buttons that he'd bought in Paris; it was vulgar, she told him, and it wasn't right to wear it in Barcelona where everyone was freezing and starving. He didn't care, he said. He had always wanted a coat like this, and if he had to die in an air raid, he would die wearing it. Not that he seemed afraid of dying—he was, Martha observed, "always very brave and always saying how frightened he was. He had none of Hemingway's bravado."

Early in December, both Martha and Capa left Barcelona for Paris. After writing up her Barcelona story for *Collier's* Martha was going on to New York, where Hemingway was waiting for her. Although she'd confessed to Herbert Matthews that she wasn't sure their relationship had a future, she needed to test it for herself. As for Capa, his coverage of the Segre campaign, coupled with the drawn-out farewells to the men with whom he, and Gerda, had experienced so much, had left him emotionally and physically depleted. When he got home to the rue Froidevaux he was, as he wrote to his mother, "so sick I had an absolute breakdown."

December 1938: Moscow

Constancia de la Mora loved Moscow. She had first visited it in the autumn of 1937, when Ignacio Hidalgo de Cisneros had suffered a stroke and she had decided he should go to Russia to recuperate ("No other country in Europe could cure Ignacio, I knew"); and now she was back, again with Hidalgo, this time on a mission to save—not her husband, but the Spanish Republic. The army had suffered huge losses, of men but also of arms and ammunition, in the disastrous Ebro campaign, and Prime Minister Negrín had sent his air force chief and his propagandist wife to beg Stalin for more war matériel. Specifically, he wanted 250 aircraft, 250 tanks, 4,000 machine guns, 650 artillery, and other ordnance and ammunition.

General Secretary Stalin invited Hidalgo and Constancia to the

Kremlin for dinner, and when the pair walked into the dining room where Stalin, Defense Minister Voroshilov, and Vyacheslav Molotov, the Russian prime minister, were sitting, all three men rose to greet them; the expression on his wife's face, Hidalgo would later say, was unforgettable. Despite this warm welcome, Hidalgo was apprehensive about asking for Stalin's help; Russian advisors in Spain had complained that Prime Minister Negrín was waging "a very expensive war."

Stalin smiled at him, that smile that could strike terror when you knew what lay behind it, and looked at Voroshilov, who smiled back.

"Your war is a very inexpensive war . . . Very inexpensive! So inexpensive and so important that we will continue to send you everything you need. Whatever you need!"

There was, of course, a price: an amount equivalent to $103 million. But, alas, of the enormous wealth—more than $500 million in gold and silver—that Spain had transferred to Moscow at the beginning of the war, there was less than $100,000 left. Fortunately, Stalin would allow Hidalgo to purchase the arms on credit, with only his signature as a guarantee.

It wasn't until, months later, some of the promised arms failed to materialize, that Constancia permitted herself the tiniest flicker of doubt. "Why didn't Stalin send us what he promised?" she wondered to a friend, Enrique Castro Delgado, one of the founders of the Communist Fifth Regiment. "Could he have tricked us?"

To which Castro confidently responded: "Stalin never tricks anyone, at least not Communists."

In the year since he had been recalled from Spain, Mikhail Koltsov had publicly thrown himself into an embrace of every official position of the Communist Party in an effort to keep the noose he feared was waiting for him away from his neck. He'd even denounced Nikolai Bukharin, Ilya Ehrenburg's friend and Stalin's former staunch ally against Trotsky, who'd been tried for treason the previous spring; and he'd toed the Party line by insisting that Andrés Nin and the POUM had been in league with Franco. But he knew he was protesting too much. "I think I'm going out of my mind," he told his brother, the cartoonist Boris Efimov. "Surely, as a member of the editorial board of *Pravda*, a well-known journalist, a parliamentary deputy, I should be able to explain to others the meaning of what is going on, the reason for so many denunciations and arrests. But . . . I know nothing, understand nothing."

Certainly he didn't know why he hadn't been included in the just-concluded meetings between Stalin, Voroshilov, and Molotov and his own old friend from Spain, Ignacio Hidalgo de Cisneros, as he told Hidalgo himself when they had dinner on December 9. He wondered what fate held in store for an antifascist like himself in a Russia where communication channels were being opened to Nazi Germany. And he was worried that only the day before, Nikolai Yezhov, whom he'd regarded as a protector, had been replaced as people's commissar and NKVD overlord by Lavrenti Beria.

On the other hand, he was riding an extraordinary crest of success and popularity: in the summer he'd been elected to the Supreme Soviet, and the serialization of his Spanish diary in *Novyi Mir* had been the talk of Moscow. Stalin himself had called him into his box at the Bolshoi to congratulate him on his achievement, and there was no talk of whether or not Koltsov might be contemplating suicide, as had been suggested in their meeting in December of '36. In fact, the general secretary had made an extraordinary and complimentary request: he had just completed a history of the Bolshevik Party, he said, and he would be honored if Comrade Koltsov would consent to introduce it with a lecture at the Writers' Union in December.

The date fixed for the lecture was December 12; and two days before that Koltsov was given another honor that filled his cup almost to overflowing: he was made a corresponding member of the Academy of Sciences. Late on the afternoon of the twelfth, in the spacious mansion in Bolshaya Nikitskaya that Tolstoy had used as the model for the Rostovs' house in *War and Peace*, he presented Stalin's party history to an enthusiastic audience of Writers Union members and their guests. At the end of the evening he went to his office at *Pravda* to take care of a few odds and ends; that's where he was when the black van, which Muscovites called a *voronka*—a crow—pulled up at the curb and the NKVD agents came for him. At the Lubyanka, where he was tortured and interrogated over a period of fourteen months, they took his glasses away. *Without glasses everything looks black to me*, he'd said to Gustav Regler in Madrid: *If they ever shoot me I'll have to ask them not to take my glasses off first.*

He didn't get the chance. On February 1, 1940, after a twenty-minute trial, he was convicted of espionage and treason—just one more of the Russian advisors to Spain, among them the generals Vladimir Gorev and Emilio Kléber and Ambassador Marcel Rosenberg, who needed to be liquidated now that Stalin had changed his mind about what game he was playing.

January 1939: New York

Claiming business in New York, where he had to discuss revisions to *The Fifth Column* with its producer, the Theatre Guild, Hemingway escaped from Christmas in Key West as soon as he decently could. Or sooner—he and Pauline could not keep from quarreling. Nor could he keep rancor out of his relations with Benjamin F. Glaser, the screenwriter the Theatre Guild had hired to adapt the not-yet-ready-for-Broadway *Fifth Column* for stage production. Glaser's contract forbade him from making any adverse criticisms of the Spanish government or the Communist Party, and required him to get the author's approval for any changes; but even so Hemingway complained to his mother-in-law that "the Jews" had so cheapened what he'd originally written that "it should be called the 4.95 Column marked down from 5." He insisted on writing new material himself to replace what Glaser had done, and although Glaser and the Theatre Guild accepted his revisions, Hemingway was by now so disgusted with the whole process that he was telling everyone he should have written the damned thing as a novel.

Even Martha's arrival from St. Louis, where she'd spent Christmas with her mother, failed to cheer him sufficiently; although he proudly (and recklessly) took her with him, silver fox and all, to a showing of *The Spanish Earth* with his teenage son Jack, on holiday from his boarding school. Afterward they went to the Stork Club, where Jack gaped at the glamorous young woman and thrilled to the four-letter words that peppered her vocabulary, without ever figuring out how his "old" father knew such a creature.

But Hemingway's inchoate anger about what had gone wrong in Spain, or gone wrong *with* Spain; his longing for Martha and guilt about Pauline; his hatred of critics who had insufficiently valued his work, and armchair pantywaists like Edmund Wilson or John Dos Passos who took issue with his politics—all these things churned in him. And on another evening at the Stork Club he was sitting drinking with the magazine writer Quentin Reynolds when a complete stranger who was himself much the worse for drink made a show of recognizing him: *Look, there's Hemingway, the big writer.* The stranger came over to the table, thrust out his hand, and started rubbing Hemingway's face. "Tough, eh?" he muttered. Seeing Hemingway's look, Reynolds warned his friend, "Give him a poke, but don't hit him too hard." Hemingway was in no mood to listen. Standing up, he raised his fists and clipped the stranger on the chin. The man went down like a felled tree.

January 1939: Paris

The winter rains had descended on Paris: every day the same gray clouds mantling the gray buildings, the mushrooming black umbrellas along the boulevards, the steady drumming of raindrops against the windows, the hiss of tires on wet pavement. At least, thought Barea, their borrowed flat had central heating, and he and Ilsa had enough translation work to keep them from starving. And when they could spare time from that he was able, at last, to finish a draft of his new book, the story of his own life, and that of his family and his city—the city that was still holding fast against Franco even as Catalonia crumbled before the Nationalist armies. The memoir ended on the afternoon he'd quit his job at the bank in Madrid, the same day the Great War broke out; and now it seemed as if another great war was about to begin. Looking at the pile of paper that was the finished manuscript, Barea felt suddenly deflated. He'd struggled to find the right voice for his story, the voice of Lavapiés and hard Castile, but it didn't sound like any book he had ever come across. Who would want to publish it? Who would want to read it?

Certainly the literary world of Paris didn't seem ready to welcome him: the few bookish gatherings a friend had taken him to had depressed him by their cliquishness and preciosity. And when he got no answer from the publisher he sent it to he was sure the book, like so much else in his life, was another dead end.

Then, miraculously, the Spanish reader from the publishing house paid him a visit, an older man, with old-fashioned taste, who told him that although he'd been puzzled, even offended by Barea's writing—*so brutal*—he'd recommended that the house publish it, because it had enormous power. Even though the publisher never followed up on its reader's advice, Barea was perversely encouraged by the man's visit: he felt as if the voice he'd worked so hard to find had spoken to *someone*. Miraculously, he had become what he had always dreamed of being: he was a writer at last.

But he and Ilsa couldn't enjoy the encouragement for long. Generosity was their downfall: they allowed a poor young émigré couple, Poles, to stay with them for one night when the couple's pipes had frozen and they were without heat or water. Suddenly the building manager had reported them to the police—they weren't permitted to have guests overnight, particularly guests who were foreigners. They'd have to get permission from the Préfecture for that.

And when they went to extend their own residence permits at the Préfecture there was more trouble: Were they refugees? No, they said. Well, said the official behind the grille, the Spanish government, which had issued their passports, was about to fall—they'd be refugees *then*, right enough. Grudgingly, he gave them new papers, for now. But they realized something they'd been trying to ignore ever since Munich: Paris was no safe haven for them. They would have to try and get away again—across the Channel, if they could, to England.

January 1939: Barcelona

By New Year's Day, 1939, Barcelona—already battered by bombs and desperate for food—was choked by the presence of tens of thousands of refugees from all over Spain, all of them fleeing the quick death of bombardments or the slower death of reprisals in what seemed ever likelier to be a Nationalist victory. The rebels had files on two million Loyalists, they boasted, and every one of them was a marked man. "There will be no mediation," Generalísimo Francisco Franco told the vice president of the American United Press syndicate, "because criminals and their victims cannot live together."

On January 3, the insurgent general Juan Yagüe's troops crossed the Ebro, and over the next few days the Nationalists continued to advance into Catalonia, while Republican attempts to counterattack in the south, near Peñarroya, and in the west, in Extremadura, were stalled or beaten back. The only thing holding the war effort together was the population's terror over what would happen to them if they *didn't* hang on.

Although he still hadn't recovered from the dysentery and depression that had plagued him since China and had driven him back to Paris in December, Capa came back to Barcelona just as the Republic's fortunes seemed to be hitting their lowest ebb. He had assignments from *Match* and *Picture Post* as well as *Life,* and safe-conducts and passes from the Spanish ministries of state and defense; but he never made it into action. The closest he came was a trip with André Malraux to photograph some of Líster's soldiers at the front on a rare day of calm; but his pictures have the look of nineteenth-century history painting, not twentieth-century war photography. Líster and his men, capes flung dashingly over their shoulders, are grouped closely together (sometimes with the black-leather-clad Malraux, looking like a solemn owl, in attendance) in front of a sweeping landscape with a low horizon line and a bright sky. In some they are peering at a newspaper—a copy of *España Republicana* with General Miaja on the front page—in others looking at what might be mail, or fighting orders, or maps. The images were elegant, sharp, striking, and would make good illustrations of the Republic's strength and resilience for articles that echoed the view of Barea's (and Connie de la Mora's) old boss, Álvarez de Vayo, who was telling Jimmy Sheean, in Paris, "Things are not so bad as the papers say. Barcelona will resist. Remember Madrid."

A more accurate portrait of what was going on in Barcelona could be seen in the pictures Capa took a few days later at a mobilization center, where the latest, last-resort wave of conscripts, citizens of both sexes between the ages of seventeen and fifty-five, was being processed. Capa's camera sought out the anxious, lined faces, the patched, worn clothes, the lingering kisses left on children's heads, the despairing laughter of a wife whose husband tries on his newly issued helmet for her—*how do I look?*—before saying goodbye, probably forever. Even in photographs of little boys exultantly clambering over the wreckage of a Heinkel bomber displayed on the Ramblas, his lens found the tight, anxious faces of their parents on the edges of the crowd, wondering if the next Heinkel would be the one that got them—or in the case of a man on crutches, with one leg missing, if this was the plane that *had* got him.

By the morning of January 14, the Nationalist army was coiled outside Tarragona, sixty miles southwest of Barcelona on the coast; refugees were pouring north on the coast road, and Capa went down to chronicle their flight. It was a bright warm day, the sort that tricks you into thinking spring might be coming sooner than you thought—*perfect bombing weather,* Martha Gellhorn would have called it if she'd been there. The refugees walked along the roads, carrying their possessions in valises, if they had them, or bundles, if they hadn't, or carts, if they'd been able to find one; some wore rough working people's clothes, headscarves, caps, overalls or bunchy skirts, others had good winter coats and silk scarves around their necks. "I have seen hundreds of thousands flee thus, in two countries, Spain and China," Capa would write. "And I am afraid to think that hundreds of thousands of others who are yet living in undisturbed peace in other countries will one day meet with the same fate."

As he was taking his pictures, a flight of Savoia-Marchettis wheeled in from the sea with the sun glinting off their silver wings and began strafing the ground with machine-gun fire. As they passed over the road they opened fire on the line of people straggling along it, including two couples helping their mule team by pushing a covered wagon up a slight incline. Seconds later the wagon had been shot to pieces, its pathetic contents strewn on the road; one of the women and both of the men who had been pushing it lay in the mud; the two mules were dead in their harness; and the remaining woman knelt on the ground, keening, reaching out for the family dog, who lay between the wheels of the cart. But he was dead, too.

Back in Barcelona, things weren't much better. If those who were fleeing were at least safe, for the moment, they were just as despairing, cloaked and huddled with their belongings on the pavement in front of refugee centers, posed as if they were figures in some grim altarpiece: young couples, old women, beautiful dark-eyed children. Capa felt his heart aching: "it is not always easy," he wrote, "to stand aside and be able to do nothing but record the sufferings around one."

On January 22, with the dust from the enemy's shells already visible behind the crest of Montjuic to the south, Prime Minister Negrín gave the order for the government to abandon Barcelona and move to Gerona, fifty-two miles north. Officials began burning documents by the drawerful—so many that minor fires broke out all over the city, their smoke mingling with that from the incessant air raids that were reducing the port area to rubble. Military convoys were pulling out, and civilians started to stream out of the city, in cars or trucks or buses if they were lucky, or on foot if they weren't. The next night, and the one after that, Herbert Matthews slept in his Minerva to prevent anyone from stealing it; he would need it when the time came to leave, but for now he and Capa, and a handful of other reporters, were holding out.

Late on the evening of January 25, word came that the Nationalist vanguard had crossed the Llobregat River and was on the slopes of Monte Tibidabo, on the city's western rim. Matthews, Capa, and a British journalist, the *Daily Express*'s O'Dowd Gallagher, went to the Censura to send their last stories. They found it a spectral place, lit only by candlelight (the power was out) and largely deserted, since Constancia de la Mora and her senior staff had left days ago for the French border. Matthews telephoned his last dispatch from Barcelona, in which he tried to sound a positive note ("While there is life, there is hope"), but Capa's photographs of the Censura, with its empty desks and flickering candles, told a different story.

After midnight the journalists went back to the Majestic through the shuttered, empty streets. It had turned cold and blustery, and propaganda leaflets and discarded identity cards skittered about in the wind. At the hotel Matthews closed up his luggage and gave tips and the last of his food supplies to the tearful chambermaids; then he, Capa, Gallagher, and another British correspondent, William Forrest, got into the Minerva and set off along the coast road for the north. Traffic was heavy. In addition to cars and trucks there were bedraggled columns of soldiers and the tragic stream of refugees trudging along the margins of the pavement. Soon after sunrise they reached Caldetas, on the coast, where American nationals were waiting to be evacuated on the U.S. cruiser *Omaha*. Stopping for breakfast at the American consulate, the Minerva's passengers learned that the editors of *Life*, concerned because Capa had no passport, had petitioned the U.S. government to allow him to be taken out of Spain on the *Omaha* as well. But Capa would have none of it. He needed to document what was happening to the refugees trying to get to the border, and he'd take his chances with Matthews and the others.

Back to the road, then, with Matthews peering through his glasses at the traffic, finding detours and shortcuts, and Capa taking pictures as if the camera were a shield against his feelings. How else could you not weep to see the little boy, his face set in a frown of concentration, his sockless bare legs exposed beneath the hem of his best wool coat, or the mother and her children sitting beside the mule cart they had to empty because the mule couldn't carry both them and their possessions?

When the Minerva reached Figueras, sixteen miles from the border, late in the afternoon, the town was in chaos. The government had already decided to abandon Gerona, and now government officials as well as foreign correspondents and a flood of refugees without passports were all milling about in the village with nowhere to go and nowhere to stay. There was an improvised press room in the back of a flat the Propaganda Ministry had requisitioned, though; in it Matthews, Capa, and Forrest found a group of censorship officials and correspondents, among them Jimmy Sheean, who had just arrived from Paris, where he and Dinah had gone the day after Bola's party in November. Sheean was in a state of growing despair. He'd been to see Prime Minister Negrín, who along with most of his government had fled to Figueras: Why hadn't they gone back to Madrid to make a stand? Sheean wondered. Why hadn't Negrín, and Del Vayo and the others, seen how dire the Republic's position was before now? Had they somehow confused confidence and courage with propaganda? But there were no answers to these questions.

Telephone service between Catalonia and France had broken down, so Matthews, Forrest, and Gallagher left Figueras and went across the border to Perpignan to file their stories. But Capa and Sheean stayed, and a few hours later Boleslavskaya made a dramatic entrance after a long and suspenseful drive from Barcelona in which she'd been stuck in a traffic jam on a village street during an air raid. "And a lot of idiots up and down the road started honking their horns, as if that would do any good," she said—the first funny thing any of them had heard in days.

That night, because there was nowhere else to sleep, those remaining all bivouacked in the press room, Bola and three or four others on a kind of *lit royal* made out of an abandoned box spring, some papers, and coats and shawls from Bola's luggage, and Capa, swearing and joking, on a pile of propaganda leaflets—*finally, a good use for propaganda!* He wanted to go back to Barcelona, which given his identification with the Loyalist cause was a nearly suicidal thing to do; and for the next two days he tried in vain to find someone to drive him there. But on the evening of the twenty-seventh a communiqué was telephoned to the makeshift Propaganda Office: "Barcelona has fallen into the hands of the enemy." By then the only accredited foreign correspondents present to hear it were Sheean, Boleslavskaya, and Capa.

The next day, France opened the border to Spain's refugees, and along with the first trickle of what would become a flood of 400,000, Capa drove through the frontier at Le Perthus for the last time.

February–March 1939: Paris

You could see them in all the newsreels and on the smudged pages of newspapers and magazines: the beaten soldiers, broken men, women, and children, struggling over the icy roads, strafed and bombed from the air, pursued from the rear by an army that would show no mercy. *An endless line of fugitives desperate for safety,* Barea thought. He had heard nothing of Aurelia and the children for months; perhaps, because they had no connection to him, they were somehow better off. Meanwhile, the word from Austria was not good: the secret police had been making inquiries about Ilsa, and her history and associations were making her family's already precarious situation worse. "These days are full of the most fateful happenings," Valentin Pollak wrote, in Vienna, "fateful for the world and for myself."

Fortunately, as dangerous as Ilsa's old socialist contacts were to her family, they were useful to her: for in England a number of old friends from her days as a socialist speaker and journalist offered to help her and Barea emigrate. Some, like the translators and editors Gwenda David and Eric Mosbacher, promised to help find work for them; others, like Henry Brinton, offered places to stay; still others extended loans to tide them over until some kind of money started coming in. For Ilsa, who had spent time in England as a girl and whose English was fluent, this seemed a promised safe haven; for Barea, it was a leap into the unknown, into a culture and a language he was completely unfamiliar with.

But they would have to go, and go at once: if and when Franco won the war, it was foolish to think that France, or Britain, wouldn't recognize the Nationalists as Spain's government, and then Republican passports wouldn't be worth the paper they were printed on. Barea and Ilsa would be stateless persons.

Astonishingly, because he rarely gambled, Barea bought what turned out to be a winning ticket for the national lottery at the corner *tabac*, and with its modest proceeds they were able to buy their passage across the Channel. They packed their bags with their few belongings and left their sublet apartment without a backward look. At the Gare St. Lazare, the plainclothes officer asked them for their passports, then barely glanced at them before banging his rubber stamp on their pages. *Is that all?* Barea thought, imagining the river of refugees backed up at Le Perthus as if by a dam: no rubber stamps for them. As he and Ilsa settled in their compartment the train gathered speed; outside, the bare fields of Normandy slid by. How long until armies fought over them, as they had fought at Brunete, at the Ebro? In Dieppe the small steamer rose and fell on the Channel chop; Ilsa went below, but Barea stood smoking on the deck, the February wind in his hair. One of the French sailors, hearing his accent, asked where he was from, and he told them. Told them about Spain's fight, his feelings of loss and betrayal at France's capitulation at Munich, his fears for the future. *What's wrong with your country?* he wanted to know. *Are you blind to what's happening? Or don't you care about your freedom?*

"Oh, no," the sailors assured him. "The others are the ones who won't fight." For a moment they all watched the French coast recede behind them. "Look, comrade," one of the Frenchmen said. "Don't go away from France in bitterness. We'll fight together yet."

"In Paris there's nothing good," wrote Capa to his mother, Julia, in New York. "Everybody is shitting in their pants and scared to death of Hitler." He'd been too tired and despondent to work for a month after returning from Spain, he went on: "I walked around like an idiot." But then he'd received a letter from his father, Deszö, in Budapest, saying he was ill— something wrong with his stomach, or maybe his liver. Capa pulled himself together enough to do some assignments for *Ce Soir* that would bring in a little money—now he could send a little something to Deszö to pay the doctor; and when the actress Luise Rainer, whom he'd met working on *The 400 Million*, asked him to escort her to a white-tie gala in Paris, he rented the requisite evening wear and went along. "Imagine how elegant I became," he joked to Julia. "Just like a Bear in Tails!"

Then in early March he began hearing reports of appalling conditions in the internment camps that the French government had set up for those members of the Loyalist army that had finally been permitted to cross the border. More than 75,000 men were incarcerated in enclosures on the beach near Perpignan, with inadequate food, water, or sanitary arrangements; but no one was covering the situation, because the entire internment area had been declared off-limits for the French press. (He didn't know that his friend Agustí Centelles, whom he'd last seen at the Despedida parade in Barcelona, was incarcerated in one of the camps, at Bram, surreptitiously taking photographs that wouldn't be seen until years afterward.) So Capa, using his *Life* credentials and identifying himself as "André Friedmann" rather than the too-well-known Robert Capa, went to the police *préfecture* in Aude on March 19 and received a permit to visit the camps at Argelès-sur-Mer, Le Barcarès, Bram, and Montolieu. Even for someone used to the privations of war, they were a revelation.

Behind fences of barbed wire through which they might be allowed a few minutes to speak to rare visitors, policed by gendarmes and mounted Senegalese troops who must have reminded the prisoners of Franco's Moors, thousands of men who had fought to the end for their country were now housed—if they had housing at all, and were not huddled in canvas tents or out in the open—in hastily constructed, unheated, and poorly insulated shacks. Filthy and emaciated, they dug holes in the sand for new huts, or lined up to receive their miserable rations. Their threadbare clothes were inadequate to the wintry wind from the nearby sea; many of them, too sick or malnourished even to stand up, lay on pallets of straw. Capa had always been prodigal with film, exposing frame after frame in the hope of finding, amid a torrent of possibilities, the perfect shot; but here he seemed overcome by what he saw and simply kept his finger on the shutter, shooting strings of images of desolation. *The truth is the best picture, the best propaganda.*

There were a few moments of gallantry and humor: he found two Basque soldiers who'd decorated their hut with wooden model airplanes and painted over the sign that bore the barracks number, 95, with the legend "Gran Hotel Euzkeldun" ("Grand Basque Hotel")—adding an image of a man squirting wine into his mouth from a *bota*; and at Bram members of a Barcelona orchestra, who'd managed to bring their instruments with them across the border, played for him. But although the cellist—a friend, it was said, of Pablo Casals—tried to smile for the camera, his eyes were full of ineffable sadness. And the smile itself revealed his missing teeth, testament to malnutrition and neglect. At least he was alive, Capa must have thought as he made his last stop, a cemetery a mile outside the camps. There a newly dug grave awaited its occupant, and a long line of white crosses marked those of the forty-four men who had already given their lives for Spain, but on French soil.

Although his photographs of the camps were featured in *Picture Post* and *Se*, a Swedish magazine, Capa felt that his trip to document them, as well as his last sojourn in Spain, and maybe even his whole Spanish experience, were "a great disaster." For the past three years he had made himself an international reputation chronicling—with compassion and immediacy—a war that had begun in hope and ended in defeat, disillusion, and personal loss. Now, he told his mother, "I am living in such a dumb manner, not knowing from one day to another what it will be . . . We are [all] walking around like dogs after the rain and trying to save our friends." It was, now, all anyone could do.

February–March 1939: Key West/Havana

When Hemingway and Pauline had first come to Key West, back in the late twenties, it had been a charmingly funky backwater, a place to fish and write and get away from the rest of the world. But the intervening years, and the Overseas Highway, had brought a new, pleasure-seeking crowd to the island; and while Hemingway was away in Spain, Pauline had made numerous friends among them. Now they were all over the place, in Hemingway's swimming pool and on his lawn and in his favorite saloon, wanting to talk or go out fishing or drinking, and he couldn't stand it. He was missing Martha, he was missing Spain, and all he wanted to do, he told his Russian translator Ivan Kashkin, in Moscow, was write. "As long as there is a war you always think perhaps you will be killed so you have nothing to worry about. But now I am not killed so I have to work."

He was already thinking about a new collection of short fiction, to be published in the fall, which would include the most recent Spanish stories from *Esquire* and *Cosmopolitan* as well as three more long ones, one about Teruel, one about an attack in the Guadarrama, and one about a

Gulf Stream fisherman who loses a huge marlin to a swarm of sharks because it's too big to haul into his boat.

But the news from Spain, in the aftermath of Barcelona's fall—like having a death in the family, he and Martha agreed, in their clandestine telephone calls—seemed to require a grander response from him: a summation or an epitaph. For even though Negrín had returned to a base near Alicante in the shrinking Loyalist zone and was urging his commanders to keep up the fight, it was clear the effort was doomed. Hemingway couldn't have known that in Moscow, Kliment Voroshilov was telling Stalin that Negrín's requests for more aid were, "at the very least, inopportune"; but he *could* read in the newspapers of how the war-weary Republican generals were seeking to make a separate peace with Franco, and how, even before the Republic could formally capitulate, the governments of France and Britain were prepared to recognize the Nationalist rebels as the government of Spain. "The only thing about a war," Hemingway said, "is to win it—and that is what we did not do." It was over, in his mind; and now, he went on, "I understand the whole thing better."

In Paris, in the fall, he had drafted two chapters of something he thought might be a novel about the war, then put them aside as too ambitious or too painful to go on with for the moment. But he was ready now, if he could get time and a place to write. Once Key West would have been the place, and Pauline would have been the muse to write for, but no longer. Dropping a thank-you note to Sara Murphy for a toy sailboat she'd sent Gregory for Christmas, Pauline remarked at how the little vessel sailed back and forth in their swimming pool, running aground as if it were trying to escape to a bigger body of water, then "setting out smoothly into the pool again . . . just like man and life." Neither she nor Hemingway was acknowledging it, but he, too, was about to sail away.

In Naples, Florida, one hundred miles north of Key West, Martha Gellhorn had been having a midwinter holiday with her mother when Hemingway asked her to join him in Havana. On February 18, she arrived to find him already established in two different hotel rooms, at the Sevilla-Biltmore for sleeping and at the Ambos Mundos for writing—"Tell everybody you live in one hotel and live in another," he joked to his bear-hunting buddy Tom Shevlin, whom he'd long ago forgiven for his comments about *To Have and Have Not*. He'd stocked the Ambos Mundos room with a twelve-pound ham and a supply of cured sausages, as if he were back in Madrid at the Hotel Florida with Sidney Franklin at the hot plate and Chopin on the Victrola.

But Martha didn't want to camp out in a hotel room, like Dorothy Bridges in *The Fifth Column*. For one thing, she hated squalor, hated it more than ever after Madrid and Barcelona; and for another thing, she had books of her own she wanted to write, beginning with a story about a reporter in Prague into which she wanted to pour all the passion and vitriol that had built up in her over the past year in Europe. She went house hunting in the country and found a tumbledown estate, *La Finca Vigía* (Watchtower Farm), on a hill in the village of San Francisco de Paula: a one-story stone house with a swimming pool, a tennis court, a huge sitting room, a library, a guesthouse, and a magnificent if overgrown garden from which, at night, you could see the lights of Havana in the distance. Hemingway thought the rent, $100 a month, was too much; but Martha took the house anyway, and planned to invest some of what she'd earned from *Collier's* in restoring and furnishing it. She was so pleased with the result that she felt embarrassed, she wrote Mrs. Roosevelt; at last she would have a place to do her own work in—a beautiful place, a place beyond her imagining—and she had paid for it all with her writing. "I have a feeling," she told the First Lady, "I ought to put up a plaque to *Collier's* magazine."

While Martha was talking to notaries and gardeners and housekeepers, Hemingway was preparing himself, like a matador or a soldier, for the work he was about to embark on. He had sketched in the background already in all the dispatches he'd written for NANA—perfunctory or grandiose, some of them, but full of useful detail. Writing them, and working with Joris Ivens on *The Spanish Earth*, he'd known firsthand the sound of bombing and artillery, the smell of granite dust and cordite, the way men made jokes before battle and then spat to show the joke was real—because, he said, "you cannot spit if you are really frightened." He'd met the commanders, and the fighting men, and the hangers-on at Chicote's and Gaylord's. And although most of the stories he might want for the foreground of his novel weren't those he knew from personal experience, he'd heard them from those who had lived through them: the tales of Orlov's *partizans*—which might allow him to use the dynamite plot he'd discarded from *To Have and Have Not*; the beautiful nurse Maria's account of being raped by Nationalists, which he'd heard when visiting Freddy

Keller in the International Brigade hospital at Mataro in the spring of 1938; the fighting in the Guadarrama that Capa had photographed and filmed with Gerda; the bloody slaughter at Badajoz that Jay Allen had described. Now all these pieces were ready to come together, not as propaganda, or reportage, but as a novel about the war that, he hoped, would "show *all* the different sides of it."

On March 1, rising early while it was still cool, he left Martha cocooned in sleep in their bed at the Sevilla-Biltmore and walked the few blocks to the Ambos Mundos. He checked at the desk for mail and then went up to Room 511. On the desk was his Royal typewriter, a supply of number 2 pencils, and two stacks of paper, one already covered with typed words and markings in his own round, almost schoolgirlish hand, the other blank, unblemished. He sat down at the desk. Taking a fresh sheet of paper from the second pile, he scrolled it into the typewriter, and began: "We lay on the brown, pine-needled floor of the forest . . ."

EPILOGUE

On March 27, 1939, Madrid—the city that Ernest Hemingway had proclaimed Francisco Franco "must" take if he were to win the civil war—surrendered without a fight to the Nationalist army. Five days later, on April 1, the Caudillo issued a final bulletin from his headquarters: "Today, with the Red Army captive and disarmed, our victorious troops have achieved their objectives." On the same day the United States recognized the Nationalist rebels as the legitimate government of Spain. Over the next few months the new government imprisoned thousands of Loyalists, or suspected Loyalists—many in forced-labor camps; of these an estimated 50,000 were executed, and the killings went on into the 1940s. Although most important Loyalist officials, including Negrín, Azaña, Indalecio Prieto, and Constancia de la Mora, managed to escape to exile, some found danger there instead of safety: Largo Caballero died after four years in a Nazi concentration camp, Azaña was being pursued by German and Vichy French agents when he, too, died in a small Provençal town, and the Catalan president Luís Companys was captured by the Gestapo in occupied France, returned to Spain, and shot.

Francisco Franco ruled Spain as a dictator until his death in 1975; but his designated heir, Prince Juan Carlos de Borbón, grandson of the old king Alfonso XIII, had different ideas than the Caudillo about the way the country should be run, and by 1978 established a parliamentary democracy with himself as constitutional monarch. Although a cornerstone of the new regime was a "pact of forgetting" that granted amnesty for all Franco-era crimes, historians and survivors of the war, or their descendants, began investigating the deaths and disappearances of the Franco years; and in 2007, with the Socialists enjoying a majority of seats in the

Cortes, the government enacted a Historical Memory law to facilitate exhumation of victims. But bitter controversy erupted when the examining magistrate Baltasar Garzón Real attempted to overturn the amnesties and prosecute wartime deaths as crimes against humanity; the result was that Garzón himself was suspended for exceeding his judicial authority. Despite the pact of forgetting, the ghosts of the Civil War have apparently still not been laid to rest.

On August 23, 1939, Germany and the Soviet Union stunned the world by doing what Maxim Litvinov had told the journalist Georges Luciani they would do: they signed a mutual nonaggression pact, accompanied by a secret map that divided Poland between the two powers in the event of a German invasion. Even though the promised partition of Poland was not public knowledge at the time the pact was signed, the news of an alliance between Stalin and Hitler filled antifascists with dismay, and drove many, including Gustav Regler, to break with the Communist Party.

On August 25, the British government signed a treaty with Poland, promising to come to her aid in the event of an attack by Germany, which by then—with Hitler blustering over the airwaves about the "harassment" of ethnic Germans in the area around Danzig—appeared almost inevitable. France already had such an agreement. A week later, with no fear of reprisal by the Soviet Union, Hitler invaded Poland, pulverizing the country's defenses with massive bombing of the sort inflicted on Madrid, Barcelona, and Guernica; two days after that, on September 3, Britain and France declared war on Germany. The general European conflict that everyone had been both expecting and hoping to avert for two decades had at last begun.

The book Ernest Hemingway began writing on March 1, 1938, became *For Whom the Bell Tolls*, the big critical and commercial hit he had been seeking for years and his most successful novel ever. The story of an idealistic young American saboteur on an abortive mission to bomb a bridge with a band of Loyalist *aktivi* that includes a beautiful young woman, a former rape victim named Maria with blond "sunburnt" hair, it was published to admiring reviews—"the best book [he] has written, the fullest, the deepest, the truest," said *The New York Times*, while Edmund Wilson proclaimed, "Hemingway the artist is with us again, and it is like having an old friend back." By six months after publication in October 1940 it had sold 491,000 copies, and Paramount Pictures had paid $110,000 for the film rights. The few critical reactions to the book came mainly from members of the Lincoln Brigade, among them Alvah Bessie, Freddy Keller, and Milton Wolff, who objected to what they felt were negative portrayals of Communists in the book, especially of the International Brigades chief André Marty, and said that Hemingway had misrepresented Russia's role in the war. (These critics would have been surprised to learn that Hemingway's relations with the Soviet Union were still cordial enough for the KGB to recruit him as a special agent, code-named "ARGO," in 1941—an assignment that apparently never resulted in any practical intelligence.)

A more substantial, and oddly sympathetic, negative appraisal of *For Whom the Bell Tolls* came from Arturo Barea, writing in the English magazine *Horizon* in 1941. "Hemingway could describe with truthfulness and art what he had seen from without," Barea said, "but he wanted to describe more. He wished for a share in the Spanish struggle. Not sharing the beliefs, the life, and the suffering of the Spaniards he could only shape them in his imagination after the Spain he knew." To Barea, the death of the hero at the novel's end occurs, "not so much because the inner necessity of the tale demands it, but because Ernest Hemingway could not really believe in his future." Hemingway, he concluded, "was always a spectator who wanted to be an actor, and who wanted to write as if he had been an actor. Yet it is not enough to look on: to write truthfully you must live, and you must feel what you are living." Barea called the article "Not Spain, but Hemingway."

Hemingway dedicated *For Whom the Bell Tolls* to Martha Gellhorn. Shortly after its publication she became his wife: he had left Pauline definitively in September 1939, and when their divorce was final he and Martha were married, in Cheyenne, Wyoming, on November 21, 1940. Robert Capa—sent by *Life* to do a story on Hemingway and the film of *For Whom the Bell Tolls*, partly illustrated with Capa's and Gerda Taro's pictures of the Guadarrama campaign—photographed the happy pair shooting game birds, reading in front of a crackling fire, and dancing together after their wedding.

Their happiness didn't last. Although Martha had been proud to list herself as "Martha Gellhorn (Mrs. Ernest Hemingway)" in the biography on the jacket flap of her Czech war-correspondent novel, *A Stricken Field*, and although she'd signed a jocular prenuptial "agreement" with Hemingway affirming that "he and his business are what matter to me in this life," she found the role of helpmeet to genius impossible to sustain. Even before their marriage she'd got an assignment from *Collier's* to cover the outbreak of war in Finland, where the Soviet Union, having previously invaded Poland in concert with its new ally, Germany, had launched an offensive; and on the way there she had seemingly, if briefly, reignited her dormant affair with the still-married Allen Grover. Although Hemingway was unaware of the dalliance (and would have been apoplectic if he had known of it), he *had* been bitter about her Finnish assignment: "she thinks now that she stood by like one of those dumb wives and abandoned her career while I wrote a book," he complained to Edna Gellhorn, "while really she went to France and Norway and Sweden and Finland to a war and made much fame and lots of money." And while he was at first grateful for her financial contributions, even telling the columnist Earl Wilson that he had been "busted" in 1940 from the economic demands of his divorce and needed her help, he grew to resent her independence and what he saw as her competitiveness. By the time she scooped him by stowing away on a hospital ship that put her on the beach at D-Day— Hemingway, who'd been ferried over on an attack transport, could only gaze at the coast through binoculars from the stern of a landing craft and didn't get on shore—the marriage had dissolved into a puddle of spite. They divorced in 1945, and he married another journalist, Mary Welsh, with whom he had been carrying on a wartime affair, who was more content than Martha to put his work ahead of her own.

In 1952 he published the story, now grown to novella length, that he had first outlined to Max Perkins before he went to Havana in 1939, about "the old commercial fisherman who fought the swordfish all alone in his skiff for 4 days and four nights and the sharks finally eating it after he had it alongside and could not get it into the boat . . ." It had taken him a dozen years to get the story right—maybe because the theme, of the fisherman fighting with and landing his treasure, only to have it chewed up by predators, felt unsettlingly like his own vision of himself, his talent, and the critics he detested. It must have seemed like justification when, in 1954, he was awarded the Nobel Prize in Literature "for his mastery of the art of the narrative, most recently demonstrated in *The Old Man and the Sea*."

But Hemingway's postwar career never brought him another success—commercial or artistic—to match the work he had done before; although it did bring him to Spain again on several occasions to follow the bullfights and revisit some of his old haunts, including the Hotel Florida. Curiously, his animosity to Franco and Francoism seemed not to act as a deterrent, either to him or to the Spanish government.

In the years after the Civil War, as he became the very icon of the Famous Writer, Hemingway lost touch with many of those who had been the friends of his youth. His relationship with John Dos Passos, in particular, never really recovered from their break over the fate of José Robles—perhaps unsurprisingly given that Dos Passos, embittered over his experience in Spain, drifted further and further to the right politically. But Dos did attempt to repair the breach, particularly in the terrible few years when it became apparent that Hemingway was suffering a prolonged mental and physical breakdown, for which he was hospitalized at the Mayo Clinic in 1960 and 1961. Hemingway never responded to Dos Passos's overtures; probably, given the suffocating silence his illness imposed on him, he *couldn't* respond. In July 1961, unable to write and in the grip of black depression, he shot himself with a double-barreled shotgun.

Martha Gellhorn was put on the masthead at *Collier's* at the end of 1939 (not in 1937 as she would later claim) at the time of her first reporting from Finland. She spent the World War II years as a front-line journalist in Finland, Asia, Italy, France, and Germany, where she was among the first to report on the liberation of the Dachau concentration camp. Afterward she covered the Vietnam war, the Six-Day War in the Middle East, and guerrilla fighting in Central America, and her name became a byword for courage and tenacity in reporting what she called "the view from the ground." She published ten works of fiction, a play (with Virginia Cowles) about women war correspondents, and several collections of reportage and travel writing, all praised for their incisiveness and eloquence, although few had commercial success.

After her marriage to Hemingway dissolved, Martha Gellhorn had relationships with a number of other powerful and attractive men, including

General James Gavin, Laurance Rockefeller, and David Gurewitsch, a physician who was also romantically linked to Eleanor Roosevelt. A marriage to the *Time* editor Thomas Matthews ended in divorce, but brought an enduring connection to his son, Alexander (Sandy), who became her executor. She adopted a son of her own, Alessandro, also nicknamed Sandy, from an orphanage in Italy in 1949; but she seemed uncomfortable in a maternal role and their relationship was often troubled. Always restless and rootless, she traveled widely and lived briefly in Africa, Italy, Mexico, and, for the last forty years of her life, England, where after her divorce from Matthews she became a kind of mentor and model to a younger generation of English journalists and novelists. Although she frequently published essays and letters to the editor in which she attempted (not always accurately) to set the record straight about the Spanish Civil War, she refused virtually all requests to discuss Hemingway in interviews, claiming that she had "no intention of being a footnote in someone else's life." In 1998, diagnosed with cancer, her hearing and her eyesight failing, she—like her first and rarely mentioned husband—committed suicide. After her death a prize was established in her honor for journalism that tells "an unpalatable truth, validated by powerful facts." The 2011 winner was the founder of WikiLeaks, Julian Assange.

Robert Capa was in Paris in 1939 when World War II was declared. Both *Ce Soir* and *L'Humanité*, as Communist-affiliated media, had been closed by the French government when the Nazi-Soviet Pact was signed; although Capa applied for accreditation as a war photographer to the Ministry of Foreign Affairs, his request was turned down because of his former association with *Ce Soir*, and it seemed possible he would be rounded up for internment as a Communist sympathizer and a former German resident. With the help of *Life* he managed to emigrate to the United States; when it appeared he would lose his visa a young woman he'd met through John Ferno suggested he marry her so he would become a citizen. He did, although the marriage was never consummated, and ended in divorce some years later. In 1941 he went to England, where he collaborated with Dinah Sheean on a photographic book about a London family surviving the Blitz; and after America entered the war he went first to North Africa, then to Sicily and Italy to cover the Allied invasions there. In 1944, landing with the first wave of troops at Omaha Beach on D-Day, he took some of the most brutal and terrifying war photographs ever shot (even though the prints were distorted by a careless darkroom assistant), then went on to chronicle the liberation of Paris (which he claimed to have witnessed from a tank driven by émigré Spanish soldiers), the Allied drive into Belgium, and the Battle of the Rhine, where he parachuted into combat with the 17th Airborne Division. In 1947, with his old friends Chim, Henri Cartier-Bresson, and Maria Eisner, and two other photographers, he established Magnum, a cooperative that became perhaps the premier photographic agency in the world.

When he wasn't risking his life taking pictures Capa spent his time seeing friends, playing poker, and chasing women. But after Gerda, he never again wanted to settle down with any of them. A two-year romance with Ingrid Bergman—whom he met in 1945, after she had starred in *Gaslight* and, following strenuous lobbying by Ernest Hemingway, as Maria in *For Whom the Bell Tolls*—foundered on his unwillingness to abandon the peripatetic and sometimes dangerous life of a photojournalist for marriage; the same thing happened with a longer-lived (though less monogamous) relationship with Jemison McBride Hammond, the ex-wife of the record producer John Hammond. Capa was always leaving to cover a war in the Middle East, the antics of jet-set skiers in Klosters or Val d'Isère, the daily lives of Picasso and Henri Matisse on the Riviera. In 1954 he accepted an assignment from *Life* to go to Indochina, where the Communist Vietminh had just taken the city of Dienbienphu from the French. "This is the last good war," Capa commented. "Nobody knows anything and nobody tells you anything, and that means a good reporter is free to go out and get a beat every day." He was out getting a beat on May 25, taking pictures of the evacuation of a fort at Dongquithan, when he stepped on a land mine and was killed.

Just over fifty years later, three cardboard boxes containing more than 165 rolls of film, shot by Capa, Gerda Taro, and Chim during the Spanish Civil War and missing ever since, were discovered in Mexico City. They had been spirited out of Paris by Capa's darkroom assistant Csiki Weiss when the Germans invaded France in 1940, and had found their way into the hands of the Mexican ambassador to France's Vichy government, who took them back to Mexico at the war's end. Somehow every one of the rolls had miraculously survived in good condition, although it took a further dozen years for arrangements to be completed for their return to Capa's and Taro's archives at the International Center of Photography, the institution founded by Cornell Capa as a memorial to his brother and his fellow photojournalists. But in September 2011, after four years of conservation work and cataloguing, ICP's exhibition *The Mexican Suitcase* made these images of the Spanish Civil War public at last.

Arturo and Ilsa Barea landed in England in February 1939 and settled in a series of rural villages—Puckeridge, Fladbury, Mapledurham—whose very names must have seemed exotic to Barea (as resident aliens, he and Ilsa were not permitted, once war had been declared, to live in London). With her knowledge of languages Ilsa found work at the BBC Monitoring Service, which eavesdropped on radio broadcasts from around the world, including hostile powers; Barea frequented the local pubs, learning English and dart-playing, tended his garden, and cooked paellas for his wife and her parents, who had managed to emigrate from Vienna at the last available moment. And he wrote—short stories, articles, a critical volume on Lorca, a short book about the Civil War entitled *Struggle for the Spanish Soul*, and most of the second and third parts of the autobiography he had begun in Paris, which would be translated by Ilsa and published as *The Track* and *The Clash*, in 1943 and 1946, respectively. Meanwhile, the first volume, *The Forge*, had been brought out in 1941 by Faber and Faber, where its editor was T. S. Eliot, and had earned Barea praise from Stephen Spender and George Orwell, among others.

In October 1940 he began broadcasting a series of fourteen-minute talks about his experiences in England over the BBC's Latin American Service, using the name Juan de Castilla, a pseudonym that both protected his family in Spain from reprisals and affirmed his identity as a son, if an exiled one, of "hard Castile," the country of his childhood. He would have preferred to broadcast over the network's Spanish Service; but the BBC, anxious to keep fascist Spain neutral during the war, didn't want to hire someone with an anti-Franco background. "We do not employ Reds," they proclaimed. The sound studio was in London, to which Barea was driven by a BBC car—a journey that filled him with anxiety and sometimes terror, especially during the Blitz and the later buzz-bomb attacks, which brought on a recurrence of what he referred to as "*mi* shell-shock."

In 1947 the Bareas moved to a spacious (if unelectrified) house in rural Oxfordshire owned by Gavin Henderson, a Labour politician and second Baron Faringdon, where their coterie of mostly left-leaning and literary friends, including T. S. Eliot, Cyril Connolly, Gerald Brenan, J. R. Ackerley, and George Weidenfeld, were always informally welcome. Ilsa collaborated with Barea on a study of Miguel de Unamuno, and wrote a novel called *Telefónica*, closely based on her experiences in Madrid during the siege, which was serialized in Vienna's *Arbeiter-Zeitung* in 1949. Both Barea and Ilsa enjoyed fishing in Lord Faringdon's private lake and Barea liked to go pheasant shooting in his landlord's woods; but he felt both worried and guilty about the family he had left behind in Spain. Aurelia and his children were living in straitened circumstances that improved only in the postwar years, when Adolfina and Victor emigrated to South America, leaving the older Carmen and Arturo behind with their own new families; his beloved brother Miguel, whom he'd disguised as Rafael in his autobiography, was imprisoned after the fall of Madrid and died after his release in 1941 or 1942. In his novel *The Broken Root*, published in 1951, Barea created a portrait of an exile whose son curses him as "the man who had left them to starve on charity lentils and on slops of water and sawdust, and had never once spared them a thought"; and writing to a friend, Ilsa spoke of the "heartbreaking" situation of Arturo's children, "double victims, of the Civil War, which interrupted their schooling, and Arturo's desertion. Surely you understand that I have to go to great lengths to help Arturo make up for it?" Barea tried hard to reestablish a connection with his children, sending them letters and monthly checks wrung from his own meager income, and cherishing the many little notes to "Querido Papa" that he received in return; but he never saw them again.

After the war he continued writing and broadcasting; the autobiography was published in one volume, entitled *The Forging of a Rebel*, in the United States and was translated into ten languages, and Barea was mentioned as a possible recipient of the Nobel Prize. In 1952 he was given a six-month visiting professorship at Pennsylvania State University, an ironic achievement for someone whose formal schooling had ended at the age of thirteen. But although his students admired him, the American Legion and other organizations labeled him a Communist and at the end of his stay his contract wasn't renewed. He had better luck on a BBC-sponsored trip to South America in 1956, where enormous audiences attracted by his books and broadcasts made him—in the words of a British consular official—"the most successful visitor we have had for many years."

In December 1957, Barea began complaining of stomach problems, and on Christmas Eve had to miss a BBC broadcast (something he almost never did) due to illness. Ilsa, too, was down with bronchitis, and during the afternoon the two of them lay on their bed, exhausted, "like a crusader and his wife on a tomb," as Ilsa described it. But she got up to do the Christmas baking with her niece Uli, who was visiting from Austria and was a great favorite of Barea's, and to decorate their Christmas tree. That night, in bed, Barea suddenly complained of pressure in his chest, then excruciating pain. He clutched at Ilsa and went limp in her arms: undiagnosed cancer had put pressure on his lungs and helped to touch off a fatal heart attack. His body was cremated, and Ilsa intended to scatter his ashes on the graves of her parents, Valentin and Alice Pollak, who were buried in Faringdon churchyard. But when she went to do this, her hands, by now crippled with arthritis, proved unable to open the urn. She had to go back to Middle Lodge and get her niece Uli to help her prise up the lid.

Moving to London, Ilsa struggled on alone, writing, translating, editing, working as an interpreter for international conferences, and publishing and promoting Barea's work in England and abroad. In 1963, Kim Philby, her former colleague from her and Leopold Kulcsar's Viennese cell, who had been working for British intelligence under cover as a journalist, was unmasked as a Soviet double agent and fled to Moscow. News accounts of his defection mentioned his service with Franco's forces during the Spanish Civil War; if she hadn't realized it before, Ilsa now understood how vulnerable her knowledge of his socialist past, which would have betrayed him to Franco, had made her to those whose job it was to protect him at all costs.

But by now she had left politics behind. For some years she'd been researching a social and cultural history of her native Vienna, a graceful and lively book that was published to admiring reviews in 1966; two years later, when she retired, she returned to the city she'd left as an exile so long ago, intending to write a biography of Schubert and to work on her memoirs. Neither project came to fruition: in 1972, she died of kidney failure, and all of the papers she had with her in Vienna disappeared. In some ways she had never recovered from the loss of her husband fifteen years earlier. "It is meaningless to say he is dead," she wrote then. "Nobody can take away from me what I had. And what I know he had. It is beautiful after all. I am grateful."

•

By the time Franco's troops entered Madrid on March 27, 1939, the Hotel Florida was virtually empty. The foreign correspondents, the International Brigaders, the fliers of Malraux's Escuadrilla España, Hemingway's "*whores de combat*"—probably even Don Cristóbal and his stamp collection—were all long gone.

During the Franco years, however, the Florida stayed open, even as its end of the Gran Via became a little shabbier, a little less elegant, with the passage of time. In 1955, Hemingway returned to the hotel, bringing his new wife, Mary, to the room he had shared with Martha Gellhorn; but the Florida's days as the center of a universe of danger and excitement were over. And no one in Franco's Spain—where the official Civil War memorial was the gigantic stone cross and underground mausoleum, built by imprisoned Loyalists, at the Valley of the Fallen near the Escorial—was interested in preserving this monument to the Siege of Madrid. In 1964 the wrecker's ball accomplished what Nationalist shells could not: the Florida was demolished to make way for a department store, Galerias Preciados—named for a nearby street, and not for anything valued or precious. Today that building is occupied by a branch of Spain's largest retail chain, El Corte Inglés.

If the Hotel Florida is gone, the Telefónica remains, just up the Gran Via, tall and white as a wedding cake. The wires and cables and switchboards have disappeared: in their places are the sleek exhibition rooms and offices of the Telefónica Foundation, showcasing art, culture, and technology of the twenty-first century. Instead of correspondents filing stories, there are concerts and art shows and lectures. But the view from the Telefónica's tower terrace is remarkably unchanged, despite the new construction of the past seventy-five years. You can still look across the Manzanares at the Casa de Campo and the hill of Garabitas where the Nationalist guns hurled their shells into the Gran Via. And on a bright autumn day the shining peaks of the Guadarrama seem so close you feel you could put your hand out and touch them.

NOTES

Unless otherwise noted, translations in these pages are those of the cited source.

PROLOGUE

3 On July 18: Luis Bolín, *Spain: The Vital Years*, pp. 20–46.

4 "This young and eager Spain": Hugh Thomas, *The Spanish Civil War* (henceforth *SCW*), p. 32.

5 Although the government managed: Nigel Townson, *The Crisis of Democracy in Spain*, p. xiv.

5 "The war in Morocco": Paul Preston, *The Spanish Civil War: Reaction, Revolution, and Revenge* (henceforth *SCW*), p. 79.

5 By the time reconquest was achieved: Thomas, *SCW*, p. 136; Antony Beevor, *The Battle for Spain: The Spanish Civil War 1936–1939*, p. 32. According to Thomas, the official Ministry of the Interior figures, released on January 5, 1935, listed 1,335 killed and 2,951 wounded. Nigel Townson, in an e-mail, points out that those killed included "priests, professionals, landowners, Catholics etc, not just those on the left."

5 one of them: Thomas, *SCW*, p. 137.

6 In February 1936: Hugh Thomas, Stanley Payne, and others refer to this confederation as the National Front; but current writers on the period (the historian Nigel Townson and others) prefer the term Anti-revolutionary Coalition.

6 "the discipline of the army": Thomas, *SCW*, p. 189.

6 however, he suggested: Preston, *SCW*, p. 96.

7 So when the hired Dragon Rapide crossed: Bolín, *Spain*, p. 49.

7 "Once more the Army": Ronald Fraser, *Blood of Spain*, p. 61. This proclamation was in fact issued by Franco before leaving the Canary Islands, which he placed under martial law; but it wasn't publicly released until several days after the uprising had taken place.

7 "There can be no compromise": Jay Allen, *Chicago Daily Tribune*, July 28 and 29, 1936, quoted in Paul Preston, *We Saw Spain Die: Foreign Correspondents in the Spanish Civil War* (henceforth *WSSD*), p. 299.

PART I: "THEY ARE HERE FOR THEIR LIVES"

11 Arturo Barea lay: In reconstructing Arturo Barea's experience of the war I have relied extensively on his own account of it in his autobiographical trilogy, *The Forging*

of a Rebel (henceforth *FR* in notes), supplementing and corroborating it where possible with other documentation. Many people in it are given pseudonyms or partial names (in part to protect them from reprisal during the Franco years) and some incidental characters may be composites. Again, where possible, I've supplied their actual names.

12 "I'm no use": Barea, *El Centro de la pista*, quoted (and translated) by Michael Eaude, *Triumph at Midnight of the Century*, p. 11.

13 the radio was playing: Thomas, *SCW*, p. 215, n. 1.

14 leaving his nostrils full: Barea, *FR*, pp. 315–16.

14 So he'd spent all night: Ibid., p. 529.

14 his politics stood in the way: Ibid., p. 407.

16 "too many of those black beetles": Ibid., p. 525.

16 It was thought that the officers: Thomas, *SCW*, p. 233, provides a fairly full account of the siege of the Montaña Barracks, which corroborates Barea's own in *FR*.

18 On Wednesday night, the government: In *FR*, Barea uses fictional names for his brothers (who were still in Spain when the book was written and published and might have been endangered by being identified); so, for example, Miguel is referred to in the book as Rafael.

18 "We led them out like sheep": Barea, *FR*, p. 542.

19 But when you're someone's houseguest: Caroline Moorehead, *Gellhorn: A Life*, p. 94.

19 an unusually favorable contract: Carl Rollyson, *Beautiful Exile*, p. 55.

19 "a constant supply": MG, letter to Gip Wells, April 26, 1983, quoted in Moorehead, *Gellhorn*, p. 96.

19 He called her "Stooge": Moorehead, *Gellhorn*, p. 92. One of the letters in MG's papers at Boston University shows a naked Wells preparing to be spanked by a disapproving Gellhorn.

20 privately admitted she was flattered: H. G. Wells correspondence notes, Martha Gellhorn collection, Howard Gotlieb Archival Research Center, Boston University (henceforth BU).

20 There she'd embarked on a four-year affair: Although some American news stories about Gellhorn at this period referred to her as being married to de Jouvenel, and although one biographer, Carl Rollyson, states that a ceremony was performed in Spain in the summer of 1933 "at the home of Colette's old friend" the muralist José Maria Sert (Rollyson, *Beautiful Exile*, p. 42), this marriage was almost certainly a fiction maintained for the sake of propriety in puritanical America. De Jouvenel never divorced his "first" wife, and Gellhorn does not seem to have ever divorced de Jouvenel, so if a wedding indeed took place, that marriage, as well as Martha's subsequent ones, was bigamous. Sert, it should be noted, was fiercely conservative, and would later be a supporter of the Franco rebellion: not Martha's kind of person at all, it would seem.

20 "there are two kinds of women": Moorehead, *Gellhorn*, p. 52.

20 "Franklin, talk to that girl": Martha Gellhorn, "The Thirties," *The View from the Ground*, p. 70.

21 "It has meant more to me": MG to BdeJ, December 2, 1934, quoted in Moorehead, *Selected Letters of Martha Gellhorn* (henceforth *Selected*), p. 31.

21 "write great heavy swooping things": MG to Hortense Flexner, April 10, 1935, in Moorehead, *Selected*, p. 33.

21 "not then or ever": Gellhorn, "The Thirties," *The View from the Ground*, p. 68.

22 Wells loved the piece: Moorehead, *Gellhorn*, pp. 94–95. Gellhorn told two versions of the story's genesis: in the first, contained in a November 11, 1936, letter to Eleanor Roosevelt, she says she never saw any lynchings at all during her time in the South, but "just made [this story] up" and sent it to her agent for submission; in the second, recounted in the 1990s to the English publisher John Hatt, the story is "based closely on fact" and Wells is alleged to have submitted it for publication without consulting Gellhorn. By that time, of course, Gellhorn had a reputation to protect, and Wells was dead and couldn't refute her; the more contemporary version seems closer to the truth.

22 "making a terrible sound": MG, "Justice at Night," in *The View from the Ground*, p. 8.

22 in North Carolina: MG to Eleanor Roosevelt, November 11, 1936, in Moorehead, *Selected*, p. 42.

23 "the mortal enemy of our nation": Adolf Hitler, *Mein Kampf*, Ralph Manheim, trans. (Houghton Mifflin, 1971), p. 367.

23 "the dictatorship of the proletariat": "Le ministère des masses," *Le Temps*, June 9, 1936, p. 1.

23 she found the atmosphere: MG to Allen Grover, August 6, 1936, in Moorehead, *Selected*, p. 38.

23 There were too many "gloomy rich": Gellhorn, "Going Home," *The New Yorker*, December 12, 1936.

23 Signs everywhere announced: Gellhorn, "*Ohne Mich*: Why I Shall Not Return to Germany," *Granta* 42, Winter 1992, pp. 201–8.

24 Disgusted, Martha decided: Moorehead, *Gellhorn*, p. 99.

24 "Europe is finished": MG to Allen Grover, October 4, 1936, in Moorehead, *Selected*, p. 41.

24 "company, laughter, movement": Moorehead, *Gellhorn*, p. 99.

24 the feeling that the War to End War: Gellhorn, "Going Home."

24 the trip had done her good: MG to Allen Grover, August 4, 1936, quoted in Moorehead, *Selected*, p. 39.

24 On Sunday, July 12: There are three ways Capa could have got to Verdun: automobile (unlikely, since he didn't have a car and couldn't drive—he failed the French license test three times, according to Whelan, *Capa*, p. 160); bus (also unlikely, since these were chartered by veterans or Peace Pilgrim groups); or train. The last-named seems the only possible method.

25 on a gray, chilly July day: G. H. Archambault, "20,000 Veterans Bow at Verdun in Oath for 'Peace of the World,'" *New York Times*, July 13, 1936; and Whelan, *Capa*, pp. 88–90. The Germans were photographed by Capa (photo at ICP).

25 Capa caught them: RC vintage prints and clippings, Robert Capa archives, International Center of Photography (henceforth ICP).

26 *Der Welt Spiegel* gave his dramatic pictures: *Der Welt Spiegel*, December 11, 1932, p. 3.

27 even if he had to ask: Leon Daniel, interview with Josefa Stuart, ICP.

27 "Why work at little things": Fred Stein, interview with Josefa Stuart, ICP.

27 When he *did* make money: Henri Cartier-Bresson, interview with Richard Whelan, ICP.

27 "like a fox": Martha Gellhorn, "Till Death Us Do Part," *The Novellas of Martha Gellhorn*, p. 302.

28 "I just have to wiggle": GT (Gerta Pohorylle) to Meta Schwarz, n.d., quoted in Irme Schaber, *Gerda Taro*, pp. 59 and 61. All quotes from this source come from its French edition and appear in my translation.

29 "the last of the great race": John Dos Passos, *1919*, p. 10.

29 he'd written Gerta a letter: RC to GT, n.d., ICP.

29 When they returned: Kati Horna, interview with Josefa Stuart, ICP.

29 "Never before in my whole life": Whelan, *Capa*, p. 74.

29 "It's impossible": Eva Besnyö interview, Richard Whelan notes, ICP.

29 Together they found a modern one-room apartment: RC to Julia Friedmann, October 22, 1935, ICP.

30 "It has a part in it": RC to Julia Friedmann, undated, ICP.

30 she spent one: RC to Julia Friedmann, November 13, 1935, ICP.

30 she had a clever gynecologist: Schaber, *Taro*, p. 135.

30 he was upset: Kati Horna, interview with Josefa Stuart, Capa archives, ICP; Gellhorn, "Till Death Us Do Part," *The Novellas of Martha Gellhorn*, p. 303.

30 Others thought she was pressuring him: Maria Eisner, Cornell Capa, interviews with Richard Whelan, ICP.

30 "What, you don't know": Eva Besnyö, interview with Richard Whelan, ICP.

30 If anyone wanted: John Hersey, "The Man Who Invented Himself," 47, *The Magazine of the Year*, September 1947.

31 "It is like being born again": RC to Julia Friedmann, April 8, 1936, ICP.

31 Not surprisingly, Lucien Vogel: Henri Daniel, interview with Josefa Stuart, ICP.

32 who had been shooting pictures herself: She also had a press pass, issued in February 1936 by the ABC Press Service in Amsterdam (in the Capa archives at ICP), but the name on the card is missing, so it's unclear what name she was using for it; and there are no records of where she published photographs, if at all. It's possible they were sold and published under the Capa byline.

33 Ilse's father, a mild-mannered school headmaster: Valentin Pollak, untitled and unpublished English-language memoir in the Ilsa and Arturo Barea Papers (henceforth BP), pp. 284–86 ff.

35 There was the business of the money: Sheila Isenberg, *Muriel's War*, p. 77, and Stephen Spender, *World Within World*, p. 217.

36 speaking of a comrade: Muriel Gardiner, *Code Name "Mary,"* p. 62.

37 The green-shuttered stone house: The total purchase price of the house is somewhat unclear, as are the details of exactly where all the money to pay for it came from. Baker and Reynolds put the asking price, which included back taxes, at $8,000; Meyers says the total paid was $12,500. This may include construction costs, and since these were considerable, I've chosen to go with Meyers's figure. No one disputes that Gus Pfeiffer paid at least $8,000 of it, and possibly more.

38 "a crazy mixture": Katy Dos Passos to Gerald Murphy, June 20, 1935, in Linda Patterson Miller, *Letters from the Lost Generation*, pp. 131–32.

38 any money in the debit column: Maxwell Perkins to EH, December 9, 1936, JFK.

38 "Bull in the Afternoon": Max Eastman in *The New Republic*, quoted in Baker, *Ernest Hemingway* (hereafter *EH*), pp. 241–42.

38 "You must finish": MP to EH, July 9, 1935, quoted in Reynolds, *Hemingway: The 1930's* (hereafter Reynolds), p. 205.

39 Why didn't he write: Granville Hicks, "Small Game Hunting," *New Masses*, November 19, 1936.

39 Although he *had* written: Ernest Hemingway, "Who Murdered the Vets?: A Firsthand Report on the Florida Hurricane," *New Masses*, September 17, 1935.

39 "so much horseshit": EH to Paul Romaine, July 2, 1932, in James Mellow, *Ernest Hemingway: A Life Without Consequences*, p. 477.

39 He wasn't going to become: ER to Ivan Kashkin, August 19, 1935, in Baker, *EH*, p. 479.

39 Set in a shabby, corrupt Key West: EH, notes for *To Have and Have Not*, item 211, Ernest Hemingway Collection, John F. Kennedy Library and Museum (henceforth JFK).

39 "What I like to feel": Arnold Gingrich to EH, July 16, 1936, JFK.

40 the accounts of the storming: EH to Prudencio de Pereda, July 23, 1936, JFK.

40 But he decided: EH to John Dos Passos, September 22, 1936, JFK.

40 Julia had always had an intensely close relationship: Interview with Gladys Berkowitz, Capa's maiden aunt, Richard Whelan notes, ICP. He did, however, begin letters to her, "My dear mother."

40 Once Julia had taken in: Cornell Capa, interview with Richard Whelan, ICP.

41 Lucien Vogel had acquired an airplane: Whelan, p. 92. Michel Lefebvre, coauthor of *Robert Capa, Traces of a Legend*, disputes this on the grounds that Vogel did not consider Taro a journalist; but John Hersey, in an article for the magazine 47 entitled "The Man Who Invented Himself," says that Vogel "took the ridiculous boy and Gerda with him" on the plane ride to Spain, and that while Vogel broke his collarbone when the plane crashed, "the boy and Gerda broke nothing."

41 On the road, they passed: Descriptions of Barcelona are drawn from Capa's and Taro's prints and negatives, ICP.

42 The Rollei's square film format tightened: Irme Schaber and Richard Whelan each describe Taro working with a Rolleiflex in Schaber, Whelan, and Lubben, *Gerda Taro*; in fact, Whelan devotes an entire essay in the book to the kind of camera Taro used. Schaber now feels that Taro may have used another medium-format camera, but has so far declined to offer documentation or details.

44 Traveling in a press car: I am extrapolating here from an account by the Austro-German sociologist Franz Borkenau, who arrived in Barcelona by train on the same day that Capa and Taro did, and traveled to the Aragon front a few days before them, accompanied by the British poet John Cornford and a French foreign correspondent. There is no reason to suppose the two photographers would have been treated any differently than the three writers. Borkenau, *The Spanish Cockpit*, p. 93.

44 "It may be the front begins there": Robert Capa, *Death in the Making* (unpaged).

44 To compensate for the lack of real action: The pervasiveness of staged photographs is discussed in numerous sources, including Philip Knightley's *The First Casualty*, and is examined with respect to Capa's and Taro's practice in Richard Whelan, *This Is War: Robert Capa at Work*, pp. 60–65.

45 "I haven't come here to play at soldiers": Barea, *FR*, pp. 549–50.

46 senior British diplomats murmured: Paul Preston, *SCW*, p. 138.

46 In the shadows: Barea, *FR*, p. 553.

47 the Communist leader Antonio Mije García: Barea doesn't identify him by his last name, but his friend is almost certainly Antonio Mije, deputy general secretary of the PCE, political editor of *Mundo Obrero*, PCE liaison between the Party and the War Ministry, and (as of October 16, 1936) deputy to Álvarez del Vayo in his capacity as war commissar.

48 The place was littered with open boxes: The story of the grenades and the grenade factory comes from Barea, *FR*, p. 566–68.

49 "show-off city": RC to Julia Friedmann, April 9, 1935, ICP.

50 Gerda, at least, wanted: GT, letter to Georg Kuritzkes, n.d., in Schaber, *Taro*, p. 161.

50 for the past several months: Leopold Kulcsar's clandestine activities on behalf of the Spanish government are detailed in Jean-François Berdah, "Un réseau de renseignement antinazi au service de la République espagnole (1936–1939): Le mouvement *Neue Beginnen* et le *Servicio de Información Diplomático Especial* (SIDE)," in Fréderic Guelton and Abdil Bicer, *Naissance et evolution du renseignement dans l'espace Européen*, pp. 295–322.

51 He'd managed to hire: Katherine Knorr, "André Malraux, the Great Pretender," *New York Times*, May 31, 2001; Louis Fisher, *Men and Politics*, p. 352.

52 Perhaps, it was suggested: In Richard Mayne's BBC Radio 3 documentary, *André Malraux: The Man and the Mask*, broadcast in 1992, Ilsa Barea tells of how she traveled to Spain with Malraux.

52 It was one of the many ironies: Chim (David Seymour) photographed the palace; photos appeared in *Regards* (November 26, 1936) and *Illustrated London News* (November 28, 1936). The building was identified as Communist headquarters in contemporary captions (see, for instance, the digital archive at Magnum Photos: www .magnumphotos.com/C.aspx?VP3=CMS3&VF=MAGO31_10_VForm& ERID=24KL53Z58C).

54 "Before they get me": Barea, *FR*, pp 574–75.

55 There, shortly after sunrise: Accounts of the battle at Cerro Muriano can be found in Borkenau, *The Spanish Cockpit*, pp. 161–65, and Clemente Cimorra, "Relato sobre la march de l'acción de Cerro Muriano," *La Voz* (Madrid), September 8, 1936. Cimorra's piece is datelined September 6 and is written in the historic present but is clearly a report of the events of the preceding day.

56 The journalists were billeted: Conclusions are based on personal examination of sites in Cerro Muriano, and on the observations of José Manuel Serrano Esparza (see, for example, elrectanguloenlamano.blogspot.com/2009/05/robert-capa-in-cerro -muriano-day-in_15.htm).

56 That was more than Namuth and Reisner: Borkenau, *The Spanish Cockpit*, pp. 161–64, and Hans Namuth, telephone interview with Richard Whelan, December 9, 1982, ICP.

56 "They were like young eagles" Gellhorn, "Till Death Us Do Part," *Novellas*, p. 306. In her fictionalized telling of the Capa story, Chim is referred to as "Lep," Capa as "Bara," and Gerda as "Suzy."

56 Coming upon them at La Malagueña: Cimorra, "Relato sobre la march." My translation.

57 So one morning he and Gerda drove: For many years it was unknown where Capa took the sequence of photographs that included what was to become known as

"Falling Soldier." In his 1985 biography of Capa and in *This Is War!* Richard Whelan mistakenly identified the site as Cerro Muriano; but José Manuel Susperregui, in *Sombras de la fotografía (Shadows of Photography)*, convincingly identified the locale as Espejo by comparing the present-day topography with that in the images. As for the timing: the hand numbering on the surviving vintage prints of the Espejo sequence (there are no contact sheets or negatives) immediately precedes that written on the Cerro Muriano refugee series, so it's possible the Espejo trip preceded the Cerro Muriano battle. However, a look at the map and the calendar suggests a more logical itinerary would proceed as follows: Almadén–Cerro Muriano–Montoro–Espejo–Andújar–Toledo.

57 just a few days earlier: Borkenau, *The Spanish Cockpit*, p. 157.

57 they ran up one of the bare hills: All these images, as described, were photographed by Capa (in 35mm rectangular format) and Taro (in 2¼-inch square Rolleiflex format). Only a handful of the original negatives survive and they were cut apart into single frames or groups of two or three soon after they were developed, then randomly mixed in with negatives of other stories, or reportages. The sequence of events, therefore, is a reconstruction, made by observation of the negatives and vintage prints for which no negatives survive, including the ultimate image, now known as "Falling Soldier." All prints and negatives are in the collection of ICP.

58 a year later a friend: "Capa, Photographer of War, Tells of 'Finest Picture.'" *New York World-Telegram*, September 1, 1937.

58 Ten years later: Capa interview with Tex McCrary and Jinx Falkenburg, on *Hi, Jinx!*, NBC radio broadcast, October 20, 1947. Capa archives, ICP.

59 one of the rebel Guardia Civil: Borkenau, *The Spanish Cockpit*, p. 157.

59 "dejected and defensive": Hansel Mieth, letter to Richard Whelan, March 19, 1982, ICP.

59 *I do not wish to hurt*: Martha Gellhorn, "Till Death . . ." p. 280.

59 this would have been a heavy one: Alex Kershaw, in his *Blood and Champagne: The Life and Times of Robert Capa*, cites a biographer of the photographer Gisele Freund, who says Freund told him that Capa claimed to have "killed" the *miliciano*; in addition, Kershaw reports an NBC radio interview given by Capa on October 20, 1947, which I have not been able to trace, in which the photographer describes *milicianos* being repeatedly struck by machine-gun fire on the hillside, but seems to say he took only one photograph (Kershaw, pp. 41–42). This story raises more questions than it answers; and like other Capa "publicity" seems designed more for effect than veracity.

59 Questioned about this possibility: Captain Robert L. Franks, Memphis (Tennessee) Police Department, in Whelan, *This Is War!*, p. 72.

60 the strips of images cut up: Whelan, *This Is War!*, p. 66. Either periodicals stopped asking for negatives (rather than prints) or Capa and Taro decided to end the practice of cutting up the negative strips, for by 1937 their rolls of film were preserved intact.

60 "The prize picture": Capa interview with Tex McCrary and Jinx Falkenburg, op. cit.

61 The transmitted version: "La defense de Madrid contre les insurgés," *Le Petit Parisien*, September 25, 1936.

62 even pregnant women: Preston, *SCW*, p. 132.

62 the cobbled main street that ran downhill: Testimony of a Lieutenant Fitzpatrick, cited in Thomas, *SCW*, p. 399.

62 "I want to shoot one": EH to AG, September 16, 1936, in Carlos Baker, *Ernest Hemingway: Selected Letters 1917–1961* (henceforth *Selected*), p. 452.

63 "living on a yacht: Carlos Baker, *EH*, pp. 266 and 612.

64 "one of the most ambitious projects": "Books: Private Historian," *Time*, August 10, 1936.

64 Shevlin wasn't impressed: Thomas Shevlin to Carlos Baker, October 3, 1963, in Baker, *EH*, p. 293.

65 After the hunting party returned: EH to AMacL, September 26, 1936, and EH to MP, September 26, 1936, in Baker, *Selected*, pp. 453–54.

65 he wrote a cheery letter to Dos Passos: EH to JDP, September 22, 1936, JFK.

68 On October 22, the first crates: These figures were reported by Louis Fischer, recounting his conversation with Negrín about the treasure, in *Men and Politics,* p. 364. Orlov and the Spanish treasury undersecretary made separate counts of the boxes; Orlov's tally was 7,900 and the Spanish count was 7,800—which suggests that one truckload of gold disappeared. Orlov, however, accepted the Spanish accounting because he feared being held responsible for the lost gold.

69 "men now in hiding": Mola quoted in Preston, *SCW*, p. 181.

69 On October 30, in an attack: Barea, *FR*, pp. 581 and 585. The bombing at Getafe has been questioned by some, notably Robert Stradling in *Your Children Will Be Next: Bombing and Propaganda in the Spanish Civil War 1936–1939*, who claim it may have been a "fictional atrocity."

69 Meanwhile, far away in Odessa: Background and details of the matter of the Spanish gold reserves are discussed in (among other places) Thomas, *SCW*, pp. 427–37, Edward Gazur, *Alexander Orlov: The FBI's KGB General*, pp. 79–99, and (in less detail) in Preston, *SCW*, pp. 190–92.

70 the woman she regarded: MG, note on her correspondence with Eleanor Roosevelt, MG papers, BU.

70 she wrote ER a chipper little note: MG to ER, November 17, 1936, in Moorehead, *Selected*, pp. 41–43. The date Moorehead gives is November 11 but this must be a mistranscription since in the letter MG talks about her appearance at the Book Fair, which took place on November 17.

70 On the evening of November 17: "The Men Smoked Pipes" (Talk of the Town story), *The New Yorker*, November 14, 1936.

71 Describing the proceedings: MG to ER, *loc. cit.*

71 It was much harder to do this: Details of Gellhorn's and others' speeches, including quotations, are from "'Local Color' Book Relegated To Past," *New York Times*, November 18, 1936.

73 one of the American correspondents: Barea identifies the man only as "the big American, over six feet and two hundred and twenty pounds or so"; Fischer, a tall and burly man, was by his own account (in *Men and Politics*, pp. 382–85) the only American correspondent remaining in Madrid on this date.

74 Henry Buckley, the slight, sandy-haired, soft-spoken correspondent: Henry Buckley, *The Life and Death of the Spanish Republic*, p. 261.

75 Barea fetched Rubio's discarded photographs: The photographs had wide and persistent impact. They were used for posters in the United States as well as Europe, were published in periodicals on both continents, were included in a British Labour Party pamphlet, and one was taken for the frontispiece of the poet George Barker's

1939 "Elegy on Spain." Virginia Woolf drew on them for her essay "Three Guineas." They can still be seen on the Internet—see for example, http://libraries.ucsd.edu/speccoll/visfront/newadd13.html.

76 For the word on the street was that Koltsov: Preston, *WSSD*, pp. 177–87. In this book, for reasons that aren't clear, Preston is highly resistant to the suggestion that Koltsov might have been more than a journalist; but the sources he quotes (including Koltsov's own published diary) seem to contradict him. See also Thomas, *SCW*, pp. 380–81, Preston, *SCW*, p. 182, etc. On the Carcel Modelo, see Preston, *SCW*, pp. 182–86, Beevor, *The Battle for Spain*, pp. 173–74, Thomas, *SCW*, p. 463.

77 Ilse felt absurdly elated: The following pages, dealing with Ilsa's and Arturo's meeting and their first days in the Telefónica, are sourced from Barea, *FR*, pp. 602–12; Ilsa Barea, *Telefónica*, a thinly disguised *roman à clef* published serially in *Arbeiterzeitung* (Vienna), May 1–16, 1949; and Ilsa Barea "Alone and Together," biographical fragment, BP. In his account of this period, Sefton Delmer (*Trail Sinister*, p. 294) says he traveled alone, on the bus, from Valencia to Madrid; perhaps he did (it certainly makes a good story), but his version seems a bit like self-mythologizing, which Delmer occasionally indulged in. All translations from Telefónica are mine, with the help of Janice Kohn.

82 "It did not seem worthwhile": Barea, *FR*, p. 612.

82 for her SAP friends at the Dôme: Schaber, *Taro*, p. 173.

83 The pilots and the tarts: Cedric Salter, *Try-Out in Spain*, pp. 108–109.

84 Regler was instantly charmed by Capa: Gustav Regler, interview with Richard Whelan, ICP. Supplementary information and confirmation in Regler, *Owl of Minerva*, pp. 281–82. The trousers story exists in many versions, the quote worded differently each time. This version is an amalgam. Whelan states, in "Robert Capa in Spain," an essay in *Heart of Spain: Robert Capa's Photographs of the Spanish Civil War* (p. 34), that Capa "had encountered [Regler] at an association of German émigré writers in Paris," and sources Regler's *Owl of Minerva* (no page given) for this information. I am unable to find any such reference in Regler's book; indeed, his account of his Madrid encounter with Capa is that of a first meeting, so I have assumed that it was.

85 "a good approximation of hell": Louis Delaprée, *The Martyrdom of Madrid* (posthumous pamphlet published in 1937 in French, English, and German), p. 40. Although Delaprée's original dispatches were in French, for the English-language edition of this book I've chosen to use the contemporary English translation of his words.

85 "the abnormal . . . had become normal": Capa, *Death in the Making* [unpaged].

85 For when Franco had found the prize: Thomas, *SCW*, p. 471.

86 And as Capa walked: Details from Capa photographs at ICP.

86 "Into the future one dares not look.": Capa, *Death in the Making*.

86 "I don't like coming up": Barea, *FR*, p. 614.

87 "the most reasonable war censorship": Lester Ziffren to EH, February 18, 1937, JFK.

87 "you must feed the animals": Barea, *FR*, p. 617.

87 Up until now it had been forbidden: Claud Cockburn, *Discord of Trumpets*, pp. 299–300.

87 The maneuver had succeeded: Barea, *FR*, p. 617; Delaprée and Alving stories cited in Preston, *WSSD*, p. 371; Capa photographs, ICP.

88 He'd hoped he might write: Pierre Lazareff, *Deadline*, p. 134. Lazareff was Delaprée's editor at *Paris-Soir*.

88 "You have not published half": Delaprée, *The Martyrdom*, pp. 46–47. The last phrase was omitted from published versions but a facsimile of the handwritten text, with Madrid censors' stamps on it, was reprinted in *L'Humanité* on December 31, 1936, and I have quoted from that version here in my own translation.

88 "I hate politics": Barea, *FR*, p. 632.

88 Neither of them knew: Virginia Woolf, "Three Guineas," p. 12; John Richardson, "How Political Was Picasso?" *New York Review of Books*, November 25, 2010.

88 When a former associate: Barea, *FR*, p. 618.

89 "*We* are here for the story": Ilsa Barea, *Telefónica*.

89 "the legendary Hemingway": John Peale Bishop, "Homage to Hemingway," *The New Republic*, November 11, 1936, p. 40.

89 pointing out where he planned: Key West *Citizen*, November 21 and 30, 1936. Although the pool was, in fact, completed, the trophy room seems never to have materialized.

89 "A man alone": Hemingway, *To Have and Have Not*, p. TK. In the first published versions the word *fucking* was excised. And Morgan's last words were added only in the very last version of the typescript, in July 1937.

89 "the old miracle": EH to Arnold Gingrich, October 3, 1936, private collection, in Reynolds, p. 240.

90 here was a letter: John Wheeler to EH, November 25, 1936, EH/JFK.

90 "I've got this nice boat": Matthew Josephson, *Infidel in the Temple: A Memoir of the Thirties*, p. 428.

91 "You were a genius": Hemingway, *To Have and Have Not*, pp. 185–86. The most obvious model for Helen Gordon is Katy Dos Passos, who shoplifted just as her fictional counterpart does; but, as her biographer Ruth Hawkins points out, it was Pauline who (Hemingway knew) had had an abortion during their premarital affair, and had suffered internal damage during her second childbirth—both sources for the rest of Helen's tirade: "Love is ergoapiol pills to make me come around because you were afraid to have a baby . . . Love is my insides all messed up . . ."

91 warm, newsy letters: Irme Schaber quotes liberally from them in her biography, although it's not clear from the book's source notes where these letters are located, and Ms. Schaber has been reluctant to share this information.

92 Georg's sister Jenny: Material on the Kuritzkes family in Italy and Gerda's stay with them from Schaber, *Taro*, p. 174.

93 The old militias: Preston, *SCW*, p. 250.

93 scores of people: Delaprée, *The Martyrdom of Madrid*, p. 14. Delaprée puts the figure in the *hundreds*, but the number seems extreme, given a total estimate of 10,000 bombing deaths for the entire war over all of Spain.

93 Barea said goodbye to his family: Barea, *FR*, p. 622; Ilsa Barea, *Telefónica*.

94 the Catholic Church had all but instructed: James L. Minifie, *Expatriate*, pp. 53–54, in Preston, *WSSD*, p. 19.

94 *The New York Times*'s front page: William P. Carney, "Madrid Situation Revealed," *New York Times*, p. 1, December 7, 1936.

95 "Simplicity is what works": Regler, *Das Ohr des Malchus*, pp. 264–67, quoted in (and presumably translated by) Hans Schoots, in *Living Dangerously: A Biography of Joris Ivens*, p. 99. The wording is slightly different in the American edition of Regler's memoirs, *The Owl of Minerva* (p. 202), but the sense is the same.

96 "like a high-school boy": John Dos Passos, *Century's Ebb: The Thirteenth Chronicle*, p. 41.

96 they'd begun talking: Schoots, *Living Dangerously*, p. 114.

96 MacLeish was captivated: MacLeish, "The Cinema of Joris Ivens," *New Masses*, August 24, 1937, p. 18.

96 So MacLeish came up with a new plan: No print exists of the finished *Spain in Flames*, so it's impossible to be certain of its final format. My account here draws on Ivens's memoirs, interviews with Helene Van Dongen in *Film Quarterly* (Winter 1976), reviews of the film in *The New York Times* (e.g.), and Carlos Baker's correspondence with the distributor, Tom Brandon, as well as Schoots, *Living Dangerously*, Alex Vernon, *Hemingway's Second War*, Virginia Spencer Carr, *Dos Passos: A Life*, and Scott Donaldson, *MacLeish*.

97 Barea's trip to Valencia: Details on the following pages, including dialogue, are from Barea, *FR*, p. 627–37, and Ilsa Barea, *Teléfonica*.

99 It was Martha's mother: Edna Gellhorn and Sloppy Joe's, Bernice Kert, *The Hemingway Women*, p. 290; Sloppy Joe's description from Baker, *EH*, p. 192.

100 "glorious idol": MG to ER, no date, in Moorehead, *Gellhorn*, p. 105.

101 "a fixture, like a kudu head": MG to PPH, January 14, 1937, in Moorehead, *Selected Letters*, pp. 46–47. In a 1980 interview with Bernice Kert for *The Hemingway Women* Gellhorn maintained she visited the house only once (p. 291).

101 mostly they just talked: EH and MG's conversations from MG to Eleanor Roosevelt, January 8 and 13, 1937, in Moorehead, *Selected*, pp. 44–46.

101 "Pauline cutie": MG to PPH, January 14, 1937, in Moorehead, *Selected*, pp. 46–47.

101 "I suppose Ernest is busy": Josephson, *Infidel*, p. 428.

101 Once, Hemingway was driving: Kert, *The Hemingway Women*, p. 290.

101 "the oldest trick there is": Hemingway, *A Moveable Feast*, p. 209.

102 "I'm a fool with women": Josephson, *Infidel*, p. 428.

102 He had let her read: MG to ER, January 8 and 13, 1936, in Moorehead, *Selected*, pp. 44–46.

102 they stayed in close touch: MG to Betty Barnes, January 39, 1937, in Moorehead, *Selected*, pp. 48–49.

103 "This is very private": MG to EH, February 15, 1937, in Kert, *The Hemingway Women*, p. 294.

103 "Me, I am going to Spain": MG to Betty Barnes, January 30, 1937, in Moorehead, *Selected*, p. 48.

PART II: "YOU NEVER HEAR THE ONE THAT HITS YOU"

108 The paunchy, red-faced general: Preston, *SCW*, p. 178, is only one of several sources for this description.

108 The Loyalist prime minister: Memo from Vladimir Gorev ("SANCHO") to Marshal Kliment Voroshilov, People's Commissar (minister) for Defense, September 25, 1936, in Ronald Radosh, Mary Habeck, and Gregory Sevostianov, eds., *Spain Betrayed*, pp. 58–63.

108 If Moscow wanted to defeat: Ibid., October 16, 1936, pp. 66–70.

109 "I could not live": Barea, *FR*, p. 642.

109 although Robles had been working: Much ink has been spilled about Robles, his motives, connections, work for the Soviet advisors, etc. I've tried to pick my way between varied (not to say opposing) versions of his story told by Paul Preston (see *WSSD*, pp. 62–92), Stephen Koch in *The Breaking Point*, and Ignacio Martínez de Pison in *To Bury the Dead*. As for Robles's movements, Louis Fischer (*Men and Politics*, p. 395) places him in Madrid on November 15; by sometime in December he was in Valencia, and in custody.

110 a sure grasp of the stakes: Herbert L. Matthews, "Spain is Battleground of 'Little World War,'" *New York Times*, published January 11, 1937. It should be noted that this story was written and bylined November 29, 1936; the *Times*'s pro-Franco night editors, Raymond McCaw and Neil MacNeil, frequently cut, spiked, or delayed Matthews's stories because they perceived them as partisan.

110 even Cockburn admitted: Claud Cockburn, *A Discord of Trumpets*, pp. 307–9.

110 After all, the rebels were issuing: The Nationalist propagandist Antonio Bahamonde "described the process whereby 'atrocity' photographs were faked" (Preston, *SCW*, p. 205); and the collector Dr. Rod Oakland points out (www.psywar.org/spanishcivil war.php) inconsistencies in such a photograph that illustrate how the process was managed.

111 the great man had told him: Barea, *FR*, p. 353.

111 a telephone call came for Ilsa: Barea, *FR*, p. 649, and Berdah, "Un réseau de renseignement antinazi au service de la République espagnole," in Fréderic Guelton and Abdil Bicer, *op. cit.*

111 She left the next day: Barea, *FR*, p. 649.

112 He'd gone to Madrid: Whelan, *Capa*, p. 109.

112 "a nest of newspaper correspondents": John Dos Passos, *Journeys Between the Wars*, in Dos Passos, *Travel Books and Other Writings, 1916–1941*, p. 460.

112 with the exiled German composer: Although there is no photographic evidence to document this trip, Irme Schaber, using Kantorowicz as a source, places Gerda, Eisler, and Kantorowicz in Valencia at this time. See Schaber, *Taro*, pp. 178–79.

112 She told Ruth Cerf: Ruth Cerf Berg, interview, quoted in Kershaw, *Blood and Champagne*, p. 52.

112 "He shared the perils": "Sur la ligne du feu," *Regards*, December 17, 1936. My translation.

113 Perkins had confessed: MP to EH, October 1 and December 9, 1936, JFK.

113 Perkins should read: Kert, *The Hemingway Women*, p. 294.

113 He visited his sister-in-law: Ruth A. Hawkins, *Unbelievable Happiness and Final Sorrow*, p. 196.

114 "If you didn't get killed": EH to PP, December 9, 1936, JFK.

114 was even more negative: PP to EH, February 9, 1937, JFK.

114 they asked Hemingway the question: The documentary evidence surrounding Hemingway's initial involvement is thin, which suggests negotiations were handled in person. A letter dated January 28, 1937, from MacLeish to "Jerry" (possibly Jerome Chodorov, one of the people named by the director Jerome Robbins to HUAC in 1953—in a marginal note MacLeish identifies him only as "a communist in NY charged with . . . agit-prop"), says that "Hemingway has joined the group" working on the full-length film "and will write the dialogue if things go as anticipated." [AMacL to "Jerry," Archibald MacLeish papers, Library of Congress.]

115 "a great fair": SWM, in Calvin Tomkins, *Living Well Is the Best Revenge*, p. 38.

115 He and Sidney Franklin left: GCM to PPH, January 22, 1937, JFK.

115 "very good reliable": GCM to EH, January 8, 1936, JFK.

116 he stopped at his bank: Michael Reynolds, *Hemingway's Reading, 1910–1940: An Inventory*, p. 28.

116 In the first months of the new year: *Le Temps*, "La Guerre Civil en Espagne," February 2, 1937.

116 Gerda and Capa clambered all over: GT and RC photos, ICP.

117 "seventy miles of people": T. C. Worsley, in Preston, *SCW*, p. 194–95.

118 he could give her his speedy compact Leica: Although the photos taken by Taro during her time on the Málaga front were made with her Rolleiflex, she appears in a photograph taken shortly after her and Capa's return to Madrid holding the Leica II, and the photos she took from this point on were made with that camera, according to research by Richard Whelan, Irme Schaber, and Kirsten Lubben (see Whelan's essay "Identifying Taro's Work: A Detective Story" in Schaber, Whelan, and Lubben, *Gerda Taro*, pp. 41–51).

118 Up to that point their photographs: Richard Whelan, "Identifying Taro's Work: A Detective Story," *Gerda Taro*, p. 46; Kirsten Lubben, "Reportage Capa & Taro," *The Mexican Suitcase*, p. 117. The stamp/credit issue is, however, something of a chicken-and-egg question: the surviving Almería prints at ICP don't carry the "Capa & Taro" stamp, but the photos were published with that credit line.

119 his cameraman and compatriot John Ferno: Ferno, born Johannes Hendrik Fernhout, used the more easily pronounced "John Ferno" for his film credits and I have followed his usage.

119 a title MacLeish: EH to Waldo Peirce, July 27, 1937, in Baker, *Selected*, p. 458.

119 "a great struggle": Ivens, *The Camera and I*, pp. 104–6. Ivens doesn't identify MacLeish by name but MacLeish described his part in the scenario to Lillian Hellman (AMacL to LH, December 24, 1936, Lillian Hellman papers, Harry Ransom Research Center). MacLeish's responsibility for the film's title is mentioned in EH to Waldo Peirce, July 27, 1937, in Baker, *Selected*, pp. 458–59.

120 conferred about it as they sailed: A letter from Hellman's secretary to H. M. Behram, December 28, 1936 (HRC), confirms she sailed with Ivens on Saturday, December 26, arriving December 31.

120 "the direction is in the hands": Ivens, "Brief aan de Groene," *De Groene Amsterdammer*, December 25, 1937, in Schoots, *Living Dangerously*, p. 119.

120 Ivens sought out Carlos and Mikhail Koltsov: Schoots, *Living Dangerously*, p. 119. Ivens's *The Camera and I* (pp. 123–24) implies these conversations took place later, in the spring, after Hemingway's arrival, but other aspects of this chronology are so confused (and confusing) as to cast Ivens's memory or his notes in doubt. See, e.g., Vernon, *Hemingway's Second War*, pp. 102–3.

120 the closest they could come: Descriptions are from *Spanish Earth* footage, various reels.

121 But *The New York Times*'s correspondent: Herbert L. Matthews, *The Education of a Correspondent*, p. 94. Other details of the battle come from Beevor, pp. 208–15; Thomas, pp. 571–78; and Buckley, pp. 280–88.

121 They found the Garibaldi Battalion on the road: Footage from *The Spanish Earth*, Reel 5; Ivens, in "Het Volk," March 6, 1937.

122 a steady rain of ordnance: Per Eriksson, from *Swedes in the Spanish Civil War,* P. A. Norstedt & Söners Forlag, 1972, on www.spartacus.schoolnet.co.uk/SPthaelmann .htm.

122 "You should hear the silence": Ivens, *The Camera and I,* pp. 114–15.

123 As the filmmakers were driving back to Madrid: Regler, *Owl,* pp. 294–96. Regler's chronology is somewhat whimsical; he claims Hemingway was present at the time of this incident, but Hemingway didn't arrive in Madrid until a month afterward. The name "Maximovich" appears to be Regler's coinage, possibly a pseudonym for Gorev.

124 the Abraham Lincoln Battalion: The Abraham Lincoln Battalion is sometimes, erroneously, referred to as the Lincoln *Brigade;* in fact, the archives of the battalion, at New York University's Tamiment Library, are called the Abraham Lincoln *Brigade* Archives. Notwithstanding, in the Spanish Civil War, a brigade was a military unit comprising four to six battalions. Thus, for example, the Lincoln *Battalion* was part of the Fifteenth International *Brigade.*

124 In Madrid, Ilsa Kulcsar learned: Barea, *FR,* p. 652, and Thomas, *SCW,* pp. 571–79. Also Beevor (p. 153) and Preston, *SCW,* pp. 195–96.

124 at least one of the resident journalists: Delmer, *Trail Sinister,* pp. 315–16.

124 Lionel Barrymore: *ABC,* February 12, 1937, p. 15.

125 Gerda and Capa headed to the Telefónica: Schaber, *Taro,* p. 181. She believes that Taro was staying with Capa at the Alianza (see below) but other sources (Whelan, Allan, etc.) say they were at the Hotel Florida. Absent documentary proof to the contrary I'm siding with the Floridians.

125 The restaurant was in the Gran Via's basement: Dos Passos, *Journeys Between Wars,* p. 470; Ted Allan, *This Time a Better Earth,* p. 103; Virginia Cowles, *Looking for Trouble,* pp. 16–18.

125 his first sight of the two photographers: Ted and Norman Allan, *Ted* (an unpublished annotated autobiography), chapter 2; this document has been published online by Allan's son, Norman Allan, at www.normanallan.com/Misc/Ted/Ted %20home.htm

126 Allan held on: Allan, *This Time a Better Earth,* pp. 31–32.

126 "couldn't say shit or sheets": Ted Allan, interview with Richard Whelan, ICP.

126 Allan turned to Bethune: Allan, *Ted.*

127 Years later, Capa would explain: Robert Capa, *Slightly Out of Focus,* p. 80.

127 he and Gerda saw the bear: Robert Capa and Gerda Taro, photographs from negative rolls 52 and 53 in the Mexican Suitcase collection, ICP.

128 There was no sign outside the "21" Club: The placing of this meeting at "21" comes from Dos Passos's *roman à clef, Century's Ebb,* pp. 40–44. The details about the appearance of "21" at the time are from Jeffre Pogash, "The Most Reputable Speakeasy in New York," *Bartender,* Spring 2008, and from "21's" website, www.21club.com /web/onyc/21_club.jsp. The phalanx of jockeys now in position wasn't introduced until later; the first jockey was donated in "the late 1930s."

128 And Hemingway and Dos Passos would each be going: Spencer Carr, *Dos Passos,* pp. 362–64. Interestingly, the essays about the Spanish and European situations that Dos Passos later collected in *Journeys Between the Wars* were published in *Esquire* and *Redbook,* not *Fortune.*

129 "one of the simplest things of all": Hemingway, *Death in the Afternoon,* p. 2.

129 Some of the participants: The account of the dinner comes from Dos Passos, *Century's Ebb*, pp. 40–44.

129 he was happy to oblige: Ira Wolfert, "Hemingway to Dig into Spanish War," *Hartford Courant*, March 1, 1937, p. 10.

130 "I'm very grateful to you both": EH to the Pfeiffer family, February 9, 1937, PUL, in Baker, *Selected*, p. 458.

130 Just before he and Katy were due to depart: Dos Passos, *Century's Ebb*, pp. 44–46; also in Dos Passos, *The Theme Is Freedom*, p. 116.

131 "a phase of prudent consolidation": *Le Populaire*, February 14, 1937, in Bernier, *Fireworks*, p. 252.

131 the high priest of French Marxism recounted: André Gide, *Return from the USSR* [*Retour de l'U.R.S.S.*], p. xv.

131 On the rue Froidevaux: Michel Lefebvre and Bernard Lebrun, "Where Does the Mexican Suitcase Come From?" *MS*, vol. 2, pp. 75–82.

132 the Associated Press reporter Lester Ziffren: LZ to EH, February 18, 1937, JFK.

133 Meanwhile, he himself telephoned: EH, dispatch 1 ("Passport for Franklin"), *Hemingway Review*, p. 13. Hemingway's dispatches from Spain were published (sometimes in slightly differing form) in a variety of newspapers subscribing to the North American Newspaper Alliance. For the sake of consistency and authority I rely on the texts as edited by James Braasch Watson and published in *The Hemingway Review*, vol. 7, no. 2, Spring 1988, henceforth referred to as *HR7*.

133 When time hung heavy on their hands: Solita Solano to Carlos Baker, January 17, 1962, in Baker, *EH*, p. 301.

133 Hemingway probably didn't understand: Schoots, pp. 120–21.

133 He even found himself trying: Joris Ivens to Jeffrey Meyers, quoted in Jeffrey Meyers, *Hemingway: A Biography*, p. 311.

134 the two men went out: Paul Quintanilla, *Waiting at the Shore: Art, Revolution, War, and Exile in the Life of the Spanish Artist Luis Quintanilla*, p. 199.

134 Twenty miles from the French border: Baker, *EH*, pp. 301–2; P. Quintanilla, *Waiting at the Shore*, p. 103; and EH, dispatch 2 (*HR*).

135 A week later, two other journalists: Whelan, *Capa*, pp. 112–13; Capa photographs, ICP.

135 The Casa de Alianza de Escritores Antifascistas: Details on the Alianza and its activities and inhabitants come from Schaber, *Taro*, p. 182; Arnold Rampersad, *Langston Hughes, vol. 1: I, Too, Sing America*, pp. 347–48; Stephen Spender, *World Within World*, pp. 245–46; Gerda Taro photographs, notebook #1, Archives Nationales de France.

136 Alberti and Maria Teresa offered to help: Alberti, "Capa and Gerda Taro," *La Arboleda Perdida*, vol. III, chapter 14, in Schaber, *Taro*, p. 244.

136 she and he had chronicled: Taro and Capa, notebook #7, Archives Nationales de France; Mexican Suitcase rolls 55 (Capa) and 56 (Taro), ICP. Neruda, whose government recalled him from Spain because of his Loyalist sympathies, wrote a poem about the destruction of his house, "Explico Algunas Cosas" ("I'm Explaining a Few Things").

137 She wasn't sure she saw a future: Kershaw, *Blood and Champagne*, p. 52.

137 Certainly she said that: Allan, *Ted*, part 2.

137 The German photographer Walter Reuter: Schaber, *Taro*, p. 185.

138 When they crossed the Jarama north of Arganda: Taro photographs, ICP; Schaber, *Taro*, pp. 194–96; Allan, *This Time*, pp. 163–201, and *Ted*, chapters 1 and 2.

139 The poor visibility produced: Thomas, *SCW*, p. 582.

139 On the fifth floor of the Telefónica: Allan, *This Time*, p. 106.

139 At dinner at the Gran Via: Spender, *World*, p. 248.

139 He'd seen what the Italians had done: Allan, *This Time*, p. 112.

139 Sitting at the telephone: Barea, *FR*, pp. 653–54. When the dispatch was published Matthews was enraged to discover that "Italian" had been changed to "Insurgent" throughout. On March 22 he cabled the *Times*: "IF YOU DON'T TRUST YOUR CORRE-SPONDENTS EITHER RELIEVE OR DISCHARGE THEM BUT EYE WONT STAY MADRID UNLESS EYE HAVE YOUR FULL CONFIDENCE" (HLM to Edwin James, March 22, 1937, Matthews papers, HRC, quoted in Vernon, p. xvi).

140 very nearly including Ted Allan and Geza Karpathi: Allan, *Ted*, chapter 1; photos from Charles Korvin photographic archive, Brandeis University.

140 abandoned Fiat tractors and Lancia trucks: Koltsov, *Ispansky dnevik* [*Spanish Diary*], p. 450, in Beevor, *The Battle for Spain*, p. 219.

140 a mailbag his men had seized: Barea, *FR*, p. 654.

140 Then, a few freezing, sodden days later: Accounts of the battle of Guadalajara mainly from Beevor and Thomas.

140 in the streets of Madrid: Allan, *This Time*, p. 129.

141 Finally, she was able to commandeer a car: Allan, *This Time*, pp. 125–26 and 137–38; Schaber, *Taro*, p. 191.

141 But she had taken "wonderful pictures": Although Whelan and Schaber both claim that Taro's photos of Guadalajara were published in *Regards* and *Volks Illustrierte* under the mistaken byline "PHOTOS WARO," it's also possible, if not probable (as Cynthia Young points out), that the credit was that of a Brussels photo agency of that name. There are no prints or negatives of any Guadalajara photographs in Taro's archives, nor any contact prints in her notebooks; possibly, whatever photos she may have taken at Guadalajara were lost or inadvertently destroyed. The only documentary evidence for Taro's presence at the battle is in Allan, *This Time*, pp. 126–39, and Schaber, *Taro*, p. 191 (which references Matthews).

141 Valencia was in full battle dress: GT photographs of Valencia, Mexican Suitcase roll 77, ICP.

142 "To win the war": Berzin to Voroshilov, copy to Stalin, February 16, 1937, Russian State Military Archive, in Radosh et al., *Spain Betrayed*, p. 127; unnamed French correspondent (presumed to be Marty), early March 1937, included in March 23, 1937, report to Voroshilov, Russian State Military Archive, in Radosh et al., *Spain Betrayed*, pp. 164–65.

142 Gerda *evolved*: Koltsov's words summarized in Schaber, *Taro*, p. 200.

143 "WE UNWANT DAILY RUNNING NARRATIVE": H. J. J. Sargint, cable to EH, March 18, 1937, JFK.

143 he told Spender he couldn't wait: Spender, *World*, p. 252.

143 Constancia, nicknamed Connie: Background: Fox, *Constancia de la Mora*, pp. 6–17 and 38–39; De la Mora, *In Place of Splendor*, pp. 1–7, 290 ff.

143 on the morning of March 20: EH, dispatch 12, *HR7*, pp. 43–44.

144 "the true gen": EH to Charles A. Fenton, July 29, 1952, in Baker, *Selected*, p. 775.

145 "the biggest Italian defeat": This and earlier descriptions of the battlefield from EH, dispatches 4 and 5, in *HR7*, pp. 20 and 22.

145 Ivens knew how important it was: Joris Ivens, interview with William Braasch Watson, in Watson, "Joris Ivens and the Communists," *Hemingway Review*, vol. 10, no. 1, September 1990.

145 Hemingway had brought two bottles of whiskey: The gathering in Koltsov's rooms and its sequelae are discussed variously in Ehrenburg, *Memoirs*, pp. 383–84; Beevor, *The Battle for Spain*, p. 205; Vernon, *Hemingway's Second War*, p. 169; Gazur, *Orlov*, p. 130, Stanley G. Payne, *The Franco Regime*, p. 137, Paulina and Adelina Abramson, *Mosaico Roto*, pp. 179–81, and LaPrade, *Hemingway and Franco*, p. 61.

146 Martha Gellhorn got out of her second-class railroad compartment: Gellhorn always insisted, and legend has accepted, that she took only a duffel and backpack to Spain. But Franklin, in his own memoir, *Bullfighter from Brooklyn*, claimed (pp. 220–21) she'd given him ten pieces of her luggage. This may be an exaggeration; but it's difficult to see how the wardrobe Martha was photographed wearing in Spain could have fit in a backpack and duffel (especially if the latter was full of canned goods, as she said it was). In addition, Ted Allan mentions many pieces of luggage. See the note at the end of this section. Gellhorn also said that she walked into Spain—an assertion her biographers and others have taken literally, assuming that she hiked over the Pyrenees. Her journal, entitled "Spanish War Notes" and lodged in her papers at Boston University, tells a different story.

147 the press department had made arrangements: Details in this section come from two versions of Martha Gellhorn's Spanish journals at BU: one is holograph, and represents her unconsidered impressions, the other, typed, with dates (March 22–27, 1937), edits some telling details out. Other sources are Cecil Eby, *Comrades and Commissars*, p. 119, Ted Allan, *Ted*, chapter 1; Gellhorn, *Face*, pp. 14–15 (the account that misleadingly suggests that she hiked from France to Spain instead of just walking across a set of railroad tracks); and Kert, *The Hemingway Women*, pp. 295–97. Interestingly, Gellhorn's contemporaneous account of her trip differs substantially from those she provided later, as well as from that in her authorized biography by Caroline Moorehead. Kert, e.g., says the locked door incident occurred on Gellhorn's second night in Madrid, but Gellhorn's journal rules this out; it must have been the first night, a conclusion with which Moorehead concurs. But Moorehead makes no mention of Ted Allan (who is mentioned in Gellhorn's diary).

147 The day before, Good Friday: Matthews, "Good Friday Quiet on Madrid Fronts," *New York Times*, March 27, 1937. This story may have spawned one of the minor canards of the war: Jay Allen, in a letter to EH dated August 25, 1937, says that at Teruel Matthews "found [POUM militiamen] playing football with the rebels," a charge Hemingway then repeated, as Allen had urged him to, in a dispatch written the next month. In fact, by the time Matthews first went to Teruel in September 1937, the POUM militia had been replaced by the Popular Army.

149 The next morning: MG, "Spanish War Notes," March 29, 1937, BU, and "High Explosive for Everyone," *The Face of War*, p. 19.

149 Ivens and Ferno went out to film: *The Spanish Earth*, Reel 4.

150 There, at the hospital: EH, NANA dispatch 8, undated but scheduled for publication on April 24 and 25, 1937, *HR7*.

151 "had no qualifications": Cowles, *Looking for Trouble*, p. 4.

151 blew in to the Telefónica: Barea, *FR*, p. 655.

151 from watering hole to watering hole: Eby, *Comrades and Commissars*, p. 119, Smith and Hall, *Five Down, No Glory*, p. 193.

151 "We were a jokey bunch": MG, interview with Michael Eaude, in Eaude, *Triumph at Midnight*, p. 18.

152 He pointed out where his mother: Barea, *FR*, pp. 655–56.

152 To begin with there was the noise: MG, "Spanish War Notes," April 3, 8, and 18, 1937, BU.

153 the charismatic colonel Juan Modesto: In her later years, Gellhorn told a story, detailed in her essay "Memory" (*London Review of Books*, vol. 18, no. 24, December 12, 1997), about Hemingway's interrupting a conversation between her and Modesto by challenging the officer to a game of Russian roulette.

153 "to understand the anti-fascist cause": Ivens, interview with William Braasch Watson, in "Ivens and the Communists," *Hemingway Review*, vol. 10, no. 1, Fall 1990.

153 "was able to sit with a bunch of men": Gellhorn, *Travels with Myself and Another*, p. 14.

153 "that it would soon be over": MG to Peter Gourevich, in Moorehead, *MG*, p. 134.

153 "skyzophrenia": EH to Sara Murphy, December 8, 1935, in Miller, p. 149.

153 "I think it was the only time": Kert, p. 299.

153 Stopping by the Telefónica: MG, "Spanish War Notes," March 28–31, 1937, BU.

154 "small, dark, square-faced": MG, "Spanish War Notes," BU.

154 a tall Swedish Valkyrie: Preston, *WSSD*, pp. 115–18; Cowles, p. 32.

154 "conceit of a beautiful woman": MG, "Spanish War Notes," April 9, 1937, BU.

154 "dirty as only places that deal with hair can be": MG, "Spanish War Notes," April 3, 1937, BU.

155 In the south, in Seville: Preston, *SCW*, p. 193.

155 in Madrid, station EAQ: Norman Bethune, J. B. S. Haldane, and Hazen Sise, *Listen In: This Is Station EAQ, Madrid, Spain*, pamphlet published by the Committee to Aid Spanish Democracy, 1937; other radio background, O. W. Riegel, "Press, Radio, and the Spanish Civil War," *Public Opinion Quarterly*, January 1937, pp. 131–36, and T. E. Goote, "Radio's Role in the Spanish Civil War," *Radio News*, January 1937.

155 suggested that Martha try her hand: MG, "Spanish War Notes," April 7 and 10, 1937, and undated fragment, "Living here is like nothing . . ." BU. It's generally assumed that Hemingway suggested MG broadcast; but it was Ilsa who was in charge of setting up such connections, and she is as likely to have made the suggestion as Hemingway.

155 Hemingway's only combat experience: Over the years the circumstances of Hemingway's wounding took on ever more colorful trappings: in some accounts he was said to have carried a wounded officer on his back for anywhere from 50 to 150 yards. This is not mentioned in his citation for bravery; and he himself used to say that the experience of Frederic Henry in *A Farewell to Arms*—"I didn't carry anybody; I couldn't move"—comes closest to his own. See, for example, Mellow, *Ernest Hemingway*, pp. 60–61.

156 he'd given expensive small leather goods: MG, "Spanish War Notes," April 8, 1937.

157 "like college kids": MG, "Spanish War Notes," April 9, BU.

157 So in chronicling: EH's descriptions of Morata and Casa de Campo from dispatch 6, *HR7*, as well as two stories, "Night Before Battle," *Fifth Column and Four Stories*

of the Spanish Civil War, pp. 110–12, and "Heat and Cold," *Spanish Front: Writers on the Spanish Civil War*. Footage of Casa de Campo and Morata—including one shot of EH at the ambulance point—is in Reel 6 of *The Spanish Earth*.

158 He wrote the dispatch out: MG's Spanish diary establishes beyond doubt that the Raven dispatch (#8) was written by April 5, when (MG notes) she proofread it and left it to be mailed, along with the note to Sidney Franklin that Baker (*EH*, p. 311) misdates as having been written on April 21. In the absence of contradictory documentation, Watson's edition of the dispatches perpetuates Baker's misdating.

158 The following morning: MG, "Spanish War Notes," April 10, 1937, BU.

159 When they returned: MG, "Spanish War Notes," April 10, 1937, BU, and Dos Passos, *Century's Ebb*, pp. 81–82. MG's journal disproves that Dos Passos was accompanied to Madrid by André Malraux, as has sometimes been claimed.

159 All Dos knew: Dos Passos, "The Death of José Robles," *The New Republic*, July 19, 1939; Martinez de Pison, *To Bury the Dead*, pp. 19–20 and 39–42.

160 "Don't put your mouth": Dos Passos, *Century's Ebb*, pp. 82–84.

161 a power play by the NKVD: Martinez de Pison, *Bury*, p. 83.

161 In the weeks since he had been in Madrid: Kert, *Women*, p. 300.

161 Whatever drove him: MG, letter to Hortense Flexner paraphrased in Moorehead, *Gellhorn*, p. 156; quotes from "Spanish War Notes," April 10, 1937, BU.

162 she'd never found *anyone*: MG, "Spanish War Notes," April 7, 1937, in Moorehead, *Gellhorn*, pp. 120–121.

162 the process of composing it: MG, "Spanish War Notes," April 15, quoted in Moorehead, *Gellhorn*, p. 123, and April 22, BU.

163 "We are launching a major attack": Simon Sebag Montefiore, *Stalin: Court of the Red Tsar*, p. 118.

163 he was summoned to the Kremlin: This anecdote, related by Koltsov's brother Boris Efimov in *Mikhail' Kol'tsov, kakim on byl. Vospominaniya* (Moscow, Sovetskii Pisatel', 1965), p. 66, is detailed in Preston, *WSSD*, p. 192.

165 "Arturo! Come away from here!": Barea, *FR*, pp. 659.

166 Quintanilla lived in an opulently furnished flat: MG, "Spanish War Notes," April 17, 1937, BU. Limoges may be best known for porcelain, but MG's journal specifies that the cup Quintanilla gave her was glass. Description of Quintanilla from Cowles, p. 30. JQ and EH's conversation about Robles, Baker, *EH*, pp. 305–6, and EH, "Treachery in Aragon," *Ken*, June 1938.

167 It was balmy, almost hot: Cowles, *Looking for Trouble*, pp. 26–27, Dos Passos, "Madrid Under Seige," "Journeys Between Wars," in *Travel Books*, pp. 470–71, and MG, "Spanish War Notes," April 17, 1937, BU.

168 "What's the matter with you?": Barea, *FR*, p. 662.

169 "But that's *me* you've killed here": Ibid., p. 665.

169 Fuentidueña de Tajo: Although both Dos Passos and the titles for *The Spanish Earth* render the spelling as Fuentedueña, I have followed most contemporary maps in spelling it with an "i."

169 to Martha Gellhorn: MG, "Spanish War Notes," April 18, 1937, BU.

169 when Archibald MacLeish screened the combat footage: AMacL to EH and JI, April 7, 1937, JFK.

170 Ivens and Ferno had discovered: Joris Ivens, in John T. McManus, "Down to Earth in Spain," *New York Times*, July 25, 1937.

170 And Dos Passos, by interviewing: Ivens, *The Camera and I*, p. 110.

170 Walking down a little dirt track: Dos Passos, "Villages Are the Heart of Spain," *Esquire*, February 1938.

170 If he thought about them at all: Herbst, *Starched Blue Sky*, pp. 150–51.

171 he and Martha somehow managed: Ibid., p. 162.

171 He and Gerda and Korvin: Schaber, *Taro*, p. 203. Schaber says (presumably on Korvin's authority) that the restaurant was Las Cuevas de Luis Candelas—impossible, since that establishment only opened in 1949. But Botín, which was opened in the seventeenth century, is only a few doors away on the Calle de Los Cuchilleros. The story of Hemingway and the paella is recounted by the establishment's present owner, Emilio Gonzales's grandson, in "Casa Botín: Mi abuelo intent enseñar a Hemingway a cocinar una paella," *La Vanguardia*, April 27, 2012. Quotes are my translations.

172 he immediately recognized in the older man: Capa, *Focus*, pp. 128–29; Herbst, *Starched Blue*, p. 151.

172 Maybe it was her fondness: Re. Dos Passos: MG, "Spanish War Notes," April 14, 1937, BU; EH on GT: Ted Allan, *Ted*.

172 Just before dawn on April 22: The story of the Hotel Florida bombardment comes from Herbst, *Starched Blue Sky*, pp. 152–53; Dos Passos, *Century's Ebb*, pp. 85–86; Dos Passos, "Room and Bath at the Hotel Florida," *Esquire*, January 1938; and MG, "Spanish War Notes," April 22, 1937, BU.

173 photographed the clean-up effort: Four prints in Capa archives labeled "Hotel Florida, Madrid, April 1937," ICP.

174 Maybe the official had been Constancia de la Mora: Fox, *Constancia de la Mora*, pp. 72–73. The conversation between Hemingway and Herbst is recounted in Herbst, *Starched Blue Sky*, p. 154.

175 at some point during those few April days: Dos Passos, *Century's Ebb*, p. 91.

176 an inadvertent chink of light: *El Heraldo de Madrid*, November 4, 1936.

176 the probable truth about Robles: Much has been written about the Robles case and what Robles did or didn't do. Many accounts, such as Paul Preston's chapter on the affair in *WSSD* and Stephen Koch's *The Breaking Point*, take somewhat politicized positions on the matter; others, such as José Martinez de Pisón's *To Bury the Dead*, seem less agenda-driven; each has something to tell us and I have drawn on all of them.

176 "They shove a cigarette": Dos Passos, "Coast Road South," originally published in *Esquire*, December 1937; in "Journeys Between Wars," *Travel Books*, p. 459.

176 "felt a heartbroken admiration": Dos Passos, *Century's Ebb*, p. 92.

177 Robert Merriman's wife found: Marion Merriman and Warren Lerude, *American Commander in Spain*, pp. 133–34.

177 after stopping in at the Telefónica: JDP to Dwight MacDonald, July 1939, in *Fourteenth Chronicle*, p. 526.

177 "late in the summer evenings": Dos Passos, "Villages Are the Heart Of Spain," originally published in *Esquire*, February 1938; in "Journeys Between Wars," *Travel Books*, p. 478. Biographies of Dos Passos and other books about the Robles matter, taking their cue from Dos Passos's "Villages Are the Heart of Spain," say that Dos Passos left Madrid, then spent some time in Fuentidueña and other villages before going to Valencia and thence to Barcelona. This is impossible: he left Madrid after

the broadcast he participated in on the night of the 24th, was seen by Ivens in Valencia on the 25th or 26th, and interviewed Andrés Nin in Barcelona on April 28 (according to a letter from Lois Orr in *Letters from Barcelona*, edited by Gerd Rainer-Horn, p. 158). The confusion is caused by the fact that he included material about Fuentidueña, which he had visited earlier, in the piece.

177 he sent Hemingway a carefully worded letter: JI to EH, April 26, 1937, JFK.

178 she spent the morning and afternoon: MG, "Spanish War Notes," April 24, 1937, BU; "A Sense of Direction," *The Heart of Another*, pp. 138–76; MG to David Gurewitsch, undated (1950?) in Moorehead, *Selected*, p. 222. MG's diary simply says Pacciardi (she spells it Patchardi) made a pass at her.

178 a correspondent for the *Manchester Guardian*: MG, "Spanish War Notes," April 25, 1937, BU; Hemingway, "Fresh Air on an Inside Story," originally published in *Ken*, September 22, 1938, in *By-Line*, pp. 294–97.

179 Hemingway was just finishing his coffee: This story is recounted, in slightly different versions, in Herbst, *Starched Blue Sky*, pp. 167–71, and Cowles, *Looking for Trouble*, pp. 30–31.

182 his last dispatch from Madrid: EH, NANA dispatch 10, *HR7*, pp. 37–37.

182 after a riotous farewell party: Baker, *EH*, p. 312, Herbst, journal, May 1, 1937, YU.

182 "His jokes told me": Barea, *FR*, p. 676.

183 he broadcast the following warning: Preston, *SCW*, p. 167.

183 "anything that might hurt": Geoffrey Dawson, quoted in Preston, *SCW*, p. 268.

183 a report by their pro-rebel correspondent: William P. Carney, "Rebels Lay Fires to Guernica 'Reds,'" *New York Times*, April 30, 1937.

183 the order to bomb Guernica: Pertinax, "Air Attack on Guernica Attributed to Goering," *New York Times*, April 30, 1937. "Pertinax" was the pseudonym of André Géraud, foreign editor of *L'echo de Paris*, ironically a conservative, Catholic-oriented newspaper. Géraud was described by the *Manchester Guardian* as a journalist who "reports today what the Quai d'Orsay denies tomorrow and confirms the day after tomorrow." (David Wingate Pike, *France Divided: The French and the Civil War in Spain*, p. 284.) The fight over what really happened at Guernica continues to the present day, with revisionist historians maintaining that the town housed several government battalions and three arms factories (Nigel Townson, e-mail to the author).

184 they'd both gone on leave: MG, "Spanish War Notes," April 14, 1937, BU.

184 "a lonely chaos of timber and brick": Cowles *Looking for Trouble*, p. 69.

184 It was May Day: "Paris Marks May Day with Demonstration," *New York Times*, May 2, 1937; "Bulletin Météorologique," *Le Temps*, May 1, 1937; *L'Humanité*, April 30 and May 2, 1937.

185 they stopped in front of a display of *muguet*: RC's photographs of GT, ICP; Schaber, *Taro*, p. 207.

186 his assertion that the anarchists and the POUM: Liston Oak, "Behind Barcelona Barricades," *New Statesman and Nation*, May 15, 1937. Martinez de Pison believes that this article was written and submitted *after* Oak left Barcelona; but given its publication so soon after his departure it seems it must have been completed beforehand.

186 a political assassin: Preston, *WSSD*, pp. 84–85; Koch, *Breaking Point*, pp. 175–77, 191–98.

187 Dos Passos had gone to interview Nin: Dos Passos, "The Defeated," in *Travel Books*, pp. 486–87.

187 he'd begged his wife's boss: "Reminiscences by Charles Orr," in Horn, *Letters from Barcelona*, p. 180.

187 he agreed with Dos Passos: *Century's Ebb*, pp. 94–95. Dos Passos also wrote about his encounter with Orwell in the nonfiction *The Theme Is Freedom*, pp. 145–46. In both places he indicates he spoke to Blair in a hotel, but a memoir in the papers of Charles Orr, an American Socialist who was in charge of arranging Dos Passos's stay in Barcelona, persuasively argues that the only time Dos Passos saw Blair was at Nin's office. (See Orr memoir in *Letters from Barcelona*, pp. 177–80.)

188 "like a tropical rainstorm": George Orwell, *Homage to Catalonia*, pp. 130–31.

189 Juan Negrín, the multilingual socialist: Thomas, *SCW*, p. 645, n. 2, cites the memoirs of Jésus Hernández, the Communist minister of education, who says he approached Negrín on his party's behalf in May 1938. Thomas also cites Walter Krivitsky's *I Was Stalin's Agent*, where the former *rezident* maintains that as early as November 1936 the Russian official Arthur Stashevsky had "picked" Negrín as a future premier.

189 "Where is Nin?": For the events of the May Days and after, including the fate of Andrés Nin, see Thomas, *SCW*, pp. 635–47; Beevor, *Battle for Spain*, pp. 263–73; Preston; *SCW*, pp. 256–62; and elsewhere.

189 Hemingway got to Paris: Details of Hemingway's trip to Paris from Baker, *EH*, p. 312; Percy Philip to Edwin James, cable May 8, 1937, HRC, cited in Vernon, *Hemingway's Second War*, p. 31; Ivens to EH, arranging plane, April 26, 1937, JFK.

190 a not-so-subtle allegory: The analysis of "The Chauffeurs of Madrid" was made by Alex Vernon, *Hemingway's Second War*, p. 63.

190 an armchair analysis: EH, dispatch 11, *HR7*, pp. 40–42.

190 "ASK YOU UNSEND": HJJS to EH, May 10, 1937, quoted in Watson, editorial note to dispatch 11, *HR7*, p. 39.

190 "There are practically no words": MG to Gunther, May 10, 1937, in Moorehead, *Gellhorn*, p. 128.

191 "irrelevant to the great drama": MG, review of Ken Loach's *Land and Freedom*, in the London *Evening Standard*, October 5, 1995.

191 Hemingway went to the Gare St. Lazare: Dos Passos, *Century's Ebb*, pp. 98–99, Ludington, *JDP*, p. 374, and Carr, *Dos Passos*, p. 372.

192 "What did you kill him for?": Hemingway, *THAHN* (Scribner Classics), p. 39.

192 "I had to go to Spain": Baker, *EH*, pp. 312–13, and note, p. 622.

192 dropping down onto the field at Sondika: Jay Allen, introduction to *Death in the Making*, unpaged.

193 whose blueprints had been smuggled: Thomas, *SCW*, p. 595; Preston, *SCW*, p. 271.

193 British and French rescue organizations: "Evacuation Work," *Manchester Guardian*, May 4, 1937; Antonio Cazorla and Adrian Shubert, *A Inmigración Española en Canada: Unha Visión de Conxunto*, Estudio Migratorios #10, 2000, pp. 32–34. The name "Carimare" is clearly visible on the hull of one of the ships Capa photographed.

193 The next day Capa headed out of Bilbao: The narrative of Capa's experience at Mount Solluve is reconstructed from the following: "Shells and Bombs Blast Bilbao Area," *New York Times*, May 8, 1937; Capa photographs and notebooks, ICP; and film fragment from Henri Cartier-Bresson, *With the Lincoln Brigade in Spain*. The

attribution of the fragment is made by Juan Salas in "Capa and Taro: Lost Footage from the Córdoba Front," *The Mexican Suitcase*, pp. 252–76.

194 There, a French plane: The story of Capa's and Allen's meeting comes from Allen, preface to *Death in the Making*, unpaged.

197 "a fear that tortured": Dos Passos, *The Theme Is Freedom*, pp. 136–37.

197 Yes, he thought, the war had been started: Barea, *FR*, pp. 670–72.

197 Barea's old friend Angel: Ibid., p. 672; AB, "Notes on Federico García Lorca," *Horizon*, pp. 192–95.

198 having lost both their business and their home: In her essay "The Eye of Solidarity" (*Taro*, p. 24) Irme Schaber says they were dispossessed in 1937; but in *GT*, pp. 272–73 she presents documentation that they had in fact possibly emigrated as early as 1935, a date she has recently confirmed in an e-mail.

198 In hiding he ran across Eric Blair: Peter Wyden, *The Passionate War*, p. 371.

199 At dusk on May 14: "Loyalist Cabinet in Spain Resigns; Valencia Bombed," *New York Times*, May 16, 1937.

199 The younger Vinding: Cowles, *Looking for Trouble*, pp. 49–50; Barea, *FR*, p. 677.

200 She sent Capa a telegram: GT telegram to RC, May 17, 1937; ICP. The telegram's receipt stamp is dated the 18th.

200 "Now I am cold sober": PPH to EH, April 25, 1937, in Kert, *Women*, p. 302.

200 "I am sick and tired": PPH to EH, in ibid., p. 301.

200 Hemingway cut it by half: EH and JI statements quoted in Baker, *EH*, p. 313.

201 MacLeish's rather timid request: AMacL to EH, May 27, 1937, JFK.

201 "The Loyalists will win": *World Telegram*, May 20, 1937.

201 she'd already negotiated: "Book Notes," *New York Times*, June 7, 1937.

201 anodyne notes: MG to EH, undated letters, BU.

201 Out in the audience: A partial report of the congress, with speeches by Hemingway, MacLeish, and others, in *New Masses*, June 22, 1937, available on www.unz.org and in Hart, ed., *The Writer in a Changing World*, pp. 69–73. EH's speech in Robert W. Trogdon, *Ernest Hemingway, a Literary Reference*, pp. 193–96.

202 "all the foreign correspondents": DP to JDP, undated, UVA; quoted in Ludington, *Dos Passos*, pp. 376–77.

203 One of those beating his hands: P de P to Carlos Baker, June 2, 1967, PUL; also in Vernon, *Second War*, p. 91.

203 "went over to the Stork Club": DP to JDP, quoted in Ludington, *Dos Passos*, pp. 376–77.

203 "A writer must be a man of action": *New Masses* and Hart, *loc. cit.*

204 "I wish we could meet": FSF to EH, June 5, 1937, in Baker, *EH*, p. 313.

204 Hemingway had come to the conclusion: EH to MP, June 10, 1937, in Baker, *EH*, p. 314. The story "Horns of the Bull" was eventually published as "The Capital of the World."

204 "I am now Joris's finger-woman": MG to EH, undated [June 1937]; BU; quoted in Kert, *Women*, p 302.

205 "Rotfront": MG to EH, telegram, June 11, 1937; JFK.

205 "send back that sheet of paper": JI to EH, June 17, 1937, JFK.

205 eager to have it repaid: EH to Ralph Ingersoll, July 17, 1937, JFK.

205 Ivens's lack: EH to AMacL cable draft [June 16], 1937, JFK.

206 immediate and poignant resonance: The Dust Bowl connection is interestingly discussed in Alex Vernon, *Second War*, p. 123.

206 Martha (as she wrote to Eleanor Roosevelt): MG to ER, [June?] 1937, BU, in Moore-head, *Selected Letters*, p. 52.

206 the roar of bombs was achieved: Erik Barnouw, *Documentary: A History of the Non-fiction Film*, p. 136.

207 Ivens was finding it: Schoots, *Living Dangerously*, p. 129.

207 "You effeminate boys": Orson Welles interview, *Cahiers du Cinéma*, November 1966.

208 On May 30 they had started: Beevor, *Battle for Spain*, p. 276; Alexander Szurek, *The Shattered Dream*, pp. 141–42.

208 "fakery in allegiance": Barnouw, *Documentary*, pp. 121–22.

209 "better there than in my heart,": Schaber, *Taro*, p. 218.

210 the agony of retreat: Szurek, *The Shattered Dream*, pp. 171–72; Capa footage from "Rehearsal for War," *March of Time* newsreel footage; Capa and Taro photos, vin-tage prints, ICP; Mexican Suitcase rolls 88, 89, 90, 91, ICP. Szurek mistakenly says that Capa and Gerda's visit was during the Battle of Brunete; but Capa wasn't there for that, and Gerda never spent the night, or had dinner, at the Brunete front.

210 By the next day: Beevor, *Battle for Spain*, pp. 276–77.

210 Instead they took pictures and shot footage: Photographs described in this para-graph have been dated by referring to Capa, notebook #1, Archives Nationales de France.

212 "His fear and his courage": Barea, *FR*, p. 678.

212 "When I was thirteen": Ibid., p. 680.

213 "the forgotten brigade": Schaber, "The Eye of Solidarity," in Schaber, Whelan, and Lubben, *Gerda Taro*, p. 27.

213 When the two photographers arrived: Kantorowicz, in Schaber, "Eye," pp. 215–17; photos of Chapaiev Battalion, RC, and GT, ICP. Chapaiev Battalion newspaper cover reproduced in Schaber, *Taro*, fig. 79.

214 In the abandoned village: GT, photographs of Valsequillo from rolls 97–99, repro-duced in *The Mexican Suitcase*, pp. 243–51; Schaber, "Preliminary Remarks on Gerda Taro's Documentation of the Defense of the Andalusian Mining Region," *The Mexican Suitcase*, pp. 239–42; Juan Sala, "Capa and Taro: Lost Footage from the Cordoba Front," *MS*, pp. 252–55.

215 So perhaps it was in Valsequillo: Photos of GT by RC, in *MS*, p. 407. Although the Capa archive has labeled these photographs "Paris, 1935–36," where and when they were taken (Spain? Paris?) cannot be determined: other than Taro's figure, all that can be seen in them is a narrow brass bed, part of a mirrored armoire door, and a rolled-up newspaper on a nightstand. Several vintage prints of the images were among Capa's possessions, and the negatives were included with the Mexican Suit-case rolls, which Capa hoped to save from the invading Germans during World War II, all of which indicates the photographs' value to him.

215 he, Ivens, and Martha: EH to Mrs. Paul Pfeiffer, August 2, 1937, in Baker, *Selected*, p. 460. Grammatical solecisms ("Joris and I") are Hemingway's.

216 Both Roosevelts seemed to feel: MG to ER, July 8, 1937, in Moorehead, *Selected*, p. 55; Schoots, *Living Dangerously*, p. 130.

216 along with Pauline: PPH to Sara Murphy, July 8, 1937, in Miller, *Letters*, p. 194.

216 what emerged from her typewriter: MG to EH, July 2, 1937, in Kert, *Women*, p. 305; Moorehead, *Selected*, pp. 132–33.

216 it was too soon: MG to ER, July 8, 1937, in Moorehead, *Selected*, p. 56.

216 having a triumph in Hollywood: Vernon, pp. 94–97, Baker; *EH*, p. 316; Schoots, *Living Dangerously*, pp. 130–31; and EH to Ralph Ingersoll, July 27, 1939, JFK.

216 wearing a dark blue suit and an expression of extreme anxiety: Anthony Powell, "A Reporter in Los Angeles—Hemingway's Spanish Film," from *Night and Day*, August 19, 1937, in Valentine Cunningham, ed., *Spanish Front: Writers on the Civil War*, pp. 208–11.

217 "THE PICTURE WAS BEYOND PRAISE": FSF to EH July 13, 1937, and FSF to Maxwell Perkins, c. July 15, 1937, in Baker, *EH*, p. 316.

217 "comradely greetings": EH to André Malraux, c. May 22, 1937, JFK.

218 The keynote speech: Koltsov's speech is reproduced in Preston, *WSSD*, p. 194.

218 Robert Capa and Gerda Taro: Descriptions of the conference from Stephen Spender, *World Within World*, pp. 261–64; Roman Karmen and Boris Makasseyev, *K Sobitiyam V Ispani* (newsreel film), July 1937; Schaber, *Taro*, pp. 221–23. My translation of Garro.

218 Capa told Ted Allan: Allan, *Ted*, chapter 2: Gerda.

219 André Chamson, in fact: Spender, *World*, pp. 265–66.

219 as the congress delegates were just applauding: Malcolm Cowley in Aznar Soler and Schneider, *Il congreso internacional de escritores antifascistas*, p. 362; GT photo, ICP.

219 "The town of Brunete": Official communiqué quoted in Matthews, "Madrid Defenders Open New Attack," *New York Times*, July 7, 1937.

220 Racing out of the auditorium: GT, photographs from Brunete, ICP; Léon Moussinac, "Hommage à Gerda Taro," *Regards*, August 5, 1937.

221 On July 8, Jay Allen: Jay Allen, intro to *Death in the Making*.

221 "a circus of intellectuals": Spender, *World*, p. 264.

221 Barea and Ilsa weren't sorry: Barea, *FR*, p. 683.

222 in his bunker: Ibid., pp. 681–82.

223 Even Gerda's anxieties: Schaber, *Taro*, p. 252.

223 Capa and Gerda went dancing: Elisabeth Freundlich, *The Traveling Years*, pp. 52–53. Schaber, *Taro*, p. 234.

224 at the end of her rope: De la Mora, *Splendor*, pp. 327–28.

224 At dinner with Claud Cockburn: Jay Allen, preface to *Death in the Making* (unpaged).

225 "Tomorrow I'll get up at six": Schaber, *Taro*, p. 237.

225 Allan had resumed his puppylike attendance: Allan, *Ted*, chapter 2.

225 "In case we do somehow get out": Whelan, *Capa*, p. 122.

226 on Sunday she asked Allan to come with her: The account of GT's experience at the battle of Brunete comes from Allan, *Ted*, chapter 2, and Schaber, *Taro*, pp. 239–42.

228 Fleeing from airborne machine-gun fire: Jacinto Antón, "Te has cargado la francesa!" *El Pais*, July 12, 2009. The driver of the first tank, Aníbal González, didn't even realize he had hit anyone.

228 "Keep her comfortable": Irene Goldin, interview, in Trisha Ziff's film *The Mexican Suitcase*.

228 Richard de Rochemont's telephone call: Except as noted, details in this section are from Whelan, *Capa*, Schaber, *Taro*, pp. 243–60, Louis Aragon, *Lettres françaises*, May 27–June 3, 1954, Eva Besnyö interview with Richard Whelan, ICP.

229 "The war photographer's most fervent wish": RC to Peter Koester, in July 27, 1938, ICP.

229 "A FRENCH JOURNALIST": *L'Humanité*, July 27, 1937. My translation.

232 the government had had 20,000 casualties: Thomas, *SCW*, pp. 693–96, Beevor, *Battle for Spain*, pp. 282–85.

233 "no middle-class child ever walked": De la Mora, *Splendor,* p. 7.

233 "She grated on me": Barea, *FR,* p. 684.

233 Constancia, however, had forbidden: Fox, *War and Exile,* p. 61, Fischer, *Men and Politics,* pp. 457–60.

235 Ernest Hemingway paid a visit: The Hemingway-Eastman contretemps is reported in *The New York Times,* August 14, 1937; "Talk of the Town," *The New Yorker,* August 28, 1937; Baker, *EH,* pp. 317–18.

236 a new contract from NANA: John Wheeler to EJH, June 8, 1937, and August 10, 1937, JFK.

236 "I promised them I would be back": EH to Mrs. Paul Pfeiffer, August 2, 1937, in Baker, *Selected,* p. 460.

237 Hemingway obligingly gave them: Baker, *EH,* p. 317.

237 "He is living in a world so entirely his own": FSF to MP, September 3, 1937, in Turnbull, *Letters,* p. 275.

237 Throughout the past month: MG, "On Apocryphism," *Paris Review* 79, p. 291.

237 Hellman wasn't in good spirits: Martinson, *Lillian Hellman,* pp. 128–29.

238 Martha didn't like Hellman: Gellhorn on Hellman, MG, "Spanish War Notes," October 15, 1937, Hellman on Gellhorn, Hellman, *Unfinished,* p. 76, Parker on Gellhorn, and Gellhorn on Parker, in Meade, *Dorothy Parker,* pp. 282 and 284.

238 Hemingway had drinks or dinner with them: SWM to EH, September 20, 1937, JFK, in Miller, *Letters,* pp. 201–2.

238 "a horse that has escaped": MG in Moorehead, *Gellhorn,* p. 133.

239 "your friends got killed": MG in ibid., p. 134.

239 Hemingway went further: EH, unpublished first-draft lede to dispatch 16, *EH Review,* p. 59.

239 a man's body had been found: *Le Matin,* September 6, 1937.

240 The NKVD's Mobile Group: Preston, *WSSD,* p. 84.

240 He made good his own escape: Gazur, *Orlov,* pp. 164–66; Krivitsky, *In Stalin's Secret Service,* pp. 181–82.

240 Franco's inner circle had been breached: Seale and McConville, *Philby,* p. 89. While Krivitsky may not have known Philby's *name,* he was aware of his mission and background.

241 He tossed off two glasses of wine: Barea, *FR,* p. 695.

241 "a dictatorship under democratic rules": Negrín in Azaña, *Obras Completas,* vol. IV, p. 786, quoted in Thomas, *SCW,* p. 750.

242 Ilsa sat at the piano: Barea, *FR,* p. 698.

243 Flying down from Barcelona to Valencia: Matthews, "Success Seen in Aragon," *New York Times,* September 8, 1937.

243 "sick with anger": MG to ER, July 3–4, 1937, in Moorehead, *Selected,* p. 54.

244 "proud as a goat": Gellhorn, "Men Without Medals," *Collier's,* January 15, 1938, p. 10.

245 There wouldn't be any inns: EH, dispatch 14, *HR,* p. 53; SWM to EH, September 20, 1937, in Miller, *Letters,* pp. 201–2.

245 Hemingway got a call: Gazur, *Orlov,* pp. 130–31.

246 Hemingway, Matthews, and Martha set off: Szurek, *The Shattered Dream,* pp. 144–48; MG, "Spanish War Notes," undated itinerary labeled "Teruel Trip," BU. William Braasch Watson, in two articles in *North Dakota Quarterly,* "Investigating Hemingway: The Story" and "Investigating Hemingway: The Trip" (Summer 1991 and

Winter 1991, respectively), proposes that instead of a trip to Alicante from Madrid in early November, Hemingway made a clandestine return trip to Alfambra to visit Chrost; but as proof he uses a safe-conduct issued for the relevant dates by the Army of the Centre (whose territory was Madrid and environs), not the Army of the Levante (whose territory was Teruel and Alfambra). In this case Occam's Razor says Hemingway did go to Alicante, not on a second run to Alfambra. Watson has, however, unearthed a wealth of relevant detail about the cars Hemingway used, what kind of mileage they got, where he garaged them, and how much it cost; for these things alone, the articles would be worth reading.

247 The correspondents spent their first night: Itinerary and dates, MG, "Spanish War Notes" ("Teruel Trip"); EH, dispatches 14 and 15, *HR7*, pp. 51–55; Gellhorn, "Men Without Medals," *Collier's*, January 15, 1938; Szurek, *Shattered Dream*, pp. 144–48; Matthews, "Loyalists Close Teruel Front Gap," *New York Times*, September 26, 1937.

248 In the lounge of the Bedford Hotel: In addition to Whelan, *Capa*, sources are "Capa, Photographer of War, Tells of 'Finest Picture,'" *New York World-Telegram*, September 1, 1937; Allan, "Aftermath," *Ted*; and Capa, *Death*.

251 They had patched up the shell holes: Matthews, "Madrid Lays Plans for Winter Siege," *New York Times*, September 25, 1937.

251 the rooms he and Martha now checked in to: William Braasch Watson, "Investigating Hemingway," *North Dakota Quarterly*, vol. 59, no. 1, Winter 1991, note, p. 67. Watson references the room receipt.

251 "dead angle": Matthews, *Education*, p. 122.

251 "you never hear the one": EH, dispatch 15, *HR*, p. 55.

251 The new, professional order: EH, dispatch 14, *HR*, p. 53; Barea, *FR*, p. 697.

252 the shops, astonishingly, were full: Matthews, "Madrid Lays Plans," *loc. cit.*

252 "the Great Adolescent": Alvah Bessie in Moorehead, *Gellhorn*, p. 136.

252 the opus 33 mazurka, number 4: Records for both these pieces are specified in Hemingway's props list for *The Fifth Column* (reproduced in the 2008 edition, p. ix).

252 To get a feel for the territory: EH, dispatch 16, *HR*, pp. 57–58; Gellhorn, "Men Without Medals," *Collier's*, January 15, 1937.

253 The lack of anything to report: MG, "Spanish War Notes," October 15, 1937; Hellman, *Unfinished*, pp. 100–103; Moorehead, *Gellhorn*, p. 135. Hellman's account of the evening comes in for withering criticism from Gellhorn in "On Apocryphism" (*Paris Review* 79, pp. 280–304), some of which is deserved and on point. However, Gellhorn maintains, incorrectly, to have never heard of Contemporary Historians, implying it is a mendacious invention of Hellman's; she also says there were no bullfights in Madrid during the war—which would have surprised General Miaja, who is shown in news photographs attending them. Sometimes her feelings get the better of her; this account is an attempt to reconcile Hellman's and Gellhorn's versions.

254 "Mr. Scrooby": MG in Moorehead, *Gellhorn*, p. 137. Much later, Hemingway and his fourth wife, Mary, used the nickname "Mr. Scrooby" for Hemingway's penis.

254 "It would be pleasant": J. Donald Adams, "Hemingway's First Novel in Eight Years," *New York Times Book Review*, October 17, 1937, p. 2.

255 "puerile slaughter": Sinclair Lewis, "Glorious Dirt," *Newsweek*, October 8, 1937, p. 34.

256 "the necessary murder": "Spain," was published as a five-page pamphlet by Faber in May 1937, with proceeds from its sale going to the British medical committee in Spain.

256 At one point Hemingway had wanted: EH, *Fifth Column* draft fragment, item 80, JFK.

257 "Don't be kind": Quotations in the preceding pages are from Hemingway, *The Fifth Column and Four Stories of the Spanish Civil War*, pp. 3, 23, 38, 39, 42, 57, 61, 65, 66, 75, 83, and 84.

257 Mikhail Koltsov mentioned it: Koltsov, *Ispanskii dnevnik* (November 6, 1937), p. 561, in Baker, *EH*, p. 624n.

257 a long story for *Collier's*: Gellhorn, "Men Without Medals," *Collier's*, January 15, 1938.

257 the second piece of hers they'd taken: Gellhorn subsequently claimed (*The Face of War*, p. 16) that after this article *Collier's* "put my name on the masthead." This is not quite true. It *was* after its publication—but not until the issue of October 28, 1939, which listed her as correspondent from Russia. In the event, she didn't go to Russia, and her correspondent credit was changed to "Scandinavia" in the issue of November 25, 1939, to reflect the assignment she then undertook to cover the Winter War in Finland. However, her name did appear, along with those of several other contributors, on the *cover* of the July 17, 1937, issue, the one in which her first *Collier's* article, "Only the Shells Whine," appeared.

258 "no ambitious woman": EH to Bernard Berenson, May 27, 1953, in Meyers, p. 318.

258 "So now the long winter": MG, "Spanish War Notes," October 26, 1937, BU, partially quoted in Moorehead, *Gellhorn*, pp. 135–36.

258 "stronger and stronger": Matthews, "Madrid Lays Plans for Winter Siege," *New York Times*. September 25, 1937.

258 Prieto, in fact, had tried: Preston, *SCW*, p. 272.

258 Hitler had recently alarmed: Hitler's "Hossbach Memorandum," in Thomas, *SCW*, p. 725, and Orlov, *The Secret History of Stalin's Crimes*, p. 238.

258 a memorandum to the Italian ambassador: Franco to Roberto Cantalupo, April 4, 1937, in Preston, *SCW*, p. 274.

259 "a brilliant gay lazy man": MG to ER, February 5, 1939, in Moorehead, *Selected*, pp. 72–73.

259 a democratic dictatorship: Negrín to Azaña and Araquistain, in Thomas, *SCW*, p. 750.

259 "This will do us a lot of harm": Fischer, *Men and Politics*, p. 422.

259 "discover the possible ramifications": Berdah, p. 19. My translation.

261 Now he listened patiently: Barea, *FR*, pp. 705–7; photographs of AB and Lobo at the Reina Victoria, Barea archives.

261 On November 7, the anniversary: In addition to MG's "Spanish War Notes" (see below) other sources here are Marion Merriman, *Robert Hale Merriman: American Commander in Spain*, pp. 184–85, and photographs and film of the November 7 luncheon provided by Alan Warren.

262 Things were merrier in Madrid: Matthews, "Gay Madrid Marks Seige Anniversary," *New York Times*, November 8, 1937.

262 That evening the Russians gave a party: Events on the following pages described in MG, "Spanish War Notes," November 7, 8, 9, 10, and 11, 1937, and Hemingway, *FWTBT*, pp. 237–38.

263 Koltsov, who had been so high-spirited: Preston, *WSSD*, pp. 196–97.

264 "And now the leaving": MG, "Spanish War Notes," December 6, 1937, BU.

265 "The frog lay on the edge": Barea, "Bombas en la huerta," *Valor y miedo*, p. 29. My translation.

265 In the darkness: Barea, *FR*, pp. 707–10.

266 which she promptly endorsed: MG to EH, December 1937, in Kert, *Women*, p. 311.

266 new, more expensive, and less satisfactory arrangements: MG to EH, undated [December 1937], BU.

266 And although Ivens had intended: JI to EH, January 28, 1938, JFK.

266 Writing to Hemingway from the boat: MG to EH, two undated letters, quoted in Kert, *Women*, pp. 311–12, and in BU; internal references to "the Yuletide season" and to her shipboard cabin place both as December 1937.

267 Ivens had sent his own letter to Hemingway: JI to EH, undated [but written on the boat train to the *Normandie*, so likely December 18, 1937], JFK.

267 the Hapag Lloyd Line's ship *Europa*: "Events of Interest in the Shipping World," *New York Times*, December 19, 1937, p. 61.

267 "Very cute and nervy": KDP to SWM, November 12, 1937, and PPH to GCM and SWM, December 18, 1937, in Miller, *Lost Generation*, pp. 203–4; PPH passport photo, December 13, 1937, in Baker, *EH*, p. 323.

268 When the news of the offensive reached Hemingway: EH had traveled to Barcelona from Madrid with Sefton Delmer and Herbert Matthews, stopping to have breakfast with Luis Quintanilla in Sitges (Paul Quintanilla, *Waiting at the Shore*, p. 209). This seems to prove conclusively that contrary to her later assertions and accounts of Caroline Moorehead (p. 140), Bernice Kert (p. 311), and others, Martha Gellhorn didn't have any kind of Christmas celebration, early or otherwise, with Hemingway in Barcelona. She was gone by then.

268 For three days: All details about EH and HLM's participation in the battle for Teruel come from Matthews, *Education*, pp. 96–105, and EH, dispatch 18, *HR7*, pp. 64–68; other background from Thomas, SCW.

270 Capa hadn't been planning: Details in the following pages from Whelan, *Capa*, pp. 129–30; Capa correspondence file, ICP; Mexican Suitcase photos, ICP.

271 At last he'd been not just a witness: EH to Hadley Mowrer, January 31, 1938, in Baker, *Selected*, p. 462.

271 "received the surrender": EH dispatch 18, and EH cable to John Wheeler, n. 5, in *EHR*, pp. 63–68.

272 it was drawn-out and dangerous: Simone Téry, "Dans Teruel, prise et gardée," *Regards*, January 13, 1938. My translation.

272 Hemingway glorying: EH to Hadley Mowrer, January 31, 1938, in Baker, *Selected*, p. 462.

272 "taking pictures of victory": Capa, *Focus*, p. 102.

272 He sought out other images: Capa's Mexican Suitcase film rolls and vintage prints, ICP.

273 The SIM agents had taken their time: Details from Barea, *FR*, pp. 710–13; identification of the Seminario, Beevor, *Battle for Spain*, p. 306, and personal observation.

275 he arrived from Teruel on Christmas Eve: P. Quintanilla, *Waiting at the Shore*, p. 210; Jay Allen in Luis Quintanilla, *All the Brave*, p. 14; Paul Quintanilla's website, www.lqart.org.

275 Hemingway stayed around to celebrate: Kert, *Women*, p. 312; Baker, *EH*, pp. 323–24; Capa photographs, ICP; EH, dispatch 18, n. 5, *HR7*, p. 68; Ehrenburg, *Memoirs*, p. 418.

276 a ragged column of men: Narrative reconstructed from Capa's film rolls in the Mexican Suitcase, ICP; Matthews, *Education*, p. 108. Other details, Beevor, *Battle*, pp. 317–18.

276 "heavy, flat-faced, brutish": Matthews, *Education*, p. 108.

278 "You're Ilse": Barea, *FR*, p. 718.

279 "Perhaps subjectively you are a good revolutionary": Katia Landau, "Stalinism in Spain," *Revolutionary History*, vol. 1, no. 2, Summer, 1988.

279 If Barea had known either of these things: Before a shell struck the car he was riding in to Teruel with three other journalists, killing all three but sparing him, Philby had felt under considerable suspicion because, as he put it, "Franco officers . . . seemed to think that the British in general must be a lot of Communists because so many were fighting with the International Brigades." (KP in Boris Volodarsky, "Kim Philby: Living a Lie," *History Today*, August 5, 2010). So Ilsa's (and Katya Landau's) knowledge of his real identity and sympathies were a danger to him, and thus unwittingly to them.

279 Kulcsar came to bid Barea and Ilsa goodbye: Barea, *FR*, pp. 715–19.

280 On December 25, Georges Luciani: Thomas, *SCW*, p. 828, n. 5; Hugh Ragsdale, *The Soviets, the Munich Crisis, and the Coming of World War II*, pp. 30–31; Coulondre to Delbos, December 27, 1937, *Documents Diplomatiques Français*, 2nd series, vol. VII, note 30, "Note de M. Luciani."

PART III: "LA DESPEDIDA"

285 On January 2: Sources for the following pages are Matthews, *Education*, pp. 109–11; Capa Mexican Suitcase photo rolls; Capa, *Slightly Out of* Focus, p. 137; Capa, "La lutte implacable dans les souterrains de la ville," *Ce Soir*, January 8, 1938. My translation.

286 "The war correspondent has his stake": Capa, *Focus*, p. 137.

287 she even became jealous: Paul Quintanilla, p. 211.

287 In their suite at the Elysée: EH and PHH in Paris and on shipboard: Reynolds, pp. 282–83; Kert, *Women*, p. 312.

287 he became enraged: EH to HRM, January 31, 1938, JFK; EH to MP, February 1, 1938, in Bruccoli, ed., *The Only Thing That Counts*, pp. 253–54.

288 He was only slightly mollified: EH interview in *Ce Soir*, December 30, 1937, reprinted in Robert S. Thronberry, "Hemingway's *Ce Soir* Interview (1937) and the Battle of Teruel," *Hemingway Review*, vol. 5, no. 1, Fall 1985, pp. 2–8.

288 He continued to fret: EH to MP, February 1 and 8, 1938, MP to EH, February 3, 1938, JFK.

288 "I don't think it necessarily follows": AG to EH, February 6, 1938, JFK.

288 a long letter he got from Joris Ivens: JI to EH, January 28, 1938, JFK.

289 He wondered if he was too close: EH to Maxwell Perkins, February 1 and [9], 1938, in Bruccoli, *The Only Thing*, pp. 253–54 and 256–57.

289 a clipping from the *St. Louis Post-Dispatch*: Clipping in EH/MG correspondence, BU.

289 "I am delighted to be back": "Hemingway Tells of War, New Play in Interview," Key West *Citizen*, February 1, 1938.

289 "I did not want to leave": EH to MP, February 1, 1938, in Bruccoli, *loc. cit.*

290 "to save the damned": MG to HGW, February 8, 1938, in Rollyson, *Beautiful Exile*, p. 88.

290 "a single cell": Rollyson, *Exile*, p. 87.

290 "called Franco a butcher": *St. Louis Post-Dispatch*, January 28, 1938.

290 "the voice, the culture": Moorehead, *MG*, p. 141.

290 the handy sum of $1,000: Herbert Matthews to his father, November 14, 1937, Columbia University.

290 "idiotic lazy cowardly": MG to H. G. Wells, February 8, 1938, in Rollyson, *Exile*, pp. 87–88.

290 she told Mrs. Roosevelt: MG to ER, February 1, 1938, in Moorehead, *Selected*, p. 57.

292 "POLDI DIED SUDDENLY": Barea, *FR*, p. 722.

292 Kulcsar had been entirely reconciled: Valentin Pollak, unpublished memoir, pp. 389–91, BP.

292 the result of intentional poisoning: Berdah, p. 20.

292 What if the NKVD was trying to eliminate: So far as I know, no one has ever directly connected Philby's placement, Ilsa's difficulties with the SIM, the persecution of the Landaus, and Kulcsar's possible liquidation; but the connection seems persuasive, especially considering the timing of Krivitsky's defection (see p. 240).

292 Things would resolve themselves: Source for the following pages is Barea, *FR*, pp. 719–27.

294 On March 18, bareheaded and without an overcoat: "Hemingway Off to Spain," *New York Times*, March 19, 1938.

294 "the fate of Spain": Matthews, *New York Times*, March 13, 1938.

294 he'd been affectionate: Kert, *Women*, p. 313.

294 "Where I go now": EH, *The Fifth Column*, p. 83.

294 he'd written an introduction: "First Hand Picture of Conflict in Spain Given by a Volunteer Here," *Washington Post*, March 18, 1938.

295 a prefatory note for the catalog: www.moma.org/docs/press_archives/437/releases /MOMA_1938_0017_1938-03-14_38314-10.pdf?2010.

295 a piece for *Ken*: Hemingway, "Dying Well—or Badly," *Ken*, April 21, 1938, and "The Time Now, the Place Spain," *Ken*, April 7, 1938.

295 "leftwing anti-fascist": Seldes cable to EH, February 23, 1938, JFK.

295 they'd reduced his pay rate: JNW to EH, May 31, 1938, JFK.

296 "I'm sorry I sent you that cable": EH to JDP, c. March 26, 1938, in Baker, *Selected*, pp. 463–65.

296 "I know the way your mind works": AMacL to EH, December 14, 1928, JFK.

297 "The news has been terrible": MG to ER, late March 1938, in Moorehead, *Selected*, p. 58.

297 "IF ANYTHING EVER STOPS": Unsigned cable, MG to EH, March 22, 1938, JFK. Michael Reynolds dates this cable as from July 1938 and interprets it as referring to a *westbound* passage. But the sailing dates and ship names make no sense in that context, whereas they *do* in March 1938, when compared with the "Mails and Shipping" lists in *The New York Times*.

297 Hemingway had told Perkins: EH to MP, February 8, 1938, in Bruccoli, *The Only Thing That Counts*, pp. 256–57.

298 They wrote to Ilsa's parents: Pollak, pp. 391–92.

298 a month of escalating threats and ultimatums: Schuschnigg, *Ein Requiem in Rot-Weisz-Rot*, quoted in Thomas, *SCW*, p. 783.

299 the streets of Vienna: "L'Armée hitlérienne a occupé Autriche," *L'Humanité*, March 13, 1938; Martin Gilbert, *A History of the Twentieth Century*, vol. 2, pp. 170–78.

299 a story about lovers: Gellhorn, "In Sickness and in Health," *The Novellas of Martha Gellhorn*, p. 251.

299 The situation in Spain: Matthews, *Education*, pp. 118–25; Thomas (*SCW*, p. 785) reports that in the raid of March 16–17, 1,300 people were killed and 2,000 injured.

300 Hemingway wasn't enthusiastic: EH to Wheeler, June 2, 1938, JFK. Hemingway claimed in his letter to have researched accreditation and transport to the Nationalist zone, and that doing so cost him the opportunity to be present when the insurgents took Lérida. This seems somewhat unlikely, since he arrived in Paris on the 24th, worked on his short story manuscript and a *Ken* article, and had to wait for Martha to arrive on the 28th. His trip to St. Jean de Luz, where he spent a total of two hours and fifteen minutes, would probably not have allowed him sufficient time to go to Hendaye, on the border, and "ascertain it was impossible" to visit fascist Spain.

300 a *Ken* article to write: "The Cardinal Picks a Winner" was published on May 5, 1938. *Ken*'s lead time was approximately a month, so he would most likely have sent the piece to New York on or around the last day of March.

300 goaded by Martha: MG, in Moorehead, *Gellhorn*, p. 130.

300 he extracted from the ambassador: Claude G. Bowers to Cordell Hull ("Confidential to the Secretary of State"), April 3, 1938, report 1475; in Shulman, "Hemingway's Observations on the Spanish Civil War: Unpublished State Department Reports," *HR7*, pp. 147–49.

300 "resist, resist, resist": Matthews, *Education*, p. 131.

300 Martha was traveling separately: In his account of the journey to the Spanish frontier in *Not Peace but a Sword*, Sheean doesn't mention Martha's presence on the train; he does, however, say that Hemingway went off in Perpignan and came back with a car, which he presumes was provided by the Spanish consulate. It seems much more likely that the car was the one Martha shipped over, and that she wasn't on the train because she was getting it to Perpignan.

300 "I don't know why you're going": Vincent Sheean, *Not Peace but a Sword*, p. 237.

301 you could nearly always find a group: Ibid., pp. 241–42. Sheean quotes Malraux as saying, "J'aime mieux les putains que les raseurs."

301 Before dawn most mornings: MG, "Spanish War Notes," April 10, 12, 15, 19, and 21, 1938.

302 they found Milton Wolff: EH, dispatch 20, *HR7*, pp. 71–72.

302 On the tenth, they lunched: EH, dispatch 22, *HR7*, pp. 76–77. In a piece entitled "Memory" in the *London Review of Books* (vol. 18, no. 24, December 12, 1986), Gellhorn, who mentions a previous encounter with Modesto in which he and Hemingway challenged each other to Russian roulette with herself being the stake, makes this meeting a similarly rivalous exchange between the two men. Unfortunately, none of the details about the earlier meeting check out, and her version of this one seems similarly creative.

303 to see for themselves what was happening: Sources for the next pages are EH, dispatch 22, *HR7*, pp. 76–77, MG, "Spanish War Notes," April 15, 1937, BU, and Sheean, *Not Peace*, pp. 72–79.

305 "The victorious sword of Franco": ABC (Sevilla), April 16, 1938.

305 the theater was crowded: "Air Raid Siren Halts Showing of War Film," *New York Times*, April 25, 1938; Sheean, *Not Peace*, pp. 248–49; EH, dispatch 26, *HR7*, pp. 84–85; Hemingway, "The Writer as a Writer," *Direction*, May–June 1939, p. 3.

306 "pig-headed": EH to John Wheeler, June 2, 1938. JFK.

307 Hemingway wrote down enough: EH, field notes for "Old Man at the Bridge," JFK, also described in William Braasch Watson, "'Old Man at the Bridge': The Making of a Short Story," in *HR7*, p. 154.

308 "THESE SHORT PUNCHES": EH to Gingrich, October 22, 1938, in Baker, *Selected*, p. 472; Gingrich cable to EH, July 18, 1938, JFK.

308 She'd wanted to do a piece: Cables between *Collier's* and MG in Moorehead, *Gellhorn*, p. 145.

308 "What goes on here seems to be the affair": MG to ER, April 24 or 25, 1938, in Moorehead, *Selected*, pp. 59–61.

308 She begged off an excursion: MG, "Spanish War Notes," April 28 and May 1, 1938, BU.

309 "history is just a big stinking mess": MG, "Spanish War Notes," April 13, 1938, quoted in Moorehead, *Gellhorn*, p. 145.

309 All he had to do was keep fighting: Thomas, *SCW*, pp. 798–99; Preston, *SCW*, pp. 284–85.

309 They'd flown down the coast: Matthews, "Madrid's Morale Found Unflagging," *New York Times*, May 10, 1938; EH, dispatch 30, May 10, 1938, EHR, pp. 91–92.

310 North had been responsible: Donaldson, *Fitzgerald and Hemingway: Works and Days*, p. 375.

310 "I like the Communists": Joseph North, *No Men Are Strangers*, pp. 143–44.

311 "Am going home": EH and PPH quoted in Hawkins, *Unbelievable Happiness*, p. 207.

311 "not exactly happy": MG to Edna Gellhorn, May 26, 1938, in Moorehead, *Selected*, pp. 62–63, Gellhorn, "Guns Against France," *Collier's*, October 8, 1938.

312 "The war in Spain was one kind of war": MG to ER, undated [March 1938?] in Moorehead, *Selected*, p. 58, and Moorehead, *Gellhorn*, p. 146.

312 Ilsa just couldn't bear: My source for details in this section is Barea, *FR*, pp. 734–36.

313 In the Avenue George V: "Le Memorial Day," *Le Temps*, May 30, 1938, p. 6.

313 At the other end of Paris: *L'Humanité*, May 30, 1938, p. 7.

314 the grave of Gerda Taro: *Ce Soir*, May 30, 1938, p. 8.

314 whether dove or falcon: Irme Schaber (in *Taro*, p. 268) identifies the bird as Horus, the Egyptian god of the sky, war, hunting, and resurrection, according to an essay by the contemporary Italian scholar Casimiro de Crescenzo, "La Tomba di Gerda Taro: un lavoro inedito di Alberto Giacometti," in *Riga*, 1991, cahier 1.

314 The person who paid that: An undated 1938 letter (probably written in July), from RC in China to Julia Friedmann, instructs her that "the gravestone (Gerda's) . . . should be paid from my money."

315 He accused Jack Wheeler: EH to John A. Wheeler, June 2, 1938, JFK.

315 He attacked Archie MacLeish: EH to AMacL, [July 1938], JFK.

315 He fought with the people: EH to Ralph Ingersoll, July 17, 1938, JFK.

315 he wrangled with Max Perkins: Perkins to EH, July 1, 1938; EH to MP, July 12, 1938.

316 The first piece he sent to *Ken*: Hemingway, "Treachery in Aragon," *Ken*, June 30, 1938.

316 a short story he'd begun in Paris: Hemingway, "The Denunciation," *The Fifth Column and Four Stories of the Spanish Civil War*, p. 97.

316 telling a gullible journalist: Key West *Citizen*, June 18 and July 13, 1938.

317 if he'd hired someone: EH to Mary Pfeiffer, date not given, quoted in Kert, *Women*, p. 118.

317 the images and tastes and sounds and smells: Barea, *FR*, pp. 738–39.

318 "march to the rescue": Gilbert, *A History of the Twentieth Century*, p. 189.

318 On the moonless night of July 25: Beevor, *Battle for Spain*, pp. 349–53; Thomas, *SCW*, pp. 815–21.

319 The club grounds: Auden and Isherwood, *Journey to a War*, p. 152.

319 "if it's not the runs": RC to PK, in Whelan, *Capa*, p. 141.

319 His new acquaintances: Auden and Isherwood, *Journey*, pp. 43–44.

320 he was sending back money: RC to PK, April 29, 1938; and July 27, 1938 bank draft from Capa's account at National City Bank to Heinrich Pohorylle, both ICP.

320 "I am the 'poor relation'": RC to PK, April 29, 1938.

321 "Unfortunately," Capa wrote Koester: RC to PK, July 27, 1938, ICP.

321 "won his English in a crap game": Whelan, *Capa*, p. 136.

321 "He was best": RC, "China phrases," fragment in 1938 miscellaneous documents, ICP.

322 At his residence in Prague: Gilbert, *History*, pp. 194–202.

322 there was no point: MG to Edna Gellhorn, May 26, 1938, in Moorehead *Selected*, p. 62.

322 "golden key": PPH to EH, September 1, 5, 10, and 28, 1938, in Reynolds, pp. 294–95.

322 they sat in the sun on the *terrasse*: Gellhorn, *A Stricken Field*, p. 288.

323 "In going where you have to go": Hemingway, preface to *The Fifth Column and the First Forty-nine Stories* (Scribner's, 1938), p. vii.

323 went pheasant shooting: Baker, *EH*, p. 334.

323 "the barbarism of Fascist interventionists in Spain": Hemingway, "'Humanity Will Not Forgive This!': The *Pravda* Article," ed. William Braasch Watson, in *HR7*, pp. 114–18. In his cable to M. M. Olgin accepting the commission, Hemingway sent regards to Koltsov, suggesting that Koltsov had something to do with *Pravda*'s request.

323 Koltsov, his teeth as bad as ever: Cockburn, *Discord*, pp. 310–14.

324 clutching her silver fox fur: George Kennan, *Memoirs*, vol. 1, pp. 90–92.

324 She, too, wanted to talk: Gellhorn, "Memory," *London Review of Books*, December 12, 1996. Gellhorn says here that Koltsov told her all about Russia's guarantees to Benes, and goes on to blame the Czech president for not accepting the challenge to fight for his people. Interestingly, she made no mention of these guarantees in her *Collier's* article, "Epitaph for a Democracy," nor in her otherwise information-packed letters to her editor, Charles Colebaugh. One wonders if the candor of Koltsov's conversation, and her indictment of Benes, were both a kind of *arrière-pensée*. Accordingly, I haven't included this point in my account.

324 after making several more vain attempts: MG to Charles Colebaugh, October 22, 1938, in Moorehead, *Selected*, pp. 67–70.

325 Stalin had agreed: G. Dimitrov and D. Manuilsky to Voroshilov, copy to Stalin, August 29, 1938, in Radosh et al., *Spain Betrayed*, p. 469. Although there had been discussions over the summer of both sides renouncing the help of outside forces, Negrín's unilateral move wasn't made until Voroshilov and Stalin had been asked for their "advice and instructions."

325 there were only about seven thousand: Beevor, *Battle for Spain*, p. 363.

325 "The only thing to say": Cockburn, *Discord*, p. 314.

325 "I've spoken about you": Barea, *FR*, p. 742.

326 they saw an old couple: Ibid., p. 745.

327 Sheean's English wife, Diana Forbes-Robertson: Richard Whelan notes, ICP. Forbes-Robertson says she met Capa when she first arrived in Spain, and that he helped her to establish herself there as a journalist. She also says, elsewhere in the same interview, that she accompanied her husband to Spain in April 1938, after he and Hemingway had tried to forbid her and Martha Gellhorn to come because it was too dangerous. Capa, however, was in China in April; and no one, including her husband in his memoir *Not Peace but a* Sword, mentions seeing Forbes-Robertson in Spain at that time. It seems more likely that she first met Capa in the fall of 1938.

327 On the sixteenth he went to Falset: Details of Capa's trips to Falset and Montblanch are reconstructed from films in the Mexican Suitcase archive, ICP, supplemented by contemporary news accounts.

329 Capa, who had dressed carefully: Agustí Centelles I Osso, photograph in the Archivos Estatales, MECyD, Centro Documental de la Memoria Histórica, Salamanca; Capa, photographs of "La Despedida" in ICP; Cynthia Young, e-mail to the author.

329 On either side of the Diagonal: Capa's photographs and notebook (#5), ICP; Matthews, "Loyalists Honor Foreign Fighters," *New York Times*, October 17, 1938; Eby, *Comrades and Commissars*, pp. 410–12, Beevor, *Battle for Spain*, p. 366; De la Mora, *Splendor*, pp. 371–73.

330 Martha Gellhorn wasn't in Barcelona: Gellhorn, "The Third Winter," *The Face of War*, p. 41. Herbert Matthews's correspondence for this period reveals that neither Hemingway nor Gellhorn was in Barcelona for the disbanding of the International Brigades: a letter to his wife, Nancie (November 8, 1938), says that Hemingway has just left Spain after a three-day visit to rejoin Gellhorn in Paris, and that she will arrive later in the month for a week's stay. As to "The Third Winter," a search of *Collier's* issues for 1938 and 1939, and of the *Reader's Guide to Periodical Literature* for 1937–1940, reveals no trace of this article. It was included under the title "The Third Winter," with a dateline of November 1938, in *The Face of War* (pp. 37–49), where the copyright page only says that "the reports on the war in Spain . . . appeared first in *Collier's*." No first publication information is given. It seems inescapable that this is the "outdated" story *Collier's* spiked (in a letter from Denver Lindley on February 8, 1939), and MG refers to in letters to Hortense Flexner (spring 1940) and Charles Colebaugh (July 17, 1941).

330 the reception for the collection: EH to Maxwell Perkins, October 28, 1938, in Baker, *Selected*, pp. 473–75.

331 "a carnival of treachery": Ibid. "Rotten-ness" is Hemingway's spelling.

331 Hemingway suddenly faltered: This incident is reconstructed from EH to Maxwell Perkins, October 28, 1938, in Baker, *Selected*, pp. 473–75; MG to David Gurewitsch, undated, in Moorehead, *Selected*, p. 222. In her letter, Gellhorn places the encounter in Valencia, which is impossible, since Pacciardi was not in Spain at the time, nor were Gellhorn and Hemingway, and neither of them was in Valencia after December 1937. On the other hand, they *were* in Paris in October 1938, and so was Pacciardi. Caroline Moorehead, in her biography of Gellhorn, mistakenly says that Gellhorn and Hemingway saw Pacciardi in the "Despedida" parade in Barcelona, which none of the parties attended.

331 "In a war": EH, preface to Gustav Regler, *The Great Crusade*, p. vii.

332 very early the next morning they set out: The November 5 Ebro incident is reconstructed from Sheean, *Not Peace*, pp. 328–38; Matthews, *Education*, pp. 138–39; Capa photographs, ICP; Matthews, "Loyalists Retain Strong Ebro Hold," *New York Times*, November 6, 1938; and Ramon Buckley (son of Henry) in Russ Pottle, "Hemingway and the Mexican Suitcase," paper presented at the 15th Biennial Conference of the Hemingway Society, June 2012. Sheean says there were two boats, one with four oarsmen, one with two, and doesn't mention the shells; Matthews mentions only one boat, and he and Buckley both cite the shellfire. Capa's photos of the boat show three or four oars.

334 On a street in the village: Alvah Bessie to Carlos Baker, February 19 and 28, 1962, in Baker, *EH*, p. 335.

334 On the night of November 6: Sheean, *Not Peace*, pp. 339–40; Diana Forbes-Robertson, interviews with Josefa Stuart and Richard Whelan, Whelan notes, ICP.

335 Hemingway got Matthews to drive him: HLM to Nancie Matthews, November 8, 1938, Columbia University.

335 Within hours he was at the front: Capa's experiences on the Segre reconstructed from photographs and newspaper clippings in the Capa archive, ICP.

337 The Segre offensive: Thomas, *SCW*, p. 833. There is considerable controversy over the final casualty counts: for instance, Beevor (*Battle for Spain*, p. 358) puts the number of dead at thirty thousand; Preston's figure (*SCW*, p. 291) is much lower, 7,150.

337 intending to write the story: MG to Charles Colebaugh, December 6, 1938, in Moorehead, *Selected*, pp. 70–71.

337 "underneath she's a lot softer": HLM to Nancie Matthews, January 30, 1939, HLM papers, Columbia University.

337 "He was my brother": Moorehead, *Gellhorn*, p. 143.

337 How could she write about suffering: Gellhorn, "Till Death Us Do Part," *The Novellas*, pp. 296–97.

338 One night he held her hand: MG interview with Richard Whelan, December 31, 1981, and letter from Peter Wyden to Ruth Cerf Berg, both in Whelan notes, ICP.

338 After writing up her Barcelona story: See paragraph that begins "Martha Gellhorn wasn't in Barcelona," p. 330.

338 Although she'd confessed to Herbert Matthews: HLM to Nancie Matthews, November 26, 1938, HLM papers, Columbia University.

338 "so sick I had an absolute breakdown": RC to Julia Friedmann, December 10, 1938, ICP.

338 "No other country in Europe": De la Mora, *Splendor*, p. 345. Her descriptions of life in the Soviet capital are idyllic.

338 he wanted 250 aircraft: Daniel Kowalski, *Stalin and the Spanish Civil War*, e-book, www.gutenberg.org, chapter 3, p. 44. Beevor, *Battle for Spain*, fn. 6, p. 372, gives the numbers as 2,150 field guns, 120 antiaircraft guns, 400,000 rifles, 10,000 machine guns, and 410 aircraft. The numbers, varied as they are, are all substantial.

338 General Secretary Stalin invited: Conversations reproduced by Enrique Castro Delgado in his book *Hombres Made in Moscú*, quoted in (and translated by) Fox, *Constancia*, p. 80. Other details, Ignacio Hidalgo de Cisneros, *Cambio de Rumbo*, pp. 297–301.

339 "I think I'm going out of my mind": Boris Efimov, *Mikhail' Kol'tsov, kakim on byl*, pp. 71–72, in Preston, *WSSD*, p. 199.

341 On February 1, 1940: See Preston, *WSSD*, pp. 173 and 197–212, for a fuller account of Koltsov's fall from grace.

341 Hemingway complained to his mother-in-law: EH to Mrs. Paul Pfeiffer, February 6, 1939, in Baker, *Selected*, pp. 475–78.

341 a showing of *The Spanish Earth*: Kert, *Women*, pp. 322–33.

342 on another evening at the Stork Club: *New York Daily Mirror*, January 15, 1939, p. 3.

342 At least, thought Barea: Barea, *FR*, pp. 746–49.

343 "There will be no mediation": Preston, *SCW*, pp. 293–94.

344 "Things are not so bad": Sheean, *Not Peace*, p. 346.

344 the latest, last-resort wave of conscripts: Beevor, *Battle for Spain*, p. 376.

345 "I have seen hundreds of thousands": Whelan, *Capa*, p. 154.

345 "it is not always easy": Ibid., p. 155.

346 It had turned cold and blustery: Josep Andreu y Abello, in Beevor, *Battle for Spain*, p. 377.

346 the editors of *Life*: Wilson Hicks (*Life* photo editor) to RC, January 31, 1939, ICP.

347 Sheean was in a state of growing despair: Sheean, *Not Peace*, pp. 347 and 360.

348 Capa drove through the frontier at Le Perthus for the last time: In addition to specific sources already cited, material in the preceding section comes from Matthews, "Constant Bombing Numbs Barcelona," January 25, 1939, and "Barcelona's Plans Upset by Apathy," *New York Times*, January 26, 1939; HLM to Nancie Matthews, January 30, 1939, Columbia University; Sheean, pp. 350–57; Capa's photographs, notebooks, and negatives, ICP.

348 the word from Austria was not good: Pollak, autobiography, p. 394.

349 a winning ticket for the national lottery: Uli Rushby-Smith, e-mail to AV.

349 the sailors assured him: Dialogue, and preceding details, from Barea, *FR*, pp. 749–51.

349 "In Paris there's nothing good": Quotes in this section are from an undated letter, RC to Julia Friedmann, early 1939, ICP. Other details, unless noted, from Capa photos, ICP.

350 using his *Life* credentials: ADA–Camp de Bram telephone log, in Marie-Hélène Meléndez, "Capa, Internment Camps, Southern France, March 1939," *The Mexican Suitcase*, vol. 2, pp. 397–98.

351 "As long as there is a war": EH to Ivan Kashkeen (EH's spelling), March 30, 1939, in Baker, *Selected*, p. 481.

352 he and Martha agreed: MG to Eleanor Roosevelt, February 5, 1939, Moorehead, *Selected*, p. 70.

352 "at the very least, inopportune": Voroshilov to Stalin, February 16, 1939, in Radosh et al., *Spain Betrayed*, p. 512.

352 "The only thing about a war": EH to Kashkin, *op. cit.*, p. 480.

352 a thank-you note to Sara Murphy: PPH to SWM, undated [December 1938?], apparently revised serially and finally sent as an enclosure with another of March 10, 1939, in Miller, *Lost Generation*, p. 219.

352 two different hotel rooms: EH to Thomas Shevlin, April 4, 1939, in Baker, *Selected*, p. 484.

353 She was so pleased with the result: MG to ER, March 18, 1939, in Moorehead, *Selected*, pp. 74–75.

353 "you cannot spit": EH, preface to Gustav Regler, *The Great Crusade*, p. viii.

354 "show *all* the different sides": EH to Ivan Kashkin, *loc cit.*

354 "We lay on the brown, pine-needled floor": EH, draft of *For Whom the Bell Tolls*, Item 83, JFK. Although the draft began in the first person, Hemingway decided by the third page to change it to third person, going back through the manuscript to change all the pronouns.

EPILOGUE

355 "Today, with the Red Army captive": Preston, SCW, p. 299.

355 Over the next few months: Preston, *The Spanish Holocaust*, pp. xi and xvii–xix. Some scholars, e.g., Michael Seidman in a critical review of *The Spanish Holocaust* in the *Times Literary Supplement*, September 7, 2012, believe that Preston errs in the spirit, if not also the letter (or number), of his condemnation. On the other hand, the historian Julius Ruiz, author of *Franco's Justice*, maintains that the number of those executed was 50,000.

357 Hemingway's relations with the Soviet Union: John Earl Haynes, Harvey Klehr, and Alexander Vassiliev, *Spies: The Rise and Fall of the KGB in America*, pp. 153–55.

357 "Hemingway could describe with truthfulness": Barea, "Not Spain, But Hemingway," *Horizon* (London 1941), pp. 350–61.

358 a jocular prenuptial "agreement": MG to EH, "Marriage Guaranty," undated, BU. Also quoted in Moorehead, *Selected*, pp. 80–81, and Kert, *Women*, p. 339.

358 Hemingway was unaware: "E wants me for himself altogether now," she told Grover, and hinted he should not write her anything that could not be shared: MG to Allen Grover, September 6, 1940, in Moorehead, *Selected*, pp. 101–3.

358 "she thinks now": EH to Edna Gellhorn, September 28, 1940, JFK.

358 he had been "busted": EW to Max Perkins, January 28, 1941, in Baker, *EH*, p. 359.

358 "the old commercial fisherman": EH to Maxwell Perkins, February 7, 1939, in Baker, *Selected*, p. 479.

358 "his mastery of the art of the narrative": EH's Nobel Prize citation is quoted on the Nobel Prize's website, www.nobelprize.org/nobel_prizes/literature/laureates/1954/.

360 "no intention of being a footnote": This much-repeated line (even used in an interview by Gellhorn's biographer, Caroline Moorehead) has proved impossible to source.

360 "an unpalatable truth": Official statement of the Martha Gellhorn Trust.

361 "This is the last good war": Whelan, *Capa*, p. 297.

362 "We do not employ Reds": Eaude, *Triumph at Midnight*, p. 114.

363 "*mi* shell-shock": AB to W. R. Wessel and William F. Stirling, June 23, 1944, BBC Written Archives Centre.

363 "the man who had left them to starve": *The Broken Root* (Faber and Faber, 1951), p. 56.

363 Ilsa spoke of the "heartbreaking" situation: IB to Margaret Weeden, November 14, 1946, IB papers.

363 "Querido Papa": Letters from the Barea children to AB, various dates, AB papers.

364 "the most successful visitor": Report from an anonymous official at the British Embassy in Buenos Aires to the BBC, May 15, 1956, WAC.

364 His body was cremated: Uli Rushby-Smith, e-mail to AV.

365 all of the papers she had with her: Uli Rushby-Smith, e-mail to AV.

365 "It is meaningless": IB to Margeret Weeden, December 25, 1957, IB papers.

GLOSSARY OF TERMS AND ABBREVIATIONS

alpargatas Rope-soled canvas shoes worn by many Spanish government soldiers

Asaltos Assault Guards, the blue-uniformed urban police of the Spanish Republic

CEDA (Confederación Española de Derechas Autónomas) Spanish confederation of right-wing groups, a Catholic political party

checa Slang term, derived from the name of the Tsarist secret police (*cheka*), for an extra-official interrogation and detention center operated by leftists

CNT (Confederación Nacional de Trabajo) Anarcho-syndicalist labor union

Comintern Communist (or Third) International, Moscow-directed worldwide union of all domestic Communist parties

Condor Legion A unit made up of Nazi German volunteers from the Luftwaffe (air force) and the Wehrmacht (Army) to fight for Spain's Nationalist rebels

Cortes Spanish parliament

Ejercito Popular The centralized Spanish government army, which superseded and replaced the militias of the early days of the Civil War

Escuadrilla España Air Squadron founded by André Malraux to fight for the Spanish Republic

FAI (Federación Anarquista Ibérica) Iberian anarchist federation

Falange Spanish fascist party founded by José Antonio Primo de Rivera

Generalitat Regional government of Catalonia

GRU Main intelligence directorate of the Soviet armed forces, the Russian military's foreign intelligence service

Guardia Civil Civil Guards, the paramilitary, largely rural Spanish national police force, known for their patent-leather tricorne hats

Junta Ruling council; in wartime Madrid, the Junta de Defensa was the committee that ran the city after the relocation of the government

NANA North American Newspaper Alliance, publishing syndicate made up of fifty major American newspapers

latifundistas Owners of huge feudal estates, mainly in the south of Spain

Loyalists Those loyal to the government of the Spanish Republic (see Republican)

Luftwaffe Nazi German air force

miliciano Member of the militias, soldiers (some affiliated with specific parties or unions) who volunteered to fight for the Spanish government

mono Jumpsuit, generally blue, worn by Loyalist militias

NKVD People's Commissariat of Internal Affairs: the Russian secret police (later the KGB)

Nationalists Those siding with the rebellion against the Republican government

PCE (Partido Comunista de España) Moscow-oriented Spanish Communist Party

POUM (Partido Obrera de Unificación Marxista) Primarily Catalan-based anti-Stalinist Marxist party

Popular Front Coalition of leftist, generally antifascist parties

Republicans Those in favor of republican government in Spain (see Loyalists); narrowly, moderate (nonsocialist) republicans

SAP (Sozialistische Arbeitpartei Deutschlands) German Socialist Workers' Party

SIM (Servicio de Información Militar) Spanish Republican government's secret police

UGT (Unión General de Trabajadores) Spanish Socialist trade union

BIBLIOGRAPHY

Allan, Ted. *This Time a Better Earth*. New York: William Morrow, 1939.

Auden, W. H., and Christopher Isherwood. *Journey to a War*. London: Faber and Faber, 1986.

Aznar Soler, Manuel, and Luis Mario Schneider. *Il congreso internacional de escritores antifascistas*. Valencia: Generalitat Valenciana, 1987.

Baker, Carlos. *Ernest Hemingway: A Life Story*. New York: Charles Scribner's Sons, 1969.

Baker, Carlos, ed. *Ernest Hemingway: Selected Letters 1917–1961*. New York: Charles Scribner's Sons, 1981.

Barea, Arturo. *The Broken Root*. Translated by Ilsa Barea. London: Faber and Faber, 1951.

Barea, Arturo. *The Forging of a Rebel*. Translated by Ilsa Barea. Introduction by Nigel Townson. New York: Walker and Company, 2001.

Barea, Arturo. *Palabras recobradas: textos ineditos*. Edited by Nigel Townson. Madrid: Debate, 2000.

Barea, Arturo. *Valor y miedo*. Barcelona: Plaza y Janes, 1984.

Barea, Ilsa. *Vienna*. New York: Alfred A. Knopf, 1966.

Barnouw, Erik. *Documentary: A History of the Nonfiction Film*. Oxford: Oxford University Press, 1993.

Beevor, Antony. *The Battle for Spain: The Spanish Civil War 1936–1939*. New York and London: Penguin Books, 2006.

Berdah, Jean-François. "Un réseau de renseignement antinazi au service de la République espagnole (1936–1939): Le mouvement *Neue Beginnen* et le *Servicio de Información Diplomático Especial* (SIDE)," in Fréderic Guelton and Abdil Bicer, *Naissance et evolution du renseignement dans l'espace Européen*. Vincennes: Service Historique de la Défense, 2006.

Bernier, Olivier. *Fireworks at Dusk: Paris in the Thirties*. Boston: Little, Brown, 1993.

Bolín, Luis. *Spain: The Vital Years*. Philadelphia: J. B. Lippincott, 1967.

Borkenau, Franz. *The Spanish Cockpit*. Foreword by Gerald Brenan. Ann Arbor: University of Michigan Press, 1963.

Brenan, Gerald. *The Spanish Labyrinth: The Social and Political Background of the Spanish Civil War*. Cambridge: Cambridge University Press, 2008.

Bruccoli, Matthew, ed. *The Only Thing That Counts: The Ernest Hemingway–Maxwell Perkins Correspondence*. New York: Simon & Schuster, 1996.

Buckley, Henry. *The Life and Death of the Spanish Republic: A Witness to the Spanish Civil War.* London: I. B. Tauris, 2013.

Bullock, Alan. *Hitler and Stalin: Parallel Lives.* New York: Vintage Books, 1993.

Capa, Robert. *Death in the Making.* Translation and preface by Jay Allen. New York: Covici Friede Publishers, 1938.

Capa, Robert. *Heart of Spain: Robert Capa's Photographs of the Spanish Civil War.* New York: Aperture Foundation, 1999.

Capa, Robert. *Slightly Out of Focus.* New York: Modern Library, 2001.

Carr, Virginia Spencer. *Dos Passos: A Life.* Evanston, IL: Northwestern University Press, 2004.

Cockburn, Claud. *Cockburn in Spain: Despatches from the Spanish Civil War.* Edited by James Pettifer. London: Lawrence and Wishart, 1986.

Cockburn. Claud. *Discord of Trumpets: An Autobiography.* New York: Simon & Schuster, 1956.

Cowles, Virginia. *Looking for Trouble.* New York and London: Harper and Brothers, 1941.

Cronin, Vincent. *Paris: City of Light 1919–1939.* London: HarperCollins Publishers, 1994.

Cunningham, Valentine, ed. *Spanish Front: Writers on the Spanish Civil War.* Oxford and New York: Oxford University Press, 1986.

De la Mora, Constancia. *In Place of Splendor: The Autobiography of a Spanish Woman.* New York: Harcourt, Brace & Company, 1939.

Delaprée, Louis. *The Martyrdom of Madrid: Inedited Witnesses (Le martyr de Madrid: témoignages inédits).* Madrid: NP, 1937.

Delmer, Sefton. *Trail Sinister: An Autobiography.* London: Martin Secker and Warburg, 1961.

Donaldson, Scott. *Archibald MacLeish: An American Life.* Boston: Houghton Mifflin, 1992.

Donaldson, Scott. *Fitzgerald and Hemingway: Works and Days.* New York: Columbia University Press, 2011.

Dos Passos, John. *Century's Ebb: The Thirteenth Chronicle.* Boston: Gambit, 1975.

Dos Passos, John. *The Theme Is Freedom.* New York: Dodd, Mead, 1956.

Dos Passos, John. *Travel Books and Other Writings, 1916–1941.* New York: Library of America, 2003.

Eaude, Michael. *Triumph at Midnight of the Century: A Critical Biography of Arturo Barea.* Brighton: Sussex Academic Press, 2009.

Eby, Cecil D. *Comrades and Commissars: The Lincoln Battalion in the Spanish Civil War.* University Park: Pennsylvania State University Press, 2007.

Ehrenburg, Ilya. *Memoirs 1921–1941.* Translated by Tatania Shebunina. Cleveland and New York: World Publishing Company, 1964.

Fischer, Louis. *Men and Politics.* Rahway, NJ: Duell, Sloan and Pierce, 1941.

Flanner, Janet. *Paris Was Yesterday, 1925–1939.* Boston: Mariner Books, 1988.

Fox, Soledad. *Constancia de la Mora in War and Exile.* Brighton: Sussex Academic Press, 2007.

Franklin, Sidney. *Bullfighter from Brooklyn.* Englewood Cliffs, NJ: Prentice-Hall, 1952.

Fraser, Ronald. *Blood of Spain: An Oral History of the Spanish Civil War.* New York: Pantheon, 1979.

Freundlich, Elisabeth. *The Traveling Years*. Translated by Elizabeth Pennebaker. Riverside, CA: Ariadne Press, 1999.

Fuentes, Norberto. *Hemingway in Cuba*. Secaucus, NJ: Lyle Stuart, 1984.

Gardiner, Muriel. *Code Name "Mary."* New Haven and London: Yale University Press, 1983.

Gazur, Edward. *Alexander Orlov: The FBI's KGB General*. New York: Carrol and Graf, 2002.

Gellhorn, Martha. *The Face of War*. New York: Atlantic Monthly Press, 1988.

Gellhorn, Martha. *The Heart of Another*. New York: Charles Scribner's Sons, 1941.

Gellhorn, Martha. *The Novellas of Martha Gellhorn*. New York: Vintage Books, 1991.

Gellhorn, Martha. *A Stricken Field*. Chicago: University of Chicago Press, 2011.

Gellhorn, Martha. *Travels with Myself and Another: A Memoir*. New York: Jeremy P. Tarcher/Putnam, 2001.

Gellhorn, Martha. *The View from the Ground*. New York: Atlantic Monthly Press, 1988.

Gide, André. *Return from the USSR*. Translated by Dorothy Bussy. New York: Alfred A. Knopf, 1937.

Gilbert, Martin. *A History of the Twentieth Century, Volume Two: 1933–1951*. New York: Avon Books, 1998.

Graham, Helen. *The Spanish Civil War: A Very Short Introduction*. Oxford: Oxford University Press, 2005.

Gunther, John. *Inside Europe*. New York: Harper and Brothers, 1936.

Hawkins, Ruth A. *Unbelievable Happiness and Final Sorrow: The Hemingway-Pfeiffer Marriage*. Fayetteville: University of Arkansas Press, 2011.

Hellman, Lillian. *An Unfinished Woman: A Memoir*. Boston: Little, Brown, 1997.

Hemingway, Ernest. *By-Line Ernest Hemingway: Selected Articles and Dispatches of Four Decades*. Edited by William White. New York: Scribner, 2003.

Hemingway, Ernest. *Death in the Afternoon*. New York: Scribner, 1996.

Hemingway, Ernest. *The Fifth Column and Four Stories of the Spanish Civil War*. New York: Scribner, 2003.

Hemingway, Ernest. *For Whom the Bell Tolls*. New York: Scribner, 2003.

Hemingway, Ernest. *To Have and Have Not*. New York: Scribner, 1996.

Hemingway, Ernest. *A Moveable Feast*. New York: Collier Books, 1987.

Herbst, Josephine. *Starched Blue Sky of Spain*. Introduction by Diane Johnson. New York: HarperCollins Publishers, 1991.

Hidalgo de Cisneros, Ignacio. *Cambio de Rumbo*. Vitoria: Ikusager Ediciones, 2001.

Isenberg, Sheila. *Muriel's War: An American Heiress in the Nazi Resistance*. New York: Palgrave Macmillan, 2010.

Ivens, Joris, dir. *The Spanish Earth*. Film. Commentary and narration, Ernest Hemingway. Photography by John Ferno. Film editor Helen Van Dongen. Contemporary Historians, 1937.

Ivens, Joris. *The Camera and I*. New York: International Publishers, 1969.

Jerrold, Douglas. *Georgian Adventure*. New York: Charles Scribner's Sons, 1938.

Josephson, Matthew. *Infidel in the Temple: A Memoir of the Thirties*. New York: Alfred A. Knopf, 1967.

Kennan, George F. *Memoirs 1925–1950*. New York: Pantheon, 1983.

Kershaw, Alex. *Blood and Champagne: The Life and Times of Robert Capa*. Cambridge, MA: Da Capo Press, 2004.

Kert, Bernice. *The Hemingway Women*. New York and London: W. W. Norton, 1983.

Knightley, Philip. *The First Casualty: The War Correspondent as Hero and Myth-Maker from the Crimea to Kosovo*. Baltimore, MD: Johns Hopkins Paperbacks, 2002.

Koch, Stephen. *The Breaking Point: Hemingway, Dos Passos, and the Murder of José Robles*. Berkeley, CA: Counterpoint, 2005.

Kowalsky, Daniel. *Stalin and the Spanish Civil War*. New York: Columbia University Press, 2004.

Krivitsky, W. G. *In Stalin's Secret Service*. New York: Harper and Row, 1939.

Langer, Elinor. *Josephine Herbst*. Boston: Atlantic Monthly Press/Little, Brown, 1984.

LaPrade, Douglas Edward. *Hemingway and Franco*. Valencia: Publicacions de la Universitat de Valencia, 2007.

Lazareff, Pierre. *Deadline: The Behind the Scenes Story of the Last Decade in France*. Translated by David Partridge. New York: Random House, 1942.

Ludington, Townsend. *Dos Passos: A Twentieth Century Life*. New York: Carroll and Graf, 1998.

Malraux, André. *Man's Hope*. Translated by Stuart Gilbert and Alastair Macdonald. New York: Modern Library, 1983.

Martínez de Pison, Ignacio. *To Bury the Dead*. Translated by Anne McLean. Swansea: Parthian Books, 2009.

Martinson, Deborah. *Lillian Hellman: A Life with Foxes and Scoundrels*. Berkeley, CA: Counterpoint, 2011.

Matthews, Herbert L. *The Education of a Correspondent*. New York: Harcourt, Brace, 1946.

Matthews, Herbert L. *The Yoke and the Arrows: A Report on Spain*. New York: George Braziller, 1957.

McBride, Robert Medill. *Spanish Towns and People*. New York: Robert M. McBride, 1931.

Meade, Marion. *Dorothy Parker: What Fresh Hell Is This?* New York: Penguin Books, 1989.

Mellow, James. *Ernest Hemingway: A Life Without Consequences*. Boston: Houghton Mifflin, 1992.

Merriman, Marion, and Warren Lerude. *American Commander in Spain: Robert Hale Merriman and the Abraham Lincoln Brigade*. Reno: University of Nevada Press, 1986.

Meyers, Jeffrey. *Hemingway: A Biography*. New York: Da Capo Press, 1999.

Miles, Jonathan. *The Dangerous Otto Katz: The Many Lives of a Soviet Spy*. New York: Bloomsbury USA, 2010.

Miller, Linda Patterson. *Letters from the Lost Generation*. New Brunswick, NJ: Rutgers University Press, 1991.

Montefiore, Simon Sebag. *Stalin: Court of the Red Tsar*. New York: Vintage Books, 2005.

Moorehead, Caroline. *Gellhorn: A Twentieth Century Life*. New York: Henry Holt, 2003.

Moorehead, Caroline. *Selected Letters of Martha Gellhorn*. New York: Henry Holt, 2006.

North, Joseph. *No Men Are Strangers*. New York: International Publishers, 1958.

Orlov, Alexander. *The Secret History of Stalin's Crimes*. New York: Random House, 1953.

Orr, Lois, with Charles Orr. *Letters from Barcelona: An American Woman in Revolution and Civil War*. Edited by Gerd-Rainer Horn. London: Palgrave Macmillan, 2009.

Orwell, George. *Homage to Catalonia*. New York: Harcourt, 1980.

Paul, Bart. *Double-Edged Sword: The Many Lives of Hemingway's Friend, the American Matador Sidney Franklin*. Lincoln: University of Nebraska Press, 2009.

Phillips, Henry Albert. *Meet the Spaniards: In Which Spain Is Seen Primarily Through the Life of the Spanish People*. New York: Robert M. McBride, 1933.

Pike, David Wingate. *France Divided: The French and the Civil War in Spain*. Brighton: Sussex Academic Press, 2011.

Preston, Paul. *The Spanish Civil War: Reaction, Revolution, and Revenge*. New York: W. W. Norton, 2006.

Preston, Paul. *The Spanish Holocaust: Inquisition and Extermination in Twentieth Century Spain*. New York, W. W. Norton, 2012.

Preston, Paul. *We Saw Spain Die: Foreign Correspondents in the Spanish Civil War*. London: Constable, 2008.

Quintanilla, Luis. *All the Brave: Drawings of the Spanish War*. Text by Elliott Paul and Jay Allen. Preface by Ernest Hemingway. New York: Modern Age Books, 1939.

Quintanilla, Paul. *Waiting at the Shore: Art, Revolution, War, and Exile in the Life of the Spanish Artist Luis Quintanilla*. Lulu Press (e-book), www.lqart.org, 2003.

Radosh, Ronald, Mary Habeck, and Gregory Sevostianov, eds. *Spain Betrayed: The Soviet Union in the Spanish Civil War*. New Haven and London: Yale University Press, 2001.

Ragsdale, Hugh. *The Soviets, the Munich Crisis, and the Coming of World War II*. Cambridge: Cambridge University Press, 2004.

Rampersad, Arnold. *Langston Hughes, Volume I: 1902–1941, I, Too, Sing America* (2nd ed.). Oxford and New York: Oxford University Press, 2002.

Regler, Gustav. *The Owl of Minerva*. New York: Farrar, Straus and Cudahy, 1959. Edited by Prof. Pierre Renouvin and Jean-Baptiste Duroselle. *Documents Diplomatiques Français*, 2nd series, vol. VII, www.diplomatie.gouv.fr/fr/photos-videos-et-publi cations/archives-et-patrimoine/publications-des-archives/article/documents-di plomatiques-francais-63592.

Reynolds, Michael. *Hemingway's Reading, 1910–1940: An Inventory*. Princeton, NJ: Princeton University Press, 1980.

Reynolds, Michael. *Hemingway: The 1930's*. New York: W. W. Norton, 1997.

Rollyson, Carl. *Beautiful Exile: The Life of Martha Gellhorn*. Lincoln, NE: Authors Guild Backinprint.com, 2007.

Salter, Cedric. *Try-Out in Spain*. New York: Harper and Brothers, 1943.

Schaber, Irme. *Gerda Taro: Une photographe revolutionnaire dans la guerre d'Espagne [Gerta Taro: Photoreporterin in spanischen Bürgerkrieg]*. Translated by Pierre Gallissaires. Monaco: Éditions du Rocher, 2006.

Schaber, Irme, Richard Whelan, and Kirsten Lubben. *Gerda Taro*. New York: International Center of Photography/Steidl, 2007.

Schoots, Hans. *Living Dangerously: A Biography of Joris Ivens*. Translated by David Colmer. Amsterdam: Amsterdam University Press, 2000.

Seale, Patrick, and Maureen McConville. *Philby: The Long Road to Moscow*. New York: Simon & Schuster, 1973.

Sheean, Vincent. *Not Peace But a Sword*. New York: Doubleday, Doran, 1939.

Smith, Richard K., and Cargill R. Hall. *Five Down, No Glory: Frank G. Tinker, Mercenary Ace in the Spanish Civil War*. Annapolis, MD: Naval Institute Press, 2011.

Spender, Stephen. *World Within World: The Autobiography of Stephen Spender.* New York: Modern Library, 2001.

Stansky, Peter, and William Abrahams. *Journey to the Frontier: Julian Bell and John Cornford: Their Lives and the 1930's.* London: Constable, 1966.

Stradling, Robert. *Your Children Will Be Next: Bombing and Propaganda in the Spanish Civil War 1936–1939.* Cardiff: University of Wales Press, 2008.

Szurek, Alexander. *The Shattered Dream.* Translated by Jacques and Hilda Grunblatt. New York: East European Monographs/Columbia University Press, 1989.

Thomas, Hugh. *The Spanish Civil War* (rev. ed.). New York: Modern Library, 2001.

Tomkins, Calvin. *Living Well Is the Best Revenge.* New York: Viking Press, 1971.

Townson, Nigel. *The Crisis of Democracy in Spain: Centrist Politics Under the Second Republic, 1931–1936.* Brighton: Sussex Academic Press, 2000.

Tremlett, Giles. *Ghosts of Spain: Travels Through Spain and Its Silent Past.* London: Bloomsbury, 2006.

Trogdon, Robert W. *Ernest Hemingway: A Literary Reference.* New York: Carroll and Graf, 1999.

Vernon, Alex. *Hemingway's Second War: Bearing Witness to the Spanish Civil War.* Iowa City: University of Iowa Press, 2011.

Watson, William Braasch, ed. *The Hemingway Review,* vol. 7, no. 2, Spring 1988.

Whelan, Richard. *Robert Capa: A Biography.* New York: Alfred A. Knopf, 1985.

Whelan, Richard. *This Is War!: Robert Capa at Work.* New York: International Center of Photography/Steidl, 2007.

Wyden, Peter. *The Passionate War: The Narrative History of the Spanish Civil War.* New York: Simon & Schuster, 1983.

Young, Cynthia, ed. *The Mexican Suitcase: The Rediscovered Spanish Civil War Negatives of Capa, Chim, and Taro.* New York: International Center of Photography/Steidl, 2010.

ACKNOWLEDGMENTS

Hotel Florida is built on the personal records of its principal subjects—Arturo Barea, Robert Capa, Martha Gellhorn, Ernest Hemingway, Ilsa Kulcsar, and Gerda Taro—and without the help of the keepers of those records, this book could never have been written. My deepest thanks go to Uli Rushby-Smith for welcoming me into her home and giving me permission to examine and use the Arturo and Ilsa Barea papers; to Cynthia Young, the curator of the Robert Capa archives at the International Center of Photography, for opening that collection (and the papers and photographic records of Gerda Taro) to me and enduring my endless questions about it; to Alexander Matthews, the executor of the estate of Martha Gellhorn, and Sean Noel of the Howard Gotlieb Archival Research Center at Boston University for granting me access to the papers of Martha Gellhorn; and to Kirk Curnutt of the Hemingway Foundation and Society, Michael Katakis, Simon & Schuster, Inc. (especially Yessenia Santos), and Susan Wrynn of the Ernest Hemingway Collection at the John F. Kennedy Presidential Library and Museum for allowing me to use material from the papers of Ernest Hemingway. I'd also like to thank the Columbia University Rare Book and Manuscript Library for making available the papers of Herbert L. Matthews, which provided a navigational third point for charting the comings and goings of some of my subjects.

For making the task of consulting all these resources easier, I'm grateful to Eugene Ludlow of the Barea archive, Claartje van Dijk at ICP, Ryan Hendrickson at Boston University, and Stephen Plotkin, now a reference archivist at the John F. Kennedy Library. Archival research is dark and lonely work, and they all helped to keep the darkness at bay.

I would also like to thank Roslyn Pachoca, a reference librarian, and others at the Library of Congress for help in tracing Ilsa Barea's *Telefónica*; the staff at the New York Public Library's cataloging and reading rooms, who guided me to obscure foreign and periodical publications; and Mark Bartlett and his colleagues at the New York Society Library, who let me treat their collection as an extension of my home bookshelves.

I owe an enormous debt to the scholars, historians, and other writers who have worked with this material before me, and in some cases are working on it still. Many are acknowledged in my bibliography and source notes, but some of them have gone out of their way to help me individually, answering my questions, pointing out my blunders, lending me books or films, or pointing me in the direction of interesting sources. I'm particularly (and alphabetically) grateful to Richard Baxell, Antony Beevor, Patrick,

Ramón, and George Buckley, Javier Cercas, Robert Coale, Mary Dearborn, Scott Donaldson, Michael Eaude, Soledad Fox, Joanna Godfry, Ray Hoff, Sheila Isenberg, Rickard Jorgensen, Stephen Koch, Anne Makepeace, José Martinez de Pison, Marion Meade, Caroline Moorehead, Paul Preston, Carl Rollyson, Irme Schaber, Patrick Seale, Peter Stansky, Nigel Townson, Alex Vernon, Alan Warren, William Braasch Watson, and Trisha Ziff; and, for help with German texts, Janice Kohn. I am also thankful for the support and probing questions from members of the New York University Biography Seminar, the first audience for early pages of this book. Without all these individuals, this book might have been written but would have been a lot less interesting, and accurate. Where it is *in*accurate, or uninteresting, the fault is mine.

There are no words to express my gratitude to my extraordinary agent, Eric Simonoff, who when I first showed him a proposal for *Hotel Florida* said the magic words "I want to sell it tomorrow." Nor to the man he sold it *to*: the equally extraordinary Jonathan Galassi, whom I've long valued as a friend and colleague, and have now come to cherish as an editor and publisher. I also thank Jonathan's wonderful team at Farrar, Straus and Giroux, including but not limited to Christopher Richards (a.k.a. Mission Control), Stephen Weil, Jennifer Carrow, Amber Hoover, Marion Duvert, Diana Frost, Jeff Seroy, Lenni Wolff, Jonathan Lippincott, Tal Goretsky, and my old Viking shipmate Lottchen Shivers; Alexandra Pringle and her colleagues at Bloomsbury, among them the ever-patient Bill Swainson and Madeleine Feeny; and my Spanish agent, Mònica Martín Berdagué, for her support and kindness.

Finally I'd like to acknowledge the friends who have graciously put up with my gossip about seventy-five-year-old events over lunches, dinners, and walks around the reservoir (you all know who you are); my loyal office assistants, Natasha and Tanaquil Stewart; and my family—Tom, Pamela, and Patrick—who teach me every day the importance of love and integrity.

INDEX

ILLUSTRATION CREDITS

Photographs by Robert Capa are copyright © International Center of Photography / Magnum Photos; photographs by Gerda Taro are copyright © International Center of Photography; photographs by Fred Stein are copyright © estate of Fred Stein, fredstein .com; and all are used courtesy of the International Center of Photography. Where no photographer's name is given, the photographer is unknown.

Arturo Barea. Estate of Arturo and Ilsa Barea
Francisco Franco. Photofest
Men and women piled on top of a car, Madrid, August–September 1936. Photograph by Robert Capa
Three World War I veterans at a peace rally, Verdun, France, 1936. Photograph by Robert Capa
Gerda Taro winking, Paris, 1935–36. Photograph by Fred Stein
Gerda Taro and Robert Capa, Paris, 1936. Photograph by Fred Stein
Ilse Kulcsar. Estate of Arturo and Ilsa Barea
Pauline Hemingway in a sailor's jersey. Ernest Hemingway Collection / John F. Kennedy Library
Ernest Hemingway fishing. Collection of the author
Martha Gellhorn. Photofest
John and Katy Dos Passos. Ernest Hemingway Collection / John F. Kennedy Library
Agricultural workers loading cart, Aragon front, Spain, August 1936. Photograph by Gerda Taro
Republican troop train departing for the front, Barcelona, August 1936. Photograph by Robert Capa
Training of the Popular Army, Valencia, Spain, May 1937. Photograph by Gerda Taro
Loyalist militiamen jumping over a gully, Córdoba front, Spain, September 1936. Photograph by Robert Capa
Remnants of apartment buildings after an air raid, Madrid, February 1937. Photograph by Robert Capa
International Brigaders firing through window, University City, Madrid, November–December 1936. Photograph by Robert Capa
Poster, "Madrid, the 'Military' Practice of the Rebels." Southworth Spanish Civil War Collection, Mandeville Special Collections Library, University of California, San Diego

Gerda Taro taking pictures at Guadalajara, Spain, 1937. Courtesy International Center of Photography

Ambulances. Ernest Hemingway Collection / John F. Kennedy Library

Gerda Taro on a bed, Paris, 1935–36. Photograph by Robert Capa

Robert Capa at the Segovia front, Spain, late May/early June 1937. Photograph by Gerda Taro

Ted Allan, book jacket photo from *This Time a Better Earth* (1939). Photograph by Sam Shaw, copyright © Sam Shaw, Inc., licensed by the Shaw Family Archives, Ltd., www .shawfamilyarchives.com, collection of the author

Air-raid victims in the morgue, Valencia, May 1937. Photograph by Gerda Taro

Burning truck, Battle of Brunete, Spain, July 1937. Photograph by Gerda Taro

Republican soldier in a tree, Teruel, Aragon front, Spain, December 21–24, 1937. Photograph by Robert Capa

Ernest Hemingway and Martha Gellhorn in fox coat. Ernest Hemingway Collection / John F. Kennedy Library

Ernest Hemingway and Joris Ivens. Ernest Hemingway Collection / John F. Kennedy Library

Langston Hughes, Mikhail Koltsov, Ernest Hemingway, and Nicolás Guillén. Yale Collection of American Literature, Beinecke Rare Book and Manuscript Library, Yale University

Father Lobo and Barea. Estate of Arturo and Ilsa Barea

Stalin and Ribbentrop. Photofest

Hemingway, Capa, Vincent Sheean, Herbert Matthews, and Hans Kahle at the Ebro, April 1937. Photograph by Henry Buckley, copyright © 2013 Patrick, Ramón and George Buckley, courtesy of the Arxiú Comarcal de l'Alt Penedès (ACAP), Fons Henry Buckley

Marineros bringing in the wounded, Rio Segre, Aragon front, near Fraga, Spain, November 7, 1938. Photograph by Robert Capa

Woman walking by a cart destroyed by fascist air bombs, along the road between Tarragona and Barcelona, January 15, 1939. Photograph by Robert Capa

Soldiers at the farewell ceremony for the International Brigades, Les Masies, Spain, October 25, 1938. Photograph by Robert Capa

Farewell parade for the International Brigades, Barcelona, Spain, October 28, 1938. Photograph by Robert Capa

Young girl in a refugee transit center, Barcelona, Spain, January 1939. Photograph by Robert Capa

Red box of the "Mexican Suitcase," the rediscovered negatives of the Spanish Civil War by Robert Capa, Gerda Taro, and Chim (David Seymour). Courtesy International Center of Photography

A NOTE ABOUT THE AUTHOR

Amanda Vaill is the author of the bestselling *Everybody Was So Young: Gerald and Sara Murphy—A Lost Generation Love Story*, which was a finalist for the National Book Critics Circle Award in biography, and *Somewhere: The Life of Jerome Robbins*, for which she was awarded a Guggenheim fellowship. In addition to writing the screenplay for the Emmy– and Peabody Award–winning public television documentary *Jerome Robbins: Something to Dance About*, she has also written features and criticism for a range of publications from *Allure* to *The Washington Post Book World*. She lives in New York City.

MUNICIPAL BONDAGE

Henry Alford

Random House
New York

Copyright © 1993 by Henry Alford
All rights reserved under International and Pan-American Copyright Conventions. Published in the United States by Random House, Inc., New York, and simultaneously in Canada by Random House of Canada Limited, Toronto.

Portions of this work were originally published, in different form, in *Mademoiselle, The New York Observer, Spy,* and *Vogue.*

Grateful acknowledgment is made to Bob Collier for permission to reprint "Affirmation" by Bob Collier. Copyright © 1990 by Bob Collier. Reprinted by permission.

Library of Congress Cataloging-in-Publication Data
Alford, Henry.
Municipal bondage: one man's anxiety-producing adventures in the big city / Henry Alford.
        p.   cm.
ISBN 0-679-41509-2
1. American wit and humor. I. Title.
PN6162.A365   1994   814'.54—dc20   93-21942

Manufactured in the United States of America
Book design by J. K. Lambert
2 4 6 8 9 7 5 3

First Edition

Contents

editor's uncanny eye for the proverbial diamond in the rough.

I bring homage to Susan Morrison, who, over the years, has proffered much encouragement and many assignments. A careful reader, a generous colleague, an individual sensitive to the subtle tensions at the intersection of syntax and word choice—a woman, in short, with many, many synonyms for *nuance*.

Writing this book required me to spend many hours sequestered within my apartment. I offer apology to those friends whose invitations I have rebuffed during the past year, fearful that the overexposure to nightlife might taint the winsome quality of my prose.

From my speeding roadster of journalistic ambition, I obsequiously tip my hat to Kurt Andersen and Graydon Carter, men of influence and suspenders.

I thank David Handelman, who assessed my raw talent and uttered the lustrous words "male model."

I thank those editors at glamorous magazines—Misses Bell, Caruso, Doppelt, and Keller, and Misters Kamp and Tyrnauer—who have helped me to slowly drain the profit margin of the Condé Nast empire.

Literary agent Laura Blake, prose stylist Jim Collins, Christie's guide Seth Flicker, mother figure Joanne Gruber, Bergdorf's shopper Michael Hainey, nubbins flack George Kalogerakis, foreign-lover enthusiast Richard Kaye, Zsa Zsa–channeler Bob Mack, poetry angel Jamie Malanowski, Democratic Convention driver Erica Marcus, food goddess Francine Maroukian, animal handler Jane McQueen-

What Is Owed

When asked by my publisher to supply this book's reading line—a reading line being the explanatory phrase that comes between a book's title and its author's name, such as "A Novel" or "A Long, Dreary History of Shoe Manufacturing in Wales by"—I submitted the accurate and quite charming "Comic Investigations and Essays." However, as the observant reader will note, it lost out to "One Man's Anxiety-Producing Adventures in the Big City"—a concession to said publisher, who felt that prospective book buyers would take one look at the phrase *comic investigations* and become instantly addled and confused in the manner of a country store clerk who has lost his spectacles in the barley.

So I would ask you to be slightly indulgent on the reading-line front. After all, not everything contained herein is anxiety-producing; the selections are not all adventures— some are essays, some are lists, and one of the selections takes place on the not-so-big-city-riddled island of Jamaica. (But these quibbles aside, let me simply say that I think this whole "One Man's" business is *brilliant*.)

I broach this topic because there is some confusion about what I do. People unfamiliar with my work have, in the past, asked me how my "skits" are progressing. Having been told that I once went to Christie's auction house and asked two employees there to appraise my bizarre, spurious heirlooms; having gleaned that I once took a cocker spaniel to the Holiday Inn at the Newark airport, where I groomed him unconventionally in an attempt to pass the National Dog Groomers Association of America's certification test, these people proceed to refer to my undertakings as "skits."

But I beg to differ. Skits, as we all know, involve a funny doorbell, bad Southern accents, and actor Harvey Korman. *Pranks, capers, monkeyshines*—call the more activity-based portions of this book what you will. But do not call them *skits*. (And if you call me a *jackanape*, I will slap you.)

I suppose I prefer to think of my contribution to the history of letters as taking the form of "investigations" because the term alludes to that aspect of my work that takes the form of investigative journalism. In almost every case, the people with whom I interact in this book did not know, at the time of interaction, that I was preparing to write about them. Posing as an individual devoid of ulterior motive, I entered these peoples' lives and allowed my innocent mien and neurotic stammerings to put them off guard.

That there is something manipulative and unsavory about this journalistic method I will not dispute; in deference to this, I have tried to write about others' professional, as opposed to private, behavior. In some instances, however, the professional/personal line is blurred, and discretion is

forced to take a backseat to journalistic vigor. Thus you will behold the clutter consultant who visited my apartment telling me about her imaginary friend, Claire; or the students at the Wilfred Beauty Academy—although they are expressly asked not to—warming up their lunches in the Academy's wig dryer.

Such disclosures may strike you as unseemly. Moreover, you may find that *my own* behavior as chronicled in this book exhibits a more-than-occasional lack of decorum. If such is the case, I would again ask for your indulgence; in vowing to push the envelope of the world around me, I have been given a compelling reason to vent many of my more unattractive personal habits.

For the record: I take responsibility for my actions; the views expressed herein—to the extent that there are views expressed herein—are my own. What I present as fact is, indeed, fact.

However, all this is not to say that the contents of th book are entirely of my own devising. No, no—mine life fairly teeming with little elves.

The Little Elves in My Life: An Appreciation

I would like to thank Random House's justly Jonathan Karp, who, after hearing me read at th Voice series several springs ago, wrote the letter that set this book in motion. Unfortunately, inquiry spelled my name A-F-F-O-R-D—a later contractual unzealousness—however,

What Is Owed

When asked by my publisher to supply this book's reading line—a reading line being the explanatory phrase that comes between a book's title and its author's name, such as "A Novel" or "A Long, Dreary History of Shoe Manufacturing in Wales by"—I submitted the accurate and quite charming "Comic Investigations and Essays." However, as the observant reader will note, it lost out to "One Man's Anxiety-Producing Adventures in the Big City"—a concession to said publisher, who felt that prospective book buyers would take one look at the phrase *comic investigations* and become instantly addled and confused in the manner of a country store clerk who has lost his spectacles in the barley.

So I would ask you to be slightly indulgent on the reading-line front. After all, not everything contained herein is anxiety-producing; the selections are not all adventures—some are essays, some are lists, and one of the selections takes place on the not-so-big-city-riddled island of Jamaica. (But these quibbles aside, let me simply say that I think this whole "One Man's" business is *brilliant.*)

I broach this topic because there is some confusion about what I do. People unfamiliar with my work have, in the past, asked me how my "skits" are progressing. Having been told that I once went to Christie's auction house and asked two employees there to appraise my bizarre, spurious heirlooms; having gleaned that I once took a cocker spaniel to the Holiday Inn at the Newark airport, where I groomed him unconventionally in an attempt to pass the National Dog Groomers Association of America's certification test, these people proceed to refer to my undertakings as "skits."

But I beg to differ. Skits, as we all know, involve a funny doorbell, bad Southern accents, and actor Harvey Korman. *Pranks, capers, monkeyshines*—call the more activity-based portions of this book what you will. But do not call them *skits*. (And if you call me a *jackanape*, I will slap you.)

I suppose I prefer to think of my contribution to the history of letters as taking the form of "investigations" because the term alludes to that aspect of my work that takes the form of investigative journalism. In almost every case, the people with whom I interact in this book did not know, at the time of interaction, that I was preparing to write about them. Posing as an individual devoid of ulterior motive, I entered these peoples' lives and allowed my innocent mien and neurotic stammerings to put them off guard.

That there is something manipulative and unsavory about this journalistic method I will not dispute; in deference to this, I have tried to write about others' professional, as opposed to private, behavior. In some instances, however, the professional/personal line is blurred, and discretion is forced to take a backseat to journalistic vigor. Thus you will behold the clutter consultant who visited my apartment telling me about her imaginary friend, Claire; or the students at the Wilfred Beauty Academy—although they are expressly asked not to—warming up their lunches in the Academy's wig dryer.

Such disclosures may strike you as unseemly. Moreover, you may find that *my own* behavior as chronicled in this book exhibits a more-than-occasional lack of decorum. If such is the case, I would again ask for your indulgence; in vowing to push the envelope of the world around me, I have been given a compelling reason to vent many of my more unattractive personal habits.

For the record: I take responsibility for my actions; the views expressed herein—to the extent that there are views expressed herein—are my own. What I present as fact is, indeed, fact.

However, all this is not to say that the contents of this book are entirely of my own devising. No, no—mine is a life fairly teeming with little elves.

The Little Elves in My Life: An Appreciation

I would like to thank Random House's justly esteemed Jonathan Karp, who, after hearing me read at the Writer's Voice series several springs ago, wrote the letter of inquiry that set this book in motion. Unfortunately, this letter of inquiry spelled my name A-F-F-O-R-D—a harbinger of later contractual unzealousness—however, I applaud my editor's uncanny eye for the proverbial diamond in the rough.

I bring homage to Susan Morrison, who, over the years, has proffered much encouragement and many assignments. A careful reader, a generous colleague, an individual sensitive to the subtle tensions at the intersection of syntax and word choice—a woman, in short, with many, many synonyms for *nuance*.

Writing this book required me to spend many hours sequestered within my apartment. I offer apology to those friends whose invitations I have rebuffed during the past year, fearful that the overexposure to nightlife might taint the winsome quality of my prose.

From my speeding roadster of journalistic ambition, I obsequiously tip my hat to Kurt Andersen and Graydon Carter, men of influence and suspenders.

I thank David Handelman, who assessed my raw talent and uttered the lustrous words "male model."

I thank those editors at glamorous magazines—Misses Bell, Caruso, Doppelt, and Keller, and Misters Kamp and Tyrnauer—who have helped me to slowly drain the profit margin of the Condé Nast empire.

Literary agent Laura Blake, prose stylist Jim Collins, Christie's guide Seth Flicker, mother figure Joanne Gruber, Bergdorf's shopper Michael Hainey, nubbins flack George Kalogerakis, foreign-lover enthusiast Richard Kaye, Zsa Zsa–channeler Bob Mack, poetry angel Jamie Malanowski, Democratic Convention driver Erica Marcus, food goddess Francine Maroukian, animal handler Jane McQueen-

Mason, unwitting investor Jane Redmond, snack-food consultant Ann Shayne, and attractive personal assistant Jess Taylor: You are *all* my children.

And, lest I overlook any names in this dizzy-making festival of cross-promotion, lest I fail to mention any single living person who might be in a position to further my station in life, I invoke two final entities.

I mention Michael Ovitz. And I mention God.

HOMESTEADING

Please Please Me

It is the curse of the single person to be a perpetual witness to the splendors and privileges of matrimony. And among the amenities matrimony lavishes upon its participants, perhaps most galling is marriage's institutionalization of gift-giving. I think of bridal-shower gifts, I think of wedding gifts, I think of anniversary gifts; I think and then I shudder. For, although I do not begrudge a happy pair the perquisites of union, there was a time when I could not help but feel that my own grim existence—an existence devoted largely to going home each night, putting on some plaintive honky-tonk music and then dancing with a mop—was the very type that would most benefit from an influx of bright and shiny objects. My married friends had both each other *and* a drawerful of sterling asparagus prongs, I thought. I had my work.

Oh, certainly, when at Christmastime family members

handed me a new appliance or a biography of Saint Ignatius of Loyola, they partly assuaged this feeling of deprivation.

But the effect was short-lived.

So it was with joyous excitement that I learned about a program within Bloomingdale's bridal registry wherein single people can register for gifts even if they are not getting married. Although self-registry is usually done by people who are moving into a new apartment, I decided that there was no reason why someone in my position shouldn't pick out merchandise simply because, as I would later tell salespeople, "I like to receive and unwrap presents."

I'm not particularly devoted to the Bloomingdale's style, so I checked to see if other stores had similar consolation-prize autoregistry programs. Employees at Saks Fifth Avenue and Alexander's told me that their stores had neither bridal nor self registries; a somewhat harried older woman at Lord and Taylor told me that her store had discontinued its registry but that it did have a personal shopper who would walk around the store with customers and help them pick out things to buy.

"And then could I have other people buy them for me?" I asked.

"No, these are things that *you* would buy," she said.

"Oh," I said. "So there's no one here whom I can tell what merchandise I'm interested in having other people buy for me?"

"No," she said, her face starting to drain of all expression.

"Could I tell *you* what merchandise I'm interested in having other people buy me?"

"No."

Chastened, I moved on. A saleswoman in Macy's bridal registry allowed me to register but seemed uncertain about the process. When I asked her if I should put my name in the space on the form marked GROOM or the one marked BRIDE, she stared at me as if her mind had suddenly and unexpectedly been transported to some very distant location. This prompted the woman who was standing behind me to suggest, "Why not put your name in both, like you're marrying yourself"—a comment discomfitting in the keenness of its perception. So I followed the woman's advice and moments later found myself racing through the store marking my selections on the form, fueled by the exciting possibilities of my burgeoning giftaganza: a microwave, an eleven-piece cookware set, a forty-five-inch rear-projection TV, a Chinese vase.

Although at Bergdorf Goodman no one had ever self-registered before, the head of the bridal registry was kind enough to get me special permission to do so. Permission granted, I was given a yellow pad and told to walk around the store and compile a list of the merchandise that I was interested in. Some thirty delicious minutes later, unable to find practical items that would suit me, I had put together a list composed of home furnishings and antiques that distinguished themselves by being both very expensive and very unappealing. But this would be a good test of friendship, I decided; for only a very *dear, dear* friend would buy me the pair of $950 Staffordshire St. Bernards or a $3000 Victorian coal scuttle.

Now I headed for Bloomingdale's. A kind woman in the bridal registry department there gave me a standard form with little boxes marked with categories like CRYSTALS, LINENS, etc., and told me to check the box on the form marked SELF. When I went off into the store to make my selections, I started to feel pangs of guilt about my indulgence at Bergdorf's and decided to try to work within a price range more realistic to my friends' incomes. A no-nonsense New York saleswoman in her late fifties took my form from me when I was finished walking through the store. She looked it over and became, in a word, *flapped.*

"Let me ask you something," she said to me, noticing that I had not signed up for any crockery. "Do you have *dishes?*"

I explained to her that I did. I asked her if they were a popular item in the Bloomingdale's registries.

"Well, it's . . ." She lost her train of thought. *"One* white plastic mug? You want someone to give you one plastic mug? Don't you ever have anyone over?"

"Sometimes," I said, not wanting to get too deep into the particulars of my private life. "But I already have one mug, so I just need the one other," I added.

She looked at me skeptically but decided to let it go.

"Garfield underpants?" she said. "You want someone to go into the boys department and . . ."

"Yes. I like them," I cut her off, anxious not to have the entire bridal registry department apprised of my taste in undergarments.

"Potato chips?" she asked, referring to my brief foray into the Bloomingdale's deli. "What do they come in?"

"A bag," I explained calmly.

"You think someone is going to buy you a *bag* of potato chips for a dollar twenty-five and then have them sent to you?" This was clearly more than she could handle. "Let me ask you something—and I'm not trying to give you a hard time here. But you've only signed up for six things here. I'm sure you have more than six friends."

I nodded.

"Well, then what is the *seventh* person going to buy?"

This seemed an odd question—first she had bullied me about my selections and now she was suggesting that I hadn't made enough of them. I explained to her that I would be very lucky indeed if six of my friends saw fit to take time off from their busy schedules and come buy me gifts. She agreed with this and, after explaining her bafflement with my selections, she ended our discussion by explaining that it would take about ten days for my selections to show up on the computer.

The following week my friend Michael went to Bergdorf's to buy me a gift. Michael expressed to the saleswoman who showed him the merchandise his surprise that my chosen objects could be quite so costly. When Michael explained that he hoped to spend something in the neighborhood of $20 on a gift, the saleswoman went to the trouble of explaining to Michael that *many* people who come to Bergdorf's can't afford the merchandise.

"I don't understand why he picked these things," a slightly confused Michael told the woman. "He . . ."

Laying her hand on Michael's arm in a sympathetic gesture, the saleswoman explained to her young customer, *"He obviously likes antiques."*

Two days later my friend Erica presented me with the bag of potato chips from Bloomingdale's. I was touched by her thoughtfulness and refrained from commenting on the absence of dip.

Michael's efforts, Erica's results—I have been paid a tribute that heretofore I would never have thought imaginable. I am witness to the breadth of my friends' affection for me and, through them, to the breadth of two New York department stores' affection for me. Although I am in other ways a pawn of the marriageocracy, I am less at odds with the likelihood that I will continue to lead a life in which non-birthday and non-Christmas gifts remain unsanctioned.

I have my friends. I have my chips.

WHAT IF UNEMPLOYED ACTORS WORKED IN BANKS INSTEAD OF RESTAURANTS?

10:14 A.M. Branch manager fires singer–dancer–teller because she wasn't making interesting "choices."

10:49 A.M. Ingenue teller decorates brass nameplate area with loathsome Pierrot dolls.

11:07 A.M. Teller gives customer ten singles, vocalizing, "Ten! Tin! Tan! Tawn! Toe! Too!"

1:28 P.M. Competition among tellers to work at window closest to surveillance camera results in tears and vicious gossip.

1:40 P.M. Security guard dons bulletproof vest in attempt to protect his "instrument."

2:31 P.M. Loan officer presses face in sand of canister-type ashtray in preliminary phase of "mask work."

2:39 P.M. Middle-aged comptroller sees his own wrinkly face reflected in bulletproof glass and wails, "I shall *never* play the Dane!"

2:45 P.M. Man in torn T-shirt enters bank; surly "Method teller" has arrived for work.

2:59 P.M. Bank robber's forceful "Put your hands up!" unleashes frenzy of precision dancing.

WHAT IF YOUR DOG DECIDED TO DO
A LITTLE REMODELING?

First Week   Dog gnaws blueprints; distributes spitty remnants amongst favorite rubber toys.

Second Week   Dog lodges snout between contractor's legs for genital update.

Third Week   Dog becomes irritable and vexed at mention of plaster's "scratch coat."

Fourth Week   Dog has all kitchen cabinet doors soldered shut in attempt to thwart chuckwagon.

Fifth Week   Dog announces he will paint whole apartment Bone.

WHAT IF THE MAFIA HAD ITS OWN
EPONYMOUS FRAGRANCE?

First Week Mobsters copyright slogan "Mafia: For all the men you are . . . and all the men you off."

Second Week *New York Post* runs front-page story with headline GOODSMELLAS!

Third Week Bloomingdale's lines up nine perfume sprayers in a row for gangland-style sprayfest.

Fourth Week Sedan barreling down Brooklyn-Queens Expressway suddenly changes direction: Carmine "the Snake" Persico has forgotten his atomizer.

Fifth Week Overapplication of Mafia short-circuits undercover cop's wire; bathroom stall in Italian restaurant becomes his grisly death crib.

Sixth Week Mob taps actress Talia Shire to be spokesperson for companion scent, Red Sauce.

Seventh Week Informant found bludgeoned to death in trunk of car, Mafia applicator wand placed in mouth.

Eighth Week Large cloud appears over Phoenix skyline: wiseguy in witness relocation program has daubed Mafia on all pulse points.

A Cluttered Existence

Optimist that I am, I have long allowed myself to believe that my life would be ameliorated by having a clutter consultant visit my home. Periodicals, mail, strange and unnecessary requests for money: my apartment is a glowing tribute to my inability to divest.

My feelings about my home are exacerbated by the fact that, having misspent a portion of my adulthood browsing through magazines and coffee-table books that extoll the virtues of the well-appointed residence, I have been bombarded with images of others' propensity and rationales for embracing a starkly minimalist or all-white aesthetic. "[W]e are fascinated by the void," one London couple said of themselves when *House & Garden* photographed their completely barren apartment. "The traditional, unhygienic houses one finds in the U.K., with fabrics and vases and cats everywhere, fill us with horror." A couple in *World of* mostly in their thirties, and was taught by a "career/stress counselor in private practice." A twinkly-eyed, middle-aged woman with ready amounts of alertness and delight, she has the perpetual look of someone who has just been given a large gift. Chief among her tenets of clutter control: Clutter is "whatever *you* think is clutter"; you should work on your clutter fifteen minutes a day, always with a specific goal; you should have folders, each with a label, with which to file loose papers (the teacher, oddly, explained that she has a file labeled "Diseases"). This whole process should be aided by *reframing*—constantly asking yourself, "Do I need it?" "Do I want it?" and "Do I love it?"

Before the class broke for intermission, the teacher encouraged us to find a "support person," someone we would call weekly to discuss clutter goals with. Neatly dodging a woman whose seven interruptions of the teacher in the first hour and a half had suggested a relationship to stackable drawers and the Hold Everything catalog far more empassioned than I thought I could feign interest in on a weekly basis, I approached a friendly-looking, slightly disheveled man who appeared to be in his early sixties. Pointing at the most attractive woman in the room, he explained that he was going to ask her out for coffee and "clutter support." However, he said that if the woman in question turned him down, he would come back to me.

Several minutes later he returned.

"No luck, huh?" I asked.

"Well . . ." he said, looking at the floor.

We exchanged phone numbers.

When the class reconvened, the teacher explained that she was going to lead us on a three-minute visualization, as had been mentioned in the course catalogue. She turned off the overhead lights. Various members of the class reached out to pull their satchels and grocery bags in close to them, the room giving birth to what sounded like several thousand candy wrappers being anxiously crinkled. The teacher encouraged us to breathe deeply. "Relax your feet . . . relax your shins . . . relax your knees," she intoned, slowly working her way up the body until we had achieved an approximation of bodily Jell-O.

Then came the visualization: we were to conjure up first a clutter "problem area" in our homes, then a successful decluttering of that problem area, and finally, the arrival of a photographer from *House Beautiful.* I encountered no difficulty bringing to mind my problem area (that part of my living room floor that my employment as a journalist has led me to saddle with large stacks of periodicals and newspapers); indeed, I even saw myself clearing the area. When the *House Beautiful* photographer arrived, we chatted and had coffee.

It all seemed quite effortless.

But a week later, my clutter remained unchanged.

=

What can be said about my ensuing relationship with my support person can also be said about Chekhov: it started slow, and then it tapered off.

In our first weekly phone call, I learned that he had been

unsuccessfully "sharing goals" over the phone with another support person for five years. When, the next week, neither of us had achieved our goals, he suggested that, if we had still not achieved them by the following week's phone appointment, that we "bookend"—tackle our problem areas immediately upon hanging up—and then call each other (or leave a message on each other's answering machine) to report that we had completed our tasks.

Suddenly the idea that another adult was going to leave a message on my machine explaining that he had moved a pile of magazines off his coffee table was profoundly irritating to me. I thought about our relationship: Did I want it? Did I need it? Did I love it?

Two weeks later, due to mutual apathy, we stopped calling each other.

=

I then spent thirty dollars to join five women at the teacher's apartment (quite tidy) for a monthly two-hour meeting of a support group. "How's this month been?" the teacher asked the three regulars who sat together on the couch.

"A nightmare," said one of them unironically. "A *nightmare . . .*"

Toward the end of the session, the teacher stood and turned off all the lights in the apartment. However, this time around, I was unable to visualize. Plunged into darkness with six female strangers in an unfamiliar apartment, all I could think of was those parties I attended as an adolescent, whereat the installation of a blacklight bulb into a lamp would suddenly render a fellow eight-grader's living room a murky, shadowy "make-out room."

This was not relaxing.

I was having problems letting go.

=

Two weeks later, realizing that I had affected no change to my apartment, I called the teacher and made an appointment for her to perform a one-hundred-dollar, two-hour consultation in my home. When she arrived, I pointed out my problem area: the fifty-five inch stack of old *New York Times*es; the twenty-three inches of *The New Yorker* and *Vanity Fair*; the twenty-two inches of *Esquire*, *The New Republic*, and *GQ*; the twenty inches of *Harper's* and *Spy*; the seventeen inches of *Entertainment Weekly*, *House & Garden*, *Mirabella*, *Vogue*, *Metropolitan Home*, and a paranoiac journal called *American Survival*; the twelve inches of *Newsweek*; the twelve inches of *Premiere*; the seven inches of *The New York Observer*; and the four inches of *Variety* and *The Village Voice Literary Supplement*.

"I'm having problems letting go," I explained.

"I can see!" she responded.

She wondered if the publications were related to my work; prevaricating, I told her no, that I tutored English and had no professional need for them.

"I was thinking that I could file to become a branch of the New York Public Library system," I told her.

She smiled indulgently.

I also tried to impress upon her my emotional attachment to the periodicals.

"It's not just a subscription," I explained, "it's a *relationship.*"

She nodded her head sympathetically.

"In fact, some of my best relationships seem to be my subscriptions to magazines," I mumbled.

After I had thrown away all the issues of one magazine that I decided I did not want/need/love (*Newsweek*), dismantled several "nests" of papers and assorted flotsam, and pledged to recycle all of the *New York Times*es, the teacher encouraged me to focus on my "one shots"—magazines that I buy individually at the newsstand.

"Like take *Mirabella,*" she said, picking up an issue of that magazine. "Is this the kind of magazine that you're going to keep and read every article, or just *some* articles?"

I explained that I had bought that issue of the magazine because it contained a profile of a favorite novelist who is not often written about.

"Are you going to keep the article or are you going to let it go?" she asked.

"I could let it go," I said. "I feel like I've done the article."

"So you're ready to let go of the magazine?" she asked.

"I . . . I think I could do that."

"Very interesting. Your words said that, but your non-verbal was a little hesitant."

Some two minutes later, we decided that I would keep the article but throw out the magazine. When the article had been put in its "home" (a folder), the teacher helped me to put all of my issues of *GQ, House & Garden,* and *Vanity Fair* on an empty shelf of my bookshelf, where she felt their smooth, white bindings would be a handsome addition.

When we had finished, I sighed deeply. It had occurred to me that it would be interesting to see how odd the nature of someone's relationship to clutter could be before it would raise eyebrows. Thus did I proceed to tell the teacher that the reason why I had had such difficulty letting go of the magazines and periodicals was because their stacks formed the playground of a special playmate.

"I've always had a little imaginary friend," I told her.

"I did, too," she responded.

"Really?" I asked incredulously.

"Oh, yes."

"He would . . . he likes to spend time here on the magazines," I said of mine, "and that was why I think it was so hard to let go."

"Because his security area was the magazines," she explained. "And *your* security area is the magazines."

"Exactly," I said. "He liked to come with his family and picnic on the back issues of *Harper's.*"

She smiled attentively.

I asked her if her imaginary friend was tied to her problem with clutter; she said no, and that she had had hers when she was young and without siblings.

"Mine is [named] Dr. Kellner," I said.

"*Doctor* Kellner?" she asked, her interest piqued.

"Yes."

"Okay."

"He's a, he's a nose and throat specialist."

"Oh," she exclaimed, "he's a real doctor!"

"He's a specialist," I reiterated.

"A specialist!"

Her expression was equal parts awe and maternal pride—in the world of imaginary friends, I had decidedly married *up*.

Shortly thereafter, we tackled my closet. Then, just before leaving, the teacher enthusiastically encouraged me to come back to the support group.

When she had gone, I cast my eye over the newly created areas of whiteness and organization in my apartment. I saw nooks and crannies where formerly there had only been effluvia and cloggage.

I smiled, experiencing a sensation of satisfaction and completion.

I had let go.

But underneath this sense of completion lurked a tinge of disquiet; disquiet and, perhaps, a touch of remorse about Dr. Kellner.

I would not fully understand these feelings until two weeks later, when I rented a video of the true crime classic *In Cold Blood* and was reacquainted with the name of the family so brutally bludgeoned therein: Clutter.

WHAT IF THE BRONTË SISTERS HAD BEEN A HEAVY-METAL BAND?

1826   Emily rejects ritual indoctrination in the domestic arts; vows to create a "towering wall of sound."

1835   Charlotte regales parsonage with blistering viola solo.

1837   After signing with P. T. Barnum, Brontë Sisters go on tour opening for the Swedish Nightingale, Jenny Lind.

1842   Anne throws sweat-drenched bonnet into seething concert crowd at Albert Hall.

1847   Emily publishes *Wuthering Heights,* Charlotte publishes *Jane Eyre;* Anne goes into jealous tailspin and starts to experiment with sherry.

1848   Brontë Sisters lock manager, Mrs. Rochester, in attic.

1849   Charlotte returns to public house to trash furniture and have sex with publican.

In Search of . . . Nubbins

Obsession begets enterprise. In the early part of 1988, I witnessed a disquieting phenomenon taking place in the pages of *The New York Times:* the otherwise admirable and level-headed restaurant reviewer Bryan Miller was, in his descriptions of various foods, making repeated use of the word *nubbin.* In one review, Mr. Miller explained that radiatore are "little nubbins of pasta with holes in the middle." At Metro restaurant, he encountered "lobster bisque holding sweet nubbins of meat." At Lutèce, he groused, "The nubbins of escargot are lost in their garlicky log of brioche."

Not numbering Mr. Miller amongst my acquaintances, I could only speculate as to what dark, sinister forces were wreaking havoc with his brain each time that he injected his prose with this term; I imagined that, after years of writing about food, he had begun to find *bit, morsel, touch, dollop, soupçon, sprinkle, smidgen, pinch, tidbit, sliver, hint, hair, sprig, dash, shred, whit, driblet, scintilla, trace, tittle, iota, fleck, gobbet, snippet, smithereen, shivereen, shive, snick, chip, nip, snip, flinder, flitter,* and *flake*—like so much of the food forced on him—thoroughly tired and overdone.

But, casting aside my preferred mode of inquiry (idle speculation), I endeavored to give my many nubbin-related questions the full brunt of my journalistic powers. I wondered: Is the term being used by other members of the food community? Is it here to stay? And does it have anything to do with television's beloved fabric-softening bear, Snuggles?

I called twenty-five New York City food experts and identified myself as a journalist hot on the nubbins trail. Neither Barry Wine, the owner-chef of the Quilted Giraffe, nor Milton Parker, the owner of the Carnegie Deli, had ever heard of nubbins. Mr. Parker was quite vehement—"Not even in Jewish. If you want to say 'a pinch,' say 'a pinch'! . . . I'm in this business fifty years, I would *never* use this expression."

Other responses evidenced the term's multiplicity of connotations. Mitchell R. Woo, the chef at the Empire Diner, said, "It sounds like a tiny nodule"; 21 Club chef Anne Rosenzweig responded, "It sounds like little ends of pinkies"; cookbook author Michael McLaughlin thought "Nubbins was a character in a Tolkien book"; Stuart Lichtenstein, the owner of Sardi's, told me, "It sounds like some sort of growth." Mimi Sheraton, Mr. Miller's predecessor at the *Times,* responded, "Nubbins has all the makings of a fast-food chain. You could serve only small, stunted, and ugly food—misshapen mushrooms, mutant potatoes, scraps from other restaurants that you dip in batter and deep-fry. You could hire a staff that looks like nubbins, too."

For Ansell Hawkins, the general manager of the Odeon, and caterer Robert Cacciola, the word had sexual connotations. Mr. Hawkins: "It sounds like duck testicles. Or what a dirty man would call his six-year-old niece: 'Come here, Nubbins!' " Mr. Cacciola: "It sounds like a small penis. It's a Mrs. Field's word. It sounds like a little snacky thing."

=

Shortly after I thought I had finished with my battery of phone calls, I remembered reading about a psychic named Christina Lynn Whited who claimed to be channeling the spirit of the late genius chef James Beard. If anyone would know the score on nubbins, I thought, it would be Mr. Beard—he wrote his first cookbook because he was so frustrated by hostesses serving nothing but what he called "doots" (hors d'oeuvres); his *New Fish Cookery* includes the immortal line, "Here are grunions at their best."

Sadly, however, when I contacted Miss Whited, she said that she would be unable to summon Mr. Beard for me— "James is off working on another cookbook and is generally not available for these kinds of interviews." But she did offer this: "I would imagine that he is familiar with nubbins. . . . Nubbins is very evocative of the fairy domain and the elfin kingdom. It might be appropriate for a childrens' and fairies' cookbook that James and I are writing for eight-year-olds." She concluded, "James's spirit is a rearrangement of other elements from the past. There is a part of us all that is eternal, that is almost always available to be channeled. Nubbins might have a more limited life span."

=

Although the majority of the responses that I received dwelled upon negative connotations, it was clear that I had touched a nerve. After publishing a magazine article in which I detailed Miss Whited's and others' responses, people—readers, friends, and family—began sending me their sightings of the word, forming a sort of unofficial *nubbin* vigil. Eric C. Trefelner, M.D., of Yale University's School of Medicine cited a reference in *Genitourinary Tract Diseases Syllabus* (1986) to a "lower pole nubbin"; a man in Seattle found a cartoon in a 1958 publication called *Six HO Railroads You Can Build* in which an exasperated model-railroad enthusiast (he is holding two ends of track that don't quite reach) cries out, "Oh, Nubbins!"

Nubbins elicited comment and response. Sightings continued to pour in; I learned that my nubbins article had been tacked up over the water cooler in the offices of *Gourmet.* When a colleague's unprompted use of the word in an article in *Rolling Stone* was followed a week later by a TV writer friend's unprompted use of the word on *Sisters,* I started to have a strange, unsettling fear. Namely, that nubbins was an alien being and I was its human host.

To my own mind, nubbins had always conjured up the

image of a calorie-rich snack food. Having misspent a portion of my adolescence in the 1970s as a witless pawn of
advertising and food trend, I was all too familiar with a
particular type of food product with which food manufac-
turers flooded the market: a tan, spreadable chemical creme
that went by the name Koogle; a boxed cake mix that, when
enlivened by water and vinegar, allowed you to make a cake
right in the mix's very packaging; a Bundt cake mix whose
squeeze packets of blackish paste yielded the disturbing
promise of a Tunnel of Fudge.

And so I latched onto the idea of turning my *idée fixe*
into a marketable, snacklike confection.

I would launch my own cottage industry.

I would be purged.

=

In its initial stage, a creative project is best approached
purely instinctively; thus can the homely offspring of impulse and whim be borne and then promptly abandoned.
This dictum at my fore, I jotted down my first approach:

Nubbins

20 Tootsie Rolls, bit in half
½ c. cornmeal
1 egg
A lot of lard

Put egg and ¼ c. water in a bowl; whisk for 1 min.
Melt lard in skillet. Soak Tootsie bits in egg mixture,

3–5 min. Roll each in cornmeal. Fry nubbins 2 min. or until cornmeal sac turns golden brown.

The best nubbin is one that is uniformly covered with a thin layer of crispy cornmeal. However, given Tootsie Rolls' inclination, when introduced to heat, to become overly relaxed, this is not always possible. Do not become alarmed when molten Tootsie bursts from its sac; simply scoop the bubbling mass up and, putting it on a plate, manipulate it into a pleasing shape. When reconstructing nubbins on the plate, the ratio between Toosie Roll and cornmeal is entirely at your own discretion; however, avoid serving anyone a big clot of burnt sac.

After diligently carrying out these instructions one afternoon in my kitchen, I discarded this recipe; its results were not delicious.

Over the next eight months I tried some nineteen different nubbin variants. Almost all were sweet; all were bite-sized. I traversed the world of yummy, snacky eatables, from corn puffs to pecan bars to marshmallow-filled profiteroles. An episode of *Nova* helped me with terminology: I learned that the texture of a snack food when it is in your mouth is referred to as its *mouth-feel;* the gradations of resistance it offers while being eaten (as measured by the electrical activity in the mouth's muscles) is referred to as its *chew profile.*

My breakthrough occurred shortly after I started making my own French bread. Buttons of French bread, each with

Although I realized that these letters were probably sent to anyone who submitted letters (when I later wrote the two companies using another name and said that I had invented a cookie called Lacey Unmentionables, Eagle expressed interest, but Brach's did not), these two missives were as sightings of land amidst an ocean of rejection. I excitedly sent off a proposal for a mass-market version of Nubbins: a canister, similar to the ones containing Pillsbury Poppin' Fresh products, would be filled with pieces of dough wrapped around disks of chocolate, which consumers would cook on a griddle.

When I had heard nothing after ten days, I upped the ante by sending Brach's and Eagle an idea for a TV ad:

Possible TV Ad for "Nubbins"

In the foreground we see a group of thirty or so hungry, waifish children dressed in rags. Dickensian squalor. In the background, Nubbins are being made by a man wearing a hat emblazoned with the Nubbins logo. The children, addressing the man, sing an impassioned version of Neil Young's rock 'n' roll classic, "Southern Man."

> Nubbins Man, better keep your head,
> Don't forget what your cookbook says.
> Nubbin change gonna come at last,
> Just keep those bread sacs from burnin' fast.

(Children undulate during guitar solo, striking poses of intense need and desire. A solo vocalist breaks loose from the rabble and sings directly to camera.)

I've had cotton candy, I've had Jax,
Appalling "Lite" ranch chips and other snacks,

(Then, suddenly drawing a bloodied knife from beneath his rags)

Swear by God I'll stab them in the back!

(Then, as the electric guitars start to pulsate and build in fiery climax, the children all rush up to the stove with looks of abject craving.)

I hear fryin'
And eggshells crackin'.
How long? How long?
Ah! Nubbins Man!

Seven weeks later I received a form rejection letter from Brach's corporate counsel; a week after that I received a letter from Eagle stating that my idea was being held "for future consideration." After waiting another month and a half, I called Eagle and spoke with a young woman in the marketing dept. In an attempt to stoke the fire, I told the woman, "I've had some interest about Nubbins from a movie studio. I'm not at liberty to say *which* studio—but it's Disney."

She explained that it was almost certain that the company would not be pursuing my idea.

"I think they're thinking along the California Raisin–Gummi Bears lines," I said, referring, in the first instance, to the wrinkly entity that went from being a food to a commercial to a TV show to a toy and, in the latter instance, to the chewy delight that went from being a candy to a TV show about and sponsored by the candy.

"We have to be really neutral and this is kind of explicit in parts," she said. "We go through an ad agency. . . ."

"They didn't like the song I submitted—they thought that was a little frightening," I said. "But I think the opportunities for ancillaries are very exciting—the T-shirt, the gimme cap, the fragrance."

She explained that my idea would be kept on file, adding, "but I don't want to get your hopes up."

"So you weren't really interested," I said, forlorn that she couldn't grasp the overwhelming beauty of a fragrance vial bearing the name Nubbins.

"The interest is always there in anything. But as to the *degree* of interest . . ."

=

When the reticence with which my brainchild was met by the corporate world began to gnaw at my confidence and enthusiasm, I decided to approach the marketplace in a more direct manner. It had long occurred to me that the Nubbins might translate well to the idiom of the street fair. Shaved ice drenched with syrups whose flavors are advertised as "cherry, lemon, or blue"; pieces of fried dough glistening with tragic dermatological consequence—this might be the very backdrop against which to showcase my Nubbins to their best advantage.

I set my sights on the Feast of San Gennaro, the street fair that draws over 3 million New Yorkers and visitors to

Little Italy each September. Knowing that I had neither the stamina nor the courage (nor, for that matter, the vendor's license) to have my own booth for the entire eleven-day run of the Feast, I decided instead that I would try to join forces with another vendor. I called the San Gennaro Society; a man with a hoarse, New Yorky rasp told me that all prospective vendors should report to the "trailer office" at 195 Hester Street between ten A.M. and five P.M. on September third, a few days before the Feast was to commence. Hying myself to this location on the appointed day, I climbed three wooden steps and knocked on the door of the trailer parked on the side of the street. A teenage boy opened the door for me, revealing a plump woman in her sixties adorned with a royal blue sweatshirt and with two pink hair curlers atop her head.

"Can I help you?" she asked, her voice a mixture of warmth and gravel.

"Yes. Is this the place where people who want to be vendors come?"

"What do you sell?"

"I've, unh . . . I've invented a new snack food."

"Oh, really?" she asked, not all that interested. "What is it?"

"They're called Nubbins. It's like French bread with melted chocolate inside it. I'm wondering if it'd be possible to supply it to someone who would sell it at his stand."

She looked concerned.

"It's French bread with chocolate?" she asked.

I nodded.

She visibly shuddered.

"Oooh," she said, grimacing, "you just sent *shivers* down my spine."

"Well, you've had croissants with chocolate inside them before, right?" I tried to reason. "It's like that." I described their appearance as "lovely."

She looked down at the floor as if averting the sight of blood. "That would be very difficult to get someone to resell."

Several seconds later, there was a knock on the trailer's door. The boy opened the door and, seeing a young Asian man, yelled, "Buffalo wings!"

The Asian man chuckled and said, "Right." The woman guided him to a table where a man in his sixties, previously unseen by me, was stationed. This older man greeted the younger man, "Hello, Buffalo Wings," and then asked him to fill out a form.

The woman returned to me and said, "Now are we through?"

I said that I supposed we were and left.

Mulberry Street was dotted with vendors' booths in varying states of readiness for the Feast. Having decided that—if given the chance—I would cook my Nubbins on a cast-iron griddle that I would put on top of a vendor's grill, I proceeded to ask three different vendors if they would let me set up shop with them. I offered them what I thought was an exorbitant amount of money—three hundred dollars a day. They all declined. Their responses: "It wouldn't work out," "I can't give up the grill space," and "I've already got the sausage."

=

Before I returned to the site of the Feast to plead my case again the next week, I changed the recipe for Nubbins. Not sure that I would be able to sell them at the Feast, I had begun to pursue getting my own vendor's license from the Board of Health's permit division. However, since the application for such prohibited the sale of "home-prepared foods," I became anxious that my home-prepared French bread might lead to my arrest. At the time, a friend of mine had taken to making the Italian bread focaccia by buying pizza dough at a pizza parlor (most will do this, charging three or four dollars for enough dough to make one pie), then taking it home and covering it with olive oil, parmesan, and herbs. Thus, engaging in the kind of last-minute retooling that can so often elevate the merely mediocre into the truly brilliant, I was now buying pizza dough at pizza parlors, wrapping hanks of it around disks of Droste bittersweet chocolate, and then cooking the resultant bundle in a little oil on a griddle.

=

When I returned to the Feast, it was with some of the feelings of anxiety and protectiveness evidenced in mothers who are interviewing prospective nannies. Having, for the past nine months, nurtured my creation within the confines of my own home, I had now reached the potentially heart-breaking stage whereat I must expose my progeny to the harsh light of the outside world. Walking down the length of Mulberry Street, I saw huge mounds of peppers and onions and coiled sausage cooking on grills; I saw photo booths equipped with zany, oversized props; I saw many, many Portosans.

But I did not see a home for Nubbins.

And then, suddenly, amidst the smoke and the jeering and thronging masses, my eyes fixated: it was Buffalo Wings. Standing at a booth emblazoned Big City Wings, he was using a squeeze bottle to lather chicken legs and breasts with an herby, oily goo. I walked over and awkwardly introduced myself to him; he was warm and friendly but did not recognize me from the trailer. I made my proposal; he was not uninterested.

"Did you get approval from the Board of Health?" he asked.

"No," I said. Then, anxious to appear legitimate, I added, "But I'm a caterer."

He suggested I return the following day with a sample, saying, "I'll try it and if we like it, I'll sell it." He cautioned, "Just bring a little. Don't bring too much."

I awoke the following day with the issues of display and presentation throbbing in my mind. I put six warm Nubbins on a plate, wrapped the samples and the plate in Saran Wrap, and put them in an unused cardboard bakery box. While making my way over to Little Italy in a cab, I nervously lifted the Saran Wrap off of the plate and flapped it

up and down so as to reduce potentially merchandise-
obscuring condensation.

When I got to Buffalo Wing's stand, he was busy with
customers; he told me to leave the samples and that he
would call me with his decision the following day. I suddenly realized that I had not yet described to him the
makeup of a Nubbin. Operating under the assumption that
the average person wants to be forewarned that, when he
bites into Food Item Number One, he will discover the
hidden presence of Food Item Number Two, I bit one of
the samples in half and said, "See, there's chocolate inside."
The part of my brain that is a storage area for unctuous
pronouncements prompted me to add, "Mmm . . . choco-
latey and good."

=

Buffalo Wings did not call me the next day. Nor the day
after that. In short, Buffalo Wings did not call me at all.
Frustrated and forlorn, I contemplated abandoning the
project altogether. I contemplated going and having a scene
with him. I contemplated filling a shopping bag with pizza
dough and then abandoning it on the #4 train to the
Bronx.

But instead I went back to the Feast. At a booth with
many colorful signs advertising Steak Giambotta, Chicken
Savoy, and fruit salad, I explained to the large, Italian-
American proprietor that I had invented a new snack food
and was eager to give it a trial run. He told me to return
in fifteen minutes and talk to his partner. When I returned,

I met the partner, a short, cocky man in his forties whom I will call Sal.

"So you think they'll do good with sausage and chicken?" Sal asked after I had made my proposal.

"Yeah," I said. "They're good. And no one else is making anything like them."

I sweetened the deal by offering Sal and his partner half of my profits. Sal said that they would have to discuss it; he told me to come back in fifteen minutes.

When I returned, Sal acknowledged my arrival but then proceeded to ignore me for some six minutes. When he had finished showing a young male employee how to make Chicken Savoy, Sal told me that he wasn't sure if he would have enough grill space for me. I explained to him the dimensions of my griddle; this seemed to calm him. Becoming increasingly aware that Sal rarely looked me in the eyes, I spent another four or five awkward minutes standing outside the booth while he alternately ignored me and asked me questions. When he finally agreed to my proposal, he said, "So come on Thursday at eleven-thirty, bring me the three, and we'll see how it goes. If it works then we'll run with it." Eager to secure the agreement, I suggested that I bring half of "the three" the following day, Wednesday, as a down payment. He agreed. When I gave him the money the next day, we decided that I would start working on Thursday afternoon. He gave me permission to put a display on the front counter, saying, "You know what you do? You get a paper plate, fold it in half, decorate it nice."

=

When I reported for work on Thursday at the appointed hour, Sal was nowhere in sight. The booth was being manned by a young man in his early twenties named Kenny. Not sure what my rights were in this situation, I timidly entered the already-crowded fifteen-by-ten-foot area of the stand and started to unpack my supplies. After putting four of my five orders of pizza dough in the stand's refrigerator, I quickly started to wrap disks of chocolate with dough. After I had fashioned twenty of them, I hung up my sign, a fifteen-by-fourteen-inch piece of white posterboard, onto which I had put two-and-three-inch-high red vinyl letters reading:

NUBBINS

THE *FRIENDLY* SNACK

Underneath this, in smaller lettering, was MELTED BITTER-SWEET CHOCOLATE INSIDE A HOT BREAD POCKET . . . 2 FOR 50 CENTS.

When Sal arrived, he did not address me directly, opting instead to mumble "Hiya" to both Kenny and me. When Kenny told Sal that the two workers from the last shift had taken the money they made back to "the restaurant" (the workers and the equipment, I would later learn, came from a restaurant in New Jersey), Sal slammed the side of the booth with his hand, causing it to rock.

"Those goddamn motherfuckers!" he yelled. "Fuckin' idiot—he doesn't know *what* he's doing!"

He then kicked a cardboard box that was lying on the floor. It crashed against the side of the wooden stand, emitting a hollow boom. I scurried to the far side of the stand, suddenly occupying myself with a piece of dough.

"Yo, Henry—you got that money?" Sal asked.

Once given the money, Sal left for about twenty minutes. While he was gone, another employee—a dark, lovely woman in her late thirties named Linda—showed up and took an interest in my wares.

"Chocolate in bread?" she asked, her eyes widening with amazement. "That's *obscene.*"

While Sal was gone, I put some Nubbins on the griddle, which was some four inches away from six or seven chicken breasts slowly cooking on the grill. I tried to work as gingerly as possible lest I incur sensitive sac rupture. I also availed myself of the opportunity to put out my display on the counter. I had taken a postcard of a dewy-eyed, sequined, choker-wearing Barbra Streisand, circa *A Star Is Born,* and, in small vinyl lettering, all capitals, written NUB-BINS across her forehead. Then I positioned this postcard into the edges of an aluminum-foil dish so that it stood straight up; I anchored the dish with three cooked Nubbins.

Both Sal and Linda had expressed a desire to taste my wares. Upon serving them each a Nubbin, I quickly returned to my griddle, anxious that my tenancy at the booth might be subject to their approval. Just then I heard Linda gasp as Sal shouted, "Goddamnit!" I winced. Sal continued, "Henry, you're out of here. Pack it up—this thing just *came* all over me!" I turned around to look, whereupon I saw Linda quickly grab a napkin and Sal—fortunately—began to laugh; he had bitten into the Nubbin too vehemently and now the treat's liquid center was spread out all over his shirt front. Moments later, Linda expressed her enthusiasm for the Nubbin's taste and asked for a second.

Between four-thirty and five-thirty, I sold only three Nubbins; however, in my own defense, I must point out that the crowd was fairly sparse.

"They're good," one of my customers enthused. "Sort of French."

At about five, Sal went outside the booth and started to wipe the front counter with a sponge. He looked slightly askance at my Streisand display. I became very conscious of the fact that my display was far more involved than a paper plate folded in half.

"Is this Barbra Streisand?" he asked.

I confirmed that it was.

"What for?" he asked dubiously.

"It'll bring people in," I said. "Curiosity."

Sal recommenced wiping, a pensive, slightly displeased look on his face. Would this, I wondered, be the last straw? Then Sal stopped wiping. He walked over to the display. He picked it up. Then, turning it so that it was facing me, he advised me, "You should have gotten one of her nude."

I nervously agreed with him, not bothering to outline for him the difficulty inherent in obtaining such a thing.

As the crowd began to swell, Kenny, Linda, and I began to yell the names of our various wares in an increasingly loud fashion. When, at one point, Linda included "Nubbins!" in her spiel, Sal whispered something in her ear, and thereafter she did not do it again.

I experienced a steady trickle of customers. About one out of every three people who came to look at the griddle or the display would end up making a purchase. I wondered if I wasn't losing customers because of the Nubbins' appearance; their casings continued to crack, causing the dark, mottled chocolate to be exuded in a manner that was unlovely. I threw many a Nubbin away. And I started to use more dough.

Taking my cue from Kenny and Linda, I also began to take an increasingly aggressive approach to sales. When a woman sidled up to the grill and, speaking to a space equidistant between Kenny and me, said, "I'll have two," I asked, "Two Nubbins?"

"No," she said. "Two chicken sandwiches, please."

"Would you like a nice Nubbin to go with that?" I asked.

"No, thank you."

"They're nice. They're hot and nice."

"No, just chicken, please."

"Maybe after dinner you'll have some."

"Yeah, maybe after dinner."

Later, when a woman in her twenties looked at my sign and said, "Nubbins? Oh God—my boyfriend's in a band called Nubbin," I tried to impress upon her the potential enjoyment to be wrought from Nubbins' use as a "gigging snack." This was not interesting to her.

=

Although Kenny and I were so closely stationed together at the grill that our elbows repeatedly rubbed against one another's, we coexisted peaceably. The lavishing of vinegar and spices onto the chicken parts was effected with a minimum of spray or fallout to my area. However, three times during the evening, Sal—who had taken to referring to my wares as "your, uh, your *muffins*"—briefly stood in for Kenny. With a dramatic flourish that I can only imagine was intended to excite comment and interest from the crowd, Sal would pour vinegar from a height some three feet above the grill. Herb-flecked vinegar would splash onto my griddle; a huge cloud of smoke would pour forth from the chicken. After several of these hot, vinegary blasts had buffeted against my face and person, I was left with the distinct impression that Sal was trying to kipper me.

=

At about eight-thirty the crowd in the street doubled, its swollen size now sometimes causing the stand to rock slightly. In my rush to keep up with consumer demand, I began to make increasingly large Nubbins—originally the size of Ping-Pong balls, they had now ballooned to the size

WHAT IF YOUR MOTHER LIVED AT THE PLAYBOY MANSION?

11:00 A.M. Mom's eyes well with tears when Miss May says her "Likes" include candles, honesty, and sharing.

11:54 A.M. Mom assumes that coke spoon she found under sofa cushion is instrument used in nail care.

12:01 P.M. Mom confuses other Mansion guests with repeated references to Hef's ex, "Barley Bensen."

3:34 P.M. Miss June cuts phone sex short when she realizes Mom is listening in on upstairs extension.

6:40 P.M. Mom leaves Jacuzzi area to get Miss January a sweater.

1:01 A.M. Mansion guests pile onto Hef's bed to screen videos; Mom launches into lengthy reminiscence about when movie admission was a nickel.

of tennis balls. One man said to me, "That's only twenty-five cents? That's too cheap. I'm not sure it will be any good." (For reasons unclear to me, this comment prompted the woman accompanying him to launch into an extended riff on the word *nuppins.*)

At one point I looked up from my griddle and saw that two women who had been admiring the picture of Miss Streisand were now eating the Nubbins that were sitting in the foil dish.

"Ladies," I said. "That's the display you're eating."

"Oh, these aren't samples?" one of them responded.

"No, you're eating the display."

The woman looked at her and her friend's half-eaten portions with slight horror.

"Are they, are they . . . okay?" she asked.

Curbing my impulse to tell her that she had just eaten a highly polished piece of wood, I assured her that she had eaten only the highest quality baked good. Then, in the name of consumer relations, I refused payment.

I had started to feel slightly guilty that some of the customers were being shortchanged. Sudden, intense waves of customers—immediately followed, of course, by long stretches of total inactivity—sometimes prohibited me from maintaining the level of quality control so essential to the production of comestibles. When a recently served customer broke through the ranks of a family of four that I was serving, showed me his sad, half-eaten Nubbin, and asked, "Is it supposed to be raw dough with a lot of, like, *burnt shit* on the bottom?" it was the harried middle-manager in me who calmly explained to him that yes, indeed, that was the desired effect.

For the most part, however, my customers were very satisfied. I had two repeat customers; one man had four portions wrapped up to take home to his wife. One of the repeat customers, having had two of the smaller Nubbins at the beginning of the evening, returned later to find that Nubbins had trebled in size. After learning that the new, larger Nubbin had the same amount of chocolate in it as the old one did, she admonished me, "You should control how much chocolate is in them."

At about ten-thirty I suddenly realized that I had run out of dough. I thought about rushing off to a pizza parlor and buying more, but somehow, having sold forty-five Nubbins, having had two repeat customers, I felt complete.

"I'm packing up shop," I told Sal.

I started to hand him the eleven dollars that was his percentage of my profit, but he told me to keep it.

=

Bit by bit, I wage my campaign. Admittedly, there is still ground to be covered: You do not see Nubbins served with coffee at the conclusion of 12-Step meetings. You do not hear kindergarten children parroting the Nubbins jingle or tag line. You do not associate the word *nubbins* with members of the law enforcement community.

But one day—one day in the not-too-distant future, if will and determination are rewarded in this lifetime—all this will change. One day you will be strolling down Aisle 3 of

your local supermarket when suddenly a large net will drop over you, and a hoary, disheveled allergist will approach bearing a platter of delectable goodies.

Embrace this man. Embrace him and his offerings. For it is only then that you will savor the fruit of obsession.

of tennis balls. One man said to me, "That's only twenty-five cents? That's too cheap. I'm not sure it will be any good." (For reasons unclear to me, this comment prompted the woman accompanying him to launch into an extended riff on the word *nuppins*.)

At one point I looked up from my griddle and saw that two women who had been admiring the picture of Miss Streisand were now eating the Nubbins that were sitting in the foil dish.

"Ladies," I said. "That's the display you're eating."

"Oh, these aren't samples?" one of them responded.

"No, you're eating the display."

The woman looked at her and her friend's half-eaten portions with slight horror.

"Are they, are they . . . okay?" she asked.

Curbing my impulse to tell her that she had just eaten a highly polished piece of wood, I assured her that she had eaten only the highest quality baked good. Then, in the name of consumer relations, I refused payment.

I had started to feel slightly guilty that some of the customers were being shortchanged. Sudden, intense waves of customers—immediately followed, of course, by long stretches of total inactivity—sometimes prohibited me from maintaining the level of quality control so essential to the production of comestibles. When a recently served customer broke through the ranks of a family of four that I was serving, showed me his sad, half-eaten Nubbin, and asked, "Is it supposed to be raw dough with a lot of, like, *burnt shit* on the bottom?" it was the harried middle-manager in me who calmly explained to him that yes, indeed, that was the desired effect.

For the most part, however, my customers were very satisfied. I had two repeat customers; one man had four portions wrapped up to take home to his wife. One of the repeat customers, having had two of the smaller Nubbins at the beginning of the evening, returned later to find that Nubbins had trebled in size. After learning that the new, larger Nubbin had the same amount of chocolate in it as the old one did, she admonished me, "You should control how much chocolate is in them."

At about ten-thirty I suddenly realized that I had run out of dough. I thought about rushing off to a pizza parlor and buying more, but somehow, having sold forty-five Nubbins, having had two repeat customers, I felt complete.

"I'm packing up shop," I told Sal.

I started to hand him the eleven dollars that was his percentage of my profit, but he told me to keep it.

=

Bit by bit, I wage my campaign. Admittedly, there is still ground to be covered: You do not see Nubbins served with coffee at the conclusion of 12-Step meetings. You do not hear kindergarten children parroting the Nubbins jingle or tag line. You do not associate the word *nubbins* with members of the law enforcement community.

But one day—one day in the not-too-distant future, if will and determination are rewarded in this lifetime—all this will change. One day you will be strolling down Aisle 3 of

WHAT IF YOUR MOTHER LIVED AT THE PLAYBOY MANSION?

11:00 A.M.   Mom's eyes well with tears when Miss May says her "Likes" include candles, honesty, and sharing.

11:54 A.M.   Mom assumes that coke spoon she found under sofa cushion is instrument used in nail care.

12:01 P.M.   Mom confuses other Mansion guests with repeated references to Hef's ex, "Barley Bensen."

3:34 P.M.   Miss June cuts phone sex short when she realizes Mom is listening in on upstairs extension.

6:40 P.M.   Mom leaves Jacuzzi area to get Miss January a sweater.

1:01 A.M.   Mansion guests pile onto Hef's bed to screen videos; Mom launches into lengthy reminiscence about when movie admission was a nickel.

your local supermarket when suddenly a large net will drop over you, and a hoary, disheveled allergist will approach bearing a platter of delectable goodies.

Embrace this man. Embrace him and his offerings. For it is only then that you will savor the fruit of obsession.

WHAT IF A FOUR-YEAR-OLD AMISH BOY GOT LOST IN THE CONDÉ NAST BUILDING?

Glamour Editor notes trend: Farmers are getting younger!

Brides Boy drools on furniture in lobby; shrieking receptionist momentarily loses fake English accent.

Self Receptionist tells boy that she wishes he were a can of Tab.

Vanity Fair Assistant editor tells boy that most Amish people are not famous.

GQ Swishy art assistant tells colleague that, yes, boy is only four, but he has the *body* of a six-year-old.

Mademoiselle Beauty editor smiles at speck of mud on boy's cheek: assumes boy has been playing with samples of new fruit-based masque.

Vogue Assistant publisher ashes cigarette over boy's head: assumes boy's straw hat is large mobile thatched ashtray.

WHAT IF YOUR LANDLORD WERE NOMINATED FOR AN OSCAR?

February 15   Elated landlord appears on local news wearing ice pack and grubby bathrobe.

March 3   Landlord buys auto-pen to sign all new leases "Love ya!"

March 29   Landlord forces tears on Barbara Walters special when asked about rent hike.

March 29   Geena Davis tells landlord she is cold; landlord bangs on pipes of Dorothy Chandler Pavilion with wrench to create illusion of impending warmth.

March 29   Landlord tells Special Effects copresenter that he will announce name of winner "gratis."

March 29   Defeated landlord attends Swifty Lazar bash; tells Shelley Winters he loved her in *The Tenant.*

2 Yrs. Later   Landlord moves to Canoga Park; takes job at Taco Bell.

Games of Chintz

Although my lack of passion and aptitude for decorating has led me to outfit most of my apartments in a style that might be best described as Early Newstand, I have long been intrigued by the earnestness and zeal with which others address themselves to the pursuit of domestic loveliness. Thus when, in the past, I have visited decorator showhouses—those events at which a dozen or so interior designers each decorate a room in a single residence no one will ever inhabit, the ticket sales to which are given to charity—it is less because I have a long-held fascination with Marie Antoinette recamiers and Louis XIV sconces than because I am loath to pass up any opportunity to overhear the promiscuous use of the phrase *yummy chintz*.

Indeed, promiscuity is the leitmotiv of decorator showhouses. Decorators who work on showhouses use their own money to pay for whatever furniture or supplies they are unable to borrow or have donated; some of them, anxious to reap the maximum benefit in publicity and job referrals, spend as much as $150,000 on a room. Given that the decorator decorates a showhouse room to his own specifications and not a client's, there are fewer constraints on his sense of the fabulous. It becomes too easy for him to ignore the little voices that admonish "Less, darling— *much, much* less": Several years ago, a decorator at a New Jersey showhouse swathed the walls and contents of an entire room in fake fur and called it the Furmality Room; at a 1993 Saratoga Springs, New York, showhouse with the theme "Let Music Fill the Air," recordings of Brahms and Beethoven emanated from a nonworking toilet. And at a recent showhouse in Massachusetts, Jamie Gibbs uphol-stered the frames of two dozen cafeteria chairs with moss, explaining "as it ages, the moss will turn gold to match the tassels."

Sometimes the excess is of a more esoteric nature. "This is not a complete room," read Thierry Despont's description of one of his two 1991 French Designer Showhouse rooms in honor of the French poet Rimbaud, "but broken pieces, a wall here, a mirror there, and then a dark cabinet that does not connect but is there, as a fragment, Rimbaud's last refuge. A flying tub, a stellar sphere, accounting books and images of slaves. The walls, the obscure cabinet, the galaxy . . . it is as if the wind of poetry had shattered a room." The larger of Despont's rooms featured a winged bathtub; the smaller contained a sink filled with spears and twigs.

Standing in the room that had been shattered by the

the Bennetts could picnic with their children, the treehouse was stocked with cookies, hot dogs, and jars filled with bugs. And for a room extolling the virtues of the equestrian life, Senator John Warner provided his own custom-made English riding boots, his riding hat and habit, suede jacket, riding silks, and a pair of velvet slippers; the decorator upholstered the walls in wool the color of jodhpurs.

The decorators are clearly entranced by their subjects. When Entertaining People asked decorator Victor Shargai to decorate a room for Kelly McGillis on the theme of "A Whimsical Dinner at Eight," Shargai created a room based on the old motorsailer that McGillis and her husband Fred hope one day to buy and restore. Shargai explained in the show's catalogue, "The on-board scenario would find Kelly in the galley (sneaking glances out the portholes at the seascapes she loves so much) while Fred and friends join her as she cooks one of her 'al dente' wonders. What a life!" (What a life, indeed—*The Kelly McGillis Story: A Passion for Pasta.*)

But of all of the showhouse rooms fueled by this unsavory form of voyeurism, few match Katherine Stephens's re-creation of the room thought to be Franklin D. Roosevelt's childhood room. Says Stephens, "Being disabled doesn't mean that you have to live in surroundings that are unattractive." According to a photo caption from *Interior Visions: Great American Designers and the Showcase House*—oddly, given that Roosevelt did not contract polio until he was almost forty—the showhouse room was outfitted with an electric bed and a remote control for the TV, curtains, and telephone. The caption added, "Below, the flat, low-pile industrial carpet facilitates movement, avoiding drag with the wheelchair; most important, it is static-free."

As the wheelchair aged, it no doubt turned gold to match the tassels.

NINE-TO-FIVING

"You'll Never Groom Dogs in This Town Again!"

Spitting is prohibited in subway cars mainly to:

a) encourage politeness
b) prevent spread of disease
c) reduce the cost of cleaning cars
d) prevent slipping

From the Telephone Maintainer civil service test

Assume that, while a [Bridge and Tunnel] Officer is collecting a toll from a motorist, the Officer sees a child tied up in the rear of the car. Of the following, the best thing for the Officer to do is to:

a) ignore what has been seen and continue collecting tolls
b) try to delay the car and signal for assistance

c) reach into the car and untie the child

d) tell the driver that he cannot use the bridge unless he unties the child

> *From a preparation guide for the Bridge and Tunnel Officer civil service test*

The proper technique for selling floral designs involves:

a) ignoring customers when they are waiting for service

b) being assertive, taking no nonsense from the customer

c) treating the customer the way you want to be treated

d) calling the customer "honey" or "dear"

> *From an exam given by the Rittner's School of Floral Design in Boston, Massachusetts*

In earlier, simpler times, you became established in a trade by following a steady path from apprentice to journeyman to master. You matured into a trusted artisan through a natural process, and you did not need to be worried about becoming "certified" and filling in computer-readable answer bubbles with a number-two pencil and responding "true" or "false" on a psychological test to the statement "I prefer tall women." No, a blacksmith was a blacksmith because he was a blacksmith; chandlers chandled and wheel-wrights wrought wheels. In today's superrationalized, post-industrial world, however, we trust numbers more than experience, so to qualify for almost any money-making endeavor, from lawyer to interior decorator to cement mason, you may be obliged to take a test. There is a Certified Picture Framers examination. There is an Aerobics Instructors test.

In an attempt to identify exactly what employers and professional organizations are looking for in their employees and members—and, incidentally, to identify exactly what work I might be suited for other than the underrationalized and basically preindustrial labor of freelance writing—I took thirty-one official or practice tests. The tests ranged from tests for bartenders, postal machine mechanics, radio announcers, and travel agents to tests for addiction specialists, geologists, foreign service officers, and FBI agents. (I did not take the exam for state troopers, however, having taken offense at some of the questions in a preparation guide for that test: "When driving a full-sized car, are you tall enough to see over the steering wheel?" "When standing next to a full-sized car, can you easily see over the top?" "Can you climb over a full-sized sedan either length-wise or from side to side?" The writers of the test seemed to suspect me of being a dwarf.)

My results were not always encouraging; I passed only three tests.

There is not yet a test for freelance writers, of course. It occurs to me that perhaps this is just as well.

SO YOU WANT TO BE A COSMETOLOGIST

In addition to a written test that includes questions on bacteriology, trichology, dermatology, and histology, aspiring cosmetologists in New York State must pass a three-hour-long practical exam. At the busy, dark premises of the Wilfred Beauty Academy at Broadway and Fifty-fourth Street, I took the first four of seven parts of the mock version of the practical exam that Wilfred students must pass before taking the state board examination.

I entered the classroom area, its air redolent with the aroma of singed hair and perfumey fluorocarbons. I joined a group of about thirty white-lab-coat-wearing students who were under the tutelage of the obdurate Ms. Valentine. A short, middle-aged Hispanic woman with full, round cheeks, Ms. Valentine has a slightly regal bearing and luxuriant blonde hair—the empress dowager of Wella Balsam. But upon introducing herself to me she explained, "They call me the Drill Sergeant."

Pleasantries dispensed with, she reached into the three-foot-tall wooden cabinet in which wigs are dried and pulled out a male rubber mannequin head with slightly chiseled, epicene facial features. Its hair was done up in curlers and covered with a hairnet. Then, with a clamping device, Ms. Valentine used her impressive strength to briskly attach the head to the worktable closest to the wig dryer.

Ms. Valentine barked out the command to begin the first part of the exam—the "comb-out"—and then urged us to be assiduous about "relaxing the set." Upon seeing that other students were "effilating" (teasing) their heads' hair with combs, I followed suit; but upon snagging and almost breaking one of the comb's teeth in the resultant tangle, I decided that this was not the proper avenue to hair relaxation. I recommenced with a brush. When a bell sounded at the conclusion of the twenty-five minutes, I had fashioned a sort of churning mass of blondeness—Gunther Goebbel-Williams after having strayed too close to an air duct. Ms. Valentine strode around the room and, jabbing her finger into some coiffures, briefly combing others, took notes. Her look of unenthused calm suggested a high level of professionalism.

For the hair-shaping phase of the exam, I was given a water sprayer, plastic clips, shears, and a female mannequin head with long, straight brown hair. Handing me an illustration of a head of hair sectioned into four quadrants and one encircling fringe, Ms. Valentine explained that I would have thirty minutes to "section, remove excess bulk, and blend." This sounded like a tall order. Indeed, it was—I spent twenty-four minutes effecting a fringe and quadrants. During this time, Ms. Valentine slunk down the aisle four times, each time yelling a new command: "Razor!" "Blunt cutting!" "Effilating!" "Thinning shears!" This was not creating an environment in which I felt I could do my best work.

Upon looking at the clock I realized that I had only three minutes left; it was with a great sense of urgency that I launched into my excess-bulk removal and shaping.

In the twenty minutes given for the permanent waving segment of the exam, I resectioned the hair and then, using wee, slippery pieces of tissue paper, put about one third of it up in curlers. At the conclusion of the segment, Ms. Valentine announced that we would break for lunch. Some ten seconds later four girls had swarmed around the wig dryer out of which they stealthily pulled the Tupperware containers full of chop suey and rice and beans that would serve as their lunches.

After lunch we fingerwaved. According to Ms. Valentine, fingerwaving—the process by which one molds hair into even, 1930s-style ridges—is the most difficult part of the exam; "Sometimes students just break down crying during it." She gave me a plastic bottle of fingerwaving lotion—a sticky, viscous substance evocative of whipped spit. I labored diligently during this twenty-minute leg of the exam; although I was unable to create the plates and ridges of hair with which the other students were transforming their heads into what looked like well-lubricated armadillos, I *was* able to create a mottled, wavy look that had its own eerie beauty.

At the conclusion of testing, I asked to see my exam scoresheet. Ms. Valentine smiled bleakly and slightly maternally. Next to where she had written that I had garnered a thirty out of a possible fifty on the comb-out, was written "too fluffy" and "removed by brushing"; next to my thirty out of a possible fifty on the hair shaping, she had written "poor." She had not even bothered to score the permanent waving or fingerwaving sections.

"So I'm not ready for my own salon," I said.

"The comb-out was the only part that was close to passing."

"Yes, I felt good about that part," I said. "But will someone hire me if I can only do comb-outs?"

"Don't worry—you will not be hired soon."

"Maybe I could specialize. Maybe I could just do comb-ou—"

Ms. Valentine extolled the virtues of a proper Wilfred training; I thanked her for her guidance and left.

SO YOU WANT TO BE A SCENIC ARTIST

The painter of theatrical scenery who is interested in gaining admittance into Local 829, the United Scenic Artists, fits into one of two categories: Track A is for scenic artists with two or more years of professional experience; Track B is for people with "more traditional design and/or painting skills." Deciding that my own painting history is "more traditional," I applied for the latter. No résumé, letter of recommendation, interview, or portfolio is required for Track B admission into the union; one must simply pay $150, successfully complete a Home Project, and pass a studio painting test.

One month before the painting test, I was mailed two 8″ × 10″ color reproductions of paintings: the Home Project. I painted larger versions (3′ 9″ × 5′ 2″ and 4′ 6″ × 6′ 0″) of the two reproductions onto cotton duck. This year's paintings were "Drapery, Molding, Marble, Wood," a picture of a marble-arched wooden door on top of which someone has carelessly draped a lot of striped fabric, and "Still Life," a picture of a typical cliffside picnic.

On the Saturday morning of the eight-hour painting test I arrived at the basement of the ABC/Capital Cities studio at West End Avenue and Sixty-sixth Street at eight-thirty A.M. I stacked my rolled-up paintings on top of the other candidates' work at the entryway. Inside the studio the test's organizers had marked out some forty-five 5' ½" × 4' ⅞" painting areas on long rolls of muslin spread out and stapled to the floor. I picked a spot and unloaded my supplies. The other candidates, most of whom were in their twenties or thirties, were hunched over their areas of canvas, applying grids. Just before nine we gathered round, and one of the union members gave us a short speech in which she welcomed us to the Track B exam, told us to "relax and enjoy" ourselves, but explained that if we didn't stop painting at five P.M., one of the test's organizers would take the paintbrush from our hands. There were three palettes of paint for our use—Muralo, Iddings casein, and Rosco Super Saturated acrylic; the paints were located in some fifty plastic buckets at the far end of the studio.

When we returned to the work area, we each had a sealed manila envelope lying on our canvas. Upon opening their envelopes to reveal lovely prints of a watercolor goldfish, most of the candidates started to frantically complete their gridding, some of them using plumb lines and one using a clear plastic sheet with gridding on it, which he taped on top of his watercolor. Others of us relied on rulers and yardsticks, calmly reasserting the "more traditional" up-bringing.

After I had gridded my own muslin, I walked over to the paint area and filled nine small plastic containers with paint. As I was carrying four of these back to my work area, a male candidate in glasses and a gray workshirt came up beside me. His self-confidence was nervous-making.

"I see you're using the Muralo," he said.

"Yes," I said, slightly defensively.

"How come?"

I had chosen Muralo because there had been fewer people in line for it. But I did not want to reveal this to this man.

"I, unh . . . I like a paint with a little *spank factor* in it," I said.

This confused the man and he went away.

As I painted, I found it difficult to capture the gauzy effects of watercolor. The man to my left, a Russian, was getting wonderful results with many thin washes of color. I emulated his style with some success.

At one-ten, although no one else seemed to be eating, I squatted at the bottom of my workspace and ate the lunch that the union's guidelines had suggested I bring. I chose not to conclude my meal with any of the Oreos or Pecan Sandies that the local had provided, loath as I am to eat anything served by someone who has just opened and stirred several hundred gallons of paint.

At about four-ten I decided to chat up one of the organizers. He told me that the work of this year's group of candidates was *much* better than last year's.

"I'm crazy about *this* guy's work," I whispered, pointing to the Russian.

"Yes, it's nice," he offered.

"*Very* Track A," I said. "My work feels . . . *flat* to me. It, it doesn't quite come up off the canvas."

"Yes," he said, warily. "You lost some of the water effects you had going. If it'd been me, I would've avoided *everything* but the Super Saturates."

"How come?" I asked.

"The undercolor doesn't work up on you."

I nodded in agreement.

I resumed painting.

At the end of the exam, I spoke to a smiley organizer.

"Do you like mine?" I asked.

"Yes, you did a nice job," she said.

"Everyone else's is much better than mine."

"No, you did fine."

"I have problems with undercolors," I confided. "I have an undercolor problem."

"Well, if you fail the test you can always take it again," she said.

"You, unh, do you think I'll fail?"

"I can't tell you that," she said warmly.

Three days later I received a form letter telling me that I had failed and that I could schedule a review of my work for the fall. There was no mention made of an undercolor problem.

The statement that proved the most difficult to respond to was a statement of the "Have you stopped beating your wife yet?" variety: "If I had had a fair chance in life, I would have been more successful." Given that I feel that I *have* had a fair chance in life, there is no way for me to answer this. I sat and thought about how I would answer variants of the statement—if I had had a less fair chance than I had, I might be less successful; if I had had a fairer chance than I had, I probably wouldn't be applying for a job at Macy's—but I was stymied by the question in its present redaction. My inability to answer began to gnaw at my self-confidence. I impulsively circled "false."

When I handed in my booklet and answer sheet, the woman who took them from me thanked me and told me that someone would call soon. But I did not receive a phone call. Two months later I called the personnel department and was told that applications are only good for thirty days and that I should reapply. "We'll be needing more people for Mother's Day," the woman whom I spoke to told me.

Upon returning, I filled out a second application in much the way I had before. The chief difference was, when queried again about jobs that I was familiar with, I thought of my *other* sister, and wrote "Primate Center Manager." When asked what the best features of the job were, I wrote, "Overseeing staff, organizing events"; when asked what the worst features were, I wrote, "Seeing chimps die."

I was not asked to take a personality test. I did not receive a phone call.

SO YOU WANT TO BE A DOG GROOMER

How do you prepare a cocker spaniel for being taken to the Holiday Inn at the Newark airport in order to be groomed for the National Dog Groomers Association of America's certification test?

There is no way, I decided. The only thing for me to do was to try to acclimate the dog to the potential vagaries of the nonprofessional grooming experience by inviting the little fellow to pass a night in my home. I called Clifford's owner and arranged to pick him up the night before the testing.

Clifford is not inconvenienced by the limitations of tact; he is a paunchy five-year-old who has heartworms and who mistakes irritability for personality. Imagine Broderick Crawford on all fours, in an ill-fitting suit. I could not allow his reputation for having bitten several people in the past to dissuade me from deciding to work with him; suffice it to say that the response to my search for a dog had not been overwhelming. That his owner has no pretensions to Clifford's being a show dog made the prospect of using him all the more attractive. Clifford was the natural choice: he had the required eight weeks, if not more, of unimpeded hair growth.

Upon arriving at my building, however, he immediately established what kind of houseguest he would be. He would not climb my stairs until jerked. He bid an upturned snout to the kibble and other savory treats offered him. He would not allow me to effilate his groin area. I did not want to press my luck with him; the more I looked over the guidelines and Breed Profiles that the NDGAA had sent me—"It is advisable when testing," one read, "to try and use a dog not sensitive to burns, so you can clip clean and close"—the more anxious I became. Indeed, when it became clear after walking him that night that Clifford's paws required washing, I prevailed upon my boyfriend Jess to lower this unpleasant battleship into the harbor of my bathtub.

Clifford spent much of the evening barking at my refrigerator. We awoke bleary-eyed the next morning at five forty-five and drove to the Holiday Inn Jetport. Going inside and confirming with the two judges that I was the owner of a Greenwich Village dog salon called Ruff Trade, I registered myself while Jess encouraged an increasingly vexed Clifford to urinate in the parking lot. The testing was being conducted in the Frank Borman Room; chairs had been stacked on the side, and large sheets of plastic had been taped to the carpeting. Two female groomers dressed in smocky, pastel groomwear had set up their tables and were talking to their uncaged dogs; I set up my table next to a power-pak, into which one of the women encouraged me to "plug-in." When I saw that the other woman's dog was a cocker spaniel whose hair was far more fluffy and lustrous than Clifford's, I nervously helped Jess guide the addled Clifford into the adjacent Chuck Yeager Room for a last-minute comb-out.

Several minutes later we took Clifford into the testing

room and eased him onto the grooming table just as the younger judge began circling the room with a clipboard to inspect each of the nine dogs. After putting her nose up to Clifford's side and inhaling, she palpated his ears. Clifford grumbled ominously. "Your dog has mats," she said. It was true; I had neglected to brush them out the evening before. "That's part of my grooming process," I explained to the woman. She wrote a note on her clipboard.

Seconds later she announced the commencement of grooming. The room whirred to life with the buzzing of electric clippers. I took my clippers and, running them along Clifford's side and back, discovered that this was not entirely pleasurable to him. He growled loudly, causing one of the other groomers to look over at us with concern. The Breed Profile for the cocker spaniel advises that one closely trim "the folds in the lower jaw area (flews), where the hair is apt to hold saliva"; I considered doing this, but decided that I was not anxious to see Clifford's reaction to my applying electricity to his saliva. Falling back on my cosmetological training, I took out my flame-tempered #10 shears and began to reduce some of the excess bulk on Clifford's legs. When I proceeded with this activity on and around his stomach, he began to make a low-pitched rumbling sound reminiscent of large aircraft. For reasons unclear to me even now, I then decided that this was the time to work on Clifford's mats. Picking up my comb, I lifted his left ear. But upon my touching said comb to the hair behind his ear, Clifford snarled and lifted his left lip, revealing a glistening incisor.

This behavior was distressing to me—as it would be, I'm sure, to any groomer. There seemed to be little that Clifford was going to allow me to do to him; surely I would fail the test if my dog exhibited no change in his appearance. Fortunately, I had had the presence of mind to bring along a few extra supplies; it was thus with a sense of professional ardor that, clamping Clifford's mouth shut with one hand, I pulled a lipstick from my bag with the other and proceeded to smear my snarly friend's snout with Clinique Citrus Pink. When I saw that the top third of the other cocker spaniel's ears were being clipped so unattractively "clean and close" that you could see the veins and skin underneath, I applied a generous daub of alcohol-free Dep styling gel to Clifford's left ear and then curled several of its long tufts of hair on his ear up into a curler. Waiting for this to set, I applied two liberal coats of Hai Karate cologne to his back and midsection.

My nontraditional grooming methods were at first almost wholly uninteresting to the judges and other groomers, four of whom were having a passionate discussion about bringing one's children along on the dog and cat show circuits.

"That's the only thing about cat cages," said one woman. "You can't fit a kid in there."

"Bet me," another countered. *"Bet* me. My friend Marie has a Siamese and she tours constantly and I've seen her put her kid in one. *Easy."*

At the conclusion of the hour-and-a-half exam period, the younger of the two judges picked up her clipboard and made her way over to Clifford and me. Silently she ran my comb through Clifford's hair. She lifted his right ear. She lifted his left ear.

"You hardly cut any of his hair," she said.

"I know," I responded. "This is what I call a Lite Groom."

She looked at me suspiciously. Then she went back to the older judge and whispered in her ear. The older judge was a muscular, compact woman who seemed to be perpetually on the boil. She walked over to us looking like a woman with a mission. After raking my comb through Clifford's right hindquarter, she said in a forceful tone, "This is totally unacceptable."

"Oh," I said, somewhat forlornly. "What about the ears? I was trying to get some *volume* with his ears."

"Not with mats you don't!" she said. She continued to look him over, wincing as she fully beheld the lipstick.

"I unh . . . I was trying to capture a sense of the unexpected," I offered.

"No, I'm sorry, this dog is not acceptable. You should familiarize yourself with our Breed Profiles." She looked again at the Citrus Pink.

"It's lipstick," I said. "It's my grooming signature. I like a dog with a *face.*"

She exhaled loudly and laid my comb down on my table next to one of the curlers. She explained that I had failed the practical part of the test but that I could take the written part.

I put Clifford and my supplies in the car and then returned to the testing room. The written test consisted of twenty-nine true or false questions and thirty-two outlines of dogs to be identified by breed. The older judge corrected my test while I waited, telling me I got a 56 percent on the written and 0 percent on the practical. The written critique of my practical work included the comment "Dog smells doggy." I declined to point out that this was unlikely since the dog was wearing a nationally distributed men's cologne. Both the critique and the older judge encouraged me to review the association's Breed Profiles and to attend more dog shows.

We drove home in silence.

SO YOU WANT TO BE A CEMENT MASON

Having mailed in an application in which I claimed to have the required "three years of full-time satisfactory experience as a cement mason, plus sufficient full-time satisfactory experience as a mason's helper," I walked to Seward Park High School on Grand Street one Saturday morning to take the written civil-service test for cement masons. About two hundred men were already waiting in line when I got there.

"It's all who you know," said the man standing in line behind me about the difficulty of getting work as a mason. "It's all Mob. Completely Mob-run."

I did not pursue this line of conversation, surrounded as we were by large Italian men.

The test consisted of eighty questions, almost all of them

specific to the trade. I did not know what screeding is. I did not know what the proper tool for preventing honeycombing is. When asked "Which two of these tools have the most similar purposes: a) strike-off rod and bull flat b) edger and jitterbug c) bull float and darby d) groover and darby," the tools all sounded to me like dance steps of the thirties and forties; however, my subsequent search for mentions of the Trunky-Doo was completely in vain.

Ever since I took this test, I have spent more time thinking about sidewalks.

SO YOU WANT TO BE A PSYCHIC

When my friend B.W. returned from Miami one day and told me that he had read about an organization that certifies psychics, something about his calm and assured tone made me think that my vocational ship might finally have come in. I called the Florida phone number he gave me and spoke to an employee of the Universal Centre in Cassadaga. A New Age seminarium with an extensive metaphysical bookstore, the Centre has three psychic readers who are available from ten A.M. to five P.M. every day on the premises or from ten A.M. to four-thirty P.M. over the phone (MasterCard, VISA, and American Express accepted). But the woman whom I spoke to knew nothing about certification; she said that the man who was in charge of it was Dr. Sekunna, the founder of the Centre. She gave me his phone number.

I told Dr. Sekunna that I was a psychic who had been

giving readings for seven years. He explained to me that people interested in becoming readers at the Centre must give an accurate reading for either Dr. Sekunna or one of the other Centre members; upon successful completion, the candidates "work with" and train under Dr. Sekunna for a period of months or even years.

I asked Dr. Sekunna if I could give him a reading over the phone.

"Sure," he said.

I paused dramatically.

"Orange," I said. "It's a, it's a color that has become important to you. It was not until very recently."

"That's true. Orange is to me a very earth color. It's an earth spiritual color. You'll find that a lot of Eastern mystics and yogis use the color orange in their spiritual work. In the past few years I've been very attracted to the color orange as a very spiritual color. If I was going to wear a robe, it would be orange."

"I'm seeing a little man with a beard who is living not in the hollow of a tree, but very close. He's very in touch with the woods. He is a sort of modern leprechaun. He has bells on his shoes."

"I'll try to explain that one to you," Dr. Sekunna said, as he began to tell me about a Centre member who had moved from Miami to the more rural Cassadaga area. "You look at this guy and you want to call him a leprechaun. He's got an impish type of personality."

I was warming to this endeavor.

"I'm sensing . . . I'm sensing *cheese,*" I intoned. "I'm

not sure if it's a Roquefort or something from the Pyrenees—but it's some kind of *blue cheese.*"

"Well, I enjoy all kinds of cheeses," he explained. "It's
what I think I shouldn't eat so much of."

"That's no doubt where it's coming from," I explained
matter-of-factly. "I'm also sensing that the underside of
tables is perhaps something that fascinates you."

"The underside of tables?"

"Yes, the underside of things," I continued calmly.
"From a *dog's* perspective."

This seemed to give him pause. But then, finally: "Yes,
I'm an investigator in life. I like to see what's on the bottom
as well as what's on the top."

When I had finished my reading, Dr. Sekunna said I was
"very highly sensitive." He gave me the name of a numerology book that espouses a simpler, "more spiritual" approach to numerology than most; although I have "an
affinity with numbers," he felt that I "get annoyed by
numbers" and that when I was studying math as a child, I
probably felt that what was being taught me was incorrect.

Twelve days later Dr. Sekunna unexpectedly called me
back. Saying he had been looking over my chart, he tried to
encourage me to go to Florida and take five hours of
palmistry lessons with him for one hundred dollars. If those
went well, I would then continue training for "a month or
two."

"The more I've been thinking about you, the more I
realize you're a touch person," he said. "If we worked on
that sensitivity that you already have, and then add palmistry

skills, we have the ability to have you make four or five hundred dollars a week."

"So you, you think I'm a touch person," I said.

"You *are* a touch person!"

"I've always wondered."

"Absolutely. You're a touch person."

Having asked me if I am "locked in to New York," he then explained that he hoped to open another Centre within a couple of months.

"This is exciting," I said. "And you think potentially you see me at this new Centre or do you think maybe there would be a spot opening at the current Centre?"

"I'll have a slot for you one way or the other."

Call me psychic.

**WHAT IF A JURY WERE SEQUESTERED
AT CAESARS PALACE?**

Voir Dire	Lawyer tries to intimidate juror with Latin phrase *Circus Maximus*.
Oath	Jurors pledge oath that they will not reveal finale of *Boylesque*.
Trial	Daydreaming juror considers alternate career as Caesars Palace wine goddess.
Recess	Juror adorns statue of Justice outside courthouse with gold lamé loincloth.
Sequestration	Juror flooded with reasonable doubt during overture to *Nudes on Ice*.
Sequestration	Bailiff elopes with waitress who is dressed as Cleopatra.
Verdict	Foreman announces, "Ladies and gentlemen, you have been a very special gallery."

WHAT IF THE U.S. GOVERNMENT WERE RUN BY TEENAGE GIRLS?

Monday President tells Pentagon official, "Fragrance is the ultimate body language."

Tuesday Speaker of the House sees Republicans passing note; humiliates junior senator by forcing her to read note aloud to joint session of Congress.

Wednesday Chief of staff slashes wrists in White House bathroom.

Thursday Vice president rushes off to Kennedy Center: first after-work meeting for *Oklahoma!* costume committee.

Friday President assigns numerical value to each letter in alphabet to predict numerologically whether recent legislation will be successful.

Saturday Secretary of state retreats to Georgetown home to curl up with clove cigarettes and *The Bell Jar.*

Sunday Commander in chief accidentally signs nuclear arms treaty "Mrs. Matthew Broderick."

WHAT IF PHIL DONAHUE ERUPTED INTO FLAMES?

4:07 P.M.   Producers of *Oprah* decide to lower Oprah into jaws of shark.

4:18 P.M.   Mario expresses relief that Phil's insides are not lumber.

4:27 P.M.   Woman in audience recounts unrelated personal anecdote.

4:42 P.M.   Woman in audience recounts unrelated personal anecdote.

4:53 P.M.   Woman in audience recounts unrelated personal anecdote.

Nackt Tonight, Darling

HYPOTHESIS: Possessed as I am of an endless fascination with the classified advertising sections of small newspapers, I often come across ads placed by nude housecleaners. Such a profession, it has always seemed, must be slightly . . . *imperiling.* Standing in the altogether while scouring a recalcitrant stovetop; wrangling ungarmented with a chunk of ice lodged in a winterscape of spilled Frogurt—these are chores fraught with occupational hazard. And, although nudism has a history rife with discipline and rigor—nudism as a philosophy started early in this century in Germany, where the *Nacktkultur* (meaning naked culture) movement prescribed calisthenics, medicinal baths, diets, and purges as the means toward spiritual equanimity and biological purity—I have always imagined the contemporary urban nudist to be an individual of slightly less gusto.

EXPERIMENT: In an attempt to test the mettle of the nude domestic, I conducted a small experiment. On two separate occasions I called a nude housecleaning service and hired cleaners—one man, one woman—to come to my home (sixty dollars an hour, with a two-hour minimum). In addition to having these cleaners perform traditional duties like sweeping and dusting, I asked them to complete tasks that I thought might prove especially challenging to those in nature's garb.

But before we turn to the data, allow me to say that both cleaners were kind, unintimidating people, neither of whom was interested in rendering me pants-less. Indeed, chief among my initial curiosities had been whether or not nude housecleaning is a euphemism for prostitution; both cleaners assured me it is not.

"The visual is okay," one of them explained to me, "but it's a hands-off policy."

DATA: I knew little about these people before they came to my home and shucked their clothing; they knew nothing about me except my name and address. I was told by the service that the first cleaner, a man, was *"very big* in all areas" (and thus, for the purpose of this report, I shall refer to him as Big); when I called to hire a second cleaner, I asked for a woman with a "fun personality" (and thus, for the purpose of this report, I shall refer to her as Fun).

"Die Vinder" (Windows)

TASK: Clean blinds-less windows looking onto busy residential street

POTENTIAL OCCUPATIONAL HAZARD: Public exposure; arrest

RESULTS:

Big: "I don't usually do windows, but it's spring and you should really be able to see out them." When told that windows had no blinds: "I don't mind. I mean, hey— *you* live here." Used newspaper and Fantastik; seemed to relish parts of task. Readjusted athletic socks throughout.

Fun, upon seeing windows: "Oh my God! Can people see me? Where are your shades?" Later, in kitchen, when asked if she'd be willing to clean windows: "Windows? I've never done windows." Did not do windows.

"Das Stoop und Grope" (Low, Hard-to-Reach Places)

TASK: Bend and stoop in order to dust low, hard-to-reach area located two and a half feet under antique desk

POTENTIAL OCCUPATIONAL HAZARD: Possible prominent display of unattractive body part

RESULTS: Both cleaners immediately got down on hands and knees, their preferred cleaning position; both deftly angled body so as to avoid aforementioned display.

Big: was particularly impressed by desk; *"That's* a nice

piece." Extolled virtues of Goddard's furniture polish—
"It won't build up like other polishes do." Volunteered
to make list of cleaning supplies necessary for gracious
living.
Fun: chatty throughout.

"Das Newspapperschmutz" (Newsprint)

TASK: Carry twenty-inch bundle of newspapers a thirty-
five-foot distance
POTENTIAL OCCUPATIONAL HAZARD: Bodily besmirchment
RESULTS: Both eluded blemishing by breaking pile down
into three loads and carrying loads out in front of body.
Big: "Do you have any twine? I can even bundle them for
you." Paid especial attention to papers' subsequent
placement. Renewed offer to make list of cleaning supplies necessary for gracious living.
Fun: "This is a lot of papers." Brief conversation about
comic-strip character Cathy.

"Die Gluetrappen" (Glue Traps)

TASK: Set glue traps in hard-to-reach location
POTENTIAL OCCUPATIONAL HAZARD: Unpleasantness aris-
ing as a result of extremity getting caught in glue
RESULTS: Both circumvented ensnarement.
Big: completed task with removal of athletic socks.

Fun: "I step in these things all the time."

Me: "When you're nude?"

Fun: "No, at home. I drag them all over the house. My nieces love this."

"Die Fireloggen" (Firewood)

TASK: Carry bundle of firewood a thirty-five-foot distance

POTENTIAL OCCUPATIONAL HAZARD: Splinters

RESULTS: Both efficiently carried the six halved logs that I had borrowed from a friend. Neither received splinters; neither mentioned that I do not have a fireplace.

Big: resembled human andiron.

Fun: "Wood is not so heavy."

"Acid in Tub" (Acid in Tub)

TASK: Unclog bathtub drain with Hot Spot, a professional-strength drain opener containing concentrated sulfuric acid

POTENTIAL OCCUPATIONAL HAZARD: Fonduelike death throes

RESULTS: Both cleaners were highly excited by my squat, deep tub. Big said, "It'd be good for groups—good for a party," and Fun enthused, "Look at this tub! You could really drown in it! I've gotta get myself one of these." They were less excited, however, about the acid.

Big: "I'll use it, but you should really just use bleach once a month. It won't eat through your pipes."

Fun: "*Sulfuric acid?* Are you crazy? This is for plumbers—I mean, this could splash in your face and make you very ugly!" Upon being told that she only needed to pour out an inch of the acid, Fun calmed down and completed the task. She poured the acid splashlessly; she does not now resemble a plumber.

CONCLUSION: My data do not support my hypothesis. With the exception of Fun's refusal to do windows, the cleaners' work was thorough and efficient. My exacting standards were met repeatedly (as was my suspicion that my visits from naked strangers might have their more awkward moments—Big, while dusting under the couch I was sitting on, at one point playfully lifted my foot up, dusted underneath it, and then let it thud to the ground; Fun, while embarking on a half-hour degrouting of my bathtub tile, asked, "Do you mind if, while I'm cleaning the bathroom, I *use* the bathroom?").

Nevertheless, I can now rest assured that, in homes throughout New York City and the state of California, domestics are busily and capably defrosting freezers, recycling rusty cans, and sharpening knives—all without the benefit of a protective layer of clothing.

Heil Nacktkultur.

WHAT IF SIGMUND FREUD HAD BEEN
A FORMER FASHION MODEL?

1894 Freud dubs new patient "Frau K." due to his inability to remember other letters in her name.

1895 Freud tries to shock colleague with confession that he was an ugly, gawky teenager.

1901 Freud disappoints Viennese intellectuals when his long-awaited "book" consists of nothing but photos of Freud pouting vacantly.

1907 Freud tells young trainee, "Catalogue work—that's your bread and butter."

1912 Jung and Adler break away from Freud, claiming he overemphasizes the importance of runway.

1914 Freud's impassioned speech to Vienna Psychoanalytical Society finds members murmuring, "Who is Coco?"

1915 Scholars reveal that *Dora: An Analysis of a Case of Hysteria* is actually about an agent at Zoli.

WHAT IF A GROUP OF PLASTIC SURGEONS STARTED PUBLISHING AN OBSCURE LITERARY JOURNAL CALLED *CONTOURS?*

Monday Fiction editor hires former patient to be assistant; introduces her to staff as "one of my rhinos."

Tuesday Contributor submits poem, "Gauzy Revelation."

Wednesday Publisher suggests that contributors' notes include "before" Polaroids.

Thursday Withdrawal of investor necessitates loss of five pages; editor announces he will "vacuum" the Sontag story.

Friday Art director borders all pages with black edging; likens effect to permanent lashlining.

Saturday Contributor submits memoir, "Low-Bleed Implants I Have Known."

Sunday Editor signs off on first issue; drives to Yaddo; slips into foam post-op girdle.

WHAT IF THE POPE WERE A DOG?

Monday   Pope rejects surplice and miter regalia; opts for simple leather collar.

Tuesday   Pope replaces ritual of "washing the feet of the poor" with licking the faces of the recently fed.

Wednesday   Pope photographed in embarrassing moment of physiological necessity when he mistakes member of Swiss Guard for yet more St. Peter's statuary.

Thursday   Pope requests meeting with actress June Lockhart.

Friday   Pope follows foreign dignitary's request to "please be seated" with demand for unspecified "treat."

Saturday   World Council of Churches meeting delayed when Pope's scratching of his belly's "skritchy spot" causes his inactive left leg to flail wildly.

Sunday   Pope attacks recently delivered newspaper; gets rubber band stuck on nose.

Drive, He Said

I have long desired to be a part of "the process." As George Bush wrote in his autobiography, *Looking Forward*, "Anything that brings the process closer to the people is all to the good"; as Tom Hayden said to Bryant Gumbel several years ago, "The process today gives everyone a chance to participate." If two minds as divergent as those of Mr. Bush and Mr. Hayden could agree on an issue, I decided, then the issue bears examination.

So when a friend called me to tell me that she had volunteered to drive VIPs to their various duties during the 1992 Democratic National Convention, I did not allow my lack of automotive brio to dissuade me from entering the fray.

Yes, I say lack of automotive brio. You see, I do not own a car; I have never owned a car. To own a car in New York, it seems, would be to fly in the face of necessity, economy, and convenience—an act tantamount to bringing a sandwich to a restaurant. Consequently, the confidence that I might have about my driving were I to do it more frequently is sorely lacking; those rare occasions when I *do* find myself behind the wheel in a metropolitan area are marked by cautiousness and a sense of impending peril. I sit very, very close to the steering wheel; indeed, in the best of all possible driving worlds, I would be seated *on* the steering wheel.

These facts notwithstanding, I called the phone number for volunteer drivers and was granted an appointment for an interview.

=

Two weeks later, in a makeshift midtown office overrun with Democrats, I wrote my name, address, phone number, and desired position ("VIP driver") on a form, whereupon a gaunt man in his sixties brought me into his office.

"Know your way around the city?" he asked me.

"Sure."

"Drive much around the city?"

"No," I confessed. "Not really."

"Well, it really doesn't matter. As long as you know midtown, it's mostly that."

He then asked me for my driver's license, explaining that he was going to Xerox it.

"You have any moving violations?" he asked matter-of-factly.

"No."

"We'll find out if you do, so it doesn't matter."

He then posed a hypothetical situation: He was a delegate who, at two o'clock on a sunny day, was exiting Madison Square Garden (where the Democratic Convention was to be held) and had one hour to see some sights. Where would I take him?

Thinking how my stepfather, when in New York, likes to go to jazz clubs in order to "listen to some sounds," I told the man that I would drive down Seventh Avenue and point out the Village Vanguard to him.

"Maybe you like jazz," I explained.

His expression suggested that he did not like jazz.

I then suggested that we continue down Seventh Avenue and make our way down to the financial district.

". . . If you have time," he cut me off. "Then you could see the Statue of Liberty and all that crap."

Although it was not my intention to gain access to political dignitaries so that I might expose them to "crap," I nodded my head so as to suggest that I am a team player.

After Xeroxing my license, the man took me to a small conference room where Ron Coleman, the Motorpool manager, was talking to small groups of applicants. On a form that listed the four days of the convention plus the weekends before and after it, I indicated that I was available on a full-time basis for all ten days. Upon exiting the conference room, I realized that I wasn't sure if I had been hired or not.

"So I'll hear from you?" I asked Mr. Coleman. "I mean, is there a test we have to take or anything?"

"No, no, you're in!" he said. "We need everyone we can get. You'll hear from us next week with an assignment."

I was startled by the ease with which I had been hired. No one had asked me my occupation. No one had administered a driving test. No one had tested my ability to lean on a horn and spew obscenities in Afghani.

=

Eight days later, at a meeting attended by some two hundred drivers, the ground plans were laid out: General Motors would be lending both the Democratic Convention and the Republican Convention 175 sedans and minivans. The DNC had comprehensive insurance coverage with $1 million liability for each accident, but drivers were responsible for all moving and parking violations. Overnight parking at Meyers Garage on Thirty-fourth Street would be paid for by the DNC upon the driver's showing his parking card; short-term parking would be paid for by the VIPs.

One of the speakers at the meeting was a short, mustachioed detective from the New York Police Department who, in a discussion of safety measures, cautioned us to be sensitive to something that he referred to as "the uh-oh feeling."

"Listen to your gut instincts," he said. "That 'uh-oh feeling'? *Listen to it.*"

=

Five days later I went to the Motorpool office and met with a well-dressed woman in her early twenties who was going to give me my assignment. Looking at a clipboard, she asked me, "What do you know about Colorado?"

"I've been there," I said. "I've never lived there."

"Hold on," she said, as she stood and left the room for some three minutes. Was she going to produce Colorado representative Pat Schroeder from the adjoining room? Would John Denver emerge looking for a ride to the Village? Was this the uh-oh feeling?

The young woman finally returned unaccompanied and said, "The guy who's about to come through the door is Ron Coleman, who's in charge of transportation."

Mr. Coleman came through the door and gushed, "Brian!"

"It's Henry," I said.

"Henry!"

"We're thinking of matching you with the governor of Colorado," the young woman said.

"Governor Romer," Mr. Coleman explained.

After the young woman had called me the next day and given me the governor's arrival time at LaGuardia the following Saturday, I did a little research. I discovered that the highly popular, twice-elected, sixty-three-year-old governor had a reputation for being unbridled. After reporters and news crews were dismissed from a meeting between President Bush and the country's governors in February 1992, Romer broke protocol by insisting that the press be allowed to stay to hear Democratic rebuttal to the president's budget and domestic policy proposals. Afterward, White House press secretary Marlin Fitzwater told *The Washington Post* that "the easiest, cheapest trick in the world is to be rude to the President to try to get into the news"; *The New York Times* later referred to the governor as "brash" and "unvarnished."

This information suggested only one thing to me: I would not be spending the convention singing rounds of *"Frère Jacques."*

SATURDAY

On Saturday morning I went to the motorpool office to pick up the keys, whereupon I was introduced to the governor's assistant campaign manager, Joan Coplan. An employee of the political consultant firm Stratton, Reiter, Dupree, and Durante, Miss Coplan is a short, take-charge woman, probably in her late thirties. She has a flat, Midwestern voice whose dial is permanently set on Resounding. We walked together to the garage and picked up our brand-new black Oldsmobile Ninety-Eight.

As Miss Coplan and I got to know one another on our way to the airport, the questions that she asked me suggested that she was expecting a driver of a more professional stripe: She asked if I drive in New York (I blithely told her, "No one does, really"); she asked, "So you've never had a car in the city before?"; she asked if I had a beeper. I started to feel more and more unsure of myself; surely these were the glimmerings of the uh-oh feeling. Indeed, when Miss Coplan went to make some phone calls in the airport waiting area, I thought that my career in politics might be rapidly drawing to a close.

However, no termination of my services was mentioned. Minutes later, the plane arrived. The first member of the Romer group to step off the plane was the governor's chief of staff, B. J. Thornberry, a warm, attractive, cherubic woman in her forties graced with bright red cheeks and an air of savvy professionalism. When I had divested her of the air travel bag that had been slung over her shoulder, I turned to find the governor looking at me with a slightly pained expression. I introduced myself first to him and then to his wife, who Miss Coplan had told me would spend most of the convention with a bodyguard named Toby. Because the governor's entry in *Who's Who in America* concludes with the rather mysterious accolade "Order of Coif."—an accolade that I could only imagine means "Order of Coiffure"—my impulse at this relatively early stage in my employment was, of course, to study his hair. It seemed highly Order-worthy; it successfully toed the line between bounce and volume.

As we headed toward Manhattan, the governor asked me what I do for a living; I told him that I tutor English and write book reviews. When he then asked how I had "hooked up with" him and his staff, I explained that they were assigned me.

"I'm glad you were assigned, Governor," Miss Thornberry joked. "No one would have picked you."

After decanting the group into the New York Hilton where they were all staying, I parked the car in a garage across the street. Then, as I had been instructed to do each day, I called the man in Motorpool who was in charge of VIP arrangements.

"They seem pleased with you?" he asked me.

"Well I guess you'll hear from them if they're not."

"I have one tip for you," he said. "And don't take this as criticism. You're wearing a blue golf shirt?"

"I'm wearing a black golf shirt and a blue blazer."

"Right. So what you should do is look at how his aides are dressed. Then dress just like them."

"Really?"

"Yeah. Try to blend in with them as much as possible. It's *mirroring* them. That way, when they go out to dinner and stuff, there's more likelihood that they'll bring you along if you dress like them."

"Both his aides are women."

"Oh."

"Yeah."

"Well you can't wear a dress. But you know what I'm saying. Blend in. Look at what the governor is wearing."

"Right."

"Just trying to let you take advantage of one of the perks of the job."

I thanked him for his advice and hung up.

Miss Coplan had instructed me to have the car waiting in the rear carport of the Hilton at six forty-five. I got permission from one of the Hilton garage's attendants to leave the car in the loading zone for what he stipulated was to be "a few minutes." Miss Coplan arrived at six-fifty and said that if I was asked to move the car that I should "tell them it's Governor Romer."

Some fifteen minutes later I was whisking the governor and his two staff members off to a reception that *The Denver Post* was holding at the Water Club for the Colorado delegates. On the way, the governor asked me if I had had to take a driving test in order to volunteer at the convention.

"No," I confessed. "I'm very raw."

Indeed, the largely intuitive nature of my driving was born out half a block later when, driving at about thirty mph, I suddenly swerved to avoid a manhole that rose some six inches above the surface of Fifty-fourth Street between Sixth and Fifth avenues.

Miss Thornberry looked slightly alarmed. "You don't normally drive in the city, do you?" she asked.

"No," I responded. "No one does, really."

The governor's staff very graciously encouraged me to attend both functions that evening: the *Denver Post* party and the Democratic National Convention Welcoming Reception, held in the lobby of Grand Central Station. I was flattered and a little surprised to be included, particularly given that I hadn't been *mirroring*.

During the parties I tried to stay outside the governor's line of vision; given that he had said nothing when the misses Thornberry and Coplan had invited me to the events, I did not want to run the risk of my presence falling under the category of the Servant Problem. However, toward the conclusion of the DNC party, all four of us discovered that, independently of one another, we had drifted down to the far end of the room where the dessert table was located. Moments later the governor scanned my person and said, "You're thin. You should eat some desserts."

SUNDAY

The following morning, I picked the car up from the garage on Thirty-fourth Street where I had been instructed by the men in the Motorpool office to park. Upon meeting Miss Coplan at the appointed hour at the Hilton, I told her that, although the luxury of parking at the hotel itself had not been offered us by the men at the Motorpool office, it appeared that other members of the convention were doing it.

"If you ever need to park here," Miss Coplan said, "Just say 'Chairman Brown, Suite 4510.' "

Before I could give much thought to the possibility of charging our parking expenses to Ron Brown, the chairman of the Democratic National Committee, I was asked to take the governor and misses Coplan and Thornberry down to Madison Square Garden, where the governor was going to use the TelePrompTer to practice the speech he would give to the convention on Tuesday night.

I pulled up to the appointed unloading zone across from the Garden, a zone that was filled two-deep with limousines and cars. The governor and Miss Coplan got out of the car and slammed their doors, whereupon I suddenly realized that I had neglected to leave enough space for Miss Thornberry to open her door. She yelled, "I can't get out! I can't get out!" Flustered and embarrassed, I shifted the car into drive; but before I could ease away from the neighboring vehicle, she had slid across the seat and exited on the traffic side of the car.

In the late afternoon Miss Coplan introduced me to Rick Reiter of Stratton, Reiter, Dupree & Durante, who would be joining the entourage. Mr. Reiter appeared to be in his early forties and was composed of equal parts warm informality and boyish excitability.

I was starting to feel anxious about the governor's schedule for that evening. Each trip between the locations on his itinerary might, with traffic, take as long as half an hour. He wanted to leave the Hilton at four for a cocktail reception honoring House and Senate Democrats at the South Street Seaport; then to East Fiftieth Street for a five- to six-o'clock reception honoring Chairman Brown at the restaurant Tatou; back to the Seaport area from six-fifteen to seven for a party for the Coloradan and Hawaiian delegates; and then, most important, be at the Garden at seven-fifteen to give a live TV interview to *Crossroads*. I decided to ask someone's advice about this last and most daunting leg from the Seaport to the Garden; I went to the Motorpool office and talked to a volunteer driver in his sixties who claimed to have been driving in New York for thirty-five years. I asked him if I should take the fast-moving but inconveniently located FDR Drive or the conveniently located but slow-moving Church Street; he favored Church Street.

"Not the FDR?" I asked.

"No, Church," he said. But at the north end of Church Street, he cautioned, "You've got to get off on Sixth Avenue, then bear left and wiggle. You know what I mean by bear left and wiggle?"

I did not bear left and wiggle—as Diana Vreeland once observed, elegance is refusal. Instead, I took the FDR. By that point in the evening—my anxiety about our lateness to the preceding three events having caused my shoulders to rise so high as to suggest the gradual retraction of my neck—I longed for a direct, uncomplicated, unmediated expanse of thoroughfare. During the ride, the conversation between the governor and Mr. Reiter turned to the recent naming of Senator Albert Gore as Clinton's running mate.

"What do you think about the Gore announcement?" the governor asked Mr. Reiter.

"You know," Mr. Reiter said, "it plays better and better."

"It does play well."

Around eight-fifteen, the governor having gone back to the hotel earlier by cab, I drove Miss Coplan and Mr. Reiter to the Hilton from the Garden. On the way, Mr. Reiter, awed by the amount of congestion and activity in the streets, turned to me and exclaimed, "All this traffic. My God. How do you get by in New York?"

Miss Coplan explained, "He doesn't drive."

MONDAY

On Monday morning at seven-fifty, I positioned the car, as Mr. Reiter had instructed me the evening before, at the garage exit. Mr. Reiter came out of the hotel some five minutes later, whereupon we reviewed the day's schedule. Then he handed me a twenty-dollar bill and three ten-dollar bills.

"Here's some money to put in your pocket," he said. "You're gonna need it to bribe parking guys."

After Mr. Reiter had gone back into the hotel, I found myself staring at the dashboard, practicing saying the phrase, *Would Abraham Lincoln ease your worries, my friend?* It did not sound natural.

However, I was trying to be more aggressive on the road. On our way to the Waldorf-Astoria, where the governor was to attend a policy issues forum of the Democratic Governors' Association, I narrowly avoided disaster when I slipped the car in front of a bus in an attempt to get out of a slow-moving lane of traffic.

"Good move!" Mr. Reiter cheered.

The governor, in the backseat, said to Rick about me, "What I've decided about his driving is either that he's too young and green to know he's doing it, or he's a pro who's got it all figured out. I suspect the former."

Mr. Reiter recounted the specifics of an equally heart-stopping maneuver I had made with a bus the day before, saying, "I thought we were going to peel paint."

The governor added, "Yes, some of your clearances are amaz—I'm a pilot, Henry. So I watch clearances."

Mr. Reiter chalked my bravado up to "New York moxie."

I explained, "It helps that I don't own the car."

My driving skills were playing better and better.

Some forty minutes later, as I was driving Miss Coplan from the Waldorf-Astoria to the hotel, trying to pass a white Lincoln Continental on my right, Miss Coplan confessed, "I could never drive in New York."

"It would make you too anxious?" I asked.

"Ye—"

Boom!

Just as Miss Coplan started to respond in the affirmative, I accidentally sideswiped the Lincoln in a textbook case of Bad Clearance. I slammed on the brakes. So *this* was the uh-oh feeling.

"Is there damage?" Miss Coplan asked.

My heart started hammering. A Long-Islandy woman in her fifties got out of the driver's seat of the car. I could see only a small scrape.

"My husband is disabled. Hold on."

Her husband, wearing pastel clothing and white shoes, got out of the car and waddled over. He surveyed the Lincoln for damage, hunching over as much as he could to inspect its chromestripping. Then, finally, he waved his hand to dismiss us.

I did not look Miss Coplan in the eyes for eighteen hours after this incident. When, back at the hotel, she made a series of calls from the pay phone, I became convinced that my services would shortly be terminated. But she never mentioned the incident.

That being the opening night of the convention, I knew we would have to be vigilant in our attempt to get close to the Garden. Avenues had been shut down, barricades had been erected; the size of the crowd of policemen outside the hotel suggested the unexpected discovery of a vault full of doughnuts. At about four-thirty, as we approached a police-man who was blocking cars from entering Thirty-fourth Street at Ninth Avenue—a location some two blocks from the Garden—I lowered my voice and said as authoritatively as possible to him, "I have the governor of Colorado, Sir." This failed to produce the desired effect; he motioned us south. We proceeded in that direction, and some six min-utes later we found ourselves circling back. When we got to another barricade at Thirty-fourth Street and Tenth Ave-nue, the governor, who at the time was being interviewed by a CNN reporter over his cellular phone, told the reporter to wait a minute; then he lowered his window and barked, "I'm Roy Romer from Colorado. I'm on the Democratic Platform Committee. How do I get into the Garden?" The policeman—perhaps out of some heretofore-inexpressible allegiance to the Platform Committee—removed the barri-cade and we zoomed down Thirty-fourth Street. However, there still remained the matter of the policeman who had rebuffed us earlier at Thirty-fourth and Ninth. Surely the fact that the other officer had let us through would give us some leverage in our negotiations; but would it be enough?

In the late afternoon I saw Ted Kennedy walk through the lobby of the Hilton; I was glad to have my own bad driving put into a historical context.

As Miss Coplan had secured me credentials to get into the convention each night—a true act of generosity, particularly given that most drivers did not get in—I was able to see Governor Romer, in his capacity as cochairman of the Platform Committee, address the convention that evening; I felt like a proud parent.

WEDNESDAY

While we drove back to the hotel after a six-thirty A.M. live interview on CNN, a cab suddenly pulled in front of us at Forty-sixth Street and Eighth Avenue. I slammed on the brakes.

"Jesus!" the governor gasped.

But the day's more knotty transportation problem was how to get the governor to a softball game in Central Park when most of the roads to the park were closed. Pitting the Coloradan delegates against the Hawaiian delegates, the game was being held on the field near the Carousel. I called four different people for directions, including the woman who organized the game and the man from the Parks Department who issued the permit for the game; I got four different answers. I ended up parking at Seventh Avenue and Fifty-ninth Street and telling the governor and his staff to walk 350 yards north.

When they emerged from the park some fifty minutes later, the governor, having removed his tie and suit jacket and put on a pair of black sneakers, was sweating profusely, his loose shirttails flapping with each step he took. Mr. Reiter explained to me that the governor had caught a line drive.

"He caught it just like this," he said, miming the governor's catch. "TV got the whole thing. You couldn't have *scripted* it better."

They got in the car, the backseat sending forth a waft of vinegary Romer-roma.

As we drove to the Beekman Tower, the governor spoke via cellular phone to a prison official in Denver. In the middle of the conversation, he asked Mr. Reiter for a pad of paper. What then happened left a permanent scar on my memory: Mr. Reiter, reaching for the clipboard that I carried each day, removed my copy of the governor's daily schedule from it, and *handed the governor the pad on which I had been keeping notes for this story.*

It is with some hesitation that I try to describe the ensuing two minutes, so inextricably linked in my mind are they with the phrase *weltering abdominal cramps.* I racked my brains trying to remember if I had torn off the last completed page of notes and put it in my jacket pocket, as I had been trying to do regularly; I could not remember. The specter of incarceration swept across my consciousness like cloud patterns on a weather map. My bowels went soft.

Finally, the governor concluded his phone call, ripped off

the page he was writing on and returned the pad, saying nothing.

On the morning of the final day of the convention, the governor's staff spent much time phoning people who might have influence over the evening's telecast. Their mission was to see that Governor Romer would be standing on the platform as part of Bill Clinton's backdrop. Miss Thornberry told someone at the Democratic Governors' Association that she had watched part of the convention on TV the night before, saying, "I think the picture that we had last night—of Tom Foley and all those Congressional people— is not the picture we want tonight. I really feel that Bill's backdrop should be the governors of this country." To a second person she suggested not that the governors of this country be on the platform, but that the cochairs of the Platform Committee of this country be. Meanwhile, the governor expressed concern that he was not "connected enough" with the Clinton campaign, saying, "If I could go over there and walk through the campaign headquarters just so they know I'm alive."

Indeed, I, too, was still having problems impressing the parking attendants and DOT workers of New York by dropping the governor's name. While I was waiting for the governor and his staff outside the Doral Tuscany, a large male DOT worker came over to the car and said that, although he didn't mind my parking in the hotel loading zone, he felt I was "inconveniencing" the truck behind me. I moved all of six feet, to the other end of the loading zone; the man returned.

"I'm waiting for the governor of Colorado and Barbra Streisand," I said.

"She's here, too?" he asked without interest.

"Yeah. She's a delegate from Guam."

"Well, you're gonna have to move."

"My problem is that Barbra is in a leotard. I don't want her to have to—"

"—You need to move, sir."

I moved.

While I later drove Miss Coplan from the credentials office to the InterContinental, she called Miss Thornberry and explained to her that the people at the Democratic Governors Association "had spoken to Ickes"—I assumed this meant convention manager Harold Ickes—and he had agreed to bring the governors up on stage after the acceptance speech. Upon disengaging the cellular phone, Miss Coplan said, "That was too easy. This can't be right."

When I had dropped the governor and staff off at the Garden, the discussion turned to whether I should run out and get the car ready during Clinton's acceptance speech, or whether I should hear the whole speech, and then run out and get the car ready.

"Listen to the acceptance speech and then come on

out," Miss Thornberry said. "You should listen to it. After all this bullshit, you deserve it."

Because Mr. Reiter had left the entourage earlier that day, I was given his credentials and was thus granted access to that vaunted location within the convention, the floor. I savored the irony that I, a driver, had gotten a floor pass when many of my journalist friends had been denied one. My interest in the proceedings of the convention trebled. What had previously seemed a fairly stock series of speeches was now, at times, truly rousing. I felt very close to "the process."

When it came time to drive the group back to the hotel, I was feeling emboldened. Flush with the dynamism of democratic ideals, I started to race the lights up Sixth Avenue. For the first time in six days, I used the car horn to admonish other drivers.

"Oh my God," Miss Thornberry said. "He's completely transformed into a cabbie."

After I had dropped the group off and bid them goodbye, I pulled into the garage. The attendant gazed at me wearily.

"Ron Brown," I said. "Suite 4510."

LIFESTYLING

How to Do Everything

As I trudge, burrolike, ever deeper into the valley of advanced age, I am increasingly struck by the realization that I have stopped developing new interests and skills. Life, it often appears, is more and more a reassertion of old and somewhat tired themes; new topics of potential inquiry are lost amidst a regimen of seeing current movies, patronizing ethnic restaurants, and making uncharitable comments about those not immediately present.

Thus, when I apprised myself of the opportunities offered by the ever-burgeoning instructional video market, I pledged to inject my torpor with the shock of the new. Indeed, be it a language, a sport, or a technique for turning travel brochures into "one-of-a-kind wearables and accessories," a huge number of endeavors can now be pursued by videotape—the aspiring ambassador of human relations can learn How to Deal with Difficult People; the aspiring angler can learn how to "locate schools of crappies and imitate their food sources."

I hastened to the Upper East Side location of New York City's How To Video Source. As I browsed through the store's more than twelve hundred titles, I fixated on the frightening illustration on the jacket of *The Art of Hair Transplantation* and the length of rope included with *Trick and Fancy Roping;* however, I put both tapes back, loath as I am to involve myself with either tweezers or chaps. But overall, I found that my selections were braver than they would have been had I been applying for a class; chief among the pleasures of video learning is the realization that you will never be forced to wear a leotard in the presence of total strangers.

In my first foray into the world of instructional videos, I chose a tape called *Blooming Visions for Beginners.* Hosted by a smiley, middle-aged woman named Carol Smith, this tape teaches you how to use Blooming Visions liquid bisque (sold separately) in order to make "beautiful, bisquelike sculpture" that does not require firing. Much of the tape consists of close-ups of Carol's glamor-length nails wrangling arts and crafts supplies that have been drenched in what looks like pudding. From the three projects demonstrated on the tape, I chose Carol's personal favorite: "Project #3, the Spilled Daisy Pot."

Per Carol's instructions, I dipped actual daisies and Spanish moss into liquid bisque, and arranged them so that they appeared to have tumbled out of a tipped-over flowerpot.

My hands thoroughly goopy, I used my elbow to turn my VCR off while I waited for my sculpture to dry. When I returned to the tape, Carol, her glamor-lengths now debisqued, showed me how to paint the flowers and moss, deftly "feathering" with a small brush, "hazing" with a large brush, and "spattering" with a toothbrush. Then she encouraged me to paint the terra-cotta pot itself with Persimmon, a color she describes as "luscious."

My resultant Spilled Daisy Pot is lovely—the arts and craft equivalent of Jell-O salad with miniature marshmallows. Given that the desired look is that of something that has been "laying out in the garden for a while," I feel that my piece is particularly successful. Carol warns the viewer never to coat cookies, vegetables, or bread with liquid bisque; I have bravely curbed this temptation.

Of the many tapes that I watched, the one that proved most difficult was the exhilarating *Curso de Rumba de la Luz*—authentic Latin instruction on how to dance the rumba. Emphasizing every third beat in its 4/4 time signature, this Cuban dance requires its participants do three things at once: rattle off highly rhythmic, tap-dance-like footwork; flourish and twirl your hands in a roiling, undulant manner; and keep your carriage erect and impervious to bounce. While you do these, your demeanor should be simultaneously tragic and urgent, as if you have been shot in the stomach and are late for an appointment. Taking my cues from the tape's *bien apasionado* male dancer, Adrian "El Chino" (Adrian "the Chinese"), I could not help but feel intensely Caucasian; I soon realized that I was at a distinct disadvantage in owning no clothing that has been shrink-wrapped to my pelvis.

Nevertheless, after honing my rumba technique for some four hours over the course of a week, I told my friend Carrie that I would make her dinner one night and then take her out to rumba. When she arrived at my apartment, her eyes widened with amazement: I had, through an application of the skills demonstrated on yet another tape, *How to Garnish,* transformed my kitchen into a winter wonderland of colorful vegetable garnishes. My kitchen table was host to ten tropically colored, canteloupe-sized Onion Mums (you slice the onions longitudinally, soak them in hot water to remove their odor, and then dip them in food coloring); in close proximity was my South Seas Island Scene featuring a Cucumber Shark and palm trees rendered with green pepper fronds atop notched carrot trunks. And, basking midway between land and sea, was my adorable Lemon Pig. "You have too much time on your hands!" Carrie gasped when she had taken it all in. Indeed, my labors may have been overkill for a casual dinner *a deux;* in my anxiety about exposing my rumba skills to the harsh light of the outside world, I may have overgarnished.

After we had supped on a delicious veal stew, I explained to Carrie that I had included in the stew's ingredients the corks from three bottles of wine. I had been initiated into this practice—it tenderizes the meat through the release of the corks' enzymes—by *Trucs of the Trade,* a tape in which various chefs proffer culinary tips and secrets, *truc* being

French for *gimmick*. Given, I suppose, that the veal was quite tender, the revelation of the wine cork *truc* did not cause Carrie to blanch; more alarming to her, it seemed, was my subsequent *truc,* wherein I pulled a crème brûlée out of my refrigerator and proceeded to brown it with a blowtorch. As Hubert Keller, the chef of San Francisco's Fleur de Lys, explains in his heavy accent on the tape, "You see it turns very, very quickly a nice golden brown color."

Located seven blocks from my apartment is New York City's premier showcase of live Latin music, S.O.B.'s (Sounds of Brazil). Thus, when Carrie and I had blithely trundled off to S.O.B.'s, it was with a note of confusion that we read, just outside the club's portals, a sign encouraging passersby to thrill to the music of a band called Raïna Raï that had come "Direct from Algeria." Our perplexity about the non-Latin nature of this offering was matched only by our bewilderment that Algeria acknowledges the umlaut. Nevertheless, we entered; I proceeded to emulate the fiery choreographic bravura of Adrian "El Chino." That I did some of my best footwork and fingerwork ever was no doubt due to my realization that, if there were ever going to be a situation in which I would feel comfortable doing the rumba, it would be deep inside a throng of gyrating Algerians.

Jugglercise came more naturally to me. This eponymous tape, which comes with three eighteen-inch-square fluorescent scarves, is hosted by an irksome man in a mortarboard and gown named Professor Confidence. We learn how to juggle the scarves (an activity more strenuous than you might imagine); the rest of the tape features folky music videos by which to juggle. Standing in front of my television, grabbing and clawing in vain at the air, I was not sure at first whether to keep my eyes on the tape or the scarves; I was reminded of the climactic scenes of *The Sorcerer's Apprentice*. However, within several hours I was able to muster a fairly steady volley of fluorescence—a sort of Dance of the Seven Veils shot through with the fragrance of peanuts and sawdust. I then moved on to the Column (scarves are thrown straight up) and the Reverse Cascade (scarves are thrown counterclockwise instead of clockwise). Indeed, I even devised my own trademark throw in which scarves originating near my stomach are thrown out in front of me; I call this throw Scarves Are Coming Out of My Body.

=

The strangest tape that I encountered was *Sybervision Bowling*. This tape, a neuromuscular approach to bowling, contains no talking or instructions, only a sonorous, *Chariots of Fire*–like music track laid over hundreds of repeated sequences, many in slow motion, of two professional bowlers continually knocking all ten pins down. According to the tape's workbook, as the viewer immerses himself in the "beautiful images of movement performed by a model athlete," his nervous system is "excited" and "reacts as if it were physically performing the skill"; this neural excitement is translated into "neuromuscular memory."

I followed the tape's 30-Day Training Program, watching part of the tape each day and then trying to reimagine it in the "imaginary screen" of my mind. (The workbook also mentions locating the "imaginary screen" in your abdomen, but I found this, like the segment in *How to Garnish* in which a carrot is thrust deep inside a hollowed-out cucumber, too upsetting to pursue.) Rewinding the tape to the section that I wanted each day was not always easy; this is not a tape whose individual scenes are startlingly unique. That the slow motion segments of the video are meant to "promote within you a feeling of confidence—'He makes it look so simple and smooth. It is simple! I can do that!'— and a desire to bowl" did not quite resonate with me; it was also difficult, when bowling, to imagine myself a "great bowler [I] admire," given that my most vivid memories of bowlers are of the other third graders at Benjie Garfield's eighth birthday party. I did, however, become all a-tingle whenever I watched the two-and-a-half-minute-long climax of the "Striking" segment of the tape, consisting of ninety rapid close-ups of the ball smashing into the pins, each close-up complete with the "sweetpot sound" of the struck pins; one day I watched this sequence fourteen times in a row and then *rushed* to the lanes (scores: 72, 110). In the end, my game improved but continued to be erratic.

Another tape that required repeated viewing was *Berlitz's German for Travelers*. After you watch two actors who play characters named Mr. and Mrs. Bell speak German in various actual settings (a bank, a café, etc.), you are then shown each scene again, only this time *you* provide both of the Bells' dialogue. Talking to my television as both man and woman was quite fun, appealing as it did to my ever-present desire to be a German transvestite; I searched my apartment in vain for photographer Helmut Newton.

One afternoon, having practiced for several days all of the scenes that involved eating or buying, I nervously headed off to Yorkville, the German area of Manhattan's Upper East Side, and found a bakery. After canvasing the bakery's offerings, I asked the dour, elderly woman behind the display case, "Voss *kone*-en zee *oonz* empf-fallen?" ("What can you recommend?"), whereupon she rattled off an intimidating series of sounds wholly unintelligible to me. She then pointed at a confection rich with frosting and cherries; I countered with a phrase from the "Shopping" section of the tape wherein the odious Mrs. Bell, looking for a blouse at a clothing store, had terrorized the sales help—"Nine, das ist *nicked* gahnz mine guh-*schmocked*" ("No, that is not my taste"). The woman gave me a sour look, as if I had personally insulted her grandchildren. "*Bit*-tuh," I added hurriedly, fearful that she was going to alert the manager to my presence, "Ick *murk*-tuh ein *shtook* hazelnut torte" ("Please, I'd like a slice Hazelnut Torte"). When she then asked me a series of incomprehensible and increasingly urgent questions, my mind suddenly filled with the graphics from a tape I had watched earlier that day, *Witness Preparation for Giving Depositions*—"Tell the Truth!" "Listen to the Entire Question!" "Don't Volunteer Information!" Finally, when it became clear that she was asking if I wanted to sit at a table, I pointed at the street and improvised,

"Nine *donk*-uh, *stross*-uh ist fear goot" ("No thank you, street is very good").

That evening, still slightly rattled, I watched the first two tapes of *Stress Management for Professionals*. After having had to rumba, jugglercise, imagine bowling, and speak German to the more interactive videos, watching this taped lecture about stress was like taking a long, hot bath. Most notable about this commonsensical series hosted by therapist Roger Mellott is the number of metaphors, mostly food-related, that he manages to fit into three hours of lecturing. People are full of "tea" (egocentrism). Like monkeys, we hold on to "bananas" (issues that we exaggerate the importance of). We are prey to the "artichoke theory" (spending too much time on the outside leaves instead of the core). We need to learn to "spend our pie" (expend our energy) more effectively by "slicing our salami" (dealing with problems one at a time). If we don't, we'll get "pizza burns" (signs of stress).

What should we do? Mr. Mellott, in addition to extolling the virtues of writing, exercising, and crying, suggests that we occasionally let go of the "marbles" (problems and stress) that we have "swallowed" by talking them through in a six-minute "verbal marble dump." He suggests that we dump on a household pet. Because I do not have a pet, I used my aloe plant. Pressing the pause button, I sat on the couch in front of my television and unloaded the burdens of my psyche on my unsuspecting plant. I was reminded of *How to Be a Ventriloquist*, wherein our host talks about how shy and introverted children often repress thoughts and feelings. "Believe me," he says, referring to his dummy, Knucklehead Smiff, "having a little partner that I could control gave me the opportunity to say many of those things and took off quite a bit of pressure." When I had put my own "little partner" back on the kitchen windowsill, I realized that, yes, I was feeling relieved; but I couldn't help but feel that there must be some more expedient means to the same end. Sex? Therapy? Keening? And then it hit me: I switched off the VCR. Then I took a crème brûlée from the refrigerator and strafed it with my blowtorch.

WHAT IF YOUR MOVING MEN WERE MERCHANT AND IVORY?

11:00 A.M. Helena Bonham Carter arrives bearing drop cloth and added spinster.

11:45 A.M. Daniel Day-Lewis puts on spats, refers to fire escape as *loggia.*

12:13 A.M. Maggie Smith announces that loose items on truck can cause "quite a kerfuffle."

1:19 P.M. Julian Sands arrives with scratch remover and local vicar.

3:25 P.M. Emma Thompson puts down packing crate; has epiphany on sofa.

4:04 P.M. Phone call: Ruth Prawer Jhabvala has been lost in baggage claim of foreign airport.

5:25 P.M. Filmmakers arrive; they reminisce, fondle wicker.

WHAT IF MACY'S WERE TURNED INTO A CORRECTIONAL CENTER?

10:03 A.M. Inmates play poker in Moderate Shoes, using mannequin heads to ante.

10:55 A.M. Lifer enters Bridal Registry; updates list.

12:21 P.M. Inmate tells social worker of desire to sodomize regional buyer.

2:40 P.M. Inmate announces to guard, "The lesbian has stolen my cigarettes."

3:38 P.M. Inmate emerges from underneath basement bargain bin carrying dirt from tunnel; surreptitiously dumps dirt on Le Petit Cafe's display of international coffees.

4:10 P.M. Group of inmates convene to hear noted gardening author C. Z. Guest discuss peat.

6:00 P.M. Inmates file into basement deli for dinner; inmate bangs crystal goblet against Calphalon in overture to riot.

WHAT IF BALLET DANCERS WERE
SUBJECT TO LEASH LAWS?

9:13 A.M. Tension from dancer's collar and leash
unsnaps Danskin crotch panel.

9:23 A.M. Dancer is momentarily asphyxiated during
a series of pirouettes.

12:20 P.M. Dancer tied to tree outside restaurant rubs
chafed neck, applies lotion.

2:46 P.M. Tourist mistakes stray dachshund for a
haggard Gelsey Kirkland.

3:30 P.M. Bitter choreographer illustrates command
"Heel!" by swatting at dancer's ankles
with heavy cane.

Circus Jerks

Although the idea of being a circus clown has held appeal for me ever since childhood, the practicalities of learning the trade have always kept me at bay: I would not enjoy getting into a tiny car and sitting very, very close to other members of my profession; I do not want to litter my friends' homes with my failed balloon art; I am not anxious to have seltzer down my pants. However, when a magazine editor told me that a singles resort in Negril, Jamaica, was, in an attempt to lure guests during the off-peak season, holding a circus workshop in which it would bring "all the excitement of the big tent to its sandy white beach on the Caribbean Sea," the inherent graciousness of resort living allowed me to abandon my preconceptions and accept the assignment. I called the resort's publicist and said, "*Les junkets—je les adore.*"

=

Two days before I was to leave, I called the singles-oriented resort and asked if there was any special circus-related clothing or equipment that I needed to bring; the woman who answered the phone said she could think of nothing.

"If I bring a broom," I asked her, "could I be the little clown who sweeps up the spotlight at the end of the circus?"

Her training had apparently not prepared her for this question. I was put on hold; seconds later the line disconnected.

I packed a broom.

Upon my arrival at the lovely, palm-dappled grounds, a young Jamaican man, one of the resort's employees, carried my bag into my room and assured me in a lilting patois, "You are going to have the ball of your life." I told him I was quite excited about the circus workshop; he smiled indulgently and said that if I maintained proximity to him throughout my stay, I would be introduced to the most beautiful of the female guests and would "definitely score." I thanked him for his vote of confidence. My room contained two mirrors—one, about five by two feet, was directly in front of the bed; the other, about five by five feet, was directly over the bed.

On the sunshiny, palm-lined beach I found a trampoline, a trapeze, and a high wire—all in excellent condition, none in use. I searched for other evidence of the circus arts but found only sunbathing and lapsed *Nacktkultur*. At dinner I thought I'd discovered an aerialist in the tubby, slightly balding man who was walking around the dining room wearing nothing but a black G-string; but someone explained to me that he was "in computers" and from Chicago. When my eyes chanced upon a woman in the dinner line wearing suspenders, I thought that I had at last found a fellow clown. But when I walked over to her I discovered that her suspenders were buoying not baggy pants but bare breasts—the better to display the shimmery gold chain that linked her two pierced nipples.

As I struck up conversations with various of the 250 or so guests during my stay, it became increasingly clear that few of them had come for the circus workshop. As it turned out, this was fortunate for them: the circus sessions for the next two days were canceled because of rain. I contemplated calling the resort's publicist back in New York but decided simply to allow events to unfold on their own.

During the rainy afternoons, the resort's employees organized group games in the dining room. In one game, volunteers from the audience were paired off with members of the opposite sex and were then encouraged to ask each other provocative questions. Thus, just as I was taking my fourth bite of delicious fresh pineapple one day, the p.a. system broadcast a giggly woman saying to a man seated across from her, "Hi. I'm Ellen from Florida. Have you ever done it in Crisco or in oil?" whereupon the man responded, "Hi. I'm Bruce from Washington. Yes, with baby oil once." Other facts that the guests deemed important to broadcast over loudspeakers included, "Do you strap on when using a big dildo?" "Have you ever been fist-fucked?" and "Have you ever licked a man's asshole?" Another game was a version of Loser's Bingo wherein players tried to be the last person standing. The categories started on a fairly tame level ("Sit down if your birthday is in July") but then, when the group was reduced to six women, became increasingly unsavory ("Sit down if you swallow"). When a forties-ish, raw-boned woman responded to the command "Sit down if you gave a blow job last night," she was accorded a smattering of applause.

=

I did not participate in these games. I was not sure how to react. I thought about my predecessors; I wondered what the immortal Emmett Kelly and Slivers Oakley would have done in my place. How would Otto Griebling, the most beloved joey to ever tramp the sawdust, have handled this situation? I did not know. All I knew was that I have certain professional limits. Which is to say, *I don't work blue.*

=

In the course of my ruminations, the dining room had given way to a toga-tying demonstration for that evening's toga party. We were reminded repeatedly that if we didn't wear a toga to dinner, we wouldn't be served ("No sheet, no eat") and that if we wore underwear under our togas, our underwear would be cut off.

I began to feel slightly anxious. A maid brought a bed

sheet to my room. As I nervously wrapped my pale body, it gradually became clear that the finer points of the toga-tying demonstration had eluded me; the toga I fashioned was melancholic and larval. I skulked into the dining room and beheld a multiplicity of elaborate toga fashions. Guests had brought accessories and props from home—one man had used a fern, sunglasses, and a necktie to anthropomorphize a three-foot-long bulbous trunk that dangled from his crotch.

Dinner gave way to the Guest Talent Show—perhaps at last the demonstration of the clowning abilities I craved. Alas, I was disappointed again. One act, the Candy Lickers, consisted of two highly Nautilized men with all-over tans wearing only G-strings and matching cowboy boots. They sashayed onto the floor to music whose lyrics were a combination of filth and bad rhyming. They coaxed three blonde volunteers out of the audience and seated them, one at a time, on a stool, then craned their heads toward each woman's crotch and commenced licking the air. By the end of her stay onstage, each of the women had mustered a tight smile or forced laughter, but even a novice clown such as myself knew that they were crying on the inside.

Later that night, after the excitement of the talent show had subsided, many guests reconvened in the dining room for the regular evening snack hour. A man placed a chair on the stage where the Lickers had done their work and proceeded to watch, mesmerized, as his female companion removed her top and danced erotically to music being played on the stereo system. He drew the woman close to him and nuzzled and fondled her breasts. About twelve guests gradually drifted away from the snack table and toward this display. Among them was the other night's publicly confessed blow-job woman, who, sitting alone, looked on while rhapsodically snacking on a tiny cheese sandwich.

A bibulous woman in her late twenties introduced herself to me and asked me my name. I told her it was Sweepy; she asked me to spell it. I did, and then she asked me whether the name was Dutch. I explained that I was a clown and that Sweepy was my stage name; she held her ground by telling me I looked Dutch.

On my next-to-last day, the weather finally permitted a trapeze workshop to be held. A mere five guests materialized. Our instructor was charming and informative: Within a couple of hours I was able, while swinging back and forth some twenty feet above the ground, to hang from the bar by my knees. I thanked the instructor and quickly retreated to my room.

Later I soaked in a jacuzzi, played squash by myself, and walked on the dizzyingly beautiful moonlit beach. I did not opt to rejoin the other guests, who continued to swing in nontrapeze fashion. As I reflected on the previous three days, it occurred to me that, with respect to this particular writing assignment, the joke had most assuredly been on me.

I longed to return to the city, to escape the predicament of having gotten a proverbial pie in the face.

WHAT IF MAYOR MCCHEESE WROTE
A TELL-ALL AUTOBIOGRAPHY?

WHAT IF YOUR CATS OPENED
A HELLENIC DINER?

2:13 P.M. Waitress-cat gives you placemat emblazoned with the history of feta.

2:14 P.M. Proprietor-cat places bust of *Born Free*'s Elsa on Ionic column fragment.

2:24 P.M. Waitress-cat explains that kitchen is out of the Bagel Fantasy and the scrod.

2:30 P.M. Dishwasher-cat enters statuary nook for licking and scratching.

3:10 P.M. Elderly waiter-cat leaves counter duty to nap at register.

WHAT IF SANTA'S WORKSHOP PRODUCED PERFORMANCE ART IN THE OFF-SEASON?

February Elf performs show utilizing African narrative, laser art, deaf signing, and piles of garbage.

March Elf arrives late to all rehearsals in attempt to create aura.

April Santa performs nine-hour show in Tibetan mime and Urdu.

May Santa calls Ottawa to place large order of yams.

June Elf uses leftover ribbon to strap Vocoder onto Blitzen.

July Rudolph offers monodrama, *Reindeer Games I Never Played: A Show About Healing.*

August Mrs. Claus walks onstage wearing beauty pageant banners and raw beef slabs.

September Elf's same five friends see his show for the forty-seventh time.

Someone's in the Kitchen

Julia Child, Shirley MacLaine, and Gerald Ford have all done it at the Park Avenue Café. The Associated Press and the Culinary Institute of America have done it at the Waldorf-Astoria. Tama Janowitz and Matt Dillon have done it at the Plaza Hotel; when they were finished, each graced the guestbook with comments rendered in an inimitable prose style (Miss Janowitz: "What a fantastic experience. As if birds, rubies, moths, and other entities descended from the sky and became food in one's mouth." Mr. Dillon: "Excellent grub.")

Enter, if you will, the stately and elegant Edwardian Room of the Plaza Hotel. Behold the high, majestic oak-and-mahogany-paneled ceiling, the walls drenched in scarlet damask, the views of horse-drawn carriages ready for hire; savor the tantalizing aroma of delicacies wafting tableward. The lovely petit-point armchair in front of you? Do not sit on it. No, come this way, please, into the kitchen—as Miss Janowitz and Mr. Dillon did, as Sting and David Lynch have, as David Hockney, John McEnroe, Dean Stockwell, Louise Bourgeois, Julian Schnabel, and the members of INXS have—past the gray and moldering mop, past the dozing busboy. It is here, amidst the heat and bustle—a step or two from the fragrant dishwashing station, hard by the plastic bin harboring soiled towels—that you will find what you are looking for: your dinner table.

=

"Is it . . . private?" I asked the Plaza employee who was taking my reservation.

"We'll just set a table for two," he told me.

"Right," I said. "But I mean, will we be able to have a private conversation? My wife has a tendency to, to sob in restaurants."

"The kitchen is a very busy place."

"But we'll be able to hear ourselves talk," I said.

"Oh, yes," he responded.

"Okay," I said. "We'll see you next Thursday."

=

It was in the dizzy 1980s, when so many people had so much money that there just weren't enough choice tables in the dining room to accommodate them all, that the Plaza solved the problem of making the important guest feel his importantness among legions of merely significant diners: Let him eat in the kitchen. Now, with evidence clear that the very people who faint at the prospect of being seated *near* the kitchen leap at the chance to dine *in* it, restaurants throughout New York City are inviting VIP customers to break bread where others are baking it.

When asked about the inclination to eat in the sweltry and clamorous kitchen of a restaurant—an inclination that can be indulged on a prix-fixed basis at the aforementioned places, as well as at Tatou and the French Culinary Institute in New York, Charlie Trotter's in Chicago, and the Raleigh Hotel in Miami—Margaret Visser, the author of *The Rituals of Dinner* and *Much Depends on Dinner,* pointed out, "In the early days of the theater, the nobility sat on the stage." Indeed; and in the case of eating grillside, sometimes the nobility *perform* on the stage: When dining in the kitchen of Arcadia (now discontinued), Burgess Meredith used to compose sonnets and sing songs of homage to the Beaujolais; when given a negligee at her birthday party in the kitchen of the Edwardian Room one year, rocker Debbie Harry shucked her clothes in a closet near the waiters' podium and, in making her way back to the kitchen, scampered through the dining room in the negligee and high heels.

In other instances, diners experience not a feeling of expansion and liberation, but rather one of entrapment. At the Park Avenue Café, David Burke's sublime, inventive food is served to diners who sit in an air-conditioned, soundproof box, two sides of which are glass. Waiters peer in from the sides to note your progress; they deposit mounds of food and then depart, quickly sliding the door shut—it's like day care, but catered. "You're in *the middle of the kitchen,*" emphasized Clark Wolf, the restaurant consultant, about dining in the kitchen of the Edwardian Room. "This one woman we were with was wearing a low-cut dress. She dropped a little bit of sauce someplace . . . *critical,*" said Wolf. "And just watched it melt."

=

"Do you think it's a little . . . weird for us to be here?" I asked our charming busboy, Balegh, midway through our meal in the Plaza's kitchen.

"Well, no," he said. "Many people find it very nice, very interesting."

"But aren't we in the way?" I asked.

"Not so much. We don't do it on the busiest nights."

"Because then we would get trampled on," I surmised.

"Yes, this could happen then."

=

Peoples' motives for enduring this particular form of hardship vary. For the food-obsessive, of course, eating in the kitchen is the ultimate insider activity, an opportunity to buy admission to the exclusivity of the ages-old chef's table, that phenomenon wherein a chef and his staff achieve commensality (meaning, literally, "togetherness arising out of the fact that we eat at the same table") by eating together in the kitchen before the dinner rush. Some partake in order to effect quality control: "I've never been served a bad dish in a restaurant's kitchen," said *Gourmet*'s New York restaurant reviewer, Andy Birsh. Some partake in order to give voice to the health inspector who lurks within: "You can see how clean the kitchen is," noted Michel Richard, the proprietor of Hollywood's Citrus.

Restaurants have other ways, of course, of accommodating Americans' fascination with the process of cooking and their need to make a celebrity of the person grilling their infant zucchini. Large pieces of plate glass at places like Citrus, Smith and Wollensky, the Tasting Room at Le Bernadin, and Brendan Walsh's North Street Grill in Great Neck, New York, afford the diners views of the chef in his domain (indeed, Citrus diners recently broke into applause at the sight of the bearded, pear-shaped Michel Richard dancing the French cancan on a kitchen counter with a customer); a sushi-bar-like "food bar" at Zoë in New York City allows diners to talk to the chef ("I don't want it," said one customer to chef Steven Levine when he saw Levine garnishing an entrée, "Your hands were on it"). Sometimes video is used to bridge the gap between dining room and kitchen—a nineteen-inch color video monitor located at the bar of City restaurant in Los Angeles captures all the splendor and excitement of the kitchen's grill area and tandoori oven; video cameras hidden in the dining room of Pierre Orsi in Lyons, France, allow the chef to gauge diners' reactions to his offerings.

But, as compared with these more dispassionate, clinical interchanges, eating in the kitchen stems more from a desire for intimacy. "It's a very ambivalent thing," said Margaret Visser. "On the one hand, diners are creating a tremendous distance between themselves and the cooks, they're being very judgmental and are expecting extreme competence and lots of entertainment; and on the other hand, they want to feel all homey."

And, of course, they want highly exciting, labor-intensive food—food that is somehow different and better than that available to the hoi polloi in the dining room. It is on this count that meals eaten in the kitchen rarely fail to deliver. During chef Kerry Simon's reign at the Edwardian Room, waiters made great ceremony of the untying of the cord that bound Simon's black squid ink lasagna in its sheath of green banana leaves; a recent meal at that same location concluded with, among other elaborate confections, delicious fresh poached apricots and apricot sorbet afloat on something called an "almond doughnut abstract."

=

"Did you say, 'almond doughnut abstract'?" I asked the dessert chef.

"Yes."

"That sounds . . . exciting," I said.

"Where did you get fresh apricots?" Erica, my dinner-mate, asked.

"We're a hotel."

"And are there other kinds of doughnut abstract?" I asked.

"You can do others," he said. "But for now it's just the almond."

=

But all standards of excessiveness pale in comparison to those of the by-invitation-only Annual Game Dinner, held in the 12,400-square-foot kitchen of the Perona Farms banquet facility in Andover, New Jersey. Attended by two hundred people in 1993, including chefs Pierre Franey, Daniel Boulud, Jean-Louis Palladin (Jean-Louis of the Watergate Hotel, Washington), Jean-François Taquet (Taquet's, Philadelphia), Gordon Drysdale (Bix, San Francisco), Francesco Ricchi (I Ricchi, Washington) and then *New York Times* restaurant reviewer Bryan Miller, the twelfth annual feast (and benefit for the National Multiple Sclerosis Society) consisted of fifty-two courses. Much of the food is hunted and fished by the guests, many of whom wear their hunting clothes; "stag" videos of the hunting and fishing expeditions that produced the food are shown throughout the meal on two TV monitors.

A variety of unusual foodstuffs has been offered over the years, including elk tacos and goose breast jerky. 1993's menu featured a veritable chorus line of the poultry world (Goose Legs Rillette, Woodcock Legs Tempura, Wild Duck Legs Salmi with Burgundy Wine, Stuffed Roasted Pheasant Legs Crêpinette); two of the watercress-based offerings were the result of one chef's highly unpleasant encounter with ducks (Watercress Salad with Duck Tongues, Watercress Salad with Duck Testicles). Jean-Louis Palladin ordered fifteen hundred shiners from the local bait shop and made Shiners Tempura; said a local who attends the dinner, "We haven't looked at our bait bucket the same since."

But it is the traditional first main course of the night that dominates the festivities. "Here they are, guys," announces Perona Farms proprietor Wade Avondoglio at about seven-thirty P.M. each year. "Get in line for the woodcock heads," whereupon, using a wax candle, he proceeds to roast the golfball-sized heads of a number of woodcocks, dip them in a veal glaze, slice the crowns of their heads off, and then hand them to diners by the birds' large beak. "You put it in your mouth and just suck out those delicious little brains," Avondoglio said, "and the eyes, too, if you want to."

As Matt Dillon noted, "Excellent grub."

—

"How was everything?" Balegh the busboy asked us as we lingered at the table in our postpayment, predeparture mode.

"Oh, it was great," I said. "The food was great."

"We loved it," Erica murmured.

"Yes—thank you," I added.

"Good, good," he responded.

He reached down to brush a few crumbs off the table, saying, "I would like now to take you on a tour of the dining room."

WHAT IF MR. PEANUT RAN A STRIP JOINT CALLED "THE PARTY MIX"?

9:50 P.M. Candee Pecan lifts part of shell provocatively; customers scream, "Shell it!"

10:24 P.M. Mr. P. introduces Whata Chestnut as "a tempest in a D-cup."

12:02 A.M. Mr. P. tells new cage dancer that pretzel-customers will do "anything for titty."

12:35 A.M. Bouncer removes raisin who has attached himself to Almond Joy.

1:04 A.M. Topless Beechnut commences novelty wrestling by entering creamed-corn pit.

1:27 A.M. Honey-slathered peanut-dancer smolders under harsh spotlight in climactic throes of the Honey Roast.

2:20 A.M. Miss Macadamia starts rumor that her competitor sleeps in dirt.

3:44 A.M. Mr. Salty and other pretzels arrive; Mr. P. runs into dressing room, shouts, "Fleet's in!"

4:30 A.M. Mr. P. removes top hat and monocle; saunters out to parking lot to fellate Brazil nut.

The Egg and Me

S he was white-haired and soft-spoken, and she was a poet. You could tell her hair color by looking and her timbre by listening, but her status as a poet—a subtler thing—was best revealed by her presence in the ballroom of the Washington, D.C., Hilton, where she was joining two thousand fellow award-winning poets—many of them also soft-spoken, white-haired ladies—at the fifth annual World of Poetry convention.

Of course, her avocation was also revealed by what she was saying to a small circle of newfound friends about the verses she composed when the space shuttle Challenger crashed. "When I sat down to write," she said, "the words just flowed." As she told the story the corners of her eyes glistened with tears. Her husband, sitting next to her, put his arm on her shoulder comfortingly. "Yep, that was a good one," he said, beaming with pride. "I had that one *laminated.*"

=

Not all of the conventioneers were feeling similarly loved. Upon their arrival at the Hilton that afternoon, several of the people new to the World of Poetry—a Sacramento-based organization that, according to its founder, John Campbell, has more than 1.1 million members and is the largest poetry society in the world—made an unsettling discovery. Having entered a poetry contest advertised in publications ranging from *The Atlantic* to *USA Today* and having received an exuberant letter of congratulations that invited them to the convention ("I'm so excited to tell you the good news! World of Poetry's board of directors has voted unanimously to honor you with our Golden Poet Award for 1989, in recognition of your poem, which you entered in our Free Poetry Contest. What is the Golden Poet Award? . . . The Golden Poet Award is to poets what the Academy Award is to actors"), many of them arrived under the impression that they alone had won.

But the World of Poetry is not a cruel, Hobbesian world in which a single winner has vanquished many lesser worthies in his dog-eat-dog climb to the top. No, no, no. The World of Poetry is a kind world, a loving world. There was not *one* winner. There were *two thousand.*

Those Golden Poets—along with anyone who bothered to respond at all—were offered the opportunity to come to

Washington at their own expense, enter a poem in the convention contest, and contend for thirty-five thousand dollars in cash and prizes and the World of Poetry poet laureateship. Some, like the frankly disappointed woman from North Carolina who had forgone paying her car insurance for a month in order to attend, decided simply to "chalk this one up to experience." Others felt more pointedly aggrieved. But to prove how loving a world the World of Poetry is, the hosts reimbursed, out of the approximately $1.7 million they had raked in, any conventioneer who felt cheated (the poets had paid a $495 fee, their guests, $425). A square deal, yes, perhaps even a loving one; still, you could not help but feel sorry for people like Elaine Martin, a woman with cerebral palsy whose friends and relatives had held a fund-raiser so that she and her sister could come from Cincinnati, or Priya Sharma, a young woman whose parents had paid for her flight from Bhopal, India.

=

The weekend-long convention was a veritable shivaree of events. Upon registering, the two thousand soon-to-be award-winning poets, along with their guests and numerous non-award-winning poets, were treated to an hour-long "Gala Champagne Reception," followed by a "Gala Afternoon Welcome." The emphasis, it seemed, was on the gala. Of the twenty-seven scheduled hours of the convention, only five and a half could be construed as poetry oriented—an hour and a half on "oral interpretation" and a four-hour period during which all the poets split into smaller groups and read their work to one another.

Much of the convention was devoted to gushy show-biz acts and shameless self-congratulation, the prime practitioner of which was World of Poetry editor and publisher John Campbell, who had himself been crowned laureate of the first convention, in 1985. Campbell's Saturday-night performance, advertised as a "one-man Shakespearean explosion!" proved to be the perfect showcase for the coy, roly-poly Campbell, who donned period costume and tested the audience's memory of the nursery rhyme "Little Miss Muffet." ("Let's give ourselves a hand for that!") Then he sat on a golden throne and read Lewis Carroll's "The Walrus and the Carpenter" while the pedestal of the throne spewed, in classic Elizabethan fashion, a large cloud of soap bubbles.

Other speakers included Bob Hope, Jayne Meadows (who at one point asked the audience, "Aren't I *marvelous?*"), poet Sonia Sanchez, and American poet laureate Howard Nemerov—yes, the *real* poet laureate. Four other celebrity poetry buffs who were advertised did not show: Helen Hayes, Tony Randall, Willard Scott, and poet Louis Simpson. Campbell made various excuses for their absence; but, according to *The Washington Post* and *The Washington Times,* darker forces had prevailed: All four had backed out upon finding out more about the World of Poetry. According to the *Times,* an agent at Helen Hayes's agency called the convention "a scandal," and the *Post* quoted Louis

Simpson as saying it was "a rip-off." Nemerov—the most prestigious speaker booked for the convention—came to the conclusion that the convention was "technically legal, but not kosher," and tried to get out of the engagement but was contractually bound. "As I can't get out of it," he said, "I'll go in with a good heart, a clean mouth, and will keep a civil tongue in my cheek. . . . It's more like P. T. Barnum than Hitler, you know."

But no matter who appeared, the audience—which, to be fair, was primarily composed of happy people returning to the convention for their second or third time—responded warmly; in the course of fifteen scheduled hours in the ballroom, no fewer than seven standing ovations were given. For many, the proceedings were an emotional whirligig, a chance to wallow in pronouncements like "We are all poets."

Nevertheless, several of the poets I talked to were dismayed by the quality of the poetry that had been recognized. "Anybody could throw words together and they got an award for it," one poet complained. "Compared with what I've heard at other poetry readings, this stuff is disgusting."

It did seem that an awful lot of, well, *chaff* had been produced by these Golden Poets. I wondered how bad a poem had to be to preclude its being recognized. With this in mind, I hastily penned the following:

I Am in the Egg; Hello? Hello?

> Orblike within my shell,
> I am a sticky placenta beach ball

I am yolkness
I am *of* yolk
Yolk yolk yolk
Yolks for sale!
        (I'll take two, they're small)
I am trapped inside a gigantic rubber egg
Please help me.

When I read this poem to my fellow conventioneers, it was met with great acclaim. "This is great," one young man raved. Another, who had won his invitation to the convention with his "Sonnet in Sympathy with Exploited Labor in South America," said, "Deep, esoteric—it's wonderful. Sometimes the realization of our own insignificance keeps us within our own shell." A similar grasp of theme was manifested by Jeanny Losey, the sixty-four-year-old Indiana housewife who had bagged the twelve-thousand-dollar grand prize and the poet laureateship in 1986. "Yes," she responded, after considering the poem at length. "It seems like we always feel like we're closed in."

Having been praised thusly, I set out in search of John Campbell to receive the ultimate validation, but he had, like one of his throne's bubbles, suddenly vanished. I settled for the teary Catherine McCord, who had just finished serving as one of three judges of the fifteen-thousand-dollar grand prize and the poet laureateship. Although it was too late to get my ovatic masterpiece into the contest, it wasn't too late to get a little helpful feedback. McCord was up on the stage, next to the judges' table, hovering on the periphery of postcoronation hysteria. I mounted the stage and squirmed through the crowd and read my poem to her. Slowly and meaningfully. She paused. She coughed. Suspense mounted. Finally, out it came: "It's wonderful. I love it. It's beautifully *crafted.*"

And soon to be beautifully laminated as well.

MOVING ON

Dread and Breakfast

The visitor to Manhattan who is in search of accommodations that might be billed as "inexpensive but lovely"
is faced with a dearth of possibilities—hotels are rarely the
former; the YMCA never the latter. Thus it was with a sense
of epiphany and joy that I opened the Manhattan Yellow
Pages and discovered, sandwiched between "Bed Boards"
and "Bed Frames (Metal)" a section entitled "Bed and
Breakfast" with some fifteen entries.

Those who have traveled Europe or back-roads America
and who have stayed at bed and breakfasts are well acquainted with the pleasures and enchantments that result
when natives with a surfeit of square footage open their
homes and their hearts to weary travelers. The paying guest
in a stranger's home is also aware of what the typical B & B
lacks—pool privileges, tiny guest soaps, a room down the
hall with several hundred pounds of free ice. No, the words

bed and breakfast are synonymous with homelike charm, with four-posters and counterpanes and a gift jar of the hostess's own blackberry jam, with clapboard houses on winding lanes and afternoon tea round the fire. Sunrise Farm, Hill & Hollow, Breezy Acres Farm, the Burton House, the Inn at Fordhook Farm, Ashley Manor—the names themselves betoken old-fashioned country comfort and delight.

And yet . . . and yet . . . happy as I was to learn that New York City, improbably, had bed and breakfasts, I was forced to ask myself whether they could provide the kind of spirit-lifting loveliness and warm human touch for which bed and breakfasts are known. Breezy Acres on West Twenty-third Street? The Inn at Fordhook on upper Broadway? I wondered.

My curiosity piqued, I set out to visit some bed and breakfasts in New York City with the hope of answering these questions:

1. Would my hosts eventually untie me and allow me to live?
2. Would I really be served breakfast?

Most travelers find Manhattan B & Bs through reservation services, of which there are at least ten. One calls a service, explains for what night and in what neighborhood one is looking for accommodations, and then answers questions as to whether or not one is able to endure cigarette smoke, more than two flights of stairs, pets, or shared bathrooms. Of course, suspicion has no place in this cozy world. None of the three services I used asked me to meet them or provide references. All they knew, and all my hosts knew, was that I was male and probably in my twenties— the precise profile of the typical violent felon.

I stayed at a handful of different bed and breakfasts in Manhattan. I asked to stay at the least expensive ones in the city, and made no demands about smoking, pets, stairs, or anything else. The price per night ran between sixty and eighty dollars, for which the reservation service takes a cut of about 25 percent. (The price for a night at a typical hotel in New York is about twice that.) My hosts said they averaged around six guests a month; and so they all had real jobs in addition to welcoming complete strangers into their homes and offering them toast.

I learned many things from my experience. I learned that even in the big, anonymous city, people are reaching out to people. And I learned that these people are very strange.

UPPER WEST SIDE STORY
Pussy Willows and Suspect Soap

An elfin woman in her early sixties who wears her hair in bangs bids me enter her dark apartment on the Upper West Side, takes my bag, and immediately and awkwardly says, "Let me show you your room." The room is small and dark and is defined on the top by a swirly stucco ceiling and on the bottom by two pieces of carpet that are both beginning to unravel. A Coke bottle filled with dried pussywillows sits on a drab wooden dresser. My host suggests that I get myself settled and then come join her in the kitchen.

As I am unpacking I notice that the transom over the door to my room has been knocked out, and suddenly I am glad that my plans for the evening do not involve having sex. I am moved, however, to check the bed linens, and I discover that they are floral-printed and are actually transparent in parts. "I could probably read *The New York Times* through these!" I think, aware that this is an accolade for croissant dough, not for bedsheets.

Moments later I walk down the hall, an area illuminated, as my room is, by naked overhead bulbs, and I pass the bathroom and another guest bedroom before entering the kitchen. The kitchen appears to be a repository for cat postcards and dried flowers and dead plants in La Yogurt containers. Its floor is clad in a hazy coffee-nougat-phlegm-colored linoleum that in one spot has begun to buckle. I join my host at the kitchen table, and we talk for about forty-five minutes, during which time she emerges as an intelligent and energetic chain-smoker. Shortly into our talk, I bring up the topic of money and say, "Should I pay you now or should I w—" whereupon, pupils practically blazing with holographic dollar signs, she cuts me off with "Why don't we get it over with now?" Her intensity resurfaces later in the conversation when she presses her finger against the red plastic tablecloth and, pinpointing a crumb, gingerly places the crumb in her mouth and swallows. I now realize that the unkempt nature of the apartment is less a reflection of lack of effort than it is of this rather time-consuming cleaning process.

When I get up to go out for dinner, my host lays out a few of the ground plans. There will be coffee, tea, and bagels on the table in the morning, and I am to help myself to them. I am free to sit in the kitchen as much as I want. There will be a couple staying in the second bedroom; my host herself will be staying with her visiting brother in the closed-off front part of the apartment. "We like to leave the bathroom door open when no one is using it," she also explains, "so no one gets stuck in the hall wondering whether or not it's okay to knock."

The next morning I am awakened by the sound of the two other guests and my host in the kitchen. Not wanting to have to interact in my precaffeinated state, I loll in bed until it sounds as though they have left the kitchen. A cursory glance around the room reveals that I have been provided with a respectable bath towel; an old but not yet fraying flesh-colored handcloth; and a sad, black-and-yellow-plaid washcloth possibly dating from the Eisenhower administration. I pad down to the bathroom, witness its grout deterioration, am vaguely repulsed by the sight of human hair and used Q-Tips in the unemptied trash can there, and decide to brave a shower. The unwrapped bar of soap in the shower looks newish but not brand spanking new; I put it between my clenched hands and lather off a good quarter inch of its potentially pubic-hair-afflicted surface before applying it to my person.

Later, once dressed, I walk out of my room, whereupon

my host, dressed in a nubbly, bright red bunny-type sleeping garment, materializes in the hallway and appears anxious to make me coffee. I tell her that I am going out to buy the paper; she oddly responds, "Oh, are you leaving now?" I tell her no, I am simply going to buy the paper and then I will be right back. This reiteration of my agenda seems to sink in, and she asks if it would be okay if she strips the bed while I am gone. I give this proposal my ready assent.

When I return, the apartment is eerily quiet. The other guests have left and I cannot find my host. With a sense of slightly anxious peacefulness, I sit in the kitchen, which is lit by a single fluorescent bulb over the sink, and drink some coffee and eat a bagel and read the paper. I've had the bed and now—breakfast!

Thirty minutes or so later, I pack and seek out my host. I knock on the door of her part of the apartment; her brother greets me and tells me she is out doing laundry, so I thank him and leave. The polite hemisphere of my brain wonders momentarily if I am meant to tip my host, but then the impolite hemisphere sniggers at the very idea.

VILLAGE VISIT
Spaciousness and a Surprise

The second apartment I stay at is in Greenwich Village, an area noted for its bed-and-breakfasty charm. The apartment features a huge living room that separates my room from the kitchen. However, my host, a vivacious, zaftig single woman in her early sixties, makes no mention of whether the living room lies within my purlieu, and thus this unavoidable area taunts me throughout the rest of my stay like a large, throbbing question mark. She does, however, make clear that I will once again share a bathroom with another guest. I accept this news with stoicism.

Uncertain of my permitted range, I confine myself mostly to my room, a twelve-by-fifteen-foot box lit by an overhead bulb shaded by what looks like a crocheted cap with tassels—perhaps an early prototype for the Shriners' fez. The door to the room, in addition to having a one-inch clearance from the floor, has a two-by-three-foot section of shutters in it, thus ensuring maximum noise carryover. At one point, while I am purposefully headed to the bathroom, my host introduces me to the other guest—a businessman from Michigan who, because he has a lot of work in Manhattan, has reserved a room with the host for Tuesday through Thursday for the entire month. The enthusiasm that the host expresses for the other guest ("A regular! All the way from Michigan!") makes me feel like a younger, less-loved sibling.

When I return from dinner that night, I can hear the news from the TV in my host's bedroom, yet she emerges from the kitchen. She tells me that she likes to listen to the news while she exercises—an activity that I can only imagine involves a lot of crouching and lotion. She walks into her bedroom, so I take the opportunity to glance briefly at some of the artwork in the outer area of the living room, still tantalizing, still unapproachable.

Later that night at around ten o'clock I decide to go outside for a walk. I grab the spare house key my host has provided me and walk out of my room. Nothing could have prepared me for what I then witness; for there, traipsing across the living room on her way to the kitchen, is my host, her calves and fleshy lower thighs unprotected by the scant yardage of her T-shirt-style nightie. In an effort to mask my nervous laughter I produce a sound that is somewhere between coughing, strangling, and revving a large outboard motor. I avert my eyes from my host's and scurry out the door.

The next morning, while I am sitting at the dining room table and enjoying my rather lavish, tasty, serve-yourself breakfast (bagels, English and blueberry muffins, coffee or tea), my host walks out of her bedroom dressed in work clothes and informs me that she has to be at work at nine but that I can stay. I thank her for her hospitality and tell her that I will leave the key on the dining room table.

Shortly after her departure I enter the living room, and I lounge victoriously on the couch for twenty minutes before heading to my office.

MIDTOWN NOCTURNE

"The Moonlight Affects Me . . . Strangely"

"Come on in. But why don't you take your shoes off," says my third host, a beatific, lovely woman in her late forties wearing a loose, tie-dyed jumpsuit. "We don't wear shoes here. This is a sanctuary." I oblige her request, walk into her immaculate midtown apartment, and behold three women lounging on the floor of the living room. It is a large, minimalist room, its whiteness punctuated only by three Turneresque paintings, two wire sculptures, a grand piano, two small chairs, and an ottoman.

I pick up my bag and ask her if I might put it in my room. She looks at me quizzically, pauses, and then, pointing to the right, says, "You'll either be in here—which is my bedroom—or in the living room on a futon. Or out on the terrace if you would like." In deference to my own personal safety, I opt for the living room.

My host introduces me to her three friends and then says, "Just make yourself comfortable. They won't be here *all* night," a statement that I find unsettling, given that the women are currently sprawled on the floor of what is to be my sleeping quarters.

I am invited to join them, so I hover briefly on the periphery of their group. They are eating chips and salsa and reading to one another from a spiritual book called *Being a Woman: Fulfilling Your Femininity and Finding Love,* and then relating the passages to their own lives. Not being a woman, I find my attention lapses and I wander out onto the terrace. Several moments later my host comes out and asks if I would like to sit out there in a chair; I say yes and she brings me a very comfortable folding deck chair. Then she goes back into the apartment and returns with a folded-up piece of fabric that she hands to me saying, "Here is a sarong. You can just slip into it. We aren't bashful here."

However, I *am*, so once she has turned and gone back into the apartment, I reach over the doorsill and lay the sarong on the living room floor. I sit and try to relax. I look at the sarong. I think, *What?*

When I go back inside an hour or so later, I discover that my host has moved my bag onto a massage table in her bedroom. I put my sneakers on and walk into the living room in order to tell her that I am going out for dinner, whereupon she stares at my sneakers and chastises me for the "negative energy" that they might unleash in her apartment.

Once outside, resentful that aspersions have been cast on my footwear, I avenge myself by going to a restaurant and eating a lot of meat.

When I return to the apartment, I slip off my shoes and enter to find that the three women have left but a new one has arrived. She and the host and I go out on the terrace and marvel at the nearly full moon. My host sets up a futon on the floor of the living room for me and explains that her bed is also portable. Then she says, "I may bring it out here and come join you. I tend to wander about in the night." I smile bleakly.

A few minutes later I follow her into her bedroom to get a pillow, and she takes the opportunity to say to me, "Don't be bashful around me."

"Don't be bashful about *what?*" I ask.

"Don't be bashful about me because I'm not bashful around you."

About an hour later her guest leaves, and twenty minutes

after that I get into bed, sure that I will awaken in the middle of the night and find myself being either raped or shaved.

The following morning, however, I arise intact and unscathed. I notice that my bag has been moved from the massage table in the bedroom into the hall. After dressing hurriedly and self-consciously in the bathroom, I am treated to a wonderful breakfast of plain and chocolate croissants, slices of melon and freshly brewed coffee. During this repast my host and I get to talking about owning things, and she says, "I don't believe in ownership. I think that I have a part of all things and all things are a part of me." I ask my host what she would do if a friend of hers were wearing a shirt that my host knew would flatter her more than her friend. My host replies that she would either ask the friend where she got the shirt or she would say, "You have had that shirt long enough and maybe I should have it for a while."

I instinctively clutch my bag, and a short while thereafter, my bag and I leave.

EAST SIDE ELEGANCE
Helpful Hints and Thoughts About Cheese

My next stay, in the East Nineties, distinguishes itself on two counts: a) the host is a male; b) he offers a snack service.

On the bedside table in my room I find a mimeographed note. "Hi," it reads. "Welcome to your home away from home. I am pleased to have you as a guest and would like you to enjoy your stay. How can I help you? Do you need information about sightseeing? transportation? entertainment? Just ask. If I don't know, I'll be glad to find out for you. Do you need an ironing board? A hair dryer? Would you care for a snack before you retire? All are available upon request. (The evening snack service is $3.50 additional to your room rate.) Breakfast will be served between 7 A.M. and 8 A.M. If that time is not convenient for your schedule, and you prefer to serve yourself at a later time, please make arrangements with me before you retire. If you need to be in and out during the day, a house key is available so you can let yourself in and out as you please. You are welcome to join us in the family room for television any evening after 8 P.M. A small radio is available for use in your room if you wish. Laundry equipment is available for your use at [Wite-Out blotch] charge. You will find extra blankets and towels on the upper shelf of your closet, should you need them. Please let me know anything I can do to make yours a very pleasant stay." I think the note is admirably comprehensive.

I don't partake of the snack service, but over breakfast the next morning (coffee, four pieces of bakery-fresh white bread, a pot of marmalade, a pot of margarine) I chat with my host—a large, bespectacled man in his fifties—about it. It is favored largely by his younger clientele. "They don't eat enough dinner, they need more. [I give them] cold cuts. An egg, a soft-boiled egg. Cheese—I keep a lot of cheese around. Or a sandwich." When he mentions the cheese, the way he says *around* faintly suggests that he uses the word literally. The rest of my stay is marked by an unshakable expectation that I will encounter cheese in some inappropriate setting.

PARTIAL PARK VIEW PLEASURES
Midway, More Soap, and An Act of Aggression

When it comes time to stay at my last Manhattan bed and breakfast, I recall the words of Bernice Chesler, as I often do in my private moments. Miss Chesler is the travel philosopher and author of *Bed and Breakfast in the Mid-Atlantic States,* among other works. With regard to the bed and breakfast, she has written that "the keynote is hospitality" and that it is "a people-to-people program." I realize that by remaining in my room too much at night and tending to avoid the living areas, I have failed to test these principles. I am now determined to become more of a people person.

My final host lives on the West Side near Central Park. She is a small, peppy woman in her early sixties, and she shows me directly to my room without mentioning her large living room. I am now a man with a mission.

I return from dinner to find that my host has gone out shopping (as she told me earlier she would) and that all the lights in the living room and adjoining dining area are off. I turn on a lamp in the living room and pull a chair up to the television. I turn the TV on and discover that the war classic *Midway* is being shown on channel five. I turn up the volume so that the soundtrack adequately mimics a sea battle.

When my host returns about twenty minutes later, she looks in on me with an initial air of distraction and confusion. But seconds later, sporting an apparently genuine smile, she asks me what I am watching. When I reply that it is *Midway,* she does not seem enthusiastic and goes into the kitchen to unpack her groceries.

Several minutes later she comes back into the living room. "I finally got some *soap*!" she says triumphantly, apparently unaware of the relative ease with which we others find and buy this product. She has bought a five-pack of Ivory and, while extolling the virtues of its subtle fragrance, encourages me to smell a bar. I do, but then quickly return to *Midway.* As the pace of the fiery maelstrom of warfare and combat starts to quicken, I decide to cheer on the battle scenes. "Bah-*bing*!" I say when a bomb is dropped on an American ship; when a Japanese plane erupts in flames I cheer, *"Bingo!"* My host looks at me slightly askance, chuckles nervously, and remarks that the *depiction* of war is so much less frightening than actual war. She then goes and sits on the couch behind me and noisily reads *The New York Times.*

At ten o'clock I stand and switch the channel to PBS, which is airing *Metamorphosis: Man into Woman,* a documentary about a man who has a sex change. My host and I watch this with rapt curiosity. When she is forced to answer the phone twice during the show, she appears slightly vexed and hurries the callers off the line.

I decide to go further. I want to see how the people-to-people program really works. Over breakfast the next morning I lie elaborately, telling my host that I am a decorator and that I have recently graduated from a community college in Massachusetts with a degree in interior design. She seems genuinely interested and asks me several questions about my schooling. Shortly thereafter I pack my bag and thank my host for her hospitality. Then, bag in hand, I tell my host that I have *rethought* the arrangement of some of the furniture in the room that I slept in. She titters nervously and expectantly and asks to see. I open the door to the bedroom and allow her eyes to take in the changes that I wrought before going to bed the night before. I have moved the queen-size bed four inches to the left, moved the dark pine Swedish modern desk fifteen feet or so across the room to where the bedside table was (and put the bedside table where the desk was), and I have switched the positions of the two framed posters.

She takes one look and says, "Oh, it's *nice*. It looks . . . it really looks nice."

"Oh, you don't mind it?" I say with feigned modesty. "I completely understand if you hate it. It's just that it's so hard for me to spend time in a space and not *interact* with it, even on the most minimal level. I didn't move *all* the pieces."

Noticing the open area created by the exchange of the

largish desk for the smaller bedside table, she says, "Oooh—it certainly makes it easier to get in here to the bathroom."

"Yes," I say, picking up her lead. "I think it really opens up the space. I was trying to create . . . *egress.*"

"Ahh," she says, apparently trying to digest this particular design element.

I walk out into the hallway, eager to leave. She accompanies me and, on our way to the door, titters, "It's *nifty* what you did in there. Oh yes, that's something."

Two days later, under the pretext of having lost a contact lens during my stay, I return to the apartment and discover that the furniture remains the way I arranged it. My host mentions that she spent the night in the guest room.

"You slept in *this* room?" I ask incredulously.

"Well, I was just concerned that with the desk so close to the bed now that it might be a little cramped, but it's not. It's good if you want to do some writing or use the desk. I really like it! I like spaciousness and this way is much more spacious."

I feel complete. I feel *loved.* But then, suddenly: "I've got some spare furniture in *my* bedroom, too; *but I'm not going to show it to you.*"

=

My sojourns at the homes of total strangers are behind me now. And although I cannot say that I have forged any new friendships or that I plan to invite any of my hosts to my own home, I have come to learn more about New York,

WHAT IF RALPH LAUREN DESIGNED COMPUTER VIRUSES INSTEAD OF CLOTHING?

"Surrey"   Virus inserts word *quite* before all of text's adjectives.

"Taos"   Screen is filled with stripes and patterns of endless Navajo blanket.

"Jockey"   All characters are reduced to ⅓ their normal size.

"Tailgate Picnic"   Printer spews cloud of deviled eggs and exhaust fumes.

"Gatwick"   Text circles screen for hours; comes out printer with portions lost.

"Old Money"   Characters cavort around screen drunkenly; disappear until following day at noon.

WHAT IF THE CAST OF *THE MCLAUGHLIN GROUP* WERE LIVING INSIDE YOUR BATHROOM?

8:30 A.M. Fred tells Pat he disagrees: creme rinse does *not* result in more volume.

8:31 A.M. Group discusses whether Tidy Bowl Man should be granted political asylum.

8:33 A.M. McLaughlin terrorizes Eleanor with towel snapping and soap horns.

8:35 A.M. Replenishing of toilet paper launches debate: over or under?

10:47 P.M. Jack lurks lasciviously near drain with blowsy Scrubbing Bubble.

11:03 P.M. Fred's tub-and-basin-region prediction provokes fiery exchange about Zud.

Foreign Objects
(How to Translate
Your Foreign Lover)

I t is inevitable that those of us who are of artistic leaning will, at some point during our urban residency, consort with foreigners. Entering international waters in the hope that some of our foreign friends' sophistication and passive involvement in the history of culture and civilization will rub off on us, we the domestic party seek a streamlined form of education: travel without the inconvenience of travel.

That these relationships are fraught with miscommunication and misunderstanding is not unrelated to why we got involved with a foreigner in the first place—after all, liaisons with foreigners offer nothing if not the swank of incompatibility. But before long, the relationship's peculiar charm begins to wane, and we realize that we are as moths attracted to a flame: Before you can inform your British lover of the whereabouts of your guest towels, he has inventoried your liquor cabinet and arranged a "drinks party" for his friend Natasha, the Belts and Accessories Editor at *Vogue;* before you can figure out what has upset your Russian lover, he is sobbing in a foreign language and arranging for his funeral to be held in Minsk.

The dire state that these relationships can reach is best evidenced by Zsa Zsa Gabor, the Hungarian author of *How to Catch a Man, How to Keep a Man, How to Get Rid of a Man.* Several years ago, my friend Bob Mack, then a fact-checker at *Spy* magazine, was asked to call Miss Gabor in order to verify the dates of her marriage to her sixth husband, an American named Jack Ryan. We pick up Bob's notes just as Miss Gabor surfaces:

ZSA ZSA: Hello, dahling. I just love your magazine, it's wonderful!

BOB: Well, thank you, ma'am, that's very kind of you. I'm sorry to intrude, but I'm fact-checking this story and I need to find out the exact dates of when you were married to Jack Ryan.

ZSA ZSA: Dahling, I was never married to Jack Ryan! I love that man, he was wonderful, a brilliant inventor, but I never married him.

BOB: Umm, the way I understand it, you married him in 1975.

(At this point, Bob was looking at Miss Gabor's entry in *Who's Who,* which, although it stated that Mr. Ryan became Miss Gabor's sixth husband in 1975, gave no divorce date.)

ZSA ZSA: Oh no, dahling! Jack lived right down the street from me. He was a wonderful man, always throwing parties in his tree house. I loved him. My husband, Mr. Rubirosa, Porfirio Rubirosa, was very jealous. I loved Jack, but I never married him.

(Stifled, Bob then dutifully listened to Miss Gabor prattle on about a number of topics, including the $2 million advance that Delacorte Press had given her to write her autobiography. Just as Bob was summoning up his courage to ask his question one more time, she blurted out:)

ZSA ZSA: Oh, dahling, you're right! I *was* married to Jack Ryan! He's such a wonderful man.

Lest, like Mr. Ryan, we allow the small misunderstandings of our relationships with foreigners to pile up to the point of total bafflement, I offer the useful guide that begins on the next page.

When Your ITALIAN Lover Says:	*What Your ITALIAN Lover* MEANS *Is:*
"You are a very kind man."	"Marry my sister."
"What a charming studio apartment."	"But where will you put Mamma and Cousin Giacinta?"

When Your BRITISH Lover Says:	*What Your BRITISH Lover* MEANS *Is:*
"You enjoy the distinction of being, as it were, paramount in our affections."	"I am wonderful."
"The manner in which you camouflage your inner pain with daft enthusiasm is quite refreshing."	"You are Liza Minnelli."

When Your GERMAN Lover Says:	*What Your GERMAN Lover* MEANS *Is:*
"I have taken many photographs of my hometown's iron foundries and dams."	"I have taken many photographs of my hometown's iron foundries and dams."

When Your JAPANESE Lover Says:	*What Your JAPANESE Lover* MEANS *Is:*
"There has always been a mythic, larger-than-life quality to Americans for me."	"Could you reach that box of cereal on the top shelf for me?"

When Your HUNGAR-IAN Lover Says:	*What Your HUNGAR-IAN Lover* MEANS *Is:*
"Words cannot express the utter rapture that I feel in your presence."	"Dahling—have we met?"

When Your MOLDA-VIAN Lover Says:	*What Your MOLDA-VIAN Lover* MEANS *Is:*
"Thank you."	"A pair of shoes! With a *buckle*!"

When Your FRENCH Lover Says:	*What Your FRENCH Lover* MEANS *Is:*
"I hate you!"	"Where are my cigarettes?!"
"I detest you!"	"Where are my cigarettes?!"

"Leave at once!"

"I do love you, darling.
It's simply that we are essentially so different—I
enjoy carrying on several
simultaneous affairs with
my bisexual cousins; you
enjoy *Roseanne.*

"But thank God for those
opportunities when I can
laugh at you and your
clothing. This striped shirt
is particularly amusing—I
am reminded of my child-
hood fascination with
clowns.

"But cheri, be a love,
won't you—Marlboros.
In a box."

WHAT IF YOUR MOTHER WERE A FORM
OF INTERACTIVE MEDIA?

Monday   MOM boots up to opening bars of favorite Neil Diamond song.

Tuesday   MOM interrupts banking program with unsolicited virtual reality tour, "Adorable Herb Gardens and Bird Sanctuaries I Have Visited with Your Father."

Wednesday   Memo from local cable system warns subscribers of likelihood that MOM will malfunction during holidays.

Thursday   MOM interfaces with neighbor's system for downloading and coffee.

Friday   MOM says that your hilarious woes of interactivity would make a wonderful Erna Bombank column.

Saturday   MOM translates sentiment "As long as you have your health" into a binary series of on-off electronic impulses.

Sunday   Sudden increase of interactive shopping programs causes MOM to crash, transmit virus.

WHAT IF MICHELANGELO
HAD BEEN HETEROSEXUAL?

1508 Michelangelo stares at mistake made in mural,
       hoping for sudden appearance of slo-mo instant
       replay.

1509 Michelangelo replaces Sistine Chapel's sibyls and
       prophets with photos of José Canseco and Kathy
       Ireland.

1510 Michelangelo and friends blow past the Medici
       Palace on bitchin' two-wheeled wagons.

1513 Michelangelo reworks sketch for sculpture *Dying
       Slave* as *Slave Guy: Keep on Truckin'*.

1514 Michelangelo's unveiling of statue causes friends
       to do the Wave.

1519 Michelangelo likens allegorical sculptures *Dawn,
       Dusk, Day,* and *Night* to a Girls of the Big Ten
       pictorial.

1523 Michelangelo develops interest in barbecuing
       and lawn care.

1530 Michelangelo's winning of bet earns him
       opportunity to throw one free punch at Pope
       Clement.

WHAT IF YOUR TRAVEL AGENT
WENT OFF LITHIUM?

First Travel agent suggests tour, "Around the World in Three Days."

Then Travel agent suggests tour, "Albania: Land of Sorrow."

First Travel agent organizes window display featuring bratwurst and dirndls.

Then Travel agent organizes window display featuring broken glass and first-aid kits.

First Travel agent sends thirteen brochures about Carnaval in Rio.

Then Travel agent sends tattered paperback of *Death in Venice.*

Beauty Through Science

Because I am five-ten and have looks more evocative of the works of Norman Rockwell than those of Giorgio Armani, I have never given much thought to the possibility of becoming a male model. However, when a colleague pointed out to me in the spring of 1993 that, given the unidealized nature of beauty then being found in the media—the underfed waifs, the grizzled beatniks, the drowsy androgynes—men no longer had to be hulks in order to be awarded lucrative modeling contracts, I suddenly realized that it was entirely possible that *even I,* with my bony frame, could be making a profit simply by posing. So I went to my bathroom mirror and savored the possibility that I might finally get to *know* the Milan airport. My moment, I sensed, was near—the moment I would walk into a modeling agency and have a large woman in a muu-muu pinch my cheek and gasp, "Ten pounds of gorgeous in a five-pound bag!"

=

But before I could go to modeling agencies and gauge the salability of my own decidedly unidealized, unchiseled looks, before I could tilt at the hydra of humiliation and rejection, I had to put together a "book"—a portfolio of photographs capturing my dizzying range of looks and attitudes.

I met with a photographer and stylist recommended by a friend. The two men's level of hipness was discomfitting: the stylist wore a lot of rumpled black clothing and a crocheted skullcap; the photographer wore an earring and leather bell-bottoms. "I'm not sure how you'll photograph," the photographer said, gazing at me skeptically. I showed them some professional portraits I had had taken a month earlier by a photographer who takes a lot of actors' headshots; the duo was unimpressed. (Photographer: "They're very Broadway." Stylist: *"Very* Broadway.")

"How's the body?" asked the photographer, alluding to the body shot required of all aspiring models; I sheepishly explained that I do not engage in formal exercise. Fortunately, the stylist said that he would put me in a wet T-shirt, the illusion of bodily definition to be created through an admixture of wetness and drapery. We also discussed a method for creating nonexistent musculature: burying your fists under your crossed arms, you widen your biceps by pushing up against them with your knuckles.

As to clothing for the shoot—a large number of couturiers' names were invoked; it was promptly decided that I was *"not* Dolce and Gabbana." (It would later turn out that I was, however, Versace, Comme des Garçons, and Fruit of the Loom.) And as to my light brown, somewhat Amish haircut—"Don't take this wrong," the stylist said plainly, "but your hair is, it's . . . *mousey*"—it was promptly decided that I would be moussed.

=

In an attempt to effect gauntness and hollows, I ate as little as possible during the next two days. The day before the shoot, I ate, in order, a Triscuit, a Triscuit, two rice cakes, an apple, a Triscuit, and three rice cakes. But then at ten-thirty P.M. I had a collapse of will and rapidly ingested two bowls of Sugar Pops served in heavy cream.

In my hunger-produced delirium, I began to fear what the modish photographer-stylist team from the East Village might do with me photographically. My mind fixated on two possible tableaux: 1) I am in my underpants; 2) A tall, naked black man is coating me with honey.

At eight A.M. the following morning, I arrived at the photographer's apartment/studio, a location whose key-notes were Donna Summer and vacuuming. We proceeded to shoot for thirteen hours, both indoors and out, creating a variety of looks—young executive, soulful outdoorsman, clubby hipster, shaving yuppie, and something that the stylist called a "little-boy grungy look" (for which they provided a pregnant model to play my hippie girlfriend). In one outdoor segment I was asked to plunge down a set of

stairs some thirty-five times while maintaining an efferves-
cent smile—a feat that bordered on stuntwork.

The last forty minutes of the shoot were devoted to the
wet T-shirt shot. Having been instructed to take a shower
with the T-shirt on, I then wrapped a towel around my
waist and proceeded to crawl along the floor while the
photographer and his two assistants (also on the floor) used
a plant mister to spray me repeatedly and liberally with
water. I felt like a vine.

At the beginning of each segment, the photographer
would coax me, "Okay, gimme some looks," but the only
expressions that seemed to come naturally were utter hilar-
ity and, increasingly, mild irritation. After ten or so hours,
my powers of adorability began to wane. When, during the
young-executive portion of the shoot, a cat walked into the
frame of the picture, the photographer told me to "work
the cat." The cat wisely fled.

=

When I had made prints of fifteen of the shots, I next went
to Devron Technologies, Inc., to make comp-cards—the
postcards, bearing my phone number, measurements, and
a composite of several of the photographs, that I would mail
or give to agencies. A young male Devronite encouraged
me to put the wet-body shot on the front of the card and
the shaving and the outdoor shot on the back. I then asked
for his advice on the name change I was contemplating,
showing him a piece of paper on which I had written the

possibilities: Dack, Ruff, Spitz, Testostero, Henry Slade, Hank Maelstrom, and Odor Johnson.

"That part I can't really help you with," he said, forgoing the opportunity to launch the career of male model Odor Johnson.

I chose the name Henry Slade, evocative as it is of danger and sexual annihilation.

Forty-eight hours later I had my comp-cards and the twelve best photographs (now placed in a slick, state-of-the-art portfolio) in hand.

Most modeling agencies ask that prospective clients either mail them pictures or attend an open call at prescribed hours; I mailed off my comp-card to twenty-nine agencies, personalizing many of the cards with notes aimed at charming the receptionists and assistants who open the mail—"I'm posed for action!," "I'd be a model client!" I also sent Polaroids of my legs and feet to Parts, the agency that represents hand, hair, leg, and foot models; I appended these, "Leg's work together soon!"

I received four calls right away: two agencies wanted to set up appointments, and two wanted me to mail them more pictures. Given that most beginning models freelance with four or five agencies, I decided to cast a wide net; I went and visited twenty-six agencies in all, sometimes going at specified open-call hours, other times simply showing up and leaving behind a comp-card. "I'm a new face on the market," I would say innocently, waifishly, to the receptionist. "I was wondering if I could show someone my book."

"No dear," responded the harried, sixties-ish reception-ist wearing a pink cardigan at Ford Models. "They'll look at your card and call you if they're interested." I skulked out of the Ford lobby. But then several days later, a Ford booker with a heavy foreign accent left a thanks-but-no-thanks message on my machine: "You don't have the look we're going for right now." At first, I did nothing, amazed that the only agency that took the time to phone rejections was also the most prestigious one. But gradually curiosity and desire began to gnaw at me; I called her back and asked her to look at my book. "It won't help," she said. "I know what we sell." I asked again, explaining how the vogue for real-looking models made me think this might be my golden moment; she responded, "They want a stronger 'character look.' " I asked yet again; she said, "It won't help. . . . You have a good look, but it's not what's selling now."

Indeed, my weak character looks weren't selling at the larger agencies and the agencies that didn't specialize in commercial work (advertising used to promote products instead of haute couture). At Thompson Model and Talent Management I waited for about five minutes with a male bodybuilder and two top-heavy women—it appeared to be Large Breast Day at the Thompson offices—whereupon a booker sniffed at me, "You're not right for me."

"Am I too . . . real?" I asked.

"Or something," he replied.

A booker at the oddly placid Maxx Men spoke the words that soon enough became the refrain of my foray into the world of fashion modeling: "You're a little . . . *small* for us," she said.

"I'm six feet," I said.

"Are you?" she asked dubiously.

"I'm *just* six feet."

"Really? You don't look it."

"I come off small in person," I explained. "But I photograph very big."

But my efforts were to no avail. Agency after agency told me I was not tall enough; I started to feel extravagantly, resoundingly wee. When the booker at Thompson became the third person in one day to assert the theme of Lilliputia, I displayed my hands to him and tried to promote myself as a hand model. There are two types of hand models—glamor (hands must be virtually poreless and have long, tapered fingers) and product (hands are more athletic looking). It had occurred to me that I might qualify in the latter category. However, the booker sitting next to the booker I had been talking to said, "Darling, your hands aren't nice enough for hand work. Look at your nails—they're *painful.*" When she told me to wave my right hand in the air, I did; she said, "Your look is very veiny." Then: "No, I am *not* encouraging you to work with your hands."

=

Not character enough, not tall enough, not veinless enough: my feelings of inadequacy metastasized into desperation. One day, having been told by a fashion industry insider that the people who run the male modeling agencies are "nightpeople," I put on a black leather jacket and black jeans and visited Omar's Men, a high-profile agency run by a hip Panamanian man named Omar. Standing in the agency's entrance I beheld a blur of cappuccino, stubble, and telephone terrorism. I walked up to a booker with shoulder-length hair and an earring; I told him that I wanted to show my book to Omar. "I can tell you right off the bat that you should go to a commercial agency," he said. So I told him, "I was talking to Matt Dillon at Café Tabac"—referring to a person I have never met, a trendy place I have never been—"and he said that I should talk to Omar."

"Well, we have a great men's department."

But no introduction to the great Omar was offered. I explained that every recent ad I had seen had used unglamorous, real-looking models: the booker responded, "That's what people are using now. But you'd do better at a commercial agency, I'm telling you."

So I went to commercial agencies. Two of them wanted me to pay them to include my picture on the poster featuring pictures of their clients—a fairly certain sign of an agency's low position in the agency food chain. At the first of these, located in Times Square, the Broadway Danny Rose–ish proprietor was literally yelling "Fuck the friendship!" into the phone when I entered. This did not bode well. At the second, located high up in the Empire State Building, the manic head of the men's division had tips for me: "You'll have to cover your blemishes with makeup when you go out on interviews," and, "Wear a Western boot with a heel." The prospect of running around Manhattan in cowboy boots and makeup was unexciting to me.

Two more legitimate-seeming agencies were equally enthusiastic. "You're a young doctor. . . . You're Dr. Kildare," an intense, vulpine booker at Formation told me. He was particularly excited about the shaving picture ("Fabulous. That's right out of an ad. That *is* an ad"). When he told me, "With your looks, your teeth, your respectability, I'd be really surprised if you weren't making thirty to forty thousand dollars a year in a year or two."

When I visited the boyish, mid-twenties booker at Foster-Fell who had called me after my mailing, the first thing he said to me was, "I've got a job for you" (what he actually meant was that he had a go-see—an audition—for a sportswear catalogue for me). In our frantic ninety-second-long exchange, during which he took two phone calls, he gave me the address of the go-see and described the desired look as, variously, "preppy gone bad," "sexy Ralph Lauren," "sexy preppy," and "preppy sexy." To be thusly described was highly flattering; although I did not get the job, it was an honor, as they say on the Oscars, to be nominated.

In the end, five agencies took two or more comp-cards from me and said that they would be "sending me out." It is with some hesitation that I report that, of these five, the one with which I felt most comfortable was an outfit called FunnyFace. "Tell me about the name FunnyFace," I said to one of the bookers. "This doesn't have anything to do with . . . *clowns,* does it?"

"Clowns?" he asked. "No."

"You don't represent circus clowns?"

The booker calmly assured me that the agency had nothing to do with that segment of the entertainment community intent on scaring children.

=

Over the course of the next month I went out on two other go-sees—one for Newport cigarettes and one for Shields Shower Gel. The drill for these two go-sees, as for the sexy preppy one, was the same—I would show up, hand over a comp-card, scout the waiting area for paragons of beauty upon whom to feast my eyes, have my picture taken, and then leave. It was fun.

But I was still not working.

=

"Give them all thirty-two flashing! If you smile long enough at someone, they'll smile back. You have to believe. You *have* to believe in yourself," the man was exhorting a class of nine of us. He pointed at his torso and continued, *"This* is the temple of the living God. Let go and let God. God is the best actor-singer-dancer there is."

Yes, I had committed an act of fashion-model hubris: I had enrolled in an acting class. To wit, "How to Get into TV Commercials," as taught by former Grecian Formula spokesman Bob Collier.

My decision to position myself at the intersection of

hucksterism and thespian blather did not stem from a need to renounce the life of bookers and comp-cards; it was simply that this model wanted *to talk*.

Thus did I follow my initial class at Bob Collier's TV Studios and Theater with four private lessons with Mr. Collier himself. Sometimes breaking into snatches of show tunes in the middle of a conversation, other times stuffing his pockets with oversized facsimiles of one-thousand-dollar bills to make the point that commercials are lucrative, Mr. Collier, part showman, part evangelist, is an affable, silvery-maned gent with a voice that is redolent of product endorsement. Our private sessions were composed of equal parts on-camera training and discussion of the Science of Success, a program of positive thinking derived from Napoleon Hill's book, *The Master-Key to Riches*. As Mr. Collier repeatedly told me, "What the mind can conceive and believe, it can achieve."

"Here," Mr. Collier said in our first session, "I want you to have this." He handed me a Xeroxed sheet and explained that twice every day—on waking and before going to bed—I should read the affirmation printed thereon out loud. (We would both also intone the affirmation out loud during each of our sessions.) The affirmation:

DAY BY DAY IN EVERY WAY, BY THE GRACE OF GOD
I AM GETTING BETTER AND BETTER AND BETTER!

I AM HAPPY!
I AM HEALTHY!

I AM TERRIFIC!

I AM IMPORTANT!

I AM BEAUTIFUL!

I AM RICH!

I AM SUCCESSFUL!

I AM CONFIDENT!

I AM A STAR!

I AM HAVING A GREAT YEAR!

I AM FILMING MY FIRST COMMERCIAL BEFORE _____!

I AM MAKING BIG MONEY IN COMMERCIALS

RIGHT NOW!

"Remember that 'I am' is the name of the God presence within you," Mr. Collier told me.

During our sessions, he encouraged me to read Napoleon Hill's book three times, explaining, "Commercials are about happiness. And that's why I'm trying to change your head by having you read the book. Because if you're not happy, how can you sell happiness?"

=

I did not chant the affirmation when I wasn't in class. I approached the on-camera portion of my tutorials with ready amounts of vigor, applying myself to the zestful blarney of ads for Rice Chex and Mitchum deodorant and Ivory soap and Band-Aid Clear Tape, but I began to feel that my ambivalence about the fundamentals of positive thinking was keeping me from truly *delivering*.

"You have to love the camera and the camera will love

you back," Mr. Collier encouraged me one day. "Give it a name if you want."

"I'd like to call it Barbra," I said.

"Then call it Barbra."

This seemed to help.

I had no disagreement in principle with the Science of Success's main tenets: Make up your mind as to exactly what you want, have a burning desire, be willing to give up other things in order to get it. What was disconcerting was the conclusions that it led to. "That's why countries who have homeless people, who have crime, who have problems—this is why they have problems," Mr. Collier told me one day. "[The countries] haven't taught them that everything they need is right in here," he said, pointing at his head.

This troubled me; people are poor for reasons other than their inability to form mental pictures of cash in large denominations.

The Science of Success also had an awkward-making interpersonal aspect in its promotion of high expectations. Mr. Collier started our second class by saying to me, "I'm feeling happy, healthy, and terrific. How are *you* feeling, Henry?"

"I'm feeling . . . well, pretty terrific," I mumbled. At the beginning of the third class, he asked, "What's your good news?"

"Oh, I don't know," I said, looking at the floor. When, at the beginning of the fourth class, Mr. Collier asked, "What's your good news?" I suddenly felt I needed to testify, as if I needed to offer up some kind of remuneration for his assiduous efforts and quite genuine charm. I proceeded to tell a white lie by explaining to Mr. Collier that, minutes before coming to class, I had splashed on some new cologne and was feeling "rather terrific" as a result.

He looked at me with slight suspicion. Then he walked closer, leaned over toward me, and took a sniff of my chest.

"It's very subtle," he said.

During our last class, Mr. Collier led us on a forty-minute-long conversation about the state of the world and various media cover-ups of the last thirty years. My teacher, it came as little surprise, was a conspiracy theorist: he avowed that E. Howard Hunt had been on the grassy knoll in Dallas and that AIDS was a vaccine formulated by the National Institutes of Health and disseminated by Citibank-financed bloodmobiles.

When our conversation had coughed to a stop in the manner of an overworked burro on the edge of the Grand Canyon, we both found ourselves shaking our heads as we stared at the floor. After a long pause, Mr. Collier finally said, "What can we do about all this?"

"I don't know," I said. "But I don't think it involves commercials."

=

Indeed, after five classes at the Collier studios, the world of television commercials held increasingly less appeal for me. I was progressing well in my studies—having taped the Rice Chex spot several times, I could see my performance shaping up into a thing of beauty, nuanced and rich with subtext—and yet it seemed that something was missing.

I realized what it was. In directing my attention to the small screen, I had unintentionally renounced the thrill of the greasepaint, the roar of the crowd, the dizzying splendor of so many thousands of theater clichés.

I had lost touch with my *craft;* I wasn't being asked to make *choices.*

So, like the film star who returns to Broadway after a too-long stint in Hollywood—granted, this star of stage and screen had yet to actually *appear* on stage or screen—I yearned to re-experience the magic of live performance. I knew that following such a plan would limit the size of my audience, would make it even more difficult to achieve carved-in-granite immortality.

But I didn't care.

I would reach for the brass ring. I would firmly grasp it. I would *hold on.*

And so I did what anyone in my position (no experience, much enthusiasm) would do: I responded to an ad in *Backstage* looking for volunteer hair models to work at a Redken trade show, to be held at the Westchester Marriott.

=

On arrival at the appointed conference room at the Marriott—a throbbing nexus of haircare implementa and large-hair-bearing women that instantly recalled a remote episode involving an ill-tempered cocker spaniel and the Holiday Inn at the Newark airport—I was handed two pieces of paper by a wonderful, husky-voiced, red-haired woman named Wanda. One was a Xeroxed letter from Redken explaining that hair shows are held for the edification of professional hairdressers and that prospective models should not be dismayed if not chosen to participate. The other piece of paper was a form we volunteer hair models were expected to fill out; at one point, it asked which of the following I was interested in—haircut and style, hair color, permanent wave, hair pieces. Not sure how willing I needed to be in order to get hired, I put a check by the first and a question mark by all the others.

After I waited half an hour, the two male Redkenites who were walking around the room and talking to each of the models approached me. Both had clipboards. The hair stylist was blond and the colorist was brunet; for the purposes of this reportage, I will refer to them as Siegfried and Roy.

Roy said to Siegfried, "He'd be a good presentation model to escort the ladies."

Siegfried murmured in agreement. Peering around the side of my head and running his right hand through the side and back of my hair, Roy said, "Tell me where you're going with your shape."

I explained that I did not have a chosen trajectory for my shape.

"Remember that haircut you had when you came back from London?" he asked Siegfried. "That would be good."

Siegfried agreed. "Very short," he added. There was mention of some kind of encircling fringe.

"I had a color treatment that I thought would be fun,

too. If we left this long," Roy continued, tugging gently on my forelocks, "I could put in bolts of color underneath. You could swish them whether you wanted to see the bolts or not."

"This is sounding kind of elaborate," I said.

"It's not. It's easy to do," Roy assured me.

Siegfried moved the hair off my forehead with his hand. "This is where we'd see the bits of color?"

"Yeah," Roy said. "Actually, more like *hunks* of color."

Siegfried okayed the plan. He said to me, "It's going to be a really different shape."

"Like a rhombus?" I asked.

"I'm gonna build in a wall," he said, patting the back of my head. "And then we'll lose the wall."

Visions of men toting Sheetrock filled my head.

Roy, who had been writing notes on his clipboard, looked up. "We need a name for this," he said, squinting artistically at the proposed hunking area.

"That's your department," Siegfried responded.

Scribbling on his clipboard, Roy said, "Let's call it Peek-a-Locks."

=

Mine is a curious profession; trouble is my business. Traipsing from situation to situation—from vendor stand to civil service test, from bridal registry to bed and breakfast—I approach the unwitting world around me as a scientist his laboratory.

Occasionally, there is doubt. Often, there is guilt. Sometimes, there is the sensation that my already-ragged karma is being eaten at by cancer.

However, let it be said that at no point in my life did I ever experience this sensation more profoundly than while standing listening to these two men discuss the near future of my hair. My ordeal with Clifford at the dog-grooming certification test flashed before my eyes, as did the governor's seizure of my notepad. I was filled with a premonition that the world had come to avenge me and that the world had chosen the Westchester Marriott as the place for the showdown.

I thought: These two men are going to dye my head a violent shade of pomegranate. And then I will go home and my friends will call me Hairdo.

=

First Siegfried cut my hair. This went quite smoothly, and the resultant shape was quite flattering, even if the front was, as one of the other twelve models would later tell me, "a little bangy." I did not cavil at this banginess; and particularly heartening was the cut's lack of encircling fringe.

Looking at my newly created shape, Siegfried said to Roy, "You're gonna have fun with that."

"Yeah, I'm gonna have fun with it," Roy responded.

But moments later, Roy said to me, "I'm not sure I'll do the underbits. I want to concentrate on the overcolors."

"Overcolors?" I asked.

He explained that he was going to practice "unidirectional tinting" on me. "It'll look like a very strong sun is hitting your head from about this angle," he explained, holding his hand about a foot away from the top of my ear. "It's a sunburst effect."

"Will this be attractive?" I asked.

"It looks great," he said.

As it turned out, however, Roy did not have time to "do me" that day, and thus suggested that I return early the following day, the day of the show.

I did. I was not sure what my duties would be during the show; all I knew was that I was meant to wear the tuxedo that I had told Wanda I would bring.

Pandemonium reigned in the Redken conference rooms. As disco music blared from a tape deck, Siegfried and Roy and two other stylists beavered away on the various models. A Caucasian model in her early twenties who had been cosmetically and tonsorially Orientalized had four curly twigs snaking out of her head; the knee-length blond hair of another model was being painstakingly transformed into a ten-inch-tall fantasia of ringlets. A model who had missed registration the day before arrived; when she was told that she could be a wig model, she began to sob softly.

While reconnoitering to see whether there were any other male models (there was only one), I struck up a conversation with a twenty-something woman who appeared to be a friend and groupie of one of the models.

"Have you done this kind of thing before?" she asked.

"No," I said. "I mostly do lobe work."

"You mean for cars and stuff?"

"No," I explained, assuming she meant lube work, "ear-lobe work. I'm an earlobe model. Like for movie posters when it's a close-up of a head but the star has bad ears."

"Wow. Do you know Tom Cruise?" she asked.

"I did his *Top Gun* ones," I said. "For the poster, I mean."

"No sir," she looked astonished. "What's he like? He's totally short, right?"

"I don't get to meet the stars," I explained. "I just, you know, get a fax of their ears about a month before the shoot and then I train accordingly."

A vague look of horror came over her face; seconds later she ran off to join her friends in the bathroom.

Moments later Roy told me that I was to be a "tech model" and that he would do my hair on the stage. I said this was fine. I changed into my tuxedo and then waited for about an hour and a half to have makeup put on. During this, an anxious Siegfried entered the makeup room and made an announcement thanking all of us models for our time and wishing us good luck. "Without you," he said, "there is no show."

=

I still didn't know what my duties entailed. Then suddenly at about noon, eight of us models—some in formalwear, some in clubwear, all having had our hair partially or fully styled—were hustled downstairs and told to wait just outside the threshold of the grand ballroom where the show was being held. When the doors were opened, we were told, we should file in past the audience of several hundred, turn to the right, and then strike poses of fabulousness and hauteur amongst the various product-laden booths the audience would soon be visiting.

A shudder of anxiety and excitement passed through the group. We could all sense it: our moment was approaching.

The doors were thrown open.

But something was wrong.

The audience had already gotten up from their seats. So instead of striding coolly before them for their inspection, we simply trudged with them over to the booths.

Indeed, even once at the booths, we models didn't seem to be so very exciting to the show's patrons.

"Do you know why I'm wearing a tuxedo?" I asked a woman in her forties who was looking at a photograph of an aerosol finishing mist called Spraye.

"Are you with the caterer?" she asked.

"No," I said. "I'm a model."

"With Spraye?" she asked.

"No, for my hair. I'm a hair model."

She looked uninterestedly at my coiffure.

"It's nice," she offered.

When I asked a second woman why she thought I was wearing a tuxedo, she said she didn't know, particularly given that the boy at the hotel's front desk was only wearing a blazer.

I was still not making modeling magic.

=

There is a part of us all that longs to be immortal, that longs to have our every utterance and movement belong to the ages. Concurrent with this desire, however, is the realization that there are not enough magazine covers, not enough Senate seats, not enough medical breakthroughs for us all to make our names on. With this realization often comes readjustment, acquiescence.

I remember once talking to an actress who had been rehearsing a play under the guidance of a Svengali-like German director. The director had burdened the rehearsals with exercises, sensory work, and assorted workshoppy digressions.

"Do you think the play will turn out well?" I asked the actress.

"In a way, it doesn't matter," she told me.

"What do you mean?"

She sighed, a note of resignation betraying her outward perk. "Well, in the end," she said, "it's really about *process.*"

A hauntingly accurate description of my career as a male model.

WHAT IF THE ROYAL FAMILY WERE PUT
ON THE ENDANGERED SPECIES LIST?

Monday Aging sex symbol makes empassioned plea on Academy Awards for preservation of royals.

Tuesday New commemorative stamp issued showing Queen Elizabeth II from four different angles.

Wednesday Prince Charles and Lady Di are shot by tranquilizer darts and air-lifted to Balmoral, where they are encouraged to roam freely.

Thursday World Wildlife Foundation issues bumper sticker: WARNING: I BRAKE FOR PRINCE WILLIAM.

Friday Japanese maintain that harvesting of royal family by factory ship is actually beneficial to species.

Saturday PBS airs documentary featuring extreme close-ups of Prince Charles perched on grass stalks.

Sunday Team of naturalists circle in on bog in hope of flushing out Sovereign.

WHAT IF A TALENT AGENT UNDERWENT TIME TRAVEL?

1880 A.D. Agent sends troubled modeling client on go-see for Rodin's *Gates of Hell*.

1307 A.D. Agent tells the first victim of the bubonic plague that her life story is *"very* M.O.W."

2114 A.D. Agent visits space colony, calls cyborg leader "dollface."

88 B.C. Agent interrupts human sacrifice to ask competitor's Druid client, "Are you happy?"

1690 A.D. Agent confuses Huguenot with use of *package* as a verb.

WHAT IF JEAN-PAUL SARTRE HAD HAD A LITTLE IMAGINARY FRIEND NAMED SNEAKERS?

1942   Sartre scours Paris for a tiny beret.

1943   Sartre pens line, "Hell is other people"; abandons Sneakers in a cardboard box on the *métro*.

Afterlife of the Party

It is the tendency of the urban resident, while waiting for his ship to come in, to fritter away his existence fantasizing about precisely how he will revel in that ship's exquisite cargo. In my own case, I have always maintained that chief among the advantages of possessing a truly lavish amount of money—besides the assurance that you would never again be forced to avail yourself of that food product that, when added to meat, makes *more* meat—is that such an existence would be the perfect basis for leaving behind a highly whimsical and elaborate will. A will that would make the distribution of moneys and personal effects an experience marked by agony and torment. A will whose dictates and codicils are so confusing that even county clerks would weep profusely.

Granted, the idea is less than gracious. It lacks charity and a fond indulgence for your survivors. However, consider this: When you die, a complicated will is the best way you have of dictating how often and with what intensity people think about you. It is the closest thing to legacy control that life has to offer. Your good deeds and interesting accomplishments are all very well, but once probate is over and the highboys and the Aubussons are dispersed to their new homes, who will attend to the eternal flame of your memory?

When I go, I want the searing anguish that only litigation can deliver. I want frayed nerves and sleeplessness and lots of intercontinental faxing. I want an otherwise meek descendant to call the executor of my estate and snarl, "Look, I just want you to know that if I don't bag the Chagall prints, my lawyers and I are *ready to mobilize.*"

=

When it comes to estate planning, I take all my cues from my grandmother. When she passed away, her heirs, eight of us, gathered to hear her will. It was written with the tenuous grasp of reality so common to those teetering on the brink of death, and so had exactly the note of vague caprice that I can only hope my own old age will engender. In it, after a fairly dry divvying up of dollars and real estate and securities, several of her more prized possessions were assigned in this fashion: "The Steinway grand . . . to a boy who plays," and "my Remington . . . to a girl who shoots." This set off a torrent of confusion—in the first instance because all five men present felt eligible for the piano, given that it was for a boy who *plays,* not a boy who plays *well;*

in the second instance because none of the women—all three of them working mothers living in the suburbs—could imagine a lifestyle that would plausibly accommodate either big game or skeet.

And then came the catalog. Several weeks after our first meeting, the bank acting as executor sent each of the survivors a booklet in which all of my grandmother's possessions not mentioned in the will were described and appraised—catalog-style—for our purchasing purposes. We could either receive one eighth of the combined value of everything in the catalog or could use that same money to buy individual items. The demotion from "heir" to "home shopper" was devastating; soon, however, we got into the spirit of the thing, and then in no time at all we were giving full vent to the more unattractive, bargain-hunting aspects of our personalities. We talked *merchandise*. We talked *items*. We talked—as a lawyer had advised us to—*intangibles*.

But then when it came time to actually go to Connecticut for the weekend and lay our claims at my grandmother's house—now a veritable yard sale of death—our consumerist impulses rammed head on with the distaste of having to even *touch* this lovely woman's memory-laden possessions, let alone buy them. This clash of opposing emotions led to a sort of grinding, manic anxiety; by the end of the first day, one family member's face was so swollen from crying that she looked like she had been boiled.

And then I realized that the catalog itself was only heightening the absurdity and confusion of the situation. The sniffy young appraiser had written it in the exaggerated and ironical fashion of a man who resented my grandmother's house for falling short of the Winter Palace. His prose style found him alternately lost in a hazy revery ("one bifurcated settee on ball and claw *pieds* . . . nineteenth-century English") and mocking with utter disdain ("one oversized papier-mâché pig . . . *probably Mexican*").

=

And so we came to fan the flames of our devotion to our dearly departed. We suffered over her loss, and we suffered over her possessions. Thereupon did I realize that there is another way to make the living tremble before a power from beyond the grave. I speak, of course, of the inappropriate bequest. A bequest of such unsuitability and incompatibility that your heirs are left scratching their heads and muttering, "What could cousin Eustacia have *possibly* been thinking?"

So when I opened *The New York Times* one chill March morning and saw an advertisement for free appraisal days at the auction house Christie's East (just below the detail of an etching of a human eye, presumably reproduced from currency, was written "Are you looking $10,000 right in the eye?"), I heard the golden bells of opportunity peal. Hying myself to 219 East Sixty-seventh Street on the appointed Sunday, I walked to the end of a line of some eighty-five people on the sidewalk. As I walked, I noticed that many people had paintings—most of which were wrapped in bedsheets or blankets; one man had decided not to cover his Renoir reproduction but rather to hold it in the thirty-three-degree air by the wire on the painting's frame. Indeed, after I further inspected others' possessions, my insecurity about the value of my own humble offerings was somewhat buoyed: the couple in front of me were banking on a wall hanging, wrought in mirror and black and pink Plexiglass, of a woman wearing a large, stylish hat; the German woman behind me clutched a screw lock that she had bought at a junk shop on Long Island.

"It's medieval," she said to a man standing behind her who looked at her dubiously. "I'm sure of it."

The general tenor of the crowd was summed up by a man ahead of me in line who, pulling a porcelain figurine out of the cardboard box he was holding, said, "Oh, I'd love to unload this baby today."

When fifty minutes later a group of about twenty-five of us was allowed to enter the building, I was ushered to a card table behind which sat a woman in her twenties with a look of mild distaste. Draped around her neck were tiny pearls; her hair's drooping bow suggested that a large black velvet butterfly had perished on her head. She asked what I was going to have appraised; seeing that she was giving each person a piece of felt in a color corresponding to the category of his possessions (Paintings, Books and Manuscripts, Jewelry, etc.), I told her, "Collectibles." Awarded a piece of felt, I was told to wait upstairs on the third floor.

When my name was called out fifteen minutes later, I was directed toward the Collectibles table, behind which sat two well-groomed, clean-shaven men in their thirties. I put down the three boxes in which I had stored my treasures.

"My aunt sent me with this stuff," I said.

"You don't look too happy about it," one of the men said.

"Well, I don't really know too much about collectibles," I offered. Then, handing over the small metal box into which I had put a bag of copper grommets bought at a hardware store for $2.39—the kind you might see at the edges of a tarp or rain poncho—I said, "This is Uncle Buzz's grommet collection." The two men peered into the box diagnostically. The right eyebrow of the man holding the box twitched; the other man's face took on a slightly suspicious cast.

"Do you know how old they are?" the one holding the box asked.

"I'm not sure. He didn't make them. He collected them. I think they might be pretty old."

He sighed. "Well, all we can really do is take Polaroids of them and maybe refer you to someone."

With that, the other man stood, and walked off with the grommets.

I next produced a wallet-size cardboard box in which I had put a house key, two pieces of chalk, a pebble, a garlic husk, and a lot of pencil shavings. The outside of the box bore a label reading, DES CHOSES INCONNUES.

"These are some things we had lying around," I said.

The man looked at these items. He shook the box lightly, causing the husk to ruffle.

He moved on to the next box.

This third box contained a shard of a chicken bone that I had dried out in my oven.

"That's a bone fragment," I said. "It's from Mrs. Filth-Winterbottom's ulna."

The man's face betrayed no emotion.

"These aren't the kinds of things we handle," he said. "What you might do, though," he continued as he took one of the pieces of paper stacked on his right, "is get in touch with Nostalgia."

On the form—a list of fourteen auction houses and galleries—he made an X next to a Long Island concern called Nostalgia Galleries. I folded this piece of paper and put it into my pocket.

"They might be interested in this kind of thing," he concluded.

"In . . . household items?" I asked.

"Yes. And they'll have themes. One week it migh stained glass, another week furniture."

"Or it might be bone fragments," I added.

"I'm not sure about that one," he smiled tigh

"It's very old," I offered. "She was pretty f was the electricity heiress."

"Oh, really?" he said, trying to remain ? you can ask them and see. See, in our ? mostly specialize in things like movie p movie cels—things like that."

When the second gentleman returr

sour expression suggested that, having subjected the grommets to his Polaroid, he was now less impressed with them than he had been before. Handing me the box of grommets, he said, "We can get in touch with Nostalgia and see if they're interested in these."

I thanked him heartily and left. As I took the subway home, I realized that the two men had issued conflicting directives—the first had suggested that I contact Nostalgia; the second suggested I wait for Christie's to contact Nostalgia. Not sure which course of action to pursue, I chose the latter, as it was more flattering to my ancestry.

=

When I had heard nothing two months later, I called the Collectibles department at Christie's East. The man who answered the phone sounded startlingly like the first appraiser.

"Hi," I said. "I came in two months ago on a Sunday when people came in with things from their house? I just wondered if you'd heard something."

"What was the piece you brought in?" he asked.

"It was a collection of grommets. It was Uncle Buzz's grommet collection."

"Yes, I think we told you at that time that that wasn't something we would handle here."

"Oh . . ."

"I think we made that clear when we gave you the referral sheet."

"Oh, right. It's just that you took three Polaroids of

them. I thought maybe they were, well . . . somehow *special."*

The man reiterated his stance; I thanked him and hung up.

=

When I discovered that the number listed on the sheet for Nostalgia was disconnected, I called the Collectibles department again and was given the name of one of Nostalgia's partners, whom I will call Ed Winston. "They split up," the Christie's employee told me, "but essentially it's the same situation as before."

Over the course of three phone conversations with Mr. Winston, I suggested four days when I would be able to drive out to Long Island and show him "some things that my grandmother left me," but our busy schedules prohibited our convening.

"What kind of stuff are we talking about?" he asked during our first conversation. "Are they toys? Are they statues?" During our third conversation he asked, "Are they Hummels? Are they porcelain? Is it Disney, is it Deco?" Each time I responded that I wasn't sure what the objects were, saying simply that they were collectibles and that I would ask my aunt to explain their significance to me.

Finally, I followed his suggestion that I send him Polaroids. Two days after I had mailed them, on a Saturday at four-thirty P.M., a rather incredulous Mr. Winston called me.

"So what's the story with these pictures?" he asked.

"Well, it's stuff my grandmother left me," I explained.

"Right, but what about these descriptions?"

"My aunt explained those to me. She provided them."

"You're telling me," Mr. Winston said, reading the label that I had affixed to the back of the Polaroid of the grommets, "that 'these hollow, copper-backed grommels were collected by Uncle Buzz, the popular children's entertainer of the thirties and forties,' and that 'he was indicted in 1948'?"

"They're not grommels," I said, hoping that this misunderstanding lay at the root of Mr. Winston's seeming skepticism. "They're grommets."

"Big difference," he said. *"Who's Uncle Buzz?"*

"He was an entertainer. He performed at society parties. I wasn't really familiar with him either. My aunt told me about him."

"Why would anyone want these? And you're telling me—" (At this point he read portions of the label I had affixed to the ulna Polaroid.)

This bone fragment is from Eleanor Filth-Winterbottom's ulna. She was, as you probably know, the eccentric British heiress who was an intimate of both Rupert Lavish and Neuralgia Crest.

She was considered to be a great beauty (although Grandmother always disdainfully referred to her as La Poitrine); she lived on a boat on the Thames during the twenties called *A Boat on the Thames During the Twenties.* She died of a skiing accident in Gstaad in 1972; she built up a lot of speed on the last stretch and then skiied *right* through the lodge.

Although cremated, she asked that her ulna be preserved and divided amongst her heirs.

"And you're telling me," Mr. Weininger was saying, "that this bone fragment belonged to someone named *Eleanor Filth-Winterbottom*?"

"Yes. The heiress."

"Who is Rupert Lavish? Is that a real person?"

"He was a poet."

"You sure you don't mean Rupert Brooke?"

"He wasn't as famous as Rupert Brooke. Look," I pointed out, "these people may not *still* be famous, but they were quite well known in their day."

"*Neuralgia Crest?*" he said, laughing. "What is that? That means, that means 'a pain in the ass'!" He started to laugh.

"And nothing on the *choses*?" I asked.

He started to read the *choses'* label: "These whatno—," but he started to laugh uncontrollably. And then, suddenly, there was a thud and a crash—it seems that he had collapsed with laughter.

For the record, the *choses'* label:

These whatnots came from my grandmother's desk. A noted court stenographer and author, she wrote the 1954 pamphlet "The Contemporary Felon: Whither Diction?"

The husks in the photo allude to Grandmother's fascination with garlic.

"I'm sorry," he said when he got back on the line. "I don't mean to make fun of your—"

"No, no, that's okay," I said. "I realize that parts of this may seem comical."

"Yeah, a little," he said.

"So, so you're sort of saying that these things have no value?" I asked.

"I don't know *anyone* who would want this stuff," he gasped, letting loose another round of laughter.

=

The city cannot accommodate all of our hopes and aspirations; there are times when it seems to exist only to steamroll our uniqueness.

Three months before my grandmother passed away, she asked me one day to take her to a doctor's appointment in Hartford. After her session with the doctor, she shuffled out to the receptionist's area, where the harried receptionist gave her another appointment for a date two months later. My grandmother, given, at this stage in her life, to black humor and dire pronouncements, looked at the appointment date and said, "Oh . . . I'm not sure I'll even be *around* then," whereupon the receptionist, clearly missing the point, chimed in, "Well, if you can't make it, *just call.*"

And this, I suppose, is the prerogative of the deceased. For once we are no longer in this life, we will no longer be free to engage in fine dining with the objects of our affections. We will no longer be available to sprawl on the hot tar roof of our building, wallowing as the cool breezes of summer curl up tendril-like against our socklessness. We will no longer be able to walk into the atrium of a sky-scraper, marvel at its accumulation of chrome panel and plashing fountain and smoky glass divider, and conclude that we have entered the depths of an enormous scotch and soda.

No, we may no longer be able to revel in any of the beguilements and enchantments that brought us to the city in the first place.

But we can always call.

About the Author

Henry Alford has written for many publications, including *Details, The New York Observer, The New York Times Magazine, Spy, Vanity Fair,* and *Vogue.* He lives in New York City.

About the Type

This book was set in Galliard, a typeface designed by Matthew Carter for the Mergenthaler Linotype Company in 1978. Galliard is based on the sixteenth-century typefaces of Robert Granjon, which give it classic lines yet interject a contemporary look.